MW00615615

INTO THE BRIGHT SUNSHINE

ALSO BY SAMUEL G. FREEDMAN

Small Victories
The Real World, of a Teacher, Her Students, and Their High School

Upon This Rock
The Miracles of a Black Church

The Inheritance
How Three Families and America Moved from
Roosevelt to Reagan and Beyond

Jew vs. Jew
The Struggle for the Soul of American Jewry

Who She Was
My Search for My Mother's Life

Letters to a Young Journalist

Breaking the Line
The Season in Black College That Transformed the Game and
Changed the Course of Civil Rights

* * *

Dying Words
The AIDS Reporting of Jeff Schmalz and How It Transformed
The New York Times
(Companion book to the public radio documentary produced by
Kerry Donahue)

Ma Rainey's Black Bottom
The Journey from Stage to Screen
(Companion book to the Netflix film directed by George C. Wolfe)

INTO
THE BRIGHT
SUNSHINE

YOUNG HUBERT HUMPHREY AND
THE FIGHT FOR CIVIL RIGHTS

SAMUEL G. FREEDMAN

OXFORD
UNIVERSITY PRESS

OXFORD
UNIVERSITY PRESS

Oxford University Press is a department of the University of Oxford. It furthers the University's objective of excellence in research, scholarship, and education by publishing worldwide. Oxford is a registered trade mark of Oxford University Press in the UK and certain other countries.

Published in the United States of America by Oxford University Press
198 Madison Avenue, New York, NY 10016, United States of America.

Library of Congress Cataloging-in-Publication Data: 2023934131

ISBN 978–0–19–753519–6

DOI: 10.1093/oso/9780197535196.001.0001

Printed by Sheridan Books, Inc., United States of America

To you, again, my bashert,
Christia Chana Blomquist Freedman
This book began with your question

*

And in memory of two mentors whom I lost along the way
Alice Mayhew, 1932–2020
Jim Podgers, 1950–2018

True freedom is to share
All the chains our brothers wear
And, with heart and hand, to be
Earnest to make others free!
                    —*Stanzas of Freedom,*
                    James Russell Lowell

CONTENTS

PROLOGUE

"30 Years Ago—Here"

Philadelphia, Pennsylvania
May 22, 1977

Hubert Humphrey, a fallen hero and a dying man, rose on rickety legs to approach the podium of the Philadelphia Convention Hall, his pulpit for the commencement address at the University of Pennsylvania. He clutched a sheaf of paper with his speech for the occasion, typed and double-spaced by an assistant from his extemporaneous dictation, and then marked up in pencil by Humphrey himself. A note on the first page, circled to draw particular attention, read simply, "30 years ago—Here." In this place, at that time, twenty-nine years earlier to be precise, he had made history.

From the dais now, Humphrey beheld five thousand impending graduates, an ebony sea of gowns and mortarboards, broken by one iconoclast in a homemade crown, two in ribboned bonnets, and another whose headgear bore the masking-tape message "HI MA PA." In the horseshoe curve of the arena's double balcony loomed eight thousand parents and siblings, children, and friends. Wearing shirtsleeves and cotton shifts amid the stale heat, they looked like pale confetti from where Humphrey stood, and their flash cameras flickered away, a constellation of pinpricks.

The tableau stirred Humphrey's memories of the Democratic National Convention on July 14, 1948: the same sweltering air inside the vast hall, the same packed seats and bustling lobby, the same hum

ix

of expectancy at the words he was about to utter. All these years later, Humphrey was standing in very nearly the identical spot.

Since that afternoon in 1948 had placed him on the national stage, Humphrey had assembled credentials more than commensurate with this day's hortatory role: twenty-three years in the U.S. Senate, four as vice president to Lyndon Johnson, three times a candidate for his party's nomination for president, and one very narrow loss as its candidate. In Humphrey's years as arguably the nation's preeminent liberal politician, he had pressed for the United States and the Soviet Union to negotiate disarmament amid the nuclear standoff of the Cold War, introduced the legislation that created and indeed named the Peace Corps, and helped to floor-manage the landmark Civil Rights Act of 1964. Relentlessly energetic, effusive to a fault, he practiced what he called "the politics of joy."[1]

Even so, five days shy of his sixty-sixth birthday, Humphrey was a dynamo diminished. Two cancers were ravaging him, one blighting his body and the other his legacy. As if entwined, each affliction had been inexorably growing over the preceding decade. Nineteen sixty-seven was the year when the escalating war in Vietnam, which Humphrey dutifully supported, deployed nearly half a million American soldiers and took more than ten thousand American lives. It was the year of the "Long Hot Summer," when Black Americans in more than 150 cities erupted with uprisings against the police violence and economic inequality that persisted regardless of civil rights laws. And it was the year when Hubert Humphrey first noticed that his urine was stained with blood.

Of the team of doctors who examined Humphrey, only one warned of incipient cancer, and he was overruled.[2] The decision suited Humphrey's congenital optimism and his yearning for the presidency, and he went through the 1968 campaign assuming good health. The next year, a biopsy confirmed evidence of bladder cancer, and after four more years without Humphrey having either symptoms or treatment, doctors discovered a spot of malignant tissue termed "microinvasive." The word meant that the rogue cells could sink roots and spread, like the plagues of thistle that overran the wheat fields of Humphrey's prairie childhood.

Subsequent rounds of radiation and chemotherapy, a regimen that Humphrey described as "the worst experience of my life," bought him three years of remission, and with it the false hope of full recovery.

For in the fall of 1976, Humphrey again spied blood in his urine, and a biopsy confirmed that the bladder cancer, far from defeated, was expanding. Humphrey submitted to the harsh and logical option of having his bladder removed and chemotherapy resumed. For public consumption, wearing a mask of willed buoyancy, Humphrey declared himself fully cured. Newspaper accounts of his stay at Memorial Sloan-Kettering Cancer Center told of him "prodding patients out of their wheelchairs, shaking hands with everyone in sight and generally infusing gaiety and hope into a normally somber ward."[3]

In fact, the disease had already invaded Humphrey's lymph nodes, the staging areas for it to advance with one nearly certain result. On the days when Humphrey received chemotherapy, he was so weak, and perhaps so humiliated, that a young aide had to roll him up into a blanket and carry him between the senator's car and the Bethesda naval hospital.[4] Humphrey was both impotent and incontinent now and reduced to relieving himself through a port in his abdomen into a collection bag. In one of the rare moments when private truth slipped out, he described his cancer as "a thief in the night that can stab you in the back."[5]

The decline of Humphrey's health coincided with the degradation of his public image. Barely had Humphrey joined Johnson's White House than the musical satirist Tom Lehrer titled one song on his Top 20 1965 album *That Was the Year That Was*, "Whatever Became of Hubert?" "Once a fiery liberal spirit," Lehrer sang in answer to his own question, "Ah, but now when he speaks, he must clear it." The clearance, Lehrer's sophisticated listeners understood, had to come from Lyndon Johnson, and its price was Humphrey's cheerleading for the Vietnam War.

Humphrey received the presidential nomination in 1968 less by competing for it rather than by having it delivered to him by tragic circumstance and machine manipulation: Johnson's decision in March 1968 not to run for re-election; the assassination in June of the next front runner, Robert F. Kennedy; and a coronation by the centrist party establishment at a Chicago convention sullied by a police rampage against antiwar protestors. Humphrey campaigned under the twin burdens of an increasingly unpopular war and the televised beating of young activists. At a more personal level, his erstwhile protégé Eugene McCarthy, the Minnesota senator who was revered on the left for his antiwar insurgency against Johnson in the early primaries, withheld his vital endorsement of Humphrey until it was too late to matter.

In defeat, Humphrey returned to the University of Minnesota, his alma mater, where the political science faculty rejected his appointment, ostensibly because he had never finished his doctoral degree. Even after the university managed to place Humphrey in a category of nontraditional faculty, the professors there banned him from their social club, the Thirty-Niners.[6]

When voters returned Humphrey to the U.S. Senate in 1971, it was as a freshman, starting over at the bottom of the seniority totem pole. And when he vied again for the Democratic presidential nomination in 1972, he lost to another protégé, George McGovern, the senator from South Dakota whose opposition to the Vietnam War made him an idealistic idol to his youthful legions. Even more humiliating, Humphrey's trademark ebullience now looked frenetic and desperate. One bard of the counterculture, Hunter S. Thompson of *Rolling Stone*, laid into Humphrey with particular rhetorical relish. To Thompson's unsparing eye, Humphrey was "a treacherous, gutless old ward-heeler," "a hack and a fool," who "talks like an eighty-year-old woman who just discovered speed." And in this insult that beyond all others clung in the popular memory, he "campaigned like a rat in heat."[7]

The calumnies were hardly the exclusive property of Woodstock Nation. Stewart Alsop, a grandee among Washington columnists, reiterated some of Thompson's barbs in *Newsweek*. Theodore H. White, American journalism's authoritative chronicler of presidential campaigns, pronounced that Humphrey "had been part of the scenery too long, as long as Richard Nixon, and had become to the young and the press a political cartoon."[8]

By the time the 1976 presidential campaign began, Humphrey was sick enough, dispirited enough, or both to stay out of it. His home city of Minneapolis, which he had made a national model of liberalism as mayor, was about to re-elect a law-and-order ex-cop named Charles Stenvig for his third term as mayor in yet one more example of white backlash against racial progress. Another of Humphrey's protégés, Senator Walter Mondale, vaulted past him into the national spotlight as the incoming vice president for Jimmy Carter. During the week of their inauguration, Humphrey was vomiting from the effects of chemotherapy.[9]

When Congress convened in January 1977, Humphrey tried one last race—running to be Senate Majority Leader. Even his longtime allies in the AFL-CIO let their opposition privately be known because he was "starting to slip fast."[10] Facing certain defeat, Humphrey withdrew. And the cruelest part of the outcome was assenting to the senator who captured the prize by acclamation. Robert Byrd of West Virginia was a former member of the Ku Klux Klan, a filibustering foe of civil rights legislation, and the very embodiment of the Jim Crow system that Humphrey had devoted his adult life to dismantling.

All of these blows, and the prospect of his own demise, put Humphrey in an uncharacteristically pensive mood—more than just ruminative, closer to depressed. After nearly thirty years in national politics, he found himself wondering what it had all been for.

"I always try to be a man of the present and hopefully of the future," he wrote in early 1976 to Eugenie Anderson, a career diplomat and longtime friend. "I am, of course, strengthened and inspired by some of the achievements of the yesterdays; but also a person is sobered and tempered by some of the other experiences that didn't produce such favorable results. I hope the experience that I have had has given me some sense of judgment and a bit of wisdom."[11]

By January 23, 1977, when Humphrey wrote to Anderson again in the wake of cancer surgery and the failed bid to become majority leader, his tone was even more despairing: "I'm no child and I surely am not naive, but I do feel that some of those I helped so much might have been a little more loyal. But I suppose it's part of human weakness so why worry about it. That's all for now."[12]

In the present moment, standing before the imminent Penn graduates and their doting families, Humphrey looked visibly weathered, even from a distance. His gown dangled from sloping, bony shoulders as if off a coat hanger. His skin had a grayish hue, the same color as the wispy hair and eyebrows just starting to grow back with the cessation of chemotherapy. His cheeks, the tireless bellows for so many speeches, were shrunken back into the bone. His chin jutted, a promontory.

Even for this celebratory occasion, even on the day he would receive an honorary doctorate, Humphrey was revisiting a place not only of triumph but rebuke. He had been picketed and heckled by antiwar protestors in this very hall in 1965, with one placard asking, "How Much Did You Sell Your Soul for Hubert?" During a presidential campaign rally in Philadelphia in 1968, the signs called him "murderer" and "killer." And after a speech on the Penn campus during the 1972 primary race against McGovern was disrupted by everything from paper airplanes to chants of "Dump the Hump," Humphrey lamented, "I've been to 192 campuses, but I've never had anything like this."[13]

So as he edged into his commencement address, Humphrey held off from the prepared text, with its survey of international affairs and its appeal for youthful idealism. He led instead with jokes that, depending how one chose to hear them, sounded either self-effacing or self-lacerating. They had the aspect of a perpetual victim mocking himself before any bully could, as if controlling the blow might limit the pain. "I've given more speeches than any man ought to be permitted to," Humphrey said. "I have bored more people over a longer period of time than any man ought to be permitted to." Then he recalled his own graduation from the University of Minnesota in 1939 and said, "For the life of me, I can't remember what the commencement speaker said, and I'll bet you that when you leave here, at least a year from now, you're gonna say, 'Who was that fellow? What did he say?' "[14]

Humphrey had the crowd laughing now, not in ridicule, but a kind of affable affinity. Maybe because the Vietnam War was over at last. Maybe because the political villain of the age was Nixon. Maybe because people felt pity for Humphrey's illness or some pang of conscience about the scorn he had endured. Whatever the reason, Humphrey seized the interval of good will and pivoted into a matter of substance and memory.

"I've been reminded . . . of the day I was here in July nineteen hundred and forty-eight," he said, his voice reedy and unforced. "Boy, it was hot, in more ways than one. I was the young mayor of the city of Minneapolis . . . but in my heart, I had something that I wanted to tell my fellow partisans, and I did."

What Humphrey said on that day preceded the Supreme Court's decision in *Brown v. Board of Education* and the Montgomery bus boycott led by Rev. Dr. Martin Luther King Jr., the two events commonly and incorrectly understood as the beginnings of the civil rights movement. What he said on that day anticipated the wave of civil rights legislation that Lyndon Johnson would push through Congress in the 1960s, addressing the unfinished business of emancipation. What he said on that day set into motion the partisan realignment that defines American politics right up through the present.

What he said on that day—with Black marchers outside the Convention Hall threatening mass draft resistance against the segregated armed forces, with Southern delegates inside the building vowing mutiny against such equal rights, with the incumbent president and impending nominee, Harry Truman, seething about this upstart mayor's temerity—followed on two sentences.

"Because of my profound belief that we have a challenging task to do here," Humphrey had declared from the convention podium, "because good conscience, decent morality demands it, I feel I must rise at this time to support a report, a minority report, a report that spells out our democracy.

"It is a report," he continued, "on the greatest issue of civil rights."[15]

CHAPTER I

BEYOND
THE MERIDIAN

Doland, South Dakota

1922–1931

Fifteen years after the Civil War ended in Confederate surrender and the Thirteenth Amendment abolished slavery, the federal census recorded the residents of John T. Cotton's home in the rolling pastureland of central Kentucky. Among them was a farm laborer named Clay Shipman, twenty-six years old, and his wife Ellen, a cook who was four years his junior. The enumerator categorized the Shipmans as "mulatto," a designation of inferior racial caste and the evidence, too, of the slave master atrocities that had been inflicted upon their forebears.

Even with the war's resolution, when Black citizenship should have been a settled matter, Kentucky resisted granting both equal rights and equal protection across the color line. Though it had been a slave state, Kentucky never seceded from the Union, and so federal troops were not deployed there as elsewhere in the South to enforce Reconstruction. The state's General Assembly rejected the Thirteenth Amendment altogether. Ku Klux Klan vigilantes attacked Black churches and freedmen's schools, assaulted Black veterans of the Union Army, and, in one instance, besieged a large iron foundry to force the expulsion of its Black workers. No sooner had freed Blacks helped to elect narrowly a Republican government in Boyle County, where the Shipmans lived, than a series of lynchings erupted and the surrounding region went on

1

to lead the state in that grim statistic.[1] A federal official trying to resettle liberated Blacks in the county faced such hostility that he declared, "Satan is loose in Ky."[2]

By the middle of the 1880s, Clay and Ellen Shipman had four children, ranging from toddler to nearly teenager, and not a single material object worth taxation. They continued to subsist on Clay's take from farm work, part of it in the form of provisions rather than cash wages, and what Ellen could make hiring herself out to white peoples' kitchens. John Cotton, for his part, descended from a slaveholding family that still owned hundreds of acres of land for grain, horses, and cattle.

In all likelihood, the Shipmans were hearing of those several thousand Black people from Kentucky and Tennessee, among other Southern states, who had headed to the western plains a few years prior, calling themselves Exodusters. The Shipmans decided to join them, taking aim at a section of northeastern Nebraska, Madison County to be precise, that had just been connected in 1880 to the transcontinental railroad. There was land there waiting to be homesteaded, land from which the American army had driven the Pawnees.

It is possible that the Shipmans traveled by horse-drawn wagon. It is possible they traveled on foot. It is possible, though improbable, they somehow gathered the necessary money to travel on the Union Pacific. Sometime and somewhere in that journey, Ellen evidently died, because all mentions of her in the public record cease. By the decade's end, Clay and his children had settled on a farm several miles outside the small town of Battle Creek, Nebraska. Thus established, Clay married for a second time in 1889, wedding a German immigrant nearly a dozen years his junior who would bear five children, all of them capable of passing as white.

Besides running his own farm, Clay ultimately managed to buy and sell 120 acres of land, and also to take regular side work on road-building teams.[3] Of the children from his first marriage, his Black children, it was the youngest one, a son named Otis, who picked up the trade. The 1910 census found Otis in Laramie, Wyoming, twenty-six years old and working as a teamster. A decade later, he and his wife Mollie and their two daughters were living in Omaha, which then had the largest Black community of any Western city except Los Angeles. Along with his unmarried older brother Leslie, Otis formed a company that graded land for the roads and rails spreading veinlike across the plains. Leslie mostly oversaw the office, and Otis led the crews—one year over in Yorktown, Iowa, the next in Elm Creek, Nebraska, and, in the summer of 1922, on a rutted, sun-cracked dirt track just outside Doland, South Dakota, a village of six hundred marooned in the state's eastern grasslands.

There, on an August afternoon, the son of a Black man once enslaved met the white son of Doland's resident idealist.

The boy, Hubert Humphrey, was a few months past his eleventh birthday, freckled and fair-skinned and a little bit feeble by the standards of the frontier. He had barely survived the influenza pandemic of 1918 and in chillier weather wore a fleece tunic to protect his weakened lungs. The folks in Doland all knew him as "Pink" or "Pinky," a nickname that referred to the way his mother had dressed him as a toddler. And he was so awkward on his gangly legs that people joked about how often he stumbled.[4]

In a community that venerated the farmer and hunter, men who contended with nature, Hubert was more of an indoor creature, the prodigy in his grade school class and the adoring son of a bookish father who ran the local drugstore. One of Hubert's jobs there was to peddle all the newspapers, some shipped from the distant East and others printed close to home. So it probably had not escaped his inquiring eye when Doland's weekly paper, the *Times-Record*, recently published this item:

> The highway construction crew is at work three miles west of town and are making good time. Those who have driven over the road say the work is about the best they ever saw in the state. The contractor is a negro [*sic*] and is doing the work exactly as called for in the specifications.[5]

Purely as a feat of engineering, the construction of U.S. Highway 212 captivated Doland. South Dakota barely had gravel roads outside its few small cities as of 1920,[6] and without them any motorist who dared the dirt routes after snow or rain risked having his automobile sink into

3

muck down to the axles and then waiting hours to be tugged free by some farmer's team of horses. People and commodities moved almost entirely by railroad, which for Doland meant the Chicago & North Western, one train a day eastbound and one headed west. That monopoly gave the rail barons control over shipping prices for grain and livestock, much to the farmers' infuriation. This newly improved road being built with federal money by Otis Shipman's crew (among other contractors) would open an alternative path to the mills of Minneapolis and the slaughterhouses of St. Paul. To the west, the highway would run twenty miles to the Spink County seat of Redfield and then, incredibly, nearly seven hundred more through the Black Hills to the national park in Yellowstone, relieving the suffocating isolation in every far-flung settlement like Doland along the way.

To the thrill of such progress was added, especially for Hubert Humphrey, the specific prospect of meeting a Black person for the first time in his life. From the perspective of Doland, with its preponderance of Protestants rooted in Germany and Scandinavia, difference was defined by the so-called "Rooshins"[7] of the Hutterite religious colonies south of town and the French Canadian Catholics clustered in the hamlet of Turton eleven miles to the north. The Native peoples had long since been pushed onto reservations halfway across the state. The small Black community composed of railroad maintenance workers in Huron, replete with its own African Methodist Episcopal church, lay forty miles of often impassable dirt road away. It might as well have been in another hemisphere.

When Hubert sought out the road crew that August afternoon, Otis Shipman must have looked as grand and strange as a Roman charioteer. He had coiled hair and tawny skin, and the relentless sun of a blistering August had darkened him even more. Beneath a broad-brimmed hat, strapping in his lace-up boots and suspenders, he directed the progress of a machine called an elevating grader as it was pulled by a team of sixteen mules. A couple of hundred feet a day, the animals dragged a wagon fitted with a wide metal blade across the grooved, weather-beaten dirt road, scraping off enough soil to leave behind a flatter surface. A conveyer belt on the grading machine then carried the soil to a trailing dump wagon. In later stages of the job, Shipman's crew would drop this harvested dirt back onto the roadway, then pack it down with a metal roller in anticipation of the final, topmost coating of gravel.

Day after day, Hubert returned to Otis Shipman and his crew, who had been personally recruited from the Black neighborhoods of Omaha. At some point, either he asked or Shipman invited the boy to sit in the dump wagon, and the crew hands fielded his incessant stream of questions. Back at home, Hubert confided the adventure to his parents. His mother, Christine, wary of the unfamiliar and protective of the boy she had nearly lost, immediately voiced her disapproval. His father, Hubert Sr., was undisturbed. He held to a favored principle: "Treat people like people. If you treat them like dogs, expect to be bitten."[8]

On Saturday nights, Shipman and his men went into town, their weekly pay in hand. Doland rarely looked more festive, even in what had been a troubled year for crops. The threshing crews that followed the wheat harvest north from the Texas Panhandle into Canada were just finishing up in the fields outside Doland and had their own money to spend. Some of them were splurging on fifty-cent-a-night rooms at the City Hotel, a few sneaking away to buy moonshine from rural bootleggers. So many farmers flocked into town that Main Street barely had a parking space to spare. Children ambled along, feasting on ice cream and popcorn, amid the strains of Doland's own sixteen-piece orchestra holding forth from the bandstand beneath the cottonwood tree.

The shops, including Humphrey's drugstore, stayed open late on Saturdays, and typically Hubert manned the soda fountain, standing on a wooden carton in order to reach the spigots. With that chore done, he headed to the rail depot to fetch bundles of the fat Sunday editions of the out-of-town papers, peddling them for his own nest egg, which he secreted in a former ice-cream carton beneath the drugstore counter.

As the Black men of Shipman's crew strolled among the townspeople, they attracted plenty of stares, somewhere between bewildered and hostile, but the men jovially hailed Hubert by name.[9] And then they bought multiple copies of his newspapers, far more than they needed, just to return the boy's uncommon kindness. Hubert trailed along as the workers made their way to Hajek's pool hall, the closest thing to decadence in a county that had gone dry a full decade before Prohibition took hold of the nation in 1919.[10] With its six tables and its complement of pipes, cigars, and tobacco, Hajek's was considered off limits for any male younger than eighteen. (Women, of course, were altogether forbidden.) But with the Shipman workers as his chaperones, Hubert gained entry to the demimonde, and they kept him happily supplied with strawberry soda pop.[11]

Then, not too many weeks later, the magic dissipated. Hubert returned to school for sixth grade. Otis Shipman had a grading job waiting for him in western Iowa, a good deal closer to his Omaha home and family. But even in the men's absence, maybe more so because of their absence, Hubert etched into his memory this brief, vivid glimpse of a world beyond Doland, and of the racial history hanging over the nation.

* * *

Hubert Humphrey Sr.—H. H. to everyone in Doland—could trace his lineage on the North American continent back ten generations to an English colonist named Jonas Humphrey, who reached Massachusetts in 1637.[12] The roots of H. H.'s intellectual and moral heritage had a more adjacent source—his mother Adeline. In the attic of their farmhouse near the central Minnesota town of Elk River, where H. H. and four siblings spent most of their childhood, Adeline augmented their schoolroom lessons with her own instruction, drawn from her readings of Dickens, Twain, Hawthorne, and Victor Hugo.[13] Those authors suited her sensibility with their combination of literary merit and humane vision. And despite the pacifism of her Quaker heritage, she joined her husband in extolling Abraham Lincoln, who had made righteous war to defeat an even greater evil. To those influences, H. H. added his own admiration of William Jennings Bryan. H. H. had heard "The Great Commoner" on the tent-show circuit re-enacting his populist "Cross of Gold" speech from the 1896 Democratic convention, which had nominated him for president and elevated his brand of "prairie populism" to national prominence.

Compared with his two older brothers, however, H. H. followed an unlikely path out of the household and into adulthood. Harry and John went on to study at the University of Minnesota, with Harry ultimately earning a doctorate from Stanford and John becoming a published poet and patent-holding inventor by his early twenties. Whether because of H. H.'s own idiosyncrasy or the drain of two sets of college tuition on the family purse, he matriculated only to a drugstore in the thousand-person mill town of Granite Falls, Minnesota. There, at the age of seventeen in 1899, he took work as a traveling salesman.

The product that H. H. peddled was a patent medicine called Peruna. Invented by a renegade doctor named Samuel Brubaker Hartman, Peruna was as lucrative as it was fraudulent. Hartman promoted the elixir as a cure for "catarrh," an excess of mucus that supposedly caused an array of diseases. Heading into the turn of the century, Peruna was the bestselling patent medicine in the country, "costing $1 a bottle at a time when 25 cents bought a full lunch."[14]

H. H. had every reason to know that his door-to-door windfall relied on a hoax. Both the Women's Christian Temperance Union and the *Ladies' Home Journal* denounced Peruna as Demon Rum by any other name. A muckraking reporter for *Collier's* magazine determined that Peruna was twenty-eight percent alcohol tricked up with a flavor cube and burned sugar.[15]

Whatever moral qualms H. H. did or didn't have, as he balanced his conscience with his sales pitch, he saved up enough money in two years on the Peruna circuit to set up a drugstore counter inside a grocery store in Lily, South Dakota, population about 175. Such operations were called "pine-board drugstores," to distinguish them from the more established and upscale "marble-floor" variety. Many of the proprietors, like H. H., lacked any formal training and worked on consignment from big-city wholesalers.[16] As far as America's physicians were concerned, by hawking their dubious nostrums these self-appointed clinicians were taking away business from real doctors and authentic medicines.

Under such pressure, South Dakota commenced a process of credentialing pharmacists, and H. H. consented by enrolling in C. W. Drew's Minneapolis Institute of Pharmacy, skipping its substantial program in pharmacology in favor of a three-month cram class for the licensing exam. Gaudy-looking diploma in hand, he returned to Lily and his next endeavor: courtship. At a Lutheran church dance, H. H. met Christine Sannes, one of eleven children of Norwegian immigrants who had homesteaded in the surrounding countryside. They made an improbable physical match—H. H. tall and rangy, Christine petite and small-boned—but shared intellectual yearnings. Rare for a young woman in her place and time, Christine had gone to college and was teaching in a rural one-room school.[17] Overriding her disapproving father, who would have preferred a fellow Norwegian, Christine wed H. H. in April 1906, and gave birth to their first child, Ralph, ten months later.

H. H. promptly shut down the Lily drug counter and moved the family back to Granite Falls. It was fivefold larger than Lily and presumably had commercial prospects to match, especially since H. H. would be operating the prescription counter at the well-established drugstore for which he'd once been merely a salesman. Instead, two years later, the store was destroyed in a fire. H. H. went back on the road, this time peddling candy from farm to farm.[18] Reversing course yet again, H. H. doubled back westward in 1911 along the expanding train lines, looking for a place where a drugstore could grow in concert with a newly planted town. He set up shop in Wallace, South Dakota, a hamlet of barely two hundred people that had recently gotten a railroad station and incorporated itself. The Humphreys' second child, a boy named Hubert, was born upstairs from the drugstore on May 27, 1911.

Meanwhile, Wallace's population barely budged, and neither did the take in H. H.'s cash register. So, in 1916, H. H. tried to make his leap into the "marble floor" echelon. He moved his brood to Doland, which had nearly triple the population of Wallace, and rented a storefront on Main Street. For once in his life of mercantile false starts, he had either chosen wisely, gotten lucky, or some combination of both.

Doland had been founded in 1882, when its progenitor, a Civil War veteran named Franklin Henry Doland, bought and then planted several hundred acres of land in the expected path of the Chicago & North Western as it moved westward into South Dakota. Sure enough, the railroad established a depot in Doland as the shipping hub for farmers in a ten-mile radius, with creameries, grain elevators, and an auction house for livestock ultimately lining the tracks. The institutions of civic life similarly germinated: general store, hotel, schoolhouse, church, post office, newspaper. Even so, entering the 1910s, Doland presented the drab picture of muddy streets and wood-frame stores, just another prairie whistle-stop.

In February 1913, three years before H. H.'s arrival, the buildings along Main Street had caught fire. Normally, a blaze causing the present-day equivalent of two million dollars' worth of damage in a town of its size would have delivered a considerable blow. Yet events halfway around the world transformed Doland's setback into an opportunity for its revival, and also H. H's.

When the Great War erupted in Europe in 1914, wheat farmers in the Dakotas literally reaped a bonanza. Bushel prices more than doubled[19] as combatant countries abroad abruptly needed to import grain. After the United States entered the war in 1917 and had to provision an expeditionary force of nearly three million soldiers, the message from Washington went to places like Doland to "plow to the fence for national defense" because "wheat will win the war."[20] For their part, the farmers called the aggressive approach "wheat-mining."[21] Planting ever more acres, and enjoying the cushion of federal price supports, South Dakota's wheat farmers saw the cash value of their annual crop leap from just below $25 million in 1913 to nearly $118 million in 1918.[22] The equivalent in 2023 dollars would be $2.3 billion.

Such sudden prosperity in a region accustomed to economic struggle meant that H. H. was moving into Doland as the town was positively booming. Downtown rose from the ashes into brick permanence. The Riley Opera House, capacity 450, screened Tom Mix Westerns and hosted touring thespians. Kitzman's auto dealership sold Buicks and Fords. There were two banks, a bowling alley, and a three-chair barbershop with the first permanent-wave machine in town.[23]

H. H. staked out his share of the jackpot. His drugstore featured the sweet snare of an ice cream parlor with a sixteen-foot burnished oak counter. He sold silverware, cut glass, pocket watches, and clocks; he touted such luxuries as Edison phonographs and diamond rings. And along with legitimate medications for both humans and farm animals, H. H. continued to stock Peruna. "Money don't get a chance to talk when you keep it in your pocket," an advertisement for his drugstore admonished customers. "Give it out."[24]

Yet H. H. was much more than a huckster. While his accomplished brothers brought their knowledge to the world—by the late 1910s, Harry was a plant pathologist for the U.S. Department of Agriculture, and John was a professor of marketing at the University of Kentucky— H. H. brought the knowledge of the world into his own tiny piece of it. He was a man of ideas, ideas he was willing to defend in a parochial place. Informed by Charles Darwin's *The Origin of Species* and Robert Ingersoll's *Why I Am an Agnostic*, H. H. considered himself an atheist in a town where the only theological debate was whether one attended the Lutheran or Methodist church. He incited the suspicious whisperings of Doland's postmaster for subscribing to the "communistic" *New York Times*.[25] In homage to his long-standing hero William Jennings Bryan and the current president, Woodrow Wilson, H. H. counted himself the rare Democrat in a Republican stronghold.

Doland was a place, after all, where the local newspaper offered the following litany of what was wrong with America: "Too many silk shirts; not enough blue flannel ones. . . . Too many satin-upholstered limousines; not enough cows. . . . Too much oil stock; not enough savings accounts. . . . Too much of the spirit of 'get while the getting's good'; not enough of the old-fashioned Christianity."[26]

H. H.'s own wife was one of those old-fashioned Christians, insisting they send their children to church services and Sunday school, despite his freethinking blasphemy. Two years after South Dakota enacted female suffrage, Christine cast her first presidential vote for the Republican candidate, Warren Harding.

H. H. had his own idea of a pulpit. In fact, he had two: his store and his home. Around the soda fountain in his drugstore, he regularly convened what passed for the elite of an egalitarian town: Zarnecke the lawyer, Doc Sherwood, the bankers Brown and George Gross. He welcomed the farmers, too, always offering free coffee to loosen up their taciturn tongues. With Prohibition having shuttered Doland's only saloon, men in search of conversation and camaraderie had few options better than Humphrey's drugstore. It was, in the words of one, "the mecca of sophistication."[27] H. H. radiated enough charm and integrity to win election to the city council in 1917, the first of his four two-year terms. Even so, there was a certain amount of behind-the-scenes grousing about the "bombastic" druggist whose voice "filled the whole store."[28]

Riding the crest of Wheat Belt bounty, H. H. was finally able to buy a home, and it was a grand one in a town of build-it-yourself bungalows from the Sears catalog. On the day after Christmas of 1918, H. H. paid about $4,500[29] for a two-story four-square house that had been custom designed for its original owner. The dining room boasted oak archways and leaded windows and a built-in stained-glass buffet. The living-room ceiling was decorated with stencils of flowers and birds.[30] A small orchard of apples and plums flanked the house. And, most extravagantly of all, nearly four hundred miles from Lake Superior and more than a thousand miles from any ocean, the Humphrey home was topped by a widow's walk.

H. H. created his sacred place in the library, packing its shelves end-to-end with history books, complete sets of Shakespeare and Dickens, and albums of classical music, his latest passion. When he got home each night from the drugstore, normally around ten o'clock, he summoned his children out of their beds for his secular sermons. The congregation now numbered four, with daughters Frances (born in 1914) and Fern (1917) joining their older brothers Ralph and Hubert. H. H.'s goal for the children, and most especially for his precocious namesake, was to be "raised in the atmosphere of the common man, yet with a cultural background unexcelled by the most privileged."[31]

Much as his mother had held forth during his own childhood, H. H. now assumed the declamatory role. Twice a year, he read aloud Bryan's "Cross of Gold" speech. He would put his two favorites, Hubert and Frances, on his lap as he recited Woodrow Wilson's "Fourteen Points," the principles for peacemaking after the Great War.[32] H. H. quoted favorite passages from Lincoln and lectured from

Edward Gibbon's *History of the Decline and Fall of the Roman Empire.*
More temporal lessons about national politics came from newspaper
columns, and H. H. sometimes punctuated them with the admonition
to his most devoted listener, "You should know this, Hubert. It might
affect your life someday."[33] The seminars only ended when Christine
appeared at the library portal to plead with H. H., "Let the children get
some rest."[34]

The paternal education of Hubert, though, only paused for the necessity of sleep. It resumed each afternoon when school let out and Hubert
reported to the drugstore for duty. If Hubert ever had an idle moment
between serving sodas and washing dishes in those vocational hours
before dinner at home, H. H. would rouse him with the command, "Ac-
ti-vi-ty, ac-ti-vi-ty."[35] From his perch at the counter, Hubert could eaves-
drop on H. H.'s conversations with customers, and it struck the boy
how his father treated the farmers—smelling of sweat and harness oil,
spiky bits of wheat stuck in their hair, gear grease staining their hands—
just as respectfully as he did the lawyer and doctor. "High-hatting any/
one," H. H. put it, "was strictly taboo."[36]

The rule applied most indelibly to Hubert's classmates. As narrow
as the range of social class was in humble, homogenous Doland, a veneer of professional people hovered above the broad middle, and a
slice of the poor languished beneath it. Their neighborhood was called
Shantytown.[37] On the east side of Doland, separated from the rest by
a creek, the area got its name because much of the housing there still
consisted of the kind of claim shanties that the homesteaders of the
1880s had thrown together with foot-wide wood planks. By the 1920s,
decades of severe weather and itinerant inhabitation later, the shacks
belonged mostly to farm laborers, some with families. Unlike most
homes in Doland, their dwellings rarely had running water and still
used backyard privies.[38] Tar paper patched the leaky roofs and newspaper insulated the walls.

Christine Humphrey was characteristically uneasy about Hubert
having friends there, much as she had been about his hanging around
with the Black road crew, and H. H. just as characteristically urged the
boy on. H. H. insisted that the ragamuffins of Shantytown be invited

to Hubert's birthday parties in the stately four-square house. On a less celebratory day, Hubert brought a Shantytown playmate into the family drugstore and informed H. H., "Jonathan here doesn't have any shoes, and his feet are so cold, they're blue." H. H. hit the NO SALE key on the cash register, extracted a handful of bills, and took Jonathan to a dry-goods store down Main Street for a set of heavy boots and wool socks. This was not an act of charity, H. H. emphasized to his son, but of "elemental justice."[39]

* * *

The ninety-eighth meridian runs almost exactly through Doland. That geographical fact carried profound meaning for the scientists of the early twentieth century who were just beginning to study the vicissitudes of agriculture in the Great Plains. The meridian carved a seemingly monotonous landscape into two versions and two destinies. East of it, rain fell and crops grew reliably; west of it, neither could be assumed. "At this *fault* the ways of life and living changed," one scholar put it, aptly employing a seismological metaphor. "Practically every institution that was carried across it was either broken and remade or else greatly altered."[40]

During the 1880s, soon after settlers first broke the sod west of Doland, the soil was so enriched by millennia of buried carbon that wheat flourished. The decade happened to be a relatively wet one, too, lending seeming confirmation to the land promoters' promise that cutting the prairie's crust would conjure the rain. The wartime boom of the 1910s fed the delusion of dependable bounty.

Good luck, however, did nothing to move the meridian or to alter the climatic realities. Doland received about twenty inches of rain a year, barely enough to sustain what was called "dry farming," which meant trying to draw on every molecule of water stored in the soil to augment the insufficiency of what fell from the sky. Just 150 miles east, the yearly rainfall reached about thirty inches, providing an essential margin to mitigate nature's whims.

While the Doland area as a whole was perched on the precipice between fecundity and desolation, each farm operated as an intricate contraption of interlocking parts. The failure of any one element imperiled the entire apparatus, which was to say a family's financial survival. The typical farm of 320 or 640 acres grew wheat to sell, corn to feed hogs, hay to nourish cows, and chickens to lay eggs. A vegetable garden supplied the kitchen table, and the "egg money" gleaned from selling crates of them at the creamery filled the household till. The modest ideal was to end the harvest with wheat seed in reserve for the next spring's planting, a year's worth of hay in the barn, a few smoked hams from slaughtered hogs socked away in airtight cans, and enough healthy livestock to sell a couple head for money to pay the property tax and mortgage and buy everyone in the family one set of new clothes.[41] "There is nothing new on the farm," wrote one chronicler. "We know it all intimately—the long hours, the sweaty, stinking heavy underwear, the debt and the mortgage, the way it feels to drag in at twilight after a day in the field and to sit on the doorstep and pull from our aching feet our brogan shoes before we eat the coarse evening meal."[42]

For the people of Doland, and for the farmers on the outskirts whose success or failure ordained the town's, 1920 began with the appearance of a record-breaking year, a year to banish all the lingering doubts. The rains came regularly. The bushel price for wheat at the Doland depot stood at $2.40, the most it had ever been.[43] South Dakota had ended 1919 with the highest per capita income of any state, $909.[44] Ordinarily frugal people felt confident spending nearly twice that on a new Studebaker. Farmers borrowed against the escalating value of their land, sinking the cash into gasoline tractors to replace their horse-drawn plows. For his part, H. H. splurged on a two-week vacation in the Upper Midwest's big city of Minneapolis with his family.

Then, for reasons both nearby and distant, the bubble began to leak. Congress allowed the federal law authorizing price supports for wheat to expire. The breadbasket countries of Western Europe, at peace again, sowed and reaped their own crops. The American military decommissioned millions of soldiers, removing yet another market for domestic grain. With all those forces driving wheat prices downward, the Federal Reserve grew concerned that banks in farming regions had overextended themselves and pressed them to call in loans. The Fed simultaneously raised the interest rate it charged major banks from four percent in 1919 to seven percent in 1920, further tightening the vise on borrowers. "The bank was the first refuge of the distressed farmer," as a federal report would later put it, but in the year 1920, 35 banks closed in the Federal Reserve district covering about 250 in Minnesota, Montana, and both Dakotas.[45]

Meanwhile, as spring turned into summer, the winds blew into Doland from the south. Most years, that weather pattern was perfectly normal; like the migrant threshing crews, the seasonal winds moved from Texas to Saskatchewan. But in 1920, as in a handful of similarly hexed years in the past quarter-century, those winds carried an inordinate amount of *Puccinia graminis*, a fungus more commonly known and feared by wheat farmers as stem rust.

The stem rust arrived in June and July, those months when the spring wheat crop was just flowering. Spores attached to the stem of a plant, and in warm, damp weather they germinated into the red pustules that gave the fungus its colloquial name. Like a leech or a tick or a tapeworm, those parasites of the animal kingdom, stem rust latched onto another living thing to nourish itself. It sank a kind of fungal spear called haustoria into the wheat stem and sucked out the nutrition—nitrogen, proteins, water—before the plant could rise upward into a stalk. Without food, wheat starved.

In untroubled years, wheat would reach chest-high by harvest time. Stalks shimmied in the wind, a faint hiss issuing from the vibrating leaves. The fields gave off a sweet, almost nutty, smell. In the years of stem rust, like 1920, the stems would be so weakened within a few days of attack that they would break and topple over—"lodged" in farmer parlance. The threshing crews who made their way through the afflicted plants would end their days so covered in stem rust they called it "red rain." At the worst, a field that could yield forty bushels an acre might produce barely five.[46]

Stem rust spoiled fully one-fifth of South Dakota's wheat crop in 1920, a toll that would not be surpassed for fifteen years.[47] The damaged land, in turn, served as a vacuum to be filled by sow thistle, a perennial plant that sank roots as much as ten feet deep, enabling it to thrive even in dry years, and spread its seeds as easily as dandelion tufts on the persistent winds. "It takes over," a reference book about South Dakota weeds put it, "and smothers farm crops."[48] Surveying its flowers and leaves, farmers called sow thistle the "yellow peril" and an "invading horde," conflating the era's anti-immigrant sentiment with an ecological scourge.[49]

Sow thistle and similarly aggressive Russian thistle—tumbleweed by any other name—afforded a feast for South Dakota's native jackrabbits. Their insatiable appetites also turned to what remained of the legitimate crops, which they would feast on down to the stubble. It was said, with a mix of exasperation and awe, that a jackrabbit could eat as much as a horse. And no matter how often farmers assembled crews to shoot or club the scavengers, their number only seemed to grow.

So as 1920 wound toward its end, the wheat lands of South Dakota resembled Egypt in the time of Joseph's prophecy—fat years brutally ended by lean years. It had its own version, too, of the plagues enumerated in the Book of Exodus, from stem rust to sow thistle to jackrabbits.

By April 1921, the bushel price of wheat at the Doland depot had slumped to $1.25, barely half what it had been a year earlier. South Dakota's per capita income, the highest of any state at $909 in 1919, plunged two years later to $312, second worst in the nation.[50] For the individual farmers outside Doland and elsewhere in the so-called Wheat Belt, the precariously interdependent household economy fell into pieces. The wheat that farmers salvaged was fetching a paltry price, and so they sold livestock to balance the books, a stopgap measure that merely shunted an ever-more-dire problem into the next growing season. Farmers who had taken loans when crop prices were soaring and land value was surging no longer had the means of paying their debts, and the ads for foreclosure auctions started to pop up in the pages of Doland's *Times-Record*.

These were the people who gave H. H. business at the drugstore. Their purchases paid for the four-square house. Their profligate ways in the boom years had been matched by H. H.'s own, the way he stocked his store with diamond rings and Victrolas and radios, such luxuries. Now the farmers' misery inevitably became H. H.'s as well. They paid him with a side of beef or a clutch of chickens, which Christine would then transform into chicken-salad sandwiches to be sold at the soda fountain. Or else those farmers just depended on the credit H. H. advanced them, partly out of compassion and partly for lack of any better choice.

With his nightly orations to his children, with his kindness to needier people like Hubert's friend Jonathan, H. H. aspired to ignore the quicksand on which he was standing. The very trait that made him a proud, unbowed dissident in his politics, that absolute faith in his own judgment, also made him stick to the "marble floor" pretensions of his store. His advertisements for it epitomized a willful optimism that barely papered over impending desperation:

> These are the days that try men's souls, the heavy laden and financially distressed will at this time shrink. But remember that he who stands it now will reap a harvest worthy of their efforts.[51]

> Brace up! Brush up! Think up! And you will get up.
> Think down! Look down! Act down! And you will stay down.
> Paint your face with a smile, advertise that you are a success, then think and work for it.[52]

As months passed and wheat prices kept falling, as farms went into foreclosure and banks shut their doors, as the 1922 growing season unfolded under blistering skies, H. H. ceased the performance. The family took in a boarder for extra income. H. H. missed the deadline for paying $150 in annual property tax. He went half a year without advertising in the *Times-Record*, surely a sign of his dwindling income, and when he resumed it was to promote utilitarian products: formaldehyde to destroy smut, which was a form of wheat fungus, and a serum to inoculate hogs against cholera, the latest curse.

America as a whole had plunged into a recession at the same time that South Dakota's had started in 1920. But by 1922, the resurgence to be known as the "Roarin' Twenties" was underway in urban America, even as places like Doland slid deeper into distress. That contrast fed both envy and resentment, the belief that somebody else—the big-city bankers and railroad barons, but also the union workers striking for better wages—was benefiting at rural America's expense. "The entire world has been desiring a 'return to normalcy,'" stated an editorial in the weekly newspaper *Dakota Farmer*. "We don't know what the term means and we doubt whether we would recognize it if we ever should meet up with it. . . . In the slump of prices on agricultural products the farming industry crashed right through normalcy into regions beyond."

For a man like H. H., seeking to imbue his children with unprejudiced benevolence, the hardening mood around Doland, no matter how justified in certain ways, presented a challenge. It was a challenge, too, to keep up his own spirits for the sake of his family, to fill Hubert with support and excitement about befriending those Black men on the road crew, no matter that Christine disapproved, no matter that the *Times-Record* cracked the periodic joke about "pickaninnies."[53] Those few days in August 1922, topped off by the Saturday night of strawberry soda pop at the pool hall, might have been the most thrilling days of Hubert's eleven-year-old life.

Two months later, another defining day arrived. It was the Friday of October 27,[54] an unseasonably balmy afternoon, when Hubert arrived home from sixth grade. The impending weekend featured a high school football game, one of the boy's favorite distractions, and the final costume preparations for Halloween. Normally, H. H. would have been in the drugstore, waiting for Hubert to begin his shift at the soda fountain, but the boy spotted his father under the cottonwood tree in the front yard of the four-square. With a grim cast to his face, H. H. was standing next to Christine, and she was sobbing. Beside both the Humphreys stood a man whom Hubert had never seen before, and he, too, had solemn expression.

"Dad has to sell the house to pay our bills," Christine told Hubert.[55]

H. H. meanwhile exchanged a few more words with the man and then signed a paper. As the man departed, H. H. began to weep. He wept, surely, for the loss of his beautiful home and for the loss of face that it meant. He could just as well have wept for having his reckless streak revealed to the son who worshiped him.

When H. H. had bought the four-square back in 1918, he had not gone to a bank or insurance company for his mortgage. He had turned instead to a wealthy farmer named Frederick Bastian, eighty years old with more than a thousand acres to his name, who had recently retired to the county seat of Redfield. Several weeks into 1919, Bastian loaned H. H. $2,500, covering more than half of the home's purchase price, but on severe terms: 7.5 percent interest, which was several points above the regional average,[56] and with all the principal due in just three years. As of October 1922, H. H. was nine months overdue without the slightest prospect of raising the necessary $2,500, not with local wheat prices now down to ninety-two cents a bushel and the Main Street economy shriveling. Frederick Bastian had died by this time, but his wife as the executrix of his estate was dunning H. H., with the looming threat of dispossession and public disgrace.

Into H. H.'s parlous situation appeared the stocky and vigorous figure of Bernard Heer, a middle-aged farmer with 160 acres outside of town. Amid the downturn in crop prices, Heer had recently auctioned off his farm equipment and livestock and rented his fields to a brother. The combination made him a rarity in Doland that awful year: someone with lots of money to spend. The paper that H. H. had signed as Hubert looked on was a deed specifying that Heer would pay off H. H.'s entire mortgage debt and add another $6,100 in cash to acquire the house. H. H. could put a portion of the money into keeping his drugstore afloat and ration out the rest in monthly rent wherever his family wound up.

Their destination turned out to be several blocks north along Iowa Street and several steps down the social-class ladder. They moved into a mail-order house barely half the size of the four-square, its upstairs bedrooms pinched by the slope of a gambrel roof. Officially designated as Style E by its maker, a Sears competitor called Aladdin, it was marketed as the "Wonder House."[57] And the build-it-yourself Dutch Colonial was indeed wonderful for families that could spend less than a thousand dollars to have their first home. But in a town as insular as Doland, the Humphreys' descent escaped nobody's view. H. H. installed his library altar, and Christine hosted dinners for the ladies' auxiliary from church. Yet they were reduced to inhabiting what one of Hubert's childhood friends bluntly dubbed "that miserable yellow thing."[58]

Not even Hubert's ebullient nature could ignore the blow. He later described it as a "total and public humiliation," and he revisited that shame periodically in his speaking and writing. "This event was probably the most profound experience of my early years. It was the moment I ceased being a child, when I began to have an adult's awareness of the pain and tragedy in life," he put it one article. "When I was very young," he confided to an interviewer, "for all practical purposes the joys of childhood came to an end."[59]

* * *

In the weeks after that teasingly clement day when H. H. sold the four-square house, the weather turned cruel. Heavy snow fell and days later melted, swamping the rural dirt roads and cutting off farmers from Doland. A chill, soaking rain ruined Thanksgiving. Then the temperature sank, and even the new gravel road of Highway 212 froze up. Typically for the bedeviled year of 1922, all the precipitation had arrived months too late to save the crops.

The growing season of 1923 brought no relief. In the summer heat, workhorses by the dozen died in the fields. Anthrax broke out among cattle. Prices for wheat sagged so low, dropping to seventy-five cents a bushel by September, that farmers fed the grain to their chickens and hogs rather than sell it at a loss. The *Times-Record*, in a front-page commentary, advised farmers to stop planting altogether: "At the present price it is a losing venture except for the speculators who are making more money than the man who grows the grain."[60]

Into the climate of despair arrived yet another opportunistic and invasive species—not sow thistle or tumbleweed, not jackrabbits, but the hooded knights of the Ku Klux Klan. As the Klan spread into the North in the 1920s, for a time controlling the state of Indiana and the city of Denver, it opened klaverns across South Dakota, some as close to Doland as the county seat of Redfield and the railroad hub of Huron.[61]

While South Dakota offered little in the way of Black people for the Klan to terrorize, there being only 832 in a state of 637,000 in 1920, the presence of Catholics and immigrants from Eastern and Southern Europe sufficed for scapegoats. Taking advantage of the economic distress in the Wheat Belt, building on the bond of fundamentalist Christianity, and pragmatically paying members for recruiting their neighbors, the Klan presented itself as utterly mainstream, in the words of one flyer, "Pro-American, Pro-Gentile, Pro-White and Protestant."[62]

By the hundreds, Klan members marched and rallied from Rapid City on the far side of the Black Hills to Sioux City on the Minnesota border. They burned crosses in Yankton, whose Black community of about 115 was the largest in the state.[63] One night in mid-August 1923, it was Doland's turn, with a cross set aflame on the outskirts of town.[64] The knights' object could have been the Catholics in nearby Turton. It could have been the "Rooshins" of the Hutterite colonies with their communal, pacifist version of Protestant faith.

Whatever its purpose, the Klan's display was not lost on H. H., who was already an alien figure with his freethinking ways and liberal politics. The approach of berobed hatred added one more element of danger to the growing list he faced. With his regular customers reeling from the worsening farm crisis, H. H. took to pushing practical items—house paint, hot-water bottles, rat poison. He enrolled in a veterinary course to learn how to concoct his own medicines for farm animals, driving out into the countryside to administer doses at a dime apiece. Things could have been worse; the Riley furniture store, which was upstairs from H. H.'s drugstore, was accepting corn in lieu of cash by the fall of 1923.[65] It closed early the next year.

H. H. vested his favored son with the adult responsibilities of tracking the drugstore's inventory and sterilizing the syringes used for animal serums.[66] Outside the store, Hubert earned three dollars a day during hunting season flushing pheasants out of the brush for shooting teams. He even sold gopher tails on the streets of Redfield for two bucks apiece. By age twelve, Hubert was buying his own clothes, saving his own money, all too aware of his father's limited ability to support the family.

Hubert's maturation included a continuing political education from his father. H. H. began nine months as Doland's acting mayor in July 1923, followed by election as city council president, more or less the high points of his local political career. He brought Hubert along to the council meetings, where, as Hubert later recalled, "He would . . . put me in a chair by the corner window, and then he'd do battle, hour after hour. Toward the latter part of the evenings, I'd doze off, but I'd wake up when Dad hit another climax."[67] The most memorable involved H. H.'s futile fight against a plan to sell the municipally owned electric company into private hands. The lesson Hubert extracted was the virtue of battling, even in defeat, for a righteous cause.

Indeed, Hubert was growing into the contours of his father's personality with its indomitable optimism. Put another way, he was learning how to avert his eyes from the travails of the household, including H. H.'s delusions of grandeur, by hurling himself into every available activity. With his sister Frances, Hubert sang at intermission of the Westerns and Hollywood romances showing at the Riley Opera House. On that same stage, he performed in elementary school operettas. Still too young to join the high school football team, he lugged its equipment to the gridiron and then prowled the sidelines as self-appointed cheerleader, taunting the rival squad as the home crowed urged him on, "You tell 'em, Pinky." When an indignant young fan of one opponent threatened to "knock your block off," Hubert tipped his cap and taunted, "You'll have to catch me."[68]

Starting high school in the late summer of 1925, Hubert became author of the "HI-SCO-PEP" column in the *Times-Record*. There he put into print his first campaign of political advocacy:

Basketball practice is now in full sway and every one is working hard. But we find as we "get-a-going" how great a difficulty we have to meet in playing in this gymnasium of ours. As everyone knows, who has ever played in our gym, or who has watched a game there, our floor space and seating facilities are absolutely inadequate. Why wait to build a new gymnasium. We must have one sometime and why not now! . . .

Our school has pep, spirit, and sportsmanship. It is one of Doland's greatest achievements. Isn't it the public's turn to show its pep, spirit and sportsmanship by building us a new gym? Does the public want Doland High School to be laughed at because of its gym? Some of our neighbors refuse to play us on our home floor. They say our gymnasium is a slam [*sic*] to the school and the community. Now let us "come to life" and all boost for a new gym.[69]

The surrounding misery, however, was ultimately unignorable. By 1925, total land value in Spink County was down to about $50 million, compared with $90 million just five years earlier; in terms of net worth, the county's farms had fallen back to their level in 1910.[70] Farm foreclosures in the county increased from 16 in 1921 to 86 in 1924.[71] Though bushel prices for wheat somewhat recovered to a statewide average of $1.35 by 1925,[72] that was still far below the coveted "two-dollar wheat" of the wartime boom. As if sensing that Doland was a losing venture, the same Chicago & North Western railroad that had established the town forty years earlier reduced service from twice daily to once—a mail train one day, a freight the next. The night watchman at the Doland depot got laid off.[73]

Yet when the conditions argued for caution, H. H. once again succumbed to his huckster's streak, his Peruna streak. It took the form now of trying to sell classical record albums. H. H. ordered dozens upon dozens of 78s from RCA's elite Red Seal label, and then he set to convincing the subsistence farmers and struggling townspeople that what they really needed was the uplifting sound of Fritz Kreisler or Sergei Rachmaninoff or Enrico Caruso. H. H. played the records on a Victrola in the drugstore for his captive audience; he loaded the records into his truck and plied the same farm-to-farm route he used for hog serum.

Invariably, he returned home with stacks of unsold albums. "Mom, they just didn't sell," he would sigh to Christine. She knew then that her modest hopes for a rug or a davenport were fruitless, and no amount of shuffling apology from H. H. reduced the sting. Trying to dispel the familial gloom, Christine would play the piano and lead her children in sing-alongs. But her sister Olga, a frequent visitor, could see Christine growing more nervous, more agitated, more finicky, wilting under the pressure of the household's unreliable provider and resenting the unending hours he spent at the drugstore with his business schemes and political dreams.[74]

H. H. had some prominent company in his ill-founded optimism. The two banks in town—the State Bank of Doland and the Security State Bank—had vastly increased their lending during the giddy years of the wartime boom, tripling and nearly quintupling their exposure, respectively.[75] All the risk appeared to be cushioned by a program begun in 1916 by South Dakota's progressive governor, Peter Norbeck, which guaranteed that the state would cover depositors' losses.[76]

But when the Great War ended and federal farm supports were removed, the price of wheat tumbled. And virtually every loan the Doland banks had made depended directly on the value of wheat or the land on which it was grown. The State Banking Commission began flagging the Doland banks as early as 1921 for "excessive loans" and pressing them to write off the most dubious altogether. Repeatedly from 1923 through 1925, the State Bank of Doland and Security State Bank were only "conditionally approved." As bank failures accelerated throughout the state—there were twenty-two in the last three months of 1925 alone from several hundred banks statewide—South Dakota's fund to compensate depositors was itself running low on money.[77]

H. H. and the other customers of Doland's banks knew almost nothing of the grim facts. Doland's banks took large ads in the *Times-Record* showing perfectly balanced books for the year 1925 and boasting of their dividends to depositors. "A Bank of Strength and Character," proclaimed the ad for the State Bank of Doland. In a local news column heralding the new year of 1926, the *Times-Record* itself attested that "these institutions are in good financial condition."[78]

Merely four days after that sunny assessment, the state dispatched an examiner to comb through the books of the State Bank of Doland. He arrived at a drastically different conclusion, citing "excessive loans," "poor and irregular cash items," and too many investments in real estate that was "heavy and slow and subject to prior encumbrances." Five months later, on June 9, 1926, state officials declared the bank insolvent and shut it down. In early August, trying to avoid the same fate, the Security State Bank suspended its operation in the hope of reorganizing.[79]

H. H. lost twice over. His entire business account, placed with the State Bank of Doland, evaporated with its June demise. He hurriedly deposited his remaining cash into Security State Bank, only to have that money frozen with the bank's suspension.[80] Even Hubert, by his adolescent's standards, got wiped out, losing the $140 he had conserved over years of peddling newspapers and magazines.[81]

Tales of instant dispossession swirled through Doland. One involved an immigrant named Oscar Schultz, who had started out as a field hand and saved and invested his money until he owned five farms and was a general partner in the State Bank of Doland. Because of that position, his property was being seized as part of paying the bank's debts. At age sixty-five, Schultz "went back to assembling farm machinery as a day worker."[82] Then there was the rumor that George Gross, president of the Security State Bank, had committed suicide. While that lurid account was untrue, Gross indeed suffered a breakdown and slunk off to Minneapolis to find work managing a pool hall.[83] It fell to the Doland's grain elevator company to cash people's checks.

In the faces of the townspeople, Hubert saw "despair . . . the look . . . of uncertainty, of unpredictability," as he later said in an interview, "a sense of fear and hopelessness which seemed to grip them." At age fifteen, he drew an adult lesson that went beyond immediate sympathy or shock for Doland's victims. For the first time, Hubert perceived the might of systemic forces, forces that swept in from a distance, like a prairie twister, and smashed the lives in their path. "One learns that no matter how competent his father may have been or how good his mother or how fine a community," Hubert recalled, "it could be destroyed or it could be wrenched or it could be injured with forces over which he or his parents had no control. That this little secure world of his home town just wasn't strong enough to fight off or resist the powerful economic and social forces that seem to be crowding in upon them."[84]

* * *

In October 1924, almost exactly midway between the Humphrey family's twin crises of losing their home and their bank savings, a new minister named Albert Hartt arrived in Doland to assume the pulpit of the Methodist Episcopal Church. Because the church parsonage stood near Doland's single school, Reverend Hartt headed there with his son Julian to register the boy for ninth grade. As the Hartts crossed the schoolyard, Julian recognized a wiry, freckled kid wearing a familiar cap. He was the same twerp Julian had threatened to punch out a year earlier for taunting the high school football team from Groton when it played Doland.

"We've met before," the antagonist said now, extending his hand. "I know who you are, but you don't know who I am. I'm Pinky Humphrey."[85]

So began the closest friendship of Hubert's youth and with it his theological education. Hubert had been baptized as a child in the Norwegian Lutheran church that his mother's family attended in Lily. When the Humphrey family had moved to Doland, Christine assented to sending the children to the Methodist Episcopal Church, as it was the only Protestant congregation in town. If she left it to H. H., she recognized, the children would all grow up as heathens. Hubert dutifully attended Sunday school and heard the conventional doctrine of temperance, purity, and salvation, the last being a kind of coupon earned on earth but only redeemed in the heavenly hereafter.

Then Reverend Hartt came to town, dispatched there as part of the Methodist program of rotating clergy every few years. Though the minister had spent sixteen previous years serving four other churches in South Dakota, he made an unlikely shepherd for a prairie flock. Hartt was a Yankee, born in Maine to a lineage of preachers, ordained as an elder by the Boston University School of Theology. In the parsonage, he kept volumes of Poe, Kipling, Washington Irving, and Robert Louis Stevenson, along with a dictionary, encyclopedia, and multiple Bibles. Reverend Hartt took the concept of citizenship seriously enough that, in his mid-forties with a wife and three children, he had volunteered as a battlefield chaplain in the Great War.

No stranger to the interplay of religion and politics, the Methodist Episcopal Church in America had fractured into northern and southern factions in 1844 over the issue of slavery. In the Civil War's wake, and amid the ostentatious wealth of the Gilded Age, a politically liberal movement began rising within Methodist and other mainline Protestant denominations, reaching its peak just before the Great War. It went by the name of the Social Gospel and its message was often distilled to the phrase, "We believe in deed, not creed."

That aphorism referred to a reversal of fundamentalist Christianity's emphases on personal piety, social conservatism, and biblical literalism as prerequisites for one's heavenly afterlife. Proponents and followers of the Social Gospel while in many cases as personally devout and theologically orthodox as their foes, stressed the doing of good works in this world. They read the Jesus narrative with more of a focus on his ministry to the oppressed than his death on the cross and maintained that establishing the Kingdom of God on earth included such practical efforts as raising wages, shortening work hours, and banning child labor. So fierce was the critique of capitalism among some adherents of the Social Gospel that they argued it was compatible with socialism.

Reverend Hartt did not espouse the Social Gospel, but neither did he denounce it. His own theology, as delivered from the Methodist Episcopal pulpit and summertime revival tents, left the door ajar just enough for progressive influences to slip inside. Decades later, as a prominent theologian himself, Julian Hartt would describe his father's style as "perfectionist piety."[86] To be a faithful Christian, Albert Hartt contended, was "to show forth kindness, humility, generosity, patience in affliction, good cheer: these as well as purity of mind and heart."[87]

Reverend Hartt's church in Doland, appropriately enough, did not have a cross in its "main room," as the sanctuary was called. The unpainted walls instead featured a list of the Ten Commandments. The minister's concern was with character—guarding against pride, pretension, artifice, and boastfulness—and with the importance of service. His biblical model of such service came from the Sermon on the Mount: "Whosoever shall compel thee to go a mile, go with him twain."[88] In plainer language, Jesus's admonition urged Reverend Hartt to do more than what is required, to put out extra effort, particularly on behalf of another person, and most especially one who is needy.[89] The formulation hardly qualified as radical, and yet it rebuked the notion shared by frontier pioneer and skyscraper tycoon alike that all failure is personal in nature and attributable to the individual shortcomings that Christianity calls sin.

At the same time, Reverend Hartt privately held the conventional prejudices of the day. Along with the *Saturday Evening Post*, he subscribed to the *Dearborn Independent*, Henry Ford's newspaper, with its weekly compendium of anti-Semitic calumnies. He reviled Irish Catholics as "the scum of the earth,"[90] blaming them for corrupt political machines and the scourge of alcohol alike. Yet, when a bootlegger outside Doland shot dead a federal agent, it was Reverend Hartt who gently broke the tragic news to the slain man's brother—a Catholic priest in the nearby town of Turton.

Under Reverend Hartt's aegis, Hubert and Julian joined the church's Boy Scout troop, which the minister puckishly named the Irregulars. On Sunday mornings, they sat together in the back row of pews, flipping through the hymnal and offering their own bits of humorous dissidence: "You better yield to temptation, because yielding is fun."[91] In truth, neither Hubert nor Julian would dare such a thing. They unflinchingly obeyed Reverend Hartt's commands not to swear, not to cheat, not to dance, not to tell or so much as snicker at a dirty joke. Drunkenness and fornication were beyond the boys' imaginings.[92]

By the standards of a remote town in the Great Plains, Hubert and Julian were a couple of hothouse flowers, unashamed of their attraction to the life of the mind. Besides the usual schoolyard games, they concocted a version of cricket using a broomstick for a bat. Their idea of fun included drawing out maps of Caesar's Gallic Wars. Both boys thrived on the nearly classical curriculum promulgated by Doland High School's three or four teachers, most of them college-educated women with no other avenue for their intellectual gifts. Hubert and Julian took four years apiece of Latin and English literature and two of civics in addition to the expected math and science. They paired up on the school's debate team, studying the Lincoln–Douglas debates to learn their rhetorical craft, and they made a complementary team. Julian could better research and present their case, while Hubert had the nimble mind and mouth for rebuttal.

The boys' friendship was paralleled by their fathers'. In Albert Hartt, H. H. found his intellectual equal. He invited the minister to his nightly symposium in the drugstore with its disputations about the League of Nations and the proposed seaway through Canada to the Great Lakes. The two men endured the same precarious sense of material security evaporating beneath them. Hartt lost all the money he had saved for Julian's college tuition in the same bank failure that emptied out H. H.[93] As the Hartt household "teetered on the line between Frugal and Meager," as Julian would later write, Doland's butcher once refused to hand over a Thanksgiving turkey until the minister paid down a few dollars of his debt.[94]

After decades as a committed atheist, H. H. converted under Reverend Hartt's influence in 1926 and soon was teaching the men's Bible study class. In this newest podium, he could wrap his progressive politics in scriptural cloth. Far more than the minister, H. H. directly addressed the concept of unmerited suffering and the imperative for society to redress it. "His emphasis was on the social imperatives of religion," Hubert later recalled. "A heavenly city, according to Dad, could be created on earth through good works."[95]

For Hubert and Julian, the righteous subversion of that old-time religion also occurred through their chapter of the Epworth League, the nationwide organization of Methodist youth. Named for the English birthplace of Methodism's founder John Wesley, the Epworth League had twenty thousand chapters in the United States by the turn of the century[96] and provided a conduit for the Social Gospel to reach young people like the Doland pair who were looking for a moral language of social reform. The league very deliberately included a Department of Mercy and Help, which helped to establish industrial schools, employment bureaus, and day nurseries.[97]

The *Epworth Herald*, the weekly magazine for chapters in the North, wrote approvingly of the interracial and interreligious clubs emerging on college campuses. It extolled Mohandas Gandhi for "preaching for the present age" in his struggle against "the exploitation of the poor by the capitalist."[98] It assailed both the Jim Crow racism of the South and, presciently amid the Great Migration, "the Northern white man [who] is apparently as hostile and as little interested in the welfare of the Negro as his Southern brother."[99] It published Harry Emerson Fosdick, the celebrated and controversial pastor of Park Avenue Baptist Church in New York, as he evoked the "thrilling" history of Christian social activism, from antiquity right up to the present:

> When Jesus headed toward Jerusalem rather than prove false to his cause, that was thrilling. When Paul said, "I have fought the good fight" that was thrilling. When [Lord] Shaftesbury made up his mind that no matter what it might cost he would redeem the British children from the mines and factories, that was thrilling. When [William] Wilberforce decided that if it meant his death he would break the grip of the British slave trade, that was thrilling.[100]

Very close to home for Hubert, a South Dakota newspaper editor named Francis H. Case used the *Epworth Herald* to deliver a broadside against "counterfeit patriotism" and "the blind reverence of the past." He argued, "America to-day is not the America of 1776 and never can be again. The America of George Washington legalized slavery. The America of Abraham Lincoln legalized the liquor traffic. The America of Theodore Roosevelt largely forbade women the right to vote. We live in a changing America, a country on the march. . . . Patriotism, genuine, means devotion to one's country's good. It is not enough to be blindly loyal; one must be intelligently, thoughtfully loyal."[101]

The question of what form America should take landed squarely in Doland, and in the friendship of the Hartt and Humphrey families in late June 1928, just after Hubert had turned seventeen and finished his junior year of high school. As the chairman of the Spink County Democratic

Party and an impending candidate for state legislature, H. H. drove to Houston for the national convention that would nominate Al Smith for president. The first Catholic standard-bearer for a major party, Smith was a "wet" on Prohibition and a product of New York's Tammany Hall machine, even though he had gone on to compile a progressive record on labor and social-welfare issues as governor of New York. His political base among urban Catholics and Jews set him starkly apart from the Democrats' faction of agrarian, Protestant populists, led for decades by William Jennings Bryan with his mixture of egalitarian economics and nativist bigotry. At the Democratic convention in 1924, when Smith had been defeated after a record-setting 103 ballots, Bryan had declared of Smith's raucous supporters, "You are not the future of this country." Unless, of course, they were.

Despite H. H.'s long-standing admiration for Bryan, he had returned from Houston smitten with Smith. He regaled the nightly drugstore convocation with tales of the speeches and floor fights from the convention. "He showed off his souvenirs as if they were holy relics," as Hubert later recalled. "His delegate badge, Al Smith posters, and a little brown Al Smith derby made of cardboard."[102]

Then H. H. made the mistake of trying to persuade Reverend Hartt to vote for Smith against the Republican opponent, Herbert Hoover, setting off a testy exchange. Why did it matter so much to the minister that Smith opposed Prohibition, when it was a "dismal and bloody failure"? To this Hartt shot back that "the Liquor interests were 100 percent behind Al the Boozer," as the minister's son Julian later recalled in a memoir. Even worse, were Smith to be elected, the Pope would "be there exercising his demonic influence."[103]

Undeterred, H. H. pressed his case. "Now look here, Albert," he said. "Al Smith was the best governor the state of New York has ever had, and that's the consensus of the people who know the score." Then he applied the intended coup de grâce. "And I suppose you don't know that Hoover is well known as a connoisseur of bourbon, which is a *whiskey*, Albert."[104]

As the presidential campaign unfolded in the fall, Hartt stopped talking to H. H., and a severed friendship was not the only price

H. H. paid for his principle. One night, the Ku Klux Klan made a re-turn visit to Doland, burning a cross on one of the few hills west of town.[105] H. H. took the ritual not only as a general warning about the peril of a Catholic president but also as a specific threat against him.

For 1928, at least, such bigots need not have worried. As one tiny part of Hoover's landslide victory—he took 41 of the 48 states and 444 electoral votes to Smith's 87—the Republican carried Doland by 183 to 81. In his own race for state legislature, H. H. managed to carry Doland, while narrowly losing overall. Uncharacteristically gloating, Hartt wrote about Smith's defeat to Julian, who was starting college at the Methodist school Dakota Wesleyan, that "popery had been met in an open field and soundly thrashed."[106]

Cold peace ensued between the Humphrey and Hartt fathers, one of them teaching the men's Bible class, the other leading Sunday worship, neither budging. Then, after some silent weeks, Hartt worked up the moral resolve to apologize for having started the rift and extended the right hand of fellowship, as it is called in Paul's Epistle to the Galatians. H. H. received it.

Moving through his senior year of high school, Hubert could extract several lessons from the falling out and the reconciliation. One was that holding to your ideals might cost you something as dear as your best friend. The other is that there was always the possibility that a decent person with some small-minded beliefs might find the path to contrition.

* * *

Some days as Hubert sat in his classes at Doland High School, where he entered his senior year in the late summer of 1928, he picked up the whistling sound of the Chicago & North Western passing through town and found his thoughts drifting far from the lesson.[107] On occasion, he walked the tracks, tracing the steel lines to the horizon, and trying to envision the state capital of Pierre some 130 miles to the west and the nation's seat, Washington, DC, more than 1,300 to the east. He yearned to travel such distances to such places, way beyond the ninety-eighth meridian.

Despite his classes in Latin and literature, despite the worldly topics his debate team essayed, despite the lectures from H. H. about ancient Rome and the Fourteen Points, despite the Social Gospel's injunction to repair America's flaws, despite that chance encounter with the Black men of Otis Shipman's road crew, Hubert's palpable world extended for only thirty or forty miles of wheat fields in any direction. Watertown to the east, Huron to the south, Redfield to the west, Groton in the north—those marked the outer rim of his trips to debate tournaments and high school football games.

The chasm between Hubert's dreams and his realities stretched dauntingly wide as he contemplated life beyond high school. There was little doubt, on the one hand, that he had laid down the academic record worthy of a fine college. He had received A's in every class except one marking period of geometry and two when the Latin class read Caesar, and those imperfections were still B-pluses. His extracurricular activities ranged from debate, oratory, drama, glee club, and the school newspaper to track, basketball, and football, the last despite weighing just 140 pounds and being "the lightest guard that played on anybody's football team."[108]

Pitted against all of those credentials was the Humphrey family's precarious financial condition. The likeliest prospects for Hubert's college looked to be either South Dakota State, a relatively inexpensive public institution that cranked out many of the state's teachers, or Dakota Wesleyan, the Methodist school favored by Christine for its religious orientation.[109] Besides, Julian Hartt and Hubert's older brother Ralph were already attending it. By the standards of a family in debt and a state in prolonged recession, having another child enroll at either college would be both a luxury and a sacrifice, as Hubert fully recognized. Neither Brookings nor Mitchell, the homes respectively to S.D. State and Dakota Wesleyan, were exactly the metropolis Hubert imagined at the end of the railroad tracks.

Even so, he moved toward graduation in the spring of 1929 with undiminished achievement. He starred in the title role of the senior play, *Captain Applejack*, portraying a bored rich man who turns adventurer. He was awarded first place in scholastic honors[110] and fêted at the annual Debate-Declamation banquet at the Doland Café. When the high school's fifteen graduating seniors assembled shoulder to shoulder in a daisy chain for their commencement exercises, Doland's weekly newspaper reported, "Hubert Humphrey, as valedictorian, in a sincere and convincing manner spoke the farewell of the class."[111]

Plenty of townspeople fervently hoped that farewell didn't mean goodbye. Farms and burgs throughout the Great Plains were losing their young people, who headed off to Denver or Des Moines or the Twin Cities looking for work. The price of wheat at the Doland depot lagged at ninety-three cents a bushel, barely above the decade's low point, and a tuberculosis epidemic had struck the region's livestock. So it sounded almost plaintive when Doland's downtown merchants, including H. H., bought a full-page ad in the *Times-Record* importuning the graduates to stay home: "As you open the door upon life, in answer to many opportunities knocking thereon, we urge you to remember that right here in this community opportunities await you at every turn."[112]

H. H., in fact, privately defied his public advice. He decided that Hubert—his namesake, his project, his brilliant boy—could enroll at the University of Minnesota in Minneapolis. H. H.'s brothers Harry and John had both gone there, after all, and a part of H. H. had never stopped wishing he had followed them instead of the siren song of Peruna. Hubert would be his scholarly surrogate.[113] Benevolent and narcissistic all at once, H. H.'s choice also carried enormous financial risk, especially with Ralph intending to transfer from Dakota Wesleyan to Minnesota. True to his impetuous nature, H. H. then went ahead and bought a brand-new, gleaming green Model A, which at eight hundred dollars cost nearly twice the average income in South Dakota, to drive his sons the three hundred miles to college.

With nearly eleven thousand students, the University of Minnesota's flagship campus in Minneapolis had triple the population of South Dakota's capital of Pierre, which had been Hubert's notion of a big city. Several days after arriving, he reported with the other thirty-two hundred freshmen to the showplace of the campus, the newly completed Northrop Auditorium. Though the welcome event was modestly called a "glad-hand" ceremony, it clearly intended to imbue newcomers like

Hubert with equal measures of purpose and awe. With its colonnade of Ionic columns, the concert hall had been very consciously modeled on an Ivy League template, Columbia University's Low Library. The procession into it on this day included the university's marching band, ROTC cadets, and faculty and regents in academic robes.[114] "No country boy," Humphrey would recall later of his introduction to the university, "was ever more wide-eyed."[115]

The culture shock quickly showed in and out of the classroom. Hubert was no longer the consensus genius of the bell jar that was Doland. Suddenly his was just one brain amid the aspirational thousands at a major university, and he managed only B's and C's in his first semester.[116] He made it onto the freshmen debate team but was turned down by the school newspaper. His collegiate home was a ten-by-twelve room in an off-campus boarding house. Though H. H. started out staking his son to ten dollars a week for living expenses, that pipeline soon closed, and so Hubert worked for twenty cents an hour washing dishes at the lunch counter of Swoboda's drugstore, where he could also scavenge leftovers for his own dinner.[117] On the weekends when a homesick Hubert returned to Doland, he traveled by thumb.

Indeed, a stark divide in social class added to the difficulty of Hubert's college adjustment. While Hubert had already endured a decade of economic struggle back in Doland, its deprivations seared into his consciousness, for many students the twenties were roaring along just fine. So many undergraduates owned cars that the regents considered banning them from campus to ease the traffic jams. When the Minnesota football team, led by its star fullback Bronko Nagurski, opened its Big Ten season at Northwestern, fifteen hundred Minnesota students rode excursion trains to the game. The pages of the student newspaper, the *Minnesota Daily*, flourished ads for Coty perfume, Finchley hats, and Rothkirk oxfords.[118] And when the campus branch of the YWCA ran a program pairing female students with young women toiling in factories to learn about those lives—exactly the sort of program that the Social Gospel and the *Epworth Herald* advocated—the *Minnesota Daily* sneered, "It is indeed coming to be a democratic world when university coeds don overalls to study at first hand the life of the 'poor working girl.' Nothing evidently can embarrass the preparing welfare worker on the much disdained way to Service."[119]

Then the New York Stock Exchange opened on the morning of Tuesday, October 29, 1929. From August 1921 to September 1929, a period when the Wheat Belt was immiserated, the Dow Jones index had increased sixfold, inflated in part by speculation buying. Then, on October 21 and 23, prices began to fall. On the Monday of October 28, the market plunged by thirteen percent. And Tuesday, soon to be branded "Black Tuesday," saw the worst rout in the stock exchange's history, with a drop of twelve percent and a net loss of $14 billion in period dollars.[120] (The modern equivalent would be $242.5 billion.)

Minneapolis and the university both responded with blithe confidence. Two days after the crash, the *Minneapolis Tribune* ran the banner headline "BUYING FLOOD LIFTS STOCKS"[121] and in an editorial assured readers that the "silver lining to the stock market cloud" is "the fact that the industrial and commercial structure of the United States is quite as strong as it ever was."[122] The *Minnesota Daily* struck a similarly Panglossian tone, opining, "As long as the injury extended no further, results of the spree are probably beneficial."[123]

The downtown skyline, easily visible to Hubert across the Mississippi River from campus, told a different story. Barely two months earlier, a utilities magnate named Wilbur Foshay had opened an eponymous tower modeled on the Washington Monument. At nearly 450 feet, the Foshay Tower reigned as the tallest building in the Midwest; Wilbur Foshay's personal office was appointed in Siena marble and African mahogany. By the end of the week of Black Tuesday, however, the company had plummeted into bankruptcy, and its creditors promptly turned off the electricity to its illuminated FOSHAY sign. That darkness was a portent.[124]

Back in Doland, the market collapse supplied a bit of schadenfreude about the city slickers getting a taste of what the Great Plains had been choking down for nearly a decade. Mostly, though, Doland shrunk into a protective crouch against the newest economic blows. "The bulls and bears wage desperate battles in the stock market," the *Times-Record* observed, "but it is the shorn lambs who usually take the punishment."[125] H. H. contributed to a full-page ad in the newspaper that pleaded, "Our churches, our schools, our business institutions, our public and private enterprises, our present and our future each and all depend on the whole hearted cooperation of every member of the community. Let us all do our share."[126]

As the year 1930 dawned, H. H.'s customers owed him upward of ten thousand dollars. He was so strapped for cash that he was fending off a law firm that was dunning him for a $350 debt. "It has been necessary for me to carry my customers for a long time owing to the continued crop failures, and it has made it increasingly hard for one to meet his own obligations," H. H. wrote as he submitted a ten-dollar payment. "[T]here is only one thing that will bring us all through and that is an appreciation of our own difficulties and indulgence in the other fellow's."[127]

When Hubert and Ralph returned to Doland for summer break, H. H. took his sons aside and explained, "I can't have you and Ralph gone at the same time. I need one of you to help me in the store." As the eldest, Ralph went back to the university first, for the fall term of 1930, supporting himself with Hubert's former job at Swoboda's drugstore.[128] Word of H. H.'s Solomonic dilemma reached his brother Harry in Washington, where he was the chief plant pathologist for the federal Department of Agriculture, and for Christmas he sent Hubert a fifty-dollar check with the note "This is something to start you back to school."[129]

With Uncle Harry's gift to help pay for tuition, Hubert resumed college in the semester that began in January 1931. By waiting tables and sweeping up at the off-campus boarding house, he got free room and board. He recovered his dishwashing job at Swoboda's and made an additional ten or twenty dollars intermittently by tutoring classmates in French.

The precarious equilibrium held only until the third week of February 1931. H. H. drove from Doland to Minneapolis, ostensibly to visit his boys. That he did, but only to reveal the true purpose of his journey. H. H. stopped by Swoboda's one night as Hubert was finishing his shift and then drove them both to H. H.'s hotel. "Son, if I'm going broke, I'm not going to do it in a small town," he told Hubert. "I've got to get out of Doland. We can't make it here."[130]

H. H. had already set his eye on a vacant storefront in Huron, a town of nearly eleven thousand people compared with Doland's six hundred. The problem was that H. H. needed more credit and more merchandise from his distributor, and the goal of the Minneapolis visit was to get both. The next day, H. H. presented himself in alternating shades of abject and upbeat to three officers of the Minneapolis Drug Company, his wholesaler for the previous twenty-five years. He rhapsodized about his longtime friendship with the owners; he pledged his life insurance policy as collateral. Everyone in the meeting already understood that if the company said no, H. H. would simply go bankrupt in Doland. So, in its only hope of being repaid at some distant later time, the company extended and expanded H. H.'s existing loan and advanced him medicines and other goods on consignment.[131]

Ralph left the university within weeks to help H. H. pack up the Doland store and shelve the hog serums and chest oils and throat lozenges and Caruso albums in Huron. Christine remained in Doland for the rest of the school year to lessen the disruption for her daughters Fern and Frances. In his last act in Doland, H. H. forgave thirteen thousand dollars in debt from his customers; with wheat down to fifty-four cents a bushel, the lowest in memory, who could have afforded to repay him anyway?

Hubert finished the winter term in Minneapolis and then dropped out of college to join his father and brother in Huron. Nearing his twentieth birthday, less than two years after riding his intellect and idealism out of Doland, Hubert was back to the ninety-eighth meridian and the straitened circumstances it marked. To save the family money, he and Ralph slept in the basement of the Huron store. Literally and symbolically, Hubert had never sunk lower.

CHAPTER 2

"HORSE-HIGH, HOG-TIGHT, BULL-STRONG"

Black Minneapolis

1931–1937

In the late spring of 1931, as Hubert Humphrey left Minneapolis, presumably forever, a farming couple in southeastern Iowa lost their life's savings in a bank failure. Entering their sixties and desperate to salvage whatever money they could, Ernest and Cora Meredith put a house they owned in Minneapolis for its rental income up for sale.[1] Soon enough, a real estate agent there found a seemingly ideal buyer. He was a World War I veteran, married for a decade, and a mainstay in an American Legion post. Best of all, amid the ravages of the Great Depression, this fellow held a steady job with the post office.

For that potential buyer, Arthur Lee, the prospects looked every bit as promising. During his years of married life in Minneapolis, he and his wife, Edith, had boarded for several years with his brother and then rented a place of their own. The home that was now available, a white clapboard bungalow, was hunched humbly in a neighborhood of Swedes and Norwegians miles south from the soot and clamor of downtown. With two bedrooms on the same floor, the Lees could sleep within earshot of their six-year-old daughter, Mary.[2] And the prospective neighbors were fitting company for a postal clerk—a foreman at a creamery, the manager of a bakery, a tractor mechanic, a tailor. So, on May 25, 1931, Arthur Lee made the four-hundred-dollar down payment on the $4,200 purchase price.

The plan involved just one unconventional element. Arthur Lee happened to be Black, as were his wife and daughter. Perhaps he did not expect race to present a problem, as his two prior residences had been in mostly-white neighborhoods, and he counted a number of white friends at his post office job.[3] The only initial impediment he faced was the standard refusal of any bank in Minneapolis to issue a mortgage to a Black person; instead, he would move into the bungalow on a "contract for deed" arrangement, meaning that he would not actually own the home until he had paid off the entire purchase price in monthly installments and could be dispossessed for a single missed payment. Merciless as the system was, it offered a Black man like Arthur Lee the only way to own a home short of building it himself.

Then word of the Lees' imminent arrival at 4600 Columbus Avenue South reached the people of the Eugene Field Neighborhood Association, apparently through the complaints of the bungalow tenant who was being evicted. The association had been formed four years earlier with the goal of racially purifying the neighborhood. Members voluntarily vowed not to sell or rent to anyone "not of the Caucasian race," and they bought out the handful of Black homeowners already in the vicinity.[4] Initially, representatives of the association tried the same diplomacy with Arthur Lee, offering him a $350 profit if he sold. The members of the association did not perceive themselves to be uncultivated; after all, their leader, Albin Lindgren, was president of a company that printed calendars.

When Arthur Lee spurned the association's offer and kept spurning it even as it escalated by hundreds and ultimately thousands of dollars, the mood of his new neighbors decidedly soured. Soon after the fireworks of Independence Day flared their last, scattered protestors began showing up outside the bungalow on a nightly basis. By the Saturday evening of July 11, 150 surrounded the home, trapping the Lees inside. The next night, even more gathered. Urged on by the grown-ups, teenaged boys spattered the Lee house with black paint and planted signs on the front lawn: "We don't want n——s here," "No n——s allowed in this neighborhood—this means you."[5]

Three thousand whites besieged the house on July 14, hurling rocks at the bungalow and shattering windows as the Lees darkened all the lights lest they be a sniper's target. Police captains fecklessly threatened to arrest the rabble for unlawful assembly. Minneapolis's mayor William Anderson, a liberal who had been elected on a wave of working-class fear and rage about the Depression, offered, equally futilely, to mediate a settlement between the neighborhood association and the Lees. And after either innocently or willfully ignoring the turmoil at the corner of Columbus and Forty-Sixth for nearly two weeks, the major newspapers blasted reports and photographs of it beneath front-page banner headlines: "HOME STONED IN RACE ROW, Police Guard Negro's Home."[6] Arthur Lee was thirty-seven years old, an unprepossessing physical specimen at five-foot-seven and 160 pounds with a fondness for bow ties. But he and Edith were both early members of the National Association for the Advancement of Colored People (NAACP), the civil rights organization that had been founded in 1909, and when a reporter from the *Minneapolis Star* afforded him an interview, Lee spoke with righteous defiance:

> Nobody asked me to move out when I was fighting for this country in France. I am not here to molest anybody. My family will not annoy any one else. They can put up a high board fence between my house and the next one if they want to. All I want is my home and I have a right to establish one and live in it.[7]

The next day, July 15, Minneapolis sweltered in 101-degree heat, and the twilight lasted until nearly ten o'clock. By then, somewhere between three and six thousand whites had thronged the streets nearest the Lee house. Drawn by the recent newspaper coverage, some had driven from as far as Hibbing, an iron-mining town nearly two hundred miles away, and the visitors took up every parking space for dozens of blocks in every direction. As if inured to the stifling heat by the unfolding spectacle, the vigilantes struck a celebratory tone. They wore button-down shirts and ties and fedoras; they wore print dresses and clutched handbags. They stood beneath the spindly trees or plopped down on the curb. Vendors moved through the assemblage, hawking ice cream from pushcarts. And, to dispel the tense tedium, they tossed firecrackers on the Lees' front lawn and hurled stones at their windows, and shouted, "Burn them out!" and "Lynch him."[8]

It so happened, however, that the all-Black American Legion post to which Arthur Lee belonged was meeting that same night at a settlement house in the city's main Black neighborhood, just north of downtown. A retired driver for the post office, one of Lee's former coworkers, burst into the meeting to declare breathlessly, "They're storming Lee's home. We should do something about it." So a delegation of war veterans drove to the Field neighborhood, picked their way amid a hostile crowd shouting death threats, and presented themselves at Lee's front door as allies. They entered the front room, all its lights off, to find another comrade, seated with a rifle across his lap. "You got any guns here?" one of the Legionnaires asked, and someone indicated several upholstered chairs. Hidden inside the cushions were enough pistols and revolvers, even a German Luger that was booty from the Great War, to arm everyone.[9]

"Now, this is Lee's home," counseled one of the Legion members, an attorney named Raymond Cannon. "This home is his castle. Lee can defend it in any way he finds necessary. But you can't do it. Don't do anything rash."[10]

As the white horde began to press toward the Lee house, the police chief on the scene issued an emergency call, summoning every available squad car and motorcycle officer in the city to help guard the house and scatter the mob. Far from defusing a volatile situation, the arrival of the cops only agitated the crowd more. One man yanked an officer off his motorcycle, and it took a half-dozen fellow cops to extricate him from a beating. Elsewhere in the commotion a woman slapped an officer.[11] As a newspaper reporter described it, "a sullen, angry semi-circle of humanity" beleaguered the protective line of police on the Lees' front walk.[12]

For Lee and his Legion comrades, barricaded inside the bungalow, the events surely brought to mind the story of Ossian Sweet. He was a Black doctor who had bought a home in a white section of Detroit six years earlier and been similarly threatened by a white mob. When Sweet fired shots in self-defense, killing one of the white attackers, the doctor wound up charged with murder. That was why Cannon the lawyer had urged caution. Instead of hoisting a gun, one of Lee's protectors lifted the telephone receiver and called in the report of a fire at 4600 Columbus Avenue South.[13] Hook-and-ladder and pump trucks soon arrived, their sirens piercing the mob's catcalls, and firefighters shoved through the crowd with their hoses. Only when the crews gained a clear view of the bungalow did they realize it was a false alarm and retreat. But something about the firemen's wedge disrupted the mob more effectively than all those police had. By two in the morning, though hundreds of white goons remained outside, the American Legion guards decided it was safe enough to leave Arthur Lee and family.[14]

In the succeeding days, both Mayor Anderson and the Lees' lawyer, a white man named H. E. Maag, suggested the family take a "vacation" to let tempers cool. When Lee refused, they next arranged a mediation session between him and the neighborhood association—essentially his would-be murderers—with the goal of pressuring Lee to sell, albeit at a profit. Anderson referred to the white riot as merely a "situation" and a "misunderstanding between individuals and groups." Such things could happen, he opined, when "the rights of one individual or group are imposed upon by the action of another group."[15] In other words, Arthur Lee had brought all this mayhem on himself.

At that point, Lee fired Maag and instead retained the leading civil rights lawyer in the Twin Cities, Lena Olive Smith. She, in turn, wrote to Walter White, the executive secretary of the national NAACP, telling him that for the Lees to surrender their home "would have no effect other than to convince the mob that their action has been successful."[16]

The NAACP raised the Lees' struggle to nationwide significance, comparing it to the Ossian Sweet case. "[W]hat you have is a composite and vivid picture of American civilization, A.D. 1931," declared an article in

The Crisis, the NAACP's monthly magazine, "not in Mississippi, not in Georgia, not in Alabama, but in the far-northern city of Minneapolis, Minnesota."[17]

By the end of July 1931, the nightly police contingent protecting the Lee bungalow had dropped from twenty-six to six. The harassment, however, persisted. When Arthur and Edith Lee's daughter Mary was to start elementary school that fall, the all-white neighborhood school refused her. Instead, she had to travel with a police escort a mile and a half to a mostly Black school. She returned home one day that fall to find that her pet dog had been poisoned.[18]

With the police entirely removed by the summer of 1932, gangs of teenaged boys resumed the nocturnal visitations, sometimes circling the block by car and bicycle, sometimes trampling the lawn. On the night of September 14, Arthur Lee finally exhausted his preternatural patience and strode into his front yard to order the boys off his property. One claimed that Lee had struck him with a stick, and the assault-and-battery case went to municipal court. There a judge found Lee guilty and fined him five dollars. Though the penalty was set so low in recognition of the yearlong tormenting of Lee, the fact remained that he was the only person ever charged with any crime related to his own persecution.[19]

Then, in July 1933, having outlasted all the physical threats, Lee apparently missed a monthly payment on the bungalow and his contract to purchase it was summarily cancelled. The Lees went back to renting, this time in a largely Black neighborhood.

* * *

As the plight of Arthur Lee rose to its volatile climax and then descended to its bitter denouement, a certain railroad porter was paying painstaking attention. His name was Cecil Newman, and in addition to working on a Pullman sleeping car for the Great Northern line out of St. Paul, he edited and partly owned a weekly Black newspaper, the *Twin-City Herald*. During short breaks in his passenger service, Newman tapped out news items on the typewriter he had secreted in a back corner of the coach.

For his editorials, however, Newman waited until the train reached his destination—Seattle if he had manned the entire route of the Empire Builder, Fargo if he had been assigned a shorter haul—and dashed from the station to each city's Carnegie Library. There, taking pencil to paper, he gave voice to all the analysis and emotion that he had tactically muted while hauling the luggage and shining the shoes and preparing the bedding of white travelers. Once finished with the essay, Newman ran again, this time to the post office to ship his commentary by air mail back to his partner in Minneapolis.[20]

"For years," Newman wrote in the immediate aftermath of the white mob's assault, "American Negroes have had to pay the cost of color, placed on his shoulders by the whites. Sooner or later Americans will realize that the cost of racial proscription and prejudice must be borne by all alike. Those who put the burden on Mr. Lee's people should recognize that they are being made to pay for wrongs against a minority group that they for years have tacitly looked upon without a murmur.

"How long does the American white man expect the colored man to accept half portions, anyway?"[21]

One year later, as Lee was being prosecuted, Newman declared, "This case is not the case of Lee alone. It is a case of the people, white and black, who believe in the fundamental laws of the country and the state. It is a case of right against wrong. It is the concern of any man, be he Jew or Gentile, white or black, Protestant or Catholic. This country will never be safe until the rights of every citizen are safe."[22]

With such words, Cecil Newman was not only passing judgment on a specific episode of intolerance. Still shy of age thirty, essentially self-educated, he was asserting his prominence in Black Minneapolis's battle for equal rights. There were other activists in the city who held titles with the NAACP or the National Urban League, founded in 1910 as both ally and rival in civil rights efforts; there were other activists who sought justice through the courts or material gains with labor unions. By way of weapons, Newman had only his newspaper and his calculatedly formal bearing. Out of his Pullman uniform, with complex connotations of both stature and servility, he invariably donned a suit and tie with steel-rimmed spectacles. His oval face and heavy-lidded eyes offered a deceptive expression of serenity, and his close-trimmed hair was precisely razor-parted. With similar exactitude, he calibrated each syllable carefully before speaking in a hushed baritone. But he was a firebrand going incognito in establishment attire. "If he had anger," a relative later recalled of Newman, "you would have read it, versus heard it."[23]

Two generations removed from slavery, Newman had been born on July 25, 1903, in Kansas City. Though neither of his parents went past eighth grade, according to their census records, and they toiled for whites as a saloon porter and a maid,[24] Horatio and Cora Newman fertilized their son's intellect from an early age. Horatio brought home newspapers and magazines that he used to teach Cecil to read, and Cora inherited a library of four hundred books from the widow of a family she served. When Cecil's segregated high school steered him toward the practical occupation of carpentry, "half-heartedly sawing boards in half and dejectedly hammering nails,"[25] he studied the history of global slavery on his own time and read deeply into the writings of the abolitionist journalists William Lloyd Garrison and Elijah Lovejoy. By seventh grade, Cecil was hand-lettering a newspaper for his classmates.

Kansas City offered Cecil repeated examples of the unfinished business of emancipation and Reconstruction, the unredeemed promises of full racial equality. His all-Black elementary school stood one block away from a white one. At age eleven, innocently presenting himself at an amusement park for its children's day, he was turned away. When he captained his high school's Junior ROTC unit, modeling patriotism for the white public to see, his company was "assigned to a tail end position" of a citywide parade.[26]

The experiences predisposed the teenaged Cecil in two foundational ways. First, he apprenticed himself to Chester Arthur Franklin, the activist editor of Kansas City's weekly Black newspaper, *The Call*. From Franklin, Cecil learned both the precepts of journalistic style and the mission of Black newspapers to champion their race. Cecil earned one of his first bylines for an article castigating the Kansas City Board of Education for having no Black administrators or clerks. Second, soon after graduating high school as senior class president, Cecil resolved to leave the racial hostility of Kansas City for what he had heard was the more tolerant atmosphere of Minneapolis. Already married and the father of a son by his eighteenth year, he rode the train northward in May 1922, carrying $1.57 and the address of his sister-in-law, with whom he would stay while scrambling for a foothold.[27] What he already understood, deep in his marrow, was his goal: "If some people shunned me because I was black, it would be my responsibility to show them that they were wrong. I knew that I was the equal of all other men and I would try to live in such a way that others would be aware of this."[28]

It took only days for Minneapolis to disabuse Newman of his favorable impression. During his job-hunting rounds downtown, he stopped into a cafe for a hamburger; as he bit into it, he reflexively recoiled from a thick coat of salt, one of the standard local methods of driving away Black customers. As for work, Newman could find only the degrading position of bellhop at the Elks Club. To plump up his meager salary of fifty-eight dollars a month, Newman began selling the Twin Cities' Black newspaper, the *Northwestern Bulletin-Appeal*, to the club's maids, bellboys, and elevator operators.[29] Before long, he was contributing items to the paper, and also stringing short articles to the *Chicago Defender* and *Pittsburgh Courier*, the nation's two leading Black newspapers. In 1924, when Newman found work through a friend as a Pullman porter, he could finally afford to bring his wife, Willa, and son, Oscar, to Minneapolis.

Even reunited, the family saw little of Newman, consumed as he was by his righteous ambition. Between cross-country trips as a Pullman porter, he heard of a printer in Minneapolis named Joshua Perry who had just opened a shop and was desperate for business. More to the point, Perry had learned the trade at a combined teachers' college and industrial school for Black students situated in Harpers Ferry, West Virginia, the site of John Brown's insurrection against slavery. The two men cut a deal: Perry would hold the title of publisher and get paid for printing, while Newman would serve as part-owner and sole editor. The maiden edition of the *Twin-City Herald* appeared on April 30, 1927, and in an editorial entitled "What of Tomorrow," Newman unleashed a critique of the city he had once envisioned as a sanctuary of opportunity:

Today we in Minneapolis with a population upwards of six thousand suffer from lack of industrial opportunity. The right to work according to ability and training is denied the Negro man or woman. No matter what the ambition, no matter what the ability, no matter what the character of the Negro man or woman may be in Minneapolis, he is condemned to work in jobs—honorable in themselves, 'tis true—but without future, without hope of advancement, without the necessity of educational equipment and therefore poorly paid. Our children face practically a futureless existence. They may go to high school—aye, to college [—] but unless they equip themselves for a profession, they will be forced to seek employment far from Minneapolis—among aliens and strangers.

As a result of this restriction of the right to work, we are forced to live on insufficient incomes and the penalty we pay is a high rate of mortality, of morbidity and a disproportionate amount of crime. This condition is more acute in Minneapolis than any city of its size in America. Nowhere is there so little chance for the colored boy and girl to work.[30]

In his weekly column, "This World," Newman approvingly used the term "Aframerican." He sardonically ranked Southern states in the "Lynch League."[31] In a list of New Year's resolutions for his readers, he started with "Support financially the N.A.A.C.P." and ended with "Tell the children about Frederick Douglass, Toussaint Louverture, Booker T. Washington . . . and other Negroes who have carved their way to fame leaving the world their debtor."[32] No sooner had Adolph Hitler seized power in Germany than Newman drew withering comparisons to homegrown hatred: "Nazis seem to seek the unenviable reputation of America who treats its black citizens like the Hitlerites want to treat the Jews."[33]

Indeed, Newman expressed little appreciation for either major party. Even though a majority of Black votes still went to "the "Party of Lincoln," the Republicans had been backing away from the racial equality promised by Reconstruction for more than a half-century. The ascendant liberal wing of the Democratic Party, embodied by Franklin Delano Roosevelt's New Dealers, had to appease Southern segregationists to win their needed votes in the Electoral College and Congress. For all his veneer of gentlemanly decorum, for all his practiced deference in the Pullman coach, Newman entered his thirties aflame with radicalism. He made no excuse for admiring the Communist Party for its legal defense of the Scottsboro Boys, nine Black teenagers falsely accused of raping two white women in Alabama, and for its nomination of a Black man, James W. Ford, for the vice presidency in 1932. One of the *Herald*'s contributors, an erstwhile postal worker named Homer Smith, even traveled to the Soviet Union to help the Black authors Langston Hughes and Dorothy West make a film about American racism. When one of the *Herald*'s readers lamented to Newman that "the entire Negro press has turned red," he stood his ground:

[T]here are many Negro editors who feel that Negroes should be allied with every political movement and party in the country, including the Communists. . . . We do not expect any of these papers to actually advocate the embracing of the Communist principles in full but most of them have assumed a friendly attitude towards this party largely because it has done something that other parties have failed to do. It has treated the Negro as a man and a component part of the American scheme.[34]

As the half-owner of the *Herald*, however, Newman functioned in a capitalist economy. He and Perry alternated in their defaults—Newman sometimes falling short on Perry's printing bill; Perry sometimes stiffing Newman on the editor's salary. Newman's effort to expand by publishing a national monthly magazine of Black arts and letters, which he grandly called the *Timely Digest* in joint homage to Henry Luce's *Time* and the *Literary Digest*, went bust in February 1932 after only ten months.

By this point, Newman's partnership with Perry was fraying on the mutually irritating pattern of unpaid debts and missed paydays. When Perry simply failed to print an edition one week in July 1934, an acute embarrassment to a newspaperman like Newman, imbued with the gospel of always making your deadline, the editor offered to buy out his partner. Perry declined.

So Newman took the sixty-five dollars from his most recent bi-monthly Pullman pay envelope and rented a storefront on the fringe of downtown's skid row. Then he borrowed several hundred dollars from his web of friends and contacts in Black Minneapolis and hired a new printer. On Friday, August 10, 1934, the *Minneapolis Spokesman* and its companion publication the *St. Paul Recorder* made their debut. In doing so, Newman situated himself among one specific part of the nation's Black intellectual elite. His subset consisted of the editors of the leading Black newspapers, hybrid journalist-activists such as Robert Sengstacke Abbott of the *Chicago Defender*, Robert Vann of the *Pittsburgh Courier*, and Carl J. Murphy of the *Baltimore Afro-American*. In a front-page editorial, Newman promised to "speak out fearlessly and unceasingly against all injustices, discriminations and all imposed inequalities."[35] Considering his first seven years as an editor, he was not bluffing or boasting but merely, in the journalistic tradition, stating facts.

* * *

Sometime in the early 1830s, a U.S. Army surgeon named John Emerson purchased a Black man who appeared in subsequent records by the name of Dred Scott. Emerson took Scott from Missouri, which allowed slavery, to the doctor's next posting at Fort Armstrong in Illinois, a free state. Two years later, in 1836, the military transferred Emerson, along with his human property, to Fort Snelling in what was then the Wisconsin Territory and would ultimately become part of Minnesota.

Under the terms of the Missouri Compromise, which had been enacted by Congress in 1820, slavery was legally barred anywhere other than Missouri that was north of latitude 36'30" in the territories of the north and central plains. Regardless, officers at Fort Snelling routinely kept slaves, and hotels in the emerging cities of Minneapolis,[36] and St. Paul did a lively business with plantation owners escaping Dixie's torrid summers. One of those slave masters was so impressed by the region that he made a loan, worth about $250,000 by current standards, to its newly founded public university.[37]

While Scott was being held at Fort Snelling, he met and married another captive, Harriet Robinson. The couple left the region's supposedly free soil in 1840, returning with Emerson's wife to St. Louis while the doctor served in the Seminole War. Several years after John Emerson's death in 1843, the Scotts sued his widow, Irene Emerson, for their freedom, arguing that their residences in Illinois and what would soon be Minnesota justified their emancipation.[38]

The Scotts' case wound its way for almost a decade through county, state, and federal district courts before landing at the U.S. Supreme Court. There, in March 1857, the justices voted 7–2 that the couple remained chattel, wherever they went, and that, more broadly, Black Americans "had no rights which the white man was bound to respect," as Chief Justice Roger B. Taney declared. In its own time, the Dred Scott decision accelerated America's path to Civil War, and in posterity it remains one of the most repugnant rulings in the high court's history.

Yet when it came to the racial saga of the North—very much including Minneapolis, whose expanding municipal borders would nearly reach Fort Snelling—Justice Taney wrote with a kind of baleful prescience. The abolition movement, he argued, persisted solely "because it was discovered, from experience, that slave labor was unsuited to the climate and productions of these States." Even in them, Taney continued, "the slave trade . . . was carried on, and fortunes accumulated by it, without reproach from the people of the States." Besides, "it could hardly be supposed that the people (in free states and territories) would have regarded those who were emancipated as entitled to equal rights with themselves."[39]

As Justice Taney contended in his sneering way, the distinction in America between Confederacy and Union, between Down South and Up North, could not be marked off as neatly as the Mason–Dixon Line or the Missouri Compromise supposed. Minneapolis offered particularly vivid evidence of how little espoused ideals and enacted laws on the subject of racial equality actually altered the human capacity for bigotry and exploitation. The symbolic descendants of Dred and Harriet Scott in Minneapolis had more than ample reason to feel similarly wrenched between liberty and oppression.

The first Black person known to have lived in the eventual Minnesota was a fur trader named Pierre Bonga, who arrived in the late 1700s and sired a son in Duluth in 1802. Regardless of the small number of Black residents over the next half-century, Minnesota's contradictory attitudes about them emerged in the very formation of the state. Suffrage was limited to white males, an 1860 bill in the state legislature to protect fugitive slaves was defeated, and two statewide referenda on granting Black males the vote failed in what one scholar a century later termed "a struggle between 'white supremacy' and 'Negro equality.' "[40] Finally, on a third attempt in 1868, the measure passed. And in 1885, the legislature overwhelmingly passed a public-accommodations law outlawing racial or religious discrimination "on railroads, in theaters, and all places of amusement or public convenience."[41]

The statute's lofty rhetoric and significant penalties—the maximum being a five-hundred-dollar fine and one year in prison—left a comforting yet entirely inaccurate impression that Minnesota had secured genuine equality even as the Jim Crow regime was sweeping through the former Confederacy. More correctly, the various actions in the Minnesota statehouse established a durable template for public policy for decades to come. Conservatives could not muster the votes to install discriminatory laws; liberals had the numbers to push through such legislation but rarely the will to meaningfully enforce it. They could, however, bask in their virtue. "White opinion makers," as a historian put it in 2015, "insisted that blacks alleging discrimination did not know how good they had it in Minnesota."[42]

However equivocal the welcome, Black migrants steadily trickled into Minnesota, raising the state's Black population from 259 in 1860 to 4,959 in 1900. Some had fled the collapse of Reconstruction in the South in the 1870s and 1880s, and others the imposition of separate-but-equal after the Supreme Court's *Plessy v. Ferguson* decision in 1896. They traveled by railroad or riverboat to the transportation hub of St. Paul. Other arrivals, having grown up on farms or in small towns elsewhere in the state, moved into the Twin Cities for job prospects, establishing their families as city dwellers. These Blacks found employment niches as whitewashers, barbers, wheelwrights, and sawmill hands; they established churches, literary societies, newspapers, and branches of civil rights organizations, from the Sons of Freedom in the late 1860s to the NAACP in the 1910s and Urban League in the 1920s. Minneapolis had its first Black graduate from the state university in 1887, its first Black doctor in 1898, and its first Black member of the State Legislature that same year. At his behest, the body even passed an expanded version of the 1885 public-accommodations law.

Yet, tellingly, that politician, an attorney named J. Frank Wheaton, served only one term in office before moving to New York. There would not be another Black person elected to the legislature for more than seventy years. The achievements of Black professionals like Wheaton, the distribution of Blacks in skilled trades, the formal legal protections accorded by the state—everything had been made possible by the fact that Black people until the turn of the twentieth century formed such a flyspeck of Minnesota's population, less than one percent, that their upward mobility and official equality presented no threat to white dominance.

It did not take much of a demographic change to exhaust the provisional goodwill. Between 1900 and 1920, the state's Black population rose from just shy of 5,000 to nearly 9,000, and Minneapolis mirrored the trend, going from 1,548 to 3,927 over those twenty years. By the standards of industrial Midwestern cities like Cleveland, Chicago, and Detroit, prime destinations for the first wave of the Great Migration of Southern rural Blacks to the urban North, the Black influx to Minneapolis was modest, and it was outpaced by the arrival of white immigrants, primarily from Norway and Sweden. With their Protestant faith and Northern European features, those newcomers passed the suitability test even for nativists. Black people, mainly transplanted from the South, spilling into hitherto white towns and neighborhoods, competing with whites for working-class jobs—they were the threat.

Racial terrorism of a Southern sort flared in the Great North, as Minnesota styled itself. In 1907, an arsonist set fire to a decades-old Black church, Brown's Chapel African Methodist Episcopal, in the town of Hastings about thirty miles from Minneapolis.[43] Thirteen years later, in the Great Lakes port city of Duluth, three Black workers in a traveling circus were arrested on the dubious accusation of having raped a white woman. A crowd of ten thousand people besieged the police station, broke into the men's cells, and hanged them from lampposts. The killers commemorated their valor with a photographic postcard of them standing beside the three corpses. Despite the initial arrest of thirty-seven whites, none were ultimately convicted of the murder of Elias Clayton, Elmer Jackson, and Isaac McGhie, even as one surviving Black man, William Miller, was found guilty of rape.[44]

While the atrocities in Duluth catalyzed Blacks in the Twin Cities to protest and organize and spurred the state legislature to pass an anti-lynching law, the spectacle also sent a favorable signal to the Ku Klux Klan about the salience of its race hate in Minnesota. The Klan's representatives first came to Minneapolis in 1921, holding meetings at several Protestant churches. More than four hundred Klan chapters opened across the state between March and July 1923, and their state-wide newspaper *Call of the North* touted "these fundamental principles of real Americanism . . . God, flag and hope."[45] The KKK even sponsored a float featuring its robed and hooded adherents at the University of Minnesota's homecoming parade.[46]

Vigilante violence was accompanied by less lethal forms of white power. A system of restrictive housing covenants had begun to spread through Minneapolis in the early 1910s, confining Black residents into three distinct districts. With the end of the Great War, returning white veterans pressured the city's factories and businesses to fire Blacks and hire them. In both the political sphere and the labor market, Minneapolis offered a stark divide. On one side stood the forces of big business and the Republican Party, most powerfully embodied by an anti-union lobby with the deceptively anodyne title of the Citizens Alliance, and on the other the burgeoning radicalism of the Farmer-Labor Party with its coalition of miners, urban unions, and agrarian populists. The one trait that both combatants in Minneapolis's civil war shared was a disdain for Black people in all but utilitarian, ideally subservient, roles. When Samuel Gompers of the American Federation of Labor (AFL) addressed a crowd of several thousand unionists in Minneapolis in 1905, he bluntly threatened, "If the colored man continues to lend himself to the work of tearing down everything that the White [*sic*] man has built up, a race hatred worse than any ever known will result."[47]

The result of such rhetoric showed in the 1920 census, which found that barely 5 percent of employed Black men in Minnesota worked in "manufacturing and mechanical industries"—compared with 18.4 percent of employed foreign-born whites. That same census tallied just 3.3 percent of all employed Black men in the professions, and even that number was misleading, as more than half were in just one field: music.[48] In a poll of more than 250 private employers in Minneapolis during the 1920s, two-thirds plainly stated that they would not hire a Black.[49] As for labor unions, only 8 of 47 had Black members, according to a survey by the economist Abram Harris on behalf of the Minneapolis chapter of the Urban League. And in only one, the Post Office Clerks' Union, did Black numbers exceed single digits.[50]

With Minneapolis's public schools refusing to hire Black teachers, such educators left the city to return to the Jim Crow South, of all places, where they at least could find academic positions. The several dozen Black students attending the University of Minnesota were banned from living in its dormitories. Department stores in downtown Minneapolis maintained such a complete embargo on employing Blacks that one woman recalled the bitter joke among her friends "not to lose your car fare downtown, 'cause you won't meet anyone you know down there." In a more serious and desperate moment, the same woman confessed, "I would pray for God to make me look white so I could get a job."[51]

One of the keenest observers of the Minneapolitan brand of bigotry was Raymond Cannon, one of the Black men who had leaped to Arthur Lee's defense. Cannon had grown up on a Minnesota farm and moved to the city for careers in pharmacy and law. From his country childhood, he knew an idiom about fences, the kind that would be impregnable and inescapable. "The discrimination," he said of his city and state, "was horse-high, hog-tight, and bull-strong."[52]

That metaphorical barrier concentrated a disproportionate share of Minneapolis Blacks into one neighborhood on the city's North side and one occupation of service. Abram Harris's exhaustive survey in 1926 determined that ninety percent of local Black men worked in such menial jobs as porter, waiter, janitor, elevator operator, and night watchman. Women hired out as maids or cooks to affluent white families. Put in material terms, the median wage in 1919 for a Black head of household in Minneapolis was $22.55 per week—barely half of what the U.S. Bureau of Labor Statistics deemed adequate for a family of five.[53]

Such numbers, however bleak, could not fully convey the assault on Black people's dignity. Blacks in Minneapolis had a literacy rate of nearly one hundred percent.[54] They were more likely than native-born whites to be in the labor force.[55] Yet to the degree that whites encountered and perceived them at all, Blacks occupied the stereotypical role of servant. The hotels in Minneapolis that had entertained vacationing slaveholders prior to the Civil War re-enacted the plantation fantasy decades after the supposed end of enslavement with a phalanx of Black doormen, bellhops, and waiters attending to an exclusively white clientele. With so many other vocational avenues closed off, such demeaning jobs qualified as a coveted form of employment.

Among the many Black men toiling beneath his true aptitude was a transplant from Oklahoma named Anthony Brutus Cassius, who had finished high school in St. Paul and completed a year of divinity studies at Macalester College. For lack of alternatives, he signed on as a waiter in the Curtis Hotel, where the rule book included the overarching admonition "Don't be a disgrace."[56] Later in his life, Cassius recounted the treatment he and other Black waiters had experienced:

If they caught you with any cream in your coffee, they charged you a nickel. If they caught you with a pat of butter, you had to pay a nickel. If you broke a glass—which, in waitering, you're bound to break something—that was all deductible. So there was no way for you to get seventeen dollars a month. Each payday for two weeks, you drew about six or seven dollars. If you didn't make any tips, you didn't have anything. "Well," I said, "this is no way of life." I discovered that the white waiters downtown at the [Hotel] Radisson, the [Hotel] Nicollet, the Minneapolis Club and the [Minneapolis] Athletic Club were all paid seventy-five dollars a month.[57]

The severity of race hate in Minneapolis could be reckoned merely by crossing the municipal border to St. Paul, which was not such a twin city in this regard. As early as 1902, St. Paul had hosted the meeting of the National Afro-American Council, bringing together such national leaders as W. E. B. Du Bois, Booker T. Washington, and Ida B. Wells.[58] Blacks formed a large share of the labor force in the Armour, Swift, and Cudahy stockyards and belonged to the packinghouse workers' union. Hiring out as dining car waiters and sleeping car porters in the railroad hub of St. Paul, they joined the Black unions for those occupations. A Black man, Charles James, even served as president of the integrated St. Paul Trades and Labor Assembly and on the executive board of the state Federation of Labor. In the professional ranks, Clarence Wesley "Cap" Wigington spent years as St. Paul's senior architectural designer.[59] The cumulative earning power and range of social classes in St. Paul's Black population infused the Rondo neighborhood, the local equivalent of New York's Harlem or Chicago's Bronzeville.

There was nothing more intrinsically tolerant about St. Paul as compared with Minneapolis; the essential difference was one of demography. With its Protestant majority and its preponderance of Scandinavians and Northern Europeans, Minneapolis conformed to the regional, indeed the national, standard of Christian whiteness and thus had no reason to compromise with its vastly outnumbered religious and racial minorities. St. Paul, however, was a much more Catholic city, the seat of the archdiocese and its cathedral, the destination that its famous archbishop, the fittingly named John Ireland, had recommended to Irish peasants fleeing chronic poverty and English oppression. By the mid-1920s, Catholics in Ramsey County (whose population was almost entirely in St. Paul) formed a 51 percent majority and in raw numbers more than tripled those of the Lutherans.[60] Acutely aware of their tenuous position within the state, especially during a period of Ku Klux Klan expansion, St. Paul's Catholics saw the pragmatic benefits of allying with the city's Black and Jewish communities. The city's Democratic machine, disinterested in the transformational goals of the Farmer-Labor Party, assembled a partnership of out-groups, harvesting votes in exchange for the practical rewards such as patronage jobs. Protecting the rights and needs of other minorities was, for the St. Paul Catholics, a way of protecting their own.

In their housing as well as their work and their politics, Minneapolis Blacks existed in infuriating proximity to privilege. By the 1920s, as restrictive covenants, mob violence, and rising prices had conspired to push them from most other sections of the city, Blacks increasingly funneled into the remnant of a formerly exclusive enclave called Oak Lake Park. A dozen blocks northwest of downtown, its Victorian homes and winding streets and shading cedar trees had been the province of 163 families listed on the Social Register in the mid-1890s.[61] But the district's nearness to clay pits, a brickyard, and the vast Munsingwear garment factory convinced the original elite to decamp for more purely residential neighborhoods several miles southward. By the 1900s, Oak Lake begrudgingly accepted Jewish immigrants from Eastern Europe, a Yiddish-speaking rabble one sociologist described as "small dealers, some rag peddlers, some fruit men, and still other dealers in junk."[62] Over the next twenty years, such Jews scraped together enough money to step up the class ladder into the nearby section of Homewood, defying its restrictive covenants in the process. The resulting vacuum in Oak Lake Park was soon filled by Blacks, to the point that nearly half the city's total clustered on the blocks anchored by the corner of Lyndale and Sixth Avenue North. In Black hands, the surrounding neighborhood was called simply the North Side, and its main commercial street "The Avenue."

The North Side contained vying currents of degradation and self-determination. Residents themselves were torn between calling attention to the neighborhood's miserable conditions, in the vain hope that city hall might respond, and decrying the newspapers' portrayal of the place as a pit of vice crime. The gabled homes of Oak Lake Park still lined the streets, but most had been carved up into multiple apartments that a maid or waiter could afford to rent. The alleys behind those houses formed their own grid of streets, where white developers practiced "back-building," throwing up crude dwellings for quick profits. The alleys also accumulated the detritus of subsistence living—the peddler's wheelbarrow, the barrel of scrap metal, the chicken coop. What was no longer useable landed, often as not, in the fetid waters of Basset Creek, a de facto sewer that slogged its way through the neighborhood. A 1925 study of the North Side by a social-service organization based in the area, the Women's Cooperative Alliance, offered a dismal tableau of "dilapidated and unpainted" houses, streets littered with rubbish and yards "piled three feet high along houses and fences."[63]

At the same time, however, the North Side also maintained a bustling business district. To believe the cops and newspaper reporters, most of its commerce involved gambling and prostitution, and they regularly waved the bloody flag of "white slavery." That provocative caricature deliberately omitted the blocks full of small shops managed by Blacks and Jews—dry goods, pharmacies, butcher stores, groceries, jewelers, beauty salons. In recognition of the North Side's restaurants and clubs, places like the Nest and the Chicken Shack, some people took to calling Lyndale and Sixth the "Beale Street" of Minneapolis, likening it, albeit hyperbolically, to the renowned entertainment district in Memphis.

The true centerpiece of artistic, intellectual, and political pursuits was the settlement house named for the Black poet Phyllis Wheatley. Founded in 1924 in a former Jewish religious school known as the Talmud Torah, the Wheatley House operated under energetic and autocratic leadership of one Gertrude Brown, an educator and administrator who held the inappropriately bland title of "head resident." Brown solicited much of the house's financial support from white Christian women, quintessential do-gooders of the Lady Bountiful sort, and then subversively applied it to myriad forms of racial uplift. The settlement house hosted meetings of the Communist Party and the Brotherhood of Sleeping Car Porters; it sponsored an orchestra and a theater troupe. When no hotel in Minneapolis would permit Black guests, Brown raised the money to build a new, larger settlement house with eighteen guest bedrooms. These welcomed the likes of Duke Ellington, Langston Hughes, Marian Anderson, and Paul Robeson, when those artists were engaged by the virtually all-white theaters downtown or at the university, and Brown persuaded the luminaries to give free presentations to her community.[64]

When it came to the exercise of political power, however, Black Minneapolis had long faltered. It lacked the sufficient numbers for mass protest and was virtually devoid of meaningful white allies. The occasional communal campaign did arise, beginning with protests against the 1915 showing of D. W. Griffith's cinematic tribute to the Ku Klux Klan, *Birth of a Nation*. Seven years later, a coalition of Black civic and religious leaders condemned the beating of a railroad porter by an off-duty cop—an incident that led to the arrest not of the police officer but, rather, of three Black men on a dubious charge of disorderly conduct.[65] Such communal efforts tended to flare briefly and then subside, leaving civil rights activism inordinately reliant on a handful of individuals who formed the local version of Du Bois's "Talented Tenth."

They called themselves the Minnesota Club and met once a month at Foster's Sweet Shop on the North Side, buying a dish of ice cream apiece in exchange for ninety minutes or so of undisturbed strategizing. The mainstays, all of them college educated, embodied a range of methods for breaking through the Minneapolis fence. Anthony Brutus Cassius was trying to organize Black hotel workers, since white unions seemed disinterested at best in having them as members. Lena Olive Smith, who had earned a law degree at age 35, after careers ranging from elocution teacher to hairdresser to real estate agent, wielded Minnesota's rarely enforced civil rights laws to litigate cases of housing discrimination for clients including Arthur Lee.[66] Nellie Stone,[67] who had grown up as a farm girl waking at five in the morning to milk thirty cows, had imbibed activism from her father's involvement with the Non-Partisan League, which sought public ownership of agricultural businesses such as mills and grain elevators, and from four uncles who belonged to the Brotherhood of Sleeping Car Porters. Moving to Minneapolis to finish high school and take classes at the University of Minnesota Extension, Stone learned most from a middle-aged, Swedish-born radical named Swan Assaron, who hung around the campus seeking recruits for the revolution. He was one of the rare whites whom Stone had ever heard refer to Blacks as equals, and she followed his encouragement into the Young Communist League.[68] Inspired to do her part for the Black component of the proletariat, Stone tried to convince her coworkers at the Minneapolis Athletic Club, where she ran the elevator, to form a union. Once the white bosses heard, she was fired, though by no means deterred.

Had the Blacks of Minneapolis been intimidated enough to remain in their designated space, geographically and otherwise, had they been long-suffering enough to endure the spasms of police violence, then perhaps a certain kind of social peace, a miserable stasis, might have prevailed. But more than any previous abomination, the mob attack on Arthur Lee and his family, who had dared to venture beyond the North Side, tore away the pretense that whites and Blacks in Minneapolis could placidly inhabit separate spheres.

In the wake of the white riot against the Lee family, a social worker in her twenties interviewed Minneapolitans of both races for a master's degree thesis at the University of Minnesota. Maurine Boie had participated in the research for the 1926 study of Blacks in Minneapolis and been on the staff at the Wheatley House. But precisely because she was white, the white people whom she interviewed for her thesis spoke with utter candor, as if assuming no one of their own race could possibly disagree. Consistent with the protocols of social science, Boie did not name her informants, identifying them by a number and sometimes a thumbnail description.

A letter from person B-11:

Don't think that this section of town is the only one that is interested in this ngro [sic] menace because the same situation is likely to arise in any part of our fair city and I am sure anybody would feel just as bitter if a negro moved in the house next door. . . . They talk about justice for the negro, how about a little justice for the white man who has put his life savings into a home. Should all the white people in this neighborhood suffer for one negro; is that justice.[69]

An interview with W-21:

That's the trouble with these Northern Negroes. They bring things on themselves. . . . They go around with a chip on their shoulders. They're like Jewish and Irish people, have an inferiority complex. They have a good neighborhood. They should be content to stay there.[70]

Such opinions belonged, too, to the supposedly enlightened. Boie quoted a newspaper column by a white minister, C-12, who portrayed himself as being sympathetic:

The Negro has used the poorest possible way to win his rights. He had become the tool of those who sought to gain personal ends by means of his martyrdom. Had he been big enough and clever enough, or had he listened to the advice of genuine friends of the colored people, he could have said, "I have a perfect and legal right to buy this property and live in it. But to do so will make my people victims of malicious, un-Christian and un-American prejudice . . . I am vacating a property . . . [to] promote goodwill and amicable relations between whites and blacks in the city of Minneapolis." . . . By such an action he would have won for his people the friendship of thousands of whites.[71]

Most emblematic of Minneapolis and its racial myopia, Boie reprinted an unpublished letter to the editor by an unnamed person she identified as W-11. After acknowledging that the law did give Lee the right to buy the home and move in, the man wrote:

During the past two weeks, these things have come to me very vividly and my own feelings and sentiments in the matter have been more clearly defined in my own mind, more clearly brought home to me, and, as a cool, calm and peaceful citizen, I want to say to you, and to all, both White and Black, that while I know that the taking of human life in any shape, form or manner has never and never can be or will permanently solve human differences, I know NOW that in defense of my home, my home community, my country, my family and race, from contamination, assimilation or influence of a foreign race, I would as a last resort, if in my power to do so, kill, destroy and annihilate the unwanted thing.[72]

By way of justifying his lethal intents, this correspondent had provided Boie with uncommonly detailed credentials. He said he had been a "fighter" for human rights for forty years, twelve of them as part-owner of a newspaper, and was a member of the Farmer-Labor Party, which, of course, stood well to the left of the Republicans and Democrats. This concise biography all but declared that the would-be murderer was Hjalmar Petersen, a Danish immigrant to Minnesota who went on to purchase the weekly newspaper in his adopted hometown of Askov, advocate for such progressive measures as an income tax, and win election to the state legislature on the Farmer-Labor line. A few years after Boie recorded his words anonymously, Petersen rose to become lieutenant governor and then governor of Minnesota. Hundreds of miles north of 36'30" and the former Confederacy, Petersen embodied the morally fatal contradiction of Minnesota's putatively unprejudiced whites. As Dred Scott had discovered seventy years earlier, the South as a geographical region could be partitioned off. The South as a dogma, as a doctrine, as a belief system of white supremacy, obliged no border.

* * *

From the moment in the late summer of 1934 when Cecil Newman pushed open the front door of his newly rented storefront downtown at 309 Third Avenue South and began producing the first issues of the *Minneapolis Spokesman*, he engaged in a simultaneous set of balancing acts. He sought readers among everyday Black folk with his entire pages devoted to "Woman's World" and "Attend[ing] Some Church on Sunday." Yet he also appealed to the community's activists and intelligentsia with his focuses on job discrimination in the city and anti-lynching legislation in Washington. From his desk behind the counter of the long, narrow newsroom, he drafted and laid out nearly every article, editorial, and column. Yet to keep the *Spokesman* solvent, he went door-to-door in the central business district selling $2.50-a-year subscriptions and stood on the bustling corner of Sixth and Lyndale on the North Side peddling loose copies for a nickel apiece. Most importantly and intricately, through the medium of his newspaper, Newman positioned himself as both race man and interracial diplomat.

"Publishing the news about our Negro community raised our morale," he later explained. "It made us feel that we were really a part of the big city. It also showed the white population that we were responsible citizens with our own rights. It helped them to understand us. My newspapers became an instrument of force, a means of hitting both sides of the problem at the same time."[73]

To help sustain Newman's endeavor, Lena Olive Smith bought a weekly advertisement for her law practice. So did the competing Black funeral homes run by the Neal and Dowdy families, as well as the Porters & Waiters Club, the social redoubt of Black railroad workers, as Newman until recently had been. He promoted the *Spokesman* to white-owned stores as a route to the collective spending of ten thousand Blacks in the Twin Cities. Tipped off by an attorney acquaintance, Newman undercut the prices charged by the established white dailies, the *Star, Tribune*, and *Journal*, for publishing legal notices in the classified ads. And he assembled a team of paperboys and papergirls, the same after-school job he'd held during his Kansas City childhood, with the promise that they could keep half of every five-cent sale and compete for the pocket watch and locket necklace that went periodically to the top sellers in each gender.[74]

Fixated on the *Spokesman* during most waking hours, inclined to retreat to his personal library when at home, Newman acknowledged, "I was a newspaper man first and a husband second." Stuck in a passionless marriage and possessed of a roving eye, he increasingly turned his attention to a young woman named DeVelma Hall, who was working part-time on the *Spokesman's* business side. Several years and one divorce later, she became Newman's second wife, as well as the de facto comptroller responsible for restoring order to the *Spokesman's* balance sheet. From his very first issue—$68 to print three hundred copies, $45 for paper, $250 for typesetting—Newman had been operating on what he called "the ragged edge . . . just one step ahead of the sheriff, who, figuratively speaking . . . was right behind me with a due bill in his hand." By the end of 1934, Newman owed his printer $5,200.[75]

In Newman's defense, there could hardly have been a harsher economic climate in which to open a newspaper, or any kind of start-up business for that matter, than that of Minneapolis in the Great Depression. The city's traditional economic pillars of flour and lumber had been crumbling for decades before Black Tuesday, and the place was already glutted with job-seeking migrants from the same kind of faltering farms that surrounded Hubert Humphrey's hometown in South Dakota. Once the effects of the stock market crash fully struck Minneapolis, the industrial sector cratered, with the annual value of manufactured goods falling by half from 1929 to 1933.[76] Private charities were so overwhelmed that destitute men at the Salvation Army's shelter shivered under newspapers because that refuge of last resort had run out of blankets.[77] And though Minnesota's voters had turned to a Farmer-Labor progressive, Floyd Olson, in the 1930 election for governor, Minneapolis stubbornly elected the conservative A. G. Bainbridge mayor in 1933, even as he vowed to require work for relief payments and to replace social workers with police officers in assessing who deserved public assistance at all. Despite such efforts to deprive the needy, the city's relief caseload rose from two thousand a month in 1930 to more than twenty thousand in 1934.[78]

The toll of economic calamity and governmental callousness, particularly under Herbert Hoover as president and Bainbridge as mayor, could be seen within blocks of Cecil Newman's office. A sociologist at the University of Minnesota, Calvin Schmid,[79] described the Gateway district, the major portal into downtown Minneapolis, as a "Hobohemia" of rescue missions, pawn shops, and flophouses.[80] Along the adjacent riverbank, squatters patched together shanties from corrugated metal, linoleum scraps, scavenged lumber, and even Coca-Cola signs, calling their encampment "Rooseveltville-on-the-Mississippi," the new president's economic recovery programs notwithstanding. Squalid as the shacks were, things could always get worse. And so they did on the day in January 1934 when police burned Rooseveltville down to the frozen riverside mud.

However much the white majority of Minneapolis was suffering, however, Blacks inevitably had it far harder. With tourism and business travel both withering, railroads laid off the Pullman porters and Red Caps who had been the core of Black Minneapolis's middle class. Hotel waiters, another staple of the community, lost their jobs from the combined effects of Prohibition and the Great Depression. Even when legal alcohol returned in 1933, hotels advertised for men of Scandinavian and German extraction to fill the revived waiters' jobs.[81] Similarly, Irish and Scandinavian women parlayed white skin and bargain prices into housekeeping jobs traditionally held by Blacks.

The cumulative effect was that Black Minneapolis, a community with an unemployment record better than whites' before the Depression, plunged into a jobless rate variously placed between forty and sixty percent—either way, well above roughly one-quarter of whites out of work by 1933.[82] Across the municipal border into St. Paul, a high school student named Gordon Parks, who had been supporting himself with a bellhop's job at the Minnesota Club, described the psychic toll for so many local Blacks as the bottom dropped out:

> The employees' locker room at the club was unusually quiet when I arrived to work one Wednesday that same month [of October 1929]. Waiters who had known each other for years were sitting about as though they were strangers. The cause for silence was tacked to the bulletin board. It read: "Because of unforeseen circumstances, some personnel will be laid off the first of the month. Those directly affected will be notified in due time. The management." ...
>
> I couldn't imagine such financial disaster touching my small world; it surely concerned only the rich. But by the first week of November, I too knew differently; along with millions of others across the nation, I was without a job. All that next week I searched for any kind of work that would prevent my leaving school. Again it was, "We're firing, not hiring." "Sorry, sonny, nothing doing here."[83]

Surveying the wreckage three years into the Depression, Newman wrote:

[T]he Twin Cities Negro, his community built largely on the success and continuance of the railroads, found himself in bad shape. . . . Homes have been lost, businesses have failed, life's savings swept away, families broken up and the little community spirit barely noticeable before, has almost vanished. Men who have worked for the railroad for 35 years find themselves jobless. . . . The churches, most of them heavily mortgaged, with only one modern structure among them, have suffered much. Most of the ministers know what it is not to receive their pay checks."[84]

Nine days after Newman published those words, FDR took the oath of office as president, vowing a "New Deal" for America's immiserated multitudes. Yet through Newman's skeptical eyes, the initial wave of legislation offered dubious prospects for Black Americans. The National Industrial Recovery Act (NIRA), passed into law barely two months after Roosevelt took office, enabled the establishment of manufacturing codes, including standards for what the president hailed as "living wages." Implementing them was the role of the National Recovery Administration, which was created by executive order. But the price that Roosevelt paid for the congressional votes of Southern segregationist Democrats was to exempt domestic and farm labor from the wage standards. The two-fold effect was the replacement of lower-paid Black workers by white ones once industrial paychecks had to be raised by federal law and the abandonment of millions of Blacks in agriculture and domestic service. Even as Roosevelt captured a majority of Black voters with his compassion and vigor in the face of widespread deprivation, African American leaders astringently defined the NIRA as the "Negro Removal Act."[85] In Minneapolis, where Black maids, cooks, and drivers in white households were routinely given $2.50 and meals for a seven-day week, Newman argued that "the domestic workers . . . need a code more than any single class of workers."[86]

The boom in union organizing and the flurry of strikes that followed passage of the NIRA left Newman similarly unimpressed. Far from being anti-labor, he belonged to a union, A. Philip Randolph's Brotherhood of Sleeping Car Porters, and even argued grievances against the Soo Line railroad on behalf of his local. From Newman's years with the brotherhood, though, he also knew firsthand how the AFL had resisted Randolph's efforts to have the union embraced as an AFL affiliate. Quite to the contrary, in the late 1920s, the brotherhood had to fight off a takeover effort by the AFL's Hotel and Restaurant Employees International Union, which permitted segregated locals and racially unequal pay. The Black worker, as Newman once put it, existed "at the mercy of exploiting capital on one side and antagonistic labor unions on the other."[87]

By way of proof, Newman needed only to stroll a few blocks from the *Spokesman* office. Out there, during the spring and summer of 1934, Minneapolis was erupting.

* * *

The eruption began in February 1934 as a seemingly unequal battle. On the political left stood the rank and file of General Drivers Local 574, an affiliate of the International Brotherhood of Teamsters that counted 175 members at best and had been long humbled by its defeat in a 1916 strike.[88] Confronting the local from the political right was the Citizens Alliance, a syndicate of several hundred executives from banking, milling, manufacturing, and other major businesses that had been formed in 1903 "to broaden and strengthen the war on unions."[89] In the decades since then, the Alliance had succeeded so thoroughly in its goal of making and keeping Minneapolis an "open-shop" city that less than ten percent of its workforce belonged to any AFL-affiliated union.[90]

Under a set of radical leaders, several of whom adhered to the Trotskyite faction of the Communist Party, Local 574 set out to forever break the Alliance's stranglehold. The effort started, strategically enough, with a walkout by coal drivers on February 7, a frigid time when cutting off the delivery of heating fuel magnified the small union's power. For added persuasion, strikers attacked "scab" trucks. Winning union recognition from coal dealers within several days, Local 574 immediately began organizing truckers and warehouse workers throughout Minneapolis, and hundreds, then thousands, of them flocked to sign up.

Atypically taken by surprise, the Citizens Alliance sprang into belated action, assembling 166 trucking firms into a coalition uniformly opposed to organized labor. The standoff prepared the stage for a citywide truckers' strike on May 16, an escalation so risky that the Teamsters' national leaders forbade it and suspended Local 574's leaders, albeit to no avail. Instead, the local expertly trained and deployed teams of picketers, along with mobile squads of enforcers, to halt deliveries to department stores, laundries, construction sites, groceries, utility companies, and nearly every other locus of daily commerce.[91] In response, the Citizens Alliance conspired with the mayor and police chief to have five hundred vigilantes deputized to augment a thousand uniformed officers.

The brinksmanship burst into full-scale combat on May 22 in the city's Market District, the center of food wholesaling. Strikers and the so-called special deputies pummeled one another with clubs, pipes, and axe handles, before the arms race expanded to knives for the picketers and sawed-off shotguns for the deputies. Two of those deputies, including the Alliance's attorney C. Arthur Lyman, died as their forces retreated in what the union instantly hailed as the "Battle of Deputies Run."[92]

A somewhat ambiguous settlement followed, with the employers agreeing on paper to recognize the union and end the open-shop policy, but in practice balking at implementation. So Local 574, by now swollen to nearly seven thousand members, declared another strike to begin on July 16. Four days later, as police accompanied a scab truck on a delivery, picketers in their own vehicle blocked its path. The cops responded by firing shotguns into the unarmed protestors, with more shooting erupting a block away. By the end of the volleys, sixty-seven people, most of them strikers and others unlucky bystanders, had been hit. One of the union men, Henry Ness, died of his wounds several days later. Local 574 now had two essential elements for mobilizing allies and winning public sympathy: a massacre, which it dubbed "Bloody Friday," and a martyr to be accorded a massive funeral procession.[93]

In the wake of the bloodbath, President Roosevelt dispatched mediators, Governor Olson declared martial law, the National Guard raided the Citizens Alliance's offices and arrested several union leaders, and, on August 22, labor and management signed an agreement that decisively transformed Minneapolis into a union town.

Cecil Newman had an intimate view of the entire spectacle. Early in the summer of 1934, as he was preparing to launch the *Spokesman*, Local 574 rented headquarters for its strike one block away from his newspaper office. Every time Newman went to the Black neighborhood on the North Side, he passed through the Market District, epicenter of the strike-related violence. So the way he responded—or calculatedly did not—revealed a great deal about the involuntary isolation of Minneapolis's Black activists between white labor and white capital.

In the second issue of the *Spokesman*, which appeared five days before the strike's settlement, Newman published an editorial that struck a tone of studied balance and wary composure. It endorsed both the union's demands for "adequate wages" and "reasonable hours" through collective bargaining and an employer's right "to protect himself against extortion by labor." For a man who had seen the closed shop often close out Black workers, the measured words were a far cry from "Solidarity Forever!" Yet, elsewhere in the same issue, Newman tartly dealt with the ongoing efforts by the Citizens Alliance to portray itself as devoted to color blindness in hiring, a self-aggrandizing way of rationalizing the common deployment of Blacks as strikebreakers across the country. "The Alliance claims that in the quarter century of its existence it has helped 400,00 men to employment," Newman wrote. "The fair ratio of this number would give 4,000 of these places to the colored people. Fine, if true!"[94]

There was no preordained reason that the drivers' strike, as an exercise in class consciousness, should have almost entirely ignored a local Black population that was almost entirely composed of the working class. Among the AFL's affiliated unions, the Teamsters had been one of the few (along with the United Mine Workers) to accept Black members in integrated locals as contractual equals.[95] Two other major strikes in 1934, those of longshoremen in San Francisco and cannery workers at Campbell Soup in New Jersey, involved substantial Black participation. And both A. B. Cassius and Nellie Stone, who had been organizing Black service workers in Minneapolis, volunteered to aid Local 574 during its struggle.

But their devotion, like Newman's more temperate support, went unrequited. Never was the disconnect more apparent than on the day in August 1934 when the Hotel and Restaurant Employees International Union, best known by the acronym HERE, assembled in Minneapolis for its biennial convention. The truckers' strike was nearing its triumphant end, and a delegation of four hundred drivers marched amid cheers into the HERE banquet at the Curtis Hotel. One of HERE's national officers, in turn, presented Local 574 with a thousand-dollar donation for its strike fund.[96]

The celebrants, as it happened, were being served by the Black waitstaff of the Curtis, one of whom was even called upon to serenade the diners with "Trees" and "The Waters of Minnetonka." The Black waiters were union members, part of Local 614 of HERE, the unit built up by Cassius. It was, however, a so-called Jim Crow local, segregated by HERE custom and consigned to lower wages than the union's white waiters made elsewhere in town. At least a few HERE members seemed to recognize the hypocrisy and proposed a resolution during the convention allowing locals to desegregate.[97] The next month, at the AFL's convention, two similar resolutions both went down to defeat. For the moment, at least, Newman looked out his window to see two brands of white people: employers who wanted to exploit Blacks and unions that wanted to exclude them.

* * *

Hours past the mid-afternoon sundown of January 3, 1936, as snow fell and temperatures outside sank into the teens, Cecil Newman tuned in Roosevelt's State of the Union address. The annual presidential oration promised to be even more eventful than usual. Roosevelt would be delivering it in the evening for the first time, modeling the speech on his folksy "fireside chats." And he had reason to be taking a victory lap after the landmark legislation he had pushed through in the previous year. The Social Security Act created a system of federally funded old age pensions and unemployment insurance. The Works Progress Administration (WPA) employed hundreds of thousands of Americans—and ultimately 8.5 million—in fields from construction to oral history. The National Labor Relations Act guaranteed the right of workers to organize and strike, energizing the union movement even more than the NIRA had.

As Newman listened to Roosevelt, he did so with at least a partially open mind. Though he had not endorsed FDR in 1932, he had seen Minneapolis Blacks streaming into the Phyllis Wheatley settlement house to apply for jobs with the WPA and the Public Works Administration.[98] When the president laced his address with criticism of rising autocracy abroad and "entrenched greed" at home, he was espousing positions that Newman also held.

Yet, at the speech's end, with the vast Democratic majority in Congress bathing FDR in applause, Newman switched off the radio, disgruntled. The vaunted new program of Social Security, he knew, excluded nearly two-thirds of Black American workers by limiting its benefits to people "regularly employed in commerce and industry."[99] Whether by nefarious design or convenient coincidence, excluding the Black staples of agricultural and domestic labor from Social Security had helped secure the votes of Southern segregationists in Congress.[100] The local branch of the Urban League, with Newman as a particularly active member, was protesting against the placement of Black Minnesotans into segregated camps under the Civilian Conservation Corps. And while FDR decried the rise of fascism, albeit without speaking its name, unlike Newman he never drew the parallel between how Nazi Germany treated its Jews and America treated its Blacks.

What Newman had heard most powerfully in the State of the Union was presidential silence. Specifically, it was silence on the subject of anti-lynching legislation, the focal goal of civil rights advocates nationwide. Various versions had been introduced and defeated for decades, even as the noose's Black death toll since the overthrow of Reconstruction surpassed 3,500. Then, in early 1935, two of FDR's allies, senators Robert Wagner of New York and Edward Costigan of Colorado, co-sponsored an anti-lynching bill that had largely been written by the NAACP. Scores of elected officials, college presidents, and intellectual leaders urged Roosevelt to push through this "must" legislation, and his own wife, Eleanor, joined the NAACP and endorsed the bill.[101] Yet the president remained mute as a filibuster by Southern Democrats in the Senate killed the bill in April 1935. And he uttered not one word now about reviving it. Newman intuited well enough the reason why: holding onto white Southern votes in Congress for New Deal legislation and white Southern voters at the polls in the 1936 election. Still fuming days later, Newman penned an editorial for the *Spokesman*'s January 10 edition:

> It is our desire . . . to call attention to the fact that the president's speech was not intended to affect the thinking of 15 millions of the Negro people whose very existence the president and his critics have forgotten, whose actions in the coming election were not considered important enough to devote a paragraph of his important message to their consideration. . . .
>
> It should not, however, close our eyes or our memories to the knowledge that 35 of our people were lynched last year; that a bill to take lawful cognizance of such happening *[sic]*, which have reached a horrifying total in this country, failed of passage largely because the president himself lent no support to its enactment; that discrimination and injustices of every kind and degree is still the accepted idea of the American people and that none of this finds a place in the president's address upon the state of the union.[102]

As Newman had put it bluntly several months earlier, "[T]he Negro must depend upon himself."[103] He showed what he meant the very next week by launching a boycott campaign against five breweries in the Twin Cities, none of which had Black workers. In so doing, Newman was following a growing model in Black communities across the country, from Chicago's Bronzeville to New York's Harlem, which went loosely under the rubric "Don't Buy Where You Can't Work." As Newman argued in his opening blast—a signed, front-page editorial headlined "Is It Fair?"—if the breweries did not immediately desegregate, then "every beer drinker in the Twin Cities (they are a legion) should stop drinking beer manufactured by the offending breweries and drink those beverages brewed by firms which do not practice race discrimination in the selection of their employees."[104]

Very much in concert with the national movement, Newman also made it plain that his fight went beyond obtaining jobs in segregated workplaces. By barring Blacks from employment, Newman argued, white businesses and unions were creating a self-fulfilling justification for bigotry. They forced African Americans onto the dependency of the bread line and then condemned them for needing the dole. "As work tightens and Negro laborers continue to lose out," Newman wrote, "the relief grows and the reputation of the Negro as a desirable citizen shrinks."[105]

Week after week through the spring and summer, with news articles and editorials and caustic cartoons, Newman pressed the issue. He pointedly dismissed the claim by brewers that unions were at fault for barring Black members. True as that was, Newman responded, "[T]here are a hundred and one places in the brewing plants concerning which the unions have nothing to say."[106] While labor and management "may fight among themselves," he observed, they "seem united on the program of 'keep the Negro jobless' or worse yet, on the relief rolls."[107]

Specifically, Newman demanded that the five offending breweries—Schmidt's, Hamm's, Gluek, Yoerg, and the Minneapolis Brewing Company—hire a total of twenty-five Black workers. And Newman stipulated they not do so by firing whites, which would guarantee a violent backlash and perpetuate the toxic image of Black worker as strikebreaker.[108] He made the rounds of nightclubs and beer parlors in Black Minneapolis urging them to stop serving those five brands. He tipped off the Black porters and waiters working trains out of the Twin Cities to recommend other brands to passengers.[109]

Newman charted a few victories in the process. An Episcopal church cancelled its order for Hamm's for its congregational picnic, ordering instead from a Wisconsin brewery that promised to hire Blacks for its Twin Cities distribution. Sure enough, Newman soon published a photo of a Black salesman-driver. The boycotted breweries either felt or feared enough of a blow to the cash register to dispatch an envoy to Newman with a contract for $1500 of advertising in the *Spokesman*. Knowing a bribe when he smelled one, Newman turned down the money, money his newspaper desperately needed.[110] By late November 1935, Newman appeared to be achieving victory; he reported in the *Spokesman* that the president of the Minneapolis Brewing Company had promised to hire two Blacks and assured Newman the other four targeted breweries would do the same. The editor, as a show of good will, toned down his critical coverage.

The brewer's promises, however, amounted to nothing. In the January 10, 1936, issue of the *Spokesman*, the same one in which Newman assailed Roosevelt's State of the Union speech, he furiously reported that none of the promised jobs had materialized. "These Firms Are Unfair!" declared the headline over a list of the breweries. Eight months into the boycott, however, Newman was howling into an abyss. Without the critical mass of Black consumers present in a Harlem or Bronzeville, Newman's campaign could only nibble away at the brewers' income. And in a city where progressive politics were synonymous with organized labor, he was bereft of white allies, because the boycott aimed at unions as much as management. That realization tasted no less bitter to Newman for being so unsurprising.

* * *

Almost two hours past the official end of a midsummer weekend, on the Monday of July 19, 1937, two Minneapolis police officers took their revelry into the Black business district of the city's North Side, the center of their home precinct. Though the cops were off duty, they caroused with the entitlement of being entrenched members of the city's rather inbred law enforcement community. Detective Arthur Uglem was the son and brother of police officers, while Patrolman E. R. Jones, whose buddies called him "Casey," was the child of a firefighter. By their rank and race, they evidently assumed that the nightlife district along Sixth

Avenue, routinely depicted in the papers as a den of sexual sin, was theirs in which to seek forbidden pleasures.

Uglem and Jones barged drunkenly into an all-night restaurant, Barney's Café, and Jones threw himself onto a Black woman there named Georgia Moore. When she resisted, he shoved her to the ground and twisted her arm till she shrieked in pain. Another customer, Willie Steele, pleaded with Jones just to arrest Moore before he killed her. Jones responded to the suggestion by turning his fists on Steele, and, hearing the commotion, a white officer walking his beat along Sixth pulled Steele away to be arrested.

Cursing the restive crowd around them, Uglem and Jones ordered the people away, and most complied. One man, however, remained at Barney's counter. He was Curtis Jordan, a sharecropper's son from Mississippi with an eighth-grade education who had migrated to Minneapolis in search of better work. It came in the form of sporadic shifts as a hotel porter. Between jobs now, he had been grabbing a solitary meal when the two cops showed up. As Uglem and Jones approached him, Jordan lay his head on his arms on the counter, and something about the pose incensed them. They yanked Jordan to his feet, dragged him out the door, peppered him with questions, and, while forcing him toward the nearest police station, beat him unconscious with their fists and flashlights.[111]

After daybreak on that July Monday, Willie Steele and another witness, Cosell Heath, went to the *Spokesman* office to tell Cecil Newman. Going into action as both journalist and activist, Newman interviewed them about the episode. Then, in defiance of the city's racial hierarchy, Newman marched into the office of the acting police chief, Fritz Ohman, to demand an investigation. Incredibly, Ohman granted a meeting the next day, and Newman appeared with twenty witnesses to attest to the cops' rampage. Then he went into print with a lead story headlined "Brutal Attack by Mill City Police Stirs Entire City," calling Uglem and Jones "Minneapolis Cossacks."[112] Over the next two weeks, Lena Olive Smith stepped forward to seek criminal charges against the men, as well to file a complaint with the Civil

Service Commission. As with the brewery boycott, Newman stood on the precipice of justice.

Instead, Curtis Jordan was the one served with an arrest warrant—two, in fact, for a vaguely defined "misuse of funds." A local judge ordered that he be picked up immediately and sent to the county work-house for up to five months. Smith reminded Jordan of his constitutional right to sue the officers; she had a sheath of affidavits from witnesses to his beating. Newman was ready to keep publicizing the case. Was Jordan, she asked, willing to proceed to trial?[113]

He confided to Smith that he was out of work and behind on his rent. He couldn't risk going to jail.

So the system went about its sanitizing way. After Smith paid Jordan's court fees, the charges against him were dropped. Uglem and Jones were transferred from their usual North Side precinct without any penalty,[114] and each man went on to serve in the Minneapolis Police Department for decades to come. Despite Cecil Newman's printed claim that this blatant, bloody case of police brutality had stirred the "entire city," none of the daily newspapers in town printed a single word about it. Their ignorance or indifference comported with a common justifica-tion that Minneapolis whites used for their bigotry, a justification that the graduate student Maurine Boie had heard often in her study of ra-cial attitudes after the mob siege of Arthur Lee's family. "Down South, Negroes understand their place and there's no trouble, but here they are always pushing in," one emblematic interviewee had told her. "I don't think we should treat them as Southerners do; they won't let them vote, you know. He [sic] ought to get the same chance in employment and civil affairs, but let them keep their family affairs to themselves. They're lower than us; let them keep to themselves."[115]

By such reasoning, because it was not a lynching, because it ended with Curtis Jordan only unconscious, not dead, the demonstrable bru-tality of two police officers was, at most, an embarrassment to be qui-etly tidied up. Justice had spurned Cecil Newman once again.

And no matter what Newman wrote at his moments of maximal pride and despair about Black people going it alone, a part of him kept searching for a just white man, even one. A few years earlier, he had extolled a white student at the University of Minnesota, Lee Loevinger, for protesting against the continuing exclusion of Black students from the dorms. "More power to Lee Loevinger," he had written, then offering the wish: "May there be more Loevingers developed in American homes and schools."[116] Lately, he had taken admiring notice of Father Francis Gilligan, a Catholic priest teaching courses in moral theology at a seminary in St. Paul, who publicly declared racial discrimination a sin. "Men like Father Gilligan who dare to tell the truth about such things," Newman wrote, "are worth their weight in gold to the Northwest where there seems to be a studied desire to even discourage discussion of such problems."[117]

Loevinger and Gilligan were men of ideals, that was true, but they were not men of great influence. Like any college student, Loevinger would eventually graduate and move somewhere else. Father Gilligan was a priest without even a parish to oversee. Against Cecil Newman's lived experience of hatred and disappointment and disinterest from the across the color line, he kept looking for that most elusive creature, a white ally who wielded both principles and power.

CHAPTER 3

A PATH OUT
OF THE DUST

Huron, South Dakota

1933–1939

Early on the Sunday morning of November 12, 1933, as Cecil Newman was preparing for his weekly pilgrimage to a Black church in Minneapolis, the Humphrey family stirred awake several hundred miles away in Huron, South Dakota, for its familiar Sabbath ritual, a compromise between piety and commerce. In recognition of H. H.'s need to make any buck that was available three years deep into the Great Depression, he and his sons Hubert and Ralph would open their drugstore for several hours starting at eight and again in the mid-afternoon. In between, the entire family would oblige Christine's faith by attending 11:00 a.m. services at the Methodist Episcopal Church.[1]

In the mercantile portion of their lives, the Humphreys were coming off what passed for a bustling day for beleaguered Huron. Saturday had been both Armistice Day, with a ceremony honoring war veterans at the Huron Theater, and Homecoming Day for Huron High School, with its annual football showdown against archrival Brookings. The festivities continued into the evening with a community turkey dinner and a student performance of *Daddy Long Legs*, a musical variation on the Cinderella theme that supplied a welcome distraction from hard times. With temperatures well into the forties even after nightfall, conditions were more than comfortable enough for Saturday-night shoppers, as H. H. strained to reach his average daily take of twenty-five dollars.[2]

Sunday morning dawned hazy and even warmer, but with the winds now shifting and gusting from the north. The temperamental weather was not unexpected, as the forecast had called for a cold front's intrusion. Even a practiced meteorological eye, the sort that could have discerned the makings of a dust storm in the gales and the parched soil outside town, might not have inordinately worried. Huron had been through such things intermittently as far back at the 1880s, when settlers began turning the sod and exposing topsoil to the incessant winds; there had been a couple of "dusters" apiece in 1931 and 1932 without lasting damage.

So, as the sun prematurely faded behind the gauzy clouds, a sight easily visible through the drugstore's east-facing display window, Hubert readied himself for the working day. H. H. had been promoting nostrums for human, animal, and vehicle in his recent ads— "Elypto-Pine" to cure poultry bronchitis, "radiator glycerine" to keep car engines from freezing, and "Humphrey's Chest Oil" for colds and the flu. Hubert often mixed and bottled the stuff himself and drove through the surrounding farmland to peddle various veterinary remedies, bartering them for beef or eggs or potatoes since hardly any farmer had money to spend.[3]

Hubert was most essential, though, behind the drugstore counter, because he was the only licensed pharmacist in the family, and therefore the only one authorized to fill prescriptions. At H. H.'s behest, Hubert had enrolled at the Capitol College of Pharmacy in Denver the preceding autumn and, by dint of his prodigious memory, completed a two-year course in six months. Then H. H. coached his son on how to flatter the head of South Dakota's licensing board. "Brag up his stores and tell him he is a big success," went the fatherly advice. "You know how."[4]

The loquacious Hubert indeed did. Subsequently endowed with official credentials and a white coat, he entered a form of indentured servitude. As the sole pharmacist in the drugstore, Hubert had to stay there for all of its working hours—seven to midnight six days a week, plus the briefer Sunday shifts—and H. H. paid him nothing for the privilege.

Only on Tuesday nights did Hubert receive a reprieve, in order to serve as scoutmaster for the Methodist church's troop. When he dared to propose hitchhiking to Chicago for the World's Fair in the summer of 1933, H. H. denied him the time off. In a rare show of filial mutiny, Hubert threatened to leave home and then settled for breaking some glasses behind the soda fountain.[5] More commonly, though, Hubert fulfilled his duties and stewed within, his life's ambitions already crushed. As a family friend had teasingly written to him, "'member what a big shot we used to plan for you to be?"[6]

Hubert's sense of obligation, however begrudging at times, also arose from genuine solidarity with a struggling father. H. H. had been a beloved fixture back in Doland; in contrast, when he opened the store in Huron, he was a stranger threatening to steal business from established competitors. Back in Doland, he could jawbone with his buddies Doc Sherwood and Reverend Hartt and entertain farmers with his impromptu lectures on American history. In Huron, the Chamber of Commerce sent an envoy to advise H. H. to tone things down—enough already with the sale prices undercutting the other druggists, and what's with those haughty radio commercials of H. H. reciting poetry. "This is an idiotic way to advertise," the chamber's president pronounced, to which H. H. replied, "It's my money. It's my time. And it's the poetry I like."[7] When the hubris faded and the store emptied out, Hubert spied H. H. "momentarily giving in, sitting head in hands, grinding life and spirit away between unpaid bills and unpaid accounts."[8]

In that despair, at least, H. H. felt at one with the rest of Huron. Though it was a college town, a railroad hub, and home of the state fair, Huron fundamentally depended on the surrounding farms for its existence. And those farms, as of November 1933, had been ravaged by three consecutive years of drought and grasshopper infestation and a recent summer of record-breaking heat. The value of crops in Beadle County, of which Huron was the seat, had collapsed by 1933 to an almost incomprehensible 1.4 percent of the previous decade's average. Beadle had more families on relief than any other of South Dakota's sixty-six counties.[9] Jobless men carried lunch buckets to disguise their unemployment. That staple of desperation-as-amusement, the marathon dance contest, filled the floor at the Band Box nightclub just outside town.[10] Most dramatically, five thousand farmers had rallied in Huron's main park in August 1932, vowing to withhold their goods from the market and blockade roads and trains to enforce the so-called Farm Holiday, unless their wheat, then selling for about thirty cents a bushel, was guaranteed a one-dollar price. "If Constitutions, laws and court decisions stand in the way of justice and human progress," the president of the National Farmers' Union declared to the approving crowd, "it's time that they be scrapped."[11]

Though H. H. and Hubert understood its cause, such rhetoric terrified them. "If a revolution were to break out, or even a violent demonstration," Hubert later paraphrased H. H. as having said, "we would be among the first attacked, not because we had so much, not because we had ever been well-to-do, but simply because, when people lose everything they have, they turn on those who have a little and are visible."[12]

As the morning of November 12, 1933, wore on, and the Humphrey family headed for church, it was apparent that a calamity other than revolution was imminent. The sky had grown nocturnally dark, and the winds were surging to nearly sixty miles an hour, driving the temperature down from the fifties into the teens within a matter of hours. Those gales whipped loose topsoil into the air and then forced the grit aloft into vast, advancing fists before it tumbled back to earth like a Stygian snowfall. Storms like this were called "black blizzards."

By the time the Humphrey men staggered back to the store, visibility in Huron was officially zero, according to the weather bureau. Winds tore off the sign at JC Penney, blew out the windows at the Farmers Union Oil station, and peeled the roof off the Huron Ice Company's warehouse. So much static electricity infused the air that car ignitions failed, radio antennae crackled, and telephone, telegraph, and electricity service ceased. Outside of town, the dust overtopped fences and obscured hunting dogs from their trailing masters. Cattle were speared by airborne two-by-fours. Inside Huron, the dust—fine as face powder, as cake flour—crept in beneath doors and around windows, defying the soaked rags people used to seal the gaps. Particles even insinuated themselves into the linotype machines of the *Evening Huronite*, halting the next edition by hours. With only slight hyperbole, the banner headline would call it the "Most Severe Dust Storm in History." Not that anyone in Huron had any way of knowing, but the storm stretched as far east as Milwaukee and as far south as Amarillo, making it the vanguard of the environmental disaster that would ultimately become known as the Dust Bowl.[13]

Just before noon on that Sunday, an amateur photographer in town named Paul K. Myers braved the blackout to chronicle the otherworldly scene. Most of his photos consisted of blackness pierced by the small halos of streetlights. In one shot, the silhouette of a police officer—charcoal against ebony—could be made out. Another showed the Humphrey drugstore, with its interior lights faintly burning and the American flag visible in the front window. After Myers printed the photo, he wrote on its borders "DUST STORM—THE TOUGHEST OF A SERIES" and "THE SANDS OF THE DESERT."[14]

Inside the Humphrey drugstore, dust wafted to the brass cash register and the varnished-oak supply cabinet and the seventeen-foot-long mirrored backbar, the furnishings that H. H. had lovingly preserved from his Doland shop. Dust covered the stools at the soda fountain and drifted into the sundae bowls. It covered the floor so that every step Hubert took left behind a footprint, soon to be filled by more dust. Not until dusk did the winds subside and the black clouds march on. By then, the damage had been done. With each succeeding storm in the months and years to come, the memory of this one would parch Humbert Humphrey's throat and turn his thoughts grim, leaving him obsessive about sweeping up any hint of dirt. He had seen, as he later put it, "the end of the world."[15]

* * *

As it happened, an especially eminent visitor had checked into a Huron hotel the night before the dust storm and ventured out by motorcar to inspect the nearby farmland during the ominous morning of November 12. Her name was Lorena Hickock, and she had spent part of her childhood in South Dakota before taking up a career in journalism, which led her to a reporter's job with the Associated Press (AP). In that role, she was assigned to interview Eleanor Roosevelt in 1928. Four years later, when the New York governor was elected president, Hickock sought and received the beat of covering Eleanor, which led to a friendship and, possibly, a love affair.

Most relevant to Hickock's arrival in Huron, she had resigned from the AP at Eleanor Roosevelt's suggestion and joined the New Dealers, deploying her journalistic skills as the chief investigator for the Federal Emergency Relief Administration. Its director, Harry Hopkins, mandated that Hickock travel the nation "and look this thing over," relaying what she found as "an ordinary citizen." By the fall of 1933, four months into her mission, Hickock had returned to her home state. She knew that South Dakota had been suffering through its own depression for much of the 1920s, but observing the hunger and poverty and drought now, she informed Hopkins, "A more hopeless place I never saw."[16]

On that epochal Sunday, Hickock and a local relief director were on the highway outside Huron, assessing the damage to crops from the grasshopper plague, when the dust storm descended. As she wrote to Eleanor Roosevelt that night:

> You couldn't see a foot ahead of the car by the time we got back, and we had a time getting back! It was like driving through a fog, only worse, for there was that damnable wind. It seemed as though the car would be blown right off the road any minute. When we stopped, we had to put on the emergency brake. The wind, behind us, actually moved the car. It was a truly terrifying experience. It was as though we had left the earth. We were being whirled off into space in a vast, impenetrable cloud of black dust.

Near the end of the letter, Hickock reached for the same metaphor as had Hubert, whose drugstore was just blocks from her hotel. "It seemed," Hickock told Roosevelt, "like the end of the world."[17]

* * *

There could hardly have been a more serendipitous situation than the presence of Lorena Hickock, an emissary from the White House itself, on the day when Huron had suffered as never before. Her letters to Hopkins and Eleanor Roosevelt ensured that the misery of families like the Humphreys would be seen and heard and felt. Those letters also ratified the hope for rescue that H. H. and Hubert placed reverentially on Franklin Roosevelt. With the New Deal programs that FDR began rolling out, the president was fulfilling the vision of activist government, compassionate government, that H. H. had first admired in Al Smith and that Hubert had absorbed from the Social Gospel.

In November 1932, not yet six months past his twenty-first birthday, Hubert had cast the first presidential ballot of his life for Roosevelt. H. H. was so exhilarated by FDR's inaugural address in March 1933 that he indulged in the luxury of a long-distance call to Hubert in Denver at pharmacy college.[18] Several weeks later, on the occasion of his fifty-first birthday, H. H. continued gushing in a letter to Hubert:

> Wasn't the inaugural great? Roosevelt shure [*sic*] told them. And he is not backing down. His record so far has been a whirlwind, and the whole country recognizes his wisdom an [*sic*] sagacity of purpose. And to think of it, he is our choice. Our democrat [*sic*]. And we can be proud of him and proud of the fact that we supported him before election as well as after, as many are now doing. I am sure he will bring us out of it.[19]

H. H. and Hubert had concrete, proximate reasons for their optimism. Huron's three banks reopened with licenses and clean bills of financial health from the Federal Reserve at the end of the weeklong "holiday" Roosevelt had declared during his first week in office, a period that also saw passage of the Emergency Banking Act. The *Evening Huronite* took note of the "broad smiles on the faces of customers and bankers."[20] By the following fall, local farmers were being paid under the Agricultural Adjustment Act for their surplus commodities and their promise to reduce future production so prices might rise. Huron received a total of $1.3 million from the Public Works Administration for relief jobs in construction. And none of the so-called alphabet soup programs earned more local praise than the CCC—the Civilian Conservation Corps—which hired several hundred teenagers and young adults from Huron for what the *Evening Huronite* dubbed the "Forest Army."[21]

Literally closer to home, H. H. and his family were spared dispossession by the Homeowners Loan Act of 1933. The law created a federal corporation to write mortgages for homeowners at risk of foreclosure, as H. H. indeed was. Amid the Depression, he had never been able to sell the family's abandoned home back in Doland, and that financial millstone dragged on the family's subsistence in Huron. In the summer of 1934, H. H. and Christine were able to take a $1,600 mortgage from the Home Owners Loan Corporation, which paid off much of their original loan and left them owing the government just $12.65 a month. In the house that H. H. was able to rent for the family in Huron, he created a shrine to his savior, hanging a portrait of FDR above the living room mantle.

The bold interventions of the New Deal could raise spirits, at least in the Humphrey household, but even truckloads of federal dollars could not fill the national chasm of need. As of 1934, nearly forty percent of South Dakotans remained on relief.[22] H. H. could see as much at his cash register. "People do not have money," he put it to Hubert, "and when they don't have money, they can't buy."[23] In his volunteer role as scoutmaster, Hubert "passed around secondhand uniforms and tried to outfit each boy from hand-me-downs of older brothers."[24]

Ever since the stock market had crashed and plunged America into the Depression—and, for South Dakotans, ever since the afflictions of stem rust, bank failures, and plummeting wheat prices had struck seven years before then—Hubert had learned one bitter truth. The bottom was never the bottom. Things could always get worse. So his adoration of FDR carried a note of fatalism. "Those were brave words, but for three long years we had heard many words, many promises," he would recall later of Roosevelt's election in the wake of the defeated and disparaged Herbert Hoover. "Could this be, perhaps, just another politician, another false prophet of better times that never come?"[25]

Nonetheless, South Dakota seemed in the early FDR years to have shed its Republican habit. Not only had Roosevelt carried the state in

1932, when the result could have been explained away as a protest vote born of desperation, but Democrats were re-elected as governor and to both of the state's House seats in 1934. By that time, South Dakota voters knew firsthand about the New Deal. Observing the partisan swing, H. H. concocted a political future for himself—a run for the state legislature in 1936, and maybe a try for governor two years later. Enabling his father's electoral fantasies demanded that Hubert stay anchored to drugstore duty. By dint of his pharmacist's license, itself the product of his father's grand plan, Hubert was the indispensable subordinate in the H. H. enterprise, irrespective of his own talents and dreams.

* * *

Finally, in the late summer of 1934, a Humphrey child left home for the gleaming possibilities of FDR's Washington. That child was not Hubert, who might have seemed most likely, or his brother Ralph, holder of the birthright. It was Frances, third in birth order and yet, in temperament, more like a peer to Hubert, even an elder sibling, than a kid sister. In childhood, she had sometimes fought against the boys who bullied Hubert, and she often accompanied him on those wistful walks along the railroad tracks, imagining a future beyond the prairie horizon. Frances had put in two years at Huron College by the middle of 1934, but considering that Hubert and Ralph had been forced by the family's struggles to drop out of school, there was no assurance she would be able to complete her degree. Money was so tight that H. H., normally generous to a fault, grew furious enough with Frances for giving away the occasional ice cream soda or chocolate malt at the soda fountain to stop speaking to her for a week.[26]

Opportunity presented itself in the form of H. H.'s brother Harry, a scientist for the federal Agriculture Department, who visited Huron in 1934 while researching a cure for stem rust. Having given Hubert money years earlier for his university tuition, Harry now offered to bring any willing niece or nephew back East with him to attend college. Frances thrust up her hand, H. H. reluctantly acceded, and soon she was riding the Greyhound bus to Washington. Her grades at Huron College had earned her a scholarship covering tuition at the George Washington University, and for spending money she made thirty-five cents an hour proofreading a plant-pathology journal that Uncle Harry edited. In exchange for housework, she boarded for free with him and her Aunt Olive, a role model with an architecture degree.

As for Uncle Harry, he was one distinctly complicated individual. A fervent Christian Scientist, he had never forgiven the Democrats for repealing Prohibition and dismissed the party's devotees in "the American proletariat" as "an emotional nonthinking mass, easily swayed by any line of argument that is in line with its prejudices."[27] For an agricultural expert, he also took a cynical view of reports about the Dust Bowl. "Those who write this or think this are, of course, only showing their ignorance," he announced. "[T]his is not the only dry cycle that the Great Plains has ever experienced, not is it apt to be the last."[28]

Harry had married an educated, professional woman, and they lived in a one-of-a-kind house that Olive had designed. There, in a Maryland town fifteen miles from Washington, she had adapted the ancient technique known as "rammed earth" to construct the home's walls and foundations from compacted soil. Harry took Frances to the first restaurant of her life and invited her to his exclusive club, the Cosmos; as a woman she had to enter through a side door. And whatever his mixture of arrogance and unconcern on some political issues, he reviled the Southern-style racial code of Washington. He and Frances rode the streetcar together, deliberately seating themselves in the Black section at the rear and ignoring the conductor's order to move forward into the white preserve.

The abrupt transplantation from prairie town to cosmopolitan capital rattled Frances at first. "The only way to do anything at all is to have perfect confidence in one's self—I wish I had that—but the bigger the place, the more the competition," she confided to H. H. "My trouble is I'm not used to being one of the 100,000—in my own mind, I've always thought of myself as being a little apart from the mob, but here one has to fight for any kind of self-expression at all."[29] She bemoaned her "need to acquire poise and become more cultured."[30]

In that pursuit, Frances studied Spinoza, Plato, and George Bernard Shaw in her courses. Outside the classroom, she wrote for the college newspaper, performed the lead in a radio play, served on the student council, and pledged a sorority, in part because then she could live there, much closer to campus. By the end of her second semester at George Washington, she was sending far different dispatches to her landlocked family:

> Oh, what an interesting, busy, mad, wonderful experience this year has been. The process of tearing down social barriers, making oneself feel felt & known, the delight of tasting a varied rich life has all been experienced by me. I live—live—live every moment, then if I tire, I sleep a bit and begin all over.[31]

Though Frances had addressed that particular letter to H. H., the entire family typically read her missives, vicariously sharing in her adventures. And, as it happened, Hubert already had plans to attend a national scouting jamboree in Washington during the summer of 1935, which would put him practically at his sister's front door.

* * *

Around the time when Frances Humphrey left her brother Hubert's immediate orbit, inspiring him from afar, another young woman became an increasing presence in his life. Her name was Muriel Buck, and Hubert had first met her fleetingly in 1932 at a dance at Huron College, where she was then a sophomore. Hubert's stint at pharmacy school in Denver interrupted the couple's nascent courtship, but after his return to Huron in the summer of 1933, they resumed dating.[32] They turned their youthful nicknames into their romantic endearment: Bucky and Pink.

Given Hubert's work schedule, what passed for a date often meant Muriel keeping him company at the drugstore. On occasion, though, H. H. issued his son a Wednesday-night furlough, and Hubert was able to take Muriel dancing. "She and I would whirl around the floor, dance after dance, until intermission," he later recalled. "We'd buy two bottles of orange pop and go out to the car and talk until the band came back."[33]

In terms of both physical appearance and social class, Hubert was punching well above his weight. He was all elbows and knees, carrying just 135 pounds on his five-eleven frame, topped off by a prematurely receding hairline. Muriel, in contrast, caught his attention with her womanly figure and the hint of elegance in her arched brows and half-moon eyelids. She had grown up affluent by Huron's standards, studying classical piano, lending her soprano to community operettas, and refining her skill at needlepoint. Throughout Muriel's childhood, even as much of South Dakota suffered, her father, Andrew, and several uncles did steady enough business as wholesalers of dairy products across a swath of South Dakota and Minnesota. The Bucks' social stature in Huron derived, in turn, from Andrew's roles as bank director, school board member, and deacon of the Presbyterian Church.[34]

Andrew Buck had the politics to match those establishment credentials, scorning even the modest relief efforts undertaken by Herbert Hoover and endorsing the conservative tonic of budget cuts and belt-tightening by Washington. At least he did until the stock market crashed and overextended banks cut off his credit, leaving him to borrow against his life insurance policy and auction off 160 acres of family land. Two days before Franklin Roosevelt was elected, Buck sold his business to an Omaha creamery at a steep loss.[35]

Precisely because she had known childhood comforts, Muriel now shared with Hubert a parallel sense of loss, of ruthless reversal of fortune. At the end of the spring term of 1932, the Bucks' financial plight forced Muriel to drop out of college, just as Hubert had done a year earlier for a similar reason. With the limited money that Andrew Buck had salvaged in selling off his business, he took the kind of wild risk for which H. H. was known, building a cluster of resort cottages on Big Stone Lake, 150 miles from Huron. He rented the cabins for $12.50 a week, offered rowboats at a dollar a day, and peddled minnows, three dozen for a quarter. His wife, Jessie Mae, conscripted in the survival scheme, did all the housekeeping. Mostly, though, the Bucks waited for whoever on earth could afford a vacation five years along in the Great Depression. Then, just a few months into the resort enterprise, Jessie Mae died at age fifty-eight.

Muriel had already been accustomed to a strikingly independent existence for a woman of her time and place. She held a bookkeeping job with a utility company and rented her own apartment instead of rooming with a family for reasons of both thrift and propriety. Now, with her mother gone, Muriel assumed Jessie Mae's former duties, cleaning the cottages at Big Stone Lake. Instead of talking leisurely with Hubert at the drugstore counter or over orange pop outside the dance hall, Muriel now depended on his getting a rare day off work to hitch-hike the ninety miles to Watertown, where she would meet him with a pickup truck to drive together the last leg to Big Stone Lake. Unwilling to sacrifice time with Muriel even for sleep, Hubert would stay up with her till three or four in the morning before hitching back to Huron for his drugstore shift.

Even in her straitened circumstances, Muriel refused to concede the future to humdrum obligation. In her high school yearbook, after all, she had chosen a motto loosely borrowed from Louisa May Alcott, author of *Little Women*: "I'll do something bye and bye, and I'll be famous before I die." The "class prophecy" envisioned her living in Hawaii by 1945 as a hotel entertainer "doing a tap dance and a boop-boop-be-doop song hit."[36] While such frivolity looked unlikely indeed from the shores of Big Stone Lake, Muriel had begun contemplating a more pragmatic escape plan: going to nursing school in Minneapolis.

As for her beau Hubert, however, the indications were decidedly mixed. One side of him joined the county branch of the Young Democrats and soon became its president. With his ongoing curiosity about Black life in America, he read Booker T. Washington's autobiography *Up from Slavery* and, even more daringly, a biography of Paul Robeson, the renowned classical actor and singer and a recent, admiring visitor to the Soviet Union.[37] In his recent letters to Hubert, Uncle Harry urged his nephew to resume college, as Frances had. Hubert's old principal from Doland High School urged him to find some fitting use for his oratorical gifts.[38]

Yet another side of Hubert, as Muriel saw firsthand, remained tethered to the drugstore counter and indentured to H. H. and all his grandiose goals. These now extended from running for statewide political office to spinning off a chain of Humphrey drugstores from the Huron model, magnifying Hubert's responsibility as pharmacist. Confiding her frustrations about Hubert's stasis to a friend of her late mother, Muriel sighed, "Hazel, there's too much family."[39] The same personality traits that made for a devoted, trustworthy boyfriend also made for a perhaps too-dutiful son.

* * *

For months during the spring and summer of 1935, Hubert anticipated only one other reward as much as he did the time he could spend with Muriel. In August, as the scoutmaster of Troop 6 from the Methodist Episcopal church, he would be part of Huron's contingent as it traveled to Washington, DC, for the first-ever National Jamboree of the Boy Scouts, a gathering of nearly 35,000 scouts and adult leaders. The *Evening Huronite* titillated its readers with details of what awaited Huron's three dozen participants during the ten-day event—excursions to Mount Vernon and Monticello, a sightseeing tour of Washington's monuments, visits to the Library of Congress and the National Zoo, and, the crescendo of it all, a "goodwill rally" featuring President Roosevelt himself. By the newspaper's awestruck tally, the jamboree would involve "3,000 faucets and showerheads . . . 70,000 quarts of garbage to be disposed of each day . . . 100,000 flapjacks for one breakfast."[40]

Then, on August 8, less than two weeks before the jamboree was to open, the scouts' national association called it off on the advice of federal public health officials. Cases of polio, that scourge of recent summers, had surfaced in and around Washington. With tens of thousands of boys packed tightly together, the jamboree would have supplied a veritable welcome mat for contagion. So scout leaders in Huron, crestfallen though they were, hurriedly put together a fallback plan for their boys, a canoe trip in northern Minnesota.[41]

Hubert, however, skipped the outing. For once indulging his own desires, he headed for Washington alone. He drove to Indianapolis, hopped a twenty-four-hour bus to Washington from there, and barely slept the whole way. Once in DC, he met up with his sister Frances, and the very next morning, August 19, they were sitting together in the Senate gallery, watching a railroad pension bill be approved and sent to the House for that chamber's vote. Robert Wagner of New York, the champion of organized labor; Robert La Follette Jr. of Wisconsin, the latest link in a family dynasty of Progressives; William Borah of Idaho, a Republican willing to buck his party in supporting the New Deal—Humphrey beheld these giants of American politics from both parties and declared himself "spellbound."[42]

By pure chance, Hubert had landed in Washington as Congress was heading into a furious final week of votes on New Deal legislation before adjourning until January. Already in the eight months of the Seventy-Fourth Congress, the body had passed the laws creating Social Security and the Works Progress Administration. Now FDR was demanding prompt action on what he called "'must' bills," covering matters from harbors to banking to farm mortgages. The president's plan was to culminate a triumphal week with a radio address to the Young Democrats of America at its annual convention, essentially launching his 1936 re-election campaign. Rarely had there been a more fortuitous time for Hubert to observe his political hero in action, even if it had come to him through the terrible coincidence of a polio outbreak.

Hubert made tourist stops at Revolutionary War sites in Virginia, rode a riverboat on the Potomac, heard the National Symphony Orchestra play an outdoor concert of Schubert, and admired Charles Lindbergh's *Spirit of St. Louis* airplane at the Smithsonian. Most of all, though, he returned at every opportunity to the Capitol for the debates and roll call votes of Congress. As he watched and listened, day after day, he did so less as a spectator and more as a student, the way a high school baseball star might sit in the Yankee Stadium bleachers not to be entertained but to be educated in the craft.[43] Or perhaps he was more like a supplicant at a shrine, thunderstruck to hear the divine command. He was so dazzled that when he wrote the first of many letters to Muriel that week, he dated it "August, 1925," off by a full decade.

This trip has impressed one thing on my mind, Muriel. That impression is the need of an education, an alert mind, clean living, and a bit of culture, which undoubtedly will come with age and learning. I don't necessarily mean more college is necessary, but I need to do more reading, more writing, more thinking, if I ever want to fulfill my dream of being someone in this world. Maybe I seem foolish to have such vain hopes and plans, but Bucky, I can see how someday, if you and I just apply ourselves and make up our minds to work for bigger things, how we can someday live here in Washington and probably be in government politics or service. I intend to set my aim at Congress. Don't laugh at me Muriel. Maybe it does sound rather egotistical and beyond reason, but Muriel I do know others have succeeded why haven't I a chance. You'll help me I know. Together we can do things I am sure. Never let me get lazy or discouraged. You be my inspirational force Muriel and always encourage me in what you feel will be right for me to do. Does this all sound ridiculous to you? Tell me, Bucky—please don't let your love for me blind your quality of reason and judgement.

Washington D.C. thrills me to my very finger tips. I simply revel and beam with delight in this realm of politics and government. Oh Gosh, I hope my dream comes true—I'm going to try anyhow, but first I shall prepare myself for the task by reading and thinking always as a liberal.[44]

From Huron, where she was helping at the drugstore in Hubert's absence, Muriel answered in kind.

When I think of you—I imagine you walking up those broad steps that lead into the Capitol Building, or in some great hall looking and wondering, or perhaps strolling beside some lake or pond under the lovely trees you describe, or just talking in your easy, earnest manner to your uncle. . . . These are the things I have not dared to dream about all summer. And now to know that you are actually doing those things thrills me more than you know. Honey, before you left I was truly frightened. It was so far and so many things, dreadful things, could happen to you that it seemed I could hardly bear to have you go. After I heard about Will Rogers and Wiley Post cracking up [in a plane crash] I wanted to go out and beg you not to go. Pink, I knew I couldn't bear it if I lost you. But that isn't the sensible way to feel about such things—I see it now. And when we are to-gether again our love will be greater for all this. And so you see, each time you are thrilled with the things you see and come into contact with, I am thrilled, too . . . I mean—it is a dream coming true for me, too.[45]

It did nothing to dampen Hubert's enthusiasm when FDR actually lost a few of the week's battles. Wary that Italy's impending invasion of Ethiopia in defiance of the League of Nations would ignite another European war and again suck in the United States, a bipartisan majority passed a neutrality bill that the president opposed. On the last night of the session, when Congress was supposed to cap it off by appropri-ating $76 million for Social Security benefits, Senator Huey Long of Louisiana robbed Roosevelt of the victory by rambling through a five-and-a-half-hour speech until midnight arrived and Vice President John Garner, as the Senate's presiding officer, adjourned the chamber until the next January with the slam of his gavel. Though the *Evening Star* lamented the "ignoble failure" on Social Security funding, the Seventy-Fourth Congress had pushed through $10.25 billion in spending, an all-time record, exceeding even the price tag of the 1933 session that included FDR's Hundred Days. And Hubert had witnessed it.

The letters from Muriel, in contrast, reminded him of the trivial doings waiting back in South Dakota—a beard-growing competition, a pet dog named Nappy going missing, the Harvest Festival with its greased-pig contest, the incessant dust piling up on windowsills.[46] For its part, the *Washington Post* ran an AP article about South Dakota having lost nearly seventeen thousand residents since 1930 as they fled drought and grasshoppers. When Hubert answered his far-flung sweetheart, on the stationery of the Willard Hotel, he was marveling at the lobby's crystal chandelier and recounting a morning pilgrimage to the White House. Though Muriel replied with a joke about Hubert planting himself in the Speaker of the House's chair, she immediately turned sober.

"Oh, Pink, I wish you would get a position of some kind so that you could stay there," she wrote.

> It would be fine for you and I think in the long run it would be better for your folks. Perhaps I am in a pessimistic mood about things today. But being here in the office and seeing the bills and bills and bills that are connected with a store and seeing business slowing down for some unknown reason even though there is supposed to be improvement in it makes me wonder if it is worth the lifetime of sacrifice, along with work, that your whole family has given it.[47]

Toward the end of that four-page letter, Muriel dared express her fantasy of a letter that H. H. would write to Hubert: "Bucky is right about all this. I need you but you must live your own life, too. Do you want to go through it always looking for a 'good crop' as I have?" Directly underneath those lines, Muriel offered an apology: "Oh, honey—I'm so nuts—but I love you and love you for your dreams and want to make them come true for you. Forgive me again for talking of the 'unmentionable' [of defying H. H.] again."[48]

But if Hubert felt that Muriel had transgressed, he did not say so in any of his subsequent letters and postcards. They mentioned how lifelike the statue at the Lincoln Memorial was, and about bumping into Huey Long in the Senate waiting room, and about his plans to visit the battlefield at Gettysburg on his way home. "One feels so rather humble and yet so proud," he summed up in one letter, "to know that you too are an American."

Emboldened, Muriel penned one last letter to Hubert before he left Washington: "I know that we can get to the top together. You were afraid I'd laugh at you for making Congress your aim? Hardly, when I have even set it higher."[49]

* * *

Nearing the most eventful week of his life, Hubert sat down on August 23, 1936, to write two letters. On August 28, President Roosevelt was scheduled to visit Huron as part of a train trip through the Great Plains to view drought conditions and public-works projects, and, not coincidentally, to campaign for re-election in November. Just three months past his twenty-fifth birthday, Hubert was on the official reception committee by dint of his leadership of the Beadle County Young Democrats. Then, on September 3, he was going to marry Muriel Buck, his partner in both love and ambition.

A year earlier, as Muriel and Hubert exchanged those letters during his Washington trip, she had joked, "Don't forget to tell the President 'hello'" from her.[50] Now, in the letter Hubert was sending to Muriel up at Big Stone Lake, he could plausibly write of FDR, "I may even get to help introduce him, and I'm sure I shall get to talk to him while he is on his train." With that missive complete, Hubert drafted a thank you letter to the president for the upcoming stop in Huron, sending it air-mail Special Delivery to the White House,[51] as if Franklin Roosevelt were anxiously awaiting the postman.

Approaching the signal date of August 28, however, the president's itinerary kept shifting and changing, with Huron finally being omitted from the litany of whistlestops. Only at 7:15 that night did word arrive via Western Union that, in fact, FDR's train would be pulling into Huron within two hours. The inconsistency in the presidential schedule may well have been fabricated for security's sake. FDR, after all, was traveling with the protection of nearly thirty Secret Service agents.

As the harvest sun set after eight, five thousand people, nearly half of Huron's entire population, thronged the platforms at the Chicago & North Western station. Huron's municipal band and a drum-and-bugle corps from the American Legion marched up the main shopping street of Dakota Avenue, right past the Humphrey drugstore, to greet the train. When Roosevelt emerged from his private car and lifted one arm aloft to acknowledge the ovation from his audience, the musicians launched into "The Star-Spangled Banner." Secret Service agents in their suits and fedoras struggled vainly to buffer the president from the encroaching wave of admirers.

Standing on the rear platform of his customized Pullman Pioneer coach, with a lectern obscuring his braced, paralyzed legs, FDR devoted much of his five-hundred-word address to the importance of agricultural planning. He had ample reason to know about Huron's vicissitudes, because one of the federal officials joining him on the inspection tour was Harry Hopkins, the federal relief administrator who'd received Lorena Hickock's harrowing account of the dust storm three years earlier. The president reminded the crowd now that wheat and corn prices were rising, and the farmers in the crowd knew that this August had been the wettest month of the year, boding well for the fall crop. "It is a fine thing to know that you people out here are not despondent the way some people back East have told us," Roosevelt said. "I have come out here to find you with your chins up, looking toward the future with confidence and courage." A moment later, with a presidential promise to "come back by daylight and see more of you," the speech was over, and FDR returned to his Pullman coach as the local bands serenaded him with "America the Beautiful."[52]

Only then did the Secret Service agents summon forward a delegation of prominent local Democrats, including Hubert and H. H., for a private audience. According to the *Evening Huronite*, FDR spoke to them mostly about the need for greater water conservation. Whether Hubert ever had the chance to introduce himself and momentarily chat with the great Roosevelt remains unclear. But, in a sense, the president had addressed Hubert most directly a year earlier, in his speech to the Young Democrats' national convention:

> While my elders were talking to me about the perfection of America, I did not know then of the lack of opportunity, the lack of education, the lack of many of the essential needs of civilization; all these existed among millions of our people who lived not alone in the slums of the great cities and in the forgotten corners of rural America—existed even under the very noses of the power of government of those days.
>
> I say from my heart that no man of my generation has any business to address youth unless he comes to that task not in a spirit of exultation, but in a spirit of humility. I can not expect you of a new generation to

believe me, of an older generation, if I do not frankly acknowledge that had the generation that brought you into the world been wiser and more provident and more unselfish, you would have been saved from needless difficult problems and needless pain and suffering. We may not have failed you in good intentions, but we have certainly not been adequate in results. Your task, therefore, is not only to maintain the best in your heritage, but to labor to lift from the shoulders of the American people some of the burdens that the mistakes of a past generation have placed there.[53]

Hubert's route to his wedding day had been a good deal bumpier than the president's rail excursion. All through the spring and summer of 1936, while officially engaged to Muriel, he had swung unpredictably between passion and prevarication. Both emotions were magnified by the 150 miles between her at Big Stone Lake and him in Huron as they wrote each other twice, sometimes three times, a day.

"You are the man I want," Muriel pledged, "so full of energy, ambition, and good honest convictions." Yet when she briefly mentioned having bumped into a former boyfriend at the county seat of Milbank, Hubert convulsed with jealousy, what he called his "devilish, nervous nature." He ordered, "NO FLIRTING WHILE IN MILBANK," in a subsequent letter. At points during the months apart, particularly after the occasional dust storm, he described himself as "depressed and blue," "sullen and upset." Trying to reduce the emotional temperature, he admitted to Muriel, "I even get kinda disgusted with life when you're not around."[54]

If the answer to Hubert's insecurity was marriage to Muriel, though, he resisted closing the deal, ashamed of how little money he could bring to the union. He squirmed away from committing to a wedding date and the lease on a marital home. It took two ultimatums—a threat by Muriel to move to California on her own and a six-page letter from her father jabbing him for treating a wedding date "same as you would a duck hunting trip, just say it will depend on weather"[55]—for Hubert to consent to a September 3 date.

Even so, he nearly forgot to pick up the marriage license, and had to beg a county employee to unlock the Huron courthouse the night before the nuptials. Early the next morning, he donned a double-breasted gray suit for the Presbyterian church ceremony, which, along with fifty dollars for a honeymoon, was Andrew Buck's present to the couple. As for H. H., he had insisted that the wedding take place at 8:00 a.m. on a weekday, so the drugstore need not be closed during lucrative hours.[56]

As Hubert's married life began, he was making radio speeches extolling FDR as often as four times a week, leaving one Huron listener to liken the improvised orations to the breakaway runs of football star Red Grange.[57] The more immediate political concern for the Humphrey family was H. H.'s race for a seat in the state legislature. Despite a notable souring in South Dakota toward the New Deal, with FDR's share of the state's vote falling by ten percent from 1932, H. H. captured a place in the Pierre state house. He conceived of it as the launching pad for a 1938 race for governor. Apparently, H. H. had not been paying much attention to the president's advice about handing the reins to the younger generation.

So at the time when Hubert should have propelled forward, he instead stalled out like one of those cars brought to a halt by the 1933 dust storm. Already thin, he grew gaunt from his long hours at the drugstore. Occasionally, he fainted, whether from exhaustion or anxiety. During the winter of 1937, their first as husband and wife, Hubert and Muriel tried to distract themselves with travel magazines about the Caribbean and Mediterranean and thoughts of saving up enough money for a cruise. Most often, though, the destination for which Hubert yearned was the University of Minnesota, the Xanadu of knowledge that financial crisis had forced him to abandon almost six years earlier.[58]

Hubert could kid around with Muriel about not being able to spoil her with a fur coat and a baby grand piano; he could joke that "our future professions are sealed—you are a scrubwoman, me a duster and dishwasher."[59] But he was also capable of more clinical, indeed unsparing, assessment. "Childish dreams—boyhood ideals—youthful enthusiasms—all these forces tended to evolve a plan of life in my mind for my future," he wrote to Muriel, "but, as is generally the case, the exact details of my plan have been lost in the mix up of these last years, and now I find that instead of living my life as I had planned from the years of 18 to 25, I have been living as circumstances forced me to . . . I lost my fondest hope of graduating from a university . . . [and] I have experienced the hardships of business depression."[60]

The reality was that H. H. kept relying on Hubert as a pharmacist to bring in money to cover the father's never-ending losses. Six years after leaving Doland, H. H. had yet to sell the family's former house there, an eyesore even in better times, and was falling behind on the monthly payments for his federal mortgage. In Huron, the Humphreys moved from one rental to another on an almost yearly basis, as if staying one step ahead of an unpaid landlord. Most recently, a competing pharmacy in Huron had installed a new ice-cream freezer, and H. H. was going $1300 dollars deeper in debt to match it, lest he lose all the soda-fountain business.

All these blows affected H. H.'s political leanings. Every bit the gung-ho New Dealer in public, H. H. privately groused about "dirty internationalists" and "money changers."[61] It was startling for a man seemingly free of prejudice to invoke phrases that were widely understood as code for Jews. At the least, H. H.'s choice of epithet attested to a new desperation in him, a need for somebody other than himself to blame.

Too loyal or too cowed to break loose from the filial fetters, Hubert turned to his one ready source of willpower: Muriel. "I've resolved again to educate myself somehow or other so as to be able to make a mark in the world," he had confided to her in a letter shortly before their marriage. "Help me honey, by encouraging our reading, our attending church, concerts and programs. I've been so used to giving up my life for my work that I know I'll need your guidance and help . . . I'm not going to be just a mediocre fellow. . . . And someday I'm going to make you proud of me—you just see if I don't."[62]

Whatever exact words of advice and inspiration Muriel provided cannot be known. Living under the same roof now as husband and wife, they had no reason to exchange letters, which could have documented their conversations for posterity. The end result of their discussions, however, became clear one evening in August 1937, as H. H. and Hubert were locking up the drugstore at midnight.

Worried about his son's fainting spells, H. H. suggested they take a drive together so they could talk without being overheard or interrupted. They climbed into the Model A, the extravagant acquisition that once had conveyed Hubert to Minneapolis for college, and headed for an isolated place. In one version of that night's events, recounted decades later, they parked the car outside H. H.'s house; in another, they went to the southeastern edge of town, where the streets gave way to wheat fields. Both accounts agree about what happened next. For perhaps the first time in the three years since Hubert had blown up at H. H. about not being able to travel to Chicago for the World's Fair, the cheerfully compliant veneer that son presented to father melted away. Hubert talked about his dark moods, his blackouts, his tormented tug of war between devotion to H. H. and the longing to test his own potential.

"Dad," he said, "I don't want to peddle pills." "Hubert," H. H. responded, "if you aren't happy, then you ought to do something about it."[63]

The dark of the August midnight was like the dark of all the dust storms that Hubert had endured, something enveloping and inescapable. But now, given this opening by H. H., Hubert at last could perceive the path out, a path lit by two women. One was his sister Frances, who had abandoned almost everything that was secure and familiar to head east to college three years earlier. By now, she had earned her bachelor's degree and entered graduate school for social work, her chosen way to improve the world. The other torchbearer, of course, was Muriel, the sharer of Hubert's secret and audacious dream of serving the nation.

As it happened, there was a month, even a few weeks more, before fall classes would commence at the University of Minnesota in late September. Hubert and Muriel had some money saved from the seventy-five dollars a month she was making as a bookkeeper. With the South Dakota legislature out of session in the fall, H. H. would have time to locate another pharmacist to take Hubert's place.

So, on one of the first mornings of autumn, Hubert and H. H. took the front seats in the Model A, with Christine and Muriel in the back, and they aimed eastward toward Minneapolis, ten hours away. If Hubert harbored doubts about resuming academic life after six years away, the passing sights eliminated any second thoughts.

"The land was sere and brown, without the lushness of a good harvest," Humphrey would later recall. "[A]nd as we bounced along the highway through the little towns that had been a part of me—I watched the gaunt faces of men standing, staring in front of buildings laminated with dust."[64]

* * *

Hubert Humphrey re-entered the University of Minnesota in a state of determined impatience. Starting his junior year at age twenty-six, he was three months older than one of his political science professors, Evron Kirkpatrick. Humphrey registered for twenty-one credits compared with the usual fifteen and ignored the undergraduate bustle of pep rallies and fraternity rushes, allowing himself the sole recreation of rejoining the debate team.

Beyond the campus, Humphrey took part-time work as a pharmacist while Muriel, alert to the bias against hiring married women, slipped off her wedding ring long enough to land a bookkeeper's job. The Humphreys stretched every resulting cent to cover tuition, books, food, and the shabby shelter of a one-room, third-floor apartment that shared a common bathroom and kitchen with tenants down the hall. When Muriel's father visited the couple, he was alarmed that their flat didn't even have a fire escape. So he tied a coil of rope to the apartment's radiator, from where it could be unspooled out the window. Above that same radiator, Humphrey hung a portrait of FDR. In the profile pose, the president appeared to be gazing toward the desk where Humphrey hunched over his nightly classwork.

During his first stint of college, nearly a decade earlier, Humphrey had struggled with the transition from being the prodigy of diminutive Doland to one bright mind among thousands. His mediocre grades admitted as much. This time, seasoned by hardship, sobered by adulthood, made ravenous for the classroom after having been denied it so long, he excelled. He aced virtually every course, from introductory surveys in political science and sociology to advanced seminars in Constitutional Law, American Diplomacy, Public Administration, and European Dictators.[65]

In the process, Humphrey attracted both mentors and allies. In one of Evron Kirkpatrick's courses, he met a farm-toughened teenager named Orville Freeman, who had been recruited as a quarterback for the college football team and ended up becoming a classroom star instead. Humphrey and Freeman tangled so often in Kirkpatrick's course that the professor took to inviting them back to his office to continue the dialogue over sandwiches. Ultimately, the odd couple—Humphrey skinny as a fence post and already balding, Freeman a blond block of muscle—competed together on the college debate team. Fittingly enough for a couple of Roosevelt devotees, they argued in favor of federal stimulation of the economy.[66]

Unlike Kirkpatrick, who was so much a contemporary of Humphrey's that he let the student call him by the nickname "Kirk," Benjamin Lippincott was a scholar of intimidating credentials. Still in his midthirties, he had already studied at Yale, Oxford, and the London School of Economics, absorbing from his mentor Harold Laski an ethos of democratic socialism. In his early years at the University of Minnesota, which hired him in 1929, Lippincott had endured a smear campaign portraying him as a communist. In fact, he believed that socialism and capitalism were potentially compatible, provided that the business community acted on the basis of "social responsibility and distributive justice."[67]

For the admiring Humphrey, Lippincott also modeled the kind of intellectual who engaged with the real world. He wrote essays about socialism, communism, and fascism for the lay readers of the *Minneapolis Star*. He taught workshops on "Building Democracy" for the local branch of the Women's International League for Peace and Freedom, a pacifist group in which his modern-dancer wife was active. He served as president of the university's branch of the American Federation of Teachers, and as a delegate to the city's Central Labor Union, socializing and collaborating with the kind of blue-collar crowd that many PhDs would shun.

"There is an idea that a teacher should be a sterilized citizen, that a teacher should not take part in political or other affairs," Lippincott told a campus forum in 1938, while Humphrey was his student. "But men who live in the ivory tower are always in danger of losing touch with the community. Too often, their scholarship is dissociated from the world."[68]

In Humphrey, Lippincott saw unrefined ore, potential greatness in need of tempering. The professor respected his student's inherent compassion and innate resistance to dogma, an earthy pragmatism that he had learned from lived experience. At the same time, Humphrey in the classroom could try Lippincott's patience. The professor taught his courses by Socratic method, orchestrating whiplash exchanges with his students. *What's a democracy? What's the rule of law? Who sets the laws?*[69] Humphrey preferred to respond with free-associative soliloquies, all those things he had been burning to say during six years of exile in the Huron drugstore, leading Lippincott at one point to declare:

> My friends, now you have just heard this brilliant speech by our older student here, Humphrey. He's been around a while and knows the drug business and has been taught politics by his father, but I've got to tell you and then tell him, that in this class, we've got to pass it around. In this class, I'm both, unfortunately, pitcher and umpire, and after three strikes, you're out. And even though it's delightful to have these excursions that my friend here has given us, I do have to give other people a chance.[70]

Lippincott was hardly alone in his exasperation. An instructor in speech class complained that Humphrey "rasped and quacked" and was "tiring to listen to for more than a few minutes." A reporter of the *Minnesota Daily* named Arthur Naftalin, coming upon Humphrey in the midst of an impromptu campus speech, shrugged him off as a "little nutty guy" who was "probably a little touched in the head." Ever eager for a pulpit, Humphrey volunteered on the spot to deliver the keynote address to a college rally against American intervention in the burgeoning European war.[71]

That speech, though, proved to be one of Humphrey's only explicit involvements with the political ferment on the campus. The University of Minnesota in the late 1930s was roiled by protests against the continuing racial segregation of student housing, a cause that engaged several of Benjamin Lippincott's other star students. A proposal by the student government to raise money for refugee students to attend the university—this coming amid the fascist triumph in the Spanish Civil War, the Japanese invasion of China, and the Nazi pogrom of Kristallnacht—set off a furious backlash from classmates that "our benevolence should start at home."[72]

So voluble and opinionated in the classroom discussions and debate tournaments, Humphrey had nothing to say publicly on such issues. And he was defensive enough about that silence to admit, in retrospect, "I didn't have much time to join a protest movement. I was concerned with being able to earn enough to eat."[73] That pressure was genuine, and it intensified a month into Humphrey's final semester with the birth of his first child, a daughter named Nancy, which meant Muriel could no longer be the household's primary breadwinner. Soon after, Muriel's father Andrew suffered a heart attack, and she went with Nancy back to Huron to nurse him.

As Humphrey donned robe and mortarboard in June 1939, he could reasonably envision a future of scholarship and public activism in the manner of a Benjamin Lippincott. FDR's "Brain Trust" of New Deal advisers, after all, abounded in people who could walk both sides of the street. Humphrey now had racked up the requisite grades to continue into graduate school, as his sister Frances had, the next logical step in his progression. Along with his diploma, he had earned magna cum laude honors, a Phi Beta Kappa key, and the William Jennings Bryan Prize for the outstanding undergraduate paper in political science. He also was essentially penniless.

For the past several months, however, Evron Kirkpatrick had been plotting his friend and protégé's rescue. First, the University of Illinois, where Kirkpatrick had earned his bachelor's and master's degrees, proposed to appoint Humphrey a "scholar in political science" for the 1939–1940 academic year. But the yearly stipend, three hundred dollars, was nowhere near sufficient for a family of three.[74] Then Kirkpatrick happened to hear from one of his own former professors, Charles Hyneman, a political scientist who had recently left Illinois to become chair of the Department of Government at Louisiana State University in Baton Rouge. Hyneman wrote that he had "enough money and a fellowship to enable a person to stay alive for a year"—specifically, $450, substantially more than Illinois was offering. Perhaps Kirkpatrick could recommend someone who "had a first-class mind and would like to come South and see what that part of the world was like."[75] Yes, Kirkpatrick could.

Two months after commencement, in August 1939, Hubert Humphrey bought a one-way train ticket to Louisiana. Having crossed only a few miles into the former Confederacy a handful of times in his life, he was bound now for the land of Jim Crow.

CHAPTER 4

THE SILKEN
CURTAIN AND
THE SILVER SHIRT

Jewish Minneapolis

1934–1939

The dense, humid heat had broken early on the evening of July 29, 1938, granting Minneapolis a breezy respite, and along the working-class corridor of Lake Street several thousand fans were heading into the Nicollet ballpark for a Friday-night game. The Minneapolis Millers, a farm club of the Boston Red Sox, were plodding along in third place, but the skinny California kid in right field by the name of Ted Williams was batting in the vicinity of .350 and lashing out homers.

A few blocks away from the stadium on that same night, a different crowd was gathering for a different attraction. They streamed into Ark Auditorium, a turreted brick fortress of respectability that was home to a Masonic lodge. For this occasion, it had been rented for a "meeting of patriotic, christian [*sic*] citizens" who were prepared to take "united action" against "the alien forces that are seeking to undermine our constitutional government, take away our right of free speech and deprive us of our liberty,"[1] as the host put it in a formal letter of invitation.

That summons brought out between three and four hundred concerned Minneapolitans. Hardly a rabble of the ignorant and unwashed, they ranged from laundry workers to merchants and business owners, nearly half of them women. A discerning eye, such as that of an under-cover informant inserted among the crowd, could even pick out some of the city's elite: George Drake, president of the school board; E. J. Somerville, head of the Real Estate Board; and George K. Belden, leader of the Associated Industries of Minneapolis, the successor organization to the anti-union Citizens Alliance that had been defeated in the 1934 Teamsters strike.[2]

Knowingly or not, these upstanding people were assembling for a rally sponsored by a homegrown fascist group called the Silver Legion of America, and more commonly known by its trademark apparel as the Silver Shirts. Very deliberately aping the Brownshirts, Adolph Hitler's militia, the legion's uniform featured a large scarlet *L* over the heart, "standing for Love, Loyalty, and Liberation."[3] Two other aspects of the legion's platform, while failing to perpetuate the alliteration, called for returning American Blacks to slavery and disenfranchising, segregating, and finally sterilizing American Jews.[4]

The Silver Shirts were the invention of one William Dudley Pelley, and he, like the group, was deceptively and dangerously easy to toss off as lunatic. Though Pelley had seen the light of the Jew-hating, Hitler-loving gospel during a series of divine visitations, or so he said, he was a main-line Protestant minister's son from New England who had done human-itarian work overseas for the YMCA during the Bolshevik Revolution and successfully freelanced magazine articles and screenplays. After founding the Silver Legion in 1933, quite consciously in the wake of Hitler's assumption of power, Pelley sold it the way one would sell magazine subscriptions, with a combination of advertisements and re-gional salesmen. In true huckster style, he wildly exaggerated the result, claiming several million followers nationwide when the hardcore mem-bership was closer to fifteen thousand.[5] But Pelley had the demagogic gift of raveling together classic anti-Semitic dogma with a proposal for a guaranteed annual income for all Americans except Blacks and Jews. What he called "Christian economics" was really a kind of social safety net exclusively for the privileged race, another concept borrowed from the Nazis and one that was undeniably tempting to much of white Gentile America as the Depression dragged on in defiance of New Deal remedies. Even as the Silver Legion stealthily sought alliances with the kindred spirits of the German American Bund and the Ku Klux Klan, it appropriated the Union's anthem during the Civil War, *Battle Hymn of the Republic*, as its own.

Once the audience members in Minneapolis took their seats, assisted by a set of well-trained ushers, they were greeted by the legion's local organizer, a confectionary salesman named T. G. Wooster. Having lost his comfortable home to foreclosure just two years earlier, reducing himself and his socialite wife to the precarious status of month-to-month renters as they entered their seventies, Wooster was a man in the market for a scapegoat, and a scapegoat was what Pelley had provided. Presumably, many of Wooster's listeners shared both his anxiety and his antipathy.

After an introductory prayer and a brief survey of Jewish perfidy, Wooster turned over the podium to the evening's main attraction, Roy Zachary, who had run a greasy spoon in the Seattle bus depot while building up a statewide chapter of the legion. As Pelley's handpicked "national field marshal," Zachary had made his way to Minneapolis by headlining rallies in cities small and large—Boise, Spokane, Youngstown, Chicago, Milwaukee, Philadelphia. Promoting the events with euphemisms about "Christian American Patriots" and "an address on communism," Zachary was able to rent out reputable settings in YMCA branches, hotel ballrooms, and fraternal lodges. People who might have recoiled from joining a movement explicitly modeled on Hitler's seemingly had few trepidations about being instructed, under the auspices of flag-waving, as to just whom they could blame for their hard times.

Admirers and opponents alike did agree about one thing: Zachary was a formidable orator. Pelley described how his protégé "gets up, pulls in his chin, shoves up the back of his head like Jiggs in the comic strips, hitches up his trousers, and forthwith lets fire. . . . The dynamic sincerity of the man explodes like a volcano, spattering his lava all over the hall."[6] The informant at the Minneapolis rally admitted that, while Zachary's content was "garbage," he "is a pretty good speaker."[7] And one with a self-effacing sense of humor, too: he joked that he was wearing a white shirt on this night because his silver one was in the wash.[8]

As legion members in their official garb patrolled the auditorium aisles, Zachary launched into a two-hour diatribe. One listener, planted there for intelligence gathering by local labor unions, subsequently reported that the field marshal "told his audience that President Roosevelt was a Jew, that he is surrounded only by Jews and that he is led and controlled by Jews. He denounced the New Deal as a Jewish contraption and blamed that race for every ill that plagues society today."[9] Similarly, the *American Jewish World*, the Twin Cities' weekly Jewish newspaper, apparently had been able to insinuate a reporter into the crowd. The resulting article described Zachary making "rambling attacks . . . on President Roosevelt, Cordell Hull, Henry Morgenthau, Frances Perkins, the United States Supreme Court, newspaper publishers and the Jews." As if the point were not sufficiently clear already, the writer added, "The latter were his 'special hate.' "[10]

In further explication of that cherished hate, Zachary aired out Pelley's most crackpot claptrap. Morgenthau, the Jew who was Franklin Delano Roosevelt's Treasury secretary, had conspired with the Soviet Union to buy silver for quarter coins, which he sold into the domestic economy at an illicit profit. President Warren Harding's death while in office was probably an assassination to keep him from revealing how the Jewish bankers of Kuhn, Loeb & Company had defrauded the American government of thirty million dollars "by forging government bonds." In the face of such skullduggery, Zachary concluded, the American people "could not combat the Jewish conspiracy through the ballot," so it must be defeated "through the organization of vigilante groups in every community to take whatever action is necessary to crush the conspiracy."[11]

Far from being put off by Zachary's antic formulations or his siren call to vengeance, the audience repeatedly and raucously applauded. When the rally ended at ten-thirty and hundreds of listeners flowed back onto the streets, a Jewish photographer was taking what he hoped would be shaming photos of the attendees. One of them, a prominent local dentist, tried to smash the camera.[12] The next day, news of the Silver Legion rally merited only a few paragraphs far inside the city's afternoon paper, the *Star*, and was overlooked entirely by the morning *Tribune*.[13]

The ovations inside the Ark Auditorium that July night had drowned out cheers from all those spectators several blocks away at the Nicollet ballpark. The Millers knocked off the Kansas City Blues by a 6–3 score, and while Ted Williams had an unusually quiet night at bat, the hero was second baseman Andy Cohen, who swatted a homer and a two-run double. Every baseball fan in town could tell that Williams would be a Minneapolis short-timer, destined soon for the big leagues. Cohen, though, followed the opposite trajectory, becoming an eight-season fixture with the Millers and a cherished local institution after his major-league career had ended. Quite possibly, he was the most popular Jew in Minneapolis. Which actually was not saying a whole lot, given the city's historic animosity toward the Chosen People.

* * *

As night fell on September 5, 1880, beginning the first day of the month of Tishrei on the Hebrew calendar, several hundred of Minneapolis's Jews gathered for a dual celebration. They were marking Rosh Hashanah, the Judaic new year of 5641, and they were doing so at the first worship service to be held in the city's first permanent synagogue, a wooden structure downtown that had been consecrated as Shaarai Tov, the Gates of Goodness. In that benevolent spirit, the congregational rabbi, identified for posterity only by his surname of Schreiber, told the faithful, "We have erected a house of worship in Israel, not only to show that the Mother of Christianity[14] is not to be despised although she is old. The Mother remembers well her duty to all of her daughters, inviting them to the universal shrine of worship."[15]

Such was the sound of an unanswered prayer. The rejection by Gentile Minneapolis of its Jewish minority did not occur instantly, to be historically precise about it. As with the city's Black population, when the Jewish enclave was new and small, it posed little perceived threat to white Protestant power. And the first wave of Jews in Minneapolis, most of them of German heritage and already Americanized by earlier residence in Eastern cities, ardently believed they could prove themselves worthy of the Mill City's embrace. In 1888, Shaarai Tov effusively recounted that its annual synagogue fair "was so brilliant and enjoyable that our local papers were united in sounding praises for the fine appearance, perfect manners and great sociability of our people."[16] By the early 1900s, the college-educated young adults of Jewish Minneapolis formed a social club named Gymal Doled after two Hebrew letters with the goal of simultaneously modeling "the highest of Jewish ideals and the spirit of American patriotism."[17]

Regardless of those aspirations, and regardless of the presence of skilled merchants and experienced shopkeepers among the German Jewish community, even the relatively early arrivals to Minneapolis got there too late for the financial bonanza. The pillars of the regional economy—lumber, milling, and railroads—were already dominated by transplanted New England Protestants at the executive and managerial levels and Scandinavian immigrants in the rank and file. "We never got anywhere near the really big businesses of this area," the adult child of German Jewish immigrants later recalled.[18]

Meanwhile, events across the Atlantic were changing the composition of Minneapolis Jewry and providing bigots a convenient excuse for maligning the entire population. The assassination of Tsar Alexander II of Russia by revolutionaries in 1881 set loose a wave of pogroms against Jews, and the next year, the first trainload of refugees reached the Twin Cities. Half of its several hundred passengers were destitute, having spent their meager funds on passage from Europe. Though the newcomers initially settled in St. Paul, where leaders of the Catholic-majority city provided public aid to them, hundreds and ultimately thousands migrated a few miles farther west into Minneapolis, often working as peddlers selling merchandise on consignment for German Jewish merchants.[19]

The continuing flow of Eastern European Jews—from Russia, Romania, Bessarabia, and Hungary—expanded Minneapolis's Jewish population from 6,000 in 1900 to 13,000 thousand in 1910 to exactly 16,260 in 1930. Nearly seventy percent of them lived on the North Side, preceding Blacks into the once-tony Oak Lake district and then the frame duplexes and brick apartments stretching northward from Sixth Avenue two dozen blocks to the edge of a working-class Scandinavian district. To a sociologist conducting fieldwork, these Jews presented the unsavory picture of "small dealers, some rag peddlers, some fruit men, and still others dealers in junk."[20] Beyond that limited portrait, Eastern European Jews also worked in garment and cigar factories, as tailors and furriers, and they opened stores of all sorts, drugstores and delis, bakeries and fish markets. In the category of *a shanda fur die goyim,* a shame in front of the Gentiles, the Jewish community also contained a share of gangsters, who took up bootlegging during Prohibition, ran gambling joints, and, in the case of Isadore Blumenfeld, aka Kid Cann, was suspected though never convicted of several murders.[21]

Collectively, Jews comprised 3.5 percent of Minneapolis's population as of 1930, and that number simultaneously managed to make them visible enough to be considered a threat and scant enough to be socially and politically powerless against the growing pattern of bias. As with local Blacks, Jews in the Twin Cities experienced a stark contrast across the municipal boundary. In St. Paul, where Jews had settled in significant numbers by the mid-1800s, they served as court commissioner and building inspector, headed the Red Cross, and were elected to the Library Board. Jews were accepted into elite clubs and upscale neighborhoods. Minneapolis, in contrast, operated under what might be called a unified field theory of anti-Semitism. Whatever social mobility Jews had achieved prior to the Great War came to a crashing halt, indeed a reversal, with the return of job-seeking Christian veterans, followed by the farm economy's distress in the 1920s, and the nativist agitation that led Congress to throttle immigration in 1924. The end product for Minneapolis Jews, as a historian later put it, was "a silken curtain which lay between them and the larger society."[22]

The city's social clubs, hospitals, public school workforce, prestigious office buildings—all of them restricted or entirely barred Jews. Despite a state law that had been unanimously passed in 1919 outlawing religious bias in selling or renting property, real estate signs routinely said "No Jewish People."[23] The broker for a coveted subdivision, which had not sold a single home to a Jew in ten years, explained that he was, in truth, protecting delicate Jewish sensibilities from feeling "out of place in a strictly Gentile [*sic*] community" where they would "have very little in common."[24] The lakeside resorts where Minneapolitans vacationed turned away Jews with the stock phrase "Gentiles Only."[25] As with Minnesota's similar law against racial discrimination, words in a statute book meant nothing without adherence and enforcement. Even one of the landmark decisions protecting the free press, handed down by the U.S. Supreme Court in the 1931 case *Near v. Minnesota*, was made at the expense of Minneapolis's Jews. In espousing a lofty principle, the court was specifically protecting the right of a scandal sheet called the *Saturday Press* to have declared without evidence that Jewish criminals, "THE RODENTS OF THEIR OWN RACE" [capitals in original], were responsible for "ninety percent of the crimes" in Minneapolis.[26]

In the Rosh Hashanah edition of the *America Jewish World* in 1923, two generations after Rabbi Schreiber's hopeful words on the holy day, a contemporary rabbi offered this grim appraisal:

> Minneapolis Jewry enjoys the painful distinction of being the lowest esteemed community in the land so far as the non-Jewish population of the city is concerned. And that is what I mean by "objective evaluation,"—the evaluation of the Jewish community by the non-Jewish population of the city. In this respect, Minneapolis Jewry is way below par of other communities in the land ...
>
> I do not believe that there is a single purely social organization in the city that welcomes Jews as members. There is not, to my knowledge, a single Jewish member in any of the numerous city and country clubs; nor are Jews solicited in the Boat Club or Automobile Club; and even the Athletic Club, I understand, has raised the barriers against any further Jewish accessions above those who were permitted to enter when its sacred precincts were first opened some years ago.
>
> Fraternal organizations too, which find their chief reason for existence in the furtherance of fellowship and brotherhood, see fit to discriminate against Jewish fellowship and brotherhood. At least, so far as I have been able to ascertain, no Jew has ever gone through the chair in either the Elks Fraternity or in any of the many Blue lodges of the Masonic Fraternity, not to speak of the honors connected with the higher degree of Masonry.

I do not know of a single Jew in Minneapolis who enjoys the privilege of sitting in at the festive board at their weekly luncheons with either the Rotary club, the Kiwanis club, or the Lions club. This is all the more strange when it is borne in mind that these organizations are devoted primarily not to social fraternization, but to civic welfare, and recruit their membership from all groups and classes, trades, industries, and professions . . . [27]

Thus walled off from the surrounding society, Minneapolis Jews enjoyed two perverse benefits. If not exactly unified, they indulged in less internal friction than did the more accepted Jews of St. Paul along the fault lines of German versus Eastern European, observant versus secular, Orthodox versus Reform and Conservative. The embodiment of Minneapolis Jewry's comparative harmony was Samuel Deinard, the longtime rabbi of Temple Israel. Though he led a Reform congregation, which had evolved from Shaarai Tov, Deinard comfortably worshiped in Orthodox synagogues on occasion; unlike the usual Reform clergy, he was Russian rather than German by ancestry, and in an era when Zionism was primarily the ideology of antireligious socialists, he not only endorsed it but also had spent his youth in Palestine.

The second advantage of their enforced isolation was that Minneapolis Jews developed a thriving neighborhood across lines of social class on the North Side, something akin to the Black hub of Rondo in St. Paul. By the mid-1930s, Jews in Minneapolis had formed nearly one hundred organizations—synagogues, burial societies, an employment bureau, lending circles offering interest-free loans, a settlement house, the afternoon and weekend Hebrew school known as a Talmud Torah, and local branches of such national organizations as the YMHA, B'nai B'rith, and the National Council of Jewish Women.[28] In commercial terms, the self-contained self-sufficiency of the North Side was typified by Solomon Brochin's deli at the neighborhood epicenter of Sixth and Lyndale, where customers could buy herring and corned beef, Russian tobacco, prayer shawls, Yiddish newspapers, and even Cunard steamship tickets for relatives intending to immigrate from the old country.

However much the North Side may have felt like a sanctuary from the hatred beyond its borders, the decade of the 1930s shattered the illusion. An unsigned editorial in the *American Jewish World* during the High Holy Days in 1933 called it "the blackest Rosh Hashana in generations." One year later, Rabbi Albert Gordon took to the newspaper's pages with an even bleaker assessment:

> That the past year has brought anguish and pain to the Jewish heart is incontrovertible. The Jew's lot, with the increase of the Hitler terrorism in Germany and the spread of anti-Semitic doctrine throughout the world, including our own land, has made us a little less certain that the Almighty who watches over the destinies of humankind still remembers His people's plight and heartache.[29]

The despair, indeed, the crisis of faith, derived from a confluence of forces—some global, some national, some local; some economic, some political, some theological. Together, they transformed the North Side, already a remote part of the worldwide Jewish map, into a beleaguered bunker. Looming over all else, of course, was the rise of Nazism in Germany and the promulgation there of anti-Jewish laws and mob violence. That Germany was an enlightened country, the homeland and cultural touchstone of Minneapolis's first wave of Jewish residents, could not help but raise the specter that even America, the *Goldeneh Medinah*, the Golden Land, might similarly mutate. And economic distress, as in Germany, could provide the convenient pretext.

The toll of the Great Depression on Minneapolis Jewry could be measured in myriad ways. With breadwinners out of work and family budgets strained, the annual fundraising drive for the local Jewish federation raised less than twenty thousand dollars in 1931; put another way, that meant there was about a dollar and a quarter on average for assistance to each Jewish resident.[30] The North Side may not have supplied the tableaux of breadlines and squatter camps so visible in and near downtown, but there were subtler signs of penury, such as the smoke rising from a family's chimney. Light gray meant the household could afford coal; a darker, oilier plume, however, indicated occupants so broke that they were scavenging and burning tar-soaked wooden blocks from the streetcar bed for heat.[31]

With any job being coveted amid an unemployment rate above twenty percent, the local branch of the National Council of Jewish Women conducted a survey of nearly one hundred Minneapolis employers in late 1931. The research documented not only the pervasiveness of bans or quotas on Jewish employment—when Help Wanted ads routinely said "Gentile Preferred," that was hardly a secret—but the fiercely held stereotypes used to justify the bias. "Many of the employers complained of Jews being too social with their own group and not always courteous to others," the study reported. "Another frequent criticism was that Jewish employees wanted raises and salaries too soon. Also there was complaint that Jews want jobs that do not require physical work. They did not take trade training. Most merchants said they could not hire too many Jewish sales people because of the danger of the place of business looking too Jewish."[32]

The epic Teamsters' strike of 1934 offered its own evidence of the particularly tenuous place of Jews in the battered local economy. While one Jew served as an officer in Local 574, another was its lawyer, and about a dozen were rank-and-file drivers, the Jewish community inordinately consisted of merchants, shopkeepers, middlemen, and the employees of such small businesses. They were, in other words, caught in a vise between militant labor and reactionary management, both of them led by Gentiles. The *American Jewish World* recounted the narrow escapes of Jewish grocers, druggists, launderers, and dry cleaners just trying to do their daily business during the strike without running afoul of the warring forces along the barricades. One Jewish proprietor, discovered with a few cases of berries, had to watch union enforcers destroy them; another, delivering laundry to customers in his own car, got hauled into strike headquarters for a beating.[33]

It was hardly that the Citizens Alliance, on the other side, offered aid and comfort. The 1934 strike fed rumors that Local 574 was run by Jews, despite the fact its leaders were Irish and Nordic; arguably the most radical ethnic group in Minnesota were the Finnish miners in the Iron Range, many of them committed communists. After Rabbi

Gordon, an experienced labor negotiator in addition to being a cler-gyman, was invited by both sides in the strike to serve as an impartial arbitrator, handbills began turning up around town with the rhetor-ical question, "Why, Rabbi Gordon, do you control the unions of Minneapolis?"[34]

Beginning a year before the strike, and continuing during and after it, top administrators at the University of Minnesota acted on the sim-ilar presumption that to be Jewish was to be alien and, quite possibly, subversive. On orders from the university president, Lotus Coffman, a running tally was kept of Jewish students, as well as Black ones, even though they amounted to well less than ten percent of the student body and were already frozen out of most fraternities, sororities, and pre-professional clubs.[35] The dean of student affairs, Edward E. Nicholson, planted spies to surveil supposed communists and sympathizers on campus. He, in turn, supplied that information to a conservative Republican politician, Ray P. Chase, who was refashioning himself as a freelance intelligence operative intent on securing "America for Americans," invoking the nativist slogan. Both Nicholson and Chase shared their findings with the FBI. And while Nicholson had not iden-tified the students on his list by religion or ethnicity, Chase sought in-formation about their "nationality,"[36] a euphemism that likely omitted white Christians. His fixation on Jews, as a later scholar put it, went beyond ideology; for him, being Jewish was "a racial marker of differ-ence . . . a category of 'otherness.' "[37]

* * *

On the Sunday morning of November 11, 1934, the Reverend William Bell Riley stood in the pulpit of First Baptist Church to declare a reve-lation. This epiphany concerned the direction of his ministry, and, more than that, a new way of understanding the world. And because Riley was among the most important and respected clergymen in Minneapolis, an ambitious and successful institution-builder, and perhaps the most sig-nificant fundamentalist Christian in the entire nation, his word carried impact well beyond his own congregation of several thousand.

Reverend Riley's sermon began with the recollection of a breakfast he had shared four years earlier with his fellow evangelist, Mordecai Ham, who was visiting from Kentucky. Reverend Ham pressed into Reverend Riley's hands a book entitled *The Protocols of the Elders of Zion* and spoke of little else for the next hour. Reverend Riley's then-wife Lillian subsequently paged through the volume and pronounced of Ham, "He has lost his mental balance." She meant it in a clinical way, for the evangelist indeed had been badly injured in a recent auto accident.

It had taken Reverend Riley until the past few months, by which time the skeptical Lillian had died, to finally read the *Protocols*. As an erudite man, the minister surely knew that the book was widely considered a forgery concocted by Russian anti-Semites. Yet as Riley read the *Protocols'* account of a Jewish conspiracy to rule the world, he found himself staggered by the prescient way it foretold the Jewish role in the Bolshevik Revolution abroad and the socialistic New Deal at home.

"Fact number one," he now informed the First Baptist congregation.

> The Jew fingerprints of the *Protocols* are in every nation on earth. Fact number two: the representatives of this race are at the elbow of every great ruler on earth, dictating national policies. . . . The *Protocols* present a definite plan to have every movement that would stall the political maneuvers of Jewry labeled "persecution" in order to blind the soft-hearted Gentile nation until the Communist coup is accomplished.[38]

Minneapolis had several other Protestant ministers who trafficked in similar trash—Luke Rader, W. D. Herrstrom, C. O. Stadsklev—but they were histrionic performers with lesser churches, rented radio time, and flocks of suspicious and resentful have-nots. Riley exuded scholarship, refinement, urbanity. He preached in a vested suit, hands clasped behind his back, studding his sermons with references to Plutarch, Plato, Kipling, and George Bernard Shaw. "NEW SORT OF EVANGELIST, THIS REV. RILEY," a Seattle newspaper had noted in a headline when he appeared there. "DOESN'T RANT AND FLAP HIS COATTAIL; LOOKS LIKE A BANKER." Reverend Riley so appreciated the compliment that he preserved the press clipping in a scrapbook.[39]

More than attire and vocal timbre set Riley apart from the fundamentalist norm. That form of American Christianity had emphasized
removing oneself from the doings of the secular world, such as voting,
and concentrating instead on achieving the personal purity that would
ensure salvation in the next world. In contrast, Riley combined the same
premillennialist theology, with its beliefs in the inerrancy of text and the
imminent return of Jesus, with a fervent call to engage with the issues of
the day. Early in his tenure at First Baptist, in fact, Reverend Riley operated as a kind of social reformer, a conservative version of the Social
Gospel proponents whom he considered heretics.

Having grown up in Kentucky as the son of a tenant farmer, working
a plow from the age of nine, Riley felt an inherent sympathy for poor
whites. Even after he had advanced himself through college and divinity
school, partly thanks to an affluent patron who saw his potential, Riley
held distinct ideas of how to create God's kingdom on earth, another
concept he shared with the Social Gospel movement. Inheriting a congregation at First Baptist that counted mill barons like the Pillsburys
and Dunwoodys as members, the new pastor did away with the system
of pew rentals that had punished if not altogether excluded the working
class. He built a Bible college next door to First Baptist, founded a
monthly magazine, more than doubled the sanctuary's size, and augmented gospel songs during worship services not only with the expected
choir but a fifteen-piece orchestra and even a harp soloist. Reverend
Riley's ferocious denunciations of the city's gambling, drinking, prostitution, crooked police, and corrupt politicians, while entirely consistent with his puritanical faith, also echoed the indictment levied by
the muckraker Lincoln Steffens in his 1903 article in *McClure's* magazine "The Shame of Minneapolis," which was subsequently included in
his acclaimed book *The Shame of the Cities*. The nation's progressive
intellectuals were hardly going to dismiss Steffens as a bluenose.

No cause engaged midcareer Riley more, however, than the battle
against teaching Darwinian evolution, an increasing challenge to the
biblical version of Creation in public school classrooms. The minister barnstormed the West Coast debating a speaker from the Science
League of America. Riley founded the World Christian Fundamentals

Association in part to mobilize Protestant clergy on the issue and in 1925 persuaded his own hero, William Jennings Bryan, to serve as the prosecuting attorney in the case of John Scopes, a high school teacher who had been charged with violating the Tennessee law banning instruction about evolution. Though Bryan actually did secure a conviction, the so-called Monkey Trial opened his brand of fundamentalism to mainstream ridicule. When Bryan died in the aftermath of the trial, Riley inherited de facto leadership of the fundamentalist movement, trying and failing in the late 1920s to push for an anti-evolution law in Minnesota.

So by the time of his breakfast with Mordecai Ham in 1930, entering his seventies, Riley was a rebuked prophet in need of a new cause. *The Protocols of the Elders of Zion* supplied it. And to the peril of Jews in Minneapolis, the cultivated figure of Riley presented an unparalleled danger. His was the reason that sanitized the contaminant of Jew hatred. He was the dapper and handsome link between the "silken curtain" of polite anti-Semitism with its quotas and covenants and the thuggery of the Silver Shirts.

"I am certainly surprised that a man of your standing, reputation and ability should help in spreading such rot," a Jewish attorney wrote to Riley. "[T]o have you heading one of the largest organizations in the city, with a national reputation that you have, you, a leader of a religious group in search with the rest of the religious groups of our country for God, to have you make these assertions, it seems to me justifies anger."[40]

So far as can be discerned, Riley never answered the letter. He did, however, respond to it at great length. That reply came in the form of sermons about how Jewish financiers had caused World War I, how Jews controlled industries and commodities in America, how Jews in Minneapolis ran all the illegal liquor and also "crowd[ed] the hall of Red Communists and head[ed] street parades of the same."[41] Riley simply ignored the intrinsic contradictions of such anti-Semitism, the way the Jew could simultaneously be capitalist, criminal, and revolutionary. And he went to pains to make it understood that he spoke this truth more in sorrow than in rage:

I disclaim all prejudice. There is no grounds [*sic*] upon which a Christian should have a mere prejudice against a Jew. We adopt his Sacred Book as our own; we give him credit for having provided the Christian's Savior through a Jewish Mother, so there could be no religious prejudice. There could hardly be a race prejudice since the Jews are a white race. . . . Socially the Gentiles have always offered to the Jew far more attention than he is willing to accept; and politically we have given to the Jew in America every right accorded to native-born Americans.

Why, then, has he become unpopular in this country? It is my profound conviction he has nobody to blame for it but himself.[42]

* * *

During the summer of 1936, a twenty-three-year-old reporter on the *Minneapolis Journal* with the byline Arnold Sevareid got a tip from what he described as "Communist acquaintances,"[43] presumably those he had met while attending the University of Minnesota. The Silver Legion was starting to organize in Minneapolis, holding secret house meetings to recruit and indoctrinate members. Sevareid somehow found a way to embed himself in a few of those sessions, perhaps because as the son of a Norwegian American banker from North Dakota, he set off no demographic alarms. Having concluded his infiltration, Sevareid told the *Journal's* managing editor what he had seen and heard. The editor considered the legion's conspiracy theories so deranged—for instance, the Jews were planning to seize control of the entire country, with Minneapolis as a key target, on their upcoming holiday of Rosh Hashana—that he could only choke them down with a strong drink. Sevareid, however, deemed the Silver Legion "a cadre of Fascism,"[44] well worth serious investigative effort.

Word of Sevareid's forthcoming articles reached some prominent members of the Jewish community in Minneapolis, and as the journalist later recalled, "A group of liberal rabbis and wealthy Jews asked the editor to withhold the story. It would all be painful to them, most undignified, and would merely drag out into the open and abet a virulent form of anti-Semitism. It would be better to ignore the madmen and pretend they didn't exist."

The editor settled on a compromise solution. Sevareid could write the articles, and they would be published, but "not as I had wanted them written, as a cry of alarm, but as a semihumorous expose of ridiculous crackpots."[45]

That turned out to be a fateful decision. In theory, the *Journal* could have portrayed the Silver Legion as a genuine danger. It could have placed the group within the context of other pro-fascist outfits like the German American Bund and the Black Legion; it could have pointed to the congruence between William Dudley Pelley's anti-Semitic belief system and that of the radio priest Charles Coughlin, who had a national audience well into the millions; it could have explored the affinity between the extremism of the Silver Legion and the widespread, socially acceptable forms of anti-Semitism that pervaded Minneapolis, embodied by such municipal pillars as Reverend Riley. The *Journal* did none of those things.

Instead, to Sevareid's frustration, the articles largely played the Silver Legion for laughs. In six front-page stories from September 11 through September 16, 1936, the *Journal* emphasized the wackiest anecdotes from the secret meetings—Franklin Roosevelt's real name as a secret Jew being Rosenfelt; the plans for a Jewish takeover of America being predicted by glyphs within the Giza pyramids; the way Henry Morgenthau, the Jew who was FDR's Treasury secretary, bought quarters for five cents apiece from the Soviet Union. (That last yarn obviously changed in a few of its details by the time Ray Zachary recycled it in the 1938 rally.) Evidently seeking to placate his editor, Sevareid employed a tone that was wry, understated, and mocking, a long way from *j'accuse*. The final installment, running on the supposedly decisive day of September 16, Rosh Hashana on the Jewish calendar that year, clucked in its headline, "Silvershirts' Dire Prophecy Falls Flat; World Goes On With A Chuckle Over Plot."[46]

The blasé public response, then, was predictable. The *Journal*'s own editorial, while conceding "this is a serious matter," expressed "pity for these misguided persons, the dupes of ambitious and unscrupulous schemers." It self-congratulatorily concluded, "The action of THE JOURNAL in letting daylight in on the fantastic Silvershirt movement should prove sufficient to dissipate it in this region." Whether out of competitive jealousy or mere complacency, the other daily papers in town essentially ignored Sevareid's scoop. Even the *American Jewish World*, in its sole editorial on the series, noted the "mingled reactions to it" among Minneapolis Jews—that the article "would serve to laugh the 'Shirts' out of existence," that "Jewish interests would be better served by silence," and that the Silver Legion would shrink away as the Ku Klux Klan had done a decade earlier.[47]

Sevareid, though, may have arranged to have the last word. The *Journal* published only one letter to the editor about the Silver Legion series. The author, Sherman Dryer, identified himself as a university student active in politics. He conveniently omitted the fact that he was a classmate and friend of Sevareid's, a fellow member of a left-wing fraternity called the Jacobins that included many leaders of the student newspaper and government.[48] So Dryer's letter served as the medium for the message that Sevareid had always intended for his articles to convey: "Most Americans do not think that it can happen here. This is what German Republicans said in 1932. But it did happen there, and it will happen here unless our citizens awake to the impending danger."[49]

* * *

Several weeks before Sevareid's articles appeared, an event that seemed entirely unrelated added power to the anti-Semitic upsurge. Governor Floyd B. Olson, the closest thing that Minnesota's Jews ever had to a political champion and guardian, died on August 22, 1936, in the midst of a campaign for the U.S. Senate. Though his own heritage was Swedish and Norwegian, Olson had grown up on the North Side, so immersed in the Jewish neighborhood that he served in youth as a "Shabbos goy," a Gentile willing to do tasks such as turning on lights that are forbidden to observant Jews as forms of work on the Sabbath. Throughout his political career, Olson deftly wielded Yiddish idioms and jokes and comfortably wore a yarmulke at synagogue events. Beyond such supportive behavior, he made good on his promises to defend Jews, as well as other racial and religious minorities. As Hennepin County attorney in the late 1920s, Olson had invoked the state's public-nuisance law to prosecute the *Saturday Press* for its anti-Semitic screeds. (The screeds also alleged that Olson himself was controlled by Jewish gangsters.) Three months into his first term as governor in 1931, he appointed a Jewish attorney, Gustavus Loevinger of St. Paul, to a county judgeship, and Olson went on to name Jews to posts in his administration. He joined several thousand local Jews at Temple Israel in early 1933 for a mass rally against Hitler's regime.[50] So Olson's death inspired both a memorial service at the Beth El synagogue and a rapturous editorial in the *American Jewish World*:

> It was this freedom from racial and religious prejudices added to his natural sympathy for the underprivileged and understanding of the problems, dreams, and aspirations of minority groups, that would have made his election to the United States Senate . . . so important, especially in these reactionary days of racial discrimination, religious bigotry and national chauvinism.[51]

Predictably enough, Olson's death set off a power struggle for his gubernatorial seat. What was less predictable, and disturbingly revealing to the Jewish community, was how much the struggle pivoted around anti-Semitic imagery, rhetoric, and insinuation. By state law, the remaining five months of Olson's term were filled by Hjalmar Petersen, the lieutenant governor. But Olson's[52] chosen protégé had been Elmer Benson, a commissioner in the state cabinet before being named to a vacant U.S. Senate seat in 1935. Benson ran for governor and won in 1936, setting up a confrontation with the spurned Petersen in the gubernatorial primary in the spring of 1938.

On paper, Petersen and Benson belonged to the same political party, Farmer-Labor. In reality, they embodied its leftist and centrist factions. Benson's stances on both foreign and domestic issues dovetailed with those of the antifascist Popular Front, a coalition of progressive groups that included communists. He also had followed Olson's example in appointing Jews to prominent positions, including the first ever to serve on the University of Minnesota Board of Regents. Though Petersen could lay claim to some major liberal achievements, authoring the state's income tax law during his years in the legislature and pushing through state unemployment insurance in his brief time as governor, he also embraced the bigoted underbelly of populism. This was the same man, after all, who had privately informed a social-science researcher that, were a Black man to move into his neighborhood, he would feel justified in killing him.[53]

Without explicitly attacking Jews during his campaign, Petersen winked in that direction. He often used the peculiar epithet "Mexican generals" to refer to shadowy, radical forces allegedly controlling Benson. Petersen did not name those insidious aliens, but he hardly needed to fill in the blank; the Jewish identity of several of the governor's advisors, including his staff secretary, was well known. In a campaign advertisement in the *American Jewish World*, ostensibly an appeal for Jewish votes, Petersen deftly deployed innuendo about dual loyalty and subversion. His primary goal was to imply that Benson was a Red, but in so doing, he was also casting the primary election as an empirical test of patriotism, as if Minnesota's Jews still had something to prove in that department:

> I know no distinction between Protestants, Catholics, and Jews, so far as their right to security, freedom and the pursuit of happiness in this free country. All I ask is that, whatever be their land of origin or their religious belief, Minnesotans should not be faithless to our State by playing with the fires of Communism, Nazism and Fascism. The time has come to say to all our people, "Be true Americans."[54]

Petersen's tactics failed, as he lost the late-June primary to Benson by about four percent, but the stink of anti-Semitism hung in the air. During the spring and early summer of 1938, even as the Silver Shirts prepared for their July 29 rally, the German American Bund began printing a weekly newspaper in Minneapolis. The Reverend George Mecklenburg, an established Methodist minister with a congregation of twenty-five hundred in the affluent Lowry Hill neighborhood, delivered a sermon on radio and in print asking the question "Who Runs Minneapolis?" He responded, in part, "There are folks who say that the Jews run Minneapolis and they point out case after case where Jews are the owners of the dives and places that violate the law."[55]

Coming amid all that, the Silver Legion meeting, with its appreciative crowd and blueblood attendees, galvanized the local Jewish community much as the white mob's attack on Arthur Lee's home had for Black Minneapolis years earlier. It was as if Sevareid's infiltration and exposé of the Silver Shirts two years earlier had done nothing but drive them briefly into hiding, cockroaches fleeing a switched-on kitchen light. Until this point, Jews in Minneapolis could believe that pigment alone afforded them some protection from exactly the sort of vigilante violence that had been inflicted on the Lees. Though Jews were "Christ-killers," as the slur put it, they still were white people, more or less. They would be denied jobs, subjected to quotas, barred from living in certain neighborhoods, but not threatened with exile or death. Or so they had long assumed. The popularity of the Silver Shirts, set against the anti-Semitic atrocities in Germany, called into doubt even such cold comfort.

A breaking point had been reached. It was no longer enough for Minneapolis Jews to snap photos and jot down license plate numbers outside legion events in the hope of humiliating members with public exposure. Confronted in an open letter by Rabbi Gordon with evidence of his attendance, George K. Belden of Associated Industries disavowed the Silver Shirts while simultaneously averring, "They have some ideas that are good." George Drake, the Board of Education president, explained that he'd gone to the rally only "out of curiosity" and found it "kind of a burlesque show."[56] In letters to the editor of the city's papers, people assailed Rabbi Gordon for having had the temerity to question Belden's behavior.[57]

It was also becoming clear, as it had been during the legion's flurry of local activity in 1936, that the city's media did not take the threat seriously enough. Even as it firmly criticized the Silver Legion in an editorial, the *Tribune* reassuringly predicted that the outfit "will probably run the same course as the Ku Klux Klan,"[58] withering away in a few years.

The Askov American newspaper, one partly owned by the Farmer-Labor politician Hjalmar Petersen, blithely opined that the group only appealed to "the simple-minded, the jealous, the ignorant and the credulous."[59] As for the Minneapolis police, the chief, Frank Forestal, explained that he couldn't do anything about the Silver Legion unless "there is violence or disorder."[60]

Such clueless consolation left Minneapolis Jews feeling both unimpressed and unprotected. They had heard it all before about how decent ordinary people would not fall for anti-Semitism. And they had heard their own rationalizations, too, that it was safer to keep your head down, not to make waves, to wait for it to blow over, all those clichés. There was even a Yiddish idiom that served up the same advice: *sha, shtil*, meaning "shh, hush." Incredible as it seemed to the city's Jews now, in the summer of 1938—after the enactment of the Nuremberg race laws, the opening of the Buchenwald concentration camp, and the Nazi takeover of Austria—there had even been times early in Hitler's reign when the *American Jewish World* had counseled German Jews to "wait for the return of calmness and sanity in the Reich."[61]

That mistake was not going to be repeated here at home. Far from recommending patience in the wake of the Silver Legion, the newspaper issued a call to rhetorical arms:

A unified, well-co-ordinated [*sic*] group should devote itself to the task—ceaseless and untiringly—of educating the general public to the real menace of fascistic groups. To speak plainly, the Silver Shirt is not solely a Jewish problem—a Jewish peril. It is an ugly, monstrous thing, masking itself as patriotic—that if allowed to spread unchecked will destroy the liberties of all.[62]

* * *

On August 8, 1938, the rising generation of Minneapolis Jewry crammed into the neoclassical temple of good works known as the Citizen's Aid Building. Along with the staples of Christian charity—the Big Sisters, the Church Federation, the Lutheran Welfare Society—it contained the offices of the Jewish Family Welfare Board. Pressed together in that air-less room on a sweltering night were 175 people representing sixty dif-ferent organizations. More important than the institutional credentials they held, these men and women were motivated by a shared impatience and indignation. Born in Minnesota, educated in its public schools, trained for professions in its colleges and universities, fluent in American pop culture and unaccented English, they collectively realized they were as vulnerable to Minneapolis's Jew hatred as the pawnbroker or scrap-metal dealer. They recognized, too, that their prior efforts at defending themselves were, "at best . . . an amateur performance, a feeble counter-measure against terrifying evil forces."[63]

Their main vehicle was an Anti-Defamation Council attached to the city's B'nai B'rith lodge. The council had no paid staff, just volunteers, and received about a thousand dollars annually from the Jewish Federation, not much fuel for the engine. And the Minneapolis council could not act without the approval of the national headquarters of the Anti-Defamation League of B'nai B'rith, a day's travel away in Chicago. These Jews in their twenties and thirties were done with taking direction from their cautious elders, however. As one participant in the meeting wrote soon after to the *American Jewish World*:

> [T]he time has come when those men who have worn the mantle of lead-
> ership in the Minnesota Jewish Community these many years must now
> turn to new blood, younger, more vigorous men for assistance. The day of
> "shah-shah" is past. By their own admission, these old leaders agree that
> the time has come when Jews must come out into the open to fight the
> enemy.[64]

The question, though, remained of how to fight. Ever since the Silver Legion had first turned up in Minneapolis in 1936, the city's Jewish gangsters had volunteered themselves as brass-knuckled avengers. "These guys will respect cracked skulls," one mobster said of the Silver Shirts to Charles Cooper, a social worker active in the Anti-Defamation Council.[65] Such boasting aside, violence was indeed bursting out, with fistfights between Silver Shirts and Jewish vigilantes outside the Silver Legion's second recent meeting, on August 2. For men like Cooper, deploying a gangster militia did not represent a plausible strategy. Jews were a tiny minority amid a hostile majority in Minneapolis, and the far tinier faction of Jewish mobsters had long provided a pretext for anti-Semitism. Yet they had tapped into a communal desire for self-defense.

The minutes of the August 8 meeting have not survived, but an account of it in the *American Jewish World* provided the essence. There needed to be a permanent, independent organization with its own staff to track and respond to episodes of anti-Semitism in Minnesota. Additionally, the current group of council volunteers had to ensure that the bigotry that had emerged during the primary election for governor not be repeated in the upcoming general election. A committee—likely led by Cooper, serving without salary in his spare time as the council's first director, and Amos Deinard, an attorney who was the son of the esteemed Rabbi Deinard—would meet with the major-party candidates to secure their promise to travel by the high road.[66]

If such a meeting ever did occur, it resulted in failure. The fall campaign between incumbent Elmer Benson of the Farmer-Labor Party and his Republican challenger, Harold Stassen, made explicit every biased double-entendre of the primary race. In the last month before the election, a political cartoon was distributed across the state, ultimately appearing on posters and billboards, as well. Entitled "Three Jehu Drivers," Jehu having been a king in ancient Israel, the drawing portrayed Benson as a donkey being ridden by three identifiable Jews—the governor's staff secretary Roger Rutchick; A. I. Harris, editor of the Farmer-Labor newspaper *Minnesota Leader*; and Art Jacobs, secretary to the speaker of the state assembly. The depictions of Harris and Jacobs each emphasized the stereotypically large Jewish nose, while Rutchick was shown wearing a sombrero, an allusion to the code words "Mexican general." As those Jews controlled the hapless Benson, the arms of "The Common Man," identified by such ancestries as Yankee, German, Irish, Italian, and Scandinavian, reached out in vain for sustenance.[67]

In the immediate wake of the cartoon, Ray P. Chase unleashed his own smear. Far from hiding his fingerprints, the entrepreneur of political espionage eagerly claimed authorship of a sixty-page booklet called *Are They Communists or Catspaws*,[68] with the redundant subtitle *A Red Baiting Pamphlet*. Chase's immediate goal was to undermine Benson's candidacy by portraying him as a communist, and the Farmer-Labor Party as a veritable creation of the Communist International. As with "Three Jehu Drivers," Chase used the time-honored tactic of fingering the secretive, seditious Jews. The purported "High Command" of Rutchick, Harris, and Jacobs featured prominently in *Are They Communists or Catspaws*, fortifying Chase's contention that they controlled Benson. (To their cabal Chase added Sherman Dryer, who had written the letter to the editor praising Sevareid's series on the Silver Legion and was now a speechwriter for Benson.) In both word and image, Chase heightened the role of the four Jews by barely mentioning the far greater number of Gentiles who were prominent in the Farmer-Labor leadership and Benson's administration. An innocuous photo of Benson surrounded by a half-dozen companions at a fraternal lodge banquet was airbrushed by Chase to look like a confidential meeting between the governor and Rutchick.[69]

Chase distributed thirteen thousand copies of *Are They Communists or Catspaws* to Republican candidates and conservative ministers throughout the state. To no avail, Jewish supporters of Benson's placed ads calling attention to the forgery and exaggeration in Chase's booklet and charging, "Jew Baiting Has Been MADE an Issue in This Campaign." Harold Stassen, meanwhile, had it both ways with anti-Semitism. The thirty-one-year-old "boy wonder" of the Minnesota GOP, he skillfully positioned himself as a "middle-of-the-road liberal" between the Farmer-Labor leftists and the Republican old guard, embracing most of the Farmer-Labor social compact while promising less patronage and tighter budgeting.[70] Yet he conspicuously refused to disavow Chase's anti-Semitic appeals, and in a complete inversion of reality, attributed "the flames of prejudice and . . . hatred" to Benson's campaign. "WE HAVE ALWAYS RESPECTED MINORITIES," a Stassen ad in the *American Jewish Week* emphatically and dubiously declared. "AND WE HAVE NEVER PARTICIPATED IN ANY MOVEMENT BASED ON INTOLERANCE OR PREJUDICE."[71]

The ballot box on Election Day, November 8, told a different story. Elmer Benson, who had won election two years prior with 680,342 votes and a twenty-two percent margin, lost to Stassen by nearly 300,000 votes, hanging on to barely one-third of the total. Benson's fervent support for striking workers and his failed efforts to expand the safety net and raise taxes may have alienated some moderate voters. The incumbent also fell victim to a national wave swamping Democrats in the midterm election, with FDR's party losing seventy-two seats in the House and seven in the Senate. But it was also undeniably true that close to 700,000 citizens of Minnesota, few of whom had ever consorted with or even heard of the Silver Legion, had proven with their votes that a candidate being supported and assisted by bigots was acceptable to them. The lunatic fringe of Jew-haters was neither a fringe nor composed solely of lunatics.

And that fact scared the hell out of the members of the Jewish Anti-Defamation Council of Minnesota. It also quickened their collective pulse. Money had to be raised, and promptly, for office space, an administrative assistant, and a full-time, paid executive secretary to run things. The upgraded organization would have to function as "a police department or a fire department or an F.B.I.," as Charles Cooper later put it.[72] For reasons that remain unclear, the hiring process for executive secretary dragged on until May 1939. But at its end, the one-man band assigned to discover and defeat Minnesota's anti-Semites was, appropriately enough, an erstwhile musician.

* * *

In the gossip column of the *American Jewish World* and the nightclubs of downtown Minneapolis, Samuel Leo Scheiner, attorney at law, was better known as Sammy Scheiner, jazz pianist. Sloppy Joe's, Curly's, the Boulevard Café, Hy Moses's Goal Post Room, the 620, the Cave—he played them all, sometimes working the keyboard alone in the stride style of James P. Johnson, the Harlem virtuoso, and sometimes leading a band playing the arrangements he bought for seventy-five cents apiece. Performing live on radio station WDGY, Scheiner reigned as the "Jazz

King of the Air." Onstage, he knew how to entice and entertain. He sported "the latest glad rags of the season," as the *American Jewish World* put it, flaunting the two-tone shoes known as "spectators" and growing a pencil mustache in the style of the Parisian guitarist Django Reinhardt.[73] When Scheiner was supposed to go silent during a horn player's solo, he just might climb onto his piano, hogging the spotlight. As a fellow musician recalled, nobody told Sammy what to do: "He was too strong-willed."[74]

Scheiner's career in jazz, much as it reflected his love for the music, also arose from some very Jewish forms of necessity. He was born in 1908 to immigrant parents from Romania who were well versed in tragedy and struggle. His father, Isadore, already had four children from his first marriage, which had ended when his wife, Jessie, apparently suffering from postpartum depression, drowned herself after slipping away from a lakeside family outing. The woman whom Isadore married a year later, Gizella Moscowitz, had reached Minneapolis in 1887 after a seventeen-month odyssey by train, foot, and steamship from her native Romania across Asia and then the Pacific Ocean. The friction between Isadore's new wife and the children from his first marriage, friction that hastened their departure, left young Sammy a kind of only child. Cosseted he was not: the family lived in an especially poor en-clave of Romanian Jews separate from the North Side and subsisted on Isadore's income from a newsstand and Gizella's shifts as a cashier. But the older Scheiner children, seeing both academic and artistic promise in Sammy, set aside a portion of their earnings for his college tuition.[75]

After graduating from the University of Minnesota, Scheiner went straight into its law school, earning his degree in 1930. Along the way, he boarded in St. Paul with a Jewish family that had lost its winemaking business to Prohibition and was filling the financial chasm by taking in tenants and bootlegging on the side. That family, the Levensons, included a daughter who was also in law school, named Sarah but Americanized to Sally. She and Scheiner fell in love.[76]

By the time they married in 1933, however, the couple's vision of se-curity and status that law school conjured had proven illusory. Sally dropped out amid the deprivations of the Depression and began clerking for a series of department stores. Sam found that his law license meant nothing to the prominent firms in Minneapolis when paired with olive skin and a Jewish surname. He rented office space as a sole practitioner and often had to take payment in barter, once accepting an outboard motor though he didn't even have a boat.[77]

The Works Progress Administration (WPA) rescued the Scheiners by giving Sam a job in 1934 as an investigator for the state Board of Law Examiners, which lasted for three years. The experience nurtured his talent for trawling through records and for poking into the obscure corners of lives. And because he kept playing nightclubs—the forty bucks a week leading the house band at the Cave easily surpassed his WPA salary—he was proximate to the demimonde of Jewish gangsters with its veneration of the *shtarker*, the tough guy.

Well before Scheiner applied to be director of the Anti-Defamation Council, he had started doing his own sleuthing into Jew haters. One of his favored methods was to deploy a front man or woman to spy on or entrap his quarry. During the summer of 1938, for example, Scheiner coached one member of a Jewish family that owned a furniture store in St. Paul, the Paymars,[78] into trying to reserve a vacation cabin at a resort believed to ban Jews. Scheiner filed away the two replies as potential evidence:

Dear Mr. Paymar:

I have your letter of July 2 and appreciate your inquiry.

Our business in the past has been affected by Jewish clientele. This is a condition beyond our control. As you wished me to be frank in my reply I hope you will pardon me for doing so.

Dear Mr. Paymar:

Many thanks for your recent inquiry. Inclosed [*sic*] is a folder which describes and gives information concerning RUTTGER'S BIRCHMONT LODGE.

All of the five Ruttger Lodges cater to a very high class of guest, and they usually object to having Jewish people amongst them. Personally none of us have anything against the Jewish race, but it is purely for the good of our business that we must discriminate.[79]

In May 1939, Scheiner began receiving his $1800 annual salary from the Jewish Anti-Defamation Council of Minnesota. Sally gave birth that same month to their first child, a daughter they named Susan. Between the financial stability and the growing family, Sam decided it was time to move from their one-bedroom apartment into a real home. He located a suitable one in St. Louis Park, a suburb on the western border of Minneapolis, and one July evening started writing up his application for a Federal Housing Administration–insured mortgage. Then the phone rang. The caller, Scheiner recounted in a letter several weeks later, "stated that he was a delegate of the neighbors in that district. He informed me that it would not be healthy for me to move out into this suburb or in this home, for the reason that I was Jewish and he and the rest of these people did not want any Jews in the neighborhood. Naturally I asked who it was that was talking and he informed me that it would make no difference, but that I had better not move out to this house."[80]

Scheiner went into detective mode. Within the month, he had determined the likely caller, a salesman for a wholesale hardware company based in Duluth. Coincidentally, in his private law practice, Scheiner had represented the company in a dispute with a state agency, succeeding in getting that agency to pay an overdue bill. So Scheiner wrote to his contact at the hardware company, its credit manager.

"I know that your company is too big, in all ways, to have a salesman working for you who expounds theories of racial hatred and prejudice," Scheiner began, offering his former client the benefit of the doubt. "I am not advocating that any drastic action be taken against Mr. R——, but I do believe that the executives of your company should call him in and ask that he send me a letter of apology for the UnAmerican [sic] thing that he did. I do hope that Mr. R——only did this because of some wrong superficial idea and not because his hatred is imbedded [sic] in his soul."[81]

The credit manager never responded to Scheiner. Nor did a letter of apology from the salesman ever arrive. Scheiner took his wife, his daughter, and his down payment, and bought a house on the southern edge of Minneapolis, a pleasant enough brick gable home, yet also the outcome of intimidation and retreat. Being the musician who didn't let anyone tell him what to do, being the *shtarker*, Scheiner should not have needed a lesson about the risks of compromise. Now he had been reminded, in the most personal way possible, that when it came to bigots, playing nice didn't work.

* * *

No sooner did Scheiner assume his duties with the Jewish Anti-Defamation Council of Minnesota than the phone started ringing and mail started mounting in his fourth-floor office downtown. The incoming reports of anti-Semitism ran quite a gamut. A hotel stopped using its usual dry cleaner when the shop was bought by two Jews. A city jailer beat up a fifty-eight-year-old Jewish man who'd been arrested for a series of unpaid parking tickets, tossing him into the cell with the exclamation, "That's the way we are treating Sheenies here." A Jewish student at the university was pressured by a top administrator into dropping out of a dental hygienist program, ostensibly because no Gentile dentist in town would hire her. Leaflets from the Minnesota Voters' Association, given to fifty thousand churchgoers in the run-up to the Minneapolis mayoral election in June 1939, declared, "When Christians Vote, They Vote Right." A streetcar motorman, his path blocked by a North Sider's car, grumbled to his passengers, "That dirty Jew, we ought to have a Hitler here." Swastikas were etched into fourteen windows of a home in south Minneapolis that had been recently purchased by a Jewish family.[82]

Assembling evidence, Scheiner sometimes took depositions longhand on a legal pad, which his secretary then typed up formally. Other times, he scrawled notes by pencil on scraps of yellow paper, his script sloppy with the haste of a man with too much to do. He assigned an index card to every known or suspected anti-Semite he could identify, along with a thumbnail description: "Coughlinite," "Will not sell Jews homes," and, on the card for Riley, Rev. W. B., "Fascist." Even when Scheiner went out to hear bands, to briefly escape into their swinging sounds, bigotry seemed inescapable. One night at the Nicollet Hotel he happened onto a touring society band—led by the Yale-educated Ben Cutler—singing in

German. Another evening, at the Magic Bar, it was the house orchestra doing a tune with the refrain "What's wrong with America?" To answer the question, one musician got decked out like a Soviet commissar only to change into the costume of an American Jew reading a Yiddish newspaper.[83]

With so many fires to fight, Scheiner darted nonstop from one to the next. He filed an official complaint to his musicians' union local about the Magic Bar band. He wrote to the voters' association leaders, urging them to rephrase their slogan. He helped file assault charges against the brutal jailer. None of the efforts brought success. Scheiner nonetheless locked his sights on one particular situation, one that conflated two different conspiracy theories about Jews: that they ran the American economy for their own benefit and that they were dragging the United States into another European war.

The twin calumnies took the form of a pamphlet that began appearing around Minneapolis in July 1939, sometimes stuffed into mail slots, sometimes slipped inside newspapers, sometimes passed out at the county courthouse, sometimes handed to customers outside drugstores and butcher shops. The pamphlet bore the Star of David on its front page and carried the name of the Committee for Relief of Jewish Refugees. There was indeed such a group, founded and funded by Minneapolis Jews, and it was indeed working frenetically to rescue Jews from the expanding domain of Nazi Europe. A couple of exiled German Jewish professors had found positions at the university, but otherwise the hoped-for influx was a trickle.

The pamphlet used a false address and told a different story. It did so skillfully, weaving together actual efforts like refugee resettlement and the proposed boycott of German-made goods with age-old libels. For good measure, the pamphlet also listed the names of several Minneapolis rabbis, Jewish communal leaders, and Jewish-owned businesses, conspirators all:

> TODAY we want to commend every Jew . . . we Jews in America have been able to care for and to find jobs for all the refugees from Europe that have come to our shores. Furthermore, we have the financial resources

and the jobs to take care of all who may come in the future, and at the present time they are coming here at the rate of 20,000 per week . . .

Therefore, we admonish you further to boycott all Gentile stores and to buy your goods only from our Jewish-owned stores so that we may soon be able to own and control all the businesses and all the industries in the United States . . .

Let us Jews never forget for an instant our vow to stamp out Christianity and to make ourselves the rulers and masters of the world.[84]

Scheiner, conveniently, already had a spy in place. The man's name was Albert Cyr, and according to all the available information he was not assisting Scheiner out of idealism. A veteran of the Great War now in his mid-forties, Cyr was struggling along as a wringer operator in a commercial laundry. His wife had recently left him, taking their teen-aged son with her, and Cyr was suffering from heart disease. It is possible that Cyr had responded to an anonymous newspaper ad that Scheiner placed offering a hundred-dollar reward for information about the fake pamphlet. With the yearly income for an American male averaging about $950 in 1939, a hundred bucks was a substantial sum, especially for a man in Cyr's financial straits. It is possible, too, that Scheiner or Charles Cooper had recruited Cyr earlier and had been keeping him on a retainer.

Regardless, Cyr paid very big dividends. Cyr was boarding with the family of a fellow war veteran named George Blaisdell, who was working as a truck driver for a WPA construction project. Either Cyr or Scheiner suspected that the pamphlet's author was T. G. Wooster, the same person who had helped organize and then addressed the Silver Legion rally a year earlier. On July 20, Cyr came to the office of the Jewish Anti-Defamation Council of Minnesota to telephone Wooster as Scheiner eavesdropped and took notes. That same evening, Cyr visited Wooster at home and was shown the pamphlet. Cyr repeated the sequence of phone call and home visit on July 29, this time bringing George Blaisdell with him. Wooster presented each man with thirty copies of the pamphlet, as well as two other circulars: "Does Roosevelt Get Net Receipts of Birthday Paralysis Balls?" and "Every Christian

American Patriot Should Have Something in Common with the Silvershirts Standing on These Declarations and Principles."

If Blaisdell was being entrapped, he took the bait altogether willingly. The next morning, he went with his eleven-year-old son George Jr. to put pamphlets on the windshields of cars parked outside St. Joseph's, a Catholic church not far from the Jewish North Side, during Sunday morning Mass. Cyr was watching the father-son outing, and Scheiner subsequently had him recount all the recent episodes with Blaisdell and Wooster in a formal affidavit.[85]

With one sting successfully completed, Scheiner launched another. He had learned—perhaps from Cyr, perhaps from some other person who answered his ad—that the pamphlet had been produced by one Cyrus Osterhus, who had a small print shop in a Minneapolis suburb. Scheiner arranged for one of the most successful Jewish businessmen in town, a feed jobber named I. S. Joseph, to show up unannounced at the printer's shop on August 2 in the company of William A. Anderson, a former mayor, current judge, and officer in the city's church federation. Though Anderson belonged to the Farmer-Labor Party and had heartily endorsed its economic agenda, he was hardly the obvious choice for an ally in the fight against bigotry. While mayor in the early 1930s, Anderson had essentially blamed the besieged Black homeowner Arthur Lee for provoking the assault by having moved into a white neighborhood, and he had incensed the Jewish community by banning Fannie Brice's musical *Crazy Quilt* as "indecent" and "sewage." (She took the revue, with its songs by those noted pornographers Rodgers and Hart, to St. Paul, where it did sellout business.)[86] But now, unlike Cyr, Anderson seemed to be acting upon principles, a sign that at least a few of Minneapolis's elites were taking anti-Semitism more seriously.

Joseph and Anderson played a charade for Osterhus, pretending that the former mayor was furious with Jews like Joseph for having written such a scurrilous pamphlet. Joseph went through the motions of indignant denial. Then Osterhus slipped and told a bit of the truth: the Jews hadn't hired him for the job. Anderson asked who had. The printer, as if realizing his mistake, turned evasive. Alright, Joseph told Osterhus, you have a choice. You can write and sign a statement telling everything you know, or Judge Anderson can go to his friend the Hennepin County attorney, "and we would haul him (Osterhus) into court and . . . he would be made an accessory to a libel or a forgery and would be exposed before the community." Osterhus asked for a day to think it over. Joseph and Anderson refused. So the printer wrote just enough to save his skin: that a man—he didn't know the guy's name, someone plain-looking and middle-aged—had ordered five or six thousand copies of the pamphlet several weeks earlier and had paid in cash.[87]

Scheiner took one final step before pouncing. On the Sunday morning of August 13, he brought a police officer with him to observe Blaisdell leafleting cars outside Ascension Church, like St. Joseph's a Catholic parish on the edge of the main Jewish neighborhood. Then Scheiner drafted a complaint, naming Blaisdell, Osterhus, and Wooster as defendants on criminal charges of forgery and libel. Besides citing the relevant legal precedents, Scheiner emphasized the broader context of the case, drawing on recent congressional hearings about the Silver Legion and other pro-Nazi groups:

> For some time there have existed, and still exist, certain secret societies in the United States of America, and in the State of Minnesota and City of Minneapolis, which, under the pretense of patriotic aims, engage in treasonable, seditious, anti-democratic, pro-fascist, race-hating and race-baiting enterprises . . .
>
> [It has been] publicly disclosed that said secret societies are part of a wide-spread secret movement in this country allied with, and supported and subsidized by the Nazi government of Germany and other Fascist powers and parties.[88]

Under Minnesota law, a grand jury was only required to consider the most severe felony charges, such as those that could result in life imprisonment. In most other alleged crimes, the county attorney would decide whether or not to indict. The records of the fake-pamphlet case no longer exist, but the only one of the three prospective defendants to be charged and tried was George Blaisdell, and that was under Minnesota's public nuisance law. The county attorney, Edward J. Goff, may have decided that the forgery and libel charges were going to be too diffi-cult to prove. *Near v. Minnesota*, after all, had established that First Amendment protection applied even to anti-Semitic tracts.

Such was the argument that Blaisdell's attorney, E. P. Willcuts, tried to make. The pamphlet wasn't promoting sedition and hadn't caused violence, he wrote in a memorandum to the municipal court judge, William C. Larson. Blaisdell had not handed pamphlets directly to any-one; he just left them on cars. It was all within his free-speech rights. The prosecution's case pragmatically relied on both Scheiner and the city cop, Stephen Dickinson, testifying to Blaisdell's actions outside Ascension Church.

For a fairly picayune misdemeanor, disorderly conduct, the Blaisdell case attracted inordinate attention. One likely reason is that on September 1, 1939, with testimony complete and Judge Larson weighing his ruling, Hitler's army invaded Poland, leading France and Great Britain to declare war two days later on the Nazi regime. Nazi sympathizers in the Mill City suddenly seemed less easily dismissable as random nuts. As the blitzkrieg neared Warsaw on September 8, Judge Larson found Blaisdell guilty. Though the punishment that he issued was light, just thirty days in the county workhouse, Judge Larson deliv-ered a four-page sentencing memorandum, way beyond the norm in a disorderly conduct case. There is, he wrote,

> no more potent breeder of public disorder than a deliberate stirring up of class against class, and race against race. There is no law-abiding element of our state or community that desires to sanction or tolerate a sowing of the seeds of strife, social dissension and public disorder among our citi-zens based purely upon class hatred.[89]

The daily newspapers in town covered the verdict and quoted the judge, with the *Journal* also publishing an editorial that explicitly drew a parallel to events in Europe:

> Racial intolerance . . . is only one manifestation of a consuming world disease. Wherever we look for the causes of a chaotic social order, of war

and conflict, of domestic discords and of international strife, we inevitably find the aggressive virus of intolerance ...

On a small scale, the distribution of anti-Jewish literature in Minneapolis represents the plague of intolerance from which the world is deathly sick today. To say that the cure lies in a greater tolerance of individuals and groups, of races and nations, is only to state a truth bedrocked in all the wisdom and experience of centuries.[90]

Sam Scheiner, not yet four months into his job, felt triumphant, so much so that he wrote to *TIME*'s editor, appending newspaper clippings about the case and urging the national newsmagazine to join in covering "the first decision of its kind anywhere in the country."[91] Whether or not Scheiner's assertion was even true, the victory was more limited than he seemed willing to admit. The judge, after all, had referred to class tensions, omitting any reference to anti-Semitism. The *Journal*, even in defending the rights of Jews, categorized them as a race, a term that implicitly and immutably separated them from the white Christian mainstream. The man most responsible for the inflammatory pamphlet, the man who was the local face of the Silver Shirts, T. G. Wooster, was never charged with any crime. He was free to keep stirring the cauldron. And George Blaisdell, however notorious he was now in certain circles, also received some emblematic fan mail from one of America's great many isolationists: "Its [*sic*] queer that when some one prints or says some thing against the jews [*sic*] he gets in trouble but when some one tries to plunge this country into war by printing anti-nazi [*sic*] propaganda that is perfectly all right."[92]

CHAPTER 5

THE JIM CROW CAR

Baton Rouge, Louisiana

1939–1940

Several days after Nazi Germany launched its blitzkrieg against Poland on September 1, 1939, plunging all of Western Europe into conflict, Hubert Humphrey rode the Illinois Central south from Chicago toward the dividing line carved by America's unending civil war. He was bound for Louisiana State University (LSU), where he would begin studies toward a master's degree in government. Nine hours into the trip, as the train pulled into Cairo, Illinois, the last major station before entering the former Confederacy, Humphrey received his first glimpse of life across that border.[1]

By well-honed ritual, a conductor moved through the Pullman coaches, ordering any Black passengers to grab their belongings and move into a different car, right behind the locomotive. This one was known as the "Jim Crow car," and it complied with the state laws along the Illinois Central route from Kentucky to New Orleans that mandated "separate cars." The entire concept of segregated rail travel had been codified by Louisiana in an 1890 law. When a fair-skinned Black shoemaker named Homer Plessy deliberately boarded a white train car two years later, only to be predictably dragged off and arrested, a challenge to the law began its path toward the U.S. Supreme Court. In its 1896 decision in *Plessy v. Ferguson*, the court not only upheld Louisiana's Separate Car Act but also enshrined the system that came to be called "separate but equal," a phrase that was accurate only in its first

144

adjective. That doctrine shaped every aspect of daily life in the South, as Humphrey was now seeing firsthand.

While he and the other white passengers on the Illinois Central could remain in their cushioned seats or stroll to the dining or parlor cars for refreshment, comforted as the stifling summer heat outdoors was cooled by air circulated from melting ice blocks, the forced migration into the Jim Crow car commenced. Depending on the precise coach being used on this trip, the Black people might be crammed in alongside baggage or spare parts or crew bunks or prisoners in the custody of a local sheriff. Instead of enjoying chilled air, the Black ticket-holders inhaled smoke and cinders that blew back from the locomotive's stack. The only food or drink available to these men and women and children for the dozen hours ahead was what they had packed or, at the best, the dining car leftovers that a porter or newsboy peddled. "The colored car is always placed ahead," the Black writer J. A. Rogers had bitterly joked a few years earlier, "so that, in the case of a head on collision, the 'Negroes' will get killed first. This, by the way, is the only instance in the South where the black man goes first."[2]

Minneapolis, of course, practiced its own brand of segregation by custom rather than law, as did the university that Humphrey had attended there. His transformational visit to Washington, D.C., in 1935 brought him to a city whose theaters, lunch counters, and hotels remained rigidly divided by race, even if the federal government's buildings and parks were integrated.[3] Yet Humphrey, so dazzled by Congress and the national monuments, seemed not to have noticed the racial separation, or not to have cared sufficiently to mention it in any of his letters to Muriel. And he had been out of college, helping his family in Huron during the Depression, when Minneapolis went through its emblematic episode of race hate, the white siege of the home bought by Arthur Lee.

At the age of twenty-eight, Humphrey's firsthand experience of Black life still consisted largely of that chance encounter with the graveling crew outside his South Dakota hometown when he was eleven. During his years at the University of Minnesota, with the sole exception of a football player named Horace Bell, Humphrey later admitted that "there was no black [*sic*] person . . . with whom I ever had a serious conversation."[4] Whatever awareness Humphrey had of civil rights as a political issue came to him indirectly, through his sister Frances in her familiar role as educator and inspiration to her nominally older brother. Having completed her bachelor's degree at the George Washington University, Frances was now pursuing a master's in social work. As part of her thesis on high school dropouts in the District of Columbia, many of them Black, she arranged to study with the political scientist Ralph Bunche[5] at Howard University, the so-called capstone of Negro education.[6] During the spring of 1939, as Humphrey was absorbed in his final semester of college work, Frances and their Uncle Harry had joined tens of thousands of people in what amounted to a mass rally for civil rights: the concert outside the Lincoln Memorial by Marian Anderson, a Black opera star who had been banned because of her race from performing at Constitution Hall, the domain of the Daughters of the American Revolution.

Though Humphrey was peripherally familiar with that controversy through Frances, and presumably aware also of the latest effort by liberals in Congress to push through anti-lynching legislation, he had been far more consumed by his chronic financial woes. With his only certain income for the next nine months a four-hundred-and-fifty-dollar graduate assistantship, he had been nervously writing his faculty advisor at LSU, Professor Charles Hyneman, for help finding a rental apartment for thirty dollars a month. Even at that rate, Humphrey would be left with just twenty dollars more each month for himself, Muriel, and their baby daughter Nancy. Those two, boarding for now with relatives in South Dakota, would not join Humphrey in Louisiana until he had suitable quarters. Meanwhile, the dean of students from Minnesota had resorted to dunning H. H. for Hubert's long-overdue emergency loan of two hundred dollars. "Now you will say, why don't you take care of your sons [*sic*] obligation," H. H. ultimately wrote back to the dean. "Nine years of dust storms and drouth [*sic*] will answer that." In order to spare his son shame, litigation, or both, H. H. ultimately consented to paying off the debt at the rate of two dollars a month.[7]

Nearly a full day after Humphrey had departed Chicago, he descended onto the platform in Hammond, Louisiana, from which he would catch a bus for the final fifty miles to Baton Rouge, the state capital and LSU's home. As he entered the handsome edifice of the Hammond station, with its Queen Anne Revival architecture and octagonal observation tower, Humphrey received one more jolt of racial reality: separate waiting rooms for White and Colored. The Illinois Central had devised and disseminated a standard blueprint for segregated train stations in its primary southern stops.[8] In both Hammond and Baton Rouge, Humphrey took note of the separate toilets and drinking fountains for the races. His response, an admittedly "naïve" one, was grounded in the only politics he had ever known, the politics of class. Having two sets of all these public facilities did not strike him as immoral on first glance; it struck him as "uneconomic."[9] Then again, his graduate studies in Jim Crow had barely begun.

* * *

Twice in his life, Humphrey had witnessed that maestro of class politics, Huey Long. Two weeks before the 1932 presidential election, the governor-turned-senator from Louisiana had swept into Sioux Falls in a Packard sedan with two accompanying sound trucks to inveigh on behalf of Franklin Delano Roosevelt. Humphrey delighted in hearing Long depict the economic inequality under Herbert Hoover, the incumbent Republican president, as "ten times as damnable as cannibalism."[10] Then, during his 1935 visit to Washington, Humphrey marveled at the spectacle of Long—"a sudden, compelling, dramatic presence in white shoes, a cream-colored suit, and an orange tie"[11]—even though the "Kingfish" with his "Share Our Wealth" platform had by then emerged as FDR's most formidable rival within the Democratic Party.

By the time Humphrey first strode onto the LSU campus in September 1939, Long was four years dead, having been assassinated by a political foe's relative in the towering State Capitol that had been erected on the governor's orders. Yet few elements of Louisiana life bore a greater posthumous imprint of Long in all his contradictions than did the state university, and Humphrey's ability to attend it was a direct result. LSU had been founded in 1860 as a military institute, which explained its nickname as the "Old War Skule," and had plodded into the 1920s with fewer than two thousand students and two hundred faculty and a middling academic program centered on agriculture and engineering. Then, starting as governor in 1928 and continuing with his election as senator in 1930,[12] Long poured millions of dollars in tax revenue that his populist program had extracted from oil and chemical companies, plantation gentry, wealthy heirs, and other economic enemies into expanding and improving LSU into a legitimate research university, and, of course, a monument to its maker.

After his years at the University of Minnesota, Humphrey was hardly a stranger to the grandiose affectations of a state's flagship campus. LSU, however, manifested all of the extravagant, lurid, inspiring, and appalling strains of Long's outsized persona. He and his successor as governor, Richard Leche, pushed enrollment to 8,500 by Humphrey's incoming semester, using an existing policy of free tuition for (white) Louisiana residents to democratize the student body. On the land of a former plantation, the Kingfish and Leche[13] had planted magnolias and live oaks, fashioned classroom and office buildings in Northern Italianate architecture, installed a three-thousand-seat Greek theater, and modeled the French House on a Normandy chateau.

Into what had been an academic backwater, Long and his handpicked university president, a Columbia Ed.D. named James Monroe Smith, recruited respected scholars. The admired poet and novelist Robert Penn Warren decamped from refined Vanderbilt University in Nashville to become an editor of *The Southern Review*, a literary journal, with the aid of a rising literary critic, Cleanth Brooks. Similarly, the *Journal of Southern History*, with its mission to bring scholarly rigor rather than nostalgia to that subject, took root at LSU. Due largely to the appeal of its programs in sugar cultivation and production, LSU was already attracting Caribbean, Chinese, and Central and South American students at a rate of several dozen a year, putting at least a small wedge into the whites-only regime. One more part of the upgrading agenda at LSU was the creation of a Department of Government, which soon evolved into a School of Government and Public Affairs, granting a master's degree. The program was chaired by Charles Hyneman, whom LSU had lured away from Indiana University, and who, in turn, had offered admission and a paying assistantship to Humphrey.

Elsewhere on the campus, high class met high crass. Humphrey's first, short-term home was a warren of dormitory rooms squeezed beneath the end zone bleachers of LSU's football stadium. Around the perimeter of the stadium stood active oil wells, a functioning sugar refinery, and the air-conditioned cage of Mike the Tiger, LSU's mascot, who was attended to by a student employee. The freshmen who were enrolling at the same time as Humphrey paid fifty cents apiece for the traditional indignity of having their heads shaved and attended the football season's first pep rally wearing pajamas. With Long himself sometimes wielding the baton as drum major, the marching band performed the fight song that he had co-written, "Touchdown for LSU."[14]

Even as a newcomer, Humphrey knew something already of the corrupt bargain that Long and Leche had exacted in return for their largesse with taxpayer dollars. During the summer of 1939, the so-called Louisiana Scandals had made front-page news in Minneapolis and been featured in the nationally syndicated columns of Drew Pearson and Westbrook Pegler. The story had broken in early June with newspaper photos of Leche's new home being built with materials and laborers appropriated from LSU. Revelations soon followed that Governor Leche and university President Smith—known to skeptical faculty members as "Jingle Money" in a sarcastic allusion to his first two initials, J. M.—had embezzled hundreds of thousands of dollars in Works Progress Administration (WPA) funds. Within the same few days, Leche resigned, claiming illness, and Smith fled to Canada. Extradited back to Louisiana, he would be standing trial later in the fall.[15] Meanwhile, the lieutenant governor who inherited the top job from Leche was none other than Earl Long, Huey's younger brother, hardly the herald of reform.

Charles Hyneman, the professor formally overseeing Humphrey's studies, denounced Louisiana as a one-party state, not a genuine democracy. "A man on the inside of the dirty doings," he put it to a student forum several weeks into the fall semester, "has no freedom to 'spill the beans.' "[16] Humphrey, however, would not join in such full-throated, public criticism. Though Huey Long had "the tongue of a demagogue" and "the muscle of a political despot," Humphrey admitted in retrospect, he also possessed "the heart of a compassionate man."[17] As a graduate student at the university that Long had willed and funded into academic respectability, Humphrey was benefiting from exactly such compassion.

* * *

After his initial days in the end-zone dormitory and a brief, unnerving residence in a rooming house with "cockroaches as big as your thumb,"[18] as he recalled decades later for an oral historian, Humphrey found an affordable apartment for his young family in a two-story frame house at the edge of downtown Baton Rouge. He paid thirty dollars a month for two rooms and a kitchenette, sharing a single telephone with the landlady's family and another set of tenants. The neighbors up and down St. Ferdinand Street were clerks and teachers and steelworkers, all of them white, and the Humphreys were conspicuous both for their college educations and Northern roots.

Even in a strange new place with an infant daughter, Muriel threw herself into the practical imperative of making ends meet. She churned out ham salad sandwiches by the bagful, which Hubert sold to fellow students. She took part-time work as a typist in Hyneman's office. With the margin of extra dollars her labor provided, the Humphreys engaged in their handful of comparative luxuries—going to the movies to see the newsreels from the European war, buying a turkey for Thanksgiving, and occasionally hiring a Black housekeeper named Maggie.[19]

By sheer numbers, Humphrey could not help but encounter Black people with a frequency far beyond anything in his parochial past. Baton Rouge alone, with about 11,000 Black residents, contained far more African Americans than did the entire states of Minnesota (9,928) and South Dakota (476), the only places where Humphrey had previously lived. Blacks formed one-third of Baton Rouge's total population, compared with barely one percent of Minneapolis's.

Every weekday when Humphrey walked or rode the main drag of Highland Road two miles from his apartment to LSU, he traversed the Black neighborhood set between downtown and the campus, known alternatively as South Baton Rouge or The Bottoms. That journey afforded an education beyond the sort that graduate school was providing. Although the Huey Long style of populism did not rely on inflaming race hate, and although the substantial Catholic presence in Baton Rouge also served to mitigate the Klan-style terrorism that was pervasive in the evangelical Protestant portions of the state,[20] The Bottoms put the inequalities and indignities of segregation on full display for anyone who cared to see. Humphrey did.

Built on nearly a thousand acres of the former plantation of Magnolia Mound, South Baton Rouge abounded in both deprivation and aspiration. Its gravel streets were lined with shotgun houses that were heated by fireplaces and lit by kerosene lamps. A 1940 survey determined that ninety percent of households lacked hot water and three-quarters an indoor toilet. South Baton Rouge's boys and girls were restricted to all-Black scouting troops. The grown-ups were forced to stand in segregated lines to receive surplus flour and lard and beans from the federal government.[21] The neighborhood's Temple Theater was not allowed to present a Hollywood movie until two or three months after it had played at the all-white Paramount downtown. The Black farmers outside of town received virtually no loans from the New Deal's Farm Credit Administration or hookups from its Rural Electrification Administration.[22]

All it took was a rare spell of freezing weather and snow in January 1940 to put Black residents' survival itself into doubt. During the cold snap, two of them were arrested for prying wood planks loose from a bridge to be burned for fuel. An elderly man froze to death in his shack, dying hunched over his empty wood stove.[23] Whether or not Humphrey happened to read the short news articles about those incidents in Baton Rouge's *Morning Advocate*, he surely noticed the inverse experience on the LSU campus, where the wintry blast was merely a novelty, providing white students the rare opportunity to build snowmen and sled down levees.

"I was dismayed by what I saw," he would write years later of his exposure to Baton Rouge's dueling racial realities. "[T]he white, neatly painted houses of the whites, the unpainted shacks of the blacks; the stately homes on manicured lawns in the white section, the open sewage ditches in black neighborhoods."[24]

Yet South Baton Rouge was more than the sum of its miseries, more than the catalyst for a white man's spasm of conscience. It exemplified, too, the achievements its people wrought in the face of implacable obstacles. Most of the neighborhood's residents owned their homes. While the women were almost entirely restricted to domestic service paying three dollars a week, the men had work in the Standard Oil refinery and the DuPont chemical factory; they were cooks, carpenters, plasterers, cement finishers, and bricklayers. McKinley High School offered a college-preparatory curriculum that included courses in Latin, and graduates could attend either Southern University or Leland College near Baton Rouge. Communal life flourished in churches and lodges, in the Good Samaritans and La Bon Ton Bridge Club. The local branch of the National Association for the Advancement of Colored People (NAACP) counted more than a thousand members.[25] Black capacity and Black assertion, in other words, were not lacking in The Bottoms' pursuit of official equality; what was missing, as Cecil Newman knew up North in Minneapolis, were open doors to opportunity and white allies truly committed to the cause.

When Humphrey's trip down Highland Road finally delivered him to the LSU campus, he entered a domain in which Black people were meant to be ever-present and yet magically invisible. Black carpenters and bricklayers, living in segregated rooming houses, had helped to build the Long-era campus. Black laborers cut the grass, cleaned the toilets, emptied the garbage cans, harvested the college farm's crops, and cooked the cafeteria meals. Yet a Black face almost never appeared in the pages of the *Gumbo* yearbook or the *Daily Reveille* newspaper. The several dozen Black spectators allowed to attend LSU football games—mostly as a reward for cleaning the stadium—were confined to rickety wooden bleachers behind the goal line. Even as LSU prided itself on its history of educating Spanish-speaking students from the Caribbean and Latin America, the closest thing to a Black student was a local peddler named Eddie Bryant, who sold vegetables grown near the campus, claiming they were more "educated" as a result.[26]

Given the deliberate and scrupulous erasure of Black people from LSU, it required not flagrant bigotry but mere passivity for a white student to accept segregation as something like natural law. Humphrey's eyes were already too open for such obliviousness. What he perceived repeatedly was a kind of paralysis that the Jim Crow system and its constantly looming threat of arrest or attack imposed on Black people, at least when they ventured outside sanctuaries like The Bottoms.

One day Humphrey and Hyneman, running an errand near the campus, spotted a Black motorist frozen in place at a street corner—unable to move forward because of a white pedestrian in the crosswalk, yet simultaneously blocked from behind by a white driver furiously leaning on his horn. "You black [sic] sonofabitch, get out of my way," the idled driver shouted more than loudly enough for Humphrey to hear. "You black sonofabitch." Another time in the lobby of a tall building downtown, quite possibly the State Capitol, Hyneman and Humphrey watched the silent torment of Black men and women fearful of walking into any elevator already carrying a white person.[27]

Segregation forced emotional contortions on white people, too, as Humphrey came to realize. One of his classmates in the School of Government, James Caffery, cut the figure of well-born privilege. The grandson of an American diplomat who had served presidents from Woodrow Wilson to FDR, the heir to generational wealth from Louisiana's sugar belt, "Jamie" had edited the LSU yearbook and been tapped by an array of social and academic fraternities before earning his bachelor's degree at nineteen. What Caffery confided to Humphrey, though, was the complex racial backdrop to his cosseted upbringing. "He told me about how he'd been brought up by a Negress," Humphrey later recalled of their conversation, "and that thing that I remembered first was how the Southerner really loved the Negro—the Negro woman that brought him up. And yet, how he held them at arm's length when they got to be adults. . . . [L]ook,' he told me, 'This woman has done more for me than my mother.' "[28]

At home after classes, Humphrey received more insight from his Black housekeeper. While Humphrey never knew or could not later remember Maggie's full name, he did listen to what she said, especially on the subject of bill collectors. When the white man came around Black neighborhoods dunning for unpaid debts, Maggie explained, "Negro families . . . would protect their own [so] the bill collectors could never find them." From that one example, Humphrey began to form a larger insight about Black resistance to "the white intruder, so to speak . . . the white police and the white politician and the white establishment."[29]

Several months into Humphrey's second semester at LSU, Muriel took Nancy back to South Dakota to help her widower father, still grieving and forlorn. Hubert began bunking with the family of a classmate to save rent money, and along with the St. Ferdinand Street apartment, Maggie vanished from his everyday life. But her moral instruction about segregation, her concrete examples of it, stayed with him. There was inevitably something clichéd and condescending about the image of the wise if unlettered Black servant kindling the white boss's conscience about the sin of racism. And yet, in Humphrey's case, the truism happened to be true. "That's the first time," he wrote later of segregation and the hate that enabled it, "I got a glimpse of that."[30]

* * *

Officially, Humphrey's academic program at LSU consisted of six courses in government, two in economics, and one in sociology, as well as the production of a master's thesis. In addition to taking those classes, Humphrey served as a teaching assistant for an undergraduate course in American government. In the process, Humphrey impressed Hyneman as being "the stand-out graduate student of the year, if not any year I was there."[31] As another professor, Robert J. Harris, later wrote, "Humphrey brought gaiety, imagination, and a sense of purpose."[32]

Then there was the informal education that Humphrey received from his classmates and friends. He moved in two overlapping circles, one populated by the dozen graduate students in government, and the other by a similar number of debating team comrades. While a few in Humphrey's crowd descended from wealth or power or both—Jamie Caffery, of course, and Russell Long, a law school student who was Huey's son and Governor Earl's nephew—most occupied an ambiguous place in the binary racial realm of the South. Not that anyone would have mistaken these young men for being Black, but neither did they carry the requisite Northern European blood and Protestant religion that defined whiteness. In their precarious position, they were kindred spirits. Or, as a displaced Harvard man on the English department faculty once said, they were "Yankee troublemakers."[33]

John Makar was a Catholic Slav from Detroit, Gus Lanzilloti an Italian Catholic from New York, and Wesley Ward a transplanted Wisconsinite. Emmett Asseff was the son of Syrian immigrants who ran a confectionary in the Louisiana town of Mansfield. The one New Orleanian in the bunch, George Carroll, had been essentially orphaned at age ten when his mother died and father moved to Ohio to remarry. At LSU, Carroll was so strapped for money that friends who were roughly his six-foot height lent him their clothes.[34]

Significantly for Humphrey, LSU was where he first got to know and know about Jews. There had been just one Jewish family in Doland during Humphrey's boyhood, occasional customers of H. H.'s drugstore, and in college Hubert's friends and mentors had all been one or another flavor of Christian. The thriving Jewish commerce in Minneapolis took place on the North Side, far from the university campus. The big downtown department stores, owned by Gentiles, would hardly even hire Jews.

Jewish immigrants from Germany and France had begun settling in Baton Rouge by the mid-1800s, and in addition to establishing communal institutions they became an accepted pillar of the city's mercantile life. Two of the biggest stores in town—Rosenfield's for dry goods and Kornmeyer's for furniture—were owned by long-established Jewish families. Both the *Morning Advocate* and the *Daily Reveille* published respectful articles about the High Holy Days, which fell during Humphrey's first semester at LSU. Along with a Methodist minister and a Catholic priest, a rabbi spoke on campus that October on the theme of "Stubborn and Intolerable Prejudice."[35]

Humphrey often bantered in the Law School building with Ed Glusman, a precocious freshman whose father had fled Czarist Russia all the way to Lake Charles, Louisiana. Partnered together for a debate tournament in Atlanta, Glusman and Humphrey belatedly realized they had left their research materials and model arguments back at LSU. Humphrey extemporized so well that the judges never knew.[36] That escapade sealed the men's bond and gave them a favorite story to tell.

The LSU debate team also included one of Humphrey's closest friends at school, a law student named Alvin Rubin. To be precise, he had been born twenty years earlier as Abraham Rabinowitz, the child of a Lithuanian immigrant who had reached America in 1906 and bounced his way through various states as a mechanic before his future father-in-law lured him to the small city of Alexandria, Louisiana, to stock shoes in a dry goods store. It proceeded to go broke during the Depression.[37]

Absent LSU's program of free tuition, Rubin might never have made it to college at all. Even so, he still had to pay for books, activity fees, and room and board. Though he affected a pipe, tweed coat, and wire-rimmed glasses for his law school portrait, Rubin lived in the stadium dorms and filled his stomach on the unlimited portions of milk, bread, and gravy available for thirty-five cents a day from LSU's Boarding Club. Some summers, he roughnecked in the oil fields.

Rubin and his buddies, probably including Humphrey, were aware enough of their difference from the LSU mainstream to create a club they called the International, Inter-religious, Inter-racial Kosher Salami Cooperative, so named for the packages Alvin got from his mother. The members included Chinese and Panamanian students, which was as close to racial integration as LSU was prepared to permit circa 1940.[38] As a sympathetic editorial in the *Daily Reveille*, written by an Irish Catholic student from New York State, put it, "Why should you, an average American, look down on the Spanish-speaking element of our campus population? It is just this which immediately causes members of this group to look at you with suspicion."[39]

As Rubin knew full well, the impact of intolerance could be far more existential. As the Nazis' Soviet allies seized half of Poland to subjugate the country completely, five of Rubin's paternal uncles remained stranded in Lithuania, a logical next target for either Hitler or Stalin.[40] Up to this point, Humphrey had understood the war only at a remove, something in headlines and on newsreels. He did make sure to read Adolph Hitler's manifesto, *Mein Kampf*, and Lawrence Dennis's *The Coming American Fascism*,[41] in which the former American diplomat argued that only National Socialism could respond to the failures of capitalism. But all of the viewing and reading connected to Humphrey only cerebrally. Being friends with Alvin Rubin was the beginning of a visceral recognition of the human toll of Nazism. The moral dimension deepened in a two-semester course drily entitled Sociology 211–212, Seminar in Social Theory, and taught by the recently arrived Dr. Rudolf Heberle, an exile by choice from the German Reich.

* * *

In the late 1920s, when Rudolf Heberle was a lecturer in sociology at the University of Kiel, he began to notice "a great deal of unrest" among farmers in the surrounding state of Schleswig-Holstein. It was a mostly rural area, stretching northward from the port city of Hamburg to the Danish border, and its economy had traditionally depended on raising cattle, growing cabbages, and exporting a fair amount of both. But with the Weimar Republic ravaged by inflation and foreign markets for German products protected by tariffs, Schleswig-Holstein rose in protest. The forms of it ranged from mass marches to blockades against farm foreclosures to attempted bombings of tax-collectors' offices.[42] Then, in the 1930 election to the Reichstag, Germany's parliament, the National Socialist Party soared to twenty-seven percent of Schleswig-Holstein's vote from a mere four percent two years earlier. The upsurge especially struck Heberle because it occurred in a region of Germany that had traditionally divided its votes between center-left social democrats and center-right conservatives, hardly a Petri dish of fanaticism.[43]

Up to this point in his career, Heberle had specialized in migration, conducting field research in Germany, the Baltic nations, and the Southern United States. He was a man of political moderation and establishment credentials—a veteran of the Kaiser's army in the Great War, and the protégé and son-in-law of the eminent German sociologist Ferdinand Tonnies. But compelled and disturbed by the abrupt shift almost literally under his feet, Heberle now turned his attention to political behavior. During the summer of 1932, he traversed Schleswig-Holstein by train and on foot, interviewing "farmers, county directors, pastors, schoolteachers, and politicians, mainly to get background knowledge, but also to find out what the grievances and problems were that had caused the radicalization of the political climate."[44] In the midst of Heberle's research, Germany went back to the polls, and Schleswig-Holstein became the only German state to award a majority of its votes to the National Socialists. By early the next year, Adolph Hitler was chancellor.

Heberle combined his fieldwork with statistical analysis of voting records and a historical survey of the far-right groups that had preceded the Nazis. By 1934, he had completed a manuscript on the subject, part scholarly discourse and part early-warning system for an imperiled democracy. Not one academic journal or publishing house dared to release it. Meanwhile, Ferdinand Tonnies had been fired from his professorship and stripped of his pension for his opposition to Nazism. He was reduced to standing beside the *Litfaßsäule*—a column covered with posters, many of them from Hitler's party—and shouting *alles gelogen*, all lies.[45] Heberle bore the burden of supporting his in-laws and his own family of five on his irregular earnings as a *Privatdozent*, a university lecturer paid directly by students. He shifted his scholarly work back into migration, hoping to avoid the kind of punishment Tonnies had suffered.

To the contrary, Kiel University's dean and rector convened an inquest into Heberle, under the guise of considering him for promotion to a full professorship. Heberle was accused of having an "underlying Marxist attitude" because he had used such words as "bourgeoisie" and "proletariat." He was accused of advocating for Germans to breed with "Mongoloids" because in the previous decade he had written about the marriages between German immigrants and Latvians in that country. Most damaging of all, when Heberle was required to produce "evidence of Aryan" ancestry, the family genealogy revealed a Jewish great-grandfather named Oppenheim. It mattered not that, well before the Nazis came to power, Oppenheim had had his children baptized as Christians. University administrators denied Heberle the promotion, and the Reich's education minister ordered him to look for another job.[46]

Heberle began hurriedly sending his curriculum vitae to American universities and appealing for help from scholars he had met there during a research fellowship in the 1920s. He found only a short-term position in New Haven, Connecticut, translating German articles on migration for a social-science journal. During those months in early 1937, while his wife, Franziska, remained in Kiel with their three young children, she received notice that the Heberles' bank account there was overdrawn. The account, she learned from a bank officer, had been shut down on command of the government, and salary payments into it halted. By the end of 1937, Rudolf Heberle was back in Kiel, broke and jobless, a political pariah, receiving letters from America that "it was a little too late to arrive in a good department—they already had all their refugees." Even more disturbing in its way, his oldest child, thirteen-year-old Juergen, was styling himself as what Franziska called "a little Nazi."[47]

Then, on April 3, 1938, a telegram arrived with a plan for escape: the Rockefeller Foundation and Louisiana State University would jointly pay for a one-year appointment in the sociology department there with the possibility of extension. The Heberle family sailed out of Hamburg, bound for Baltimore, that June. They moved into their rented home in Baton Rouge on, as Heberle would always point out in years to come, July 4, Independence Day.

This independence, however, was of an equivocal sort. As German nationals, the Heberles had to register and be fingerprinted as "enemy aliens." A neighbor spotted Heberle on his porch poring over maps, which were actually for his students' fieldwork placements, and informed the FBI. Agents showed up within days to confiscate the professor's shortwave radio and Leica camera on suspicion of spying. It did not help that when one of Juergen's classmates said the Nazis "were good for nothing," the Heberle boy responded, "Not even my friends?" Soon his unchosen nickname was "Hitler."[48]

Yet, simultaneously, Rudolf and Franziska Heberle feared being branded disloyal for their actual, genuine opposition to the Nazis and their desire for America to join the war against fascism. "Some of us German refugees would have liked to enter the discussion on foreign policy while there was still a question whether this country should go to war or not," Heberle confided to a purged German Jewish professor who had landed at North Carolina State University. "And yet, many of us probably felt that we should not appear as war-mongers, at a time when there was still a strong isolationist sentiment."[49]

Indeed, now that the Soviet Union was allied with Nazi Germany, every political compass point in Baton Rouge from the America First right to the Popular Front left espoused isolationism, whether it was cast in terms of avoiding a foreign war or a capitalist one. As Congress debated a Roosevelt proposal to lift America's arms embargo as a means of aiding Britain, the *Morning Advocate* commended the "time-honored policy of mere neutrality and isolation by sheer physical advantage." On campus, the *Daily Reveille* declared that students "do not want war and above all . . . do not want to cross the ocean to fight in a general conflict." A professor at Louisiana Tech, who had spent the summer of 1939 in Europe, reported to the *Reveille* that the German people "were very cordial and impressed me greatly with their friendliness," notwithstanding the "swastika arm bands" and shop "signs prohibiting Jews."[50]

As much as the Heberles appreciated their American haven, and apprenticed to Louisiana life, with its barn dances and bayou picnics, they privately despaired not only for their former country but also for their adopted one. "I would like to know what my friends there, who last year thought fascism was quite outrageous, think now," Franziska Heberle wrote to relatives. "We haven't delved into politics here yet, but sometimes I think: Brüning era. [Brüning was last chancellor of the Weimar Republic.] I still find it strange that we now have such a placid life. The contrast to our last years in Germany is unfathomable. They'll develop their own problems here with time."[51]

Rudolf Heberle had his own way of drawing the same parallel, making the same point. He did so in the Seminar in Social Theory. The course consisted of only a dozen students, including Humphrey, many of whom had been directed to Heberle by professors in the School of Government. Each week Heberle delivered one daytime lecture in the classroom and held an evening discussion section, often at his home. In those settings, beyond discoursing on theory, Heberle finally gave public voice to the prescient research he had conducted back in Schleswig-Holstein on the rise of Nazism. Very much contrary to the stereotype of *Herr Doktor Professor*, imperious and remote, Heberle also spoke candidly of his own family's experience of persecution and dispossession.

The Nazis' regime of murderous extremism came to power, in Heberle's analysis, not by a coup from the armed fringe but thanks to "mass support . . . from middle layers of society." Reasonable people were entirely capable of acting in morally unreasonable ways and rationalizing away their actions. Heberle had seen and heard it during his fieldwork. For working-class voters in Schleswig-Holstein who had been Social Democrats for economic reasons, the Nazi movement touted opposition to tariffs, which it conveniently blamed on Jewish businessmen seeking to profit off German misery. For upper-class voters who had relied on the Conservative Party to protect their wealth, the Nazi movement presented itself as a useful cudgel against socialism and Marxism. Across class lines, amid the depredations of the worldwide Depression of the early 1930s, the Nazis "offered a psychic outlet for the repressed ambitions and emotions of rural youth" and "lent prestige and authority to persons of mediocre or subordinate positions."[52]

The story that Heberle was telling, too late now to save Germany, was a story that Humphrey understood from intimate experience. He had seen the farms of the Dakotas eviscerated by falling prices abroad and then literally picked clean by stem rust and grasshoppers and dust storms. His own family had lost its home and store. Whether in the form of the Ku Klux Klan burning a cross outside Doland or the Farmers Union rally in Huron denouncing government itself, he had witnessed the appeal of terror and insurrection when the center could no longer hold. Heberle was warning Humphrey, in so many words, where such impulses led.

From his round of research in the American South in the 1920s, Heberle could also draw parallels from Nazi Germany to the former Confederacy. The peasant villagers in the farming belt of Schleswig-Holstein reminded him of "the Southern hill-billy [*sic*] or redneck." The affluent farming class in the German state "represented the . . . equivalent type of Southern planter philosophy."[53] The elite controlled the rabble in part by manufacturing resentment against some readily identifiable enemy, some threat to the pure blood of the *Volk*. For Heberle to draw such comparisons between Germany and America was implicitly to liken one nation's scapegoat to another's.

A thousand miles from Minneapolis, Heberle was suggesting what Cecil Newman had been writing about for years in the *Spokesman*: the Jew in Germany was the Black in America. This analogy was entering Humphrey's consciousness at the same time he was encountering flesh-and-blood Jews and Blacks in a daily, personal way he never before had.

Heberle considered Humphrey "the most intelligent student he had ever encountered."[54] For his part, Humphrey learned from Heberle "the dangers of dictatorship and the tragedy of totalitarian rule." On a campus gripped by willful innocence, in the form of pep rallies for the football team and peace rallies against intervention, Heberle "opened our eyes to the real world of 1940."[55] In his exile, Heberle embodied one example, albeit far from the worst, of what happened when hatred was permitted to triumph. More than anything else from Heberle's course, Humphrey remembered a particular conversation around the seminar table, a moral challenge, really. It occurred one night when the professor drew his gaze across the dozen students and flatly stated, "Out of this group, there wouldn't be over two of you that would have resisted Hitler."[56]

* * *

On June 3, 1940, as the German Luftwaffe bombed Paris and the final British troops were evacuated from the beaches of Dunkirk in defeated Belgium, LSU issued diplomas to 1,136 graduates. Under the floodlights of the football stadium, with the gridiron now filled with chairs and adorned by bamboo and magnolia, the commencement speaker decried Nazi aggression while still calling for America to stay home. That the message came from George Zook, formerly the commissioner of education in FDR's administration and now the president of a national higher-education association, added to its disturbing import.

Though Humphrey had already posed in gown and mortarboard for his yearbook portrait, he was not, in fact, among the graduates, and he feared he never would be. For much of the academic year, he had sparred with his faculty advisor, Professor Alex Daspit, over the content and tone of Humphrey's master's thesis. Now completed under the title *The Political Philosophy of the New Deal*, the manuscript struck Daspit as insufficiently objective and scholarly.

By traditional standards for an advanced degree, Daspit had a strong case. As elegantly, eloquently, and knowledgeably as Humphrey wrote about the New Deal, he did so less as an intellectually independent analyst than as a worshiper defending his deity. Certainly, Humphrey stood on secure ground in presenting the New Deal not as a revolution against capitalism but as a rescue mission to save it from its excesses. Similarly, he made a trenchant point about how the New Deal aspired not to aggravate class tensions, as its critics claimed, but to ease them by bringing economic security to the poor and working classes. Yet in its scores of pages, in its tens of thousands of words, Humphrey's thesis found not a single significant fault with FDR and the New Deal, not even in the president's catastrophic attempt to pack the Supreme Court with justices friendlier to his program. Humphrey diminished the New Deal's failure to extend its full benefits to tenant farmers and unorganized laborers, many of them Black people whom Southern Democrats demanded that Roosevelt exclude in exchange for their votes. Most of Humphrey's footnoted sources led to Roosevelt's own speeches and sympathetic accounts by journalists and historians, a convenient way to rig the laudatory conclusion.[57]

Charles Hyneman, though, proceeded to do some rigging of his own. He delayed consideration of Humphrey's thesis until late June. By then, Daspit would be at Harvard working toward his doctorate. With the nemesis gone, Hyneman packed the court of Humphrey's thesis committee with favorably disposed government professors. During Humphrey's oral exam, though, one of them could not resist playing a parting trick.

"Hubert, I've decided I'm going to fail you on this examination," said Norton Long in a deadpan tone.

"Why?" Humphrey shot back in alarm.

"Well," Long explained, "if we give you a degree, you're just as likely as soon to end up a college professor. And if we flunked you right here and now, you'd go back to Minnesota and run for the United States Senate, and you'll amount to something."[58]

Possessed now of an A on his thesis and a master's degree, Humphrey still aspired to the academy. Princeton University had admitted him to its doctoral program in political science, but without enough financial support to sustain a family of three in the comparatively expensive East. So Humphrey instead headed back to the University of Minnesota, where his mentor Evron Kirkpatrick had arranged a teaching assistantship paying six hundred dollars for the academic year and a two-hundred-dollar-a-month summer job administering adult education courses in the WPA.[59]

In the early summer of 1940, the season of the Democratic and Republican national conventions, and the grim days with France newly conquered and London under nightly assault by German bombers, Humphrey boarded the Illinois Central once again. On the train's northbound route, as it stopped in places like Macomb and Grenada and then Memphis, the Jim Crow car filled with former sharecroppers and housekeepers bound for the imagined freedom and factory jobs available at the terminus in Chicago. Such people had been streaming into the city for nearly twenty-five years by now, increasing its Black population by more than two hundred thousand, part of the so-called Great Migration from the rural South to the urban North. After the train crossed the Ohio River—or as Chicago's Black newspaper, the

Defender, called it, "the River Styx"—the Black passengers could begin to move into regular coaches, which in Illinois and the rest of the North were allowed to be integrated.

Humphrey's trip required transferring in Chicago to another train aiming toward Minnesota and the Dakotas, places seemingly distant from matters of racial conflict. Yet Humphrey could not unknow what he now knew. White as he was, he had spent ten months in what amounted to the Jim Crow car, the American South. He had not been its captive passenger, but its acute observer, its attentive student. The lessons about racism of The Bottoms, of Maggie, and of Jamie Caffery, and those about other forms of bigotry from Alvin Rubin and Rudolf Heberle, accompanied Humphrey as psychic baggage. "No one, I thought, could view black life in Louisiana without shock and outrage," he later recalled. "Yet its importance to me was not only what I saw there and what my reaction was to southern segregation. It also opened my eyes to the prejudice of the North."[60]

CHAPTER 6

VESSEL AND VOICE

Minneapolis in Wartime

1941–1944

Six days before Thanksgiving of 1941, as the season's first blizzard bore down on South Dakota, H. H. Humphrey disengaged from the family drugstore in Huron long enough to type out a letter to his namesake son. In his characteristic blend of erudition and self-absorption, H. H. devoted most of the five single-spaced pages to sentimental memories of his prairie childhood, one blessedly free of such modern contraptions as electric lights and automobiles. He decried "our pursuit of the Golden Calf, our worship of things material rather than things spiritual," as if he were not an essentially agnostic businessman reliant on modernity's machinery and quite eager to make a buck.

Elsewhere in the missive, with its mixture of elegy and jeremiad, H. H. pointed to the more immediate causes of his concern about the state of the world. He referred to the string of Nazi conquests, from Poland to France to Greece, and he lamented the American politicians still espousing isolation, even with half the globe on fire. Then, toward the letter's end, H. H. finally turned his attention to Hubert, and his fatherly tone softened into one of reassurance. "Your sense of honor, your integrity, industry, your unselfish outlook upon life, your passion for the truth, and singleness of purpose, coupled with unusual mental capacity and remarkable gift of expression . . . will make [you] a power among men," H. H. wrote. Then he added for emphasis: "<u>Keep your ship of destiny out of the shoals of doubt and discouragement</u>."[1]

With that allusion to wavering confidence, H. H. either understood or guessed accurately the state of his son's mind. More than a year after returning to Minneapolis from graduate school at LSU full of righteous purpose, Humphrey had bogged down. Already past thirty, and abashed that his "accomplishments are not extensive,"[2] he still had not resolved the dilemma that his professors had joked about in assessing his master's thesis. Was his future in politics or the academy? Instead of deciding, Humphrey strained to keep a foothold in each, taking courses toward his doctorate at the University of Minnesota, and meanwhile supervising the Works Progress Administration (WPA) Workers' Education Program. For an ardent New Dealer, who had always resisted the Republican caricature of the WPA as so much goldbricking, Humphrey found himself disconcerted at his staff's lassitude, ultimately firing some of the teachers he oversaw.[3]

Even so, Humphrey's bigger worry was that the WPA might shut down altogether, because he and Muriel needed every cent of the $150 monthly salary. With the couple's daughter Nancy now two and a half, Muriel was several months' pregnant with a second child. The family had recently rented an apartment in a fourplex near the university campus, and Hubert bargained down the monthly rent from fifty-five dollars to forty by serving as the building's caretaker, scrubbing the hallway toilets, and sweeping out the furnace ashes. He had to borrow money from his undergrad buddy Orville Freeman to afford a used car and scavenged the refrigerator that another classmate was throwing out.[4]

Beyond the daily strain of balancing the books, Humphrey fully shared his father's anger and fear at the direction of the larger world. FDR and the New Deal seemed to be running out of electoral gas, at least in Minnesota. The president had carried the state by just three percent in 1940, having coasted to a thirty-point landslide just four years earlier. Republicans won eight of the nine Congressional races and held both of the state's Senate seats. One of those senators, Henrik Shipstead, had jumped parties from Farmer-Labor to the GOP, in part to give full voice to his isolationism. When William Bell Riley, the Minneapolis minister of copious anti-Semitism, delivered a sermon against American

167

intervention, Shipstead had it read into the *Congressional Record*.[5] (In typical fashion, Riley found a way, in the midst of a biblical exegesis about pacifism, to drop in an admiring reference to *The Protocols of the Elders of Zion*.) Even at the University of Minnesota, that seat of enlightenment, nearly eighty percent of students in an opinion poll opposed America entering the war against Nazi Germany.[6] All the while in the autumn of 1941, the German army was advancing on Moscow, Hitler having betrayed his notional ally Stalin by invading the Soviet Union in June.

Inspired by Rudolf Heberle's lessons on the imperative of confronting fascism, Humphrey cast about for some way to join the ideological battle. When he approached the local chapter of the Committee to Defend America by Aiding the Allies, a pro-intervention group, he struck a plaintive tone: "I have had considerable speaking experience and fairly wide training in international relations, and whatever talent I may have shall be yours for the asking." There is no record of the committee having taken up the offer.[7]

Then came the morning of December 7, 1941. As the *Minneapolis Star Journal* put it in an editorial, "The United States, a sleeping giant, has been stabbed awake."[8] Throughout the Twin Cities, private planes were grounded, guards posted at power and sewage plants, and soldiers at Fort Snelling put on alert. The Minneapolis branch of the Federal Reserve froze the assets of a hundred Japanese nationals in the area, while the FBI arrested four German citizens on suspicion of espionage. Students filled Northrop Auditorium at the university to hear the broadcast of Franklin Roosevelt's declaration of war against Japan, and some of them joined the record-breaking number of young men enlisting to fight.[9]

The Blacks and Jews of Minneapolis, like their brethren throughout the nation, had required no such wake-up call. Outcasts alike in a white Christian city and country, fellow subhumans in the Nazi cosmology, they had long seen in Hitler's Germany disturbing parallels to Jim Crow and Jew-hatred at home. The Nazis themselves made no secret of having drawn inspiration from America's style of racial segregation and its eugenics movement. For Blacks and Jews now, to be able to take up arms against the Reich was to offer patriotic sacrifice on the battlefield abroad in exchange for the prospect of genuine equality at home.

The first Minneapolitan reported dead at Pearl Harbor was a Jew, Ira Weil Jeffrey, a twenty-three-year-old naval ensign who had once been president of the Junior Congregation at Temple Israel. In its first issue after the attack, published just before Hanukkah, the *American Jewish World* conflated the modern fight against fascism with the ancient one against Judea's Hellenist rulers. "Forward in the Maccabean Spirit!" declared a front-page editorial. A week later, the newspaper featured a full-page illustration of an American GI brandishing a rifle in one hand and the Jerusalem temple's menorah in the other.[10]

Cecil Newman similarly devoted the *Spokesman's* latest edition almost entirely to war news. Even as one article quoted a half-dozen Black Minneapolitans supporting the war, another piece pointedly noted that five local men trying to enlist had been turned away by the army and told to try signing up in some other city.[11] The sting of that snub informed Newman's own front-page column, in equal parts a promise and a warning:

> As we Americans prepare to defend our country, it might be well that we take stock and make a start toward making every citizen glad he is an American.... Our leaders in civil and military affairs wherever they can will do this country a favor by ending as much of the Jim-Crow in civil and military war preparations as is possible. Mind you, the Negro is not going to let previous mistreatment affect his loyalty to America, but that loyalty, strong as it is, would be much stronger if in the nation's hour of extreme need there would be a cessation of race discrimination.[12]

By the time Humphrey wrote to H. H. a week after Pearl Harbor, the United States was at war with all of the Axis powers, not only Japan. In the existential struggle, he found both national and personal clarity, and what would prove to be common cause with the Blacks and Jews in his midst. "Last Sunday . . . sure put an abrupt stop to all argument over foreign policy," Humphrey wrote to H. H. "We are in war up to our eyebrows, and before long all of us shall feel the effect of total war. . . .

We may have lost a military & naval engagement at Pearl Harbor, but we gained a tremendous victory of national unity at home."[13]

By the summer of 1942, the WPA had appointed Humphrey the state-wide chief of the War Services Project, which aimed at building morale on the home front. In that role, he almost instantly became a ubiquitous public speaker. All of the debating skills he had sharpened on the teams in high school, college, and grad school; all of the impromptu orations he had inflicted on passersby outside classroom buildings; all of the unsolicited commentary that had driven even admiring professors to exasperation—that boundless if undisciplined supply of intelligence and volubility now had both a direction and a waiting, willing audience.

Humphrey delivered his standard speech, variously titled "Total War and Total Victory" or "Total War and Its Challenge to America," from the Kiwanis Club to the Knights of Columbus, from Local 292 of the International Brotherhood of Electrical Workers to the PTA of Ericsson Elementary School, from the Duluth Chapter of the American Institute of Banking to the Minnesota League of Poets. In one typical version, given at the Minnesota Library Association's annual conference, Humphrey set forth his challenging thesis. America had "closed her eyes" to the "danger of a militant and brutal Fascism" [sic] and had "slept while our enemies worked overtime." Even winning a battlefield victory would not fully destroy fascism. Democracy needed also to defeat the very idea of it, lest it "infect our lives until we have lost the faith of a free people."[14]

The response was effusive. "You certainly had the members of the Minneapolis Lions Club sitting on the edges of their chairs last Wednesday," a member wrote to Humphrey about the "Total War" speech. "It was one of the most stirring programs we have had in recent years."[15] A Rotary Club listener hailed the speech as "a beacon in these seas of confusion."[16] After another Humphrey stop on the rubber-chicken circuit, chicken being one of the few meats not subject to war-time rationing, an audience member exulted, "When a group of hard headed business men will get up and cheer a speaker it is a sure sign that he deserves to be cheered and that his message touched something in their hearts."[17]

The praise must have reassured Humphrey that he was doing something important for the war effort, for he did not have to look far for much riskier examples of service. His brother Ralph had quit the family drugstore to enlist in the navy. His sister Frances's new husband, Ray Howard, was a military doctor on troop ships braving Nazi U-boats in the North Atlantic. Frances herself had been plucked straight from graduate school by Eleanor Roosevelt to assist her with employee services in the Office of Civil Defense. Herb Gosch, who was married to Hubert's other sister, Fern, was training with the Army Air Corps. Orville Freeman had volunteered for the Marines. Even the kids whom Humphrey had led as Boy Scouts back in Huron were grown up enough now to be donning a different kind of uniform.

By the time a somber version of July 4 fell in 1942, with American troops struggling to reverse Axis gains in the Pacific and North Africa, Humphrey was thirty-one and the father of a second child, a son christened Hubert III. The military may not have wanted Humphrey under such circumstances, but at least audiences on the home front did.

Their ovations and adulation took him by surprise. When one listener asked for a copy of a particular speech, Humphrey had to admit he didn't have a written text. "I'm busy beyond belief," Humphrey confided to H. H. "[T]here is so much to do that I scarcely know where to turn. Letters pour in, telephone calls, speech requests, meetings."[18] As Humphrey's rounds continued through 1942 and into 1943—the appearances before the American Legion and the Twin Cities Apparel Association, the broadcasts on radio station WCCO—he was making a choice, even if he was not entirely aware of it. Humphrey was building contacts and connections in town. His name was becoming known. As much by coincidence as intention, the late starter was assembling the rudiments of a political career.

It included an almost literal version of a kitchen cabinet. When Humphrey burst through the door of his apartment after an evening's speech or speeches, still abuzz from the thrill of the podium, he often found five people waiting for him. In addition to Muriel there were two couples—Evron and Doris Kirkpatrick, and Arthur and Fran Naftalin. Too strapped to afford beer or whisky, the friends socialized over ginger ale and popcorn, rounds of gin rummy, and plenty of political strategizing.[19]

Kirkpatrick tied together the group, both personally and ideologically. He had taught both Humphrey and Naftalin in political science classes several years apart and in the spring of 1942 invited Naftalin to hear Humphrey speak to an adult education group. "I know that windbag," Naftalin had sourly observed, recalling one of Humphrey's impromptu declamations on campus in the late 1930s. Still, he agreed to chat with Humphrey at a nearby ice-cream parlor after the adult ed session and found himself surprisingly "captivated . . . fast friends."[20]

More than Humphrey or Kirkpatrick, Naftalin brought street smarts to those late nights in the living room. He had started working on newspapers straight out of high school in his hometown of Fargo, North Dakota, earning enough money to enroll at the University of Minnesota, and become a reporter on the *Minneapolis Tribune* after graduation. Working nights on the city desk, he knew the municipal underbelly of gangsters and gamblers, crooked politicians and bought-off cops. As a Jew, he was acutely aware, as he later said, of the "sharp segregation between the gentile population and the Jewish population."[21]

A scholar who appreciated rather than scorned the practice of politics, Kirkpatrick supplied his acolytes with an overarching analytical framework. Even as the Democratic Party held national power, the New Deal remained vulnerable in Minnesota. The state's non-conservative votes were divided between the Farmer-Labor and Democratic parties, allowing Republicans to win elections with a mere plurality. Each anti-Republican faction, in turn, contained its own inherent flaws—the machine chicanery and Catholic identity of the Democrats, and the utopian vision and communist influence of the Farmer-Laborites. Kirkpatrick sought an activist government free of both corruption and illusion.[22]

What Humphrey brought to the mix was political talent. He could spellbind a crowd in a way that Kirkpatrick and Naftalin could not. He had a personal touch that could not be taught. He had a wife of public deference and private wisdom, capable of making peace with the couple's rapid transformation from companionate marriage to the more conventional arrangement of housebound mother and workaholic father. Judging by Humphrey's speaking schedule, he ran on an engine of passion and ambition that was made for the round-the-clock demands of a campaign. The open question was, a campaign for what?

* * *

Three months before Pearl Harbor, with the United State supposedly neutral in the world war, Cecil Newman released his latest issue of the *Spokesman* with the front-page headline "HITLER MUST BE LAUGHING!" The accompanying article consisted largely of a statement, formally notarized by Newman himself, from a local Black man named Melvin Stone, a mechanical draftsman who had studied at the University of Minnesota. Stone had applied for a job with the Minneapolis field representative of a West Coast aircraft manufacturer, only to be informed there were "strict orders from the main office . . . not to consider any Negroes for any technical work under any circumstances."[23]

Newman carried over the public shaming into his editorial column. Under the headline "Giving Aid to Hitler," he asserted his own definition of treason: "It's Hitler's theory that this country does not practice what it preaches. It is his theory that certain races are inferior. . . . It is his practice that such races be barred from the professions, the skilled trades, etc. Those who practice these things in America must believe as he does."[24]

Such words marked a continuation of Newman's long-standing concern not just with the immorality of racism but its material consequences. He was decrying Stone's treatment for the same reason that in the prior decade he had orchestrated a boycott of Twin Cities breweries for refusing to hire Blacks. Yet Newman was also altering his familiar argument for equal employment, applying leverage he had never before had. It was the leverage of war—the war that indeed arrived one Sunday morning in December.

As a former Pullman porter and a current newspaper publisher, Newman entered the war years personally involved in two nationwide movements for Black rights. Even before the United States joined the Allies, the leader of Newman's longtime union, the Brotherhood of Sleeping Car Porters, had successfully faced down the president. A. Philip Randolph had threatened a March on Washington, one hundred thousand strong, if Roosevelt did not end segregation in the fast-expanding defense industries. Though FDR had resisted previous appeals from Black activists, white liberals, and even the First Lady to support anti-lynching legislation and to integrate the armed forces, he capitulated this time in a tacit exchange for Randolph calling off the march. Executive Order 8802, issued just a week before the protest's July 1 date, put hiring at defense plants on government contracts under the oversight of a Fair Employment Practices Commission (FEPC). It was to that very commission that Newman submitted the case of Melvin Stone.

One of Newman's peers in the elite ranks of Black publishers, P. L. Prattis of the *Pittsburgh Courier*,[25] soon supplied the image and slogan for the bargain that Black Americans were willing to strike with their hypocritical country. The process began when the *Courier* published a letter in February 1942 from a young man quite similar to Melvin Stone. James Gratz Thompson had found work in an aircraft factory, a Cessna plant in Wichita, Kansas, but only in the cafeteria. Executive Order 8802 notwithstanding, skilled labor was for whites, servility for Blacks, and even at that Thompson had just been denied a nickel-an-hour raise. "Should I sacrifice my life to be half American?" Thompson asked in his letter. "Would it be too much to demand full citizenship rights in exchange for the sacrificing of my life?"[26]

Then Thompson delivered what was, in effect, the advertising campaign for an ideal. He chose the phrase "Double V," with "the first V for victory over our enemies without, the second V for victory over our enemies within." The icon that Thompson had in mind, one that would have been familiar to millions of Americans, was Winston Churchill's two-fingered salute of pluck and resolve. As the Double V campaign captivated Black America, as well as sympathetic whites, with songs, posters, sweaters, and contests invoking the theme,[27] Cecil Newman added his fervency to the movement.

Throughout the first year of U.S. involvement in the war, Newman relentlessly reported and editorialized on the duplicity of American democracy—lynchings, whites-only primary elections, discrimination in defense plants as far afield as Oregon, segregation in Minnesota's own Home Guard units, and the harassment of a local Black minister's wife by a Southern sergeant posted at Fort Snelling. Again and again, Newman linked homegrown bigots to Hitler and Himmler. Again and again, he posed the same kind of question that a *Spokesman* reader named Charles Beasley did in a letter to the editor: "It is a fine country, in fact the best, but what has this country done for us?"[28]

One white person in Minneapolis providing an answer was Charles Horn, the president of Federal Cartridge, a company that manufactured bullets for sport hunting. In the spring of 1941, with the goal of aiding Britain even if the United States did not enter the war, the army had contracted with Horn to operate a massive ammunition factory to be built just north of Minneapolis. Heeding Roosevelt's executive order, Horn hired five Black men as security guards that fall and promoted one to supervisor. By the spring of 1942, with Twin Cities Ordnance running round-the-clock shifts and cranking out bullets by the million, Horn turned to Cecil Newman for help finding Black workers.

The men had met more than a decade earlier during Newman's time as a Pullman porter. When Newman launched the *Spokesman*, Horn became its first white subscriber.[29] That decision hinted at Horn's background. Though he held the conventionally conservative stances on economic issues of a corporate executive, he was the grandson of an abolitionist involved with the Underground Railroad, and he had worshiped all his life in Quaker congregations, though he was not formally of that faith. In April 1942, Newman accepted Horn's offer to serve as a de facto recruiter[30] on two conditions—that he receive no salary[31] and that all Black job-seekers be screened by the Urban League. Then Newman passed day-to-day control of the *Spokesman* to his wife, DeVelma, though her own expertise was in bookkeeping rather than journalism, and the inexperience soon showed in the paper's clumsy layout and reliance on syndicated articles.

However painful it must have been for Newman to step away from his creation, the choice allowed him and Horn to collaborate on a social experiment the likes of which Minneapolis had never seen. When white foremen objected to Horn about the growing number of Blacks on the job, the boss stuck by Newman.[32] Nor did Horn quail when Newman's own personnel file revealed that the FBI considered him a communist sympathizer.[33] At its peak, Twin Cities Ordnance employed nearly twelve hundred Blacks among its twenty-six thousand workers. (In addition, nearly two-thirds of the workforce was female.) Horn refused to segregate employees by race, and he mingled them not only on the factory floor but in the plant's choir, sports leagues, and cafeteria. With promotions based on aptitude tests rather than kinship networks, that staple of all-white unions, Blacks rose to positions as foreman, engineer, accountant, and stenographer. "It is important in this battle for democracy," Horn wrote to Newman, "that the Negro be recognized."[34]

On the Saturday night of September 19, 1942, Horn issued an order for a full complement of workers to report. Certainly, the Allies needed all the war materiel possible, with Germany having driven into Egypt and toward the Soviet city of Stalingrad. But even by the standards of Twin Cities Ordnance Saturday night was usually slow, and employees wondered why they were being summoned. Then a train pulled into the rail spur that served the plant, and out of one coach rolled a custom-built Lincoln convertible called the Sunshine Special. It carried President Roosevelt.[35]

FDR's secret visit to Twin Cities Ordnance was part of an eight-thousand-mile tour of defense plants, the workshops of what the president had famously called "the arsenal of democracy." In Roosevelt's two-hour tour, Horn guided him through one factory that made .50-caliber ammunition for the Browning Automatic Rifle and another that produced .30-caliber shells for the M-1, the semiautomatic service weapon that was the staple of the infantry. Spotting FDR, one worker was so shocked that he dropped his wrench. Another employee, one of the thousands of women who had been hired, handed the president a clip of cartridges as a souvenir.

In deference to wartime security, news reports of Roosevelt's visit did not appear until two weeks later. When they did, and in lengthy subsequent articles about Twin Cities Ordnance, no mention was made of the Black workers and their thorough integration into the factory. Photo essays in the Minneapolis and St. Paul papers almost entirely omitted Black faces. Only in the *Pittsburgh Courier* was the achievement of Charles Horn and Cecil Newman hailed as a "model for the entire country."[36]

The disinterest, or willful ignorance, on the part of the Twin Cities' white press was outdone by the refusal of local defense contractors to follow Horn's lead. As Newman pointed out in the *Spokesman*, Northern Pump counted just three Blacks in a workforce of seven thousand. American Hoist & Derrick had none among its fourteen hundred employees.[37] Minnesota Mining and Manufacturing (3M) did not get around to hiring its first Black worker until late 1942, nearly eighteen months after Executive Order 8802 had taken effect.[38] Nationwide, as of mid-1942, only three percent of defense plant workers were Black.[39] As admirable as Charles Horn's partnership with Cecil Newman was, it served as the color-blind exception that proved the discriminatory rule.

All the contradictions of Black service in America's war effort turned more personal than ever for Newman in early 1943, when his son Oscar received an induction notice from the army. Despite Cecil Newman's divorce five years earlier from Oscar's mother, Willa Mae, father and son had remained close. Oscar handled distribution of the *Spokesman*, and he followed the paternal example of leadership, being elected president of a Black group called the Minneapolis Young People's Forum. In one incident in August 1940, Oscar paid the price for Cecil's activism in what was almost certainly a case of mistaken identity. As Oscar was pulling away from Cecil's house with a load of *Spokesmans* to deliver, one white man ordered him out of the car at gunpoint and another beat him with a blackjack.[40] The chin scar noted on Oscar's draft card was the permanent record of that attack.

On Friday January 31, 1943, four days before twenty-one-year-old Oscar was to report for duty, Cecil and Willa Mae threw him a send-off party at a Black social club, the Rawjess.[41] There was plenty of music and dancing and a turnout of dozens of Oscar's friends. The celebratory mood, however, did not last long with Cecil. From his own articles and those he likely had read in the *Pittsburgh Courier* and the *Chicago Defender*, he held no illusions about the hostility Oscar would face. Black soldiers often rode in Jim Crow train cars to the vast military bases in the South, where they had to serve under bigoted white officers. Like Oscar, who would be assigned to the Quartermaster Corps, Black GIs were restricted to "noncombat service units" that moved supplies and constructed such military facilities as barracks, landing fields, and telegraph lines. Not even the Black aviators being trained at Tuskegee Institute thanks to the advocacy of Eleanor Roosevelt were yet permitted to fly combat missions. The Red Cross's military blood banks segregated donations by race—despite the fact that one of the world's experts in plasma donation and storage was a Black American doctor, Charles Drew—and Black military nurses were allowed only to treat patients of their own color. Though nearly a half million Black men and women were serving in the U.S. armed forces by the time Oscar entered them (and the number would ultimately peak at 1.2 million), the American military suppressed publication of photos of Black soldiers deployed overseas.[42]

Weighing the future promise of Double V against the abysmal reality of the present, Cecil Newman delivered his send-off in the form of an editorial headlined "War Gets Close to Home":

> Now that our pride and joy is wearing a uniform, getting ready we hope to do his best, for the greatest nation on earth, our personal approach to the war and victory is no longer academic . . .
>
> It's a task to talk to a Negro boy who has been south and who has seen how people of his race are treated, or who is cognizant that democracy means one thing for whites and another thing for Negroes, though America hypocritically contends the same democracy embraces all its people. Attempting to give a Negro boy headed for the Army or Navy . . . a pep talk filled with platitudes that sound empty, that are empty, is a task which is great . . .

Sure, son, we don't expect you to fight for what your people are receiving today, but fight, pray and hope that the sacrifices you and others will make will help raise our common country in reality to the lofty heights described and prescribed in our Bill of Rights, our Declaration of Independence and our Constitution.[43]

* * *

One of Humphrey's myriad speaking engagements during the autumn of 1942 took him to the Saturday Lunch Club, a weekly gathering of educators, attorneys, journalists, and other public-spirited Minneapolitans. Having hosted the likes of Jane Addams, Louis Brandeis, and William Jennings Bryan over the years, the club's podium put Humphrey in rarefied company. The person who mattered most in Humphrey's audience, though, was more privately influential than publicly famous: Vincent Day, a local judge who had been executive secretary to Floyd Olson, the late and beloved Farmer-Labor governor.

Several days after Humphrey's address, which most likely would have been a version of "Total War and Total Victory," Day invited him to the courthouse for a chat, which culminated in the unprompted proposal that Humphrey run for mayor.[44] On its face, the idea was ridiculous. By his own later description, Humphrey was a married father of two with a still-unfinished doctoral dissertation, a couple of WPA jobs, and no money in the bank.[45]

Besides, the looming opponent in the 1943 mayoral campaign would be the Republican incumbent, Marvin L. Kline, a fixture in Minneapolis politics after six years as a city council member, two as its president, and another two as mayor. An architectural engineer by training, Kline had begun his political career as a college athlete running for campus office—and being accused of stuffing the ballot box in the process.[46] With his matched sets of floral ties and pocket squares and his penchant for gag photographs—holding a starting pistol over three aldermen in a mock race, chomping on a Victory Garden carrot as big as an ear of corn[47]—he retained a certain raffish charm as mayor. Though Kline represented the conservative interests of big business and Christian churches in Minneapolis's officially nonpartisan elections, he navigated the city's political divides deftly. As one foe begrudgingly put it, Kline "had no enemies . . . plenty of money . . . and just hadn't done anything against anybody."[48] The expected candidate from the opposition, a co-alition of liberals and labor unionists, was T. A. Eide, the manager of a workers' cooperative creamery, who had narrowly lost to Kline in 1941. Where exactly did Humphrey even fit in? In the wake of their explora-tory conversation, Day and Humphrey each engaged in some political depth soundings to find out.

Day floated the idea of a Humphrey candidacy to several established leaders in the city's Central Labor Union, which, compared with the Trotskyites and communists in town, embodied the relatively moderate politics of the American Federation of Labor (AFL). Even so, these were men who worked with their hands, made things, and passed on their tactile skills to younger apprentices. The judge found them wary of backing some grad student who had no track record beyond a bunch of speeches. "The man on the street," one of Humphrey's own friends later recalled, "didn't know his name from a lump of hay."[49]

As for Humphrey, late one bitterly cold night in December 1942, he telephoned his compatriot Arthur Naftalin. "I talked to some folks," Humphrey explained, "and they want me to run for mayor." Clad only in a bathrobe, Naftalin impatiently shivered as he listened. "Do you think," Humphrey continued, "I'll get shot?" Familiar from his reporting days with Minneapolis's history of mob killings, several of them aimed at muckraking journalists, Naftalin replied, "We'll talk about it."[50]

So far as most of Minneapolis knew as the May 10 mayoral pri-mary drew closer, Hubert Humphrey had nothing to do with it. Eight other challengers to Kline ultimately filed, an eclectic assortment, ran-ging from Henry Soltau, a minister obsessed with stamping out demon rum, to Vincent Dunne, a leader in the 1934 truckers' strike who was presently appealing his 1941 conviction for sedition as a member of the Socialist Workers Party. Amid such extravagant company, T. A. Eide looked to be Kline's chief challenger, especially given Eide's support from the left-leaning Congress of Industrial Organizations (CIO) unions. As long as Eide finished second in the primary, he would advance to a one-on-one runoff against Kline in June.

Away from public view, however, Judge Day had lined up the Central Labor Union behind Humphrey. The union, in turn, would supply rent and a small paid staff for campaign headquarters, as well as a reservoir of volunteers. With its line of credit, the union could purchase postcards and placards and newspaper ads. Arthur Naftalin and Evron Kirkpatrick were on board as campaign advisor and publicist, respectively. The pool of incipient volunteers featured a former journalist and union organizer named Feike Feikema, whose politics had been formed by a youthful rejection of Calvinist asperity. On April 19, three weeks before the primary election, Humphrey filed.

For the most part, the city yawned. Public attention clung to the impending Allied invasion of Sicily. Thousands of potential voters were serving in the military or toiling in defense plants, far from their local ballot boxes. Amid the unfolding revelation of Hitler's atrocities against European Jewry, the Twin Cities' *American Jewish World* newspaper barely reported on the mayoral race. Cecil Newman in the pages of the *Spokesman* tersely observed, "City elections have never paid Minneapolis Negroes any dividends. A look around city hall and a study of municipal payrolls will convince one of this fact."[51] Even Minneapolis's bookies, setting Kline as a 4–1 favorite, bemoaned a "new low mark" in betting on the election.[52]

The mundane mood of the campaign afforded a long shot like Humphrey his opening. The friends and union allies in his inner circle pooled their rationing coupons so there was enough gas to drive Humphrey to three or four speaking events a night. Naftalin booked fifteen-minute slots on radio station WLOL for Humphrey, and in an appropriate contrast, the liberal candidate's talks often followed the broadcast sermons of Reverend Luke Rader, who peddled an even cruder version of William Bell Riley's Jew-hatred. When Humphrey's campaign determined he was still trailing T. A. Eide for a spot in the June runoff against Kline, Feikema hastily concocted an impromptu poll of about fifty people, and on that sketchy sample, it predicted Humphrey finishing second. Then Naftalin planted a press release about the poll on the desk of Minneapolis's reigning political reporter, M. W. Halloran, who in turn touted it on the eve of the primary as a "scientific survey, taken a la Gallup."[53]

As for Humphrey's platform, much of it was prosaic and some was deliberately fuzzy. He droned on about juvenile delinquency, government reorganization, and that mainstay of municipal handwringing, the gangsters downtown with their gambling and liquor rackets. Humphrey derided Kline as a "do-nothing mayor" with a "do-nothing philosophy,"[54] not an entirely fair criticism, given that the municipal charter made the city council far more powerful than the mayor. In Humphrey's ads, he made sure to mention his English and Norwegian background, assuring the city's white Protestants he was one of them. The letters to the editor that Humphrey partisans seeded in the *Tribune* and *Star Journal* emphasized the generational angle, depicting him as "young and clean and untagged." The campaign slogan similarly declared, "THE MAN FOR MINNEAPOLIS! YOUNG! HONEST! VIGOROUS!" And because the election was nonpartisan, Humphrey left more than a few hints that he might even be a closet Republican, seeking crossover votes by implying with utter implausibility that he had voted for Wendell Willkie against FDR in 1940.[55]

While the anodyne tone of Humphrey's campaign attested to an accidental candidate taking too much advice from supposed experts, there were still several moments when listeners got to hear the unmediated Humphrey, the one who had been so exhilarated by his 1936 trip to Washington, the one who had observed American racism and studied German fascism during his pivotal year at LSU. In a meeting with Bradley Mintener, a Yale-educated blueblood who was the general counsel for Pillsbury, Humphrey placed race relations second only to law enforcement in a list of civic problems.[56] Humphrey castigated Kline for refusing to endorse an equal rights law that was being debated in the state legislature and was supported by Cecil Newman of the *Spokesman* and Sam Scheiner of the Jewish Anti-Defamation Council of Minnesota, among others.[57] While Eide and Kline spoke frequently of the necessity of winning the war, as if it were even remotely in their power to affect the battlefield, Humphrey warned against postwar complacency and a resurgence of isolationism and intolerance. "The present mayor has been conspicuously silent on the real issues of war," Humphrey told an audience of union members at a Honeywell plant. "He has not understood, apparently, that this is not merely a military struggle but also a war against the idea of fascism."[58] In Humphrey's last radio speech of the primary campaign, he struck a sermonic tone to make the same point: "[M]an must have a moral philosophy. He must be convinced of the necessity of tolerance, the equality of men, the essential dignity of men; yes, the divinity of men."[59]

When the primary votes had all been counted, one prediction was proven correct. Turnout slumped to 74,474, barely one-third of registered voters and the lowest total in any mayoral election since 1931. As the one energetic candidate in a listless race, however, Humphrey captured second place and another chance at Kline in the runoff. True, he lost to the mayor by the humbling margin of nineteen percent, but he did what he had to do in edging Eide by three percent. In that close contest, Humphrey's pursuit of Black and Jewish votes surely mattered. As the *Star Journal* marveled, "[L]iterally an unknown to the general public scarcely a month ago," Humphrey had "come dashing out of nowhere to stage a colorful, fighting campaign to win this high honor."[60]

Marvin Kline, for one, appeared neither impressed nor distressed. Soon after the primary, he left Minneapolis for a week-long working vacation in New York and Washington, ostensibly to raise money for a local polio-treatment center. During Kline's absence, he even received the endorsement of his two-time rival, T. A. Eide. They shared a sneering consensus that Humphrey was just a bookworm and a gasbag, when in reality "it takes more than oratory to qualify for mayor."[61] Kline returned from his road trip to administer a lesson in practical politics, the better to dispose of Humphrey the annoyingly persistent naïf.

Toward noon on May 25, Feike Feikema went to Snyder's Drugstore to pick up the early edition of the evening papers. His gaze swerved to the front-page headline in the *Minneapolis Daily Times*,[62] "Racketeers Back Rival, Kline Claims." The accompanying article distilled a speech the mayor was to deliver on radio that night. Without the cumbersome baggage of truth, Kline was going to claim that Minneapolis's mobsters—and it hardly needed to be said that the most notorious, like Kid Cann, Yiddy Bloom, and Dave Berman, were Jews—"are back in this campaign, upon the side of my opponent, armed with vicious and diabolical schemes."[63]

Feikema was so furious that he tracked down Humphrey speaking to a women's group downtown and informed him of the smear. Instead of becoming angry, though, Humphrey the first-time candidate betrayed "kind of a crushed, devastated look, like the world had come apart." Almost timidly, Humphrey asked what to do. "We ought to go down and get that bastard and make him put up or shut up right in his office," Feikema shot back. "[G]et out the horsewhip. I would just go in there and raise the devil."[64]

For moral support, Feikema grabbed Arthur Naftalin out of a grad school class on campus. They both alerted a group of reporters and photographers to the imminent showdown in city hall. Initially, Humphrey played his indignant part well, since it was a part he genuinely believed in. He shoved a copy of the *Daily Times* at Kline, he wagged a finger in reproach, and he dared Kline to name one, just one, mobbed-up supporter. Kline conjured up George Murk, president of the local musicians' union, member of the city's Charter Commission, and purported owner of a crooked nightclub.

"Isn't Murk going to be your chief of police if you're elected?" Kline claimed.

"He has as much chance to be chief," Humphrey retorted, according to the *Minneapolis Daily Times*, "as Mahatma Gandhi has to be president."[65]

Then, in the tradition of Minnesota propriety, however insincere, one of the press photographers asked for Kline and Humphrey to shake hands and make up. So instinctually amiable, Humphrey foolishly complied, and the photo appeared in the next day's *Tribune*, undermining Humphrey's indignant words. Meanwhile, Kline went ahead as planned with the radio address, recycling the calumnies about Humphrey the mob's puppet. Humphrey was left to keep pressing by telegram and letter for a public debate on the charges. Kline went on dodging it.

But by the Memorial Day holiday weekend, two weeks before the election, Kline had become sufficiently concerned about Humphrey to open a campaign headquarters belatedly. It was too late for him now to play catch-up on Humphrey's tireless speaking schedule, from the roughnecks of the Railroad Brotherhood to the patricians of the Commonwealth Club, from the Jewish group called the Maccabees to the Polish National Alliance. Kline splintered off a few dissenting union leaders from the Humphrey camp, but Humphrey inherited the CIO endorsement that Eide had received in the primary.

Something else was happening, something new in Minneapolis's electoral history: the mobilization of the Black vote. Anthony Brutus Cassius, the activist who had organized the hotel waiters' union, donated five dollars to the Humphrey campaign—not a large sum, but an unmistakable signal to the Black community at large.[66] Though Cecil Newman was largely absorbed in recruiting and placing Black workers at Twin Cities Ordnance, he had been taking notice for several years of Humphrey's performance with the WPA, and specifically his insistence on hiring and promoting Black employees. As if supplying Newman with a news peg, Humphrey scheduled a speech on the last Saturday night of the campaign to the Working Girls' Council at the Phyllis Wheatley House, the signature institution of Black Minneapolis. Newman did not issue a formal endorsement of Humphrey, though he would later claim he had, but in several news articles he ensured that the *Spokesman* conveyed that essential message. One item saluted Humphrey's "unusually fair treatment of Negroes during the period he held several executive positions with the WPA."[67] Another praised his "honesty and understanding when dealing with Negroes' problems."[68]

In a sign of panic about Kline's complacency, the state Republican Party took partial control of his campaign in the race's final week.[69] Then, three days before the election, Humphrey was hit with one more dirty trick. Vincent Dunne—the unapologetic Trotskyite already convicted of sedition, the mayoral candidate who had taken less than two hundred votes in the primary—endorsed Humphrey as "a step forward against reactionary capitalist politics." Humphrey scrambled to repudiate the endorsement, accurately calling it a "kiss of death."[70]

Privately, he seethed that Kline had engineered the whole thing, an un-proven but logical assumption.

The attacks on Humphrey, however groundless, succeeded in stir-ring establishment doubts. None of the city's three major newspapers endorsed Humphrey, and a *Star Journal* editorial echoed the innuendo that Humphrey would not be "FREE to serve the whole community" (capitals in original). Minneapolis already had a "much-better-than-average" mayor in place, and while Humphrey "might make a much better mayor than Marvin Kline—he might make a much worse one."[71]

Heading toward Election Day, Humphrey wrote to H. H. in the tone of a hayseed who'd just gotten jumped in the big bad city:

> The opposition is continuously circulating filthy rumors, painting me as a Communist, as a Fascist, as immoral, as incompetent, etc. The latest one is that the Eastern bankers are supporting me . . . I understand that all these rotten rumors are going to be gathered together in a final scandal sheet which the Mayor's coherts [sic] will circulate throughout the city the day before the election . . .
>
> I don't even have the active support of the churches . . . I had my good friend, Rev. Nye,[72] call me this morning and inform me that he must no longer support my candidacy since if he continued to do so, his job would be jeopardized and many members of the church would be outraged. I told Nye I appreciated his position and at the same time gave him a sermon on the unchristian attitude of his membership and the filth and dirt that some of them were carrying around about me.
>
> It doesn't really disturb me except that I want to have a chance to fight back.[73]

At another point in the letter, however, a different side of Humphrey emerged, a tougher and more competitive side. For all his seeming inno-cence, for all his genial and deferential nature, he had honed this other side as a champion debater, a winner. It was the side, too, of his youthful exposure to the Protestant theology of "muscular Christianity," the belief in a literal sense that there was nothing weak about being good: "Well, Dad, put this down in your book. We are going to give this fellow a good licking. I get so damn mad at him that I don't know how to get tired any more and have but one desire—to prove to this city that political deceit and treachery are no longer good politics."[74]

Humphrey very nearly made good on that vow. In the June 14 election, he came within six thousand votes and five percentage points of toppling Kline. Humphrey almost tripled his own vote total from the primary, and the excitement he generated pushed voter turnout from less than seventy-five thousand in the primary to more than one hundred fourteen thousand in the runoff. Suddenly the newspapers were full of speculation about Humphrey's future. Might he run for Congress in 1944? Might he become a Republican? Even the condolence letters that Humphrey received looked forward.

"Bravo for the race you ran," said one such missive, "and tears for the less than 3,000 votes that went the wrong way! . . . In school we learned 'success is never final; failure is never fatal.' You are now known, and liked and admired by so many thousands here, we look and hope for bigger and better things under your leadership in the future."[75]

* * *

On May 16, 1942, a Saturday about a year before the mayoral election, Private First Class Samuel Tucker donned his olive drab uniform and left his base at Fort Snelling for a double date. The couples wound up at a tavern just north of St. Paul, the Wagon Wheel Inn. Soon after the foursome took seats, a waitress asked for their nationality, not the usual greeting for a customer. "Jewish," Tucker and his friends answered. Whereupon the waitress refused to hand over any menus. Tucker demanded to speak with the manager, only to be informed that the waitress was the manager. "I told her she could not refuse to serve a uniformed soldier of the United States Army," Tucker recalled soon after. "She said she could serve whomever she pleased." Unserved and incensed, Tucker and his friends drove away.[76]

Word of the confrontation reached the chaplain at Fort Snelling and after passing through several ascending levels of officers somehow found its way to Sam Scheiner of the Jewish Anti-Defamation Council of Minnesota. Scheiner persuaded Tucker to sign a complaint against the manager, one Mae Belle Perlstrom, for violating Minnesota's anti-discrimination law, and she even spent a night in jail before being released on bond. In the end, though, a county judge dismissed the charge, leaving Tucker with a letter of apology from Perlstrom[77] and Scheiner with the most recent example of the painful paradox of American Jews during World War II. For plenty of white Christians, Scheiner could see, fighting against Hitler was not at all inconsistent with continuing to discriminate against the Jews in their midst. Scheiner's mission on the home front was to expose such moral hypocrisy, to make it untenable, indefensible.

As Jews streamed into the American armed forces, ultimately forming five hundred thousand of the nation's sixteen million men and women in uniform, none of them ever coined a phrase as evocative as "Double Victory." Yet the same concept that animated Black soldiers—defeating bigotry both abroad and at home—inspired Jews, as well. Fighting and dying, particularly in a war against fascism, would forever banish the stereotypes of the Jew as coward, as conniver, as money-grubber, as special pleader for his tribe alone. Or so they were tempted to believe.

In Minneapolis, the *American Jewish World* touted the community's service and sacrifice in a weekly column, "With Our Fighting Men." The Passover edition in March 1942 featured a cover illustration of Moses and FDR together parting the Red Sea, and vanquishing Hitler, Mussolini, and Hirohito in the waves. In a grim coincidence six months later, Minneapolis conducted a citywide blackout on one night of Rosh Hashanah, when the Judaic liturgy asks who shall live and who shall die. As if to answer the ontological question, the *American Jewish World* reported in its Rosh Hashanah edition the toll from the first nine months of global war: two local Jewish boys killed, three missing in action, one a prisoner of war, and 780 men (as well as three women) serving. By Rosh Hashanah in 1943, the death count had risen to eight and the number serving to thirteen hundred.

"My only hope," wrote Marvin Hork, a private in the Army Air Corps, "is that the spirit shown by us in the war effort will forever blast away the myth that a Jew in the Army has to have an office job; I hope that we will forever blast away the theory that the quartermasters' corps is the "Jewish infantry." We are out there to do our best—to be a credit to our race and to our country."[78]

Scheiner knew better than to assume victory on that front. For him, the first figurative shot of the war at home had been fired nearly three months before Pearl Harbor. On September 11, 1941, Minnesota's homegrown hero, Charles Lindbergh, addressed an audience of supporters of the America First Committee. "The three most important groups who have been pressing this country toward war," he told the crowd in Des Moines, Iowa, "are the British, the Jewish, and the Roosevelt Administration." On the subject of the Jews, Lindbergh nodded in brief sympathy toward the "persecution they suffered in Germany," before more characteristically warning that the "greatest danger to this country" was not Hitler's fascism but rather Jewish "ownership and influence in our motion pictures, our press, our radio, and our government." That influence, Lindbergh prophesied, could "lead our country to destruction."[79]

Within three days of the Des Moines speech, Scheiner drafted a response, which would be issued under the name of the anti-defamation group's chairman, Arthur Brin. The letter asserted that the "Jews of this country yield to no one in their patriotism," and on that basis it demanded that the America First Committee repudiate Lindbergh's "balderdash," "canards," and "threadbare falsehood[s]."[80] Scheiner's ultimatum thrust his obscure organization—three years old then, with a staff consisting essentially of him alone—into the national spotlight. It pitted the council against an isolationist organization deeply woven into America's corporate and political mainstream. America First's national chairman was Arthur Wood, a retired general who now led Sears Roebuck. A Harvard-educated attorney, Jacob Holtzermann, headed the committee's Minneapolis chapter.

In one respect, Scheiner succeeded. Newspapers as far afield as Philadelphia, New York, and Los Angeles carried a wire service article about his letter. Otherwise, the response served as yet another reminder of Scheiner's isolation. It was predictable enough that he received hate mail reviling "your rotten, filthy race."[81] It was not surprising that the

America First Committee stood by Lindbergh, its star attraction. But Scheiner also received a dressing-down from the national leadership of the Anti-Defamation League, his presumed allies, for having dared to "initiate independent action on matters of very important national policy."[82] The *shtarker*, the tough guy, needed to know his place.

The coming of war did little to alter the fundamental struggle that Scheiner faced. Even as the United States took up arms against racial and religious supremacy in both its German and Japanese versions, Scheiner surveyed—and surveilled—a fervid pageant of anti-Semitism in his own city and state. In a confidential report to his board in 1942, he estimated that he had investigated five hundred complaints about anti-Semitism in the previous three years. That summer, the anti-defamation group streamlined its name to the Minnesota Jewish Council, and Scheiner announced the desire for it "to become more an educational and constructive agency rather than a purely defensive one."[83] Events proved him far too optimistic.

As the war dragged on and the extermination of European Jews continued, Scheiner sent informants, some of them idealistic young Christian volunteers, to attend and stealthily note the content of worship services and revival meetings led by various anti-Semitic ministers. He kept track of the companies that advertised in the bulletin of a local German American group. He added dozens of names to his card catalog of local extremists, and in the most worrisome cases tipped off the FBI or the Minneapolis police, albeit to uncertain effect. He distributed tens of thousands of anti-discrimination pamphlets at the state fair and union picnics, lined up Jewish war veterans to give radio addresses on patriotic holidays, and pleaded with newspaper editors to stop publishing hateful letters in the interest of "free speech." If Scheiner thought a particular bigot could be reasoned into tolerance, he would correspond with or even meet the person, devoting innumerable hours to changing just one mind. Such an approach, however admirable, was an absurdly inefficient way of improving society as a whole. Often enough, Scheiner failed in his entreaties, anyway. "No wonder Hitler chased you out of Germany," said a man who had come to Scheiner's attention for insulting the Jewish owner of a furniture store. "A Jew would do anything for a dollar more."[84]

Amid the parallel wartime struggles of Minneapolis's Blacks and Jews, a common front began to develop between them, with Scheiner and Cecil Newman among its most integral participants. Scheiner reported to the Minnesota Jewish Council that he "cooperates very strongly" with organizations such as the NAACP on "many matters of mutual interest" and "maintains a close friendship with the editor of the Negro papers in the Twin Cities."[85] The men swapped podiums and audiences, with Newman addressing the Gymal Doled Club and Scheiner speaking to the Urban League. The *American Jewish World* hailed the emerging alliance by invoking the groups' common foes of the Ku Klux Klan and the America First movement: "Anti-Jewish sentiment is as freely expressed as anti-Negro views. The tyranny of economic and political obscurantism is the menace to the American way of life. Jews should be the first to understand it and to fight it."[86]

Newman framed the bond in both historical and literary terms. Alluding without naming them to men like Scheiner, Humphrey, and Charles Horn, Newman harked back to the abolitionists as the model for those few white people "who labor in the vineyard of causes which champions on the underdog."[87] At his most despairing, Newman continued, he took solace in a century-old poem by James Russell Lowell, "Stanzas on Freedom," quoting the final verse in the *Spokesman*:

> They are slaves who fear to speak
> For the fallen and the weak;
> They are slaves who will not choose
> Hatred, scoffing, and abuse,
> Rather than in silence shrink
> From the truth they needs must think;
> They are slaves who dare not be
> In the right with two or three.

The coalition embodied by Scheiner and Newman faced its most significant public test in the late winter and early spring of 1943. Prodded by a liberal member from Minneapolis, and doubtlessly affected by the wartime climate, the state legislature sought to amend an equal rights law dating back to 1927. The existing statute barred discrimination in public accommodations on the basis of race; the amended version, partly drafted by Scheiner, would also outlaw bias on the basis of "national origin and religion." It would, to put it another way, protect both Blacks and Jews. Considering how rarely the original law had ever been enforced, expanding its scope hardly qualified as an act of moral courage. Even so, in certain white quarters, the prospect stirred the primordial fear of miscegenation.

"Well Mr. Scheiner just because you want to sit at the table with a negro thats [sic] no reason why all of us must do the same," one anonymous correspondent wrote to him. "[H]ow would you like to have your daughter marry one of those negroes—<u>huh</u> well think it over. I hope she does."[88]

After the State Senate passed the bill, it landed in the House's Judiciary Committee to be neutered. The committee refused to advance the bill to the full House, and ultimately Governor Harold Stassen, unless violations were reduced from a gross misdemeanor to a simple misdemeanor and the five-hundred-dollar civil fine was eliminated. As the bill languished in the Judiciary Committee for weeks and the legislative session plodded toward its close, newspapers from the *Spokesman* to the *Star Journal* to the *American Jewish World* raged. A columnist in the *Tribune* took the satiric tack of writing in the voice of the Grand Cyclops of the Ku Klux Klan:

> Yes, Sir-ree, I'm proud to see Minnesota lining up as a state which ain't afraid to be intolerant. . . . You can see that they pretty much agree with Hitler in a lot of his racial and religious ideas and, when you come right down to it, Hitler is a pretty smart guy even if we do happen to be fighting him right now. I sometimes wish we had a Hitler in this country.[89]

Privately, Scheiner felt torn. Even a diluted equal rights law would enshrine the principle that Jews (and, for that matter, Catholics and other minority religious groups) deserved legal protection from discrimination. Stiffer penalties could be built in later. It even seemed possible, Scheiner confided to a council member, that "these bigots in the House of Representatives" would conveniently rely on Black protest to "kill the bill . . . so that they can crawl out from under this mess."[90] Yet supporting the bill in its diminished form meant selling out the Black allies whom Scheiner had only recently developed and accepting a law even more toothless than the original. It meant being divided and conquered.

So Scheiner joined the interracial delegation that successfully pressed Governor Stassen in mid-April to throw his popularity and national ambitions behind the original iteration of the bill. Within a week, legislators had maneuvered the bill away from the hostile Judiciary Committee, restored the penalties for violation, and moved it to a floor vote. Cecil Newman extolled the Black and Jewish collaboration in "the most hectic battle for democracy and tolerance" in Minnesota's history.[91]

What looked like overwhelming approval—a vote of 83–11 in the House—was less impressive considering that forty legislators abstained. No sooner did Governor Stassen sign the bill into law on April 23, mere weeks before the summer vacation season, than the proprietors of Minnesota's lakeside cottages replied. They swapped out their "Gentiles Only" signs and brochures, newly illegal, for such euphemisms as "A High Class Clientele," "Mutually Congenial Clientele," and, pun intended or not, "Resort for Discriminating Families."[92] Bigoted business went on as usual. As Sam Scheiner had seen for years by now, from T. G. Wooster of the Silver Shirts to Mae Bell Perlstrom at the Wagon Wheel Inn, having a law on the books was one thing. Having the will to enforce it was quite another.

So Scheiner tried one more gambit: subjecting Minneapolis to national notoriety. In the summer of 1943, he had learned that a liberal journalist named Selden Menefee had been traveling the country to write a book on its wartime mood. Menefee had previewed some of its findings in an article in the *Nation*, where he regularly published, singling out Minneapolis as the only city in the Middle West that had a "serious problem" with anti-Semitism.[93] It turned out that Menefee had based that conclusion, however accurate, on just one day's visit to Minneapolis and a single informant who was not even Jewish. In a flurry of correspondence with the author, Scheiner hastened to fill the gap, feeding Menefee material that could be squeezed into the almost-finished book:

> It might interest you to know that Minneapolis is the only city in the United States where the Service [sic] clubs, as for example the Rotary, Kiwanis, Lions, and Automobile Club does not allow Jewish membership. That is also true of the Toastmasters' Club here . . . I am firmly convinced that Minneapolis is the only large city in the United States where this is true.
>
> By way of contrast, it might interest you to know that the Saint Paul Automobile Club has a Jewish president . . .
>
> It might also interest you to know that a month ago, in a certain select suburb of Minneapolis, a shotgun shell was fired through the home of a Jewish individual, in an attempt to get him to remove from the neighborhood.[94]

When Menefee's book *Assignment: U.S.A.* appeared in November 1943, reiterating Scheiner's information and warning of the potential for violence against Jews in Minneapolis, it drew review attention in the *New York Times*, among other major newspapers. Scheiner bought fifty copies to give to influential figures in Minneapolis. Yet the papers in the Twin Cities almost willfully ignored the book's critique. Even a journalist whom Scheiner had expected to be sympathetic, editorial editor Gideon Seymour of the *Star Journal*, blithely replied, "I don't doubt the truth of what he says about anti-Semitism here so much as I doubt that Minneapolis is worse than, or as bad as, a number of Middle Western cities in this regard."[95] Meeting with a group of local rabbis at Scheiner's behest, Seymour vowed to write an editorial objecting to the book's conclusions.[96] Just as the Minneapolis press had dismissed how deep and entrenched local bigotry was during the earlier upsurges of the Ku Klux Klan and the Silver Shirts, portraying them as the marginal acts of marginal people, so it turned off the alarm that was Menefee's book and rolled over back to sleep. In another worthy cause, Scheiner had been rebuffed again.

As 1943 concluded, Scheiner received two newly official designations. First, he was named by incoming Governor Edward Thye as a policy advisor to a newly formed state commission on interracial relations. Several weeks later, Scheiner received his induction notice from the U.S. Army, with a reporting date of February 8, 1944. Exactly a week before then, the Gymal Doled Club hosted a farewell party, with speakers including Cecil Newman and Hubert Humphrey.[97] Portly and bespectacled at thirty-five, the father of a four-year-old daughter, and the husband of a pregnant wife, Scheiner hardly presented a martial profile. Given his musical experience, he expected to be placed in a military band, maybe to play USO shows. Instead, the draft board sent Scheiner into the infantry. He could not help but wonder if that posting was payback for being such a troublemaker about equal rights.[98]

* * *

In the aftermath of his near-miss at the mayoralty, Humphrey found himself politically ascendant and materially earthbound in the summer of 1943. He traveled to Washington to meet with Democratic National Committee (DNC) officials about merging the state party with its Farmer-Labor rivals, the better to beat the already unified Republicans. An admiring article in the *New Republic* several months later gave Humphrey his first blast of national publicity.[99] (Readers outside Minneapolis, of course, had no way of knowing that the encomium's author, Feike Feikema, was a personal friend and campaign volunteer of Humphrey's.) Only thirty-two, Humphrey already loomed as a potential candidate in the Minnesota governor's race in 1944 and rising star in the post-FDR generation of Democrats.

Despite that glistening public profile, Humphrey was worse than broke. He owed thirteen hundred dollars for campaign expenses, mostly printing bills. Having resigned his position with the War Manpower Commission to run for mayor, he was now jobless. The landlord of his fourplex was threatening to fire him as caretaker, and take away the fourteen-dollar break on the monthly rent, because Humphrey had been so busy on the speaking circuit and campaign trail that he'd stopped washing the windows, cleaning the basement, and raking the leaves.[100] Humphrey needed every one of those speeches, though, because the honoraria of ten or twenty dollars apiece supplied the only reliable money coming into the household, and Muriel was pregnant by the late summer of 1943 with the couple's third child.

So Humphrey went after an open faculty position in the political science department at Macalester College in St. Paul with something like desperation. His anxiety only increased when the college's president, C. E. Ficken, questioned whether Humphrey "would be too greatly inhibited by the degree of objectivity and undogmatic presentation which is essential . . . both inside and outside the class room."[101] Beneath the lofty prose, Ficken was raising the same warning that the *Star Journal* had in refusing to endorse Humphrey—that this callow young greenhorn was controlled by corrupt, radical labor unions. It took a three-page, single-spaced letter, a promissory note for scholarly detachment, to land Humphrey a one-year appointment without the prospect of permanence or tenure.[102] Every so often, Humphrey's landlord interrupted class with a phone call to the college demanding that the caretaker get home to fix a toilet.[103]

Humphrey taught courses in political philosophy and world affairs to a combination of standard undergraduates and Army Air Corps cadets. Very much in the spirit of his mentor at LSU, Rudolf Heberle, he devoted particular attention to the totalitarian models of German and Italian fascism, Soviet communism, and Japanese militarism, all of them military and ideological challenges to democracy. He recounted the saga of American isolationism, tracing a path from the country's refusal to join the League of Nations to the day when Hitler's troops marched into the Sudetenland. To stand on history's sidelines at such times was nothing less than "great treason."[104]

As if to ratify Heberle's influence, another German exile appeared in Humphrey's academic circle. The erudite child of a prosperous Jewish family in Berlin, Theodore Mitau had fled the Nazi regime in 1938, leaving his entire family behind, ultimately to be sent to concentration camps. By 1943, Mitau was pursuing his doctorate at the University of Minnesota and instructing alongside Humphrey in Macalester's political science department. Mitau found himself touched, and also startled, by Humphrey's compassion.

"I had just been a young refugee from the Old World and here was this man speaking right out of my heart almost . . . showing this deep concern for the victims of fascism," Mitau later recalled. "That made an enormous impression on me . . . I mean, how should this young fellow from South Dakota know anything about the pain and suffering of persecution and refugeedom?"[105]

Humphrey's deep concern reflected the year that he had spent in Baton Rouge as Heberle's student and Alvin Rubin's friend. It also derived from his increasing contact with the Jewish community in Minneapolis. During the fall of 1943 alone, Humphrey addressed the Women's League of Adath Jeshurun, the United Jewish Brotherhood, and the local chapter of Hadassah, whose president called Humphrey "fearless in your expression."[106] Some months later, at a time when much of America remained willfully or otherwise ignorant of the Nazis' mass murder of European Jews, Humphrey received one of the earliest full reports on it. The *Black Book of Polish Jewry* was the product of a year of secret research and documentation, including firsthand accounts by escapees and refugees, that had to be smuggled through German lines before being compiled into its final form. The book estimated that one million Polish Jews had been systematically killed since the blitzkrieg invasion in 1939, a figure that ultimately proved to have been too low.[107] "You can be assured," Humphrey wrote back to the St. Paul branch of the American Federation of Polish Jews, which had given him the *Black Book*, "that I will find ample opportunity to use the contents in my public speeches and writings."[108]

Humphrey's sensitivity arose, too, from his experience as a committed Christian. Since his childhood years under the influence of Reverend Albert Hartt, he had essentially been a foot soldier in the civil war within American Protestantism between the devotees of the Social Gospel and of fundamentalism. Reverend William Bell Riley set the dominant tone for Christianity in Minneapolis from his pulpit at First

Baptist Church. By the time Humphrey returned to the city from LSU, however, the Social Gospel's alternative was gathering force in other congregations. One of them was First Congregational, the church that Humphrey and his family joined in the early 1940s.

Though Humphrey had been born and raised a Methodist, his family lived walking distance from First Congregational, and its membership over the years had included three presidents of the University of Minnesota and countless professors, imbuing it with the kind of intellectual pedigree that would have appealed to him. The church's pastor, Reverend Philip Gregory, viewed himself as a "protagonist of liberalism in theology and politics," even when that meant clashing with the conservative faction of his congregation.[109] Humphrey brought to First Congregational his speaking talents, whether delivering his "Total War" speech to the Pilgrim Federation of college students or teaching a course of "The Post-War World" in the Adult Forum. In turn, what Humphrey received during worship every Sunday morning at eleven went beyond the Social Gospel's concern with economic and social equality to advocacy for interracial and interreligious unity. As the Sunday bulletin of First Congregational put it in an essay entitled "A Creed for an American," "I believe . . . in an America fashioned from the fibre [sic] of many races and people, where none shall know discrimination and all shall have respect."[110]

To back up those words, First Congregational incorporated into its services both Black spirituals and the lyric poetry of James Weldon Johnson, the NAACP activist who also composed the so-called Negro National Anthem, "Lift Ev'ry Voice and Sing." The church's Sunday bulletin approvingly quoted the Black author Richard Wright from his book *12 Million Black Voices*: "We want what other people have, the right to share in the upward march of American life, the only life we remember or have ever known."[111]

Just as significantly, First Congregational grew deeply involved with the Minneapolis chapter of the National Conference of Christians and Jews (NCCJ). The organization had been founded in 1927 in response to the anti-Catholic bigotry heaped on Al Smith during his failed 1924 race for the Democratic presidential nomination—including, as

Humphrey recalled, the first of several cross-burnings outside his hometown of Doland. The NCCJ went on to promote what would become
Brotherhood Week and to devise a format called the "Tolerance Trio,"
in which a rabbi, a priest, and a minister would appear together for
the interfaith cause. Reverend Gregory participated in many Twin Cities
versions of the event, including a radio broadcast during Brotherhood
Week in 1942 when the trio warned of "the present crisis in human
relations."

Such fears were well-founded. Within Minneapolis, Reverend
Riley denounced the NCCJ for "sell[ing] Christ afresh for less than
thirty pieces of silver."[112] Not content to trot out that venerable anti-
Semitic slur, he likened Christian "modernists" to the Nazis for their
shared belief in evolution.[113] At the national level, the American military was sufficiently concerned about discord in its religiously diverse
ranks that it invented the "Judeo-Christian tradition" as the basis for
common purpose. It even provided a martyrology for the fighting faith,
sanctifying the deaths of four military chaplains—two Protestants, one
Catholic, and one Jewish—in the German sinking of the transport ship
Dorchester in early 1943.[114]

For his part, in First Congregational's pulpit, Reverend Gregory
went so far as to liken the experience of refugees—even if he did not
specify that most were Jewish—to the homelessness of Jesus, Mary, and
Joseph in the Nativity narrative. Addressing the congregation on the
first Sunday of 1943, he strove to present the Other as the Familiar:

No words can describe and no mind can imagine the suffering and agony of
the refugees. If those of us who are here this Sabbath morning, in the peace
and quiet of the sanctuary of God, would enter into the pain and distress
of the refugees, we might imagine ourselves out on a highway . . . escaping
from a merciless enemy who had invaded Minneapolis and St. Paul.
We carry in our arms a few treasured possessions we have been able to
quickly gather together from our homes; but much that is precious has
been left behind, and in some instances, the bodies of our loved ones lie
amid the debris of our ruined homes. Such has been the experience of
the refugees. Millions of people have lost their homes, their farms, their

property and means on subsistence. They have been cold, hungry, forlorn, frightened and desperate. They have been in peril of starvation and pestilence, and some of them, of arrest and execution.[115]

As a reliable churchgoer, Humphrey almost certainly would have heard that sermon and others like it. Reverend Gregory meant them as a form of Christian witness, a cumulative answer to his own question, "What can church do for our nation in saving it from hate?"[116] Humphrey adapted the theology to his political ideals, espousing public policy through the use of moral rhetoric. Such hybrid language came in very handy as he prepared to confront his dark doppelganger.

* * *

Like Hubert Humphrey, Gerald L. K. Smith grew up in the early decades of the twentieth century as the prodigy of an isolated and parochial place, which in his case was the countryside of southwestern Wisconsin. Like Humphrey, Smith excelled as a youthful orator, winning public-speaking contests and memorizing William Jennings Bryan's "Cross of Gold" speech. Like Humphrey, Smith was the adoring son of a financially struggling father, who put his political faith in Populists to protect the little guy from the ravages of unrestrained big-city capitalism. And like Humphrey, Smith left the Upper Midwest in his twenties for that living experiment in Populism, Huey Long's Louisiana.

For Smith, an ordained minister by that time in the early 1930s, the attraction was not graduate school but a call to pastor Kings Highway Church in Shreveport. Amid the Depression, Smith set to shaking his prosperous congregation out of its smug comfort. He publicly demanded that Shreveport's wealthy donate accordingly to the Community Chest. He befriended the state president of the AFL, ultimately becoming the union's chaplain. He fed and housed teachers who were going unpaid. He traded pulpits with a local rabbi, each preaching to the other's flock, and the rabbi was so moved by the experience that he wrote, "We are co-religionists, worshippers at the same shrine."[117]

Then Smith's path veered away from Humphrey's, beginning the journey that would turn them from analogs to adversaries. The pivotal event, at least in Smith's own telling, occurred when one of his congregants was threatened with foreclosure for having fallen several hundred dollars behind on his home mortgage. Huey Long came to the rescue, vowing to destroy the lender's business if he did not relent. But even with disaster averted for the church member, it was not lost on Smith that the lender was a Jew. That fact comported with the grievances that Smith had long heard from his father that Jewish bankers were the cause of his financial woes, that they indeed were at the heart of the entire rapacious financial system.[118]

When Smith left Kings Highway Church in 1934 to become the national organizer for Long's Share Our Wealth Society, he could preach his new gospel to far larger flocks. Standing six feet tall, packing a solid two hundred pounds, casting his blue eyes across rapt crowds, he was both a more commanding physical presence and a more eloquent speechmaker than the Kingfish. By the end of that year, Smith had addressed a million listeners "wherever he could round them up," as a historian later put it, "in pastures, in fields, in courthouse squares, and on city street corners." Along the way, he had also found enough time to correspond with Dr. Hugo R. Fack, a physician of fascist sympathies who wrote treatises about "money power." "I am anxious to get in touch with his Honor, Adolf Hitler," Smith wrote in a letter that caught the notice of the FBI. "I am convinced that the Jews are trying to rob American people just as they attempted to do in Germany."[119]

After Long was assassinated in September 1935, Smith was freer than ever to seek the national limelight. First in New York and then in Detroit, he refined his pitch as a foe of communism and the New Deal, which he considered all but synonymous anyway. He dropped his former support for organized labor in favor of testaments to free enterprise and private property. Then he conflated right-wing politics with American nationalism and Christian fundamentalism, playing to what he variously called "old-fashioned," "God-fearing," "ice-cream eating," "baby-having" Americans. As he explained in one notably candid moment, "Religion and patriotism, keep going on that. It's the only way you can get them really het up."[120]

Smith's nascent organization—initially called the Committee of the Ten Thousand and then aggrandized to the Committee of One Million—flourished on donations from executives in the chemical, asbestos, oil, trucking, and broadcasting industries. Smith was even welcomed to lunch by Arthur Hays Sulzberger, the Jewish publisher of the *New York Times*. He was invited by senators who shared his isolationism to testify before the Foreign Relations Committee. Henry Ford supplied Smith with money, bodyguards, and intelligence files on supposed Reds, as well as recommended reading in the form of *The Protocols of the Elders of Zion*. Thanks partly to Ford's largesse, Smith was able to syndicate his weekly radio show over the same forty-eight-station network that had previously been Father Charles Coughlin's electronic megaphone.[121]

The Pearl Harbor attack may have chastened certain isolationists, but even as Smith's own son went on to serve in the American military, Gerald L. K. clung to his formula. As a first-time candidate in his new home of Michigan, he drew more than thirty percent of the vote in the Republican primary for the U.S. Senate in 1942. That same year, he started publishing a magazine, *The Cross and the Flag*, which soon attracted twenty-five thousand subscribers. At a convention of five hundred supporters in January 1943, Smith launched the America First Party, which he envisioned as the vehicle for Charles Lindbergh to run for president.

Smith calibrated the party's message to stay just within legal lines. Three of his kindred spirits in white Christian nationalism—William Dudley Pelly of the Silver Shirts, the Kansas minister Gerald Winrod, and the writer Elizabeth Dillig—had already been convicted of sedition or were standing trial for it. Smith managed to embed his pro-Nazi sentiments in code words rather than uttering them outright. His party platform hung onto just enough of Huey Long's economic populism, reserved for the preferred racial stock of white Gentiles, while promising to bar immigrants, resettle Blacks in Africa, and investigate the devious, disloyal Jews.[122]

In these efforts, Smith also became a very regular visitor to the hospi-
table climes of Minneapolis. He had allies there with the Protestant ministers C. O. Stadsklev and W. D. Herrstrom, who shared Smith's belief
that Anglo-Saxons were the true descendants of the ancient Hebrews.
In a broader sense, William Bell Riley had prepared the anti-Semitic soil
for Smith, and Riley's diminishing public role as he entered his eighties
made him less of a competitor for bigotry's limelight. With the demise
of the Silver Shirts as a local force, its large Minneapolis contingent
was ripe for being recruited by Smith, who himself had once been a
member of Pelley's group. The nativist element within the Farmer-Labor
Party also cottoned to Smith's message of shadowy forces rigging the
economy and luring America into Europe's war; Norma Lundeen, the
widow of longtime U.S. Senator Ernest Lundeen, was Smith's most
prominent establishment patron in Minnesota.[123] Four times in January
and February 1943, Smith spoke in either Minneapolis or Saint Paul,
attracting crowds well into the hundreds.

On most of those occasions, the audience included Sam Scheiner's
informants. He had been tracking Smith for at least a year, partly by
signing up to attend speeches under the Germanized pseudonym
S. L. Schleiner, and sharing the information he gathered with local
journalists, law enforcement agents, and even the syndicated columnist
Walter Winchell. The reports that Scheiner received from his spies made
it clear that Smith enjoyed a broad, enthusiastic following. An unsigned,
handwritten account of a Smith rally at the Ark Lodge, the former redoubt of the Silver Shirts, noted the crowd "filled every seat, jammed the
aisles, and overflowed onto the stage."[124] The young Jewish man whom
Scheiner sent to observe Smith at a St. Paul event came away "just about
scared . . . out of my britches." As for the reason why, he reported: "The
crowd was certainly 100% with Mr. Smith, and continually broke into
applause. This solidarity—plus suspicion of a stranger—made it rather
difficult to take notes in a nonchalant manner. . . . There was nothing
specifically anti-Semitic in his talk. . . . But he did constantly use the term
Christian-American."[125]

When Smith returned to Minneapolis on February 24, 1944, several
weeks after Sam Scheiner had departed for military duty, he attracted

a thousand listeners, who jammed the Leamington Hotel's ballroom and lobby. As usual, Smith adroitly avoided directly attacking Jews. He merely had to refer to the Supreme Court justice Felix Frankfurter or the labor leader Sidney Hillman for everyone to get the point. He only needed to decry the wartime alliance with the Soviet Union for everyone to be reminded that all the communists were Jews and the only Jews who weren't communists were international bankers. To this stock liturgy, Smith added a scheduling note. He intended to return to Minneapolis on April 20, and he intended to speak for the first time in a public facility, the Municipal Auditorium. That decision put Humphrey and Smith, so similar and so divergent all at once, on a collision course.

Under the weak-mayor system of government in Minneapolis, Marvin Kline could remain safely irrelevant to the controversy. The decision on whether to rent the auditorium to Smith rested with the city council, and the first step in the process would be a public hearing by its five-member building-and-grounds committee. It set that hearing for March 23, and Smith moved back the date of his prospective rally until May 24.

Meanwhile, each side mobilized and staked out its ideological grounds. For Smith, the one and only issue was free speech. In a rally on the night before the hearing, Smith cannily wrapped himself in the First Amendment, declaring, "When the time comes that the enemy is so desperate that the only way they can stop us is to deny us the use of free speech and radio—then their strength is weakening."[126] One of Smith's local supporters made the same point in a letter to the building-and-grounds committee: "For any group to try and have a tax supported building closed to any person or persons who wish to speak—such a group is denying 'freedom of speech' to others, while usurping all the freedom for themselves."[127] Even the Minneapolis police inspector in charge of surveilling subversives, Ed Ryan, opined that people should be able to "listen to Smith rant" and then "make up their own minds."[128]

From college students, labor leaders, GIs, and Black and Jewish residents flowed a torrent of letters, postcards, and petitions framing Smith in a wartime context. "Our boys are fighting overseas to destroy race hatred," wrote one Jewish woman. "Please do not destroy what our boys are fighting for."[129] A committee of employees in local defense plants echoed that point: "Hitler's secret weapon is expressed in the doctrine of racial superiority, in anti-Semitism, anti-Negroism, and anti-Catholicism. One of Hitler's agencies is Gerald Smith and his so-called America First Party."[130]

By the time the clock tower of city hall tolled 2:00 p.m. on March 23, every seat in the council chambers was filled, and the walls were lined with news photographers and undercover cops. The opposition speakers testified first, most of them reiterating the arguments they had already made in writing. For his part, Humphrey ridiculed Smith for being "as mixed up as an octopus's tentacles." He tried to disarm the free speech issue by affirming Smith's right to speak in any private setting, and by invoking the quote (erroneously) attributed to Voltaire, "I disapprove of what you say, but I will defend to the death your right to say it." On the subject of rights, Humphrey added, "It is the tactics of fascists who cry out for civil rights that the first thing they do after they get control is to take away civil rights." By the rhetorical standards of the hearing, which one newspaper later described as a "free-for-all," such criticism of Smith fell on the tepid side.[131]

Smith handled the rebuttal with a well-honed display of feigned innocence. How could he be called anti-Negro when he and Huey Long had supported education for children of all races? How could people say he was pro-Hitler when his own son was serving in the army? Were people going to start calling him anti-Episcopalian because he was anti-Roosevelt? As for those allegations that he is anti-Semitic, Smith went on, "I'll tell you what this accusation business is. It's the old Communist Party line." Just to be fair and reasonable, Smith proposed turning over the decision on auditorium rental to "three leading rabbis or three Negro divines." Then he singled out Humphrey. Smith would gladly debate Humphrey one on one, right there in the Municipal Auditorium. Why, he'd even split the rent.[132]

There was a reason that Humphrey, of all the speakers, seemed to have especially irritated Smith. It likely had relatively little to do with the Humphrey comments that were quoted in newspaper coverage of the hearing. Rather, alone among the critics of Smith, Humphrey had taken aim at the minister's version of Christianity. Humphrey had said words to the effect that Jesus was Jewish, and because Jesus was Jewish, then no genuine Christian could be an anti-Semite. Smith, in other words, blasphemed.

From a lifetime in Social Gospel churches, Humphrey would have been familiar with this line of thinking. One of the most important theologians of the movement, Walter Rauschenbusch, had written of Jesus as the continuation of the Hebrew prophets with their insistence on a just society rather than empty ritual or individual purity. "The greatest of all prophets was still one of the prophets," Rauschenbusch asserted in his 1907 manifesto *Christianity and the Social Crisis*, and "the religion of the prophets was part of his life, too."[133] Churches like First Congregational also took inspiration from the Confessing Church in Nazi Germany, the devout Protestants who courageously opposed fascism's persecution of Jews. The dissident Lutheran pastor Dietrich Bonhoeffer, who was imprisoned for his political heresy, had described Jews as "brothers of Christians" and "children of the covenant." That both Rauschenbusch and Bonhoeffer nonetheless believed that Jews should ultimately accept Jesus did not obviate the impact of their words on American Christians committed to interfaith activism.

Though Humphrey's exact words have been lost—there is no existing transcript of the council committee's hearing—one particularly detailed piece of hate mail plainly alluded to his theological attack. That letter, sixteen pages in length, came not from a crackpot but from a retired schoolteacher named Ida Schoening, who resided in an upscale neighborhood near the Lake of the Isles:

> Mr. Humphrey—what makes you a Christian? When did you become a Christian? What did you do to become a Christian? . . . Jesus Christ <u>has no place for a counterfeit Christian in his ranks</u> . . .
>
> You belong to that <u>Modernist outfit</u> who <u>do not believe in the Bible</u>. . . . The Modernist preachers have reduced Jesus the Christ to a mere man, putting him in the same place the Jews have placed him . . .

Mr. Humphrey—everyone who knows the Bible knows that Jesus was not a Jew. Jesus is God's only begotten son. Certainly, no one would have the stupidity to say that God is a Jew ...

Mr. Humphrey—if Jesus is a Jew as you claim, then pray why don't the Jews bestow a bit of their brotherly love on Him? .... Answer me that ...

What's more, it is just about time that this anti-Semitic bugaboo were [sic] dragged out in the open & exposed for what it is—a big lie—cooked up by the Jews themselves to make it seem that other Americans are picking on them & and then by doing a lot of whining and shouting of "anti-Semitism" draw sympathy to themselves & through it gain political advantage.[134]

Eight days after the public hearing on Smith's request for a speaking permit, the full city council convened and refused it in a voice vote. Humphrey got around to replying to Schoening's letter, averring with icy decorum that "name-calling is a terrible thing, and I do not wish to participate in this sort of cheap talk."[135] His fuller response to Schoening and her ilk, the Christian nationalists who were so numerous in Minneapolis and in Smith's nationwide following, took the form of a lecture to a Reform Jewish congregation at its Friday night worship service several weeks later.

What Christianity calls a sermon or a homily is known in Judaism as a *d'var Torah*, a word of Torah, the Torah being the first five books of the Hebrew Bible. Strictly speaking, Humphrey did not draw upon the weekly passage from the Torah, as a rabbi would have, but in teasing out modern meaning from ancient words, he could not have been more Judaic. Humphrey expounded on the prophets Amos, Hosea, Isaiah, and Jeremiah, knowledgably citing verses in pursuit of his overarching theme:

We have relied on ritual, on pious pronouncements, rather than action. Faith is only as strong as its believers. We have failed to believe. We just accepted! ... The ancient prophets all cried out against injustice— proclaiming the doctrine of social justice. (Underlining and punctuation in Humphrey's original manuscript.)

Then he propounded his own Ten Commandments, applying the biblical injunctions to the crises of contemporary America, ranging from the exploitation of labor to gender inequality to racial and religious discrimination. "I am the Lord thy God," went one of Humphrey's commandments, "but thou shalt remember I am also the God of the earth. I have no favorite children. The Negro, the Hindu, the Chinese, Russian, and Mexican are all my beloved children." He redefined the commandment against bearing false witness to proscribing the "malicious propaganda" of bigotry against "the Negro in America, the Jew, the Japanese-American."[136]

* * *

The secular side of Humphrey's life accelerated immediately in the wake of his showdown with Smith. Suddenly he was a player not only in statewide politics but on the national scene, as well. In mid-April of 1944, Humphrey helped negotiate a merger of the Democratic and Farmer-Labor parties in Minnesota, with the fusion becoming instantly known by the initials DFL. The achievement reflected both the practical imperative of defeating Republicans and the wartime alliance of the United States and the Soviet Union. If Uncle Sam could fight alongside Uncle Joe, as Stalin was now being styled, then it was acceptable for urban machine hacks, Iron Range Reds, clannish craft unionists, CIO fellow travelers, and campus intellectuals to set aside their conflicts.

At the party convention that consecrated the new unity, Humphrey delivered the keynote address and was answered back with spontaneous chants of "We Want Humphrey!," urging him to run for governor. He spurned them in part because he considered the moderate Republican incumbent, Edward Thye, too strong to topple in the coming November's election, less than seven months after the DFL conclave. Even so, Humphrey whined to his former professor Charles Hyneman, "Never in my life did I feel so emotionally upset . . . I don't suppose I'll ever have such a [sic] unanimous support again."[137]

With his heightened profile, Humphrey attended the Democratic National Convention in Chicago as a delegate that summer and even

delivered a seconding speech for the failed renomination of Henry
Wallace as vice president. The national party nonetheless hired
Humphrey to run the statewide campaign for FDR and his new, more
conservative running mate, Senator Harry Truman of Missouri. After
1940's close call against Wendell Willkie, Humphrey's efforts helped
FDR more than double the margin of victory in Minnesota against his
GOP opponent, Governor Thomas Dewey of New York.

This sequence of events, the sheer velocity of upward mobility, must
have dazed Humphrey. By the fall of 1944, he was only a few years
removed from being the scuffling grad student begging for speaking
gigs and apologizing for his paltry achievements. And the abrupt prominence did nothing to solve the central dilemma that he now faced: how
to get into the military. He fully recognized that, as he had written to
Hyneman in April 1944, "if a fellow is going to have any political future,
he had better be in the Armed Services."[138] Marvin Kline had trotted
out the image of Humphrey as a draft dodger during the 1943 mayoral race. Even Humphrey's brother Ralph, visiting Minneapolis during
that campaign while on leave from the army, chided Hubert about it.
Humphrey literally pulled down his trousers to show Ralph the truss he
was wearing then for a double hernia, the injury that had resulted in a
draft deferment.[139]

Beyond political calculus, Humphrey had both proximate and personal reasons for wanting to serve. "Don't you know there's a war
on?" went the accusatory question for any suspected malingerer. In
Minneapolis, the fervent response took the forms of Boy Scout troops
collecting scrap metal, grammar school kids filling up a "Paper for
Victory" wagon, the Victory Garden stakes in vacant lots, and the
scarecrow mascot for the USO's Barn Dance. Amid those reminders,
Humphrey was acutely aware of how greatly his friends and family
members already had sacrificed. Orville Freeman had been wounded so
severely in the jaw and arm during the invasion of New Guinea in late
1943 that he was ultimately reassigned to a desk job at Marine headquarters in Washington. Frances Humphrey's husband Ray Howard
had been the ship's doctor on the Coast Guard cutter *Comanche* as it
accompanied American convoys across the North Atlantic. When the

Dorchester was torpedoed and sunk in February 1943, causing the death of nearly seven hundred service members, including the four chaplains, the *Comanche* dispatched Howard to tend the barely two hundred survivors. Though he ultimately reached the coast of Greenland with them, he had been missing and presumed dead for six months before being rescued. Then, in the week before Christmas of 1944, Humphrey learned that one of Muriel's cousins had perished as a Marine aviator patrolling the Philippines.

Beginning in autumn 1943 and continuing twenty times through 1944, Humphrey applied for an officer's commission in the Naval Reserve and, failing that, tried to enlist as either as a pharmacist's mate or an apprentice seaman. In each effort, he was rejected for color blindness, the unrepaired hernia, and calcification of his lungs—the latter doubtlessly being the remnant of his nearly fatal childhood bout of influenza. When Humphrey was finally classified as 1-A in July 1944, the draft board deferred him because of his age and family size.[140] Humphrey even traveled to Washington to plead his case with Navy and Marines officials whom Orville Freeman knew. That gambit, too, proved futile. "I can remember putting him on a train one night when he was just literally crying," Freeman later recalled. "He was so frustrated and unhappy and was trying in every way he could to get in the service, and he just couldn't get in."[141]

As a reluctant civilian, Humphrey drew his last paycheck from the FDR campaign in December 1944 and opened a public-relations office with Arthur Naftalin to cobble together some income and ponder the next move. Events, as it turned out, had some ideas of their own for him. It was apparent by this time that the Allies were going to win the war. The U.S. Navy had invaded the Philippines as it island-hopped toward Japan, the Red Amy had liberated the Majdanek death camp on its westward march to Berlin, and the British-American push across France since D-Day had liberated Paris. With victory nearing—albeit, at the ultimate toll of more than four hundred thousand American lives—the question loomed over the home front of what kind of country postwar America was going to be. Having defeated fascism abroad, what if anything was to be done about racial and religious bigotry at home? Was all that blood spilled just so life could return to the Jim Crow, Jew-hating, anti-Catholic normal? To put the question in Minneapolitan terms, what was the proper response, verbally or legally or even physically, to a William Bell Riley or a Gerald L. K. Smith? To the crowds who had thronged the Silver Shirts rally at the Ark Lodge and the mob that had besieged Arthur Lee's home? To the vigilantes who had threatened Sam Scheiner for trying to move into a Christian neighborhood and who had beaten Cecil Newman's son, mistaking him for their intended target, the Black publisher? All of those people were still around, and so were their toxic beliefs.

Again and again during the war years, Humphrey heard the call, not the call of God to faith but the call of humanity to service. There were people from throughout his life who recognized something in him—skills, yes, but something larger, a kind of destiny—more than he recognized it in himself. He was their vessel and their voice, the vessel in which to pour their passion for a more just America and the voice to amplify that passion insistently enough to affect a nation whose soul was very much at stake.

* * *

Hans Israel Neumaier had grown up in the German city of Frankfurt surrounded by culture and entertainment, with a mother who sang opera and a father who had a film-advertising agency. That cocoon of refinement was shattered once the Nazis took power. Hans dropped out of school in 1934, at the age of thirteen, to be spared the beatings being inflicted on Jewish students. His father Otto's Gentile partner seized sole control of their business. His mother, Leonore, was banned from performing. After the family's synagogue was burned to the ground during *Kristallnacht* in 1938, the Neumaiers scrambled to escape. An adult son from Otto's decades-earlier first marriage, now working as a doctor in Minneapolis, sponsored the elder Neumaier in 1939. Hans managed to contact family friends in England, who brought him over in that same year on the pretext of being a farm laborer. Leonore, marooned, would ultimately be dispatched by the Nazis to Majdanek.[142]

By March 1940, Otto was able to pay for Hans Israel's passage to New York, and at age eighteen he entered the United States, using the Americanized name of John. Once in Minneapolis, he began working in a nuts-and-bolts factory and studying philosophy at the University of Minnesota, using the English he had begun learning in childhood. His American girlfriend, Virginia Bratman, introduced Neumaier to her father, Sam, a Romanian Jewish immigrant who managed catering for the Nicollet Hotel. And it was through Sam Bratman that Neumaier met Humphrey, one of the Nicollet's regular customers, and ultimately volunteered in the 1943 mayoral campaign.[143]

Several months later, in October 1943, Neumaier enlisted in the Army, and in early 1944, it assigned him to Camp Robinson in Nebraska to interpret for German prisoners of war. Humphrey wrote a letter to Neumaier that March filled with enthusiasm about the prospect of entering the military. When those plans were dashed, Neumaier responded not with sympathy, or even with congratulations, but with the summons to a different kind of duty in the war at home:

> I believe that you could do a lot more good outside the army than inside. For, as you can imagine most of your personal initiative would be taken away, even though you might be assigned to an executive position. And if you should be assigned into some line outfit, I dare say, with all due respect to your possible shooting abilities, that a man of your abilities and liberal attitude can fight fascism on the home front better than on the battle field . . .
>
> In the barracks opinions run as follows: "It's all the fault of those goddamn Jews" or "you have to show those sons of bitches n——s where their place is" [or] "We're just in this war to save the British empire." . . . Many of them are usually militantly intolerant.[144]

Humphrey received a similarly dire report from one of his former students at Macalester, a young Jewish woman named Jean Ann Rosenbloom. She had taken part in protests against one of Smith's Minneapolis speeches and subsequently moved to a Black section of Indianapolis to live in a settlement house, in effect an interracial and interfaith commune. Her letter to Humphrey partly exulted in being among "twenty-nine other energetic individualistic people of all colors and beliefs" and partly recounted the "education" of "learning how to effectively use roach powder and spray for bedbugs." But Rosenbloom turned grim and unflinching when she described the corrosive power of racism, even on white people of good will:

> One thing—It is the wickedest blot (or one at any rate) on the white people in this old country that when you see a Negro on the street—you smile—it [sic] smiles, but beneath that smile is hatred and bitterness. Sincerity in itself won't do. They distrust white people. They hate white people. And, by gum, lots of them feel that if they can go over to Europe and do killing and fighting for democracy, they can do a little fighting here at home for the same thing.[145]

Rosenbloom was writing in the aftermath of two outbreaks of racial violence that had similarly given lie to the American promise of democracy for all. In mid-June 1943, the shipbuilding city of Beaumont, Texas, convulsed with rioting provoked by that staple of race hate, the allegation that a Black man had raped a white woman. A prospective lynch mob of about four thousand whites surged toward city hall in search of the supposed perpetrator before turning its destructive attentions instead on hundreds of Black businesses, homes, and passersby. Less than a week later in Detroit, another industrial center of the "arsenal of democracy," wartime tensions over racial discrimination in housing and employment, fanned by yet another rape rumor, exploded into two days of street battles between whites and Blacks. By the time that six thousand armed troops halted the violence, forty-two people, all of them Black, were dead, seventeen at the hands of police.

Cecil Newman, not surprisingly, paid close notice to the riots and to the national sickness they revealed. As a regular reader now of the *Minneapolis Spokesman*, and a periodic visitor to its office to chat with Newman, Humphrey may well have encountered such caustic sentiments. Even if they weren't directly addressed to him, like Rosenbloom's letter, they might as well have been. Newman, for instance, printed a guest editorial written by Sergeant Arthur Williams of St. Paul, one of the Black airmen trained at Tuskegee and finally mustered into combat as the segregated 99th Pursuit Squadron. "The States are going to be forced to recognize us in spite of our color," he asserted, "because we who have fought and sacrificed are not going to accept the low place reserved for us before the war. The riots in the cities prove to us that the supposed superiors are not ready to give it to us so we may be forced to fight for it just as we are fighting for democracy now."[146]

Several months later, Newman published a columnist, Dan Gardner, who all but recommended an armed uprising, if that's what it would take to achieve Double V. "Sooner or later," he wrote, "this country has got to take time out to dispose of the problem of 'Crackerism' or suffer a revolution, bloodless or economic, approaching the scale of the great Russian revolt. . . . The revolution will come when over a million Negro fighting men, augmented by thousands of whites who know the score, return to this country and demand something far better than what they left when they went into the service."[147]

Even as one of those whites already inclined to "know the score," Humphrey could not conceivably have endorsed, much less joined, Gardner's revolution. Yet he also understood that complacency and self-satisfaction about the "American way" only augured more intolerance at home once the last ticker tape had fluttered down on the returning troops. He had been saying as much in the boldest of his wartime speeches. And the most powerful reinforcement for his moral instincts and future direction, all the more powerful because of how it echoed the words of Neumaier and Rosenbloom and the *Spokesman*, may have come from Humphrey's cherished friend and ally Orville Freeman. In the weeks before the invasion of New Guinea that nearly cost his life, Freeman wrote from a forward base "somewhere in S.W. Pacific":

Dear Hubert:
I am sitting here long after Taps trying to read by inadequate candlelight. I am thinking about war & peace, about what the future offers. I know that you are making many speeches. I wish you would include this letter in them.

People at home are trying to help the war effort & the boys over-seas. The biggest way they could help is in preparing themselves intelligently for the peace to come. Many of the long lonesome nights we spend . . . clustered around fox holes waiting to dive in when the bombs start to fall are devoted to discussing post war world problems. And we would like to feel that those at home are trying to prepare themselves by intensive study. And I mean study and not the palliative of "too busy" . . .

This is by no means intended to be an emotional plea, far from it. But only thru the Dem process can we hope for peace, and to participate intelligently people must study & think. That is what we ask of you. We need supplies, also we need spiritual sustenance that you can give us by our knowing you appreciate what goes on & are working to lay the foundations for the peace we fight for today.

[A]ll of us here, differently tho [sic] we may express it, pray that this will truly be the war to end wars. With your help we can & are winning it. But we ask more—we want to win the peace, we need your help, & want to know you are seriously preparing yourself.[148]

Hubert Humphrey's hometown, the hamlet of Doland, SD, (Top Left), was created in the late 1800s around a rail station to ship grain and livestock to the Twin Cities. When the first gravel road reached Doland in 1922, young Hubert befriended the Black crew led by Otis Shipman (Middle) that built it. Amid the wheat boom of the 1910s, Doland thrived, and the Humphreys bought one of the fanciest homes in town (Bottom). Hubert, his younger sister Frances, and his older brother Ralph stand on the front lawn.

Courtesy of Mick Caouette/South Hill Films.

Courtesy of Lesley Unthank.

From *Hubert Humphrey: An Inventory of His Photographs*, Minnesota State Historical Society, St. Paul.

Hubert's parents, H. H. and Christine (Left), shared intellectual ambitions even as they differed on politics and religion, with her more conservative in both areas. As a high school student in Doland, Hubert met Julian Hartt (Right), a Methodist minister's son who would become his best friend. The center of Hubert's youthful life was the family's drugstore (Bottom), where H. H. often held forth on national politics.

Courtesy of Hubert Humphrey III.

Courtesy of Mick Caouette/ South Hill Films.

Courtesy of Hubert Humphrey III.

Hubert enrolled at the University of Minnesota (Below) in the fall of 1929, just weeks before the stock market collapsed and plunged the nation into the Great Depression. After the Humphrey family lost both their home and store in Doland, H. H. started anew in the small city of Huron, (Middle) about forty miles away, and Hubert dropped out of college to become the store's pharmacist. It was his sister Frances (Bottom right) who managed to leave Huron for a college education at George Washington University.

Courtesy of Mick Caouette/South Hill Films.

Courtesy of Mick Caouette/South Hill Films.

Courtesy of William Howard.

While Hubert was hundreds of miles away in Huron, Minneapolis exploded into racial turmoil after the family of a Black postal worker, Arthur Lee, bought a home in a white neighborhood. Mobs besieged the home and threatened the family (Top left). In the aftermath, Lee's wife Edith and daughter Mary Lee stood outside the vandalized bungalow (Middle). Among the journalists who covered the episode was a young Black reporter and editor, Cecil Newman (Bottom Right).

Used by permission of the *Star Tribune*.

Used by permission of
Hennepin County Library,
Minneapolis, MN.

Courtesy of Tracey
Williams-Dillard.

In the fall of 1937, Hubert finally returned to the University of Minnesota, now with his new wife Muriel (Top right). On the school's debate team, Humphrey teamed up with Orville Freeman (standing to Humphrey's left in Middle), who would become one of his closest political allies. Muriel helped keep the Humphrey household financially afloat by sewing all her own clothes and talking her way into office jobs that employers normally denied to married women (Bottom right).

From *Hubert Humphrey: An Inventory of His Photographs*, Minnesota State Historical Society, St. Paul.

Courtesy of Mick Caouette/South Hill Films.

Courtesy of Hubert Humphrey III.

Humphrey's idealism was informed by mentors and allies. As a graduate student at Louisiana State University, he studied with the exiled anti-Nazi Professor Rudolf Heberle (Top right). In Minneapolis afterward, Humphrey learned about the city's rampant anti-Semitism from the local Jewish activist Sam Scheiner (shown with his daughter Susan in Left). No person had a greater effect on Humphrey than the journalist Cecil Newman, here (rear row, second from right in Bottom right) attending a convention of Black newspaper editors and publishers.

Courtesy of Antje and Edward Kolodziej.

Courtesy of Susan Druskin.

Courtesy of Tracey Williams-Dillard.

Along with his allies, Humphrey had his foes. One of the most established ministers in Minneapolis, Reverend William Bell Riley of First Baptist Church (Top right), put a refined, erudite face on virulent anti-Semitic canards. Both before and during his mayoralty, Humphrey confronted Gerald L. K. Smith (Bottom), the national leader of the America First political party and Christian Nationalist movement.

Courtesy of the UNW Archives at the Berntsen Library, University of Northwestern, St. Paul, MN.

Photograph by Arline Roe, used by permission of the *Star Tribune*.

Having narrowly lost his first race for mayor in 1943, Humphrey mounted an energetic campaign (Top right) to win by a landslide in 1945. Muriel and a group of supporters from labor, business, and the religious community gathered to congratulate him (Bottom left). Humphrey threw himself into the mayoralty with nearly round-the-clock effort (Bottom right).

From *Hubert Humphrey: An Inventory of His Photographs,* Minnesota State Historical Society, St. Paul, MN.

Courtesy of Hubert Humphrey III.

From *Hubert Humphrey: An Inventory of His Photographs,* Minnesota State Historical Society, St. Paul, MN.

The mayor's fervent advocacy for civil rights and opposition to anti-Semitism brought him both national acclaim and local controversy. Left-wing protestors broke up a speech by Gerald L. K. Smith in 1946 (Top left). One of the Smith adherents who blamed Humphrey for the outbreak, Maynard Nelsen (Top right), is almost certainly the person who tried to assassinate Humphrey several months later. Though never charged in that shooting, Nelsen was arrested for anti-Semitic vandalism and found to have a trove of firearms and propaganda material (Bottom).

Used by permission of Hennepin County Library, Minneapolis, MN.

Used by permission of Hennepin County Library, Minneapolis, MN.

Used by permission of Hennepin County Library, Minneapolis, MN.

The issue of civil rights surged in importance as the 1948 presidential election approached. The Democratic incumbent, Harry Truman, took the unprecedented step of addressing the NAACP at the Lincoln Memorial in June 1947 (Top left). But when Truman then began backing away from his own legislative agenda, especially the call the desegregate the armed forces, the civil rights leader A. Philip Randolph (right in Photo in the top right) testified to Congress that he would organize massive draft resistance by young Black men in protest. Meanwhile, on the other side of the racial and political divide, Mississippi governor Fielding Wright (Bottom right) began planning a mutiny of Southern Democrats from the national party, who would become the "Dixiecrats."

New York World-Telegram and the *Sun Newspaper* Photograph Collection, Library of Congress, Washington, DC.

Photograph by Abbie Rowe, National Park Service. Harry S. Truman Library, Independence, MO.

New York World-Telegram and the *Sun Newspaper* Photograph Collection, Library of Congress, Washington, DC.

The battle over civil rights came to a head at the 1948 Democratic National Convention in Philadelphia. Just thirty-seven years old, and only three years into elected office, Humphrey delivered the impassioned plea for Democrats to march "into the bright sunshine of human rights" (Left). His father H. H. (Right), a delegate from South Dakota, was there to cast his state's votes for a civil rights plank to the party platform. After its adoption, the Mississippi delegation, along with half of Alabama's, walked out of the Convention Hall (Bottom).

From *Hubert Humphrey: An Inventory of His Photographs*, Minnesota State Historical Society, St. Paul, MN.

Courtesy of William Howard.

Used by permission of Harry S. Truman Library, Independence, MO.

On Humphrey's return to Minneapolis from the Democratic convention, thousands of supporters turned out to salute and congratulate him.

Photograph by Wally Kammann. Used by permission of the *Star Tribune*.

CHAPTER 7

"WE MUST SET THE EXAMPLE"

A New Mayor in Minneapolis

1945

On the icy and overcast Thursday of January 18, 1945, deep into the Minnesota winter, Hubert Humphrey signed an affidavit and handed it to his wife Muriel for safekeeping. The affidavit would certify Humphrey's candidacy for mayor that spring in an anticipated rematch against Marvin Kline. Tellingly, Humphrey did not intend to submit the paperwork until he locked down several integral elements of his campaign. From the neophyte who had been almost passively inserted into the 1943 election, he had grown in just twenty months into a politician of sufficient savvy and clout to dictate his terms for entering this next race.

Soon after passing the affidavit to Muriel, Humphrey left Minneapolis for a doubly strategic trip to the East Coast. In the coming ten days he would meet with several big-city mayors, including the renowned Fiorello LaGuardia of New York, to discuss plans for addressing the housing shortage and industrial decline expected during postwar readjustment. In Washington, Humphrey would attend the inauguration of Franklin Delano Roosevelt (FDR) for a fourth term, with the young visitor's status as a rising star confirmed by additional invitations to a White House tea honoring Eleanor Roosevelt and a cocktail party featuring the U.S. Army's chief of staff, General George Marshall. Outside of such lustrous settings, Humphrey was scheduled to consult privately with Robert Hannegan, who held joint titles as postmaster general of the nation and chairman of the Democratic National Committee. He had also been an advisor and confidante for Humphrey since helping to orchestrate the merger forming the Democratic-Farmer Labor (DFL) Party.[1]

As Humphrey traveled, he waited for one last poker chip to be added to his pile. He had decided not to declare for mayor unless all of organized labor in Minneapolis endorsed him, avoiding the divided union vote that had hindered him in 1943. The official announcement of that backing came through on January 24—from the Hennepin County CIO, the AFL-based Central Labor Union, the railroad brotherhoods, everyone but the contrarian Teamsters—and the next day Muriel presented herself, her children, and the affidavit at City Hall. In time for the afternoon edition, a photographer from the *Star Journal* was on hand to snap the calculatedly cute scene of two-year-old Skipper, as Hubert III was called, handing the city clerk a ten-dollar bill to cover the filing fee.[2]

As the first candidate in what would become a primary-election field of fourteen, Humphrey took full advantage of the early start. His campaign set up volunteer organizations in all thirteen wards and among various interest groups. Fifteen thousand dollars from unions paid for Humphrey's name and image to blanket the city, adorning the wraparound billboard on his headquarters downtown, a tent for "G-I Wives and G-I Joes," a horse-drawn stagecoach, and a forest of lawn signs. Arthur Naftalin crafted a series of radio speeches in which Humphrey laid out detailed plans to attract postwar industry, crack down on crime, and serve as a bridge between labor and management. The speeches, in turn, were promoted almost like an entertainment product, touted on sandwich boards with the lure "Have You Heard Humphrey?" and advertised alongside movies in the daily papers with the slogan "Everybody Is Talking About the Radio Addresses."[3] Hubert was getting even more local ink than the spring's other Humphrey, meaning Bogart, who was starring in *To Have and Have Not* and preparing to wed his bombshell costar Lauren Bacall.

More than pizzazz separated Humphrey from his competitors. Nearing his thirty-fourth birthday, he embodied a generational passage and with it an attitudinal one. His de facto running mates in the campaign included a Jew (Rubin Latz) and a Black (Nellie Stone), both seeking citywide office on the Library Board. Humphrey made plans with the local chapter of the National Association for the Advancement of Colored People (NAACP) to send campaign literature and a personal letter to every member.[4] With his endless energy, and the invisible toil of a wife who would stay up late washing diapers by hand while Humphrey made the nightly speaking rounds, the campaign trail led to the Young Voters League, Junior Hadassah, the DFL Women's Study Club, and just about any garage or basement that could hold a dozen listeners. "[O]rdinary people . . . used to sort of hold onto him and just loved what he was saying . . . having to do with civil liberties, civil rights, equality, sympathy for the oppressed, sympathy for the needy," one campaign aide later recalled. "It just spilled out from him."[5]

Whether Humphrey was extolling the United Nations as it met in San Francisco in late April or appropriating the popular song "Accentuate the Positive" as his campaign anthem, he was evoking a future of promise and possibility. The college students and returning vets who volunteered in the race proudly dubbed themselves "the Kiddie Corps." That overarching sense of transformation even reached the Philippines, where Corporal Sam Scheiner had been fighting with the 96th Infantry in the Battle of Leyte Gulf. "Go to it," Scheiner urged Humphrey by V-mail, "and lick the old Tories once and for all."[6]

If anyone doubted how fast the present was hurtling into the future, the proof came in the form of two sequential events during the primary campaign: the death of Franklin Roosevelt on April 12 and V-E Day on May 8. "We are part of one world," Humphrey said in a radio address delivered between those two defining occasions. "We are living in a time that has forced upon us great responsibilities. We cannot escape our destiny for greatness or for chaos. Every American, every citizen of this community, must grow to understand the community around him. We blundered into the war, but we must not blunder into peace."[7]

Marvin Kline, in contrast, entered the campaign both weary and wounded. His twelve years as a council member, council president, and mayor had covered almost the entirety of the Great Depression and the Second World War. At his most adroit, he had finessed the balancing act of governing a city that was prurient and puritanical in equal measure. Kline had maintained the support of Christian fundamentalists like William Bell Riley even while providing gangsters, Jewish and otherwise, sufficient latitude for their vice crimes. But in December 1944, a county grand jury had nearly indicted Kline and his police chief, Elmer Hillner, in a probe of illegal liquor sales.[8] Later that same month, a local scandal sheet called *The Public Press* unloaded its new issue with the banner headline "KLINE ADMINISTRATION MOST CORRUPT REGIME IN HISTORY OF THE CITY."

The entire staff of *The Public Press* consisted of Arthur Kasherman, the latest in a series of journalistic provocateurs in Minneapolis. Outside of the established daily papers, they sporadically published tabloids (in spirit, if not page size) that walked an indistinct line between muckraking and rumor-mongering, The first two such editors, Howard Guilford and Walter Liggett, had been assassinated, presumably by mobsters, in the mid-1930s. Kasherman presently met the same fate, ambushed and shot dead outside a downtown cafe on January 22, 1945. Not entirely surprisingly, Kline's police chief failed to solve, or even seriously investigate, the murder.[9] For public consumption, the mayor and chief did force a temporary shutdown of a number of gambling parlors and after-hours clubs.

As a political matter, however, Kasherman's killing was not so easily managed. It focused and intensified years of suspicion that Kline and much of his police force were on the take. The FBI already had concluded that Kline was "controlled by racketeers."[10] One of the city cops known to be honest, Inspector Ed Ryan, later said of the Kline administration: "[W]henever racketeering is going on, exists in the community, large or small, there has to be a payoff. It's that simple. I don't give a Goddamn who's the mayor, the chief of police. If God were sitting in there, and if racketeering is going on, then He's on the take. It has to be that way."[11]

So there may have been good reason for Kline to waver before formally joining the mayoral race. He waited until April 26, less than three weeks before the primary election, to even open campaign headquarters. By then, he faced a problem beyond the allegation of corruption and a public disgrace besides Kasherman's murder. The trail of that problem and that disgrace traced back to the exact day when Humphrey had signed the affidavit to run for mayor.

* * *

On the editorial page of the January 18, 1945, edition of the *Star Journal*, in a regular column devoted to correspondence from soldiers, there appeared a letter from a naval radio technician named Jay Golfus. The headline read, "Anti-Semitism in the United States." In fact, Golfus was writing specifically about anti-Semitism in Minneapolis, a detail that the newspaper editors seemed to have preferred to elide. Golfus recounted a recent evening when he had come into barracks after duty, wanting only to flop onto his bunk and read the daily letter from his wife. He proceeded to quote from it:

> Rather frightening things have been happening here of late. Gangs of boys have been attacking Jewish boys here in the vicinity. Last Wednesday or Thursday my young brother and two of his friends were skating. Towards the end of the evening one boy came up to him and asked if he was Jewish. He asserted that he was. Then this boy called another boy and finally a gang of 15 or 20 boys gathered and started calling him and his two companions names. They just ignored the insults as they didn't have a chance against a gang like that. When they got home, they reported to the police, but of course then it was too late.
>
> Last night my uncle's son who is the same age as [my brother] Butz (14) was walking with another boy about 1 a.m. and they were attacked by a gang. My cousin had two teeth knocked out. My brother and his cousin say that the boys in these gangs are about 18 and 19 years old and they usually pick on younger boys. There has been quite a bit of it. It frightens me. What do you think we should do about it?[12]

The letter marked the first public recognition of a wave of attacks against Jewish boys and girls on the North Side that had been going on for nearly a year. Jewish children had been kicked, punched, jumped, beaten, slashed, robbed, called "dirty Jews" and "hook noses," and subjected to chants of "Heil, Hitler!"[13] Not only had the daily newspapers ignored the episodes, so had the *American Jewish World*. Even when it finally took up the subject a week after Golfus's letter appeared, the Jewish newspaper sought to assuage readers that "these unfortunate occurrences are not the result of an organized group" and "the police are dealing effectively with the hoodlums."[14] It was the familiar defensive reflex of *sha, shtil*, don't make waves. And Sam Scheiner, fighting the Japanese a hemisphere away, was in no position to trouble the waters.

Organized or not, the attacks continued unabated, and the police proved manifestly ineffective. The Jews of Minneapolis, of course, were well experienced in anti-Semitism, mostly in the form of bans, quotas, restrictive covenants, and hateful rhetoric. The North Side neighborhood had endured Silver Shirts rallies in North Commons Park during the 1930s and spasms of fighting on the border between Jewish and Scandinavian districts. Yet this iteration of intimidation and this rash of beatings felt like something different, because the world around them was different.

Virtually every week through February and March 1945, the *American Jewish World* reported on the local Jewish boys who had died in combat: Morley Horowitz, whom everybody remembered from the 1939 championship team in the American Legion baseball league, dead in Belgium; Willy Billig, the refugee from Nazi Germany who'd prayed to be sent to Europe to avenge his parents' murders, dead in the Pacific; Morris Silverstein in France; Daniel Goldblatt on Iwo Jima; Sam Scheiner's hometown comrade in the infantry, Julius Margulas— the one who folks called "Tully," the one with a baby girl named Beverly Jo—perished in the Leyte Gulf.

Even as the fallen were buried at a distance and mourned with shiva at home, definitive and irrefutable word was reaching Minneapolis and the rest of America of the Nazi project of Jewish extermination. The advancing Red Army had brought Soviet photojournalists into the liberated Majdanek death camp in the summer of 1944 to chronicle the piled corpses and the skeletal survivors. When Western publications largely ignored even those images, Soviet leaders opened the ruins of Majdanek to American and British correspondents. William H. Lawrence of *The New York Times* wrote in the opening sentence of his dispatch, "I have just seen the most terrible place on the face of the earth . . . a veritable River Rouge[15] for the production of death."[16] The *Minneapolis Tribune* quoted his report in its own article in early September 1944. On the Sunday after Thanksgiving, the newspaper's front page carried an Associated Press article about the estimated death toll of 1.5 million at Auschwitz-Birkenau, which Soviet forces would liberate in late January 1945. "All U.S. Should Read and Understand This," read the headline, paraphrasing a statement from FDR's War Refugee Board.

Then, on the night of March 22, an unfamiliar car trawled through the North Side. First its four occupants pulled up to surround and batter a fifteen-year-old Jewish boy, leaving him with a broken nose. Then they rammed a car containing four Jewish teenagers. For a change, a police squad car gave chase and ultimately caught up to the attackers, arresting four who were subsequently described as "white, gentile, Protestant, with an Anglo-Saxon or Scandinavian name."[17] The victims swore out complaints to ensure that the case moved forward. The next morning, however, the police released the assailants without either charges or explanation. At that point, the Jews of Minneapolis exhausted their collective patience with the law-enforcement system in a way they had not since the Silver Shirts' 1938 rallies.

On the Sunday evening of March 26, two nights before the beginning of Passover with its evocation of ancient oppression, local Jews and their allies packed all 1,604 seats in the auditorium of Lincoln Junior High School, with hundreds more thronging the aisles and lobby. On the stage sat the immediate targets of their ire, Mayor Kline and police officials from central headquarters, the North Side precinct, and the juvenile division.

One of the eight rabbis present, S. L. Levin of Sharei Zedeck Congregation, bluntly asked, "What are the boys overseas fighting for, anyway?" His fellow rabbi David Aronson of Beth El Synagogue, whose own son had been beaten the previous year, followed up: "I want to make it clear that these incidents are neither the product of the imagination of nervous children or of nervous parents. Some people tell us, "Let the kids fight it out." I say it may be alright to strike a match in a normal situation, but strike a match when there is dynamite around and it may be very serious indeed."[18]

After the crowd's applause swelled and then subsided, Lieutenant Magni Palm of the juvenile division waved away such concerns. "I think it is regrettable that a mass meeting should have been called for such a silly thing," he said. "I can't in the past year recall more than eight complaints, and each one was promptly investigated." Besides, he went on, what could the police do without sufficient witnesses and evidence?

"How about the brass knuckles in the car?" someone shouted.

"Three signatures!" hollered another voice from the crowd, referring to the sworn complaints. "There were three of us who signed the paper."

Near tears, a woman named Hildegarde Bearman recalled having two of her sons jumped near North Commons Park and waiting twenty-four hours for the cops to start investigating. "I am not speaking as a Jew," she concluded. "I am speaking as an American."

The onslaught left Kline mute and Palm sputtering. He granted that the attackers suffered from "an inherited prejudice which children absorb from home, streets, and ministers." Then he reverted to the same old script: "Everybody makes mistakes. . . . [I]t was no organized gang. . . . Not even premeditated. It was merely the animal sense of youth."

Enraged by the officer's excuses, Jewish men began pushing toward the stage, some screaming denunciations, others still muttering about Palm's condescending "silly thing." Teenaged boys started talking about getting some knives of their own and some muscle from the Jewish gangsters. Mayor Kline threatened to call in more police to control the meeting. It ultimately took Rabbi Aronson to restore a semblance of order.

Mayor Kline consented to increase police patrols in the neighborhood. Then, in one last dismissive gesture, he excused himself long before the meeting had run its three-and-a-half-hour course. People in the audience were still hectoring the police brass when the school janitor turned off the auditorium lights.

The response of the Minneapolis establishment, as expressed on the editorial pages of the daily newspapers, was characteristically tepid. The *Tribune* laid responsibility for the attacks on inadequate parenting. The *Star Journal*, while decrying intolerance, also echoed justifications for it: "Jews are different in some respects than Gentiles. Most of them practice another religion. Many have definite facial characteristics, as do many Scandinavians. Perhaps the Jews do not join so easily in the amalgam of the melting pot."[19] In a letter to the *Star Journal*, one reader asked, "Do Jewish leaders warn their people against self-pity and a persecution complex? Those emotions . . . start wars as well as race riots."[20]

By all existing accounts, Humphrey did not attend the mass meeting, or at least did not speak during it. But in its wake, he repeatedly addressed its concerns and plainly shared the Jewish community's belief that the problem went way deeper than mere hoodlums. For the first time in Minneapolis's decades-long history of racism and anti-Semitism, a political candidate was placing those issues at the center of a campaign.

Humphrey issued a five-point plan for addressing "racial intolerance and violence in any section of the city." The police would have to recognize "the magnitude of the problem." A citywide conference of religious, labor, business, and social services leaders needed to be immediately convened. The outgrowth of it should be a formal organization, presumably a branch of the city government, devoted to combating bigotry. "It is not sufficient," Humphrey concluded in the prepared statement, "for the mayor to give but a feeble pledge of 'co-operation' in putting down the attacks and curbing violence."[21]

Unlike the white Christian editors in town, even those who considered themselves models of tolerance, Cecil Newman in the *Spokesman* quoted Humphrey's campaign speech about the North Side attacks at great length. At one point, Humphrey harked back to Selden Menefee's book *Assignment: U.S.A.*, the one that Sam Scheiner had tried to call attention to three years earlier. Menefee's prediction that anti-Semitism in Minneapolis could turn violent, a prediction that had been largely scoffed at or ignored by the city's media, was now being borne out. In demanding that Minneapolis confront such violence, Humphrey drew yet again on what he had learned from Rudolf Heberle about how an enlightened society can turn barbaric: "Let us not fail to remember that minority persecution is the first sign of social disintegration. Let us not fail to remember that wherever dictatorship has gained control, its first attack was on a racial or religious minority."[22] Events both near and far soon justified Humphrey's warning. Despite Mayor Kline's promise of heightened policing, a group of drunken young men, one of them serving in the Merchant Marine, set upon several Jewish boys who had just left a movie theater in South Minneapolis. After one attacker pushed a boy through the plate-glass window of a nearby candy store, leaving blood stains on the ground, another in the gang exulted, "Here's the damn Jew's blood."[23] That episode took place on April 15. Over the next two days, the *Star Journal* published front-page photographs of the Ohrdruf concentration camp, the first such images to reach the American media. The Allied commander, Dwight Eisenhower, had personally ordered that journalists be brought to Ohrdruf soon after its liberation on April 12. "I felt that the evidence should be immediately placed before the American and British publics," he later wrote of the decision, "in a fashion that would leave no room for cynical doubt."[24]

* * *

On the day before the May 14 primary, the most reliable local poll showed Humphrey in a tight three-way race with Kline and T. A. Eide, a warhorse running for the fourth consecutive time.[25] The survey could hardly have been more wrong. In a crowded field, Humphrey nearly captured an outright majority, taking forty-nine percent of the vote, winning 12 of 13 wards, outpolling Kline by almost two to one, and tripling his vote total from the 1943 primary. His coattails helped Nellie Stone make it into the runoff for a Library Board seat, one step closer to becoming the first Black person to ever win citywide office. The leading political reporter in Minneapolis, M. W. Halloran of the *Star Journal*, raved that Humphrey "upset all tradition and threw all precedent to the winds" in compiling "the most amazing vote record in a primary election in recent city history."[26] Kline sheepishly admitted that throughout the campaign his own doorstep had been deluged with Humphrey literature and nearly devoid of his own.[27] Both the *Star Journal* and the *Tribune* soon endorsed Humphrey in the general election, and the candidate himself shifted his standard stump phrasing from "If I'm elected" to "When."[28]

Indeed, it was all over except for the bile. Kline reached back to the 1938 gubernatorial race to reconstitute Ray Chase's innuendo about communists and cat's paws. It did not matter that Elmer Benson, the candidate who had been smeared back then, was not running for mayor of Minneapolis. The mere fact that, in the newly formed DFL, he embodied the left-wing faction with its Popular Front politics provided justification enough for Kline to declare, "[A]ll the Communists in Minneapolis and Minnesota—and there are many of them—are behind my opponent's campaign."[29]

For good measure, Kline trotted out William Bell Riley, now in his mid-eighties and no longer even a resident of Minneapolis. "My whole tendency is against the communistic trend of the day," Reverend Riley compliantly pronounced. "I fear it for my city and also for my country. Those leaders in the CIO and some kindred unions, tinctured with its doctrine, are not to be trusted."[30]

As for Humphrey, as much as he stuck to his multi-part plans and appeals to civility and ebullient flesh pressing, he also displayed a previously untapped capacity for ruthlessness. In pursuit of an idealistic agenda, he proved willing to engage in some dirty tricks and innuendo of his own. Two years earlier, Humphrey and his political allies had arranged for his 1943 campaign aide William Simms to be transferred from his day job in the county welfare department to one as an investigator for the county attorney. What the Humphrey crew most wanted Simms to investigate was inside evidence of Kline's corruption. In the aftermath of Arthur Kasherman's unsolved murder, the county attorney assigned Simms to delve into the publisher's safe-deposit box. There, folded into a copy of *The Public Press* with the front-page headline decrying Kline, Simms found three fifty-dollar bills. Or so he claimed and so the Minneapolis public was told. Flourishing the bills as proof of a bribe, Simms appeared in a front-page photo and article in the *Star Journal* under the titillating headline "Kasherman 'Hush Cash' Discovered."[31]

The newspaper conveniently failed to mention that Simms, far from being an impartial sleuth, was closely tied to Humphrey. Nor did any law-enforcement authorities ever identify the source of the supposed payoff, whether Kline or a mobster enjoying the mayor's hands-off attitude. Humphrey, however, beat the drum of insinuation from the time the article appeared in late February until the mid-June general election. Again and again, unencumbered by specifics, Humphrey alluded to "the mysterious and insidious influence that seems to have the key to the mayor's office."[32]

With or without that rhetoric, Humphrey was clearly going to hold those keys very soon. The enormity of his triumph, though, came as a revelation. He buried Kline by more than thirty thousand votes and twenty-two percent, rolling up the largest margin of victory for any Minneapolis mayor since 1931. His momentum helped carry Nellie Stone to a seat on the Library Board. Cecil Newman in the *Spokesman* saluted the breakthrough in an editorial entitled "It Did Happen Here." Citing the fact that only one percent of registered voters in Minneapolis were Black, he dared a bit of optimism: "There must be hope for the unity of people when people from all walks of life here in Minneapolis . . . go to the polls and elect a Negro American woman to public office."[33]

Indeed, Humphrey had not only won big but won different. Minneapolis liberals in the past had staked their appeals on class solidarity and labor interests, only incidentally including the city's small communities of Blacks and Jews. Against electoral logic, Humphrey had elevated the battle against discrimination, and the interests of racial and religious minorities, to a prominent role in his campaign. He was formulating his own answer to the question of what kind of country postwar America should be. The *Minneapolis Tribune*, which had been slow to warm to Humphrey, now expressed a sense of destiny about him: "No mayor of Minneapolis in this century has taken office with such a chance to give the city real leadership toward a bright future as Hubert Humphrey will have. . . . That isn't just day-after-election rhetoric."[34]

Humphrey heard similar congratulations from Orville Freeman, from his former professor Charles Hyneman, from his pastor Reverend Gregory at First Congregational, and even from a childhood friend from Doland named Clair Lovelace, who wrote from the front lines in Okinawa, "Pink it's guys like me who can do things like this. But it's fellows like you that can help see that this was not done in vain."[35]

The weight of responsibility descended on Humphrey in an even more personal way. On the very night he won the election, he received a call from H. H. Five weeks after V-E Day, the family had just learned that Herb Gosch, the husband of Hubert's sister Fern and father of their two children, had been shot down and killed during the last stages of aerial combat in Europe. "I don't know where to start picking up the pieces," Fern wrote to Humphrey soon after his election. "I keep looking for a miracle to happen, I guess. I just can't believe that everything that made life beautiful for me is completely gone. I know I must do something, but I don't know where to start."[36]

Six days before his inauguration as mayor, Humphrey replied by special delivery. "I need not tell you that these are tragic days—days of waiting and days of sorrow for many, many people," he wrote. "It is all part of a terrible price that thousands of people in this country are paying due to the madness of a few people who became drunk with power and who refused to recognize the real truth of what has been going on in the world for the last twenty years. Unfortunately, you were one of the many young people who had to grow up because of the blunders of those of the older generation."[37]

In his inaugural address on July 2, 1945, a speech suffused with the knowledge and burden of America's battlefield sacrifices, Humphrey enumerated the various concrete improvements he intended to seek in postwar Minneapolis. He reserved his greatest emotion, though, for the place where statecraft and soulcraft intersected. "We have pointed with pride to the fact that men and women of all races and creeds are fighting side by side in the cause of freedom," he stated. "Yet there are disturbing signs of disunity and intolerance which must command our attention.

Government can no longer ignore displays of bigotry, violence, and discrimination. . . . We must dedicate ourselves to the true ideals of democracy, wherein every person is accepted as a human being with dignity and worth, regardless of race, creed, or color."

Then, as if turning his gaze to the nation, he concluded, "We must set the example."[38]

* * *

When Muriel Humphrey brought her son Skipper to visit city hall for the first time, she issued one piece of advice: don't touch the side of the building. For all the granite grandeur of the building, with its Romanesque features and a clock tower modeled on Big Ben, the external skin was covered in soot. The Milwaukee Road station and railyard spread along the Mississippi just two blocks away, and decades of coal smoke had even turned city hall's clock face blurry with grime.[39]

The filth, undisturbed for years if not decades, supplied an apt metaphor for the overarching demands on Mayor Humphrey: to clean things up, to make a fresh start. He did so literally, ordering that the city hall clock be scrubbed, and he set about doing so figuratively. He hung a portrait of FDR above the mayoral desk, and he set symmetrical stacks of correspondence, policy papers, and relevant books on its corners. As always with Humphrey, his ravenous appetite for information was mediated by his phobia, going back to the dust storms in Huron, of any sign of disorder. He approached the workload very much like the veterans flocking to college on the GI Bill, impatient about the lost years, scornful of distractions, perpetually in a hurry. Humphrey ate dinner at home with his family perhaps once a week. More often, the workday led into a public meeting or a speaking engagement or two, and afterward, Humphrey would return to the mayor's office. There he read through every piece of the day's mail and memos, jotting down directions for how he wanted Arthur Naftalin or William Simms or some other staffer to follow up in the morning, invariably with the word *RUSH*. The office lights went out toward 2:00 a.m.

Every manner of request or concern surged at the new mayor. He fielded appeals to lower taxes, to build veterans' housing, to put

"The People Sing" show back on radio, to help a woman in ravaged Czechoslovakia find a distant relative in Minneapolis, to arrange a local pen pal for a boy from New Zealand, to halt the bingo games at the Minneapolis Athletic Club as a form of illegal gambling, to find a suitable tenant for a blind homeowner with a bedroom to spare. Salesmen were pitching Humphrey life insurance policies and homes for sale and even patented rattraps.[40] (He did buy a house, the first he ever owned, in a neighborhood near the university campus. As for the rattraps, the historical record is unclear.)

"Nothing was off his desk," Arthur Naftalin later recalled. "Everything was before him, and we would criticize him for this, because those of us who worked with him found it just almost too much, because he never quit and he expected that none of us ever quit."[41]

One task above all others preoccupied Humphrey during his initial weeks in office. He held the power to appoint a police chief; in fact, appointing one was among the few direct powers that the city charter granted the mayor. While Humphrey had emphasized law and order in his campaign, Minneapolis's gangsters had heard such pledges before and managed to bribe their way to continuing business as usual. According to several different accounts—from Humphrey himself, William Simms, Ed Ryan—the Kid Cann and Davie Berman mobs dispatched trusted lieutenants to talk money with Humphrey. These retrospective tales all end with Humphrey delivering a crushing riposte and sending the crook scuttling away. As such, the anecdotes sound just a bit too rehearsed. A different, more credible recollection came from Humphrey's boyhood friend, Julian Hartt, who visited city hall soon after the election. Humphrey told Hartt about having found a sealed envelope on his desk and opening it to find five $1,000 bills and a note promising more if the new mayor let mobsters choose the next police chief. "People think the big job is making sure they elect the right man," Humphrey confided to Hartt. "I'm not sure they want to know how quickly the punks move in—they figure *their* work has just begun."[42]

Until Humphrey did name a police chief, he had one trusted guide in handling the underworld's emissaries. During the 1945 campaign, he had grown close to Fred Gates, a child of Syrian immigrants who operated a pinball arcade downtown. In that line of work, which some people suspected extended to slot machines, Gates brushed up against mobsters and their suborned cops on a daily basis and, as Humphrey later wrote, "understood the netherworld of floating card games and after-hours whiskey joints."[43] Perhaps because the pervasive lawlessness offended his own values, or perhaps because he was sick and tired of being forced to pay protection, Gates lent his knowledge of the demimonde to Humphrey's campaign and his nascent mayoralty. He insisted, for instance, on verifying the identity of anyone contributing money to Humphrey to ensure that none of it was tainted.

Even as Humphrey revered Gates as a "one-man intelligence bureau," however, he could not possibly approximate a police chief. For that position, Humphrey quickly settled on Ed Ryan, a detective and former inspector in the police department. At six-foot-four and 220 pounds, Ryan stood out from the corps for more than his imposing physique. The typical Minneapolis cop was poorly trained, high school educated, and socially inbred with the white working class. Ryan, to the contrary, cut a sophisticated figure. He had married a French woman he met during his World War I service and lived in France for several years, becoming fluent in the language. After returning to Minneapolis in the mid-1920s to become a park policeman and then a beat cop, he earned a promotion to detective with the top score on a qualifying test, the result of "reading a Funk & Wagnalls legal guide that was kept at the station."[44] Thanks to public-speaking classes at the University of Minnesota, he was a polished and in-demand orator on law-enforcement topics. And alone in the Minneapolis department, Ryan had studied at the FBI's National Police Academy, graduating as vice president of his class.[45] In fact, J. Edgar Hoover himself recommended Ryan to Humphrey as the one definitively honest cop in town.

Yet Ryan excited opposition almost as fervent as his support. Liberals and leftists in Minneapolis had never forgiven him for testifying in favor of Gerald L. K. Smith's bid to speak in the Municipal Auditorium the previous year. Ryan's tolerant attitude toward the reactionary Smith sharply contrasted to his vigorous surveillance of actual or supposed communists when he had led the police department's internal security bureau. One of Humphrey's most important labor backers, Robert Wishart, chairman of the Hennepin County Congress of Industrial Organizations (CIO), informed the mayor that Ryan and his witch hunts were unacceptable. That stance imperiled Humphrey's chance of getting his choice approved by the city council, on which Humphrey's liberal faction held only a 14–12 margin and could ill afford any dissent. One council member predicted of Ryan, "He won't get enough votes to form a basketball team."[46]

With Ryan installed as acting chief, pending a council vote, Humphrey put his coalition-building skills to their biggest test yet. He created a Mayor's Committee on Law Enforcement, something within his limited powers since it required no budget, and appointed to it both Wishart and Bradshaw Mintener, the corporate attorney who was Humphrey's most prominent ally among the business elite. Then the mayor more or less locked Wishart and Mintener together in a committee meeting like a couple of feuding siblings enduring joint paternal punishment. After a very long night in the second week of July, they reached a 2:00 a.m. accord on Ryan. Mintener was able to persuade Wishart that cracking down on communists was not tantamount to cracking down on organized labor. Wishart made it clear to Mintener that labor saw the benefit of uprooting organized crime, which was trying to grab control of certain union locals.[47] With both political flanks now covered, Humphrey brought Ryan's appointment to a city council vote, and it sailed through by 21 to 4.

Ryan vaulted into action, seizing liquor licenses from known gangsters, busting bookie joints and brothels, and in one case making a public spectacle of having a thousand-dollar roulette wheel smashed in front of press photographers.[48] The new chief also consented to Humphrey's command that police officers not take sides during strikes—as the cops had done most notoriously during the 1934 drivers' strike, when officers collaborated with hired goons in pummeling union pickets. Humphrey raised police salaries to diminish the appeal of criminals' payoffs. To follow the progress of his reform efforts, the mayor rode along in squad cars and appeared unannounced for midnight shift changes. "When it comes to your reputation or mine, God damn it," Humphrey told Ryan with a rare flourish of profanity, "I'm looking out for mine."[49]

Not only did violent crimes such as murder and assault start to decline, so did a whole shadow economy that had been built around pervasive gambling. At one point, a representative from Western Union complained to Ryan that, with so many bookies being shut down, he was losing the customers who rented ticker-tape machines for sixteen dollars a month.[50] An inmate at the state penitentiary in Stillwater offered perhaps the ultimate compliment, writing to Humphrey, "There is a large delegation from Mpls, and the consensus among them is that your Police Chief cannot be bought. I guess they should know as many of them have been here several times."[51]

Humphrey's dilemma was that a cop could be incorruptible in terms of money while being entirely immoral in how he treated the public. Even as the reform effort proceeded, complaints to the department piled up—a drunken cop groping a veteran's wife in open court, a doctor being stopped for speeding on the way to the hospital to deliver a baby. No community in Minneapolis suffered more such harassment than the Black neighborhood on the North Side. For years, precinct police on the take had allowed vice crime to flourish there, despite the outcry from leaders like Cecil Newman. Then the morals squad used the presence of that same vice crime as the pretext for brutality.

The coexistence of cash honesty and abusive performance took vivid human form in Eugene Bernath. Unmistakable with his barrel chest, scarred nose, and the residual accent of his Swiss childhood, Bernath had racked up thousands of arrests as a patrolman and then a homicide detective before Ryan named him deputy inspector in charge of the morals squad. Humphrey considered Bernath the "most aggressive single individual" on the force, "a real detective's detective."[52] The mayor almost gleefully authorized him to "knock off every gambling joint in this town, and I don't want it done with kid gloves . . . I want them smashed. I want to have tables ripped up and ripped apart."[53]

* * *

In Black Minneapolis, however, Bernath was developing a rather different reputation.

In the predawn hours of August 29, 1945, the Minneapolis police received the report of a fatal shooting in a Black section of the North Side, and from the outset it conjured all the primal fears of miscegenation and "white slavery." The victim was a twenty-seven-year-old Black man, Marvin Lewis, and the suspected killer was a white woman of eighteen, Jeanette Faltico. As the daily newspapers recounted the events, Faltico had moved onto the North Side with several other white women because they were "nuts about jitterbugging" and Blacks are "a hundred times better than the best white dancers and musicians."[54] Lewis and Faltico had met during a night of drinking and, by her version of events, he had begun to slap around one of her white girlfriends. At that point, she grabbed a gun he was wielding and shot him to protect herself.

By the evening of August 29, Deputy Inspector Bernath was on the case, retracing Faltico's path in the hours leading up to the shooting. One of those stops, or so Bernath contended, had been a restaurant and club several miles away from the North Side crime scene. The Dreamland Café was more than a place that served steaks and chops and the weak beer known as "three-point-two" for its minimal alcohol content. It was as swanky a setting as Black Minneapolis had to offer in a city where Black customers were still barred from the fancy hotels and restaurants downtown, and in which Black restaurateurs had no chance of receiving a bank loan or liquor license. Anthony Brutus Cassius, the Black labor and civil rights activist, had opened the Dreamland in 1939 with years of his savings as a hotel waiter and situated it in a section of South Minneapolis, where a small but emergent Black middle class was buying homes and founding businesses. The Dreamland Café supplied the sort of racial haven that turned up in the *Green Book*, the national guide for Black travelers seeking food or lodging without the indignity of being turned away or directed to the back door. When touring Black stars like Lena Horne performed in Minneapolis, they dined at the Dreamland.[55] So did interracial couples, relieved to have a sanctuary from harassment.

Bernath barged in on the evening of August 29, accompanied by nearly a dozen plainclothes and uniformed officers from the morals squad. On the pretext of searching for clues to the Lewis murder, they frisked the patrons, forced the men to produce their draft cards, and demanded that the women open their purses. Two women refused to so much as give their names until they were told the reason for being investigated. Bernath instead ordered them arrested, stuffed into a squad car, and driven to the lockup downtown.

Under normal Minneapolis circumstances, the episode would have ended the usual way, with humiliation and an upcoming court date and roiling Black rage that had to be swallowed back down. On this occasion, though, the police had chosen the wrong targets, and not just because the Dreamland's regulars had nothing to do with the Lewis murder. The two "girls without names," as the cops sardonically called them, both had ties to Cecil Newman. Anita Bloedoorn had worked as a nurse at Twin Cities Ordnance, the defense plant where Newman recruited Black employees for Charles Horn. Emma Crews managed the office of the *St. Paul Recorder*, Newman's companion newspaper to the *Minneapolis Spokesman*. In between rounds of interrogation by Bernath, Crews placed her one permitted phone call. She placed it to Cecil Newman.[56]

He was both an avid and indignant listener. Newman had been exposing examples of police brutality for nearly twenty years already, incidents as egregious as the beating of Curtis Jordan by two cops on a drunken rampage back in 1937. More recently, he had begun stopping into police headquarters and the municipal court nearly daily, finding out who had been arrested and why and how they had been treated. Sometimes his front page carried photographs of the latest Black face swollen from a police beating. For his efforts, Newman endured broken windows at his home and newspaper office, sugar in the gas tank of his car, threatening phone calls, and the beating of his own son.[57] What Newman had never received, however, was justice.

This time, Newman and his wife DeVelma headed straight to police headquarters. Before leaving, he called a dozen community leaders to meet him there. And he also rang Mayor Humphrey at home, just as he was preparing for bed.

By the time Newman reached police headquarters, Bernath was also on the phone with the mayor. After hanging up, Bernath asked Newman to talk things over with him and the police captain in charge. Newman brought his wife and entourage with him, and in the captain's suddenly crowded office, tempers rose immediately. Bernath claimed Humphrey's own law-enforcement committee had pushed for the raid. And why, the deputy inspector went on, was Newman trying to intimidate him? Bernath walked out of the meeting—so much for conciliation—and Newman followed. He helped himself to a phone and called Humphrey again. The mayor summoned a squad car to drive him to police headquarters.

When Humphrey arrived, not yet two months into his mayoralty, he faced two men he considered essential allies and the irreconcilable choices they embodied. Bernath was Humphrey's righteous fist in battling mobsters and the cops they corrupted. Newman was the mayor's moral conscience on matters of race. "If I were walking down the street with your wife," Newman told Humphrey now by way of example, "*we* might well be stopped for questioning."[58]

There was no middle way for Humphrey that would placate both men. He had to decide. And as new as he was to elected office, Humphrey understood something about the power of a political leader's personal example. He had learned this from his sister Frances. Though Frances by this time was living at Fort Leavenworth in Kansas, where the military had posted her husband, Ray, in the early war years she had been a protégé of Eleanor Roosevelt. In that role, she had joined the First Lady in a spontaneous act of desegregation, showing up at the restaurant of Washington's all-white Shoreham Hotel with a racially mixed group of civil-defense employees for lunch. The hotel manager had no option but to capitulate to the First Lady.[59]

Humphrey did throw one crumb Bernath's way, saying that underage drinking at any bar or club should be probed. Then, in the kind of fiat that Eleanor Roosevelt might have appreciated, he ordered Bernath to release Crews and Bloedoorn from their cell and to drop charges against them. In that one middle-of-the-night moment, Humphrey chose the principle of racial equality over the word of "the most effective police officer I have ever known."[60] Whereupon, at two in the morning, the mayor treated the two women and Cecil Newman to coffee in an all-night cafe. No one dared object to seating or serving an integrated group that included the mayor.

When Newman led a delegation of Black business owners from the Dreamland Café's vicinity to meet with Ed Ryan the next day, the chief rebuffed their charges of discrimination.[61] Then, it seems, Humphrey had some words directly with Ryan, because the chief hastily scheduled a speech to the local NAACP on the theme "Together We Build." The mayor also reminded Ryan in a formal letter that the Police Department must, among its other duties, "protect human rights," a concept not previously associated with its corps. Cecil Newman in the *Spokesman* wrote an editorial under the admiring headline "Humphrey Came Through."

Meanwhile, however, the white newspapers in town reiterated Bernath's version of the Dreamland raid. No journalist appears to have ever pursued the question of why the morals squad had been assigned a murder case unless there was some other agenda. A grand jury refused to bring charges against Faltico in Lewis's killing. And in the wake of Japan's formal surrender on September 2, ending the world war and returning home soldiers by the millions, one Minneapolis veteran wrote Humphrey to recommend a specific program of race relations for peacetime: "Let's get a little tough with the negroe's & keep this white man's country—as it always had been.—For instance we could give a negroe twenty-four hour's to get out of the city & state & stay out for good—this being for any crime & disorder caused by such negroe—A 30 year sentence for his illegal entry back into the state would be stiff enough to keep them away once they were out."[62]

* * *

As Minneapolis headed toward its first postwar holiday season on November 9, 1945, the vast and ornate Orpheum Theater

downtown unveiled its new double bill. The main attraction, a film entitled *First Yank into Tokyo*, was a hurriedly assembled potboiler about
an American secret agent whose face is surgically altered so he can pass
for Japanese, infiltrate the country, and expose its efforts to build an
atomic bomb. Two weeks since the movie's debut on the East Coast, it
had already been dismissed by a *New York Times* critic as a "fishy little
fiction."[63] *First Yank into Tokyo* was preceded on the Orpheum's screen,
however, by a short subject being released nationally by RKO on that
very day, *The House I Live In*.

The film starts with footage of Frank Sinatra and a big band in a recording studio doing the ballad "If You Are but a Dream." As the singer
steps outside for a cigarette before the next cut, the onscreen action
starts to look a lot like events on the North Side in the preceding year.
A gang of about a dozen teenagers chase a younger boy down an al-
leyway, pinning him on a windowsill and threatening to beat him for
being a Jew. Interposing himself between the mob and its quarry, Sinatra
tells a couple of war stories—about a pair of Jewish and Presbyterian
aviators who bombed a Japanese destroyer, about the blood banks for
wounded soldiers that took and infused plasma based on need alone.
Then he delivers a plain-spoken homily:

> Look, fellas: Religion makes no difference. Except maybe to a Nazi—
> or somebody as stupid. Why, people all over the world worship God in
> many different ways. God created everybody. He didn't create one people
> better than another. Your blood's the same as mine; mine's the same as
> his. [Sinatra then indicated the Jewish boy.] Do you know what this won-
> derful country is made of? It's made up of a hundred different kind of
> people. And a hundred different ways of talking. And a hundred different
> ways of goin' to church. But they're all American ways. Wouldn't we be
> silly if we went around hating people because they combed their hair dif-
> ferent than ours? Wouldn't we be a lot of dopes?[64]

For his encore, Sinatra shifts into song, voicing words that had been
written by Abel Meeropol,[65] a white, Jewish radical who had also done
the lyrics for Billie Holiday's anti-lynching elegy, "Strange Fruit":

What is America to me?
A name, a map, a flag I see
A certain word, democracy
What is America to me?
The house I live in
A plot of earth, a street
The grocer and the butcher
And the people that I meet
The children in the playground
The faces that I see
All races and religions
That's America to me

The House I Live In has its sour notes. While decrying prejudice, the script repeatedly refers to "Japs." Sinatra's anecdote about blood donations ignored the military's practice of segregating plasma by race. One lyric extolling "my neighbors black and white" had been cut from the title song to keep the film palatable for Southern white audiences.[66] Even so, the film became an instant classic, earning both a special Academy Award and a Golden Globe. That response ratified a very deliberate effort by Sinatra, the progressive screenwriter Albert Maltz, and the Anti-Defamation League of B'nai B'rith, which sponsored the film, to harness the mass media of pop music and the movies to an ethical cause.

Indeed, *The House I Live In* crystallized a moment in which American letters and popular culture sought to provoke a national reckoning with racial and religious bigotry. The body of journalism, art, and entertainment produced within the space of barely five years during and immediately after World War II amounted to its own kind of Double V campaign, insisting that the United States live up to its rhetoric about democracy, its paeans to the newly invented "Judeo-Christian tradition." Taken together, those books and songs and films and comics repositioned the definition of American identity from white Christianity, or even the melting-pot ideal of submission to that

WASP model, to the newer concept of cultural pluralism with its embrace of difference.

Though deeply affected and inflected by the world war against fascism, the corpus had its origin a year before Hitler's invasion of Poland. In 1938, the Carnegie Corporation had engaged a Swedish sociologist named Gunnar Myrdal to conduct a study of Black Americans. A friend and colleague of Humphrey's mentor Rudolf Heberle, Myrdal had done some fieldwork in the United States in the late 1920s, but he was selected largely because his foreignness was deemed a guarantee of intellectual objectivity. Over the next four years, Myrdal plunged into both qualitative and quantitative research, at one point interviewing Cecil Newman over lunch in Minneapolis, while extensively depending on the most accomplished Black social scientists in America, among them Ralph Bunche, E. Franklin Frazier, Charles Johnson, and Kenneth Clark.

An American Dilemma: The Negro Problem and Modern Democracy arrived in 1944 with the dimensions of a cinder block—more than fourteen hundred pages in two volumes, with exhaustive footnotes and charts documenting aspects of Black life from voting behavior to out-of-wedlock births to sawmill employment—and the blunt force of one, as well. All the data notwithstanding, Myrdal presented American racism as fundamentally an affliction of the conscience. Discrimination and inequality unbearably contradicted both "the entire American Creed of liberty, equality, justice and fair opportunity for everybody" and the Christian "ideals of human brotherhood and the Golden Rule."[67] Putting his words in italics for emphasis, Myrdal wrote in his introduction:

The American Negro problem is a problem in the heart of the American.... It is there that the decisive struggle goes on.... Though our study includes economic, social and political race relations, at bottom our problem is the moral dilemma of the American.[68]

While the critical and commercial response to *An American Dilemma* built gradually, it became formidable over the growing months and years. White reviewers in mainstream publications likened Myrdal's exploration to Alexis de Tocqueville's in *Democracy in America* and lauded the book as "monumental" and "overwhelming." The more politicized newspaper *PM* effused that *An American Dilemma* "blows to smithereens the hatemonger's cherished delusions of white supremacy." W. E. B. Du Bois termed Myrdal's work "unrivaled."[69]

Besides its own virtues, *An American Dilemma* also benefited from the literary landscape around it. In the several years immediately before and after Myrdal's book appeared, so did popular works that prepared the soil for his exhaustive study. Richard Wright's memoir *Black Boy*, Lillian Smith's novel of interracial love *Strange Fruit*, and Ashley Montagu's anthropological argument against *Man's Most Dangerous Myth: The Fallacy of Race* all reached wide audiences. All, too, represented the testimony of long-ignored voices in the American conversation. Wright was a Black American, Smith a dissident white Southerner, and Montagu a Jew born under the name Israel Ehrenburg.

As Myrdal appealed to the better angels of American heritage, the bestselling author with the nom de plume John Roy Carlson went incognito into the nation's hateful underground. As an Armenian American actually named Avedis Derounian, Carlson had undoubtedly been sensitized by the Turkish genocide against his ethnic forebears, a mass extermination that Hitler considered as a model for his own Final Solution to the Jewish problem. Carlson's 1943 book *Under Cover*, which Humphrey cited in many speeches, was the product of his investigative immersion into pro-Nazi groups in the United States. Carlson followed it up in 1946 with *The Plotters*, plumbing the netherworld of right-wing extremists in America such as Gerald L. K. Smith, who personified the homegrown, postwar threat to democracy:

> We've won the military war abroad but we've got to win the democratic peace at home. Hitler is dead, but incipient Hitlerism in America has taken on a completely new star-spangled face. It follows a "Made in America" pattern which is infinitely subtler and more difficult to guard against than the crude product of the Bundists. It is found everywhere at

work in our nation. It's as if living embers had flown over the ocean and started new hate fires here while the old ones were dying in Europe.[70]

A similar message in dissimilar form reached America's young people just before dinner time on June 10, 1946, airing in Minneapolis on station WLOL. The *Superman* radio show launched a new series that would stretch for sixteen shows over the next three weeks, culminating just before Independence Day. The character of Superman had been invented a decade earlier by two Jewish teenagers from Cleveland, Jerry Siegel and Joe Shuster, and the superhero started out as a crime-fighter in the mode of the FBI's G-men, albeit with X-ray vision, the ability to fly, and so forth. During World War II, however, *Superman* comics featured him directly battling Hitler. Now, in the postwar years, Superman turned to a domestic villain—a secret society called the Clan of the Fiery Cross, plainly meant to be the Ku Klux Klan.

The storyline begins with the competition between two teenaged boys to be the starting pitcher for their baseball team in Metropolis's youth league. The coveted spot goes to one named Tommy Lee, the Chinese American son of an immigrant. His white rival Chuck Riggs, in turn, is enticed to take vengeance through the Clan, whose Grand Scorpion is the boy's uncle. Within the norms of comic-book derring-do, with its requisite cliffhangers and narrow escapes, the radio shows present an unflinching portrayal of terrorism driven by bigotry. Clan members first try to kill Tommy by placing a bomb under the seat of his bicycle, then beat both him and his father, and finally plot a mass shooting at the baseball championship game. Predictably enough, Superman flies to the rescue, intercepting every fatal bullet in midair. What was less typical for the cops-and-robbers genre were the words the winning players received along with their trophies: "You've not only proved that you're the best baseball team, but you proved that youngsters of different races and creeds can work and play together successfully—in the American way."[71]

Four months later after *Clan of the White Cross* concluded, the November edition of *Cosmopolitan* magazine brought a similar message into the mailboxes of its own, very different target audience: America's fashionable young women. The cover illustration characteristically enough showed a young blonde woman as she coquettishly toyed with an autumn leaf. Beneath the image, though, appeared a splash of bold type promoting the issue's major article. "'Gentleman's Agreement,'" it read, "the novel all America will be talking about." Prior to its publication in early 1947, the book by Laura Z. Hobson was being excerpted in *Cosmopolitan*.

Though her married surname obscured the fact, Hobson was the daughter of two Jewish immigrants of socialist leanings, and the Z stood for her family patronymic of Zametkin. *Gentleman's Agreement* told its own story of blurring identities, and it relied on a version of Avedis Derounian's undercover sleuthing as John Roy Carlson. Hobson inverted the tactic by having a Gentile journalist, Philip Green, pretend to be Jewish in order to write a magazine exposé about anti-Semitism. And while Derounian revealed the virulent and violent style of Jew-hating embodied by Silver Shirts, the German American Bund, and their ilk, Hobson used the fictive Green to unveil the polite, socially acceptable anti-Semitism of the country club and exclusive hotel and restricted neighborhood, the so-called silken curtain. Through Green, Hobson also fingered the "nice people" who are the bigots' "unknowing helpers and connivers."[72]

Cosmopolitan's prediction about *Gentleman's Agreement* proved correct. The novel soared to the top of the bestseller list, and the film adaptation in 1948, starring Gregory Peck, earned three Academy Awards and five more Oscar nominations. With its immense mainstream success in print and on screen, *Gentleman's Agreement* also brought to a crescendo this five-year period when the myriad forms of mass culture, culture usually concerned with profitable popularity above all else, instead combined to speak as the national conscience. The works of that brief, fervent period radically redefined what it meant to be American—and, in contrast, un-American.

CHAPTER 8

"WE ARE LOOKING IN THE MIRROR"

Postwar Reckoning in Minneapolis and America

1946–1947

Hubert Humphrey and the rest of Minneapolis spent the final night of 1945 celebrating the first New Year's Eve since the world war had ended and he was elected mayor. Nobody was deterred by the temperature dropping to eleven below, not after having waited since Pearl Harbor for such a catharsis. Humphrey and Muriel were going to a house party, mostly likely with their favorite couples the Freemans and Naftalins and Kirkpatricks, and no longer restricted to the graduate student menu of popcorn and ginger ale. Bourbon was the choice of the evening, at least for Humphrey.

In the city over which he now presided, every hotel room was booked, and every nightclub table reserved. At midnight, the sounds of whistles, gunshots, and church bells vied to declare the new year. The city's first baby of 1946 was born just five minutes later, appropriately enough to an army lieutenant's wife. After the bars shut down at 1:00 a.m., revelers poured into the downtown streets and kept the hoopla going past 3:00 a.m. Drunks toppled into snowbanks, tipsy drivers crashed their cars, and it took triple the usual police contingent and thirty ambulances to handle the human toll of all the excess.[1]

Humphrey shared the exhilaration. Six months since his land-slide victory, he plainly thrived on being mayor, whether in the serious pursuits of building housing for veterans and expanding the municipal airport, the audacity of proposing Minneapolis as host city for the 1948 Olympics, or the showmanship of posing with beauty queens during the Aquatennial festival. He had landed the police chief he wanted, Ed Ryan, and one of Ryan's last decisions in 1945 had been to remove Eugene Bernath from the morals division, his base for harassing Black Minneapolitans as at the Dreamland Café. No longer suffused by the purity of powerlessness, Humphrey had been discovering the perks of being mayor—the gifts of sports tickets or pheasant meat or lingerie for Muriel from people wanting city hall favors.

Not unlike his constituents thronging the streets downtown, Humphrey commenced 1946 in dissolute fashion. "[A]t about 2:00 a.m., returning from a hilarious house party, I had to lean out the window and give forth of that wonderful bourbon," he admitted to a friend from Huron.[2] To another buddy, this one stationed in Okinawa, Humphrey reported, "The New Year's celebration was one that this country won't forget for many a year. In fact, I won't be able to forget mine for at least two days. I still feel the effects."[3]

In more ways than one, in fact, Humphrey started the new year with overreach and embarrassment. That he did so in the worthy cause of ending racial and religious discrimination in employment did not di-minish the damage. Just weeks after his election, Humphrey and Naftalin had traveled to Chicago to meet with Mayor Edward Kelly about that city's proposed law mandating fair employment practices. When Chicago enacted it, in August 1945, Cecil Newman put the story on the *Spokesman's* front page, where Humphrey read it and kept a copy for his mayoral files.

Two months later, in October, Humphrey had floated the idea of a similar law for Minneapolis, barring discrimination on the basis of race, religion, or national origin. The precise contours of the ordi-nance kept changing from covering only government contractors, as the nation's wartime Fair Employment Practices Committee (FEPC) did, to extending to labor unions and private business, as well. At moments Humphrey indicated that he wanted the statute to impose fines for violations, and at other times he backed away.[4] He was improvising.

Finally, three days into 1946 (and presumably done with his New Year's hangover), Humphrey arranged for several witnesses to testify in favor of the proposed law to the city council's committee on ordinances and legislation. The most potentially persuasive speaker, or the one least likely to be accused of special pleading, looked to be a white woman with a professor husband and a fashionable home overlooking the Mississippi. Her name was Genevieve Fallon Steefel, and, appearances notwithstanding, she had grown up as the child of Irish immigrants, put herself through Radcliffe, and remained faithful to a hardscrabble heritage by devoting herself to labor and civil rights causes. Steefel described the pervasive racism and anti-Semitism in the Minneapolis job market, culminating with the question "Do you know of a Negro teacher or clerk in our public schools?" She then pointed to the influx of another minority group—several thousand Japanese American soldiers who had trained as linguists, translators, and codebreakers at Fort Snelling and decided not to return to their hostile home cities on the West Coast. Yet in the supposedly more tolerant confines of Minneapolis, Steefel informed the committee members, a hospital with a staffing shortage had refused to hire a Nisei nurse.[5]

Having been thus challenged, the council committee proceeded to humiliate the mayor publicly. It kicked the proposed ordinance over to the municipal attorney to study its legality. In part, the council was registering its opposition to the concept that private industry and labor unions might actually have to answer to the public and to the law about their long-standing favoritism for white Protestants. More personally, the council was slapping some tarnish on Humphrey's shine, reminding him that under the city charter the mayor was mostly a figurehead.

The ritual repeated itself on February 13. This time, Humphrey assembled an even lengthier array of speakers—J. T. Wardlaw and William Seabron of the Urban League, columnist Nell Dodson Russell from the *Spokesman*, the local CIO's attorney Douglas Hall, as well as himself and Steefel. The council's legislation committee listened for two hours "without major dissent."[6] Once again, however, consumed by idealism and innovation, Humphrey had neglected the fundamental political task of counting votes. By a three-to-two margin, the committee again refused to move the fair-employment ordinance forward for consideration by the full council.

"I think he favored these programs and ideas but he had no hope of being able to ever implement them," one of Humphrey's closest advisors later recalled. "He had no money, he had no resources, there was not a party who had gone out and picked him out. So it was something that had to be fashioned and fabricated, and bit by bit."[7]

* * *

For civil rights supporters, both locally and nationally, no issue loomed larger at the war's end than did job discrimination. It had surpassed even anti-lynching legislation as the front line in the struggle for racial equality. However reluctantly Franklin Roosevelt had created a wartime Fair Employment Practices Committee covering the defense industries and however begrudgingly those corporations had submitted to it, the results were demonstrable. The combination of federal oversight and a labor shortage pushed the percentage of Black workers in defense plants from three percent in 1942 to eight percent in 1944. By that same year, the Black portion of the federal workforce in Washington reached nearly twenty percent.[8] The availability of wartime jobs in the urban North had attracted Black migrants by the millions from the rural South and in the process remade the political map of the nation.

So, once Allied victory was within reach, the future of the FEPC became the test case for preserving and expanding Black economic progress and the expanded equality it augured. The "Red Summer" after World War I in 1919 and the recent riots in cities such as Beaumont, Detroit, and Mobile had borne bloody testament to the conflict between Black Americans seeking to hold onto wartime improvements or to lay claim to them as military veterans and whites expecting a return to the Jim Crow inequality that had previously prevailed in workplaces in both the South and North. To go back even deeper into American history, the battle over the FEPC recalled the nation's abdication of Reconstruction with the removal of federal troops from the former Confederacy in 1877. A decade's worth of Black political progress, with sixteen members of Congress and more than six hundred in Southern state legislatures, vanished in short order with the reassertion of white supremacy and the application of white terrorism.

"We talk about reconverting from a war that ended in 1945," the syndicated columnist Marquis Ball wrote of the FEPC issue in the *Star Journal*. "We are still, it seems, reconverting—the word they used then was reconstructing—from a war that ended in 1865."[9]

The opposition bloc in Congress—primarily composed of Southern segregationists in the Democratic Party, but also Republicans trying to roll back the New Deal's activist government—were not able to kill the FEPC in a 1944 vote but managed to cut its funding in half the following year. The mere existence of the committee, Southern senators warned, would inexorably lead to a "communistic dictatorship" and a "mongrel race."[10] On the other side, the same civil rights leader who had forced FDR's hand in creating the FEPC, A. Philip Randolph, headed a national committee agitating for the agency to be made permanent. His cause attracted support from the periphery of the White House—from Eleanor Roosevelt, the Republican presidential candidates Wendell Willkie and Thomas Dewey, and Commerce Secretary and former Vice President Henry Wallace, the progressives' hero in Washington—without getting more than a tepid endorsement from the accidental new president, Harry Truman.

Randolph made repeated visits to the Twin Cities, raising money and mobilizing volunteers to lobby Congress. Mass rallies packed liberal churches and Black settlement houses in the Twin Cities, as if somehow the fervor might make some difference in Washington. Randolph's allies in Minnesota ranged from the moderate Republican Senator Joseph Ball to Jewish union activists like Rubin Latz to the Catholic priest and educator Reverend Francis Gilligan to Cecil Newman at the *Spokesman*.

From his role in recruiting Black workers for Federal Cartridge, Newman acutely understood what Black people had to lose. Total employment at the company plummeted from a high of twenty-six thousand to three thousand by 1944, and its factories closed down entirely in August 1945 as Charles Horn converted several industrial buildings to veterans' housing. Franklin Roosevelt may have been deified in life, and even more so in death, by most of the New Deal coalition. But coming after all of FDR's calculated refusals to press for racial equality—by endorsing anti-lynching legislation, outlawing the poll tax, desegregating the military, extending Social Security to agricultural and domestic workers—the precarious state of the FEPC brought Newman to a breaking point with a Democratic Party. "Chanting the Roosevelt name will not be enough, we are afraid," he wrote, not sounding fearful in the least. "If Democrats are not careful in approaching the Negro voter, they will orate 'Roosevelt' to death, just as their Republican adversaries have worn threadbare the name of the revered Lincoln."[11]

Despite such warnings, neither the Truman Administration nor its congressional majority delivered so much as one last extension of the temporary FEPC. With its money gone and its staff laid off, the committee withered away by the summer of 1946. Whatever progress was going to be achieved in ensuring fair employment was going to be made in discrete states and cities. That otherwise disappointing reality meant that Mayor Hubert Humphrey, having bungled the issue twice already through either a newcomer's arrogance or naivete, was going to have another chance.

* * *

On the deliberately chosen occasion of Abraham Lincoln's birthday in 1946, Humphrey welcomed to his mayoral office a deliberately chosen clergyman, the Reverend Reuben Youngdahl. Youngdahl was a phenomenon among the young Christians of Minneapolis, having taken the pulpit of Mount Olivet Lutheran Church in 1938 at the age of just twenty-seven and built its congregation from three hundred to well beyond two thousand. Reverend Youngdahl cut the trim, athletic figure of the basketball star he once had been, and his homiletic skill "removed the gray beard from God and replaced this image with the picture of a buoyant and companionable God," as a journalist later put it.[12] The pastor entitled one sermon "Going God's Way," a nod to the Bing Crosby movie about a young, unconventional Catholic priest, and liked the phrase so much that he went on to use it as the title of a book and radio show. Beyond all that, Youngdahl had connections. One of his brothers, Oscar, had served two terms in Congress and another, Luther, currently sat on the state supreme court as an associate justice and was considered a potential candidate for governor. Though Youngdahl had to stay publicly noncommittal, his family's political leanings were moderate Republican in the Harold Stassen and Wendell Willkie mode.

Humphrey had invited Youngdahl on this afternoon in February in order to announce the creation of the Mayor's Council on Human Relations and to introduce the minister as its founding chairman. The official "Statement of Purpose" described the council's goal as assuring "all citizens the opportunity for full and equal participation in the affairs of this community." It decried the "destructive character . . . and undemocratic nature of all discriminatory practices."[13]

Such lofty rhetoric, of course, meant nothing without action. Political leaders often established advisory bodies to siphon off public discontent and to drag out a response so long that hardly anyone remembered what the original question was. Minnesota's governor, Edward Thye, had named an interracial council several years earlier, in fact, and in 1945 it had produced a report on *The Negro Worker*, which went on to have zero direct effect on public policy.

Humphrey intended for his Human Relations Council to be a cudgel. He would use it to circumvent the city council, building up public pressure for progress on civil rights. Then the mayor would wield that pressure against the recalcitrant aldermen, especially on a fair employment practices law. The blessing and curse of Humphrey's plan were that his limited powers as mayor allowed him to form the human relations group without city council approval while providing him no municipal funds to pay for it. When it came to the financial part, Humphrey reverted to the huckster side of his father H. H. He'd find the money somewhere, somehow, sometime; meanwhile, it was time, as the old man always put it, for *ac-tiv-i-ty*.

The choice of Reverend Youngdahl as chairman signaled Humphrey's strategy of assembling a wide-ranging coalition, as he had in pushing through Ed Ryan's appointment as police chief, so that bold stances against racial and religious discrimination would look more like a common-sense consensus. Over the coming weeks and months, the Human Relations Council's eighteen-member board took final shape, stretching from corporate executives like Durward Balch, the counsel for General Mills, to left-wing activists such as Douglas Hall and Genevieve Steefel, to the Minneapolis superintendent of schools, Walter Anderson. To ensure favorable coverage in the newspapers, Humphrey appointed Bradley Morison, editor of the *Daily Times*, the spunkiest of the city's dailies. Racial and religious minorities were represented by Cecil Newman, the Jewish attorney Hyman Edelman, and a Nisei pastor, the Reverend Daisuke Kitagawa.

To these official members, Humphrey informally added a newly decommissioned GI: Corporal Sam Scheiner of the 96th Infantry. After combat in the Philippines and Okinawa, Scheiner had returned to Minneapolis in January 1946 twenty-four pounds lighter and visibly haunted by the death of his comrade Julius Margulas. The day Scheiner showed up at his in-laws' home in St. Paul, his daughter Susan did not even recognize him. He had seen his twenty-month-old son only once while on leave before shipping out. And Scheiner had lost the family's Minneapolis home in his absence, leaving his wife and children to move back in with her parents, because his military pay fell short of the mortgage.[14]

However distracted or morose Scheiner often appeared at home, he swapped his uniform for a coat and tie and reported for duty at the Minneapolis Jewish Council's office. "Don't fail to let me know if you hear anything that I ought to put a stop to," he told his old contacts. Scheiner renewed his fake-name subscriptions to extremist magazines, compiled the latest brochures from Gentiles-only resorts, and coached a local rabbi into applying for membership at the Minneapolis automobile club, just to prove that even the most respectable Jew would be turned down for membership. With wartime savings, Scheiner bought a lot in South Minneapolis to have a home built for his family. The neighbors arranged to have the property's water supply cut off so Scheiner's contractor could not mix concrete for the foundation.[15]

The work of Humphrey's human relations group, meanwhile, proceeded fitfully. He could not raise enough money to fund a study of discrimination in Minneapolis, as he had hoped. Strains emerged between the ideological factions on the council, testing the durability of the mayor's common front. Even as Edelman and Hall, both from the left-liberal side, were drafting a model fair employment ordinance to be resubmitted to the city council, the more conservative members were objecting. Durward Balch of General Mills asked: Weren't Negroes and Jews better off in Minneapolis than elsewhere? Shouldn't changes in employment practices be voluntary instead of compulsory? Stuart Leck, a member who ran a construction company, similarly equivocated, suggesting that the council recommend no ordinance until studying the handful already enacted in other cities and states. When the journalist and author Carey McWilliams sat in on a council meeting in March 1946, during research for a magazine article about Minneapolis, he warned that voluntary efforts like Humphrey's could wind up being "centers of organized local futility."[16]

Struggling for unanimity, chronically short of funds, the Human Relations Council operated more situationally than strategically as the spring and summer of 1946 rolled by. It reacted more than it acted. It swerved from topic to topic, controversy to controversy, with a wavering attention span. In that respect, the council very much resembled its creator, the mayor.

Less than one month into the council's existence, Ed Ryan announced he would resign as police chief in April in order to run for Hennepin County sheriff. His imminent departure imperiled Humphrey's efforts to reform the police department, both in terms of corruption and discrimination. No one else in the department could match Ryan's integrity and credibility and expertise. Cecil Newman feared that Humphrey might still offer the position to Eugene Bernath, once the mayor's favorite cop, after the disgrace of the Dreamland Club raid. Newman sent up a warning flare by letter, assailing Bernath as a "race prejudiced man," one especially inflamed by interracial couples. At a time when Minneapolis needed "the appointment of a person with broad knowledge and experience with the race problem," Newman wrote, "the greatest blow to interracial relations in the community, in my humble opinion, would be the naming of Eugene Bernath as chief."[17]

Humphrey heeded the admonition, appointing a career officer named Glen MacLean. MacLean was not notorious among minority groups as Bernath was, though nothing in his twenty-four-year track record suggested any particular talent or capacity for intergroup relations. So the mayor sent several officers to the University of Minnesota to receive training in that subject from Joseph Kluchesky, the former police chief in Milwaukee and a national expert in the field. When complaints kept coming in about the force—two Black men groundlessly arrested while eating lunch in a downtown park, a fifteen-year-old girl yanked out of a high school class on the false report that she was pregnant, even a white man pummeled with a nightstick for not producing his draft card as the cop had ordered[18]—the Human Relations Council convinced Humphrey to dispatch a larger contingent of police to Kluchesky's classes.[19] Humphrey ultimately ordered MacLean to give every single officer a copy of Minnesota's 1943 anti-discrimination law at morning lineup. He kept the pressure on his chief with a letter that he pointedly shared with Cecil Newman, Sam Scheiner, and several radio stations in town:

> Every citizen, regardless of his race, color, or creed, is worthy of the full protection of the law and equal application of it. . . . A police officer, in order to fulfill this responsibility, must know his community.
>
> There is no particular group in this city that has a monopoly either on decency or lawlessness. There are good and bad people in all sections and areas of our community. We deal with people as individuals, not as races, creeds, political or religious beliefs. We believe in the principles of equal opportunity and human equality. There is no room in [a] modern democratic system for persons who are bigoted or intolerant of their fellowmen.[20]

Even as Humphrey and the Human Relations Council kept prodding a resistant police force toward some modicum of tolerance, they were drawn into the local front of a national battle against housing discrimination. The proximate conflict began in June 1946, when fifty war veterans, many of them attending the University of Minnesota on the GI Bill, formed a co-op to buy home lots in a development just being platted on the grounds of a former cemetery in northeast Minneapolis. One of the veterans happened to be Nisei: Takushiro Matsuo, who with the Americanized name of Jon had served three years in the Army. Now he was married, the father of an infant daughter, and the waterfront director of a summer camp, sharing the aquatic skills he had refined as a varsity swimmer in college.

Matsuo was also, to the developer of the Oak Hill subdivision, an abomination. His potential residence in Oak Hill would violate its restrictive covenant, which permitted the sale of homes to Caucasians alone. In the face of protests by Matsuo's fellow veterans, the executive secretary of the Minneapolis Board of Realtors opined that such a covenant was consistent with the ethical code of the profession. That code, he went to pains to emphasize, did not set out to separate people by race or religion but merely "aimed at fostering cohesive neighborhoods."[21] For that matter, the New Deal's housing initiatives—the Home Owners Loan Corporation and the Federal Housing Authority—relied on a system of rating neighborhoods that considered Black or integrated districts high risks for mortgages.

To quell the protests and muzzle the bad press he was getting in the local papers, the Oak Hill developer offered a putative compromise. He would assign the Matsuo family a lot at one distant corner of the development, leaving the other forty-nine home sites contiguous and still covered by covenant. To this Matsuo's wife Ruth retorted, "When I think of how many young Nisei fellows in relocation camps stood up against their elders in defense of America and democracy and how they entered the army, which previously had excluded them . . . we're almost obligated to see this through." For its part, the Minneapolis chapter of the American Veterans Committee wielded the favored progressive phraseology of the time to condemn restrictive covenants as "undemocratic and un-American."[22]

By early July, Humphrey and the Human Relations Council had jumped into the case, voting unanimously to denounce covenants and successfully pushing the city's planning commission to urge the Board of Realtors formally to stop using covenants in the future. These efforts spurred the *Minneapolis Tribune* to do something that no local journalist had done before: expose the pattern of thousands of existing covenants and describe housing discrimination as systemic rather than anomalous. By the *Tribune*'s estimate, the restrictions affected fifteen hundred Nisei and six thousand Blacks in Minneapolis. The newspaper also pointed out that although existing state law barred covenants based on religion, a variety of euphemisms barred Jews, too.[23]

Meanwhile, 660 miles down the Mississippi River, a case parallel to Matsuo's was making its way through the legal system, bound eventually for the U.S. Supreme Court. J. D. and Ethel Shelley had fled the vigilante violence in their native Mississippi to move to St. Louis in 1939, and J. D. had found wartime work as a mechanic in an ammunition factory. After several years of boarding with relatives, the couple set out in 1945 to purchase a brick duplex in a neighborhood with a covenant against "people of the Negro or Mongoloid race." To evade it, a realtor arranged for a white woman named Fitzgerald to buy the house and then sell it to the Shelleys at a profit of twenty-five percent. No sooner did the couple and their six children move in than the neighborhood association served an eviction order. Then one of its members, Fern Kraemer, sued in city circuit court to have the property seized from the Shelleys and returned to Fitzgerald, preserving the racial sanctity of the neighborhood and the legal principle of restrictive covenants. By the summer of 1946, with the Shelleys having won in a lower court, Kraemer had appealed to the Missouri Supreme Court, one step closer to the nine justices in Washington.

As for Jon and Ruth Matsuo in Minneapolis, the city council that August passed a resolution barring the Real Estate Board from including covenants in home sales. The measure, however, did not erase the restrictions already in place. It was the latest in a series of partial victories and incremental advances for Humphrey and his Human Rights Council. The Matsuos and their fellow veterans had to content themselves with pulling out of the Oak Hill deal and living elsewhere. Within two years, the Matsuos had left Minneapolis entirely.

* * *

Only three days before Humphrey had begun assembling his Human Relations Council, Joseph Stalin rose before an audience at the Bolshoi Theater in Moscow to deliver a campaign speech for an election to the Supreme Soviet in which, of course, he was running unopposed. Much of Stalin's oration consisted of salutes to the achievements of Marxist-Leninism in agriculture, industry, and armaments that had enabled the USSR to defeat Nazi Germany. While Stalin acknowledged the "antifascist coalition" with the United States and Great Britain, he placed the responsibility for both world wars on "the capitalist system of world economy." Moreover, he predicted that capitalism would once again provoke "general crisis and military conflicts," for which the Soviet Union would need to remain militarily prepared. Without explicitly using the term, Stalin was anticipating World War III.

In the immediate aftermath of Stalin's speech, the American chargé d'affaires in Moscow provided an analysis in the form of an eight-thousand-word telegram to the State Department. That diplomat, George Kennan, dismissed the prospects of a "permanent peaceful co-existence" between East and West. The Soviet Union, in his view, was bent on territorial expansion and ideological battle, and it would respond "only to logic of force." The punctuation to Kennan's "long telegram," as it came to be known, was delivered several weeks later in Fulton, Missouri. With President Truman at his side, Britain's wartime prime minister Winston Churchill declared of the Eastern European nations now controlled by Moscow, "From Stettin in the Baltic, to Trieste in the Adriatic, an iron curtain has descended across the continent."

As much as any set of events, those two speeches and one diplomatic cable marked the transformation from the Grand Alliance to the Cold

War. The tremors went on to affect Humphrey's current political career and future ambitions in direct, linear ways. As Truman adopted the policy known as "containment" and his Secretary of State, George Marshall, proposed a program to rebuild Western Europe as a bulwark against Soviet influence, the Democratic-Farmer-Labor (DFL) Party, along with the New Deal coalition as a whole, cracked into adversarial halves. Even while liberals and leftists concurred on the Rooseveltian social compact as a domestic agenda, they were bitterly divided on international politics, meaning primarily whether the Soviet Union loomed as a beacon of human equality or a murderous and belligerent dictatorship. In Minnesota the geopolitical question boiled down to whether the DFL would be controlled by its Popular Front faction, including communists and sympathizers, or more traditional liberals.

At the end of the same month that had begun with the Iron Curtain speech, the party held its first major convention since the 1944 gathering during which Humphrey had helped engineer the merger. In a mirror image of the fission of wartime Allies, the DFL delegates separated into combative sides, one embodied by former Governor Elmer Benson and the other by Humphrey. For the Benson faction, the prevailing rule of political conduct was "no enemies to the left." The phrase went back to both French Jacobins and the Russian revolutionary Alexander Kerensky, and in its present connotation meant no questioning the possible communist allegiance of any DFL member or any collaboration with possible front organizations.

Between Humphrey's accommodating personality and his inclusive brand of politics, he had previously managed to sidestep the party's infighting. If anything, he himself had been the object of Red baiting, such as from Kline during the 1945 mayoral race, far more than the author of it. This time, as keynote speaker, Humphrey supplied the Left's target. His very success at enlisting businesspeople, clergy, and Republicans into efforts like the Human Relations Council was proof of his perfidy. So was his association with Evron Kirkpatrick, an outspoken anticommunist. From his own student days at both Minnesota and LSU, Humphrey held a reflexive mistrust of communists, vividly remembering the party loyalists whose preferred American policy toward Nazi

Germany pivoted from opposition to isolationism to intervention as the changing Comintern line dictated.

The speech that Humphrey had prepared for the convention began by striking many notes of unity and conciliation. It called for "all truly progressive forces in the state of Minnesota [to] be brought into the folds" of the DFL, and it lacerated the "same old gang" of Republicans in Washington for their "reactionary political leadership" and devotion to "corporate power and special privilege." A quarter of the way through his sixteen-page text, however, Humphrey stepped into a minefield. Without mentioning the Soviet Union by name, he declared, "Large areas of our world today is [sic] cursed by the enslavement of untold millions of human beings through the suffering and agonies of war, starvation, totalitarian state control, and the supremacy of brute force." And without mentioning the Benson faction in the DFL, he decried "the right of any minority of any select group to dictate its will over that of the majority."[24]

If all hell did not proceed to break loose, then enough of it did. Humphrey was spat on and hooted, heckled as a "fascist" and "warmonger," and warned by a sergeant-at-arms, "Sit down, you son of a bitch, or I'll knock you down." For probably the first time in his voluble life, Humphrey could not finish a speech. By the convention's conclusion, Benson's forces had won control of the DFL executive committee, making Humphrey an outcast in his own political party and a pariah to many suddenly former friends.

The next blow to Humphrey came at the hands of his erstwhile hero, Henry Wallace. Humphrey had modeled one of his home front speeches for the War Mobilization Board on Wallace's address "Century of the Common Man." At the 1944 Democratic Convention, Humphrey had delivered a seconding speech for Wallace in his failed bid to be renominated as vice president. "I regard Henry Wallace not only as a real friend but, even more important, as one of our great liberal leaders," Humphrey put it in a letter to a DFL ally later that year, anticipating a Wallace presidential run in 1948. "God only knows there are damned few of them."[25]

During a visit to Minneapolis in 1946, with Mayor Humphrey as his official host, Wallace averred in a speech that "the peoples of

Eastern Europe have always been governed by semi-authoritarian regimes which never allowed the Four Freedoms." He was referring to Franklin Roosevelt's call in his 1941 State of the Union address for freedom of speech, freedom of worship, freedom from want, and freedom from fear. The pro-Soviet governments at least deserved credit for addressing "freedom from want," Wallace contended, and "trying to help the common man as against the small group of rich barons and industrialists."[26] Back in Washington as commerce secretary to Truman, Wallace objected in writing to the president's adversarial stance toward the Soviet Union. Then, in New York's Madison Square Garden on September 12, Wallace painted a sunny future of "friendly peaceful competition" and mutually respected spheres of influence between East and West. "On our part we should recognize that we have no more business in the political affairs of Eastern Europe," he told a supportive audience, "than Russia has in the political affairs of Latin America, Western Europe, and the United States."[27]

Within a week, Truman had demanded and received Wallace's resignation from the Cabinet. By the end of 1946, Wallace had led about twenty Popular Front organizations into the creation of the Progressive Citizens of America, the functional equivalent of a third party. Wallace's break with the Democratic Party left Humphrey without his political lodestar, the expected inheritor of FDR's mantle. And the local version of the Truman-Wallace rupture, the schism within the DFL, presented Humphrey with the challenge of pushing a liberal agenda against opposition from both flanks.

"A fellow sort of gets himself into a peculiar predicament," Humphrey wrote to Orville Freeman. "I know damn well there are people in Minneapolis who go around calling me a Red and a Communist and what-have-you, and then I know there are other people who are on the so-called left side who in recent months have called me everything from a Fascist to a downright screwball. I might be guilty of the screwball title but the other ones are all wrong."[28]

* * *

One day in mid-July of 1946, a young woman traveled nearly two hundred miles from her family's dry goods store in Viroqua, Wisconsin, to Sam Scheiner's office in downtown Minneapolis. Helen Marsh Felix had some disturbing news to share. Viroqua would be celebrating its centennial on August 18, and the keynote address was to be delivered by the town's most famous son: Gerald L. K. Smith. Being one of the handful of Jews in Viroqua, Felix was terrified.[29]

As Scheiner sprang into investigative action, he discovered the implications of that Viroqua event for Minneapolis, its mayor, and the Human Relations Council. For one thing, a Methodist church in Viroqua had invited Reverend Youngdahl—chairman of the council and brother of the Republican candidate for governor—to preach on the morning of Smith's address. The coincidence, apparently unknown to Youngdahl, was meant to imply his approval of Smith's bigoted versions of both Christianity and Americanism. Alerted by Scheiner, Youngdahl wrote to the Methodist minister in Viroqua to cancel "due to the fact that I cannot subscribe to his [Smith's] philosophy and I do not in any way want to be connected with him and that philosophy."[30]

Defusing that potential embarrassment, however, only began Scheiner's work. It turned out that Smith's Viroqua speech would serve as the prelude to an address in Minneapolis three nights later. With his America First Party a whopping failure in the 1944 election and his anti-Semitism politically radioactive in the wake of the Holocaust, Smith had taken to booking hotels under an alias and reserving speaking venues through cover groups.[31] The auditorium of the Leamington Hotel in Minneapolis had been retained for the evening of August 21 by a previously unknown outfit called the Northwest Pioneers.

The two skills that Smith continued to refine were playing the martyr and shaking the money tree. His recent speeches in Dayton, Kansas City, and Cleveland had drawn nearly as many picketers as listeners. By depicting his persecution at the hands of communist Jews in the pages of his weekly bulletin *The Letter* and magazine *The Cross and the Flag*, Smith tapped into a growing stream of private, confidential contributions. His wife kept twelve thousand dollars' worth hidden in their belongings when the couple traveled.[32] (The equivalent in 2022 would be nearly one-hundred-and-eighty thousand dollars.)

Minneapolis afforded Smith a reliable source of cash and the opportunity to exercise his animus against Humphrey. Smith had been stewing about Humphrey ever since receiving that lecture about Jesus being a Jew. Now, more infuriatingly, Smith's nemesis was mayor. But Smith knew the truth—that Humphrey was a "Jew left wing stooge" with a "cabinet of Stalin lovers" and "revolutionary" plans for a fair-employment law.[33] All the perfidy and treason would be revealed, with lucrative donations to follow, if Smith could just provoke Humphrey into overreacting. Based on the events of 1944, Smith expected that misstep would take the form of Humphrey refusing him a speaking location, which Smith could then portray as denying him a First Amendment freedom.

Smith had tried and failed once already during Humphrey's term, with a Minneapolis speech in October 1945. Humphrey did not object to Smith's rental of a private hall, and dozens of picketers marched outside, with the police monitoring the whole situation. In the days leading up to Smith's August 21 speech, however, Humphrey found himself straddling a widening fissure among his own allies. While the Minnesota Jewish Council and NAACP recommended ignoring Smith and his waning loyalists, the American Veterans Committee, the county CIO, and the Central Labor Union argued for confrontation. The Trotskyites of the Socialist Workers Party, whose taste for street battles went back to the 1934 truckers' strike, added their followers. "[T]o picket," Humphrey pleaded, "would be to play into the hands of those who were looking for trouble or a dramatic scene."[34]

On the morning of August 21, Smith showed up at police headquarters to demand that Chief MacLean provide protection from the expected protestors at the evening's speech. MacLean assured him of it. When Smith and his audience of several hundred appeared at the headquarters of the Hennepin County Republican Party, they were met by an equal number of picketers, filing up and down the sidewalk with placards saying "Race Hatred Is Fascism," "Don't Be A Sucker for

Gerald L. K. Smith Poison," and, most resonantly, "We Fought Hitler Over There! We Don't Want a Hitler Here."[35]

Smith found the doors of the Republican offices locked, the result of the party chairman belatedly learning who had rented the premises. Prepared and unperturbed, Smith shouted to his admirers to move on to the Leamington Hotel. In the pages of *The Cross and the Flag*, Smith had already promised his devotees a speech on the prospects for a third-party coalition between Southern segregationist Democrats and Northern isolationist Republicans. The goal, he had written earlier in *The Letter*, would be to hand an indecisive presidential election in 1948 to Congress to resolve, which it would do by installing "a Nationalist, a conservative, and one who has a high regard for American Traditions, racial purity, and is dead-set against Communism."[36]

Before Smith could begin, protestors surged into the hotel, shoving past the several cops on duty. As several dozen of the most incensed picketers pushed against the ballroom doors, Smith's minions fortified the entrance with folding chairs. To the sound of wood cracking, the protestors breached the barricade and began hurling chairs into the crowd. Smith himself was nowhere to be found. On the way over from Republican headquarters, he had taken refuge in a hotel room across the street, a general abandoning his troops.

Three or four minutes of mayhem later, enough police arrived to restore order. Then Chief MacLean, surely acting on Humphrey's instruction, extended a remarkable invitation. The picketers were welcome to reassemble in the mayor's reception room in city hall. Three hundred did so. It could be that Humphrey had offered his premises, and the implicit approval it connoted, simply as a way of defusing the violence. It could also be that, after his years of prickly history with Gerald L. K. Smith, he was not entirely displeased that the "minister of hate," as a later biographer would call Smith, had been muzzled.

If so, the guilty pleasure faded quickly. Smith re-emerged from his veritable bunker to hold an impromptu press conference, telling reporters, "Just remember this was done by Jewish terrorists. This is the result of thirteen years of Roosevelt."[37] In a subsequent edition of *The Letter*, he enlarged the indictment: "The Mayor and the entire administration, although sympathetic to the hoodlums, evidently now find themselves in a very embarrassing situation."[38]

With a kind of devious genius, Smith had analyzed the situation correctly. Humphrey's fears about violence by protestors ceding the moral high ground to Smith and his rabble had been borne out. In the aftermath of the melee, Humphrey humbled himself to apologize that "1,000 Christian Americans have been denied the right of peaceable assembly."[39] In so doing, he even parroted Smith's wildly exaggerated estimate of the audience's size. The *Star Journal* laid into the mayor it had endorsed for election. "The display was a disgrace to the city," an editorial declared. "A mob is a mob, whether the target is Gerald L. K. Smith or an Alabama Negro."[40]

In a letter several days later, Humphrey put his quandary into the form of a broader political analysis, one that arose from his experience with the Cold War and the DFL's schism. While he pilloried "the 'extreme Right'" for instigating and exploiting "disorder and violence" for political gain, he extended the indictment to "a militant minority . . . who are on the 'extreme radical Left.'" They, too, "caused great trouble and confusion to those who would live by democratic principles."[41]

Certainly, the trouble and confusion adhered to Humphrey, and potentially to his initiatives on civil rights. His whole purpose in assembling the Human Rights Council with a white Protestant minister at its helm and a share of businessmen on its board had been to present civil rights as a mainstream cause, as the American way. Now that council felt compelled to condemn formally both Smith and the violent picketers, implying a moral equivalency between bigots and at least some of their foes. At the same time, as September 1946 commenced, the Human Rights Council also faced practical problems. It had only $104 in the bank and debts of nearly $800. The surrounding political climate was turning forbidding for the New Deal coalition, with Harry Truman's popularity rating at thirty-two percent, and large gains by Republican conservatives anticipated in the November midterm elections. Gerald L. K. Smith's vision of a bipartisan right-wing coalition looked entirely, and dismally, possible.

After fourteen months as mayor, Humphrey was staggering under the burden. Even as he maintained an ebullient and effervescent public face, ever the salesman's son, he understood the toll. Already an infrequent presence at the family dinner table, Humphrey barely joined Muriel and their children for that Minnesotan tradition of a midsummer week at the lake. "I am going to warn my younger friends," he wrote to a political associate, "that if they really want any family life, or enjoy just being a 'good fellow,' they better stay out of this game."[42] In a rare and revealing bit of humor, he confided to a woman friend, "I'm too damn tired to even do work here in the office, much less under the covers. So my wife says."[43]

The self-effacing joke was not exactly accurate. As Muriel herself wrote to her husband from the family's vacation cabin, "Gee honey— When are you coming again? Your schedule looks so full. We miss you terribly and want you to come just as soon as you possibly can. Wasn't it fun [last] Sat nite? Or Sunday AM—I mean?? Hurry back for some more."[44] She signed the note, "Your Bucky," an endearment that went back to their courtship years, when she had been the girlfriend urging on his improbable hopes of political life, rather than the wife who paid the price of their fruition.

* * *

Periodically during the mid-1940s, as an itinerant lecturer on the subject of race relations, Carey McWilliams alighted in the Twin Cities. He spoke to the Urban League chapter, the State Council for Social Work, and students at Macalester College and the University of Minnesota, displaying an idealism that had complicated roots. McWilliams had grown up as a white Protestant in Colorado, absorbing and espousing conventionally bigoted views of Jews, Mexicans, and Chinese. The twin crises of his father's death and expulsion from the University of Denver impelled him to move to Los Angeles,[45] and the combination there of a newspaper job, then law school, and finally the Great Depression radicalized him in the manner of a religious conversion. As if to expiate his younger self's sins, McWilliams devoted his writing life to exposing the myriad forms of American inequality. His book about migrant farmworkers, *Factories in the Field*, appeared within months of John Steinbeck's parallel novel, *The Grapes of Wrath*. McWilliams went on to devote volumes to Black Americans (*Brothers Under the Skin*, 1943) and to the Japanese-Americans then being incarcerated as potential traitors (*Prejudice*, 1944).[46] During his visits to the Twin Cities, he heard repeated accounts of Minneapolis's anti-Semitism.

The sum total of those gleanings, in the form of a magazine article entitled "Minneapolis: The Curious Twin," hit the city in September 1946 like an anvil dropped from a rooftop. "One might even say, with a measure of justification, that Minneapolis is the capitol [*sic*] of anti-Semitism in the United States," McWilliams wrote. "In almost every walk of life, an 'iron curtain' separates Jews from non-Jews in Minneapolis. Nor is this 'iron curtain' a matter of recent origin; on the contrary, it seems to have always existed."[47]

Realistically, McWilliams's article should not have made much impact. It appeared in a liberal quarterly, *Common Ground*, with only nine thousand subscribers nationwide. Everything McWilliams said—not just his conclusion but the supporting examples of intolerance in service clubs, the job market, churches like William Bell Riley's, and Jew-baiting political campaigns—had been said many times before. Rabbi Maurice Lefkovits had written it in *American Jewish World* on Rosh Hashanah in 1923. Cecil Newman had been citing such examples in the *Spokesman* since the early 1930s. Arnold Sevareid[48] had raised the subject with his articles about the Silver Shirts in 1936. Sam Scheiner had file cabinets full of examples of anti-Semitism. Selden Menefee had levied the same indictment as McWilliams just three years earlier in *Assignment: U.S.A.* In one way or another, every one of those Cassandras had been ignored or tut-tutted in proper Minneapolitan circles.

This time, however, the shame stuck. Perhaps it stuck by dint of sheer repetition. Perhaps it stuck because the Holocaust had demonstrated the linear extension of even "silver curtain" anti-Semitism. Perhaps it stuck because McWilliams—unlike Lefkovits, Newman, Sevareid, and Scheiner—was a white Gentile writing for a national audience. Perhaps it also stuck because Hubert Humphrey had elevated the fight against bigotry of all racial and religious kinds to the top of his political agenda. For whatever combination of reasons, the *Star Journal* published a lengthy condensation of McWilliams's article and accompanied it with an editorial headlined "Capital of anti-Semitism?" As the question mark implied, the newspaper was not quite ready for Minneapolis to plead guilty, but it did acknowledge McWilliams's reputation for "competence and objectivity."[49] When Rabbi David Aronson issued a searing response in *American Jewish World*, the *Star Journal* took the rare step of reprinting it verbatim, ensuring that the grievances of the shtetl would be heard on Gentile Main Street:

> Now that Minneapolitans know the facts what are they going to do about it?
>
> What are the decent citizens and moral and spiritual leaders of the community going to do about it? What are our educators, our responsible editors and the Christian ministers, who are sincere in their preachments of a God of Love, doing?
>
> They can no longer plead ignorance of the situation even as an extenuating excuse. Now that the facts are public, silence on their part means consent, and inactivity will be interpreted as acquiescence.[50]

The mayor had a ready answer. Humphrey had already been seizing upon the McWilliams article as the means to resuscitate his Human Rights Council and its proposed survey of prejudice in Minneapolis. He summoned several hundred supporters to a public meeting at the Curtis Hotel, decrying the postwar resurgence of the Ku Klux Klan and despairing of another wave of race riots. Sermon complete, he did what preachers do and passed the collection plate, reaping $2471. The donation fell far short of the thirty-five-thousand dollars that the council's operations, including the survey, would require. But it qualified as a windfall at a time when Humphrey had fallen a thousand dollars behind on paying the council's director, Wilfred Leland, who was on the verge of losing his home as a result. Rescued from dispossession for the moment, Leland addressed a YWCA audience four nights later, assailing the Minneapolis mindset as "smug, complacent, apathetic, and hypocritical." Reverend Youngdahl followed up with a speech to the League of Women Voters, warning, "This may be our last chance to build a new world. We must begin by building a new community."[51] More than ever, such gatherings and such words made it onto the front pages of the city's newspapers.

Humphrey was a politician who functioned on the basis of visceral reflex, of personal encounter, and the evidence of Minneapolis's bigotry landed repeatedly on his desk. One day it might be an editorial by Cecil Newman jabbing that the municipal workforce of nearly eight thousand included just fourteen Blacks. Another it was the complaint from a Jewish doctor who'd been denied a hospital residency on the specious claim that it would violate the merit system. Another it was an Urban League officer being refused service at a downtown restaurant. Another it was a Jewish war veteran getting a dubious speeding ticket from a cop notorious for staking out Olson Boulevard, the main drag through both the Black and Jewish sections of the North Side.[52] And another it was a three-page, handwritten letter, carefully proofread and corrected, accompanied by a three-cent stamp for Humphrey's reply.

"I am 22 years of age," the letter began.

I am a Negro. I have had 4 years of high school 4 years of college in which I majored in Biology, and 3 months training in X-ray technique. I come from a respectable Christian home and I have some of the highest character references that can be given in many states. My problem is that in spite of my education, references, and experience I can't get a decent job, at present the best job I can get is at the Northland Bus Station as a bus washer. Here there is no need for education, self respect or anything. To be frank. I am strictly disgusted with my working conditions. While I am at work the only conversation I can get is only about how many girls I went out with or how much whisky I drank and I don't do either, it is just degrading. I tried to better my conditions but to no use. So my wife suggested my writing you as my one and only solution.[53]

In the short term, Humphrey scribbled a note for his aide, William Simms: "<u>Bill</u> call this fellow in—see him—we must help this man."[54]

(There is no existing record of the outcome of that meeting.) In the longer and broader frame, Humphrey was depending on the discrimination survey to build the case for systemic change, change with the force of law. The first step toward it would be assembling the incontrovertible evidence, the social science data. Though Humphrey himself used more temperate language, the essence of the task meant grabbing Minneapolis by the back of the neck and grinding its face into its own prejudice. In so doing, by the mayor's design, Minneapolis would be taking direction from a Black man.

* * *

At the age of 53 in the autumn of 1946, Dr. Charles S. Johnson quite possibly knew more about race relations in America than any person alive. He had started learning experientially as the child of a Baptist minister in Virginia, working after-school jobs in a barbershop and hotel that placed him within earshot of white bigotry being casually expressed. Then, as an undergraduate at the segregated Virginia Union University, he began to link his instinctive curiosity to the practice of social science. In graduate school at the University of Chicago, he became a protégé of Robert E. Park, who had taught under Booker T. Washington at Tuskegee Institute and returned north to help pioneer the discipline of urban sociology. Johnson made his name as an emerging scholar when he served as associate secretary of the commission that studied the Chicago riot during 1919's "Red Summer," helping to write its detailed inquiry into the city's pattern of racial inequality, *The Negro in Chicago*.

After joining the faculty in 1928 at Fisk University, a church-affiliated Black college in Nashville, Johnson produced prolific and wide-ranging research into African Americans. He investigated the lives of cotton sharecroppers and college graduates, delivered papers on racial issues to presidents Hoover and Roosevelt, and authored or contributed to more than a dozen books over the next seventeen years. He investigated reports of slavery and enforced servitude in Liberia on assignment from the League of Nations and advised Japan on reforming its education during the postwar American occupation, unofficially receiving the rank of brigadier general.

In the process, as chair of the Department of Social Sciences at Fisk and then director of its Race Relations Institutes [*sic*], Johnson made the university an unparalleled repository of data about American Blacks. Fisk hosted interracial summer workshops for scholars on race relations and produced an authoritative digest on incidents of discrimination, *The Monthly Summary*. Johnson's personal ties stretched from the white philanthropists of the Rosenwald Fund and the American Council of Race Relations, who underwrote much of his work, to the Black intelligentsia of Arna Bontemps and Mary McLeod Bethune.

World War II refocused Johnson's energies from academic research to the active pursuit of racial equality and from the overt oppression of the Jim Crow South to the comfortably complicit North and West. "A considerable portion" of white people there, he asserted, "is insensitive on matters affecting the Negro minority and uninterested unless threatened and challenged."[55] As Johnson told a race relations conference in Chicago in 1944, "In practically all the cities or states in the North there are civil rights laws, but in no state that I know of is it easily possible for these protective laws to give easy, normal protection ... of Negro members in their civil rights. ... [I]t is certainly contrary to the tradition or to the American creed which we are trying to review and reinforce."[56]

Having studied outbreaks of racial violence during the war—in Beaumont, Detroit, and Mobile, among other cities—Johnson began devising a method of identifying and addressing incendiary conditions before such explosions. He called this method the "self-survey," and it relied upon what a later biographer called "quiet confrontation."[57] If a given city requested Johnson's involvement and could demonstrate a critical mass of local support, he sent a team of sociology researchers, virtually all of them Black, to guide a months-long survey of racial disparities in categories from education to employment to religion. The actual fieldwork would be done by local volunteers, most of them white. And it would proceed under the aegis of Christian good works, specifically the American Missionary Association of the Congregationalist

Church, an interracial organization whose activism traced back to the abolitionist movement.

Part of Johnson's purpose was to provoke a "psychological crisis of considerable significance" when the white interviewer "is required to go into the Negro ghetto and knock on the door of a strange and unknown house," initiating "the first contact that white persons have had with individual Negro families in their family setting."[58] The point of such shock therapy was neither guilt nor moral awakening. It was to compile information and wield that information to compel tangible change. Johnson's first self-survey, undertaken in San Francisco in 1944, helped to stave off the imposition of restrictive covenants in housing and wedge open union jobs for Blacks in the city's shipyards.

Humphrey had begun following Johnson's work during the mid-1940s, if not earlier, and had always intended for it to be the centerpiece of the Human Relations Council's program. With Minneapolis now nationally reviled for its intolerance by Carey McWilliams, and with a few thousand dollars of donations in hand and the prospect of several thousand more from Sam Scheiner's Minnesota Jewish Council, Humphrey contracted with Johnson in October 1946 to mount a self-survey of Minneapolis. A week into November, Johnson came to Minneapolis with the protégé who would oversee the on-site, day-to-day research, a doctoral student in psychology named Herman Long. In their meeting, the mayor told Long that he "considered this the most significant project undertaken in this city during his administration."[59]

By the end of December, Humphrey had selected Bradshaw Mintener, his preferred ally in corporate Minneapolis, to chair the study. The mayor soon turned over his twice-weekly radio show to Mintener, Youngdahl, and Wilfred Leland to appeal for community involvement.[60] More than three hundred volunteers soon stepped forward to serve as interviewers, investigators, and clerical workers, with the number ultimately reaching nearly a thousand. The topmost echelon, those on the survey's sponsoring committee, typified Humphrey's kind of coalition—"labor leaders, leading industrialists and business men, outstanding social workers, teachers, ministers, religious workers, newsmen, radio professionals and minority group leaders," as an internal report noted.[61] Many of the foot soldiers fit the profile of what Johnson considered his secret weapon. They were women of education and ideals with precious few opportunities to put them to use amid the postwar return to domesticity. Herman Long recruited them from the PTA, the League of Women Voters, even the Junior League.

"As a matter of philosophy," Long explained, "the survey is not so much concerned with how people feel about minority groups as it is with what they do toward them."[62] Genevieve Steefel, the foremost woman in the self-survey effort, described its goal as producing an "objective statement" about the extent of discrimination "not as a protest or accusation, but as evidence."[63]

Not every woman in town bought the concept. The widow of a university dean, having heard about the self-survey at the Woman's Club, informed Humphrey, "As I would never knowingly discriminate in my own thinking, I would find it hard to be a party to the proposed survey. It would seem to me that it would but stir up conflicting thinking."[64] Columnist Nell Dodson Russell at the *Spokesman*, normally an admirer of Humphrey, had earlier warned him, "I believe . . . the whole issue of inter-race relations is shrouded in pessimism. Too much emphasis is being placed on the negative aspects such as job discrimination, etc., and not enough publicity is being given to the good things that are being accomplished."[65]

Framed in national terms, the self-survey was taking place in the crosscurrents between mass culture's messages promoting tolerance and mass politics' swing to the right. The midterm elections of 1946 had thrown the New Deal coalition out of congressional power, as Republicans gained twelve seats in the Senate and fifty-five in the House to seize control of both chambers for the first time since 1932. Whatever the shortfalls on race relations under Franklin Roosevelt, and now Harry Truman, those presidents had offered far more commitment than the tacit alliance of Southern segregationist Democrats and free-market, anti-union Republicans now in charge of the Capitol.

Nonetheless, Herman Long readied his troops. The first stage of the survey involved interviews with Black, Jewish, Nisei, Slavic Catholic, and Native American residents, to compile the anecdotal evidence of bias against them. On the Wednesday morning of January 29, 1947, with the winter's first heavy snowfall approaching, the volunteers clasped their pens and note pads, bundled into their overcoats and mittens, and started to knock on those unfamiliar doors of which Charles Johnson had written.

Both the *Tribune* and the *Star Journal* sent a photographer along with the emblematic face of the self-survey, Lisa Gunhild Murphy, the Swedish-born wife of an engineering company's buyer. At thirty-three, Murphy knew something about life's disappointments. Her first marriage had ended in divorce, and just a year earlier her first child with her new husband had died at birth. The newspapers' photos showed her patiently listening and jotting down notes as she met families across the color line—a Black draftsman, Melvin Stone, and his wife Opal; a Nisei mother named Sachi Doi, who had moved from California with her machinist husband Thomas; Gladys Patterson, a Black homemaker whose husband William was at his job waiting tables. All of the pictures included the families' children, looking on expectantly at their white visitor and lending the amiable aura of a kaffeeklatsch to what was, at bottom, a dead-serious inquest into entrenched bigotry.

Only in later months would researchers submit detailed survey forms to thousands of Minneapolitans in power—real estate agents, teachers and principals, clergy members, hospital administrators, business owners, union officers—to cull statistical data to be analyzed. Those results would not be fully released until 1948. But even in its first phase, fortified by favorable coverage on radio and in print, the self-survey generated the groundswell of support that Humphrey had been seeking for his human relations agenda.

After gestating for a full year, the proposed fair-employment ordinance moved forward, and it did so in a bolder form than the measure that had failed in 1946. Humphrey's allies on the city council introduced a statute that would outlaw racial or religious discrimination in virtually every workplace—government, labor union, private company with more than two employees. Moreover, unlike existing municipal and state fair-employment laws elsewhere, the Minneapolis version would fund a city commission to oversee compliance and impose penalties of up to a one-hundred-dollar fine and ninety days in the county workhouse.

The city attorney continued to oppose the proposed law as an illegal intrusion into hiring, and several members of Humphrey's own Human Relations Council from the business community voiced opposition. On January 15, 1947, after presentations by speakers, including Sam Scheiner, Genevieve Steefel, Robert Wishart of the CIO, and William Seabron of the Urban League, the measure squeaked through the city council's committee on ordinances by a vote of three to two. Even the alderman who cast the deciding vote, J. W. Straiton, worried aloud that "you can't change the hearts of people by legislation."[66]

By the time the full council took up the ordinance on January 31, the federal government's wartime fair-employment commission was staggering toward extinction, and the liberal minority in Minnesota's legislature was struggling to move forward a state law, which ultimately would die in committee. But against the backdrop of Lisa Murphy and the rest of Charles Johnson's female brigade going door-to-door in pursuit of a more equitable city, the council voted to enact the fair-employment law by the convincing margin of twenty-one to three.

Humphrey maintained the momentum by naming a deliberately diverse set of fair-employment commissioners—Raymond Cannon, a Black attorney whose activism traced back to the mob assault on Arthur Lee's home; Amos Deinard, also a lawyer, a fixture in the Jewish community; George Jensen, an executive at Kelvinator who was a leader in ecumenical efforts; and Lawrence Kelley, a Catholic and former president of the Junior Chamber of Commerce. The mayor received requests for copies of the Minneapolis ordinance from San Francisco, Dayton, Omaha, Los Angeles, Philadelphia, and New York City. The *New York Times* wrote about the law. Less than six months after Carey McWilliams had presented Minneapolis as the epitome of bigotry, Hubert Humphrey had transformed it into the national model of enlightened progress.

"As one zealot to another," Genevieve Steefel said in a handwritten note to the mayor, "I wish I could do more! More strength to you, and may it all come in the form of green cheese. You deserve a generous slice of the moon and I suspect you may get it!"[67]

* * *

The hate mail and telephone threats began arriving in November 1946, not coincidentally in the aftermath of Carey McWilliams's article and Humphrey's first public meetings about the self-survey. Along with the letters and calls appeared placards, tacked to trees on the University of Minnesota campus. One declared, "Kill Jews." Alluding to "The Curious Twin," another boasted, "When they start talking of racial equality, pull the safety catch on your gun. Hail to Minneapolis, capital of anti-Semitism."[68] The posters bore the *Sieg* rune insignia, a hybrid of lightning bolt and uppercase S, which Adolph Hitler had used as the symbol of his *Schutzstaffel* paramilitary, the SS. The letters came on stationery from a group called the Democratic Nationalist Party (DNP), which stipulated, "The United States was founded of, by, and for the people of European-Caucasian descent only." As for the mayor, "If you oppose us and serve as a tool of the Jewish Communist interests, we will promise you here and now that on the day of judgment, our day of victory, you will meet your just retribution."[69]

Whoever sent the ultimatums did so with tactical care. He did not often menace Humphrey directly. Rather, from late 1946 into the first weeks of 1947, he touched the circle of colleagues and allies around the mayor, as if doing so would magnify the aura of danger. He wrote to Reverend Youngdahl, chair of the Human Relations Council, and to Charles Bolte, national chairman of the American Veterans Committee, which had alerted Humphrey to the Matsuo housing discrimination case.[70] He advised J. L. Morrill, president of the university, to "rid the campus of all Catholics, Jews, Negroes, Communists, and other inferior persons to uphold the purer race and save the United State for democracy."[71] He dialed the private office line of Bradshaw Mintener, soon to be chair of the self-survey, and the Pillsbury executive had the presence of mind to start recording. "[L]isten carefully, you Jew Communist bastard," the voice told the Protestant Republican. "Just cease . . . any human relations activities whatsoever. Because if you don't, something might happen. This is a final warning by the DNP."[72]

Mintener turned over the recording to the St. Paul field office of the FBI. So did Gideon Seymour, editorial page editor of the *Star Journal*, after receiving a letter with the most detailed accusation yet, one that echoed the rhetoric of Gerald L. K. Smith:

> [T]wo of the fundamental parts of our Bill of Rights, namely Freedom of Speech and Freedom of Assembly, are abrogated by the local city administration, under the leadership of the infamous Jew and Negroe [*sic*] lover, Hubert Humphrey. Mr. Humphrey is a traitor to his people, and consequently the local group of the DNP has officially condemned him. At the proper time he will meet his just retribution. This is no idle threat, for we of the DNP have the resolute determination to obey the official pronouncements of our Supreme Party headquarters.[73]

The FBI submitted the letter to its national lab to search for fingerprints and determine the typewriter model. Agents from the St. Paul office met with an undercover informant for any tips he could provide. No leads initially emerged. The agents also passed along the Seymour letter to the assistant U.S. attorney for the region, Linus Hammond. He decided not to pursue an investigation because "the threat was only a veiled one."[74]

Not every law-enforcement official shared Hammond's blithe attitude. Ed Ryan, now the Hennepin County sheriff, had surveilled extremists both right and left during his days in the internal-security division of the Minneapolis Police Department. He evidently kept up his contacts, because one night in either late 1946 or early 1947, he got a tip that Humphrey was going to be shot.

Ryan tracked down the mayor and Muriel out for dinner in the Twin Cities suburbs with William Simms and his wife. Ryan called the restaurant, had Humphrey summoned to the phone, and told him, "We've just received word there's going to be an attempt on your life. Would you please get back to town as fast as you can? I'll send men out to meet you on the highway."[75] Humphrey did as instructed, and a squad car and several motorcycle officers escorted him and Muriel back to their home. Then either Ryan or Glenn MacLean, his successor as Minneapolis chief, placed an armed bodyguard in a police car outside the house every night for several weeks.

By the beginning of February, though DNP posters kept popping up on the university campus and outside a liberal Presbyterian church, the threats to Humphrey had subsided and his protection was removed. Over the nearly three months since the first warnings from the DNP had surfaced, even as some coverage appeared in the daily papers and the *American Jewish World*, Humphrey had clung to his normal schedule, with its council and committee meetings, its speeches and ribbon cuttings, and most of all, the push forward on the self-survey and the fair-employment ordinance. For Skipper Humphrey and his siblings, family life proceeded with its routine of peanut butter sandwiches and piano lessons and beef vegetable soup, with no sign from either parent that anything was amiss.

Thursday, February 6, unfolded as a typically hectic day of the Humphrey mayoralty. He attended a meeting of the charter commission that he kept hoping would persuade voters to grant the Minneapolis mayor more authority. He added five professors from the university to the self-survey research team. He split the evening between an AFL dinner at the Radisson honoring local teachers—knowing his audience, he used the occasion to call for increased school funding—and a banquet at the municipal auditorium for the start of Boy Scout anniversary week.

As midnight neared, Humphrey rode toward his home with several aldermen in a police car piloted by his regular driver, officer Vern Bartholomew, who was packing a .38. Normally, Bartholomew walked Humphrey to the front door, just to ensure that the mayor got inside safely. But it was miserable outdoors even by Minneapolis standards— below zero, a furious northwest wind, imminent snow—and Humphrey told Bartholomew to stay at the wheel and take the other passengers to their homes.

Oddly, the nearest streetlight to Humphrey's house was out. The moon, more than half full, was blotted out by storm clouds, and the only availably light seeped from a glass panel in the front door. Humphrey hunched over the lock and squinted at the keyhole, chilled fingers trying to guide the key. Hearing him at the door, Muriel opened it from the inside. Then, either from a stand of shrubbery or the side yard, a bullet whizzed past, followed by two more, clinking into the siding as they struck wide of their target. Humphrey ducked into the entry hall, blurting out, "Why would anyone shoot me?"

Then he and Muriel tried to piece together the sequence of events. Humphrey rummaged through the bushes, looking for spent shells. Muriel recalled having heard the gunshots, and assuming the sound was a car backfiring. And there was one more thing. Just before the noise, the family's dog Tippy had barked at something. It seemed possible, in retrospect, that the canine alarm had rattled the would-be assassin just enough to make him miss.[76]

Not until the next morning did Humphrey inform Glenn MacLean, ordering the police chief to keep the shooting incident out of regular crime reports "to avoid any publicity."[77] As an investigation belatedly commenced, Humphrey and Muriel coordinated a response of both personal and political stoicism. Skipper awoke to find a cop sitting in the living room, a shotgun across his lap. Bartholomew commenced nightly walks around the neighborhood to spot anything or anyone suspicious. For public purposes, however, Humphrey succeeded in keeping news of the shooting out of the papers and off the radio. When Hubert and Muriel arrived tardily to a planning meeting for his re-election campaign on the morning after, she presented their inner circle of advisors with the picture of poised nonchalance, explaining, "We're sorry we're late, but somebody took a shot at us coming down."[78] Before long, however, she began suffering migraine headaches that would plague her for decades to come.[79] Two weeks after the attack on Humphrey, the family dog, Tippy, inexplicably vanished.

Finally, on March 18, news broke of the assassination attempt, with the *Tribune* running the banner headline "3 SHOTS FIRED AT HUMPHREY." Even then, Humphrey refused to confirm the attack on the record. The article attributed the details, all of them factually accurate, to an "informant."[80] Whatever public sympathy for Humphrey the story may have stimulated, it also compelled his unknown assailant to disguise his crime through disinformation.

The day after the *Tribune* article, a letter reached Humphrey at city hall. It said the mayor's life was still in danger and pointed an accusatory finger at Jewish mob associates of a local nightclub manager, Rubin Shetsky, who was standing trial for the 1945 murder of a union organizer. The same correspondent wrote to Muriel at home three days later. Very cunningly, compared with the impeccable grammar and lexicon in letters from the DNP, this one adopted an ignorant affect:

Tell your Husband to be very carefull, I work for a Jewish Familie, I over heart a Conversation in an other Room ther was no name mention but I know it was sent for him. 4 big Jews goin to pay $5000 to bump somebody of, it is about the Gambling. They don't make enough money . . . keep this out of the Papers. The Papers is a Jew outfit tha Jews do anything for Money. wer there is Jews ther is Murder and Crime. They control every thing . . .

this is from a real Friend.[81]

Certainly, the Jewish gangsters of Minneapolis had more than enough blood on their hands to make plausible suspects. And there was a deep enough reservoir of anti-Semitism in Minneapolis to find ready believers for this theory of the case. There was, however, a glaring failure of logic on the writer's part. It was inconceivable that Kid Cann and his ilk, who considered themselves proud and legitimate members of the Minneapolis Jewish community, would try to kill a mayor who was cherished by their brethren for his battles against anti-Semitism. The mobsters might try to buy off Humphrey; in fact, they already had tried, to no avail. But murdering a popular mayor would have been really bad for business.

The FBI, in any event, was pursuing a very different sort of suspect. More than a thousand miles from Minneapolis, a neo-Nazi named Homer Loomis was on trial in February 1947. Despite the establishment pedigree of a prep-school diploma and admission to the Ivy League, Loomis had managed to be expelled from Princeton and blow apart two marriages. Still in his early thirties, he had headed South in 1946 to reinvent himself as a white supremacist. He joined forces in Atlanta with a Ku Klux Klan veteran to form a uniformed, goose-stepping troop dubbed the Columbians. Its intimidation and vigilante attacks against Black residents exceeded what Georgia's governor Ellis Arnall, a racial moderate by regional standards, would tolerate, and Loomis was charged with incitement to riot and usurping of police powers.

In the course of building the case against Loomis, investigators in Georgia discovered letters to the Columbians from the DNP of Minneapolis. The FBI proceeded to match fingerprints from those letters to ones on the hate mail sent to Humphrey, Gideon Seymour, and others in Minneapolis. Weeks later, linking the prints to a particular selective service record, agents determined that the fingers in question belonged to one Maynard Orlando Nelsen. Minneapolis detectives arrested him on April 23 in his parents' home in South Minneapolis.

In the process, the police found a German Luger, a .38-caliber pistol, bullets, a blackjack, and a pocketknife. They also found posters, pamphlets, and a logo stamp from the DNP. And they found letters to Nelsen from Mississippi Representative J. E. Rankin, one of the most outspoken bigots in Congress, and a copy of the conspiratorial book *The Red Network* by Elizabeth Dillig, who had been tried for sedition as a Nazi sympathizer.[82] From arms to ideology to propaganda, Nelsen possessed the complete toolkit of a terrorist.

As for Nelsen himself, he cut an unprepossessing figure. He was short and slight, with the fair features of his Norwegian-immigrant parents. After graduating from high school as an honor student, he had enlisted in the army and served in the Signal Corps. It was there, investigators later learned, that Nelsen began nursing resentments when soldiers whom he considered racially inferior were given the combat duty he craved. Discharged from the military and enrolled in the University of Minnesota, he had tried to attend the Gerald L. K. Smith rally in August 1946 that was broken up by left-wing protestors.[83] Like Smith himself, Nelsen laid the blame on Humphrey.

Nelsen unhesitatingly told police he was a "troop leader" for the DNP and had hung the racist and anti-Semitic posters on the university campus. Those disclosures earned him a charge of breaching the peace, the prospect of six months in the county workhouse, and a court-ordered psychiatric exam. He ultimately posted the thousand-dollar bond required to be released from jail.[84] By the late spring of 1947, Nelsen had decamped for Northern California, saying he planned to attend Stanford Law School. He was also reported by an informant of Sam Scheiner's to have ordered the replica of a Nazi uniform from a San Francisco clothier.[85]

By all the available records and press reports, Nelsen appears never to have been intensively investigated for Humphrey's shooting. Realistically, that oversight could only have had one cause: that Humphrey himself did not want the case prosecuted. Such a directive would have been consistent with his initial decision to hide the incident from public knowledge, to go about his mayoral duties as if nothing had ever happened. A high-profile trial surely would have risked providing Nelsen with a martyr's platform. It would have stolen time and energy from Humphrey's work on the self-survey and the new fair-employment law. Beyond all those factors, Humphrey may have considered Nelsen a lone crackpot rather than an ongoing threat, part of a larger malignancy in America.

Back during the mayoral campaign in 1945, no less an expert in white hatred than Cecil Newman had worried aloud that Humphrey was moving too far and too fast on civil rights for Minneapolis to tolerate. He didn't want Humphrey to abandon those positions, just to "soft-pedal" them temporarily for fear of the backlash.[86] In the days after the assassination attempt was revealed in the papers, a former Macalester colleague wrote to Humphrey, "The world is crazy enough without those who can and will give leadership getting themselves dead!"[87] A Jewish pharmacist urged the mayor, "Don't give a 'crank' an opportunity he is looking for. In as far as I am concerned—I'm sure in as far as many of your friends are concerned—I would much rather have a poor, shriveled worn out college professor called Hubert Humphrey than some illustrious national figure whose life is in constant danger."[88]

* * *

When Minneapolis went to the polls on June 9, 1947, the only drama in the mayoral race concerned the margin of Hubert Humphrey's victory. He outdid even his landslide of two years prior, driving record turnout, winning every ward, taking sixty-six percent of the vote, and running up a fifty-thousand-vote cushion over Frank Collins, playing the role of sacrificial lamb. Even that longtime scourge of liberalism, Reverend William Bell Riley, had recently written to Humphrey to recant his previous denunciations of the mayor. Nearing the end of his life, Riley was busily grooming his chosen successor, a Baptist prodigy in his twenties named Billy Graham.

The pressing question for the day after the election was how long Humphrey would stay in city hall. Minnesota would elect a governor and one senator in November 1948, and with both positions currently held by Republicans, Humphrey topped the list of prospective challengers. He was already building a national profile in terms of both public service and media coverage, even vaulting into discussions of future presidential timber after only two years as the mayor of a city of half a million people. The *New Republic* titled its feature article on Humphrey "Young Man in a Hurry" and predicted that "his debating talents and showmanship are admirably suited" to the Senate.[89] The Yiddish-language *Forverts* (Forward), the newspaper of record for generations of Jewish immigrants, speculated whether "this phenomenally successful" young mayor "is truly made of the stuff required of a national figure and national leader."[90]

Accustomed by now to the relentless demands of the mayoralty, perversely invigorated by them, Humphrey was an indefatigable figure whether mediating the strike at a tractor factory or arranging the construction of Quonset huts for veterans' housing or following the Fiorello LaGuardia playbook by reading the funnies over the radio when a polio quarantine was restricting home delivery of newspapers. He was a natural campaigner, a tireless flesh-presser with an incomparable memory for any voter he'd ever met, and a speechmaker easily capable of stemwinding three or four times a night. More than anything else, however, Humphrey's growing national stature arose from his prominence in the cause of civil rights.

The track record of Humphrey's two major civil rights efforts was actually rather mixed, though national journalists and politicians did not seem to notice. The municipal FEPC limped through 1947 without adequate funding, a paid staff, or any office besides a couple of desks in the city Welfare Department. The committee fielded only nine complaints between May and December 1947. Nell Dodson Russell, writing in the *Spokesman*, cast doubt on whether private employers would even follow the new ordinance: "Now that Minneapolis has an FEPC law, seems to me it's about time for some of those 'liberals' who do the hiring and firing to either put up or shut up. This business of spouting brotherhood all over the banquet circuit provides a good smokescreen but the real proof of the pudding is the number of brownskins on the payroll."[91]

As for the Human Relations Council, despite now being an official part of the city government, it still depended on outside donors. After all of Humphrey's fervent appeals to labor unions and corporations and individual philanthropists, the council reached the end of October 1947 $3,819 in debt and counted $7.42 in its bank account. The council still owed $850 in back salary to the executive director, Wilfred Leland, and more than eleven hundred to his secretary, Sally Stevens, who hadn't been paid in seven months, as well as another thousand to Herman Long and his team of researchers from Fisk. As a result, the timetable for completing the self-survey kept getting pushed back, now into the middle distance of 1948.[92] It was fair to wonder whether Humphrey's seeming achievements resembled the movie-set Main Streets in the Westerns he had watched as a kid, with all those bustling storefronts hiding the empty space behind them.

Yet, however fragile and precarious and nearly bankrupt the fair-employment commission and Human Rights Council were, their mere existence mattered in concrete ways. Minneapolis stood as virtually the only city in America where a wronged job applicant could count on the government as an ally. Put another way, racial fairness no longer depended on a lone savior like Charles Horn at Federal Cartridge. The law applied to bigots and humanitarians alike, and, in a rarity for Minneapolis and Minnesota, Humphrey's administration actually meant to enforce the law.

In its early months, the commission investigated the cases, among others, of a Black woman denied a job at Dayton's department store, a Nisei woman seeking work at Archer Daniels Midland, and a Jewish man who'd been rebuffed by a handbag factory. Laundries, factories, insurance agencies, hotels, the phone company, the Veterans Administration—the commission looked into the hiring practices of all of them.[93] The implicit pressure of the commission's presence lent sudden leverage to the Urban League, which had long been the main organization battling job discrimination. Sometimes all it took was for William Seabron, the league's industrial secretary, to quote the fair-employment statute to an obstinate boss.[94]

Barriers collapsed or were knocked over. At the start of the 1947–1948 school year, Minneapolis hired its first-ever Black public school teacher. Woolworth's employed its first Black waitress. The Veterans Administration in Minneapolis took on nineteen Black people as clerks, typists, and messengers, meriting front-page coverage in the *Spokesman*. Under scrutiny from the Human Rights Council, the city's housing agency increased the number of Black families being placed in public housing. A bartender who had spit in the glasses of two Black customers was arrested and faced a five-hundred-dollar fine—the equivalent of two months' income for the median American family—before pleading guilty in exchange for a lower penalty.[95] The *Tribune* followed the whole saga, magnifying the public humiliation.

For Humphrey, these local accomplishments translated into national recognition. Early in 1947, he became chair of the National Committee for Fair Play in Bowling, which was a lot more important than its name suggested. In the wake of Jackie Robinson breaking the color line in pro baseball in April 1947, the committee took on the segregated tournaments of the American Bowling Congress. Bowling was the fastest-growing recreational sport in America in the immediate postwar years, a nearly billion-dollar industry. Teams in local leagues were portrayed as American egalitarianism incarnate, next-door neighbors and factory-floor buddies racking up strikes and spares in friendly competition. The gaping flaw in that picture was that the American Bowling Congress, which held almost monopolistic power over tournaments and championships, still hewed to an 1895 "eligibility clause" limiting teams to members of the "white male sex."

There was no single Branch Rickey on hand to desegregate bowling as the Brooklyn Dodgers' owner had prised open baseball. Rather, the National Committee's leadership amounted to a *Who's Who* of civil rights and organized labor—Walter Reuther of the United Auto Workers, Walter White of the NAACP, Philip Murray of the CIO, and A. Philip Randolph of the Brotherhood of Sleeping Car Porters. The vice chair was Betty Hicks, a professional golfer and committed feminist. The committee aimed both to shame the American Bowling Congress by branding its tournaments with proper-noun labels like "Jim Crow," "Intolerance," and "Prejudice," and to outflank it by inviting interracial teams to a series of "All-American" bowling tournaments. Humphrey assembled one in Minneapolis just weeks after Robinson first trotted onto Ebbets Field. Like Robinson, he soon heard the bigoted catcalls of the crowd:

> So—the Jews have gotten to you and Miss Hick's [*sic*]. I'm an ex-G.I. who fought for America—but I know now these Jews & Communists are pouring money into a pot for Equality—its [*sic*] stupid Christians like you and Miss Hicks that Jews would not spit on . . . I'm also a Damn Yankee—but I'll be with the South when the Civil War comes. . . . Wake up, man.[96]

Most important to Humphrey's national standing, he found an ideological home for his form of liberalism, endangered as it was by the surging energies of Right and Left alike. This haven, this base, was an organization recently renamed the Americans for Democratic Action (ADA), and it owed its existence to the dual challenges posed by GOP conservatism and Progressive radicalism. Under its original name, the Union for Democratic Action (UDA), the group had puttered along through the war years as a kind of very junior partner in the Democratic Party, never sharing the tolerance for communism practiced elsewhere in the Popular Front and accruing fewer than ten thousand members coast to coast. Paradoxically, it was Henry Wallace's rupture with

Harry Truman, and the subsequent founding of Progressive Citizens of America, that breathed life into the UDA and supplied it with a compelling raison d'être.

The executive secretary of the UDA, a scholar of Romance languages named James Loeb, had come by his anti-communism the George Orwell way. Like the novelist, Loeb had aided the Republican[97] cause in the Spanish Civil War and was outraged when the Stalinist faction turned against its anarchist and socialist comrades in what was supposed to have been a unified struggle against Franco's Fascists. The mission statement of what would become the ADA took the unlikely form of a letter to the editor of the *New Republic*, in which Loeb posed three essential questions: Were the geopolitical tensions of the Cold War entirely due to "the imperialistic, capitalistic, power-made warmongering of Western democracies?" Would economic security be the only goal of the progressive movement and human freedom secondary? And should progressives work in political organizations that include Communists? The answer to all three, Loeb concluded, had to be *no*.[98]

One of Humphrey's DFL allies, Eugenie Anderson, brought the letter to his attention, and in August 1946, Loeb came to Minneapolis to meet with Humphrey, Anderson, Naftalin, and Kirkpatrick.[99] Three months later, Loeb invited Humphrey to join a planning meeting in Washington scheduled for early 1947. "There will be no speeches at the conference," Loeb assured him, "but a real effort to reach agreement as to where the non-Communist liberals are going at the present time and how they are going to get there." Referring to the midterm elections a week earlier, in which Republicans had retaken both houses of Congress, he added, "Surely, after these elections, we have a responsibility to think through our whole problem."[100] That problem, as the journalist and ADA leader James Wechsler put it in retrospect, was a political landscape composed of "a rising Republican reaction, a pro-Communist Left and nothing in between except the still inept, bumbling presidency of a man who wishes he wasn't there."[101]

Propitiously, the ADA conference took place in Washington's Willard Hotel less than two weeks after Henry Wallace had launched Progressive Citizens of America, positioning the organizations as direct rivals. The meeting on January 4, 1947, brought together what Eleanor Roosevelt hailed as "the best brains of liberalism."[102] Those brains belonged to, among others, Walter Reuther, Walter White, theologian Reinhold Niebuhr, garment union leader David Dubinsky, historian Arthur Schlesinger Jr., and attorney Joseph Rauh. Typically for Minnesota in January, a snowstorm grounded Humphrey's flight to Washington and he missed the founding meeting. Even in absentia, though, he was named to the ADA's organizing committee and soon rose to the position of national vice chairman. Humphrey also stood out among the ADA's inner circle of intellectuals, theoreticians, and interest-group executives as an elected official, someone who genuinely knew how to sell ideas, win elections, and pass laws.

Not surprisingly, the nascent ADA framed many of its goals in terms of global competition between East and West, between Marxism and liberal democracy. It had to demonstrate, in Reuther's words, "whether it is possible to feed, clothe, and house people without putting their souls in chains."[103] There were fissures within the ADA itself over how large a role anti-communism should play in its public persona, on whether it should devote more of its limited resources to battling the American right, and on how exactly it should engage or dispute with the Truman Administration. From the outset of the ADA, however, one portion of its domestic agenda was clear and consensual and fully attuned to Humphrey's own priorities: civil rights. The organization's document of "General Purposes" called for America to achieve "equality before the law and freedom for all persons to speak, to write, to worship and to vote as they choose, without regard to race, creed, color, or economic status."[104]

* * *

For the first time in more than a decade, when he had been an awestruck visitor from the South Dakota prairie, Hubert Humphrey entered the neoclassical grandeur of the U.S. Capitol. On that earlier trip, he had witnessed Congress during one of the most fruitful years of New Deal legislation, and the experience had ignited the audacious dream of serving in Washington himself. Now, on the cloudy Thursday morning of June 19, 1947, he returned not as a tourist but a participant, preparing to testify in favor of a proposed federal law on fair employment.

For all of Humphrey's recent stature as a big-city mayor, a rising national star, a politician synonymous with civil rights, he was encountering a hostile political atmosphere. In place of FDR's congressional majority back in 1935, Republicans now dominated, and on the very day of Humphrey's testimony, the House was in the process of overriding President Truman's veto of the Taft–Hartley bill with its rollback of labor union rights. From the other political direction, Henry Wallace had drawn more than ten thousand listeners to a Washington speech just three nights earlier, with some chanting, "Wallace in '48!" Such was the vise squeezing Truman, Humphrey, and the ADA, on whose behalf he was appearing.

Midway through the morning, in a hearing room on the ground floor of the Capitol, Humphrey took his seat before a five-member subcommittee of the Senate's Labor and Public Welfare Committee, which was considering Senate Bill 984. The measure would create a permanent federal Fair Employment Practices Commission, the preeminent goal of civil rights activists nationwide. In theory, Humphrey might have expected a favorable reception, given that the bill had been co-sponsored by the subcommittee's chair, a liberal Republican from New Jersey, H. Alexander Smith. Humphrey had come prepared with a lengthy statement, describing Minneapolis's efforts with the self-survey and fair-employment ordinance, and offering that statute as a proven model for a federal law. But he made it no further than the recitation of his academic credentials before the confrontation began.

It emanated from one specific senator, Allen Ellender of Louisiana, whose interest had been piqued by the mention of Humphrey's graduate studies at Louisiana State. Ellender was a protégé of Huey Long's, even assuming the Kingfish's former Senate seat, and he had been an ardent enough New Dealer to vote for FDR's court-packing plan. At the same time, Ellender's devotion to segregation never wavered. Perhaps he had been intending to disparage Humphrey as an arrogant Northerner, willfully ignorant of the South's cherished values. Instead, he swiveled to another angle, inviting Humphrey the former Louisianan to affirm that "the people of both races lived together pretty well, and agree amicably, do they not?"

To which Humphrey replied, "I have great admiration for the people of Louisiana. I just think that they are actually injuring themselves by not permitting . . . all people, regardless of their race, their color, national origin, or ancestry to fullest participation in the civic life of this community."

"You would advocate . . . for social equality?" Ellender asked a moment later, uttering the polite euphemism for what bigots more commonly termed "mongrelization of the races."

"I am," Humphrey answered.[105]

Having failed twice already to ruffle Humphrey on the subject of Louisiana, Ellender turned his focus to the Twin Cities. How many Negroes (his word) lived there? What was the total population? Humphrey supplied the estimates.

"That is about two percent," Ellender announced. "What if you had a fifty-fifty ratio?"

"Discrimination for one or a hundred is just as bad."

The dialogue continued along these lines as the other subcommittee members remained silent. Was it true, Ellender wanted to know, that there was anti-Semitism in Minneapolis? Plenty of it, Humphrey admitted. And who hates the Jews, the Louisiana senator persisted, isn't it the Negroes? Aren't Negroes prejudiced, too? Every population group, Humphrey conceded, contains a share of intolerant people. But the greatest amount of bigotry, he added, whether bigotry against Blacks or Jews or Catholics or Japanese, came from the majority group. Everybody in the hearing room knew full well that Humphrey meant white Christians, in Minneapolis and in America. Not for the first or last time, he was indicting his own people. As Humphrey had said of the self-survey earlier in his testimony, "We are looking in the mirror. We want to see our own reflection."[106]

Eventually, Ellender grew tired of badgering Humphrey and turned the hearing over to Smith. He, in turn, spoke all too belatedly in defense of his own bill and expressed gratitude to Humphrey for supporting it.

Then it was time for the next witness. Humphrey, however, was not yet done. He handed over the text of his undelivered testimony so it could be entered into the official record of the hearing. On page 445 of the subsequent transcript, those words describe a battle larger than any one particular piece of legislation and the domain of one city's mayor, something more like the struggle for the national soul:

> [O]ur conscience in America has become corroded and encrusted with a bitter feeling of guilt, because we profess a belief in justice and equality of opportunity, but we practice injustice and discrimination against the members of minority racial, religious, and nationality groups in every one of these United States . . .
>
> This is a problem of national morality. . . . We cannot hold up our heads as self-respecting American citizens, and we certainly cannot successfully aspire to leadership in world affairs, as long as we make mockery of our high-sounding talk about justice and democracy by practices of discrimination which destroy the dignity and deny the rights of millions of our fellow citizens.[107]

CHAPTER 9

THE COMING
CONFRONTATION

Civil Rights and the Democratic Party

October 1947–June 1948

In the fall of 1947, the Americans for Democratic Action (ADA) put Hubert Humphrey on the road to Philadelphia, where the Democratic Party would hold its nominating convention the following July. Humphrey's autumn itinerary bounced him from California to Connecticut and back, wherever the ADA was trying to build a local chapter and piece by piece expand its influence in the party. So dependent was the ADA on Humphrey as its public face, so reliant on his eloquence and charisma, that something like panic ensued when illness interrupted the speaking schedule. "What Massachusetts did to Sacco and Vanzetti is nothing to what will happen to us if anything should prevent your being in Boston Saturday evening November 8," wrote Joseph Rauh and James Loeb in a joint telegram. "We are figuratively and literally down on our knees."[1]

Early October found Humphrey delivering four major speeches within eight days to union and education conventions on the West Coast. After stops in Sacramento, Los Angeles, and Santa Barbara, Humphrey landed in San Francisco to address the American Federation of Labor on October 8. While Humphrey had commonly given three or four speeches in a single day ever since Works Progress Administration (WPA) days in the early 1940s, the California events all promised audiences in the thousands and national, even international, attention.

Civil rights served both principled and strategic purposes for the ADA. By the organization's thinking, a strong stand on racial equality would help the Democrats stave off the expected third-party challenge from Henry Wallace and compete against the prospective Republican candidate, Thomas Dewey, both of whom were firmly associated with the cause. In the global arena of the Cold War, American influence in Asia, Africa, and Latin America suffered when the persistence of segregation in both its statutory and vigilante forms handed the Soviet Union a propaganda weapon. So breaking the grip of Southern Democrats on the party fit squarely into ADA's ethos of liberal anti-communism.

Along with that broad mandate from the ADA, Humphrey held particular goals for the American Federation of Labor (AFL) speech. While ADA prided itself on selectivity and self-discipline, not unlike the communist front groups it despised, the AFL could provide both blue-collar credibility and foot soldiers for mass campaigns. In lining up political support for the civil rights program that Harry Truman had begun to lay out—much to the ADA's surprise and satisfaction—Humphrey sought to win over an alliance of craft unions that had historically practiced segregation and discrimination.

On this mission, Humphrey traveled with two key companions. One was his wife Muriel, freed briefly to resume her role as confidant and advisor while Orville and Jane Freeman babysat the children back in Minneapolis. The other was Andrew Biemiller, the political director of the ADA, its chief on-the-ground strategist, and at forty-one a seasoned veteran of the factional wars on the American left.

Biemiller had grown up in the industrial city of Sandusky, Ohio, where his introduction to the concept of racial equality took place at the double desk in grade school that he shared with a Black classmate and on the youth baseball team, with four whites and five Blacks in the starting lineup.[2] After college and several years as a professor, Biemiller veered into labor organizing and left-wing politics, even managing several states for Norman Thomas's Socialist Party campaign for president in 1932. Settled in Wisconsin by then, Biemiller won election to the state legislature in 1937 as part of the Progressive Party before shifting to the Democrats in protest of the Progressives' isolationism and winning the congressional seat from a Milwaukee district in 1944.

Very much like Humphrey, Biemiller operated within a precarious middle ground, simultaneously attacked as being too radical and not radical enough. He lost his congressional re-election in 1946 to a Red-baiting Republican who "wondered whether Stalin would have voted any differently than Biemiller."[3] Yet Biemiller had been part of the fervently anti-communist Union for Democratic Action almost since its inception, and while campaigning for Humphrey during the 1947 mayoral race, he had observed Elmer Benson's Popular Front wing dominating the Democratic-Farmer-Labor (DFL) Party. When it wasn't easy for any liberal to be a Truman man, Biemiller still considered himself one.

He was a Humphrey man, too. Three months before the AFL speech, Biemiller had drafted a "Memo of Political Recommendations" for the ADA. Assuming Truman's renomination for president, Biemiller contended, "The fights in the Democratic convention will be on the vice-presidency and the platform." Only victories there, he went on, could spare the party "a conservative front."[4] Barely two years into elected office of any kind, Humphrey was integral to both prongs of Biemiller's plan, as an advocate for civil rights during the platform wrangling and as a potential candidate for vice president.

Biemiller knew and understood the criticisms—Humphrey the gasbag, Humphrey the know-it-all, Humphrey the glutton for approval. Biemiller happened to disagree. "Now, a lot of people used to be mad at him because they claimed he was talking too much about too many things," Biemiller later recalled. "He actually *knew* those things." And as a campaigner, "[H]e was inspired by people. The more he associated with people, the stronger he got. I mean even physically stronger, you got the impression. Now that's rare."

Even so, it took no small degree of commitment to Humphrey and civil rights for Biemiller to be chaperoning these California speeches. He was paying out of his own pocket for the trip, because the ADA had fallen hundreds of dollars behind in reimbursing him.[5] Humphrey struck a similar note in an October letter to an ADA leader in Rochester,

Minnesota: "We have never kidded ourselves about the difficulty of the job we are undertaking. We are under-staffed, under-financed and overworked."[6]

The day of Humphrey's speech to the AFL could hardly have unfolded with more disruption. During the morning session, the union's combative general counsel, Joseph Padway, was midway through a tirade against the Taft–Hartley Act when he collapsed with a brain hemorrhage and slipped into a coma. Another oversized personality, President John L. Lewis of the United Mine Workers, upheaved the next order of business when he publicly refused to sign the non-communist oath required of union leaders under Taft–Hartley. Whether Humphrey realized it or not, he mounted the rostrum of the Civic Auditorium that afternoon to face a distracted, unsettled audience, and a contingent of newspaper reporters who already had decided upon their next day's leads based on the turbulent morning.

Oblivious to the mood of the room, Humphrey launched into a meandering excursion through family history, Depression economics, voter turnout in the 1946 midterms, postwar inflation, the New Deal, reactionary Republicans, and that reliable villain for a union convention, Taft–Hartley. Thousands of words issued from Humphrey, and several ovations interrupted him, and on and on he spoke. When he finally arrived at the issue for which the AFL most needed his persuasive talents, civil rights, he was forty minutes into the oration, and he zigzagged from concentration camps to the Minneapolis Fair Employment Practices Committee (FEPC) to a strained analogy involving entrenched prejudice and the ulcers he had treated customers for as a young druggist. No longer cheering, the AFL delegates sat restlessly at long tables covered with their newspapers and fedoras. Nearly lost in Humphrey's thicket of verbiage was a passage in which he nodded to the unkept promise of Double V: "America can no longer afford to keep certain people from participating. We need their help these days. We needed them to die for democracy, didn't we? We needed them when we had to fight for democracy. I submit to this audience that we need them when we live."[7]

With that appeal made, Humphrey assured the audience, "Just a few more words and then I will conclude my remarks." Instead, he went on for another fifteen hundred words, and the applause at the end of his fifty-minute disquisition may have arisen from relief as much as enthusiasm. Humphrey, however, was sure he had wowed them. Back at his hotel with Muriel and Biemiller, expecting an effusive answer, Humphrey asked, "How did I do?"

"Well, Hubert, look, great," Biemiller replied gingerly. "But, Jesus, what a chance you took. An AF of L convention, anybody gets cheers at the end of twenty minutes, they'd better quit. Thirty-five minutes, you certainly should have quit."

Humphrey fumed.

"Goddamn it," he shot back to Biemiller. "They listened, didn't they?"

"Yes, they did."

Then Muriel, who had been subjected to Humphrey's logorrhea since their courtship days, and who usually saved her political advice for the confidentiality of pillow talk, interjected: "Hubert, some day you must learn that to be immortal, a speech does not have to be eternal."[8]

Humphrey returned with Muriel to Minneapolis "somewhat battered and torn,"[9] as he wrote to Franklin Delano Roosevelt's son James Roosevelt, and with out-of-town speeches in Chicago and Omaha looming. The whirlwind schedule left him with pneumonia and Biemiller "on the verge of nervous exhaustion."[10] Humphrey's physician admitted him to a hospital and ordered doses of sulfa and penicillin along with two weeks of rest, no speaking engagements allowed. Not since his childhood siege of influenza had Humphrey fallen so ill. It was appropriate that his mother, Christine, who had endured the harrowing experience of a child's near-death, had been warning him for months by now, "I always hope and pray you not give so many speeches. It's too much for you. You can't do justice to the speeches or to yourself."[11]

Temporarily and uncharacteristically idled, Humphrey also had to reckon with the price of being a political comet. In the preceding months, Orville Freeman had railed about Humphrey's habit of double-booking his schedule and missing key appointments. His daughter Nancy had taken to writing pleading notes for him to come home for dinner. Most embarrassing of all, Humphrey had forgotten to thank his sister Frances for the box of Christmas gifts she had sent to the family. The woman who had so inspired and influenced him, who was still trying to do so now as a social worker among the poor in Georgia, was just another unchecked item on the to-do list. "[I]t's rather hard to accept a status of complete non-communication between our two families," Frances had written Hubert few months earlier. "It's doubly difficult for me, since we once were so close in interests & affection. I think it would be strange indeed if I did not keenly feel the loss of our friendship. I realize that you have grown in stature as a man and as a citizen of our great country, but surely such intelligence and spiritual growth does not mean that you completely cut off old ties and contacts."[12]

Humphrey had replied with contrition—"Letters like yours make me realize what a jerk I am"[13]—but he stuck with the life he had chosen. Recovered from pneumonia, he climbed back into the centrifuge, simultaneously playing mayor, ADA vice chair, spokesman for fairness in both bowling and employment, and prospective candidate for senator or governor or vice president. The 1948 presidential election drew closer by the day, and with it the pressure on Humphrey to deliver some kind of breakthrough on civil rights. Even though the Republicans and Democrats would not formally nominate their presidential tickets until the next summer, Henry Wallace announced his Progressive Party candidacy three days before the end of 1947. "We are not for Russia and we are not for Communism," he declared in a radio address, jabbing at liberal foes such as the ADA, "but we recognize Hitlerite methods when we see them in our own land."[14]

Humphrey had an especially astute grasp of the electoral challenge that Wallace posed. Regardless of how relentlessly the ADA depicted Wallace as a Commie dupe, he commanded vast support among Black voters. Humphrey knew as much from being Cecil Newman's friend and reading each week's *Spokesman*. Far from being put off by Wallace's alleged ties to Communist Party members, Newman had appreciated the party's involvement in civil rights as far back as the Scottsboro Boys case in the 1930s. When the Democratic establishment dumped Wallace in favor of Truman as Roosevelt's running mate in 1944, Newman had condemned it as "political appeasement that will live in infamy along with Munich."[15] The editor's admiration only grew as Wallace traveled through the Deep South in late 1947, defying segregation laws to address interracial crowds in Atlanta and Norfolk, appealing to listeners at Black churches and colleges, shattering barriers as no major-party candidate ever had. On the day before announcing his candidacy, Wallace spoke in Tulsa before the national convention of Alpha Phi Alpha, a Black fraternity that claimed such members as W. E. B. Du Bois and Paul Robeson and fought for voting rights under the slogan "A Voteless People Is a Hopeless People."

Newman made sure to cover that speech in the *Spokesman*, and he approvingly quoted Wallace telling the Alphas, "The abolition of Jim Crow must have top place on the agenda of a program for national defense. Until it is abolished, the words 'democracy' and 'freedom' and 'justice' used to glibly support our foreign policy will ring hollow throughout the world."[16] Three weeks later, Newman put Wallace back on the front page for his meeting with fifty Black leaders. The week after that, a cub reporter named Carl Rowan[17] reported on the *Spokesman's* straw poll of Black voters statewide. Wallace took sixty percent of the vote with Truman in third place, behind Dewey, at nineteen percent. "The other parties will have to do battle for these voters, and tagging Mr. Wallace with the 'Red' label will not demolish their faith or cool their ardor," predicted an editorial that Newman reprinted from the National Association for the Advancement of Colored People's (NAACP's) magazine *The Crisis*. "They are accustomed to being mis-labeled, mis-represented, and mis-treated because they want their rights. To use their language, Wallace is 'straight on our question.'"[18]

* * *

Seven days into 1948, Harry Truman ascended the podium to deliver his State of the Union address to a joint session of Congress. Only pallid, polite applause, even from his own party, had acknowledged the president's arrival in the House chamber. As Truman moved toward a bank of microphones for the nationwide radio broadcast of the speech, those twin embodiments of Republican control of Congress, the Speaker of the House and President Pro Tempore of the Senate, sat behind and above him in stony silence. Truman's approval rating in the Gallup poll was in the midst of plummeting from the low sixties to the low forties, the consequence of postwar inflation afflicting the economy and conservatives from both parties blocking the president's "Fair Deal" legislative agenda.[19] As for the senators and representatives, Truman had predicted in his diary the previous night, "They won't like the address, either."[20]

Much of the five-thousand-word speech amounted to familiar pleas for continuing a New Deal style of social compact, and the response met Truman's low expectations. He went twenty-six minutes into a forty-one-minute address before receiving the first smattering of applause from the Democratic side of the aisle, and the ritual was repeated only five more times, mostly in response to Truman's calls for tax credits and a strong national defense.[21] The next morning's newspapers echoed the same conclusion. "Congress Hostile," read the headline in the *New York Herald Tribune*, "Congress Cold to Message" in the *Washington Post*, and "COLD RECEPTION GIVEN TRUMAN" in the *Des Moines Register*.

Amid the desultory performance, however, Truman had struck one daring note, and it surely was part of the reason he had anticipated the disgruntled reception. The very first topic that Truman took up in the speech, preceding the typical State of the Union wish list of legislation, was what he pointedly called "the essential human rights of our citizens." Harking back to the Bill of Rights, and also to his predecessor FDR, Truman saluted the United States for protecting the freedoms of speech, worship, and thought. Yet despite the nation's "deep concern for human rights," he went on, America continued to deny those rights, and equal protection under law, to "some of our citizens." To make his meaning explicit, Truman declared, "Whether discrimination is based on race, or creed, or color, or land of origin, it is utterly contrary to American ideals of democracy."[22]

This was neither the first nor last time of the Truman presidency that he advocated for civil rights. Yet the insertion of such language in the

State of the Union address, what one advisor termed "the opening gun" of the 1948 campaign, essentially put civil rights in the "Democratic platform, five months before his party's Philadelphia convention," as the *Washington Post* put it.[23] And the near-silent response from the congressional audience attested to two realities: the unlikelihood that Truman's program would ever be enacted and the unlikelihood that he would be the one to propose it.

Truman had grown up in the border state of Missouri as the descendant of two grandfathers who owned Black human beings and an uncle who had fought for the Confederacy. For most of his life, he privately told racist jokes and used the most notorious racial slur about Black people. Given the necessity of competing for Black voters during his evolving political career in Kansas City, Truman had taken stances in favor of a federal anti-lynching law and a permanent Fair Employment Practices Committee. Still, as he told the National Colored Democratic Association in 1940, "I am not appealing for social equality for the Negro," adding in condescending fashion, "The Negro himself knows better than that." Six months into his presidency, Truman defended the decision of his wife Bess to be fêted by the Daughters of the American Revolution (DAR) at the same time when the DAR, in a replay of the Marian Anderson controversy, was barring the Black jazz pianist Hazel Scott from performing in Constitution Hall.[24]

The transformation of Harry Truman on racial issues began, as much as it did in a single time or place, when a Greyhound bus carrying a newly discharged sergeant named Isaac Woodard pulled into Batesburg, South Carolina, on February 12, 1946. Woodard, a Black man, had been feuding with the white bus driver about being able to use a bathroom during stops, always a fraught event in the segregated South. The driver ordered Woodard off the bus in Batesburg, and the decorated veteran, still in his uniform, was soon confronted and beaten by the town sheriff, Lynwood Shull. Woodard managed to wrest away Shull's blackjack, only to have to release it when another police officer threatened to shoot him. Shull resumed the beating, driving the tip of his blackjack repeatedly in Woodard's eye sockets. When Woodard awoke in jail the next morning, he was blind.[25]

Over the next six months, Woodard became the emblem of America's undiminished race hate. While there were similar attacks on returned Black veterans during the same period—men who were lynched, shot, whipped, or beaten for such affronts as voting in a primary election or removing a Jim Crow sign from a streetcar[26]—the photograph of Woodard in his uniform with dark glasses shielding sightless eyes provided an icon of intolerance. Prompted by Walter White of the NAACP, Orson Welles devoted several episodes of his radio show to Woodard's case. A benefit concert for Woodard at City College in New York, co-sponsored by the boxing champion Joe Louis, drew more than twenty thousand spectators to hear musicians including Billie Holiday, Cab Calloway, and Woody Guthrie, who wrote a protest song for the occasion.[27] Woodard himself spoke across the country, including a stop in St. Paul that Cecil Newman covered in the *Spokesman*. Instead of the fulfillment of Double V, as Woodard told the audience at City College, "I spent three-and-a-half years in the service of my country and thought that I would be treated like a man when I returned to civilian life, but I was mistaken."[28]

With Woodard's blinding as its prime example, the National Association of Colored Women's Clubs picketed the White House to demand a federal investigation of attacks on Black veterans, and the NAACP dispatched six members of its National Emergency Committee against Mob Violence to meet with Truman on September 19, 1946. Walter White described the growth of extremist groups targeting Catholics and Jews, then the series of attacks on Black veterans, and finally, in unflinching detail, the torture of Isaac Woodard. It activated some nerve of personal decency in Truman. "My God!" he told White. "I have [sic] no idea it was as terrible as that! We have got to do something."[29]

Truman did two things. The Justice Department brought criminal charges against Sheriff Shull on September 26, 1946. Then, safely past the disastrous midterm elections in December, Truman followed the urgings of his aide David Niles and Attorney General Tom Clark to appoint a presidential Committee on Civil Rights. Very much in the model of Humphrey's Human Rights Council, Truman headed the panel with a corporate executive of centrist politics, General Electric president Charles Wilson, and populated it with painstaking diversity. "Noah's Ark," as newspapers wryly called the committee, contained pairs of women, Jews, Catholics, Blacks, labor leaders, moderate Southerners, and business people.[30] Part of the committee's mandate under Executive Order 9808 was to investigate the state of race relations in the United States, much as the Minneapolis self-survey would begin doing several months later, and part of it was to determine which local, state, and federal laws "may be strengthened and improved to safeguard the civil rights of people."[31]

While the committee embarked on its mission, Walter White kept Truman visibly and audibly tied to civil rights by inviting him to address the NAACP, the first American president to do so. Standing before the Lincoln Memorial in the company of Eleanor Roosevelt, facing a crowd of ten thousand, Truman implicitly evoked the previous decade's pinnacle of civil rights activism—Marian Anderson's concert for a vast, interracial audience. While she had expressed the quest for equality through the spirituals of the Black Church, Truman struck a register of eloquence quite distinct from his usual plodding style with a prepared text:

Our immediate task is to remove the last remnants of the barriers, which stand between millions of our citizens and their birthright. There is no justifiable reason for discrimination because of ancestry, or religion. Or race, or color.

We must not tolerate such limitations on the freedom of any of our people and on their enjoyment of the basic rights, which every citizen in a truly democratic society must possess.

Every man should have the right to a decent home, the right to an education, the right to adequate medical care, the right to a worthwhile job, the right to an equal share in the making of public decisions through the ballot, and the right to a fair trial in a fair court . . .

Many of our people still suffer the indignity of insult, the harrowing fear of intimidation, and, I regret to say, the threat of physical injury and mob violence. The prejudice and intolerance in which these evils are rooted still exist. The conscience of our nation, and the legal machinery which enforces it, have not yet secured to each citizen full freedom from fear.

We cannot wait another decade or another generation to remedy those evils. We must work, as never before, to cure them now.[32]

Passionate as Truman's rhetoric was, the force of his committee's report surpassed it. Released on October 30, 1947, *To Secure These Rights* delivered a moral indictment of America, the national equivalent of the unsparing community surveys that Charles Johnson and Herman Long had been doing in cities across the land, including Humphrey's Minneapolis. The report's preface bluntly stated that the committee "almost exclusively focused our attention on the bad side of our record," that it viewed individual atrocities as "reflections of deeper maladies," and that the problem of bigotry was national in scope even if "many of the most serious violations of civil rights have taken place in the South."[33] Lynching, police brutality, the poll tax, restrictive covenants, infant mortality, and more—*To Secure These Rights* painted a withering portrait with data and charts in addition to anecdotal evidence.

To fulfill the promise of American democracy, the committee set forth a package of laws and a vision of the federal government serving as the "friendly vigilant defender of the rights and equalities of all Americans."[34] The recommendations—including laws against lynching, the poll tax, police brutality, and restrictive covenants; a permanent FEPC; equality in public accommodations; the creation of both an ongoing Commission on Civil Rights reporting to the president and a standing committee on civil rights in Congress—amounted to the boldest, most comprehensive federal action on racial inequality in the seventy years since Reconstruction had been abandoned.

"It may be impossible to overcome prejudice by law," the report asserted, anticipating the coming objections, "but many of the evil discriminatory practices which are visible manifestations of prejudice can be brought to an end through proper governmental controls. . . . The Committee rejects the argument that government controls are themselves threats to liberty. This statement overlooks the fact that freedom in a civilized society is always founded on law enforced by government. Freedom in the absence of law is anarchy."[35]

In one respect, *To Secure These Rights* backed Truman into a corner, saddling him with the choice of polarizing the country with a second Reconstruction or hypocritically disowning the very report he had authorized. In another way, though, the prospect of Truman pursing civil rights through a combination of legislation and executive orders made electoral sense.

One month after *To Secure These Rights* was released, Truman received a more private assessment bearing on civil rights. It was a forty-three-page memo surveying the state of the 1948 presidential race, largely written by the former FDR aide James Rowe, known as an antagonist of Truman's and therefore likely to be ignored. So it officially bore the name of presidential counselor Clark Clifford. The segregationist South and labor-oriented West would remain safely Democratic, the memo predicted, and so the election would hinge on such swing states in the Northeast and Midwest as New York, Illinois, Ohio, Pennsylvania, and Michigan. In those states, Black voters held a pivotal portion of votes. Truman's expected Republican opponent, Governor Dewey of New York, had a proven appeal to Black voters based on his enactment of a state fair-employment law and consistent support for civil rights. Truman could not passively expect that the Black voters who had gradually been migrating from the party of Lincoln to FDR's New Deal coalition would stay put. The "rising dominance of Southern conservatives" in Congress, with their implacable opposition to civil rights, was unacceptable. "Unless there are new and real efforts (as distinguished from mere political gestures which are today thoroughly understood and strongly resented by sophisticated Negro leaders)," the memo warned Truman, "the Negro bloc, which, certainly in Illinois and probably in New York and Ohio, <u>does</u> hold the balance of power, will go Republican."[36]

In the international sphere, too, Truman had pragmatic reason to move forward on civil rights. American diplomats in Moscow had been pointing out since the previous year that state-controlled Soviet newspapers such as *Trud* seized the moral high ground simply by recapitulating factually accurate articles from the "progressive American press" about lynching, job discrimination, and other bigoted practices. In the battle between East and West for what was then called the "developing world," as well as in the struggle between the communist left and social democrats in Western Europe, the Soviets could plausibly argue that "American professions of liberty and equality under democracy were a sham."[37] The press in countries ranging from Ghana to India to the Philippines critically portrayed American racism. In the United States, Black activists from both the National Negro Congress and the NAACP petitioned the United Nations in 1946 and 1947, respectively, for "relief from oppression." The NAACP document, largely written by W. E. B. Du Bois, asserted, "It is not Russia that threatens the United States as much as Mississippi; not Stalin and Molotov but Bilbo and Rankin; internal injustice done to one's brothers is far more dangerous than the aggression of strangers from abroad."[38]

With both the national and global implications in mind, Truman delivered his State of the Union address. However lofty it was as a statement of his ideals, it clearly crashed as a political appeal, even to his own party. Not quite four weeks later, on February 2, 1948, Truman returned to the Capitol to address a special joint session of Congress on the sole topic of civil rights. "They no doubt will receive it as coldly as they did my State of the Union message," he wrote in his diary. "But it needs to be said."[39]

Building on his commission's report, Truman called for Congress to enact a ten-point program. Among other goals, it would outlaw lynching, establish a permanent FEPC, ban segregation in interstate travel, end the poll tax, and create both a Division of Civil Rights in the Department of Justice and a joint congressional committee on civil rights. Truman vowed to use his own executive authority to halt discrimination in federal employment and have the defense secretary "take steps to have the remaining instances of discrimination in the armed forces eliminated as rapidly as possible." While Truman stopped short of directly attacking the entire edifice of Jim Crow, and while he invoked deliberately vague language about "protecting more adequately the right to vote," his program far exceeded anything Franklin Roosevelt had ever attempted and outdid any Republican president since Ulysses Grant. "We shall not . . . finally achieve the ideals for which this Nation was founded," Truman declared, summoning the full weight of history, "so long as any American suffers discrimination as a result of his race, or religion, or color, or the land of origin of his forefathers."[40]

One of Truman's intended audiences reacted as he had hoped. The *Chicago Defender*, the nation's most influential Black newspaper, hailed his speech as "a courageous attack upon racism in America and a noble declaration of principles." In the *Pittsburgh Courier*, the newspaper that had created the Double V campaign, columnist George S. Schuyler wrote, "President Truman went all the way in demanding an end to racial bias. Such words give hope and comfort to those who have been battling for the application of Christian principles to race relations for many years."[41] But the *Spokesman* made only cursory mention of Truman's speech, one more indication of Cecil Newman's support for Henry Wallace.

On the white side of American politics, everything from passive resistance to prospective mutiny quickly developed. Predictably enough, Southern Democrats in Congress denounced the speech as "the platform of the Communist Party."[42] The syndicated columnist David Lawrence skeptically dismissed Truman's address as a "clever piece of politics" to pander to Black voters. Truman submitted the language for a civil rights bill to Alben Barkley, the Kentucky Democrat who was minority leader in the Senate, whereupon Barkley, anticipating a Southern filibuster, never even introduced it.

The direness of Truman's predicament appeared most vividly on what was normally the occasion for Democratic celebration, Jefferson–Jackson Day on February 19. When Truman rose to speak that evening to an integrated audience in Washington's Mayflower Hotel, the table for South Carolina's contingent, located directly in front of the podium, sat pointedly empty. Press photographers clicked away at the visual insult to the president. No sooner had Truman uttered the standard greeting, "Mister Chairman, fellow Democrats,"[43] than half of the eight hundred Arkansas Democrats listening by radio linkup in a Little Rock banquet hall stood up and marched out. The United Press International article on their protest made front pages nationwide.[44]

Even though Truman continued to embrace his civil rights agenda when he announced on March 8 that he would seek re-election, the cumulative message had gotten through. Jim Rowe and Clark Clifford just might have been wrong in their memo. When those Arkansas partisans had walked out, was it bluster, a show of leverage, or an actual threat? In a presidential election, it was true, the South was hardly going to embrace Republicans, the historical enemy. But in the internal struggle for the Democratic nomination, a South solidly aligned against Truman posed a palpable risk. Even before the July nominating convention and November vote, Truman needed Southern votes in Congress to push through the Marshall Plan. As for the general public, eighty-two percent of respondents to a Gallup poll in early March opposed passage of Truman's civil rights program; a mere nine percent supported it.[45] Breaking the promises in his congressional address, Truman never moved forward with executive orders to desegregate the military and ensure fair employment in the federal workforce. In a private meeting with a delegation of Southern governors four days after the Jefferson–Jackson Day protests, Democratic Party national chairman J. Howard McGrath assured them that Truman's 1948 campaign platform would reiterate the deliberately ambiguous plank on civil rights that the segregationists had accepted in 1944.

"There was some question in everybody's mind as to whether the President would get the nomination if he didn't back off a little," Truman's advisor on civil rights, Philleo Nash, later recalled. "I think it was an estimate of political reality." Blacks, Jews, and liberals like Humphrey and the ADA would just have to be satisfied with "a report and a strong message," mere symbolism. "The strategy," as Nash put it, was to "backtrack after the bang."[46]

* * *

Thirteen days after Harry Truman delivered his 1948 State of the Union speech with its appeal for civil rights, an inaugural parade coursed through the teeming streets of Jackson, Mississippi. Bombers from the state's National Guard streaked through the overcast sky, thirteen marching bands strutted, and in the atypically flamboyant setting of a red convertible, a career politician named Fielding Wright rode toward the State Capitol to be sworn in. From a platform adorned with patriotic bunting, with the backdrop of 350 Mississippi colonels in uniform, Wright droned through sixteen legal pages of past achievements and future promises, a litany ranging from road construction to public education to forestry and agriculture.

Finally, he arrived at what the thousands of spectators had come to hear. Point by point, Wright objected to the laws that Truman's Committee of Civil Rights had proposed in late 1947—federal bans on poll taxes and lynching, a fair-employment commission. Then Wright let fly. "These measures, and the proposals of this Committee are deliberately aimed to wreck the South and our institutions," he thundered. "But they are far more sinister . . . for, hidden under their misleading titles and guarded phraseology, are elements so completely foreign to our American way of living and thinking that they will, if enacted, ultimately destroy this nation and all of its freedoms." The time had come to defend tradition, which for Wright included racial segregation and white supremacy, "with all means at our hands."[47]

In essence, Wright had threatened another Southern secession, this one from the Democratic Party rather than the nation as a whole. The *Jackson Clarion-Ledger* captured the tone and import in its three-deck, front-page headline the following day: "Governor Flays Party / Suggests Bolt from Democratic Party by South/ Inaugural Address Most Militant in Many Years."

If the tone of the speech was shocking, even more so was the man who gave it. The grandson of a planter and son of a country sheriff, Wright had fought in the Great War, played semipro baseball, and practiced law before entering the state legislature in his early thirties. As he rose to be Speaker of the state house and then lieutenant governor, he reliably represented the interests of the prosperous planters of his homeland in the Mississippi Delta. When it came to race, they wanted a reservoir of quiescent, dependent cheap Black labor. The populists whom Wright opposed, Senator Theodore Bilbo and Congressman J. E. Rankin, were the ones who serenaded the small farmers and shopkeepers of the hill country with calls for both economic justice and racial intimidation. With a public demeanor as gray as his hair, Wright would never have become governor had not the sitting executive, Thomas Bailey, died in November 1946, leaving his lieutenant to inherit the position. For someone who loathed Harry Truman, Fielding Wright had more than a little in common with him as an accidental leader.

The event that challenged the unequal equilibrium of the Jim Crow South and radicalized Wright was the Supreme Court's decision in 1944 to declare Texas's all-white primary elections unconstitutional. By implication, the ruling in *Smith v. Allwright* applied to every other state, including Mississippi, with similar state laws or Democratic Party rules. Nowhere did white dominance face a more immediate threat than in Mississippi, which had the largest percent of Black residents (49.2) of any state. For a politician like Wright, whose own home county was less than one-third white, Black enfranchisement augured the return of Reconstruction. Only four months into his partial term as governor, he convened a special session of the state legislature to determine some means of circumventing or defying the Supreme Court. "[T]here is a spirit of hostility in the air," he warned the solons, "one which we cannot ignore and to which we cannot submit."[48]

Wright's inaugural speech, followed less than two weeks later by Truman's address on civil rights, instantly transformed the obscure governor into "a national figure whose name is on many tongues," as the *Memphis Commercial Appeal*, a major regional newspaper, put it. When Southern Democrats in Congress issued their formal denunciations of the president's program, "[E]veryone referred to Governor Wright's courageous leadership." An article reprinted in several Mississippi newspapers predicted, "If southern states and southern voters should heed his advice, they can become an instrument powerful enough to command respect for their views in the halls of Congress, or anywhere elsewhere where they may raise their voices."[49]

More privately, segregationist politicians were not so quick to sign up for Wright's revolt. By coincidence, the Southern Governors Association had a meeting scheduled for February 7 and 8, less than a week after Truman's speech. The original agenda involved setting up a regional graduate school for Black students, a "separate but equal" means of keeping the all-white state universities racially pristine. Instead, Wright pressed his fellow governors to unite as "true Democrats" in opposition to Truman. But he lost the argument to the younger, more moderate governor of South Carolina, J. Strom Thurmond, who proposed diplomacy with the White House. During a forty-day "cooling-off" period, the governors would hew to a tone of "dignity, self-respect and restraint." A public rift with the Truman Administration could well deprive the governors of federal funds, patronage jobs, and public works projects. Franklin Roosevelt had punished Huey Long in precisely that way during the mid-1930s. Unswayed and indignant, Wright spurned a place on the governors' negotiating team, and he and Thurmond veered in their separate directions.

Thurmond had reason to believe he could reason with Truman. During his political career as a legislator, judge, and now governor, Thurmond had cultivated the image and track record of a liberal, at least by Deep South standards. In practice, this version of liberalism meant perfecting a balance of progressive and bigoted stances. On the one hand, Thurmond had proposed tax exemptions for Ku Klux Klan property and a whites-only workforce for all state buildings.[50] On the other, he had promoted literacy campaigns, supported union rights, pushed for a statewide minimum wage, and, in his 1947 inaugural address, even called for ending the poll tax. To the greatest national acclaim, Thurmond had insisted on a vigorous investigation by state police into the torture and execution in February 1947 of a Black man, Willie Earle, who had been jailed and was awaiting trial for murdering a white cab driver. "We in South Carolina," Thurmond declared, "want the world to know that we will tolerate no mob violence."[51]

With the FBI also on the case, a South Carolina court ultimately tried twenty-one men for Earle's killing. Predictably enough, an all-white jury acquitted them, but Thurmond's reputation survived even that injustice. The *New York Times* approvingly wrote that Thurmond had "earned the enmity of the purveyors of race hatred," and the *Christian Science*

Monitor lauded him as part of a new generation of white Southerners, "young voices crying in the cold."[52] Thurmond fancied himself the living proof that a generation of enlightened modern Southern leaders could contain the bloodiest excesses of Jim Crow and thus keep federal hands off the legal architecture of white supremacy.

None of those credentials mattered when Thurmond and his delegation of governors sought a meeting with Truman. He rebuffed them and shunted them off to J. Howard McGrath, the newly installed chairman of the Democratic National Committee. As an agitated Thurmond paced the room, the governors issued their demands. Truman must disavow his own civil rights program, allow a state's rights plank in the party platform, and return to a prior rule requiring a two-thirds vote of delegates for any presidential nominee. Acting on the president's behalf, McGrath held fast on each one, offering the sole concession of maintaining the 1944 plank on civil rights. However much that proposal incensed civil rights supporters, it did nothing to placate Thurmond's crew.

Meanwhile, back in Jackson, Wright had been going his own confrontational way. On Abraham Lincoln's birthday, the governor welcomed four thousand true believers, whom the *Jackson Clarion-Ledger* saluted as "white Mississippians, blood of the Confederacy and of true Jeffersonian democracy."[53] With Confederate flags waving and rebel yells echoing, Wright once again threatened mutiny: "[If these so-called civil rights laws which would deprive us of our rights are imposed upon us, then we shall have been virtually driven out of the party and would be driven to the necessity of protecting ourselves as best we could, even to the extent of temporarily withholding our electoral votes or using them in favor of some southern Democrat considered suitable."[54]

Four days later, the States' Rights Democrats Campaign Committee set up shop in Room 916 of Jackson's Heidelberg Hotel. At a meeting there the following week, volunteers from seven states pledged more than sixty thousand dollars to seed the insurgency. By the middle of March, Democratic state committee leaders in both Mississippi and Arkansas had formally endorsed Wright's plan to hold a conference of States' Rights Democrats in Jackson. With Thurmond's alternative strategy of cool heads and restrained rhetoric a near-total flop, Wright solicited his rival to become his partner. The first step would be for Thurmond to issue under his own name a philippic composed by Wright. It recapitulated the Southern grievances from the governor's February speech and raised the ante by playing on the Cold War fears being felt throughout the nation: "This so-called civil rights program, which bears a striking resemblance to Communistic doctrine and method, is aimed primarily at the Southern state but is in fact a threat and a menace to the reserved rights of all the people and of all the states."[55]

Stars-and-bars flags festooned the streets of Jackson on May 10, 1948, as twenty-five hundred zealots from twelve states and the District of Columbia crammed into the Municipal Auditorium. The nascent States' Rights party was in the process of raising two and a half million dollars, setting up county units, and establishing a women's division, all precursors to an as-yet-undeclared national campaign. Wright willingly bestowed the chairman's position on Governor Ben Laney of Arkansas and the role of delivering the keynote address on Thurmond. Putting his own imprint on the civil rights issue, Thurmond struck alternating notes of sorrow and anger, potency, and victimization. He placed himself among the "forward-looking and liberal-thinking men and women on the South," those who understood that racial separation was in the mutual interest of both whites and "decent and self-respecting Negro[es]." Southerners were not revolting against the Democratic Party, he explained; the Democratic Party was revolting against Southerners, visiting the schemes of "big-city bosses" and "hacks" on the most loyal voters who had ever lived. "We are here because we have been betrayed in the house of our fathers," Thurmond declared, "and we are determined that those who committed this betrayal shall not go unpunished."[56]

Wright had successfully shaped the amorphous Southern rage at Truman into a precise, bellicose strategy. The conference adopted a resolution that no Democratic delegates from the twelve states vote to nominate a candidate for president or vice president who supports civil rights or to approve a platform with a plank endorsing civil rights legislation. If those efforts fell short, then the States' Rights Democrats would gather in Birmingham, Alabama, on July 17, three days after the

Democratic Convention would end, to select their own candidates. Far from envisioning a gallant and ill-fated protest, yet another Lost Cause, Wright perceived a path to victory. Coincidentally or not, it was similar to the strategy that Gerald L. K. Smith had been propounding for several years in his speeches and articles. A States' Rights candidate could win nearly 120 electoral votes, depriving either Truman or Dewey of a majority and throwing the final decision into the House of Representatives. There, Wright and his allies assumed, Northern Democrats would sooner vote for a Southern Democrat than any Republican, and Republicans would prefer a Southern Democrat to a Northern one.

The Dixie minority would hold its rightful place in the appropriately named White House.[57]

* * *

Having waited months for the opportunity, A. Philip Randolph strode with a delegation of Black leaders into his favored venue for issuing an ultimatum: the White House. By this point on March 22, 1948, Harry Truman was two weeks past declaring his candidacy and nearly a month from beginning to back away from his own civil rights program. Unfortunately for Truman, he had promised Randolph this meeting before changing direction and was obliged to keep his word.

For a man denied legal and social equality in his own nation, Randolph conducted public life as if he controlled the levers of power. For a quarter-century by now, as founder and president of the Brotherhood of Sleeping Car Porters, he had stood at the vanguard of civil rights activism, equaled in stature only by W. E. B. Du Bois and Walter White, one of Randolph's companions on this day. Eight years earlier in the Oval Office, Randolph had accomplished the unthinkable, wielding the threat of a hundred-thousand-strong protest march to pressure Franklin Roosevelt into desegregating the defense industries during wartime.

On this return visit, in his role as treasurer of the Committee against Jim Crow in Military Service and Training,[58] Randolph had only one item on the agenda. It was an unfulfilled demand he had made of

Roosevelt in a second White House meeting: ending segregation in the military. While Truman's own commission had called for such action in *To Secure These Rights*, the president had noticeably omitted that element from his civil rights address to Congress. The nation's present and former top brass—generals Omar Bradley and Dwight Eisenhower, Army Secretary Kenneth Royall, Secretary of State George Marshall—considered integrating the armed forces anywhere from inadvisable to objectionable to abhorrent. Several of those leaders explicitly deemed Black soldiers racially inferior, capable only of lesser duties, a view that was also pervasive in the ranks. As Eisenhower would later put it, "When you pass a law to get somebody to like you, you have trouble."[59]

Randolph had been willing to relent on the issue during wartime, banking on Double V to be achieved. Instead, a draftee named Winfred Lynn sued the Selective Service over military segregation in 1942, losing both at federal district court and in a 1944 appeal. Returning veterans such as Isaac Woodard were terrorized, disfigured, or murdered. In the peacetime army since V-J Day, Black soldiers continued to be separated by race, invariably commanded by white officers, and disproportionately stationed on bases in the Jim Crow South. Given the nation's gratitude to its victorious military, and the army's consequent influence on civilian society, Randolph believed that desegregating it held "the basic key to smashing all discrimination."[60]

Even before hearing what Randolph had to say in the White House, Truman weighed some calculations of his own. His party's Southern wing, that reliable source of electoral votes, was revolting against him for being too liberal on civil rights. His presumed opponents on the Progressive and Republican ballot lines, Henry Wallace and Thomas Dewey, boasted longer records on civil rights than did his latecoming self. So Truman faced two ways of losing: with too much Black support or with too little. And Randolph had no intention of making the dilemma any easier.

"Mr. President," he told Truman as the meeting commenced, "the Negroes are in the mood not to bear arms for the country unless Jim Crow in the armed forces is abolished."[61]

"Mr. Randolph," Truman replied, "I wish you hadn't made that statement."

Undeterred by the crackling tension in the room, Randolph persisted. Black soldiers were sick of being "the objects of affront and insult all over this country," he lectured the president. They "have fought and bled in every war, but they have not gotten adequate recognition and consideration."

So, Truman asked, what did Randolph want? An executive order. "I agree with you," the president conceded, "but this is something I have to think about—how we are going to do it." Randolph pressed for a timetable. Truman said he couldn't provide one. What hovered in the air as the meeting ended was the boldest and riskiest threat of Randolph's career. As the Committee sgainst Jim Crow expressed it in a press release about the White House encounter, American Blacks would not "shoulder another gun for democracy abroad when they are denied democracy here at home."[62]

Eight days later, on March 30, Randolph ensured that white America at large heard his message. As part of the Truman's Administration's plan to bulk up American forces for the Cold War, the Senate Armed Services Committee was holding hearings on a bill to resume "universal military training and service" for eligible men. Randolph viewed that legislation as providing the greatest opportunity outside of an executive order to mandate integration of the military. And if Congress quailed, as he suspected it would, then he had his plan.

Hands clasped before him, vein rising on his forehead, Randolph launched into his testimony, deploying the baritone voice, precise elocution, and deliberate pace that he had developed decades earlier as a Shakespearean actor. He reiterated his statements to Truman. He invoked Mohandas Gandhi's successful campaign of civil disobedience against the British rulers of India. He reminded the senators and journalists of the way American racism nourished Soviet propaganda. Then he spoke truth in the manner of a prophet, someone expecting to be rebuked and disbelieved: "I can only repeat that this time Negroes will not take a Jim Crow draft lying down. The conscience of the world will be shaken as by nothing else when thousands and thousands of us second-class Americans choose imprisonment in preference to permanent military slavery."[63]

Randolph's words proved too much even for one of the Senate committee's more liberal members, Wayne Morse of Oregon. He asked: Wouldn't draft resistance by Black men provoke white violence? Randolph agreed it would, but such violence was a price worth paying. And if America were summarily attacked, Morse went on, alluding to a Cold War version of Pearl Harbor, would Randolph still counsel Black men not to serve? Yes, he would. In that case, Morse concluded, "the law of treason would be applicable."[64]

In the aftermath of Randolph's testimony, even some of his normal allies feared he had overstepped. One Los Angeles minister, active in civil rights since the Scottsboro Boys case, cautioned Randolph that "being interpreted as unpatriotic will get Negroes in serious trouble . . . and will eventually cripple your own usefulness." Walter White of the NAACP, while assailing Morse's treatment of Randolph, said the NAACP would not advise draft resistance if the United States were endangered. The *Pittsburgh Courier*, the newspaper most associated with the Double V campaign, vowed, "The Negro has never produced any traitors, and we do not believe he ever will."[65] On the front page of the *Spokesman*, however, Carl Rowan reported on a local groundswell of support for Randolph. Delivering a speech on the subject "Democracy at Home" to a Lions Club meeting in the largely white Minneapolis suburb of Hopkins several weeks later, Cecil Newman echoed Randolph, a man he had known for more than twenty years. "We cannot explain [away] to the rest of the world," Newman warned his listeners, "such things as lynchings, restrictive covenants which create racial and religious ghettoes, job discrimination, Jim Crow cars, segregated and unequal schools, segregated military establishments and discrimination in public accommodations. All of these inequalities bring racial tensions. There is not a man in this room who would not rebel if subjected to any of these restrictive conditions that I have enumerated."[66]

Randolph and the Committee Against Jim Crow proceeded to raise the temperature on Truman. Randolph led a picket line outside the White House on May 7, passing out buttons reading, "Don't Join a Jim

Crow ARMY." He helped arrange and then testified before a "commission of inquiry" holding public hearings throughout the country on "the effect of segregation and discrimination on the morale and development of Negro servicemen." The NAACP meanwhile conducted a survey of more than two thousand students at Black colleges and found that seventy-one percent favored Randolph's demand for desegregation and half would refuse to serve if the military remained racially divided.[67]

None of these efforts moved Truman or Congress. When one sympathetic Republican senator, William Langer of North Dakota, introduced a desegregation amendment to the Selective Service Act, even most Northern liberals voted against it, confirming Randolph's assessment that "we have found our white 'friends' silent, indifferent, even hostile."[68] The bill passed with the Jim Crow system intact, and Truman signed it into law on June 24. Two days later, Randolph's committee spun off a parallel group, the League for Non-Violent Civil Disobedience Against Military Segregation. It provided a pledge form for young Black men to sign, promising "not to register or be drafted for jimcrow [sic] military service or training" and to "encourage others of all races with similar convictions to follow the same course." The league established chapters in ten cities, including Chicago, Philadelphia, and Washington, and it began lining up fieldworkers to recruit draft resisters and attorneys to defend them.[69] Inspired by Randolph's campaign, a veteran who had served four years before returning home to Arkansas wrote to him:

I was eager and anxious to see for myself if there had been any conditions improved for the so called "Negro Veterans"—no not one have I found. I have found the Negro Veterans having to go in the back of white cafes just as they had always done, I have found them having to sit in segregated coaches on the trains just as they had always done, I have found them having to ride in the back of buses as they had always done, I have found them having to Mr. & Miss white boys and girls that they reared and played with just as they had always done, I have found them still being beaten and kicked around by white folks and white cops just as they had always done, I have found them still having to live in a designated and segregated area called "n——r town" just as they had always done, I have found them still having to attend school in a segregated school which is far below par just as they had always done and worst of all I have found them still having to go to church in a segregated church and serving God as if He were a prejudiced God just as they had always done. Nothing that I have had an opportunity to observe have [sic] I seen any difference in now and what it was before the war . . .

You have the solution already—just don't go.[70]

To ratchet up the pressure on Truman even more, Randolph made plans to lead protest marches outside the Democratic Convention in mid-July. And if that spectacle would discomfit the president, exposing the chasm between his espoused ideals and concrete actions, then Truman could not say he'd never been warned. Randolph had done so, under oath, in his testimony to the Senate committee: "Something has got to be done to stop America going on its hypocritical course of professing one thing and practicing another. If the Negroes, who are the most downtrodden in the country, have got to do it, then that is the history as put upon them, that responsibility and obligation, and the Negroes must not shirk that responsibility."[71]

* * *

No sooner had Harry Truman announced his presidential candidacy in early March 1948 than Hubert Humphrey found himself embroiled in a vigorous ADA debate about whether to challenge the incumbent. The names of those prospective opponents ranged from Dwight Eisenhower to Supreme Court Justice William O. Douglas to two relatively liberal Southerners, Florida Senator Claude Pepper and Georgia's former governor, Ellis Arnall. The common bond, however, was that not a single one of them had indicated any intention of seeking the Democratic nomination, and Eisenhower's political views were so ambiguous that Republicans and renegade Democrats like Strom Thurmond were also nursing fantasies of having the war hero at the top of their ticket.

"[I]t was a body blow," James Loeb wrote to Humphrey of Truman's decision to seek a full term. "There is still talk of finding some way to put up another candidate. . . . Our general feeling is that the matter is so serious as of now that we have to think and act without too much delay."[72] Chester Bowles, an advertising executive and New Deal administrator before joining the ADA, worried that even if Henry Wallace lost half his present support, he'd drain away enough Democratic voters to cost Truman the election and damage the entire liberal project. "This leaves people like ourselves in a bad dilemma," Bowles wrote to Humphrey. "A Republican victory . . . would be disastrous and we cannot accept a third party in which the Communists carry a major influence." Better to break with Truman now, he advised, than to stand loyally beside him "as, I suspect, he gets a bad pasting in November."[73] Yet Humphrey's closest partner in the ADA, Andrew Biemiller, repeatedly warned that instead of devoting its energies to toppling Truman, the organization ought to concentrate on shoring him up against Wallace.

In the weeks leading up to the ADA's National Board meeting in Pittsburgh on April 10, Humphrey wrestled with his response. He admitted to a "soft spot in my heart for Truman" and went to pains to assure Democratic National Committee (DNC) officials that "I am not part of the 'ditch Truman' movement."[74] At the same time, Humphrey feared that "without any first-rate dramatic personality on the national level," liberals would pale next to the "oversimplified emotional appeal of either the extreme right or the left."[75] He hardly needed to mention the names of Wallace and Thurmond for anyone in the ADA to understand the allusion.

Literally closer to home, Humphrey had decided to run for senator rather than governor. Not only did the Republican incumbent in the state capitol, Luther Youngdahl, share Humphrey's views on civil rights; his brother Reuben chaired the mayor's Human Relations Council. But the GOP senator up for re-election, Joseph Ball, was vulnerable to a liberal challenge on two core issues. He had abrogated his previous support for a permanent federal FEPC and vigorously pushed the Taft–Hartley bill that was anathema to organized labor. Even so, Humphrey's prospects of defeating Ball would be imperiled by association with a listless, losing Truman campaign. With the DFL still controlled by the Popular Front faction, it was even conceivable that the party would award its ballot line to Wallace rather than Truman and deny Humphrey the DFL endorsement for Senate. As if daring his friend Humphrey directly, Cecil Newman in the *Spokesman* scoffed at whether the ADA really had the guts to confront Truman or would fold in the end, betraying the cause of civil rights in the process.[76]

Sifting through the competing voices and variables, weighing personal ambition and moral principles alongside party fealty, Humphrey sent a telegram to Loeb on the opening morning of the ADA meeting:

IN MY JUDGEMENT IT WOULD BE A MISTAKE FOR ADA AT THIS TIME TO ENDORSE ANY PRESIDENTIAL CANDIDATE FOR THE DEMOCRATIC NOMINATION . . . WE SHOULD MAKE IT CLEAR TO THE PUBLIC THAT INSOFAR AS ADA IS CONCERNED NO PERSON HAS PRE-EMPTED THE FIELD . . . LET'S HAVE THE DEMOCRATIC CONVENTION ONE THAT IS WIDE OPEN FOR POLITICAL LEADERSHIP[77]

The following day, the ADA National Board formally called for an open convention. An internal poll of forty-seven ADA chapters found Truman the choice of only two, with Douglas selected by sixteen and Eisenhower by fourteen.[78] (The remaining fifteen were undecided.) In a subsequent tally of convention delegates, Loeb estimated that barely one-quarter were firmly bound to Truman.[79] All of these developments fed dreams in the ADA hierarchy that Douglas could be enticed off a lifetime seat on the court or the general won over by a "Draft Eisenhower" movement. So flagrantly did the ADA break from Truman, and so little did the group seem to fear political retribution, that when the president went on a speaking tour of the Pacific Northwest later in the spring, ADA partisans unrolled a twelve-by-seven-foot banner in the path of his motorcade:

Mr. President
PLEASE
REHABILITATE the DEMOCRATS
Nominate
W.O. DOUGLAS![80]

The most significant outcome of the ADA's national meeting for Humphrey concerned his signature issue of civil rights. In essence, the ADA resolved to fight for Truman's program even while fighting against Truman the candidate. And it fell to Humphrey to square that particular circle by convincing prominent Democrats to sign a statement calling for Truman's civil rights proposals to be written into the Democratic Party platform, to which any nominee would be tethered. Out of both duty and belief, Humphrey circulated the statement to a targeted group of about fifty party heavyweights, ranging from big-city bosses such as Jacob Arvey in Chicago and Ed Flynn in the Bronx to labor leader William Green of the AFL to that embodiment of the New Deal's legacy, James Roosevelt.

As public antagonists of Truman, the ADA inner circle were unlikely to have had access to the Rowe-Clifford memo about the pivotal power of the Black vote. But by the end of May, Humphrey and his cohort almost certainly would have encountered the same argument in a new and widely discussed book with the arresting title *Balance of Power*. The author, Henry Lee Moon, had worked as a journalist and a CIO organizer before becoming public relations director for the NAACP. In that capacity, he had been closely watching both the uptick of Black voter registration in the hostile South and the growing support for civil rights among Democrats, Republicans, and Progressives in the North. With the prospective size of 3.5 million by November 1948, Black voters potentially held the margin of victory in sixteen states with 278 electoral votes. That number, not coincidentally, was enough to win the entire election. "Unlike the southern vote," Moon cautioned, "the Negro vote today is tied to no future political party. It cannot be counted in advance."[81]

All the while, from the midwinter through the early summer of 1948, Humphrey received a parallel set of urgings on civil rights from his own family. For someone whose politics were personal and visceral, such pleadings had to matter. They replenished Humphrey's own sense of civil rights as an ideal, a value, not just an instrument to be deployed on behalf of urban machines or the broader liberal agenda. There was a reason that Humphrey resorted so often to the language of religion— the words "sin" and "guilt" and "conscience" recurred in his speeches and letters—when he advocated for the equal rights of Blacks and Jews.

Humphrey's sister Frances had followed her husband Ray's military postings to Savannah, Georgia, where she was doing casework for the Family Service Association. The position afforded her a front-row seat to exactly the sort of white backlash that Fielding Wright was so successfully orchestrating across the South. "This is a conservative reactionary place," Frances wrote to her brother. "The "Haves" are so afraid of the "Have-nots" that anyone who believes in old age security, A.D.C., Aid to the Blind, or the Social Security Act is a Communist—I mean it— it is awful. People here not only believe that the "poor whites" and "n——s" ought to stay poor—they say it openly in public & in the press."[82]

Several months after receiving her letter, Humphrey read one from his Uncle Harry, the soil scientist for the federal Department of Agriculture. Much of the letter simply recounted a recent visit to Washington by Humphrey's parents, H. H. and Christine, with a recitation of the sundry monuments seen. Then, abruptly, Harry turned to the subject of race, and with a fervor decidedly apart from his usual scientist's detachment and conservative leanings:

After we had shown your father and mother the bright side of the shield,[83] we showed them a residential street near the Center-Market, then drove down one of the streets of S.W. Washington and within 2 blocks of the magnificent and imposing Capitol building itself. The contrast presented by what is superbly beautiful and complete in every particular essential on the one hand and what, on the other hand, is sordidly wretched, filthy, run-down, and drab, was most depressing to look at.

What such housing conditions must mean to those who, for no good reason, must put up with them I shall leave to your own lively imagination. Who owns these hovels? White landlords. Who lives in them? Colored people—Americans, all of them—putting up with every inconvenience, fire hazard, and menace to public health . . .

Things will never be right here nor anywhere until we change the direction of our thinking about these other Americans. As Booker Washington once said: "He who holds his brother down in the ditch must stay there, himself." Our attitude toward and treatment of minorities in general and Afro-Americans in particular are curses that ever rise to damn us and raise hell with our happiness and sanity. Some day, I trust, we shall have become so enlightened as to make it impossible to tolerate such conditions anywhere in the U.S.A. That happy day, however, cannot come until we have learned to live above and beyond discrimination against our brother, be he white or black or of whatever color. . . . The big and the initial problem is not theirs, but ours.[84]

Girding for the civil rights battle at the Philadelphia convention, Humphrey also was starkly reminded that it was a truly national issue. In fact, probably the only viewpoint he shared with the likes of Wright and Thurmond was that the North had no reason to sneer down at the South from a summit of moral superiority. The results of Minneapolis's self-survey, being compiled in May 1948, could disabuse any Yankee of such arrogance.

On May 26, the day before Humphrey would turn thirty-seven, the Black social scientists and mostly white volunteers who had collaborated on the study gathered in the Citizen's Aid Building to release its preliminary findings. Somehow, amid all the hours and days that Humphrey had been devoting to the ADA and his impending Senate campaign, he had kept his word about raising enough money to keep the Human Relations Council and its survey afloat. Against political logic, Humphrey had staked his mayoralty, along with his national prospects, on forcing Minneapolis to confront its ugliness.

The survey spared no aspect of the city from its indictment. Of 523 companies that were studied, nearly two-thirds explicitly hired only white Gentiles, and a mere three percent demonstrably employed Jews, Blacks, and Nisei. Private hospitals resisted hiring Jewish doctors and treating Black, Nisei, and Mexican patients. Labor unions rarely placed Black members into the apprenticeship programs that led to higher-skilled, better-paying jobs and feared opposition from their white rank-and-file if they fully integrated workplaces. Across categories, from recreation to welfare services to education to religion, the survey identified a characteristically Minnesotan brand of bland, even-tempered obstinance. There was little adherence to the "expressed policy of no discrimination," there was a "somewhat passive attitude toward . . . the

322

practice of inclusiveness," and there was an "almost total absence" of dealing directly with race relations.[85]

As for the color-blind hiring in defense plants like Federal Cartridge and the testimonials to Double V and the Judeo-Christian tradition, in the survey team's analysis, none of those wartime gains made by Blacks and Jews had lasted long beyond war's end. Plainly, too, the progress achieved by Humphrey's fair-employment law and commission had only chipped away at the mass of inequality that had been calcified by decades of discrimination. Knowing this infused Humphrey with humility and shame and responsibility before he pointed an accusatory finger toward the South.

As often and eagerly as Humphrey had shouldered the issue of civil rights, he was still struggling for that one single unforgettable phrase to frame the crusade. Back in the summer of 1947, the Human Rights Council had partnered with the CBS radio network's affiliate in Minneapolis, WCCO, to produce a six-part series on discrimination entitled *Neither Free Nor Equal*. Humphrey reserved the final segment for himself, and he went through several variations of a call to moral arms. One draft drifted into the prolix and pedantic:

> You will hear people ask if we are not moving too fast in trying to change the bad habit of intergroup relations that too many of us have accepted with smug complacency for the past many years; but I say that we are more than one hundred fifty years late in according to some of our citizens that equality of civic right and human dignity guaranteed them by our American Constitution.

An alternate version pared down the wordiness and adjusted the time reference: "People sometimes ask me if we are not rushing things. I reply that we are some one hundred and seventy years late."[86] Almost a year past then, Humphrey was still tinkering with the language of his sermon, waiting for an appropriate pulpit.

* * *

Exactly one month before the Democratic National Convention would open in Philadelphia, Humphrey attended another partisan gathering that promised comparable discord. It was the biennial convention of the Democratic-Farmer-Labor Party, which had essentially split along Cold War lines into two combative factions, each claiming legitimacy. The Popular Front group, which had controlled the DFL since 1946, looked to Henry Wallace as the herald of conciliation with the Soviet Union. The Humphrey bloc, identified by default and disdain as the "right wingers," supported the anti-communist foreign policy of the Truman Doctrine and Marshall Plan while remaining ambivalent about the president himself. That ambivalence stopped well short, however, of wanting Truman pushed off the DFL ballot line, and Humphrey along with him.

For more than a year leading up to June 12 and 13 in the central Minnesota city of Brainerd, Orville Freeman had been acting as Humphrey's enforcer, a suitable role for a football star and Marine veteran. Freeman had been the one dissident to hang onto a seat on the DFL executive committee amid the Popular Front's convention sweep in 1946, and early in 1947 he started to use that position to construct a kind of parallel universe. To compete against the left-leaning DFL Association of local activists, Freeman created the DFL Volunteers. To dispute the party's official publication, *Minnesota Leader*, Freeman launched the *DFL Independent Newsletter*.[87] While the movement's leadership core consisted largely of ADA diehards—Arthur Naftalin, Evron Kirkpatrick—Freeman's efforts also drew a combination of AFL union members and campus politicians. (Among them were a Macalester College student named Walter Mondale and a College of St. Thomas professor, Eugene McCarthy.[88]) The single requirement for participating, as a later historian put it, was the willingness to "work to destroy the Popular Front."[89]

To that end, Freeman's wife Jane set about researching the past involvement of prospective DFL delegates in communist front organizations, forming the basis for what came to be called a "squeeze out" list. Through the vehicle of the DFL's steering committee, Freeman and

Naftalin pushed through a resolution barring "third party adherents" from the DFL.[90] In a flyer that Freeman produced subsequently, he adopted the Red-baiting lexicon so often deployed by conservative Republicans: "Will the D-F-L Party of Minnesota BE A CLEAN HONEST, DECENT PROGRESSIVE PARTY? OR WILL IT BE a Communist-Front Organization?"[91] Even Humphrey, as much as he preferred playing the nice guy to Freeman's heavy, turned strident and sarcastic, taking a potshot at his former hero Wallace: "We too believe in the century of the common man. But we are not prepared to see the century of the common man become the century of the Comintern."[92]

The vitriol, of course, flowed in both directions. The *Minnesota Leader* mocked Humphrey as "window dressing for the Wall Streeters and militarists behind Truman."[93] Popular Front activists tried to paint Humphrey as an anti-Semite until Sam Scheiner heard of it and vouched for his friend's values. Humphrey was reviled in leftist circles as a traitor and a hypocrite. "What would you politicians do if you did not have this communistic bunk to rave about?" one DFL veteran asked Humphrey. "Why don't you politicians ever have anything to say about fascism? You know there are so many Fascists and you would lose too many votes."[94]

The struggle for control of the DFL proceeded during the spring of 1948 through more than two thousand precinct caucuses and then eighty-seven county conventions. Freeman mobilized volunteers, trained them in the abstruse caucus rules, and then ran a set of mock caucuses a week before the real thing. Most importantly, he just plain got his people to show up, which meant obtaining a majority in the great many precincts with chronically low turnout. During the period for county conventions in May, the Popular Front and the Humphrey–Freeman bloc were holding separate meetings, electing rival slates of delegates for the state convention, and swapping charges of election fraud.

By the time that convention opened in Brainerd, most of the Popular Front delegates had determined not to attend, sundering the DFL's wartime alliance of leftists and liberals. The several dozen Wallace supporters who tried to be seated soon walked out in defeat and joined about four hundred like-minded delegates holding a counter-convention at the Labor Temple in Minneapolis. There, in an auditorium adorned with a "Wallace In '48" sign, they booed Humphrey's name and passed a resolution hailing the Soviet Union as "our ally in the fight against fascism."[95] Behind the scenes, unknown to many members of the Popular Front contingent, the Communist Party's national leadership had directed its Minnesota cadre to push for separating from the DFL and aligning with the Progressive Party.[96]

Having secured command of the DFL, along with its endorsement for Senate, Humphrey faced one more intraparty battle of consequence. Where did the DFL stand on Harry Truman? Humphrey answered that question with a resolution echoing the ADA's position nationally. Truman should be commended for his stands on labor, civil rights, and the Cold War, and the DFL delegates "voice our sincere appreciation and gratitude . . . for his courageous leadership."[97] But as the next morning's banner headline in the *Minneapolis Tribune* accurately parsed things, "DFL Refuses To Indorse [sic] Truman."

* * *

In the weeks between Humphrey's triumph at the DFL assembly and the opening of the Democratic National Convention in Philadelphia, he traveled to a lakeside cottage about thirty miles west of Milwaukee. Regardless of the sylvan setting, this was not a pleasure trip but, rather, a working vacation. The Dutch-hipped-roof house in Okauchee, Wisconsin, once the property of a prosperous butcher, belonged to Andrew Biemiller and served as his seasonal base each summer. While the rest of Biemiller's family swam or gardened or took out the rowboat—one summer his wife even raised chickens—he sat inside and devised political strategy. Once a lean five-foot-eleven, Biemiller had spent so much time in the past year exercising only his brain that he'd become the steady customer of a tailor who "let out" his suits.[98]

Humphrey's visit clearly indicated a strategy session for the upcoming convention. While the ADA leadership was exhausting Biemiller's patience with its dump-Truman efforts, and he would soon resign in protest as political director,[99] he was certain to attend the convention as a Wisconsin delegate, and he held a seat on the Platform Committee. So did Humphrey himself as part of the Minnesota delegation. The Platform Committee was the logical place for liberals to introduce and fight for their civil rights plank, and considering the dual opposition it would face from Truman's party regulars and the incensed Southerners, Biemiller and Humphrey needed a plan to surmount or circumvent their foes.

Exactly what the two men discussed during their time in Okauchee was not preserved for the historical record, but the signs point to a mixed message. In a handwritten note to Humphrey a week or so before meeting, Biemiller had promised that "I am . . . in the position to do a little scrapping" for a strong civil rights plank.[100] Yet in a recent analysis that Biemiller had prepared for the ADA, entitled "Notes on the Democratic Presidential Nomination," he had urged the organization to make its peace with Truman and appreciate the benefits of that alliance. Didn't the ADA agree with the president on the Marshall Plan and the Truman Doctrine of containment? And surely, no liberal could "desert" him amid the Southerners' revolt on civil rights. At most, Truman might be persuaded to retire "for the good of the nation, his party and the liberal movement." But "[o]pen talk of ditching him simply strengthens his stubborn streak and makes him more determined than ever that he will run."[101]

Whatever effect Biemiller's realism had on Humphrey, it failed to persuade the ADA's leaders. Less than two weeks before the first gavel in Philadelphia, national chairman Leon Henderson predicted an "open convention" in which two-thirds of the delegates would not be bound to Truman. "[W]e are satisfied," Henderson's statement continued, "that the convention will now call on men like General Eisenhower or William O. Douglas to head the Democratic ticket." For an organization that prided itself on intellectual rigor and unsentimental evaluation, the ADA was fiercely clinging to its fantasies, facts be damned.

Humphrey returned to Minneapolis desperately trying to line up signatories for the ADA statement endorsing Truman's civil rights program. As July drew near, the letter only had forty-nine confirmed names. It was problematic enough, though not exactly surprising, that only two signers were from below the Mason–Dixon line. More disconcerting was the response from the supposed liberals of the North. Presumably under pressure from Truman, New York Mayor William O'Dwyer withdrew his prior commitment.[102] The president of the Ohio-based Brotherhood of Railroad Trainmen, A. F. Whitney, refused to sign because the union's Southern members would object. Helen Fleek Marty, a DNC member from Wisconsin, turned down Humphrey because her family owned a summer resort with a "restricted" policy on guests. The Democratic Party's chair in Iowa, Jake Moore, curtly informed Humphrey, "I cannot see where we will benefit by again bringing up this issue."[103]

On July 4, Humphrey released a statement vowing to "actively seek" a platform plank to enact the civil rights plan that had been espoused in *To Secure These Rights* and then alternately embraced and ignored by the president. "The issue of civil rights," the statement asserted, "is in the worthiest tradition of our party."[104] The best Humphrey could do in the end was fifty-three signatories, a mixture of labor, liberal, and big-city machine people, drawn almost entirely from a dozen Northern states. Having fifty-three names was a long way from a groundswell in a convention that would have more than twelve hundred voting delegates. Yet it was more than enough, as the *Minneapolis Tribune* put it, to serve as the "[o]pening gun of a sure-fire fight."[105] Hate mail started to flow into the mayor's office the next morning, and by no means were all of the missives from the South. A correspondent with a return address in Peoria, Illinois, advised Humphrey: "You or no one else will be successful in breaking down the Jim Crow laws in the South, the South will fight before they allow a filthy crowd of n——r lovers to dictate to them, as to how they shall live."[106]

Duly warned, and surely not surprised, Humphrey packed his bag for Philadelphia. So did Andrew Biemiller and James Loeb, and Fielding Wright and A. Philip Randolph, each of them with a stake in the coming confrontation.

CHAPTER 10

INSIDE AGITATOR

The Democratic National Convention

July 1948

As Hubert Humphrey boarded his flight at the Minneapolis airport late on the afternoon of July 6, bound for Philadelphia, the temperature had just cracked the hundred-degree mark, the highest point yet in a week-long heat wave. Winds whipped through the city at forty miles an hour, kicking up the dirt from gutters and parched gardens and bare baseball diamonds into a dusty haze. This was weather that killed people or damn near tried. Around Humphrey's city that day, one man fell dead doing yardwork, another collapsed unconscious at the edge of a fire stoked by the arid gales, and an eight-year-old boy drowned while seeking relief in the waters of Lake Nokomis.[1]

For Humphrey, the blistering heat and incessant winds and gauzy sky must have summoned memories of the "Dirty Thirties" back in Huron. Even fifteen years later, the experience of drought and dust storms kept him obsessed with cleanliness and order, the way he stacked paperwork on each corner of his mayoral desk, the way he swept the floors and reorganized the pantry shelves and hunted for stray cobwebs at home, regardless of how meticulous a housekeeper Muriel already was. A day like this one could not help but evoke that Sunday in 1933 when the airborne silt kept sneaking its way into the drugstore as the noontime sun vanished into a mud-brown sky.

Such dire recollections would have suited Humphrey's mood as he flew toward the Democratic National Convention. Awaiting him there was a man-made crisis. From Southern segregationists of the Strom

Thurmond variety to big-city bosses like Jacob Arvey in Chicago and Frank Hague in Jersey City to the anti-communist liberals of the Americans for Democratic Action (ADA), nearly every feuding faction of the Democratic Party agreed on the single precept that because Harry Truman would be annihilated in the November election, he must be replaced by somebody, anybody, at the top of the ticket.

James Roosevelt and Leon Henderson on the ADA had been promoting a "Draft Eisenhower" movement for months by now, unencumbered by any interest on the general's part. It barely dented their rescue fantasy when, on the night of July 5, Eisenhower explicitly stated that he would not "accept nomination for any political office or participate in a partisan political contest."[2] The next night, as Humphrey traveled eastward, ADA activists in New York led a torchlight parade to Eisenhower's current residence as president of Columbia University, trying and failing yet again to persuade him. Henderson then turned to William O. Douglas, reaching the Supreme Court justice on vacation in Oregon. Two Southern moderates, Senator Claude Pepper of Florida and Governor "Big Jim" Folsom of Alabama, offered up themselves as presidential timber. In the White House on the night of July 6, Harry Truman wrote in his diary of the ADA crowd, "Doublecrossers all."[3]

Humphrey arrived in Philadelphia with the funereal mood palpable. The only signs and banners in town touted Eisenhower. The only hoopla on the street emanated from the marching bands parading for a different convention, that of the Benevolent and Protective Order of Elks. Several hundred rooms remained vacant in the convention hotel where Humphrey was staying, the Bellevue-Stratford, even as preliminary party meetings were about to begin.[4] The ultimate absence, of course, was that of Franklin Delano Roosevelt, whose personal magnetism and New Deal social compact had defined every Democratic convention since 1932 and held together the party's improbable coalition. Among the living, the presidents of the American Federation of Labor (AFL), the Congress of Industrial Organizations (CIO), and the Teamsters had all made it known that they would not attend the 1948 convention, keeping their distance from a presumed fiasco. Eleanor Roosevelt was skipping it. A mordant joke making the Democratic rounds had a delegate calling room service to order a bottle of bourbon. Told it's sold out, the delegate then asks for a bottle of Scotch. Again, sold out. "Well, then," the delegate says, "send up a bottle of embalming fluid. If we're holding a wake, we might as well do it right."[5]

Joseph and Stewart Alsop, writing in their nationally syndicated column, saw nothing worthy even of gallows humor in the "sullen, squalid, depressing" convention. "[I]f Truman is nominated, he will be forced to wage the loneliest campaign in recent history," they predicted. "It is difficult to imagine the total lack of enthusiasm in which the campaign will be fought.... No one knows what the private reactions to all this of the stubborn, mild-mannered President may be. But there is little doubt that he underestimates the extent to which his own party has already repudiated him."[6]

For Humphrey, the problems only started with the disgruntled, dyspeptic state of the Democratic Party. Because of the looming battle over civil rights, the convention perversely promised to be simultaneously dreary and explosive, listless and flammable. The eyes, and the hopes, and also the fears of many Black Americans now rested on Humphrey as much as on any single political leader. With only 10 Black voting delegates among more than 1200 at the convention, civil rights activists had little choice but to push from outside the party apparatus, whether through A. Philip Randolph's brand of mass protest or the National Association for the Advancement of Colored People's (NAACP's) earnest advocacy or the Black press's thunderous editorials and investigative reports about American racism. Humphrey, however, was that rarest of things: an inside agitator.

"We are at a crossroads," an NAACP leader in Florida wrote to Humphrey in the runup to the convention. "Either we must face the facts and work earnestly for a practical application of these democratic ideals that we have preached to the rest of the world, or we must shamefully admit that our American Democracy is little more than 'sounding brass or tinkling cymbal.'"[7] A devout Christian like Humphrey certainly recognized the phrase from First Corinthians, describing an insistent, useless noise.

Walter White himself telegrammed Humphrey apoplectic at rumors that the ADA crowd might cynically collaborate with Fielding Wright's self-described "States' Rights Democrats" to deny Truman enough votes for nomination. "COALITION WITH SUCH ELEMENTS," White warned, "MEANS COMPLETE SACRIFICE OF ALL CIVIL RIGHTS MEASURES." On his first full day in Philadelphia, a flummoxed Humphrey replied, "I have had no correspondence with these men. I have never met them and undoubtedly they will be a bit perturbed with my position on civil rights. . . . Please don't turn your fire on those of your friends until you know just where they stand. I want to work with you and I need your help and guidance."[8]

Historians and journalists were busily drawing parallels between the 1948 convention and two past Democratic disasters, each caused by seismic rifts within the party. During the 1924 convention, delegates had deadlocked for sixteen days and more than a hundred ballots in the irreconcilable struggle between Al Smith, a Catholic who embodied the urban, ethnic side of the party, and William McAdoo, a Southern Protestant unwilling to repudiate the Ku Klux Klan. The compromise candidate, John Davis, went on to be pummeled by his Republican opponent, Calvin Coolidge, in the general election. The Democratic convention of 1860, when the party cracked apart over the issue of slavery, provided an even more alarming analog to 1948's gathering. The Northern faction ultimately nominated Stephen Douglas for president and adopted his concept of "popular sovereignty"—letting voters in each newly admitted state decide if it would accept or reject slavery. The Southern faction, fearing that such free choice would reduce the spread of enslavement and dilute their region's political power, broke with the national party and moved toward secession and armed revolt.

If anything, the political geometry of 1948 surpassed that of its two precursors for complexity, and that complexity largely revolved around civil rights. Whether or not Southern Democrats deserted the party, both the Progressives and the Republicans by their actions were daring the Democrats to take a definitive stand on civil rights. From the outset of his campaign, Henry Wallace had staked out the issue and insistently pursued Black voters. Opinion polls in early July showed his national support slipping to five percent,[9] but five percent subtracted from a Democratic candidate could be decisive in a close presidential race. As for the Republicans, they had convened in Philadelphia in late June and achieved just about everything that was eluding the embittered, divided Democrats. New York's governor, Thomas Dewey, won the GOP nomination on a unanimous third-ballot vote in a vivid display of party unity and then addressed an effusive crowd of ten thousand from his balcony at the Bellevue-Stratford (which was, for the Republican convention, sold out). Forming what one party leader called "a dreamboat of a ticket,"[10] Dewey selected California Governor Earl Warren as his running mate. Between them, the two candidates dominated home states that contained more than one-quarter of the electoral votes needed for victory. Without any significant constituency in the white South to placate, the Party of Lincoln wrote into its platform an unflinching plank on civil rights:

> Lynching or any other form of mob violence anywhere is a disgrace to any civilized state, and we favor the prompt enactment of legislation to end this infamy ...
>
> The right of equal opportunity to work and to advance in life should never be limited in any individual because of race, religion, color, or country of origin. We favor the enactment and enforcement of such Federal legislation as may be necessary to maintain this right at all times in every part of this Republic.
>
> We favor the abolition of the poll tax as a requisite to voting.
>
> We are opposed to the idea of racial segregation in the armed services of the United States.

To put it starkly, the Republican Party sounded more like the Harry Truman of *To Secure These Rights* than did Truman himself. The GOP plainly intended to lure back the Black voters who had in growing numbers cast ballots for FDR. Meanwhile, as the initial activities of the Democratic Convention commenced in Philadelphia, an embattled Harry Truman remained in Washington, absorbing the advice of his counselor Clark Clifford. There was "no need to mortify the

South" with a firm endorsement of civil rights. Doing so could "only hurt President Truman's chances." And raising the issue on the convention floor, as Hubert Humphrey and Andrew Biemiller were prepared to do, if necessary, was "the wrong time, the wrong place, and the wrong way."[11]

* * *

On the morning of Wednesday, July 7, Humphrey took his seat in the Rose Room of the Bellevue-Stratford Hotel, the setting for three days of hearings on the Democratic Party platform. Humphrey held one of the coveted eighteen seats on a committee responsible for writing a preliminary draft of the document. That version would be submitted the following week to the full, 108-member Committee of Platform and Resolutions, which included both Humphrey and Biemiller, for discussion, amendment, and adoption. The platform's last stop would be on the convention floor, sometime after plenary sessions began on Monday, July 12. Despite the trappings of democratic process, the Truman loyalist who chaired the Platform Committee, Senator Francis J. Myers of Pennsylvania, made it clear that the president would have the "final say."[12]

Even so, the drafting committee offered the setting for the opening skirmish over the civil rights plank. Much of the testimony during the initial six-hour hearing, though, involved issues other than civil rights, focusing instead on planks concerning agriculture, business, veterans, foreign relations, and national defense. Those subjects enabled the pretense of Democratic harmony, as committee members took turns cuffing around one particular witness, the president of the National Association of Manufacturers, for his support of tax cuts and the Taft–Hartley law. For the most part, as a photograph in the *Minneapolis Tribune* showed, Humphrey sat tight-lipped and listening intently.

Shortly before the lunch break, one of the first witnesses on civil rights appeared before the panel. A white woman in her mid-fifties, Helen Hall had begun her professional life as a social worker in settlement houses before serving in the federal Office of Price Administration during the

New Deal and the Red Cross during World War II. If the panel had thus been expecting some sort of Lady Bountiful, all good works and soft words, Hall shattered the illusion as soon as she referred to lynching as "a survival of barbarism." The four Southerners on the subcommittee visibly "ignored" her and "voiced no expression," as a newspaper reporter recounted.[13]

Hall's words, and the echoing silence that greeted them, set a tone that carried over into the following day. The hearing on Thursday, July 8, belonged to several of the most important civil rights leaders in the nation. There was Walter White of the NAACP. There was Roy Wilkins, a graduate of the University of Minnesota who had gone on to succeed W. E. B. Du Bois as editor of the NAACP's magazine *The Crisis*. There was Channing Tobias, a minister and YMCA executive who had served on Truman's Committee on Civil Rights. Before the drafting committee, he represented a coalition of twenty major Black organizations—labor unions, professional organizations, religious denominations, fraternal groups—claiming a total membership of six million.

Through hours of testimony, these Black witnesses and several others voiced arguments ranging from the moral to the pragmatic, from the domestic to the geopolitical, for the Democratic Party to solidify and specify its commitment to civil rights. White declared, "The day of reckoning has come when the Democratic Party must decide whether it is going to permit bigots to dictate its philosophy." Wilkins likened the Southern defenses of white supremacy to "those of the unlamented Adolph Hitler." Paying lip service to equality, witness after witness asserted, no longer sufficed. "The Democratic Party, if it chooses, can continue to tolerate their little men of evil," Wilkins testified. "Or it can rise to the challenge before it, this time no mere oratorical challenge." Tobias submitted a statement from his coalition castigating Northern and Western Democrats, as well as Republicans, for blaming their own inaction on Southerners in Congress. "Even under the archaic rules of the Senate," the coalition contended, "a filibuster can be broken if there is a will to do so." The minimum required, the bare minimum, would be a permanent Fair Employment Practices Committee (FEPC), an anti-lynching law, the end of the poll tax, and, invoking A. Philip Randolph's slogan, "No Jim Crow Army." Anything less would drive Black voters to either Thomas Dewey or Henry Wallace. Anything less would enable the Soviet Union to continue portraying communism as the system that abolished bigotry and American democracy as the one that perpetuates it. "This propaganda is having enormous effect," the coalition uncompromisingly stated, "for the simple reason that these charges against the United States are true."[14]

In the wake of this righteous whirlwind, not a single member of the drafting committee, not the Southerners surely infuriated by it, not the liberals like Humphrey inclined to affirm it, not one of them said a consequential word. Truman's man at the head of the drafting committee, Senator Myers, had evidently imposed a policy of no response. The *Philadelphia Inquirer* wrote of a "tacit agreement not to argue the controversial civil rights issue publicly." The *Washington Post* reported that there was an agreement among the committee members not to even ask questions of the witnesses, lest any queries lead to public disagreement.[15] For Black Americans, who had dared to think they were being heard, who had dared to expect something like progress, the soundless chamber of the Rose Room blared the answer. As the *Baltimore Afro-American* put it, "A strange silence greeted the sharp testimony. . . . The other members, during the barrage of platform demands, merely sat back and smiled. They had no questions. From here it looks like a deal has already been made. . . . It doesn't look too hopeful."[16]

That deal almost certainly entailed a promise by Democratic National Committee (DNC) chairman J. Howard McGrath, implicitly with Truman's approval, to reiterate the vague, equivocal language of the civil rights plank from the 1944 Democratic platform.[17] That plank consisted of just one single paragraph. Even as it expressed the party's conviction that "racial and religious minorities have the right to live, develop and vote equally with all citizens and share the rights guaranteed by our Constitution," the plank declined to propose any legislation to achieve such equality. Crucially for the South, the platform only stated, "Congress should exert its full constitutional powers to protect those rights." What sounded encompassing in that language was actually constraining, at least in the view of segregationists. They believed that under Article X of the Constitution any powers not explicitly assigned to the federal government, including the entire architecture of the Jim Crow system, belonged to the sovereign states.

The signs of capitulation continued after the drafting committee concluded its hearings on Friday, July 9. That evening, McGrath hosted a dinner for party leaders and Truman Cabinet officials at the Bellevue-Stratford. The talk was all about party unity. The band played "Dixie" and "Swanee River" to great applause from Southern delegates. McGrath informed reporters covering the event that he expected a platform that "Southerners will not walk out on."[18]

A mile and a half down Walnut Street from the hotel, dozens of ADA members were moving into the Alpha Sigma Kappa fraternity house near the University of Pennsylvania campus, which they had rented for the week. Leon Henderson, delusional as ever on the prospects for ditching Truman, had hired painters to produce "Douglas For President" signs. It barely deterred him when the Saturday morning papers on July 10 carried the decisive word from Douglas: "No matter under what terms, conditions or premises a proposal might be couched, I would refuse to accept the nomination." For good measure, Douglas also spurned a feeler from Harry Truman to be his vice president, tartly explaining that he didn't want to be a "number two man to a number two man."[19]

By that Saturday morning, after three and a half days in Philadelphia, Humphrey had said little and accomplished nothing, other than dropping a lot of weight from long hours in sweltering rooms. By all the available evidence, Truman was going to be the nominee, and the 1944 civil rights plank was going to be in the platform. In both ways, Humphrey had landed on the losing side of an insurrection, which was hardly the way to advance his political career.

Just to add to the ignominy, the national media was now blaming the ADA rather than the Southern states' righters for destroying the convention and with it Truman's hopes for November. "[T]hese party wreckers," an editorial in the *Washington Post* scolded, "even after General Eisenhower's refusal, continued to fasten their hopes on the miraculous appearance of a tin god." In a similar vein, the *New York Herald Tribune* cast Humphrey's crowd as petulant and ungrateful:

"[S]o far as the liberal wing of the party is concerned, the only charge against Mr. Truman is his weakness. In every major issue, both of domestic and foreign policy, he has aligned himself with the Roosevelt tradition. . . . There is a difference between a defeat and a rout—between going under in a good fight and in confusion and mutual recrimination throwing away the shield."[20]

* * *

At the Humphrey family home in Minneapolis, Muriel spent part of that same morning of July 10 composing a letter to Hubert. She had been following coverage of the convention in the *Tribune* and *Star Journal* and with a bit of loving boosterism told her husband, "You've certainly let them know you are there with plenty to say and do about the things you believe in." More candidly, she wrote, "I'm so terribly lonesome for you."

Knowing that Hubert would return from the convention with his Senate race awaiting, the Humphreys had been planning a family vacation before campaign season went full speed after Labor Day. In previous years, the Humphreys had rented a cabin along the St. Croix River, an hour's drive east of Minneapolis. For this summer, Muriel had discovered an appealing alternative, one reminiscent of the lakeside resort she had run with her father years ago in the Dakotas, back when she and Hubert had been young and courting.

The place was called Beecher's Resort, and it consisted of a set of whitewashed wood cottages, each with its own screen porch, on the shore of Clearwater Lake, fifty miles northwest of Minneapolis. Word was that the lake teemed with sunfish, crappies, and northern pike, and the resort's resident cook would fry them up for guests as a favor. The lodge building, done up in green and white stripes, hosted evening Bingo games and screened movies like *It Happened on Fifth Avenue*. Loyal guests returned each year from as far away as Omaha.

Muriel had stumbled onto just one problem. A few nights earlier, she had visited with Jane Freeman while her husband Orville was in Philadelphia for the convention. When Muriel mentioned Beecher's, it caught the attention of Freeman's mother, Frances Shields, who was also in the house. A friend of hers, Shields said, had recently tried to rent a cottage at Beecher's and been presented with a questionnaire asking for all sorts of personal details and saying something about the clientele being "restricted."

Sam Scheiner of the Minnesota Jewish Council had spent years before and after the war compiling exactly these kinds of brochures and firsthand testimonies. He had arranged special showings of the film version of *Gentleman's Agreement* to try to get across his point about the dangers of even "polite" anti-Semitism. Yet as close as Scheiner had been to Hubert, and Hubert was to Muriel, the notion that the Humphrey family had naively selected such a vacation spot hit her with a wallop. White skin and Protestant faith and middle-class money had cushioned the Humphreys with layers of protection from bias. Now, though, Muriel was realizing that there was no such thing as being an innocent bystander, not when bigotry was concerned. You discriminated, you were discriminated against, or you closed your eyes and let it happen. Unless you objected and fought back. With the visceral decency and political wisdom that Muriel had maintained all through the years, even if most folks just saw her as the aproned housewife in all those press photos, she wanted to share that insight with Hubert. What was it he had asked of her in a letter from Washington back in 1935? *You be my inspirational force Muriel and always encourage me in what you feel will be right for me to do.* Inspiration and encouragement might come in handy in Philadelphia.

"If it's cool enough tomorrow," she informed him, "I'll take the boys and drive up for swimming and relaxing and have a chat with Evelyn [Beecher, the co-owner with her husband Artis].[21] . . . If this is true, we cannot go up there for our three weeks stay. It is morally wrong to go there when we believe as we do. Besides, politically it could hurt us. So I just plan to cancel out if it's true—but I want to ask them personally about it first. Am I right about this? It's made me quite unhappy."[22]

* * *

When Saturday afternoon arrived in Philadelphia, and Humphrey had expected to be writing a provisional platform with the drafting committee, Francis Myers pulled his next maneuver to muzzle dissent. From the eighteen members of the committee, he handpicked five loyalists and sent them into seclusion at the Chateau Crillon, a swanky highrise apartment building half a mile from the main convention hotel. Thus hidden away, the five would formulate a platform suited to Harry Truman's desires and deliver it several days later to the full Platform Committee as a fait accompli.

More disturbing to Humphrey, while nearly one-third of the drafting committee members were confirmed liberals, Myers had plucked centrists and conservatives likely to follow his lead. One was Scott Lucas, a member of Congress for thirteen years and most recently Truman's Democratic whip in the Senate. Another was Dan Moody, the former governor of Texas, who supported states' rights. The so-called secret five discussed and drafted straight through till three in the morning on July 11 and resumed again at one that afternoon. When reporters discovered their lair at the Chateau Crillon, Myers's fivesome fled and stealthily relocated to a high floor of the Bellevue-Stratford. In the process, Myers expanded the group by two more members, including another Southerner, former Alabama Governor Chauncey Sparks.[23]

By the end of Sunday night, this secret seven had broadly agreed to reiterate the 1944 civil rights plank. Moody indicated that the party's Southern wing could accept the language if it was accompanied by an affirmation of states' rights. In a spirit of compromise, party chairman McGrath averred that such an addition was possible, as long as it "did not nullify the principles of a civil-rights plank." His goal for the convention was to "reduce floor discussion to a minimum."[24]

All the clandestine dealmaking demonstrated that the price of achieving unity among white Democrats was going to be selling out the constitutional rights of Black Americans. Just as Social Security had omitted agricultural and domestic workers, just as mortgages under the G.I. Bill and Federal Housing Administration had redlined[25] nonwhite neighborhoods as risks, the Democratic Party's civil rights program would have to be tailored to Southern sensitivities. Which meant, of course, that it would be the equivalent of that "sounding brass or tinkling cymbal."

Humphrey and the four other liberals on the drafting committee exploded with indignation. To them, the secret committee had been "stacked" to do the White House's bidding. Emanuel Celler, a Jewish Congressman from Brooklyn with a quarter-century track record of fighting against racism and nativism, asked, "What do they think we are—a bunch of boobs?" The *Herald Tribune* described the liberals as the "out-in-the-cold contingent," but the group had its own preferred name: "the vigilance subcommittee." As such, they convened a rump meeting at the Warwick Hotel on Sunday afternoon, vowing a floor fight over civil rights if necessary.[26]

After atypically holding his tongue during the drafting committee hearings, Humphrey fired away. "We can't have double-talk," he told the vigilance meeting. "To use the 1944 plank over again won't appease anyone." Ideally, the platform should incorporate Truman's ten-point civil rights program, the one that had never even received a congressional debate or vote. But the bottom-line essentials were the same four elements that Channing Tobias had cited in his testimony before the drafting panel: permanent FEPC, anti-lynching law, ban on the poll tax, and desegregating the armed forces. "The convention is going to renominate [*sic*] Mr. Truman," Humphrey went on. "Let's give him the plank he enunciated himself in his message to Congress."

Humphrey did something else as he spoke. He threw in a rhetorical fillip, one of those phrases he had lately been trying to perfect. "We don't want to be the party to fight in the shade of state rights," he declared, "when it should fight for human rights."[27]

Most of the press, white reporters writing for white readers, overlooked those particular words. But the two most important Black newspapers, the *Chicago Defender* and *Pittsburgh Courier*, both paid attention. The *Defender* quoted Humphrey at length, while the *Courier* marveled at such a "vigorous" and "forthright" call for civil rights coming from "the Swedish Mayor of this Minnesota city with a Negro population of less than 5,000."[28]

Humphrey proved clairvoyant with his prediction that the 1944 plank wouldn't "appease anyone." Even as the "vigilance subcommittee" was holding its rump meeting, five hundred politicians from twelve Southern states gathered at the Benjamin Franklin Hotel. These men, the troops that Fielding Wright had begun inspiring and assembling six months earlier, put no faith in McGrath's notion that the platform might be able to endorse both civil rights and states' rights. They were not passively waiting for whatever platform language the secret seven would deign to provide. By the time the full Platform Committee convened, on Tuesday, July 12, it would be too late.

When the Southerners spotted Truman posters, they turned them upside down. By the time the election was over, they joked, the symbol of the Democratic Party would be just one end of the donkey, and that didn't mean the head. The Southerners were still looking for their own man to nominate, and Arkansas Governor Ben Laney had just declined. But Walter Sillers Jr., the speaker of the Mississippi House, was drafting a states' rights resolution for the full Platform Committee to consider and Strom Thurmond supplied the rhetorical fire. Harry Truman, he declared to the crowd at the hotel, had "destroyed the South" and "stabbed us in the back" with his "damnable proposal." Then, playing both victim and aggressor, he added, "We have been betrayed and the guilty shall not go unpunished."[29]

* * *

Four hours before the Democratic National Convention officially opened at noon on Monday, July 12, A. Philip Randolph led a procession of forty-five protestors outside the main entrance of the Philadelphia Convention Hall. He was coming off a weekend rally for eight hundred supporters of his campaign of draft resistance to the "Jim Crow Army." On the next Saturday night, he intended to deliver a speech in the heart of Harlem urging young Black men to refuse registration or induction when national conscription resumed in mid-August. With such a public act of defiance, Randolph was deliberately daring the federal government to arrest him for treason, as Senator Wayne Morse had suggested during Randolph's testimony to Congress four months earlier.[30]

During this week, however, Randolph harbored the single goal of pressuring the Democratic Party to desegregate the armed forces. A committed socialist for most of his adult life, he had excluded Henry Wallace's followers from the picket line, lest it be smeared as a communist-front operation. Randolph provided the marchers with a personal example of radical politics robed in professional respectability—double-breasted suit, pocket square, fedora, necktie firmly knotted even on a stiflingly muggy morning. His right hand held a sign stating, "Prison Is Better Than Army Jimcrow [*sic*] Service." The picketers who followed behind, most of them Black but a few white, brandished their own placards or sandwich boards: *We Want Free Men Not Jim Crow Slaves. Our Brother Died At Anzio But They Can't Sleep For Old Jim Crow. We Will Not Register Aug. 15.* One young woman's slogan specified, "No Button No Date," the button being one for Randolph's League for Non-Violent Civil Disobedience Against Military Segregation.

As delegates began to filter slowly into the Convention Hall, Randolph and the others handed out leaflets challenging them. "The Truman civil rights program has become meaningless," the flyer said. "Neither the President nor the Democratic members of Congress have taken action. The Democrats' devotion to civil rights began and ended in words." Randolph had also provided the marchers with his standard reply to any young man facing a draft decision and asking for advice: Why would a Jew in Nazi Germany have joined Hitler's army?[31]

Randolph's fearless posture belied the fragility of his endeavor. He had put up the entire eight-hundred-dollar budget for the league to mount its campaign for civil disobedience, and with that money already spent, the operation was a thousand dollars in debt. Barely three hundred Black men of draft age had signed the league's pledge of resistance. The greatest asset Randolph had, then, was the panicked overreaction of white America, which elevated his act of virtuous bluffing into a formidable threat, one that could only be disarmed with concessions.[32]

The picketers also supplied about the only passion of any kind as the convention commenced. Delegates filled barely half the seats on the convention floor, and a sprinkling of spectators roamed the upper galleries as Pennsylvania Senator David Lawrence gaveled the proceedings to order. A new Roper poll showed Dewey ahead of Truman 50.5 percent to 28.2 percent, with 4 percent for Wallace, and the remainder undecided. Those numbers underscored the recent claim by syndicated columnist Drew Pearson that the Republicans considered Truman the easiest of possible Democratic nominees to defeat. "What is so strange about it all," the *Washington Post* observed, "is that the heirs of Jefferson and Jackson . . . seem to have given up the fight before it has started. . . . It is not even defeatism; it is a creepy, funereal mood that baffles all who are veterans at these conclaves. Perhaps it should be called the 'cry-baby convention.' "[33]

In an effort to energize the disconsolate delegates, the local Democratic Party arranged for the Philadelphia social clubs collectively known as the Mummers to replicate their traditional New Year's Day parade with its string bands, comic skits, and lavishly feathered costumes. But as the five thousand celebrants strutted down Broad Street, a truckload of donkeys meant to be part of the parade got loose, trotting haphazardly down Broad Street. One of the Mummers' theme songs, "Oh! Dem Golden Slippers!," could be traced back to blackface minstrel shows, not exactly a helpful reference during a convention torn apart by the issue of civil rights. The delegates needed plenty of cajoling to join the sing-along outside the Bellevue-Stratford, unconvincingly chorusing, "Keep your sunny side up, hide the side that turns blue."[34]

Thus admonished, the delegates returned to Convention Hall for the evening session of the first day. The program essentially settled one lingering question, that of the vice-presidential nomination. In his keynote address, Senator Alben Barkley delivered a soaring defense of the New Deal and a scathing denunciation of the Republican-controlled Congress, earning a prolonged ovation from delegates eager for anything worth applauding. The speech instantly situated Barkley as the presumptive choice to be Truman's running mate. It also, however, advanced the efforts by Truman, McGrath, and Myers to marginalize the ADA liberals and reach a truce with the rebellious South. Barkley was a white Southerner of a certain age, born in Kentucky the same year that Reconstruction was abandoned, and his progressive politics on economic issues cohabitated with consistent opposition to civil rights. When Barkley spoke briefly in his keynote about the equality of all people, he couched the concept in the words of Jefferson, the segregationists' favorite Founding Father. Never did the noun *civil rights* pass Barkley's lips.

The next test of Truman's plan would be the release of the civil rights plank, which had to occur sometime before the afternoon of July 13, when the full Platform Committee was scheduled to convene. In anticipation, Humphrey and the ADA contingent assembled in the overnight hours at their frat house. Even diehards like Leon Henderson and James Roosevelt had to admit by now that the Democratic Party and the liberal movement were going to rise or fall with Harry Truman as the default standard-bearer. The one and only battle left was the one for which Humphrey and Biemiller had been preparing: a sweeping and effective civil rights plank. As for how to wage that battle, an ADA leader in upstate New York had just sent a letter to Humphrey. It began with a typed headline: "<u>THE CONVENTION NEEDS LIGHTNING OR A BOMB-SHELL!</u>"[35]

* * *

At three-thirty on the morning of Tuesday, July 13, after the secret seven had been sequestered in a hotel suite for more than fourteen hours, Francis Myers flung open the door to announce the language of the civil rights plank. With Truman's blessing, he had ultimately refused to include any reference to states' rights. The president, in fact, had disregarded the advice of Clark Clifford to weaken the 1944 plank.[36] Myers's group had even added a few sentences with the intent of making the plank sound more forceful, albeit without actually specifying how any of its lofty goals were to be achieved.

The Democratic Party is responsible for the great civil rights gains made
in recent years in eliminating unfair and illegal discrimination based on
race, creed or color.

The Democratic Party commits itself to continuing efforts to eradicate
all racial, religious, and economic discrimination.

We again state our belief that racial and religious minorities must have
the right to live, the right to work, the right to vote, and full and equal
protection of the law, on a basis of equality with all citizens as guaranteed
by the Constitution.

We again call on Congress to exert its full authority to the limit of its
constitutional powers to assure and protect these rights.

When Humphrey trudged toward his room at the Bellevue-
Stratford at 4:40 a.m., he found seven liberal delegates and strategists
awaiting him. Another batch arrived at seven in the morning. This
caucus, that delegation, civil rights activists by ones and twos—the
retinue of petitioners stretched into the dozens, the scores, the hundreds, all of them urging Humphrey to find some way to rescue civil
rights.[37] Meanwhile, Andrew Biemiller and Joseph Rauh, probably
the most skilled attorney in the ADA contingent, set about composing
an amended version of the Truman plank to be introduced to the
Platform Committee. All 108 members gathered shortly after lunch on
July 13 in the rooftop garden on the nineteenth floor of the Bellevue-
Stratford, a suitable altitude for all the rising heat, both meteorological and political.

By the time Humphrey began his testimony to the committee,
Biemiller had offered the amendment that he had written with Rauh.
It accepted the first three paragraphs of the Truman plank verbatim.
But because the fourth, final paragraph still included that troublesome
phrase about the "limits of its constitutional powers," the phrase that
Southerners had always seized upon as a loophole allowing states'
rights, the Biemiller-Rauh replacement language linked the general precept of congressional power directly to four points listed in Truman's
program:

We again call upon Congress to exert its full authority within the limit of its constitutional powers to assure and protect those rights, providing all our people with personal safety from the brutal crime of lynching, mob violence, equal opportunity in employment, full and free political partici- pation, and equal treatment in the armed services.

Reading the room, Humphrey could already tell that the amendment, as written, would fail in humiliating fashion, drawing four or five votes at best. A solid core of Southerners and Truman loyalists opposed any re- iteration of the president's civil rights program—not ten points, not four points, only no points. Even many moderates and liberals were uneasy with the emotional tone of "brutal crime of lynching." At the microphone, on the spot, Humphrey had to improvise a sales pitch. He reminded the committee of the risk that a weak plank would tell voters "that we do not believe in the President's civil rights program." He reminded the com- mittee of the way Republicans would campaign on the GOP's unstinting plank. He said he was ready to drop the phrase "brutal crime" in order to salvage the rest of the amendment. Biemiller himself would accept the revised, toned-down version, with the invocation of the four civil rights initiatives left intact. Then Humphrey set about closing the deal.

Friends, I want to get this across to you. I have been saying to my friends on this platform [committee] that this is an irreducible minimum for a large number of people in this convention—an irreducible minimum. There isn't any use kidding yourself about it. I don't think any peace- maker in the house can prevent the convention, to be held up here in this fine auditorium, from having a minority report one way or another. I don't think there is any way it can be stopped . . .

I say it should go to the convention. Then people will have a chance to have their say. Frankly, my good friends, America needs to have some ed- ucation on these problems from both points of view. And I think it would be a distinct service to this country if our friends from the South have their chance to tell the story to America over a radio hook-up that covers every home in this name. [And] I think it would be a distinct service, if you please, for those persons who are proponents of this amendment to have a chance to tell their story.[38]

On and on Humphrey talked. During the initial part of his presentation, he was being questioned by a friendly moderator, Emanuel Celler, the Jewish congressman from Brooklyn. Celler made sure to guide Humphrey through an explanation of why the four specific civil rights elements were necessary for the party to "compete with the opposition platform and underwrite what we know to be in our hearts." By dropping the "brutal crime" wording, Celler suggested optimistically, "we could get all factions to go along." Besides, as Humphrey put it, "We have compromised down to the cellar."

Once Celler turned over the microphone, however, any pretense of comity vanished, and it did so as much for generational reasons as ideological ones. Here was Hubert Humphrey, thirty-seven years old, the mayor for just three years of the nation's seventeenth-largest city, telling the Democratic mandarins what to do and how to do it. Senator Scott Lucas, a committee member from Illinois, had been born twenty years before Humphrey and elected to Congress in 1935, when Humphrey was still making ice cream sodas and peddling hog cholera medicine at the family drugstore in Huron. Francis Myers was a decade Humphrey's senior and had begun serving in Washington when Humphrey was a college senior. "Who is this pipsqueak who knows more than Franklin Roosevelt knew about Negro rights?" Lucas scoffed. Myers repeatedly asked in exasperation, "Will the gentleman yield?" Instead, Humphrey disparaged the Truman plank as a "bunch of generalities" and a "sellout to states' rights."[39]

None of Humphrey's rhetorical gambits worked. When the amendment to the civil rights plank went up for a vote, it lost by a more than two-to-one margin. The blow set Humphrey spinning even faster. As the Platform Committee deliberated on through the evening, he reclaimed the microphone with yet another variation on the liberals' amendment. It would omit any reference to lynching, mob violence, equal employment, and voting rights in return for one mere sentence: "We call upon our defense authorities to afford equal treatment in the armed services to all citizens." The amendment failed thirty-six to twenty-eight.

And still Humphrey talked on. He was losing his audience, losing control, just as he had in the speech to the AFL. Awash in his own grandiloquence, he careened from appeal to appeal. He wasn't trying to desegregate theaters or dance halls, after all. He wasn't asking for interracial marriage. He knew the South was making economic progress. He knew lynchings also happened in the North. Didn't the Democrats want freedom for the people of Poland and Estonia and Czechoslovakia? Didn't they want the new nation of Israel to be able to defend itself? So what about some democracy in America's military? Would the Platform Committee at least be willing to state that "we stand for" racial equality in the armed forces? "I plead with you," Humphrey implored. "I am not used to begging people. But this time I beg you to give us support."[40]

Myers shut him down. "The subject matter has been passed upon." He then called for a voice vote on approving the Truman plank and reported, "The 'ayes' have it."

After nearly twelve hours of disputation, the Platform Committee adjourned at 12:50 a.m. on Wednesday, July 13. Both the states' rights faction led by Dan Moody and the civil rights proponents headed by Biemiller and Humphrey were signaling their intent to introduce minority planks before the full convention that night. In a last set of warnings, Scott Lucas went on the radio to accuse the ADA of trying to "wreck the Democratic Party." As for Humphrey's political future, party chairman J. Howard McGrath informed him, "This will be the end of you."[41]

* * *

While Humphrey was fighting his losing battle in the Platform Committee through the afternoon and evening of July 13, a parallel struggle for civil rights was being waged in the Credentials Committee. Humphrey knew it would be happening, because his father H. H. sat on that committee as a delegate from South Dakota. Hubert knew, too, that the result of the credentials deliberations would provide a valuable clue as to how a liberal plank on civil rights might fare on the convention floor. What Humphrey had no way of knowing, captive as he was to the platform debates on the Bellevue-Stratford rooftop, was what exactly was going on for all those hours with H. H. and the Credentials Committee.

The confrontation there involved two dueling slates of delegates from Mississippi. One had been assembled by Fielding Wright and pledged fealty to the states' rights cause, vowing to vote against any platform or candidate endorsing civil rights. As such, they formed part of the Southern movement that Wright titled the States' Rights Democrats but was unofficially and commonly dubbed the Dixiecrats. The other Mississippi slate, calling itself the Loyal Democrats and promising to support Truman, was the product of a white Episcopal minister who was making a career out of principled futility.

His name was Charles Granville Hamilton, and he had grown up as a preacher's son in Berea, Kentucky. The geography mattered, because Hamilton attended Berea College, an institution founded by abolitionists and committed to having an interracial student body. By the mid-1930s, a decade past graduation, Hamilton found himself pastoring St. John's Episcopal Church in Aberdeen, Mississippi, a county seat that had been a hub of cotton trading during the Confederacy and the site of periodic lynchings since Reconstruction.

Amid that hostile climate, Reverend Hamilton stuck out as "a rare specimen in the Deep South with reference to the Negro people," as a Black minister once put it. Hamilton pressed his fellow Episcopal ministers to support anti-lynching legislation, associated with the National Committee to Combat Anti-Semitism, and volunteered for the Southern Conference for Human Welfare as soon as that civil rights organization was founded in 1938.[42] He attended the 1940 Democratic National Convention as a fervent backer of Roosevelt, even being pictured in *LIFE* magazine leading an FDR parade. Back in his home state, though, Hamilton managed to serve just one term in the state legislature before being decimated as the liberal rival to the flagrantly racist J. E. Rankin for Congress.

When Fielding Wright formed the States' Rights Democrats in February 1948, Hamilton had the temerity to speak in opposition. He was shouted down, and his own father-in-law subsequently sent him a cautionary letter: "I sincerely hope you have sense enough to accept this repudiation and keep out of this mess. You are a minister and a teacher & a good one at both & I would like to see you devote your intire [sic] time to both. The People of Miss don't want you in their Politics."[43]

Far from heeding such advice, on the very night of the States' Rights Democrats meeting, Hamilton gathered attendees from about half of Mississippi's counties who shared his opposition to Wright's impending break with the national party. They chose their own set of delegates, who were united less by a commitment to civil rights than to Truman and the party establishment, and Hamilton traveled to Philadelphia to present their case for being seated. And until they were seated, Hamilton would not release his delegates' names, for fear that premature exposure would cost them their jobs back in Mississippi.

Precisely because Hamilton was not a recognized delegate in Philadelphia, he needed someone who was already on the Credentials Committee to make motions on his behalf. Fortune presented him with one of the finest Black attorneys in America, fresh off a victory in a landmark civil rights case before the Supreme Court. The descendant of enslaved people, the product of a Black college and law school, George Vaughan had entered political life in St. Louis in the 1920s as a Republican and shifted to the Democratic Party during the New Deal. His partisan loyalty ultimately earned him the position of assistant attorney general. His fame and impact, though, arose from his private law practice. He represented J. D. and Ethel Lee Shelley, the Black couple who had been denied the right to purchase a home in a St. Louis neighborhood due to its restrictive covenant. Vaughan argued their case through lower courts for two years, earning the sobriquet "Fighting George" from the *Pittsburgh Courier*, before the Supreme Court agreed to hear it in early 1948. On May 3, the nine justices handed down a unanimous decision declaring that restrictive covenants violated the Equal Protection Clause of the Fourteenth Amendment.

Thanks to his steadfast support for Truman, Vaughan was named an at-large delegate to the Philadelphia convention and rewarded with a seat on the Credentials Committee. When that panel convened in a meeting room at the Bellevue-Stratford on the afternoon of July 13, a series of challenges to all-white delegations from the Jim Crow South quickly emerged. One of those controversial slates, from South Carolina, included Strom Thurmond. Within the previous two weeks, a judge in South Carolina had ordered that Blacks be allowed to vote in the Democratic primary. On that basis, two different interracial slates of delegates—the Progressive Democrats and the Citizen's [sic] Democratic Party—sought to replace the Thurmond group.[44] It was the product, they asserted, of the exact sort of all-white voting that now was prohibited. But the competition for primacy between the two civil rights slates, in addition to the prospect of uprooting white delegates for Black ones, doomed the challenge. The Credentials Committee voted by 25–2 to seat Thurmond's segregationists.

That kind of rout, relying on votes from Northerners as well as Southerners, liberals as well as conservatives, boded ill for the Loyal Democrats from Mississippi. Except that Hamilton's slate was presumed to be all white, making their investiture somewhat less controversial. In addition, Vaughan and Hamilton depicted the Fielding Wright delegates as the actual insurgents, for they had sworn to defy Truman unless he capitulated on state's rights. Finally, though, Hamilton did raise the issue of racial discrimination. It was four years by now since the Supreme Court had outlawed all-white primary elections. Yet Blacks "are denied the right to register, vote or participate in government in Mississippi," the minister said, and on that basis Wright's delegates had not been democratically chosen. To this Fielding Wright fumed that Hamilton was "deliberately stirring up racial hatred for political gain."[45]

The arguments flew back and forth as four hours elapsed, and the committee could not vote because it was one person short of the twenty-seven required for a quorum. The chair, a protégé of New Jersey Democratic powerhouse Frank Hague's named Mary Ann Norton, asked Hamilton and Vaughan if they would agree to suspend the rule.

They did. The subsequent vote ended in a deadlock at thirteen apiece for seating or rejecting the Loyal Democrats, a shocking blow to the segregationists. It was also a problem that Norton somehow had to solve. As she proposed that debate resume before trying a second ballot, two absent delegates, one from Alabama and the other from Mississippi, returned to the committee room. Meanwhile, two liberal members left, in either an example of terrible timing or last-minute cowardice.[46] Norton called for another vote, and Wright's slate was affirmed by 15 to 11.

Being the kind of lawyer he was, envisioning the chess board several moves ahead, George Vaughan announced he would resume the battle before the full convention that same evening. In order to do so under convention rules, he required a formal request from ten delegates of ten different states. He had already locked up all ten, including H. H. Humphrey of South Dakota.

When Norton stood at the Convention Hall rostrum soon after 9:00 p.m. for her designated thirty minutes of speaking time, she immediately yielded ten of them to Vaughan to present the minority report—that is, the case for evicting Wright's slate and installing Hamilton's. The boos began right away, and Alben Barkley, as temporary chair of the convention, banged down his gavel for order. Vaughan proceeded with his prosecution, reciting the exact wording of two resolutions that the Mississippi Democratic Party had adopted at its party convention three weeks earlier. These bound the delegates not only to oppose Truman and a civil rights plank, unless both were weighted down with the formal approval of states' rights, but also to walk out of the convention. Then Vaughan introduced his own resolution: "We recommend that the delegation from the State of Mississippi be not seated by reason of the acts of the Convention held in that State."[47]

More hoots and catcalls surged from the Southern delegations, and Barkley hammered down his gavel again. Undeterred, Vaughan continued, "Harry S. Truman has not advocated a single proposition in his Civil Rights program but what is contained in the Constitution." So furious were the Southerners at those words that, as a newspaper reporter described it, "An air of violence lurked around a corner, hung over the great hall as Barkley pounded his heavy gavel and pleated [*sic*] for order."[48]

Raising his voice, lifting his arms, Vaughan proclaimed the litany of Jim Crow in Mississippi: lynching, mob violence, the poll tax, under-employment, inferior education, segregated trains and buses, exclusion from the entire political process. "[A]s long as they do not participate in government," he declared, "Black men could never have their rights."

Incensed, delegates poured into the aisles, as Philadelphia police strove to force them back into their seats. In the Alabama, Mississippi, and Texas sections, delegates stood on their chairs and bellowed out rebel yells. One Southerner made it all the way to the rostrum, posting a sign saying, "Don't be unbrotherly, BROTHER." A Florida delegate shouted at Vaughan, "Sit down." Amid the "angry roars of disapproval and shattering boos," the delegates' faces purpling with rage, Barkley's gavel was "busier than a blacksmith's hammer at a horseshoeing."[49]

After Vaughan concluded, the police cleared the aisles, and Barkley imposed a semblance of order, Mary Ann Norton returned to the microphone to grant five minutes of her time to Carl A. Hatch, a New Mexico senator on the Credentials Committee. Personally sympathetic to civil rights, Hatch nonetheless did his partisan duty, recommending that Wright's delegates be accepted. Even after the fury of the previous fifteen minutes, he was hewing to the McGrath plan for a placid convention. With similar obedience, Barkley called for a voice vote rather than a roll call, first on the Credentials Committee's majority report seating Wright's slate and then on Vaughan's minority report impaneling Wright's dissidents.

Cacophony ensued.

No sooner did Barkley announce that "the ayes have it" than the former mayor of Chicago, Edward Kelly, ran forward from the Illinois section to demand that his delegation's votes for the minority report be recorded. Delegates from New York and California shouted out the same order. Just as an Illinois delegate began to speak, probably to insist upon a roll call, all the floor microphones went mysteriously silent. Muted, the liberals on the convention hall beseeched Barkley by wildly waving their banners. Presumably as a way of appeasing the civil rights forces, Barkley asked every willing delegation to send a tally of its votes to the podium.

The final tally showed that 503 delegates had voted for the minority report, for throwing out the states' rights slate from Mississippi.[50] The Democratic convention had fallen just 115 votes short of breaking Southern power.

* * *

Disheveled, exhausted, and coated in sweat, Humphrey slogged into his fourth-floor room at the Bellevue-Stratford toward one in the morning on July 14. He had lost a dozen pounds over the past week with its endless meetings and unrelenting stress, and he was still suffering from the same double hernia that had led to his draft deferment years earlier. Howard McGrath's threat to end Humphrey's career was fresh in his mind. At a minimum, the Democratic National Committee could punish Humphrey's insolence by cutting off the party's financial support for his senatorial campaign.

Regardless of Humphrey's woes, physical, fiscal, or psychic, a decision had to be made about introducing a civil rights plank and waging a floor fight. Two of Humphrey's most trusted allies in the ADA and the Democratic-Farmer Labor (DFL) Party, Orville Freeman and Eugenie Anderson, joined him in the hotel room. So did Andrew Biemiller. Eventually, the entire Minnesota delegation crowded in. Humphrey's brother Ralph, who had accompanied H. H. to the convention, stocked the bathtub with ice and beer, the fuel of choice for the delegates' all-nighter.

From his passionate, desperate, flailing performance before the Platform Committee, Humphrey recognized that whittling down the liberal plank, whether by settling for more general language or a single commitment to desegregating the military, would not win over Truman's loyalists. The only option, besides giving up entirely, was to return to language more like Biemiller's tougher version. And the near-victory of George Vaughan in his floor battle pointed to the possibility of defeating Truman, McGrath, and their "Watered-Down Plank," as a banner headline in the early edition of the *Philadelphia Inquirer* disparaged it, with a frontal assault. "We were inherently stronger than Truman's followers believed," Humphrey's ADA ally Paul Douglas, a candidate for senator in Illinois that fall, later recalled having thought. "Perhaps we were even stronger than Truman himself."[51]

Even so, Humphrey quailed at bringing the civil rights plank to the full convention. Biemiller and Rauh would write it, true, but it was Humphrey who would have to stand there at the podium, in isolation, and sell racial equality to delegates who considered it snake oil, just as worthless as the Peruna that H. H. had long ago peddled door to door. And who was Humphrey, after all, to defy a president? He was the "boy mayor," as the newspapers put it. He was a "pipsqueak," at least compared with the party elders. How could taking on Harry Truman turn out to be anything but a suicide mission?

Orville Freeman and Eugenie Anderson spent three straight hours in the predawn darkness prodding and pleading with Humphrey to make the speech. In their plank, the liberals would propose replacing just the final paragraph of the Truman version, the paragraph that included the deliberately imprecise call for Congress to "exert its full authority to the limit of its constitutional powers." In its place, the Biemiller amendment would restate the "irreducible minimum": racial equality in political participation, employment, and military service, and "the right of security of person."

Humphrey resisted each importune, fearful of losing his political life. Then Anderson spoke up. A pianist by training, and the wife of a wealthy man, she had been awakened to political activism by a visit to Nazi Germany in 1937. Back home in Minnesota, she rose through the League of Women Voters to the DFL and the ADA.[52] And because of Humphrey's reliance on the political advice of his sister Frances and wife Muriel over the years, he was an uncommon man for his generation: one willing to listen to a woman as an equal.

Having Humphrey's ear, Anderson proposed a solution brilliant in its simplicity. Everyone in Humphrey's camp knew full well that their plank was reiterating exactly what Harry Truman had proposed in his own address to Congress five months earlier. So why not say so? Instead of trying to outpunch Truman in a floor vote, why not immobilize him in a bear hug? Anderson laid out one sentence to be included as the penultimate paragraph in the liberal plank: "We highly commend Harry S. Truman for his courageous stand on civil rights." Humphrey could include a similar statement, Anderson added, in his speech.[53]

"All right," Humphrey said, persuaded at last. "I'll do it."

By this point, it was nearly 5:00 a.m. and the midsummer sun was rising. The afternoon session of the convention, with the Platform Committee on the agenda, was scheduled to begin at noon. Over the next seven hours, the ADA had to mobilize sympathetic delegates, Biemiller had to secure speaking rights to introduce the liberal plank, and Humphrey had to write the most important speech of his life.

Before beginning, he turned to his two closest companions in the world. First was his father H. H., right beside him in the hotel room. H. H. had shared Hubert's wariness of openly challenging the Truman plank, and father and son talked through the pros and cons. A dozen years earlier, Hubert had struggled to break free of H. H. and the drugstore in order to chase his own future; now he was asking for the patriarch's blessing.

"This may tear the party apart," H. H. finally said, "but if you feel strongly, then you've got to go with it. You can't run away from your conscience, son. You've got to go with it."

Hubert asked, "What do you think will happen?"

"I don't know," H. H. answered honestly. "But you'll at least have the eight votes of the South Dakota delegation."[54]

Then Hubert telephoned Muriel in Minneapolis. He pondered the consequences of his choice. He could end up "an outcast." He could lose "my chances for a life of public service." Such setbacks, needless to say, would carry obvious, material risks to their entire family. It had not been so many years since Hubert was moonlighting as a janitor to help the couple make their rent. Unwavering, Muriel told her husband that he was doing the right thing and he should see it through.[55] Even as she spoke to Hubert, a letter from her to him was en route to Philadelphia. It contained a kind of real-life parable about the insidious nature of prejudice:

We drove up Sunday [July 11, the day before convention started] to Beecher's Resort & talked to Evelyn & Art about their "Restricted Clientele"! It's true—they have felt they had to do it or quit the business. They hate doing it—feel it's wrong—it's not what they (Evelyn, at least) believe in—but feel that their resort and one or two others in taking the whole burden can't solve the problem. They have tried several times to get other resort owners in the association to relax their restrictions but with no results. They said that they had three cabins that day with Jewish people at the resort and that the only reason they have that word in their literature is that it cuts down on the hundreds of calls and people they have to turn down to keep the types of people and customers they have well balanced. It's all the "pat" excuses again.[56]

Humphrey went into the bathroom to shower and begin to mentally compose his speech, speaking passages aloud to an ADA volunteer who was within earshot taking notes. Andrew Biemiller, meanwhile, set about deploying a few of the parliamentary tricks he knew. When Biemiller had been elected to Congress in 1944, he had made it a point to cozy up to Sam Rayburn, who was at that time the Speaker of the House. Rayburn learned of Biemiller's background in labor unions and Wisconsin's state legislature, both of which operated under their own parliamentary rules, and he urged Biemiller to study the House's procedures closely. "Only the Southerners know the rules, and I'm having my troubles," the speaker told Biemiller. "And if you ever show me that you're right about a rule, you'll get notice, and you'll get my attention, and you'll get what you need."[57]

That same Sam Rayburn was now minority leader in the Republican-controlled House and, more relevant to the moment, permanent chairman of the Democratic National Convention. Biemiller telephoned Rayburn on the chairman's private line.

"What are you calling about?" Rayburn said. "Civil rights, I suppose?"

"That's right, Sam."

Biemiller thought he heard a grunt of disapproval. As one of Truman's men, along with Barkley and Lucas and Myers and McGrath,

Rayburn had subscribed to the impossible task of shepherding a fiercely divided party through a calm, unruffled convention. That convention just happened to function under the same parliamentary rules as the House of Representatives. And Biemiller just happened to have become an expert in those rules, at Rayburn's own behest. As Rayburn all but admitted, Biemiller surely knew the intricacies of being recognized to submit a minority report before the full convention.

"Well, all right," Rayburn told Biemiller. "I'll see you on the platform. Quarter to twelve."[58]

* * *

At the designated time, Hubert Humphrey approached the Convention Hall. He had spent a week in Philadelphia without once setting foot inside the auditorium, having been consumed instead by the plotting and infighting at the ADA frat house or the Bellevue-Stratford Hotel. From the outside, the Convention Hall resembled a vast stone aircraft hangar, a gray rectangle topped with an arched roof. Its one grand embellishment was a set of bas-relief sculptures, which wrapped around the building much like the famous friezes of the Parthenon. The Philadelphia carvings traced a saga of inexorable progress from antiquity to modern America in fields ranging from art to engineering, commerce to construction, and they collectively told a triumphal story of enlightenment and prosperity. The friezes simply omitted a particular portion of the America story—the African captives who had first reached its shores before the Mayflower, and their descendants bound in slavery for the next 250 years, and the succeeding generations who were emancipated and yet unfree. These were the people for whom A. Philip Randolph was picketing, and these were the people for whom Humphrey was about to speak.

After several days of paltry attendance, the floor and galleries inside were packed with fifteen thousand delegates and spectators, drawn by the promise of political combat. As many as sixty million listeners would follow along on radio, and in a first for the Democratic convention, perhaps ten million viewers would watch on television, thanks to the coaxial cable that had been newly installed along the Northeast seaboard.[59] The air inside the auditorium was stifling already from a week's worth of swampy heat, and the television networks' klieg lights only magnified the discomfort. Delegates futilely waved cardboard fans for relief and wiped their sweaty foreheads with handkerchiefs and even the long end of neckties. One man brought his own thermometer. Up on the rostrum, where Humphrey and Andrew Biemiller were bound, the temperature surpassed ninety degrees.

The two men presented themselves to Sam Rayburn, who asked Biemiller, "You sure you got your rights protected?"

"Absolutely," Biemiller replied.

Rayburn summoned Clarence Cannon, a Missouri Congressman who was serving as the convention's parliamentarian. Cannon was nearly twice the age of Biemiller and Humphrey and a chronic curmudgeon besides. A "no" from him would end the liberal insurgency.

"Clarence, Andy got his rights protected?" Rayburn asked.

Oddly, Cannon smiled, or so it seemed to Biemiller.

"Three different ways, Sam."

"Oh, my God, alright." Rayburn sighed. "The fat's in the fire."

As if to show just how hot the fire was going to be, Dan Moody from the Southern faction walked up to Rayburn.

"I got a minority report," Moody said, meaning an amendment to introduce.

"What now? States' rights?"

"Of course. What did you expect?"

Rayburn repeated, "Oh, my God." Then he called over Biemiller and Humphrey to join Moody. Did each side want a roll call? Yes, they did.[60]

There was no way now for Rayburn to keep a lid on the rancor between the civil rights and states' rights forces. The Democratic Party had not been through a comparable floor fight since the 1924 convention, when the platform plank at issue would have condemned the Ku Klux Klan. Rayburn knew how that debate had turned out for the party, with sixteen days of trench warfare at the convention and a crushing defeat by the Republicans in November. The most he could hope for now was that both dissident amendments would be voted down and the delegates would revert to the middle course of Truman's plank.

Out on the convention floor, the ADA's Joseph Rauh had spent the morning bargaining with a series of big-city bosses—Ed Flynn of the Bronx, Jacob Arvey of Chicago, and David Lawrence of Pittsburgh. Temperamentally, they hewed closer to Truman's machine instincts than to the ADA's cerebral liberalism. Pragmatically, though, each boss presided over a city whose Black population had soared with the Great Migration. If the Democrats didn't take a strong stand on civil rights, Rauh argued, then a lot of those Black voters would defect to Henry Wallace and the Progressive Party. Not only would Truman lose; so would the Democratic candidates for local and statewide offices.

On his rounds, though, Rauh also ran into David K. Niles, Truman's advisor on minority affairs. The liberal plank, Niles predicted, would be lucky to get fifty votes. "And all you'll do," he added, "is ruin the chances of the number-one prospect for liberalism in this country."[61]

As the afternoon session neared, Humphrey sat at the rear of the rostrum, taking an editing pencil to the typewritten draft of his speech. He underlined here and crossed out there and scribbled in some of the phrases he had been trying so hard to perfect.[62] In an arena filled to its rafters, amid the horns and chants and shouts, he bent over the pages as if it were just one more of those very late nights in city hall, reading the mail and marking every letter "RUSH." All the while, he worried whether he should deliver the speech at all. "I didn't want to split the party," he would recall later. "I didn't want to ruin my career, to go from mayor to 'pipsqueak' to oblivion." Then he noticed Ed Flynn sitting nearby him, and almost timidly showed him the text of Biemiller's plank.

"Here's what we're asking," Humphrey said. As much to convince himself as Flynn, he added, "It isn't too much. I'm sure we don't really have much chance to carry it, but we ought to make the fight."

Flynn read the plank, and then he threw his arms around Humphrey.

"You kids are right," Flynn said, referring to both Humphrey and Biemiller, who was also seated on the rostrum. "You know what you're doing. We should have done this a long time ago."

Flynn sent a runner onto the convention floor to find Arvey, Lawrence, and Frank Hague of Jersey City and bring them up to the rostrum. "This is the only way we can win this election—stir up the minorities," Flynn told them, recasting Rauh's pitch in a coarser way. "Can't you fellows swing your delegations? I can swing New York."[63]

* * *

The afternoon session of Thursday, July 14, commenced with a series of symbolic gestures to appease the party's liberal wing. A Black minister offered the opening prayer, the Black Congressman William Dawson of Chicago delivered a speech likening Franklin Roosevelt to Moses, and FDR's son James, having failed at ditching Truman, was permitted to lambaste the Republicans while barely mentioning the president. After nearly two hours of such preludes, the convention program arrived at its true focus: the platform. Truman's legatees on the Platform Committee, senators Scott Lucas and Francis Myers, each addressed the delegates, and Myers recited the committee's approved platform. Its four temperate paragraphs about civil rights appeared near the end of the forty-five-hundred-word statement, tucked between planks on antitrust legislation and refugee resettlement, as if the subject of race could have possibly slid by unnoticed.

Rayburn had apportioned sixty minutes of time for presentation of the minority reports. In addition to Moody, two other Southern delegates—Cecil Sims of Tennessee and Walter Sillers of Mississippi—had reserved the right to introduce their own versions of a states' right plank. Each plank would then receive a supporting speech. So six opposing speakers, plus Biemiller unveiling the liberal plank, would have cut into the available hour before Humphrey could even begin. Under such constraints, it would be foolhardy to stemwind and improvise in his usual fashion. For one of the rare times in Humphrey's speech-making career, he had to stick to the script and mind the clock. Then again, what was it that Muriel had told him after the AFL convention? *Hubert, some day you must learn that to be immortal, a speech does not have to be eternal.*

As Humphrey tailored his text, Rayburn came to the podium microphone and asked the question to which he and nearly everyone else in
the Convention Hall already knew the answer: "Does any member of
the Committee on Platform and Resolutions desire to offer a minority
report?"

Dan Moody stepped forward as the first and the most politically
complex of three Southerners slated to introduce states' rights planks.
If any of those men could make inroads with party regulars outside the
South, it would be him. Decades earlier, Moody had been both a wun-
derkind and a racial progressive. As a district attorney in central Texas
in the 1920s, he had successfully prosecuted five Ku Klux Klan members
for flogging a white traveling salesman. At just thirty-three, he rode
that crusading image into election in 1927 as the youngest governor in
Texas history. During the New Deal years, though, Moody had turned
against many elements of Roosevelt's program, and his conservatism
hardened when he left electoral politics in the 1940s for a private law
practice. Still, like Strom Thurmond, he could portray himself as the foe
of both vigilante violence and a federal role in civil rights. With fourteen other Southern delegates from the Platform Committee, Moody
had framed a highbrow defense of Jim Crow, one in which respect for
the Constitution rather than commitment to white supremacy was the
principle to be upheld:

> [T]he Constitution contemplated and established a union of indestruct-
> ible sovereign States. . . . Traditionally it has been and remains a part of
> the faith of the Democratic Party that the Federal Government shall not
> encroach upon the reserved powers of the States by centralization of gov-
> ernment or otherwise.[64]

Even so, Moody's proposed language proved too moderate for the
two Platform Committee members who would speak after him, Cecil
Sims of Tennessee and Walter Sillers of Mississippi. Sims compared
federal enforcement of civil rights laws to an invasion, while Sillers
declared that the Truman platform espoused more freedom for foreign

lands under Soviet domination than for America's own South, the home of "Jeffersonian Democracy."[65]

Then it was Andrew Biemiller's turn. On behalf of himself, Humphrey, and the Platform Committee's vice chair, Esther Murray, he recited the two new paragraphs to be considered. The one that Eugenie Anderson had composed, the one commending Truman, attracted notably more applause than any of the states' rights planks had. Maybe there was some reason for the liberals to hope.

As the minutes in the designated one hour waned, Moody, Sims, and Sillers returned to the microphone a second time to advocate for states' rights, as did one more Southerner, former Alabama Governor Chauncey Sparks. In their wake, another former governor, Maurice Tobin of Massachusetts, made the case for Truman's centrist plank. "For the good of America, I plead with my fellow delegates," he told the audience, sounding nearly abject, "to leave the platform as it is."[66]

Now Francis Myers, in his role as Platform Committee chair, stood at the podium. He and Humphrey had been scrapping and sniping about the civil rights plank for eight straight days by now. For this public purpose, however, Myers muted his hostility and exuded decorum. "I now yield ten minutes," he announced, "to a delegate to this Convention, a member of the Committee on Resolutions, the Mayor of Minneapolis, the Honorable Hubert H. Humphrey."

Humphrey stepped to the microphone in as formal a suit as he had worn since his wedding. On his left lapel hung his delegate's badge, and on the right was a campaign button with capital letters spelling "TRUMAN." In the steamy indoor air, under the relentless television lights, a sheen of sweat coated Humphrey's face, making it glisten. He looked wan and almost haggard in his double-breasted jacket and knotted navy tie, and the truss for his hernia sealed in the damp heat, heat that on this national stage he had to pretend not to feel. Humphrey had sought this kind of pulpit, after all, since that life-changing visit to Washington in 1935, and now he occupied it, with all the awe and fear it provoked. The presidential seal decorated the rostrum beneath him, and portraits of Harry Truman and Franklin Delano Roosevelt loomed above him on the gallery railing. As far as Humphrey could see into the middle distance, not one vacant seat remained. All was bunting and banners and the cardboard standards marking each state delegation's section on the convention floor. The faces of the delegates, row after row, were squeezed together like mosaic chips, and those faces all peered toward Humphrey. In the Illinois contingent, seated just below the ros-trum and to Humphrey's left, sat his liberal comrade Paul Douglas. "No braver David," Douglas later recalled of Humphrey in those last word-less seconds before the ten minutes began ticking down, "ever faced a more powerful Goliath."[67]

This particular David began by flattering Goliath. Or to be more ac-curate, two Goliaths: the Dixiecrats and the party establishment con-trolled by Truman. Civil rights, Humphrey acknowledged at the outset, was "a charged issue . . . an issue which has been confused by the emo-tionalism on all sides of the fence." He did not have opponents on the issue, but rather "friends and colleagues of mine . . . who feel just as deeply and keenly as I do . . . and who are yet in complete disagreement with me." As for the vitriol and bitterness of the previous week, all that just added to Humphrey's "respect and admiration" for the "sincerity, courtesy, and forthrightness" of his foes.[68]

Humphrey seemed to be willing himself to speak more deliberately than usual, to grant each word its own careful enunciation. The pace was of a piece with his appeals to fellowship and reason. He was drawing on the conciliatory skills he had honed in managing his expansive mayoral coalition. And now, having painted an attractive and wholly inaccurate portrait of the convention, Humphrey turned the rhetorical corner:

> Because of this very great respect, and because of my profound belief that we have a challenging task to do here, because good conscience, decent morality demands it, I feel I must rise at this time to support a report, the minority report, a report that spells out our democracy.
>
> It is a report that the people of this country can and will understand and a report that they will enthusiastically acclaim on the greatest issue of civil rights.[69]

With that phrase uttered, a tide of boos began to wash forward from the Southern delegations, mingling with the cheers from Illinois and New York and New Jersey, all of those contingents being seated closer to the rostrum. Philadelphia cops were already trawling the aisles, on alert for a replay of the chaos during George Vaughan's speech the previous night.

Amid the audible proof of an irreconcilable regional divide, Humphrey denied its very existence. The civil rights plank, he declared, was intended for no single region or race or religion or class. Every state has "shared in our precious heritage of American freedom," and every state has seen "at least some infringements of that freedom." All racial groups "have been the victims at times in this nation of vicious discrimination." Humphrey even portrayed Alben Barkley, that opponent of civil rights, as the clarion voice of racial equality, quoting the Kentucky senator's few sentences on that subject from his keynote address.

Humphrey was dissimulating, of course, and even patronizing the Southerners with their notion of white victimhood. Yet he was speaking a version of truth, too. From his years as mayor of Minneapolis, he recognized the Northern brand of Jim Crow. From his city, he recognized, too, the way racial discrimination ran parallel to anti-Semitism, one form of hatred reinforcing the other. He understood that no place in America was untainted by such sin.

Now he started to hurry the pace, to shift from the cadences of a Social Gospel minister to those of a radio announcer calling a close ball game. He slashed the air with his right hand. He shook his fist. He widened his eyes and lifted his brows and trumpeted out his tenor's voice through a mouth stretched open to its limits. The Democratic Party had accomplished great things in civil rights, made "great progress in every part of this country," but it was not enough. There must be "the realization of a full program of civil rights to all." To advance it, Humphrey invoked the two presidents whose portraits hung above him. "[W]e can be proud of the fact that our great and beloved immortal leader, Franklin Roosevelt, gave us guidance, and we can be proud of the fact that Harry Truman has had the courage to give to the people of America the new Emancipation Proclamation."[70]

Once again, a single phrase provoked both applause and derision, and Humphrey orated on, piercing through the clamor. He was six minutes into the speech by now, burning up his allotted time with each word, each clause, each sentence, and still with three or four pages of text left to deliver. Overtired and anxious, he channeled his ragged energy into a vibrating, thrumming tone. Earlier in the speech, he had entreated the Dixiecrats and party regulars with the generous language of mutual respect, civil disagreement. Now he set about shattering any hopes of reconciliation:

> Yes, this is far more than a party matter. Every citizen in this country has a stake in the emergence of the United States as a leader in the free world. That world is being challenged by the world of slavery. For us to play our part effectively, we must be in a morally sound position.
>
> We cannot use a double standard. There is no room for double standards in American politics. Measuring our own and other people's policies, our demands for democratic practices in other lands will be no more effective than the guarantee of those practices in our own country.[71]

As fifteen thousand people listened to Humphrey in the Convention Hall, some sixty million more did on radio throughout the country. They listened from Bridgeport, Connecticut, to El Paso, Texas; from Milledgeville, Georgia, to Rivera, California, from Oklahoma City to Brooklyn to Seattle. They listened in a hospital bed, in an idling car in a city park, in a segregated YMCA, in a corner drugstore, in a church parsonage, in a dance-band rehearsal room.[72] Cecil Newman listened in the offices of the *Spokesman* as he worked against deadline for his next edition. Muriel Humphrey listened in her living room in Minneapolis.

All of them, at every compass point, then heard Humphrey proceed:

> Friends, delegates, I do not believe that there can be any compromise on the guarantees of the civil rights which we have mentioned in the minority report. In spite of my desire for unanimous agreement on the entire platform, on top of my desire to see everybody here in unanimous

368

agreement, there are some matters which I think must be stated clearly and without equivocation. . . .

There will be no hedging, and there will be no watering down, if you please, of all the instruments and the principles of the civil rights program.[73]

Then Humphrey turned from a typed page to a sheet of paper he had written in looping longhand barely an hour earlier, sitting at the back of the rostrum, contemplating disaster. The page started with his newest iteration of a phrase he had first tested a year earlier on the WCCO radio series *Neither Free Nor Equal* and had continued revising in the intervening months. He double-underlined the last three words of it, cuing himself to raise his volume and lower his pitch, a veteran debater's device for imparting emphasis. When Humphrey spoke the words now, his voice sounded like something being strafed, being shredded.

To those of you, my friends, who say that we are rushing this issue of civil rights, I say to them, we are 172 years late.[74]

For a second or two, silence filled the arena, as if every single listener were registering what Humphrey had just said, absorbing the impact of such a censure. Then the response rolled forward in two parts, the tinny staccato of rapidly clapping hands and the guttural roar of disgust.

As the din subsided, Humphrey moved onto the next handwritten paragraph. He had been revisiting a particular phrase in this one, as well. He had wanted to draw a contrast between light and dark, the classic metaphor for good and evil, and when he tried out a version during a drafting committee hearing, he had used the word *shade*. Yet *shade* wasn't quite right; shade was where you found relief on a scorching day. The word that had come to Humphrey since then was *shadow*. Humphrey certainly knew the Twenty-Third Psalm with its evocation of the "shadow of the valley of death." In fact, he was going to quote from it later in this speech. But he had an association with shadows beyond the psalm, the lived experience of that dust storm in Huron in November 1933, the enveloping shadow of noontime darkness that had felt to him like the end of the world. And he could recall, too, the radiant sunlight that returned to the Dakota sky the next day with its reassurance of survival. He shouted now in that fraying, insistent voice:

> To those who say, to those who say that this civil rights program is an infringement on states' rights, I say this, that the time has arrived in America for the Democratic Party to get out of the shadows of states' rights and to walk forthrightly into the bright sunshine of human rights.[75]

The dueling sounds of acclamation and revulsion battled in the air once again. Humphrey had no more than a minute, minute and a half, left. With that bit of time, he soared into in his last late addition to the speech. Modeling it on Eugenie Anderson's revision to the platform plank, he declared, "I ask this Convention to say in unmistakable terms that we proudly hail and we courageously support our president and leader, Harry Truman, in his great fight for civil rights in America."[76] Then Humphrey was finished, with nine seconds to spare.

From his seat in the Illinois delegation, Paul Douglas gaped in astonishment at "hard-boiled politicians dabbing their eyes with their handkerchiefs."[77] He hollered "Here goes!" to one of those politicians, Chicago's former mayor, Edward Kelly, and then hoisted the Illinois standard to lead a delegates' parade. California's contingent followed suit, lofting the Bear Republic flag. Delegates from Michigan, California, and Pennsylvania surged into the aisle, along with those from New Jersey and Massachusetts and Ohio, everybody blowing horns and waving hats or just standing on their chair and whooping. The celebration went on for eight minutes before Sam Rayburn darkened the lights and Francis Myers urged the delegates back to their seats.[78]

The hoopla, though, was just a deceptive sideshow. All Humphrey had achieved so far was a rhetorical triumph. The actual votes on the minority reports—first states' rights, then civil rights—had to wait until later in the afternoon. Which still left Harry Truman's people a final chance to marshal his delegates against it. Clark Clifford, the president's counsel, bemoaned the speech precisely because it was so "eloquent." Easy for Hubert Humphrey to play the righteous zealot; he probably figured Truman was going to lose anyway. Clifford was the one who had to make sure the party regulars didn't abandon ship.[79]

Back in Minneapolis, Cecil Newman had already sent his editorial about the convention off to the print shop to be typeset. He had no way of knowing how the vote on the civil rights plank would turn out. He could only extrapolate from what he had read and heard of the convention thus far and what he had lived through in forty-five years as a Black American. In the editorial, Newman extolled Humphrey for making a "strong fight for a strong stand on civil rights." He favorably compared the Democratic Party's "vigorous young men like Humphrey" with the "reactionary Southern Bourbons and corrupt machine bosses." But when it came to venturing a prediction, Newman wrote, "In all likelihood he will not be successful."[80]

* * *

At 3:40 p.m., an hour behind his own preferred schedule, Sam Rayburn announced that voting on the four minority reports would begin. The first to be considered was Dan Moody's, and he displayed enough support from the floor to receive a roll call vote. As the state delegations reported their tallies, the results reflected a strict regional line, the Deep South versus the rest. In the end, Moody's plank lost by 925 to 309. Alben Barkley, doing his duty for Truman, compelled even Kentucky's delegation to vote against states' rights. So did the delegation from the president's home state of Missouri, a state whose adoption of slavery had helped kindle the Civil War.

With the most formidable of the states' rights planks so overwhelmingly rejected, Rayburn dispensed with the Sims and Sillers versions by voice votes. In their wake, Rayburn moved on to the civil rights plank, which he described as "the resolution presented by the delegate from Wisconsin, Mr. Biemiller." Then Rayburn hastily called for a voice vote, which would have left him, a Texan and a Truman ally, the sole arbiter of the outcome. Instantly, the chair of the California delegation, John Shelley, requested a roll call and delivered the required one-fifth of all delegates to rise in support.

Paul Douglas in the Illinois section was growing increasingly apprehensive. Just then, for a second time, Rayburn called the plank "the Biemiller resolution." The entire convention hall associated the civil rights plank with Humphrey, thanks to his speech. Douglas suspected that the convention chairman was hoping to confuse enough delegates for the liberal plank to fall short of a majority. If it did, then Truman's plank would probably be approved. Taller than six feet to begin with, Douglas grabbed hold of Jacob Arvey and lifted the bald, diminutive boss atop his shoulders, where Arvey would be nearly at eyeball level with Rayburn.

"Is this the Humphrey amendment?" Arvey asked the chair.

"The what?" Rayburn replied.

Now angered, Arvey shouted, "Is this the Humphrey amendment?"

Still dodging, Rayburn answered, "The resolution was offered by the delegate from Wisconsin, Mr. Biemiller." He paused and then conceded, "The Chair is under the impression that the Mayor of Minneapolis spoke in favor of it."

"That," Arvey shot back, "is all we want to know."[81]

The vote on Humphrey's plank, it quickly became clear, was not going to adhere to the regional lines that promised success. As the convention clerk went alphabetically through the states, Arizona and Idaho from the West voted nay. So did the border states of Delaware and Maryland, even though both had rejected the Moody plank. Barkley's Kentucky and Truman's Missouri obediently went against the civil rights resolution. States that had fought for the Union or had not even existed during the Civil War—Maine, Nevada, New Hampshire, New Mexico—voted almost unanimously with the nays.

In the Minnesota delegation, Orville Freeman was adding up the numbers, and the numbers so far were disturbingly indecisive. Even with the full support of the large delegations from California, Illinois, and Massachusetts, even with Humphrey's own state of Minnesota having voted by that point, the civil rights plank led by only 341.5 to 329.5. It needed at least 618 to be carried.

Then Ed Flynn, as promised, delivered New York's 98 votes, the largest single bloc in the convention. David Lawrence did the same with

Pennsylvania's 74, including that of Humphrey's week-long tormentor Francis Myers. Amid a series of opposing votes from South Carolina, Tennessee, and Texas, H. H. declared South Dakota's eight delegates for civil rights. Finally, when Andrew Biemiller's Wisconsin added its 24 ayes, the civil rights plank crossed the threshold of a majority. In the end, it won by 651.5 to 582.5.

In the White House, Truman had irritably watched the whole hullabaloo on television. Preparing to leave Washington for a train to Philadelphia, the president fumed in his diary, "Platform fight in dead earnest. Crackpot Biemiller from Wisconsin offers a minority report on civil rights. . . . The Convention votes down States Rights and votes for the crackpot amendment to the Civil Rights Plank. The crackpots hope the South will bolt."[82]

Indeed, no sooner had Rayburn announced the final tally than one of Alabama's delegates—a police commissioner from Birmingham named Eugene Connor and nicknamed "Bull" for his hyperbolic tendencies as a sportscaster—climbed onto his chair demanding to be recognized. As a newspaper from the state capital of Montgomery described it, Connor was "hollering like the devil's own loudspeaker" with his "mighty vocal cords swelled up, blue and purple and scarlet in his open shirt."[83]

Rayburn had failed to protect Truman's compromise plank on civil rights, but at least he could stave off a Southern walkout for the moment. Ignoring Connor, Rayburn recognized one of his congressional colleagues, John McCormack of Massachusetts, who moved that the convention be recessed until 6:30. Delegates shouted out their assent.

"We'll be back tonight," Connor bellowed. "And go out the first chance we get."[84]

* * *

The interregnum allowed the journalists and activists time to begin comprehending and assessing what they had just witnessed. The NAACP called passage of the civil rights plank "the greatest turning point for the South and America which has occurred since the Civil War." One of the nation's preeminent political columnists, Arthur Krock of the *New York Times*, wrote that the former Confederacy had suffered a "second Appomattox." The *Philadelphia Inquirer* editorialized: "Not because of anything the leaders did, but in spite of them, the Democratic platform possesses at least the merit of a plank committing the party to support Mr. Truman's program against lynching, poll taxes and segregation and in favor of equal employment opportunities for minority groups."

And Austin Norris in the *Pittsburgh Courier* envisioned a transformed South, with "rich, conservative elements eventually turning Republican and the underprivileged masses, both black and white, taking over the reins of the Democratic Party."[85]

* * *

After the invocation and requisite denunciations of the Republican Party by Utah's governor and one of Connecticut's senators, Sam Rayburn brought the evening session on July 14 to its fundamental purpose: the roll call for presidential nominations. Making good on Bull Connor's promise, the chair of the Alabama delegation, former lieutenant governor Handy Ellis, immediately asked to be recognized "to speak on a point of personal privilege." Ellis proceeded to announce that half of Alabama's twenty-six delegates would leave rather than cast their convention votes for Harry Truman and a platform with the present civil rights plank. While Ellis had the floor, he also spoke on behalf of the Mississippi delegation, all twenty-two of whom would join the walkout.

"We bid you goodbye," Ellis stated into a floor microphone before turning to head down the aisle with his mutineers in tow. One Alabama delegate brandished a Confederate battle flag, and one of Mississippi's lofted the state flag with its Confederate stars and bars in the upper-left corner. Most of the twelve hundred remaining delegates sent the deserters off with a rousing chorus of boos, and the Southerners emerged from the Convention Hall into a downpour. "We leave with no feeling of animosity," Fielding Wright insisted to newspaper reporters, "but with the sincere feeling of having served the Mississippi and the South."

For his part, Sam Rayburn said in the aftermath, "Those Dixiecrats are as welcome around here as a bastard at a family reunion."[86]

Quite deliberately, Strom Thurmond had not joined the exodus. Had South Carolina's all-white delegation left, he worried, the interracial slates of the Progressive Democrats or Citizen's Democratic Party stood ready to claim their seats. Similarly, Senator Lister Hill of Alabama remained inside the Convention Hall. Like so many other political moderates in the segregated South, Hill had carefully balanced his support for the New Deal with the reflexive opposition to civil rights required to keep being elected. In that spirit, he now contrived to help nominate a similarly minded senator, Richard Russell of Georgia, for the presidency.

Recognized by Rayburn because Alabama was called first in the alphabetical order of states, Hill yielded his time to Charles Bloch of Georgia to actually enter Russell's name as a favorite-son candidate. This bit of parliamentary maneuvering allowed the several hundred Southerners still in the Convention Hall to launch a twenty-minute celebration to the tune of "Dixie," and for Bloch to relitigate in his nominating speech the myriad degradations suffered by the white South at the hands of the federal government. Near the close of his soliloquy, Bloch declaimed a variation on William Jennings Bryan's famous metaphor: "You shall not crucify the South on a cross of civil rights."[87]

The crucifixion nonetheless went forward. After Truman had been nominated and numerous seconding speeches had been offered for each candidate—Orville Freeman providing one for Truman, and a young Alabama legislator named George Wallace doing the same for Russell—the mathematical march to the obvious result commenced. Truman received 947.5 votes and Russell 263.

Fielding Wright had already reserved several Pullman coaches to transport the Southern delegates directly from Philadelphia to Birmingham, Alabama, for the nominating convention of the States' Rights Democratic Party, which began on July 17. As always, more comfortable slightly outside the limelight, Wright accepted the nomination as vice president on the Dixiecrat ticket. The presidential spot predictably went to Strom Thurmond. Surrounded by true believers,

Thurmond readily threw off the dignified image that he had long cultivated, telling the delegates, "There's not enough troops in the Army to force the Southern people to break down segregation and admit the n—— race into our theaters, into our homes, into our churches."[88] Such was the Dixiecrat version of a civil rights plank.

It was two in the morning on Thursday, July 15, when Harry Truman delivered his acceptance speech to the weary delegates in Philadelphia and any insomniacs across the country who were still glued to the radio or television. Truman struck the pugnacious tone that would typify the rest of his presidential campaign, vowing, "Senator Barkley and I will win this election and make those Republicans like it. Don't you forget that." He promised to call Congress back into session on July 26 in honor of a Missouri holiday known as Turnip Day[89] to pass an array of bills that the Republican majority had never enacted. One part of that package, Truman specified, would be civil rights legislation. And as if it had not taken Hubert Humphrey and Andrew Biemiller and Eugenie Anderson and all the big-city bosses to corner the president with his own bravest words, as if that same president had not conspired with Sam Rayburn and J. Howard McGrath and Francis Myers to bury the whole subject of civil rights in pablum, Truman matter-of-factly told the convention, "Everybody knows that I recommended to the Congress a civil rights program. I did so because I believe it to be my duty under the Constitution."[90]

A week or so after the Democratic National Convention panted to its conclusion, Truman's special assistant Philleo Nash was recuperating by tending to his family's cranberry bog in Wisconsin. There he received an unexpected phone call from Clark Clifford. The president's counselor asked Nash to return to Washington and retrieve two pieces of official paper from "the deep freeze." These were executive orders that Nash had written months earlier at Truman's request to desegregate the armed forces and the federal workforce and that the president had then backed away from issuing.[91]

The decision to revive the orders now was less an act of resurgent idealism on Truman's part than a concession to the post-convention political reality. "After the adoption [of the Humphrey plank] you had no choice but to pursue a strong civil-rights position and hope this would enable you to bring out a big minority vote in the key urban industrial states," a Democratic Party strategist for the Truman campaign later recalled. "[T]here was no point at that junction of trying to placate the South. . . . [F]or better or worse, you've taken the fork to try to get the Negro vote."[92]

On Turnip Day of July 26, 1948, in addition to summoning Congress back to work, Harry Truman issued Executive Order 9980, ordering a "policy of fair employment in the Federal establishment," and Executive Order 9981, mandating "equality of treatment and opportunity for all persons in the armed services." The two orders supplied the most concrete evidence that Truman actually meant to run on the civil rights platform, even as segregationists in Congress threatened to impeach him and the Army's chief of staff, General Omar Bradley, complained that the military was not in the business of "social reforms."

Cecil Newman put Carl Rowan on the story and composed a front-page editorial himself. "Time, if not common sense and a belief in moral as well as verbal democracy," Newman wrote, "will soon convince Mr. Bradley that the American Army, the 'great purveyor of Democracy,' cannot sugar-coat the world with freedom talk while it exists half-slave and half-free." The *Chicago Defender* greeted the news of Truman's actions with an Extra edition. The two-deck banner headline read, PRESIDENT TRUMAN WIPES OUT / SEGREGATION IN ARMED FORCES. Not far from it on the front page was an article datelined Hazelhurst, Mississippi. Its headline served as a reminder of all the other struggles for equality that lay ahead: "Under 'States' Rights'/ Posse, Bent On Lynching, / Searches Woods For Prey."[93]

* * *

As for Hubert Humphrey, he left Philadelphia after the convention ended on Friday, July 15, and took an overnight train to Chicago. There on the morning of July 17, the same day when the Dixiecrats were convening in Birmingham, he transferred onto the Burlington *Zephyr* for the final leg home. When the train pulled into Winona, Minnesota, a little over a hundred miles down the Mississippi River from Minneapolis, Muriel and their sons Robert and Skipper climbed aboard for a family reunion on the last two hours of the journey. "WE WERE THRILLED WITH YOUR SUBERB SPEECH," she had telegrammed Hubert in Philadelphia only moments after it concluded. "I AM TERRIBLY PROUD OF YOU. ALL MY THOUGHTS ARE WITH YOU."

As the *Zephyr* rattled northward along the riverbank, a motorcade to greet Humphrey formed at the Municipal Auditorium, the focus of Humphrey's first public battle against Gerald L. K. Smith. The sedans and coupes and roadsters then drove through downtown to the Great Northern railroad station. Most of the vehicles were adorned with placards: *Humphrey Fights For Human Rights! Humphrey Champion of Human Rights. Humphrey Fights For The People.* Two thousand people carrying hundreds of similar banners were already crammed in the station by the time the motorcade arrived. The turnout, the *Minneapolis Tribune* would report the next day, "made the station's biggest wartime crowds look puny."

When the *Zephyr* glided to a halt and the doors slid open and Hubert and Muriel and the boys stepped onto the platform, the Police Department band burst into "For He's a Jolly Good Fellow." A group of teenagers lifted Humphrey onto their shoulders and escorted him to a waiting convertible, which rolled past hundreds of spectators on Nicollet Avenue to the Nicollet Hotel. The place had long been a favorite of Humphrey's due to his friendship with the catering manager, Sam Bratman, a Russian Jew who had made it to America as a stowaway.[94] "I have a really bad throat," Humphrey rasped from a podium at the hotel. "I just came back from a lot of shouting in Philadelphia."[95]

Over the next several days, going through the accumulated mail and telegrams in city hall, Humphrey began to fathom the full consequences of his speech, the plank victory, and the Dixiecrat walkout.

There were, of course, expressions of profound thanks. From a Black minister in Baltimore: "NEVER HAS ANY SERMON FROM ANY PULPIT SURPASSED YOUR SPEECH TODAY." From a civil rights attorney in North Carolina: "YOU AND THE DEMOCRATS SUPPORTING THIS REPORT [for the civil rights plank] ENDEARED

YOURSELVES TO THOSE AMERICANS WHO LOVE LIBERTY AND JUSTICE FOR ALL STOP YOUR PRESENTATION WILL GO DOWN IN HISTORY AS ONE OF THE LANDMARKS OF OUR PROGRESS TOWARD A BETTER WORLD." From Walter White of the NAACP: "THANKS TO YOU ON MAGNIFICENT VICTORY FOR CIVIL RIGHTS."[96]

Other letters and telegrams spoke in terms of moral awakening. From the mother of two sons in a St. Louis suburb: "I heard you on the radio at the convention and you really changed my attitude on things. We are all southerners, all our ancestors were in the Confederate Army and I am a very active member of the United Daughters of the Confederacy, but I think you're wonderful. . . . Thanks a million for your efforts in behalf of our party and on President Truman, bless his heart." From Reverend Edward Hughes Pruden of First Baptist Church in Washington, D.C., which President Truman attended: "[T]ruly I was inspired . . . Though I am a southerner by birth and training, I belong to a younger group of men who is utterly ashamed of the attitude of many southerners on the race question."[97]

Another trove of correspondence, however, vented blame and condemnation. Not surprisingly, a good deal of the hate mail bore postmarks from the South—Nashville, Jacksonville, New Orleans, Houston. A self-described "Southern Woman" sent a postcard adorned with the painting of a siskin bird by the British artist and naturalist John Gould. On the back of that refined image, she wrote to Humphrey, "We should do all we can here in the South to see that all the n——s get transportation to Minneapolis—Since you want them so badly you shall have them—and you'll learn something you didn't know when you spewed like a sewer."[98]

The attacks on Humphrey emerged also from the North, from Spooner, Wisconsin, and San Bernardino, California, and Scranton, Pennsylvania. Some writers, such as a banker in Missouri, assailed Humphrey for costing the Democrats the fall election. Others, including an attorney in South St. Paul, Minnesota, echoed the states' rights gospel: "Where do you find in the Constitution or in American thinking any discussion of "human rights" or that might makes right? Is a resident of Mississippi to be damned because he is white? And where in the Constitution do you find any reference to 'social equality' "?[99]

The caustic letters and telegrams repeatedly made two points, both erroneous: that Minneapolis obviously had no Blacks or else Humphrey would have known better than to propose integration, and that Humphrey must have no knowledge of the South, or he would have appreciated the diligent efforts of the many decent people there to up-lift the ignorant darkies. At one point, Humphrey lost his own temper enough to reply. He reminded the letter writer that he had spent some time in the South and been an instructor at LSU.[100] "Frankly, my heart went out to the people of the Southland," he continued. "Never in my life have I seen such poverty—such lack of spirit. This not only applied to the colored folks, but it applied to the white people as well. I am sure that you want to see such conditions erased."

Humphrey added a few sentences averring that he wasn't advocating for intermarriage, only economic opportunity. But then, as if regretting that tactical retreat, that spasm of pandering to a potential voter, he fired away:

> I must add that for those persons who are deeply concerned about the mixture of the races, that most of the mixing has been done by the whites and not on the basis of social equality but on the basis of exploitation of the human body.

After that barb, Humphrey indulged in a tone of performative polite-ness that had been imported to the Upper Midwest by Scandinavian immigrants and would come to be known as "Minnesota Nice." "These are just my thoughts," he signed off. "I may be wrong and, believe me, I am anxious to be better informed."[101]

Out of all the correspondence that Humphrey received, whether laudatory or contemptuous, the very first piece to be sent was a telegram from Cecil Newman. The Western Union time-stamp froze the moment of transmission at 1:32 p.m. Central Standard Time on Wednesday, July 14, 1948. Newman had even beaten Muriel Humphrey by twenty-eight minutes. On that afternoon in the *Spokesman* newsroom, most of Newman's upcoming edition was already in the typesetting process. Newman was furiously trying to overhaul the front page to incorporate Humphrey's speech and the impending vote on the civil rights plank. He paused just long enough to dictate these words to the Western Union operator:

ADDRESS WAS MAGNIFICENT. MOST OF MINNESOTA IS PROUD OF YOUR COURAGEOUS FIGHT FOR HUMAN RIGHTS. MAY GOD BLESS AND STRENGTHEN YOU.[102]

It took Humphrey nearly two weeks to finish answering the flood of mail about his speech. He saved the most personal responses to his oldest and dearest friends for last. One of those letters, dated July 30, went to Newman. No human being had taught Humphrey more than Cecil Newman about the imperative of racial equality. And no white man in Newman's life had ever put his racial privilege so completely at risk for that sacred cause. The gravel road out of Doland and the train tracks from Kansas City had somehow delivered them both to the appointed place and time in history.

"You know that the Philadelphia victory was ours—not mine," Humphrey wrote. "It's people like yourself who have labored patiently in the vineyards for years who prepared the moral climate that made my speech and its acceptance at Philadelphia possible."[103]

EPILOGUE

"The Unfinished Task"

Six Moments in Time

Harlem

October 29, 1948

One year to the day since Harry Truman had received *To Secure These Rights* from his Civil Rights Committee, he became the first president to deliver a speech in Harlem, the symbolic capital of Black America. It was the last Friday of the 1948 presidential race, with only four days remaining until the nation cast its ballots. Throughout the preceding two months of fervent campaigning, while giving more than three hundred speeches and traveling nearly thirty thousand miles,[1] Truman had not devoted a single address to civil rights. Even when he had spoken in Newark and Pittsburgh and St. Louis, all cities with large numbers of Black voters, he had not raised the subject, relentlessly focusing instead on economic issues and withering attacks on the "do-nothing Congress." It was as if he were once more backing away from his own stance on civil rights, distancing himself even from the executive orders he had issued on military desegregation and fair employment. When the *Pittsburgh Courier* made its presidential endorsement under the banner headline "NEGRO VOTE FOR DEWEY!," that mandate shared the front page with an article pointedly titled "President Truman Ominously Silent on Civil Rights."[2]

That calculated silence was about to end. The last Gallup poll of the campaign showed Truman still trailing Thomas Dewey by four points, 45.5 percent to 49.5 percent. The president's prospects depended on the pivotal electoral votes in swing states, such as California, Illinois, and Ohio, that had substantial Black populations. In one promising sign, Cecil Newman's final survey of Black voters in Minnesota showed Truman surpassing Henry Wallace for the first time and leading Dewey, as well.[3] Behind the scenes, Clark Clifford had been urging Truman for weeks to deliver a civil rights speech, ideally in Harlem, and within the last few days senior adviser Philleo Nash had composed one reaffirming the president's commitment to his own program. After Truman read a draft of it, he told Nash with genuine if excessive enthusiasm, "Well, anybody who isn't for this, ought to have his head examined."[4]

By 10:00 in the morning on October 29, nearly six hours before Truman was to speak, thousands of people began pouring into a public square named for Dorrance Brooks, a Harlem-born hero of World War I. Truman arrived to find the crowd swollen to sixty-five thousand, covering every inch of the square, pressing against the police sawhorses, and filling the adjoining park that rose up a hillside toward the City College campus. A few of those listeners were white students from the college, holding placards with the campaign's slogan "Give 'Em Hell, Harry!" The overwhelming majority in the audience, however, were the Black people of Harlem. Officially, they were attending a public worship service organized by an alliance of Black ministers, who would be bestowing on Truman the Franklin D. Roosevelt Memorial Brotherhood Medal from this, their outdoor pulpit. When Truman moved to the microphone, the congregants went silent and dropped to their knees in prayer.[5]

After all of his fits and starts on the matter of civil rights, after all the careening between boldness and prevarication, Truman used every one of the 1,156 words he declaimed on this day to stake both his name and campaign on the issue:

> It is easy to talk of unity. But it is the work that is done for unity that really counts.

The job that the [President's] Civil Rights Committee did was to tell the American people how to create the kind of freedom that we need in this country.

The Civil Rights Committee described the kind of freedom that comes when every man has an equal chance for a job—not just the hot and heavy job—but the best job he is qualified for.

The Committee described the kind of freedom that comes when every American boy and girl has an equal chance for an education.

The Committee described the kind of freedom that comes when every citizen has an equal opportunity to go to the ballot box and cast his vote and have it counted.

The Committee described the kind of freedom that comes when every man, woman, and child is free from the fear of mob violence and intimidation.

When we have that kind of freedom, we will face the evil forces that are abroad in the world—whatever or wherever they may be—with the strength that comes from complete confidence in one another and from complete faith in the working of our own democracy.[6]

Truman reminded the Harlem crowd of his two executive orders. He pointed out that, in the Supreme Court case of *Shelley v. Kraemer*, his Department of Justice had opposed restrictive covenants. Then he made his parting promise. "Our determination to attain the goal of equal rights and equal opportunity must be resolute and unwavering," Truman declared. "For my part, I intend to keep moving toward this goal with every ounce of strength and determination that I have."[7]

That vow, and the ovation it received, radiated out from Harlem to every corner of Black America. In the words of Benjamin Mays, the leading Black educator in the nation, Truman had "stood like the Rock of Gibraltar" against the Dixiecrats in his own party. And by "winding up his campaign in Harlem, he reaffirmed his faith in civil rights."[8] Even Cecil Newman, skeptical for so long about both major political parties, and so deeply affected by Henry Wallace's courageous campaign trips through the South, rushed to publish a last-minute, front-page endorsement of Harry Truman on the day of the speech.[9]

The iconic photograph of the 1948 election showed the victorious Truman on the morning after, brandishing an early edition of the *Chicago Tribune* with the headline "DEWEY DEFEATS TRUMAN." Indeed, Truman defied every prediction of disaster by outpolling Dewey 49.6 percent (with 24,179,345 votes) to 45.1 percent (21,991,291 votes). The president captured 303 electoral votes against 189 for Dewey, while Thurmond received 39, carrying Alabama, Louisiana, Mississippi, and South Carolina.

It was Cecil Newman's headline in the *Spokesman* that grasped the key reason for the epic upset: "TRUMAN'S CIVIL RIGHTS STAND WINS." The columnist Dan Burley in the *New York Age*, one of the city's several Black newspapers, described the phenomenon in touchingly human terms:

> I'm not writing about ratios, pluralities, and all that jive. I'm talking about what went down when the stevedores, the kitchen mechanics ... the soda-jerkers, the pushwagoneers, folks in the Amen Corner . . . started marching into them polling places.
>
> I'm talking about the cab drivers, the bartenders, the cooks, waiters, horse players, porters, reporters, and "exporters." . . . [They] cheered like they holler at a Joe Louis fight [and] Wednesday morning showed the election box score with Truman leading the field like Citation.[10]

Altogether, Truman carried 77 percent of the Black vote, bettering even Franklin Roosevelt's best performance of 71 percent in the 1936 election.[11] More critically for Truman, Black voters turned out for him in the right places. They gave Truman 70,000 votes in California, which he won by 18,000; 85,000 votes in Illinois, which he won by 33,000; and 130,000 in Ohio, which he won by only 7,000.[12] Cumulatively, those three states provided Truman with 78 electoral votes, the decisive bloc. Had Dewey captured those states, neither major candidate would have held a majority, and the election would have been decided in the House of Representatives with the Southern segregationists holding the pivotal votes. It would have been precisely the scenario envisioned by Gerald L. K. Smith and Fielding Wright.

Instead, Black support for Truman proved that the Democratic Party could win nationally without the "Solid South." The fundamental internal contradiction of the New Deal coalition—its illogical alliance of labor, liberals, and white supremacists; its inability to extend its progressive stance on every other domestic issue to civil rights—had been resolved for the moment by those Black voters. With the benefit of hindsight, a scholar in the early 1970s assessed the impact.

"[T]he election of 1948 legitimized the issue of civil rights," wrote Harvard Sitkoff, a respected historian of both the New Deal and the civil rights movement.

Once the almost private domain of Negro protest groups, leftist clergymen, and Communist-dominated unions and front organizations, civil rights became part of the agenda of respectable urban liberalism in 1948 and was identified with both national parties and the President of the United States . . . Truman's identification with the civil rights movement in 1948 sparked a whole new set of expectations. It increased the pressure on future Presidents, especially Democrats, to support civil rights. It made it easier for liberals of both parties to speak out for civil rights, for the Supreme Court to revitalize the Fourteenth Amendment and reverse a century of law unfavorable to the Negro, for civil rights partisans to receive a respectful hearing at the White House and for Negroes to believe that they would soon share the American Dream.[13]

As for Hubert Humphrey, he won a seat in the U.S. Senate on the same dramatic day when Truman was elected president. Not only did Humphrey become the first Democrat ever elected to statewide office in Minnesota, but he also helped Truman carry the state by a wide margin. Just outside Washington, Humphrey's sister Frances had joined her Uncle Harry in his home to listen together to the election returns on the radio. From South Dakota, H. H. wrote to his namesake, "Everything that I have ever desired is wrapped up and delivered in you. You have given expression to my innermost desires & longings. You are a great liberal and fighter for the right. Keep it up, Hubert, speak the voice of the people and some day you will find yourself as Chief of this Nation."[14]

H. H. died less than a year later.

Within weeks of entering the Senate, Humphrey hired for his staff a Black veteran of World War II who was studying public administration at American University. That aide, Cyril King, was the first Black person ever to work on a senatorial staff. In the manner of sister Frances and Eleanor Roosevelt at the Shoreham Hotel, Humphrey soon took King to lunch in the Senators' Dining Room, thereby desegregating another Washington institution.[15] On the legislative front, success proved far more difficult. Within Humphrey's first three months as a freshman senator, he introduced bills to outlaw lynching and to create a federal Civil Rights Commission. Both were dead on arrival in a Senate still dominated by the Southerners, who led major committees and wielded the filibuster against any civil rights legislation. No matter that Humphrey had triumphed over the Dixiecrats at the Democratic National Convention, no matter that Truman had won election without the Solid South, no matter that the president had issued executive orders on civil rights, in Humphrey's new home at the Capitol the segregationists still held the levers of procedural power. Many more battles, with no certainty of triumph, lay ahead.

* * *

Miami Beach, Florida
August 3, 1965

Hubert Humphrey stood before the annual convention of the National Urban League on August 3, 1965, at the pinnacle of his career. He would be speaking as Lyndon Johnson's vice president and indispensable junior partner in pushing through the most important civil rights laws since Reconstruction. Finally, after sixteen years of failed efforts and compromises on half-measures, the promise of racial equality inherent in Harry Truman's 1948 election was about to be realized.

Much of the reason, of course, had more to do with activists like the Urban League members than with sympathetic political leaders such as Humphrey and Johnson. The mass movement that A. Philip Randolph had started building in the 1940s evolved in subsequent decades into a series of galvanizing public protests by Black Americans, sometimes joined by white allies: the Montgomery bus boycott led by the Reverend Dr. Martin Luther King Jr. in 1955; the lunch counter sit-ins begun by four college students in Greensboro, North Carolina, in 1960; the Freedom Rides in 1961 to integrate interstate transportation in the South; the marches headed by the Reverend Fred Shuttlesworth against segregation in Birmingham, Alabama, in 1963; and, finally, Randolph's own March on Washington for Jobs and Freedom at the Lincoln Memorial on August 28, 1963, when Dr. King delivered his "I Have a Dream" speech.

All those televised spectacles of principle and courage—and the brutal response to them by Southern whites, most notoriously Birmingham police chief Bull Connor, instigator of the Dixiecrat walkout in 1948—built pressure on the overwhelmingly white legislative and judicial structures. Even when the federal government had responded to the moral challenge of racial inequality, as in the Supreme Court's 1954 decision in *Brown v. Board of Education* to declare segregated education unconstitutional, it had failed to implement and enforce the law thoroughly in the face of the Southern strategy of "massive resistance." The civil rights bills passed by Congress in 1957 and 1960 were diluted enough to satisfy Southern Democrats and conservative Republicans.

Ultimately, it had taken the spectacle of Bull Connor turning fire hoses and police dogs against the freedom marchers in Birmingham, many of them schoolchildren, for then-President John Kennedy to submit a civil rights bill to Congress in June 1963. Then it took Kennedy's assassination the following November for Lyndon Johnson to become president. Once in the White House, Johnson was able to apply his legendary legislative skills and underestimated idealism to a bill that Kennedy in all likelihood would have lacked the savvy or guile or clout to have seen through into law. In that effort, Humphrey was Johnson's right hand.

Thirteen months before the Urban League speech, while serving as Democratic whip in the Senate, Humphrey had helped to floor-manage the Civil Rights Act of 1964, breaking a Southern filibuster after the longest debate in the upper chamber's history. So consumed was Humphrey by the effort that he remained in the Capitol even as his son

Robert underwent surgery for a cancerous tumor in his neck back in Minnesota.[16] For the rest of his life, Humphrey kept the tally sheet on which he had marked the senators' votes on cloture, the procedure that ended the filibuster and brought the bill to its successful enactment.

The Civil Rights Act banned discrimination on the basis of race, color, religion, sex, or national origins in employment, public accommodations, and federally funded programs. In order to enforce the rules on hiring, firing, and promotion, the bill also created the Equal Employment Opportunity Commission, essentially a national version of the similar body that Humphrey had established as mayor of Minneapolis nearly a generation earlier. The fact that the Urban League was convening at a hotel in Miami Beach, a city that had long barred Black people from staying in its resorts, even the Black performing artists headlining in its nightclubs, attested to the impact of the civil rights law.

For all of its virtues, however, the Civil Rights Act had largely omitted voting rights in order to enhance its chances of passage. To press for action on that issue, Dr. King led a march from Selma, Alabama, toward the state capital in Montgomery on March 7, 1965. Barely had the procession crossed the Edmund Pettus Bridge when state troopers both on foot and horseback attacked with tear gas, billy clubs, and trampling hooves, forcing the marchers into bloody retreat. That tableau compelled Johnson to introduce voting rights legislation just eight days later.

Now, after more than five months of legislative maneuvering, on the very day of Humphrey's address to the Urban League activists, the Voting Rights Act was in the process of being passed by the House of Representatives. The bill would go before the Senate, with approval assured, the next day. Johnson would sign it into law on August 6. Ninety-five years after the Fifteenth Amendment had granted Black men the right to vote, federal law would finally ensure the franchise by prohibiting any denial or restriction on the right to vote based on race or color. Moreover, federal examiners would be permitted to register voters in any resistant Southern states, and those states could not change their own voting laws without federal approval.

So on that midsummer night at the Eden Roc Hotel, with passage of the Voting Rights Act imminent, Humphrey had reason both to acknowledge his debt to civil rights activists and to feel part of their triumph:

> We have, at long last, witnessed the virtual elimination of legalized prejudice and discrimination in America. Many brave and courageous people—both colored and white—have risked their lives, and, yes, sometimes lost their lives, in carrying forward this assault upon the barriers of legalized discrimination. And we can look with pride upon the dignity and compassion—yes, even the love—which has characterized the efforts of these courageous Americans. Their actions have demonstrated that freedom still lives on these shores. They have shown us that the quest for freedom is the strongest and most compelling force in the world.[17]

Humphrey had no way of knowing it, but his speech in Miami Beach was also closing a circle in his life. One of the Urban League members listening to him was a sixty-five-year-old physician from Portland, Oregon, named DeNorval Unthank. He had moved to the city in 1929, just three years after Oregon had changed a state law banning Black people from being permanent residents. Like another Black doctor of this time, Ossian Sweet in Detroit, and like the Black postal worker in Minneapolis, Arthur Lee, Unthank had his home besieged by a white mob, and he was forced to move four more times within Portland before finding tolerant neighbors.

As the only Black doctor in Portland for many years, Dr. Unthank had welcomed the Asian, Black, and Native American patients who were otherwise denied treatment. He campaigned during World War II for Blacks to receive a fair share of jobs in nearby defense plants. Once, when the tap dancer Bill (Bojangles) Robinson was in Portland for a performance and had been turned away by every hotel, Dr. Unthank took him in. And, most relevant to Dr. Unthank's presence in Miami Beach on this night, he had helped to found Portland's chapter of the Urban League in 1945, sometimes holding meetings in his patients' waiting room. He never missed a national meeting.

Dr. Unthank's companion in both marriage and activism, until her death in 1959, was Thelma Shipman. And Thelma Shipman was the daughter of Otis Shipman, who had run the road-building company that laid down the gravel for Highway 212 outside Doland, South Dakota, back on the day in August 1922 when eleven-year-old Hubert Humphrey showed up to watch and ask questions. DeNorval Unthank, in other words, was the descendant by marriage of the first Black person whom Hubert Humphrey had ever known, the person whose own family lineage had traced back into enslavement.

As his speech to the Urban League made apparent, Humphrey held no illusions that the struggle was over. "The time has come," he said, "to recognize that although our laws are more just than ever before, true justice is for many a distant and unrealized promise." Humphrey contrasted the rising enrollment of Blacks in college and professional schools, as well as the growth of the Black middle class, with the worsening plight of the Black poor. The overall rates of unemployment, infant mortality, median income, and poverty for Black Americans, he explained, lagged farther behind those of whites than they had in 1948. Humphrey painted this disturbing picture not as cause for despair but for even greater government action, an array of programs that Johnson envisioned as his own expansion of the New Deal, what he called the "Great Society."

In an implicit homage to the Jewish friends and allies in his life, Humphrey closed with his variation on the famous formulation of the Talmudic sage Hillel: "If I am not for myself, who will be for me? But if I am only for myself, what am I? And if not now, when?" Humphrey followed with his own question, "Yes, my friends, if not now, when?" And then he concluded with a handwritten sentence he had added to the prepared text: "I believe <u>we agree</u> that the <u>only</u> answer is NOW!"[18]

On the morning after Humphrey's speech, he received laudatory coverage in both of Miami's daily papers, the *Herald* and the *News*. The local press also prominently featured the House's approval of the Voting Rights Act. Interestingly, however, the *News* did not put Humphrey on the front page. There, its lead story, filed from Washington by the Associated Press, bore a headline related to a different part of Humphrey's and Johnson's legacy: the undeclared war in Vietnam.

Almost exactly a year earlier, just weeks after passage of the Civil Rights Act of 1964, Congress had approved the Gulf of Tonkin Resolution. The measure was named for the body of water where North Vietnamese warships had supposedly attacked two American military vessels, and it empowered the president to "take all necessary measures to repel any armed attack against the forces of the United States." The attacks and responses in Vietnam had only escalated since then. Now, as the *Miami News* headline stated, "LBJ Asks $1.7 Billion, 340,000 More GIs."[19]

* * *

Crosstown Service Road, Minneapolis
December 22, 1977
On the day after the Winter Solstice, D. J. Leary pulled his car onto the shoulder of a service road just outside the landing field for the Minneapolis airport and lifted his gaze toward the overcast sky. He was looking for Air Force Two, the plane reserved for Vice President Walter Mondale, which was bringing Hubert Humphrey back home to die.

Humphrey had been part of Leary's life for thirty of his now-forty years, ever since D. J's boyhood in St. Paul, when he had leafletted for Humphrey in the 1948 Senate race. After college and the military, Leary had stomped through the snow for Humphrey as a volunteer in the 1960 Wisconsin primary against John Kennedy. He had signed on as an advance man in the 1968 presidential race against Richard Nixon, that excruciating near miss, and then handled statewide media during Humphrey's successful runs for the Senate in 1970 and 1976. Leary still loved telling the story of Humphrey on a helicopter trip to a bunch of small-town events during the 1970 campaign. When the long day of speech-making and flesh-pressing was finally done, and the men were flying back to Minneapolis, Humphrey noticed one more gaggle of people on the ground below—a bunch of skeet shooters, as it turned out—and ordered the pilot to land so he could give them his pitch for their votes.[20] After all that electoral warfare, all the heartbreak and the triumph, Leary could not bear for his last encounter to take place at Humphrey's deathbed.

Through the windshield of his idling car, Leary eventually spotted the C-137 jet descending to the tarmac. It would then taxi to a hangar at the Air National Guard base so as to avoid the general public. Leary zipped up his overcoat and put on his favorite Navy baseball cap, so different from the leisure suits he favored on the job and that Humphrey always teased him for wearing. He leaned against the rear fender of the car and peered down the westbound lane of the service road. From past experience, he knew that the limousine taking Humphrey to the family home in Waverly would have to pass this way. Sure enough, after about thirty minutes, Leary caught sight of the vehicle, black as a hearse. It streamed past him, then abruptly stopped and backed up. As Leary walked to the car, Humphrey opened the rear passenger door, and said, "Old friend, old friend."

Humphrey's journey to this final meeting had begun, in a certain sense, on August 18, 1977. On that day, less than three months after returning to the scene of his "bright sunshine" speech to deliver the commencement address at the University of Pennsylvania, Humphrey had undergone surgery at the University of Minnesota hospital for a bowel obstruction. The doctors instead found that his bladder cancer had spread through his entire pelvis and was both inoperable and terminal.

After convalescence and chemotherapy, Humphrey returned to Congress on October 25, receiving a five-minute ovation and a half hour of spoken tributes by his fellow senators. No less a nemesis than Strom Thurmond supplied a hug.[21] In early December, a similar outpouring of affection and respect from leaders in both politics and business took place at a fundraising event for the eponymous public-affairs institute that Humphrey intended to establish at the University of Minnesota. All these accolades for a man who had been so relentlessly criticized and ridiculed over the preceding dozen years could not help but sound just a bit tinny. As the journalist Aaron Latham put it in a profile of

Humphrey for *Esquire* magazine, "Everybody loves him now that they know he is dying."[22]

The reality was that Humphrey's last effort at major legislation, a bill to guarantee full employment, had been rattling around Congress for three years already and was still stuck in committee. In the process, the bill had already been watered down to appease Jimmy Carter's administration, dropping the very provisions for public-sector jobs programs that were meant to echo Franklin Roosevelt's New Deal and Lyndon Johnson's Great Society. More broadly, Humphrey had no illusions about the damage that his support of the Vietnam War had inflicted on his reputation. His hawkish stance had estranged him not only from liberals in general but also from cherished friends and mentors such as Joseph Rauh of the Americans for Democratic Action and Rudolf Heberle at Louisiana State University. Asked by Latham about his greatest regret, Humphrey was candid:

I think the misjudgment of Vietnam. At the time I did what I thought was right. It was not because Johnson was forcing me. I had very serious doubts in the beginning. Yet living and working in the White House atmosphere, I became convinced that we were doing the right thing.[23]

Even Humphrey's defining achievements in civil rights had been abraded over time. As he had presciently warned in his Urban League address, Black America was simultaneously expanding rapidly in two disparate directions, one part toward education and prosperity and the other toward entrenched poverty and despair. A treacherous gap was opening between the expectations of equality raised by civil rights laws and daily life on the street.

Just five days after Lyndon Johnson had signed the Voting Rights Act, the confrontational arrest of a Black motorist by a white police officer in the Watts section of Los Angeles exploded into violence that would be variously described as a riot or a rebellion. By either name, it caused thirty-four deaths and $40 million in property damage over nearly a week. The Watts turmoil helped catalyze a backlash by white voters that led to the Republican Party winning forty-seven seats in the House of Representatives in the 1966 midterm elections, effectively throttling the idealistic ambitions of Johnson and Humphrey. The following year, during the so-called Long, Hot Summer of 1967, a nationwide wave of unrest reached the North Side of Minneapolis. Although its genesis involved an alleged incident of police brutality downtown, much of the violence took aim at Jewish-owned stores on the North Side, along with the nearby home of a Jewish member of the City Council, imperiling the Black–Jewish partnership on civil rights that Cecil Newman and Sam Scheiner had embodied.

Both of those Minneapolis allies of Humphrey's had died after suffering, like him, late-in-life blows to their reputations. Newman was felled by a heart attack on November 8, 1976, at the age of seventy-two. Humphrey mourned him as someone who "did more for human rights than any man I know or have known," as someone who "not only inspired but advised and counseled me, helped sensitize me to civil-rights issues."[24] Newman had broken the racial barrier of the Minneapolis Club and served on bank boards and as a Democratic Convention delegate. But in the last decade of his life, a time of ascendant Black Nationalism, Newman's brand of interracial partnership could not help but seem naive and outdated to younger activists. The fearless radical of earlier decades went to his grave being disparaged by his political descendants as an "Uncle Tom."

Less than a year after Newman's death, Sam Scheiner also suffered a heart attack, dying on April 7, 1977, at the age of sixty-eight. After nearly forty years of battles on behalf of Minneapolis Jewry, Scheiner did not rate even a full obituary in the *American Jewish World*, just a couple of paragraphs in a rundown of the previous week's deaths. During the heyday of the civil rights movement, Scheiner had taken particular delight in combining his musical and ideological interests in presentations to schoolchildren. Seated at the piano, he would start to play the "Star-Spangled Banner" using only the white keys, and the kids heard it as a random spray of notes. Only when Scheiner then played the black keys as well did the anthem sound recognizably itself. But the 1967 rioting on the North Side had damaged, if not broken, something in Scheiner's spirit. In its wake, he had increasingly focused his scrutiny on anti-Semitism in the Black community, compiling file folders on the subject, as if he considered it a form of personal betrayal.

If Humphrey's image were ever going to be rehabilitated, he would not live to see it happen. As Christmas 1977 approached, Muriel flew back to Minnesota to prepare the Waverly home for Hubert's arrival. Their daughter Nancy stayed in the couple's Washington apartment, a hospital bed now its centerpiece, to help Hubert manage. Embarrassed by the way the disease had wasted him, he swathed his "scrawny neck" with a scarf and covered his wispy hair with a Tyrolean hat. Even thus costumed, his head looked "like a skull on a stick."[25]

Still, Humphrey willed himself to walk across the tarmac to the waiting jet at Andrews Air Force Base for that final flight, refusing to let the world spy him in a wheelchair.[26] On board with his protégé Mondale and his sister Frances and a few other intimates, Humphrey roused himself from an in-flight nap long enough to put in a phone call to Cal Stoll, the University of Minnesota's football coach, whose Gophers would be playing in a bowl game that night. "I'll be shouting," Humphrey promised, as if he were still the scamp taunting opposing teams from the gridiron sidelines in Doland.

When the C-137 landed, Mondale grasped Humphrey's hand as he limped down the aircraft stairs, wearing bedroom slippers, one hand gloved and the other bare. For the next ten minutes, Humphrey held forth in the hangar, regaling the reporters and camera crews for posterity's sake. "My shirts are a little smaller than they used to be, in case any of you were planning on sending one," he joked, and only a scattering of awkward laughter followed. Asked if he would remain in the Senate, Humphrey cheerily retorted, "I'm not resigning from anything. I may even join something."[27] Then the crowd broke into full, genuine applause, some of the last that Humphrey would ever hear.

As usual on visits back home, Humphrey was being picked up by Fred Gates Jr., the son of the pinball-arcade owner who had helped him steer clear of the downtown gangsters back when Humphrey was the do-gooder greenhorn running for mayor. In Gates Jr.'s limousine,

Humphrey caught sight of Leary on the roadside and said, "That's D.J." He asked Gates to put the car in reverse for a reunion.

When Leary reached into the car to hug Humphrey, the senator's arms felt "like twigs." He worried that the embrace itself would hurt. If so, Humphrey betrayed nothing.

"How are you doing?" he asked Leary.

"I'm the one to ask you," Leary replied. "I wanted to come and wish you a Merry Christmas. I didn't think all the other people needed to be around."

"I began to wonder why nobody had you here," Humphrey said, referring to the welcoming committee at the airport. "I didn't think I was really going to get a chance to see you."

The two men chatted for perhaps four or five minutes. Then Leary said softly, "I don't want you to use any extra energy."

"It's so good to see you," Humphrey said. "It's so good to see you."[28]

Leary stepped away from the car. The passenger door closed, and the limousine drove off toward the western horizon, as if trying to outrun the oncoming dusk. Twenty-two days later, on January 13, 1978, Hubert Humphrey died at the age of sixty-six.

* * *

The Druskin apartment and the *Spokesman* office
August 11, 2017, and May 25, 2020
On a summer evening forty years after Sam Scheiner's death, his daughter Susan Druskin was proceeding through her Friday rituals, a mishmash of sacred and secular. At six o'clock, she had gone to her synagogue to sing with its choir in the *kabbalat* Shabbat service, which welcomes the Sabbath. Then she returned to her high-rise apartment near downtown Minneapolis for dinner with her husband Len. After the meal, they began channel-hopping between CNN and MSNBC, not seeking anything in particular, just keeping up with the news.

In retrospect, she could not recall which station she had been watching at the time, and which sight or sound had first frozen her attention. Was it the video of all those young white men in parade formation bearing torches? Was it their chant of "You shall not replace us," which soon became "Jews shall not replace us"? Was it when they began reciting the Nazi slogan of "blood and soil"?[29]

The spectacle, Druskin soon learned from the broadcast, was a march in Charlottesville, Virginia, by several hundred white supremacists and neo-Nazis in advance of the next day's "Unite the Right" rally. The professed reason for that gathering was to protest against the impending removal of a statue of the Confederal General Robert E. Lee. In the two years since a white supremacist had shot down nine worshipers at a Black church in Charleston, South Carolina, Confederate monuments throughout the South had become flashpoints in America's unending Civil War.

On the day after the torchlight march, a white supremacist who had traveled from Ohio for the Unite the Right barreled his car into a group of antiracist counterprotestors, killing a thirty-two-year-old paralegal named Heather Heyer. During the subsequent week, President Donald Trump equated the white supremacists with the antiracists, telling reporters that there "were very fine people on both sides."[30]

Druskin was disturbed by everything she saw and heard, but she was not shocked. She had grown into adulthood in a Minneapolis and America that appeared to have not merely accepted Jews but embraced them. In the mid-1960s, Hubert Humphrey's longtime aide Arthur Naftalin had been the first Jew elected mayor of Minneapolis; since then, Minnesota had sent a series of Jews to the U.S. Senate—Rudy Boschwitz, Paul Wellstone, Norm Coleman, and Al Franken. Druskin's own lengthy career as a social worker in the Minneapolis school system attested to the vocational doors that had been opened to her generation of Jews.

Even so, the scenes from Charlottesville transported her right back to childhood memories. She thought of the movie-house newsreels of Nazi marches in Germany and of the anti-Semitic magazines that her father had subscribed to under assumed names. One time, frighteningly enough, the editor of one showed up at the Scheiners' door, asking if he could stay overnight. ("Sorry, wrong address," Mrs. Scheiner told him.) All these decades later, here were the same conspiracies about Jewish control of the world, the same veneration of Aryan purity.

"It reminded me of my father's adage," Druskin said later in recalling the August night. "He always said, 'Don't sit on your laurels. Don't rest on your laurels. It will all be back. It never goes away.' He said, 'It goes below the surface of society and is dormant. The minute somebody permits it, it re-emerges.' It's like I was just kind of waiting. I've always known it was there. It was like a smoldering fire that flames up when it's permitted."[31]

Not quite three years later, and several miles south of the Druskin apartment, Cecil Newman's granddaughter, Tracey Williams-Dillard, was catching up on work as the publisher of the *Minneapolis Spokesman*. May 25 was a federal holiday, the Monday of the Memorial Day long weekend, so Williams-Dillard had the newsroom and offices to herself. She wasn't much for celebrating holidays in general, and this solitude was especially welcome amid the Covid pandemic.

The low brick building had been the *Spokesman's* home since the late 1950s, and it qualified as a kind of historical site in the Black section of South Minneapolis. A mural on the outer wall featured Cecil Newman, photographs of him adorned the interior hallways, and his old manual typewriter sat on his granddaughter's shelf. Diagonally across 38th Street stood another landmark, the former Dreamland Café, Anthony Brutus Cassius's place, the club that the cops had raided on that night in 1945 when Newman called for help from Mayor Hubert Humphrey.

Late in the afternoon, Williams-Dillard finished up and drove to her home in the suburb of Burnsville. Sometime into the evening, her phone rang with a call from Mel Reeves, her community editor, one part activist and one part journalist. He told her that a man had been killed by the cops a few blocks down 38th Street from the *Spokesman*. There was video of it on social media. It showed a white cop with his knee on the neck of a Black man who was lying prone and face down on the street.

Tracey Williams-Dillard did not fully grasp the consequences of George Floyd's killing for the next day or two. There had been other local Black men killed by police in recent years—Jamar Clark in North Minneapolis, Philando Castile in the suburb of Falcon Heights—and protests had come and gone. Nobody had ever been convicted. In all of America, the list of Black people killed by police officers or wannabes in the past decade alone seemed endless: Trayvon Martin, Michael Brown, Eric Garner, Tamir Rice, Breanna Taylor, Ahmaud Arbery. For that matter, Williams-Dillard was old enough to recall Rodney King, battered senseless by the Los Angeles police in 1991. Just like George Floyd's death, that beating had been captured on video by a bystander. And the evidence hadn't made a bit of difference to the jurors who acquitted the cops.

When Williams-Dillard drove back to the *Spokesman* over the succeeding days, two different and nearly simultaneous sights made her realize that George Floyd had been the breaking point. One was the presence of so many white people taking part in the Minneapolis marches and rallies for racial justice, white people chanting, "Black lives matter." The other was the scorched ruin of the police precinct house on Lake Street, and the ransacked stores all along that commercial strip. In terms of both principled protest and visceral rage, Williams-Dillard had seen nothing like it in Minneapolis in her life.

"What does come to my mind," Williams-Dillard said later, "is after all these years of us African Americans being suppressed, and for all the coverage that my grandfather had done to try to right the wrong, that we're still writing the same story. Even with George Floyd waking the world up, it's as though everyone's been asleep for hundreds and hundreds and hundreds of years."[32]

Hubert Humphrey and Cecil Newman and Samuel Scheiner were all long dead, of course, by the time of Charlottesville and George Floyd. Yet the sense of *déjà vu* that Susan Druskin and Tracey Williams-Dillard experienced, their encounters with the intractability of prejudice and hatred, raises questions about legacy. In Hubert Humphrey's years as mayor, he had transformed Minneapolis from a national example of bigotry into a beacon of progress against discrimination. Now, seventy-five years later, Minneapolis was once more notorious, with the image of George Floyd's lifeless body under Derek Chauvin's knee circulating around the globe. After a history of electing such advocates of racial equality as Harry Truman and Lyndon Johnson, and in the immediate wake of making Barack Obama the first Black president in American history, the nation in 2016 had chosen Donald Trump. He was both the beneficiary and the architect of a reactionary coalition of Christian nationalists and unreconstructed racists, the metaphorical descendants of William Bell Riley, Gerald L. K. Smith, and Strom Thurmond.

So do the shadows and dust storms triumph over bright sunshine in the end? Does the arc of the moral universe, contrary to Dr. King's prophecy, just as easily point away from justice as toward it? Or, as A. Philip Randolph eloquently put it, is America continuously engaged in "the unfinished task of emancipation"?[33] The national endeavor to achieve a full, inclusive democracy proceeds not with inexorable advancement but through cycles of oppression, resistance, liberation, reformation, and retaliation. Ground can be lost, but ground can also be gained, inches at a time, and with tenacious effort it can be held. For all his flaws and failures, Hubert Humphrey had committed his life to the grinding work of trying.

* * *

Lakewood Cemetery
Autumn 1981
Toward the end of September 1981, Solomon and Alyene Slaughter put in for three vacation days apiece from their jobs, hers as a social worker for the state of Indiana and his at the blast furnace of a steel mill in Gary. The Slaughters shared a love of both travel and history, and they had made it a marital project to visit all fifty states. From their upbringing in Birmingham, Alabama, they held particularly deep feelings about the civil rights movement. Alyene had been a student at Miles College in the late 1950s and early 1960s, when that Black school was a hub of Birmingham activism and a major source of foot soldiers for the freedom movement. She had marched on the days in May 1963 when Bull Connor let loose with the fire hoses and police dogs.[34]

From their tidy brick bungalow in Gary, the Slaughters headed northwest, driving nearly 450 miles to Minneapolis. There would be one travel day going, one coming back, and one day to accomplish their goal: visiting the grave of Hubert Humphrey.

Humphrey had been buried in Lakewood Cemetery, 250 acres of softly rolling hills near the southeastern corner of what was then called Lake Calhoun.[35] The grounds held the remains of a hundred thousand people, a notable few of them Humphrey's kindred spirits in activism. Floyd Olson, the Farmer-Labor governor who had grown up among the Blacks and Jews on the North Side and been their greatest champion until Humphrey came along, lay beneath a polished granite headstone. The grave of Lena Olive Smith, the leading civil rights lawyer in the Twin Cities for most of her eighty-one years, was set near a tranquil pond. Reverend Reuben Youngdahl, the minister whom Humphrey had appointed to lead the Human Relations Council, was interred in the Garden of Praying Hands. And the casket of Cecil Newman rested on Tier 4 of Room 218 in Garden Mausoleum D.[36]

The Slaughters found their way to the Humphrey family plot, overarched by the gnarled arms of three oaks and flanked by the gardens of Faith and Reflection. In a cemetery filled with its requisite share of grandiose monuments, Hubert Humphrey's final resting place had only a simple brass marker with his name and the dates 1911—1978. The empty space beside it on a square of well-tended lawn awaited his widow Muriel. Behind Humphrey's grave stood a low stone wall, etched on the front with his signature and the four distinct seals of Minneapolis, Minnesota, the Office of the Vice President, and the United States of America. The top surface of the wall, where someone had recently laid a rose and carnation, carried a quotation from Humphrey, in a sense his final, and shortest, speech:

I have enjoyed my life, its disappointments outweighed by its pleasures. I have loved my country in a way that some people consider sentimental and out of style. I still do, and I remain an optimist, with joy, without apology, about this country and about the American experiment in democracy.

On the frigid afternoon in January 1978 when Humphrey had been buried, the mourners stood for hours at the graveside, a few even enduring frostbite in their determination to pay homage. For days afterward, as many as two hundred cars every hour rolled slowly past the site.[37] But now, more than three years later, the Slaughters were nearly alone in attendance.

The only other person nearby, as it happened, was a reporter from the *Minneapolis Tribune* named Ruth Hammond. She had grown up near a cemetery and still felt a certain affinity for them, so she had decided to write a feature article about Lakewood. She watched as Solomon sat down on the wall, his legs bent alongside Humphrey's signature, while Alyene took his picture. Then they reversed positions, and Aylene reminded Solomon to move his finger away from the camera's lens. Learning the distance that the Slaughters had traveled, all to spend barely five minutes at Humphrey's grave, Hammond asked them why.

"I appreciate what the man has done for me and for the race," Solomon answered. "That's the least I could do, if I could come up to show my condolences and respect."[38]

ACKNOWLEDGMENTS

In the dedication to this book, I wrote that it began with a question from my wife Chris. She asked that question of our friend, the historian Julian Zelizer, at a launch party in early 2015 for his book about Lyndon Johnson and the Great Society legislative program. Having lived for about twenty-five years in Minnesota, Chris was curious about what role Hubert Humphrey had played as LBJ's vice president in pushing through those laws. In the course of answering, Julian mentioned the underappreciated importance in civil rights history of Humphrey's speech at the 1948 Democratic National Convention. The proverbial light bulb went off for me at that moment. But before doing anything about it, I needed to be certain that Julian himself did not intend to write about Humphrey, 1948, and the "bright sunshine" speech. To my immense relief, Julian told me he was already deep at work on a book about Newt Gingrich and Jim Wright. So my foundational acknowledgment in this book must be to Julian, for inspiring the idea, for being generous to a fellow author, and for modeling the role of a public intellectual.

One of my earliest steps in the research process was to contact Skip Humphrey—officially, Hubert Humphrey III, but no one calls him that—in his role as executor of his father's estate. From our first conversation, Skip offered unceasing support for the book, including granting me access to the treasure trove of Humphrey's personal and family papers at the Minnesota Historical Society. Unlike Humphrey's public and political files, the familial collection is only accessible with explicit permission, and in it I found so many keys to understanding Hubert Humphrey.

Besides Skip, several other members of the Humphrey extended family and political circle bestowed their time, insight, documents, and artifacts on me. I am deeply grateful to William Howard, Julie Howard, Anne Howard-Tristani, Walter Mondale, Norman Sherman, and D. J. Leary. Mick Caouette, the writer and director of the definitive documentary film about Humphrey, *The Art of the Possible*, unstintingly shared his knowledge and visual and audio materials.

The bulk of research for this book took place at the Minnesota Historical Society (MHS) in St. Paul, and I am especially indebted to its team for soldiering on through periods of partial or total shutdown to in-person research during the Covid pandemic. Among the past and present executives, archivists, reference librarians, and desk staff, I bow down to Kent Whitworth, Jenny McElroy, Anne Thayer, Jennifer Wagner, Chris True, Erin Schultz, Heidi Heller, Hamp Smith, Debbie Miller, Jennifer Kleinjung, MacKenzie Ryan, Brigid Shields, Ellen Jaquette, Katie Jean Davey, and Sarah Quimby. May Jah forgive me if I inadvertently omitted any names from the exceptional MHS team.

As readers of this book will discover, my intent was not to write a conventional biography of Humphrey but to surround him with his allies, influences, and adversaries, and to place him in the context of Minneapolis's disgraceful history of racism and anti-Semitism. In those pursuits, I was immeasurably educated by two scholars at the University of Minnesota, each of whom has developed a remarkable digital repository. Riv-Ellen Prell produced the groundbreaking scholarly investigation into the university's own practices of racial and religious bigotry, "A Campus Divided." Kirsten Delegard has overseen two related websites—"Mapping Prejudice," about the pervasive use of restrictive covenants in the Twin Cities, and "Historyapolis," a kind of local encyclopedia of what Herbert Gutman famously called "history from below." Riv-Ellen and Kirsten both read and commented on substantial portions of my manuscript and answered innumerable questions and emails of mine as I sought to raise my work to their level.

Another outstanding scholar of Minneapolis history, Laura Weber, rigorously vetted all of the chapters in this book that dealt with the city, and I'm thankful for her scrutiny.

In telling the story of Cecil Newman, and hopefully restoring him to his deserved prominence in both African American and journalistic history, I received consistent support and enthusiasm from his granddaughter, Tracey Williams-Dillard, who continues to publish the *Spokesman*. Similarly, my ability to portray Samuel Scheiner was greatly enhanced by the support of his daughter, Susan Druskin, and of Steve Hunegs, executive director of the Jewish Community Relations Council, the successor organization to Scheiner's Minnesota Jewish Council. During the direst months of the pandemic, Mordecai Specktor bravely allowed me to sit (with social distance) in his editor's office at the *American Jewish World* so I could read the bound volumes of that newspaper from the 1930s and 1940s. When conditions improved somewhat with the advent of Covid vaccines, I moved that research to the Upper Midwest Jewish Archives at the University of Minnesota, where I benefited from the expertise of Kate Dietrick and Mary Blissenbach.

In my homage to other archives and archivists, let me also give shout-outs to: Chelle Somsen, Halley Hair, Kimberly Smith, Sara Casper, Virgina Hanson, Matthew T. Rietzzel, Kevin DeVries, and Nicole Hosette at the South Dakota State Archives; Germain Bienvenu and Barry Cowan at the Hill Memorial Library at Louisiana State University; Gregory Rosauer of the Berntsen Library at the University of Northwestern; Jenna Jacobs, Bailey Diers, and Ted Hathaway at the Hennepin County Library Special Collections; Shaun Stalzer, Laura Heller, Mike Allard, Jeff Giambrone, De'Niecechsi Layton, Erin McCain, Andrew McNulty, Ally Mellon, William Thompson, and Archie Skiffer at the Mississippi Department of Archives and History; Lisa Moore at the Amistad Research Center; Robert Spinelli at the Fisk University Archives; Jim Armistead at the Harry S. Truman Library; Bridgett Pride and Jack Patterson at the Schomburg Center for Research in Black Culture; John Pettit at the Temple University Archives; Amanda Rindler at the Indiana University Archives; Alan Weirdak at the George Meany Labor Archive at the University of Maryland; Erik Moore at the

University of Minnesota Archives; Samuel Herley at the South Dakota Oral History Center; and Daniel Smith at Garrett Theological Seminary.

During nearly eight years of research on this book, I was beyond fortunate to have some invaluable, expert assistance. Elizabeth Gomoll, the GOAT of genealogists, went far beyond assembling family trees, excavating way into the social, cultural, and historical roots of dozens of individuals. Her enthusiasm for this project nourished my own. Cynthia Maharrey, a specialist in African American genealogy, and Dan Sullivan, a gifted historian and author based in Omaha, contributed greatly to my understanding of the Shipman family and its history. Joanna Arcieri, a doctoral candidate in journalism at Columbia University and a former student of mine there, put her passion for political history into the service of this book. Abigail Goldberg-Zelizer, an apple that fell very near the tree of her historian parents Julian Zelizer and Meg Jacobs, helped me get a detailed sense of Hubert Humphrey's 1948 race for Senate. Under great time pressure, Jan Hillegas spelunked through the archival records of Rev. Charles Hamilton in Mississippi. Jacob Torkelson provided invaluable expertise in helping me understand the architectural intricacies of structures from the build-it-yourself houses in Doland to the Convention Hall in Philadelphia. A. J. Goldmann, an accomplished arts journalist based in Munich, steered me to Alexander Pearson, who translated Franziska Heberle's remarkable wartime letters from their original German into English. Aliza Hornblass and Gabriel Fisher were vital in transforming my markups of various secondary sources into digital files.

I have been blessed to have two academic homes during my lengthy periods of research and writing this book. At Columbia Journalism School, where I have been on the full-time faculty since 1993, I've been supported and inspired by deans, professors, and administrative and technical staff. Once more at the risk of forgetting someone in a brain freeze, let me deeply thank: Dean Jelani Cobb; former deans Steve Coll and Nick Lemann; faculty homies Michael Shapiro, Ari Goldman, Alisa Solomon, LynNell Hancock, David Hajdu, June Cross, Kia Gregory, Dale Maharidge, and Kerry Donahue; current and former administrators Winnie O'Kelley, Sheila Coronel, Melanie Huff, Elena

Cabral, Laura Muha, Jane Eisner, Melissa O'Keeffe, and Chanel Roche; tech wizards Andrew Lynagh, Jeff Sieben, Andre Wood, Carlos Ivan Cruz Rijos, Nicholas Mistretta, and A. J. Mangone; librarian Kristina Vela Bisbee; and the beyond-category Debi Jackson, Tanya Mottley, Ryan Neary, Thaddeus Craddock, Derek Gano, and Scott Osborn. Then, of course, there are my students in the Book Seminar every spring semester, whose presence and promise keep me bringing my best game.

The other pole of my academic life has been at the University of Minnesota. In 2019, the then-dean of the Humphrey School of Public Affairs, Laura Bloomberg, generously appointed me to a research scholar's position, which provided me with the huge assets of office space and library privileges. Now that Laura has gone on to become president of Cleveland State University, her successor at the Humphrey School, Dean Nisha Botchwey, has very kindly extended my tenancy. From the larger community of "the U," I want to thank Andrew Elfenbein, Elisia Cohen, Kate Solomonson, Elaine Tyler May, John Wright, Tonisha White, Sherri Holmen, Pam St. Michel, Brian Gjerde, and Julian Fradda.

Beyond the university itself, Minneapolis has been a welcoming second home for Chris and me. Among the people who have enriched our lives here, and have kept me personally in functional mental and physical health for this marathon of a book, are: Rabbi Morris Allen, Dr. Phyllis Gorin, Steven Foldes, Jim (Frenchy) Lefebvre, Kathryn Quaintance, Kate Parry, Nan Blomquist, Melissa Falldin, Sharyn Jackson, Dr. Jon Finnoff, Dr. Jeffrey Payne, Dr. Dinesh Goyal, Joshua Mayhugh, Jack Goldenberg, and Austen Kordosky.

For sundry reasons—reading portions of the manuscript, pointing me in fruitful directions, digging out documentary evidence, and just plain being a mensch—I am also indebted to Joseph Crespino, Robert Mann, Timothy Thurber, Davis Houck, Don Mendel, Tip Myles, Roberta Widman Ganz, Tim Mulligan, David Stone, Dan Egan, Dave Huft, Ken Skorseth, Kam DesLauriens, Rev. Dr. David Gushee, Kevin Kephart, Neil Foster, Paul Maccabee, Volker Berghahn, Jeff Smith, Mia Bay, Joan Quigley, Sarah Tittle, Deborah Lipstadt, Ann Juergens, Jay Weiner, Antje and Edward Kolodziej, Bill Blomquist, Michael Bobelian, Sheraz Farooqi, Robby Luckett, Sid Bedingfield, Dr. David Kaufman,

Dr. Britt Zimmerman, Michael Lansing, Greg Kaster, David King, John Wareham, Mary Lockhart, Molly Rozum, Justin McCarthy, Dave Krajicek, and Jason Myles.

Barney Karpfinger has been my devoted agent and my dear friend for going on forty years. His fervent belief in this book has helped sustain me throughout the journey, and he has been steadfast during an entire career in which I've insisted on playing the music inside my head, no matter what the marketplace says. Hopefully, with this book, we will have proven all the naysayers wrong.

Tim Bent, my editor at Oxford University Press, entered my writing life with some extremely large shoes to fill. Those belonged to the late Alice Mayhew, the legendary editor at Simon & Schuster with whom I had worked on four books over a twenty-five-year period. Adding to the challenge that Tim faced, the Covid pandemic struck less than a year after he had acquired *Into the Bright Sunshine*, meaning that we were rarely able to meet in person over the next two and half years as we tried to build up the necessary mutual trust between an author and editor on their first joint project. Tim more than hit the mark, whether it was adjusting my deadline when important archives shut down for public health reasons, talking through structural and conceptual questions, or providing precise and incisive line edits. In an overarching way, he made me feel that this book mattered.

Elsewhere at Oxford University Press, Brady McNamara designed a book cover that I had concocted in my imagination but could not quite believe a designer could put in material form. Ris Harp at OUP and Jubilee James at Newgen smoothly oversaw the production process. Gabriel Kachuck and Leah Paulos put their energy and expertise into publicizing this book.

My family has been the source of so much joy, and also some very necessary distraction, during the making of this book. It's been an ongoing pleasure to see my son Aaron and my daughter Sarah find both their professional paths and great personal happiness. And it's been inspiring to see my children continue to fight, as Humphrey did, for a more equitable and just society. While it's true that no one gets to choose their family, I could not have asked for better siblings than my sister Carol and my brother Ken or for a cousin as close to us all as Yoni Neirman. My aunts Fannie Stevens and Jacqueline Freedman are cherished, living links to the wartime and postwar years at the heart of this book.

I dedicated this book to Christia Chana Blomquist Freedman. But that gesture is insufficient, because what I really dedicate to her is all of my life, whatever I have to give. May it be worthy of her.

Samuel G. Freedman
October 9, 2022

NOTES

Prologue

1. "Announcement of Candidacy," April 27, 1968. HHSTF 310.G.14.3B, Box 32.
2. For the account of Humphrey's entire illness: Ralph H. Hruban et al., "Molecular Biology and the Early Detection of Carcinoma of the Bladder— The Case of Hubert H. Humphrey, *New England Journal of Medicine*, Vol. 330, No. 18, May 5, 1994; Christopher Hartman, and Robert Moldwin, "Hubert Humphrey's Bladder Cancer," *Journal of Urology*, Vol. 191, No. 4S, May 19, 2014; "Medicine: H.H.H.'s Cystectomy," unsigned, *TIME*, Oct. 18, 1976; Dr. W. Britt Zimmerman, author interview.
3. "The Ebullience of Hubert Humphrey," unsigned editorial, *Washington Post*, Aug. 23, 1977.
4. Pat Gray, author interview.
5. Humphrey on *Today* show, NBC, May 27, 1977.
6. Hy Berman, author interview; Hy Berman with Jay Weiner, *Professor Berman*.
7. Hunter S. Thompson, "More Late News from Bleak House," *Rolling Stone*, May 11, 1977.
8. Theodore H. White, *The Making of the President 1972*, p. 120.
9. Culver oral history, HHOHP.
10. Andrew Biemiller oral history, HHOHP.
11. Humphrey letter to Eugenie Anderson, Jan. 6, 1976, HHPFP Box 148.A.18.18F.
12. Humphrey letter to Anderson, Jan. 23, 1977, HHPFP Box 148.A.18.18F.
13. "Students Picket Hubert Humphrey at Convention Hall Appearance," *Daily Pennsylvanian*, Oct. 28, 1965; "300,000, Confetti Hail Nominee," *Philadelphia Inquirer*, Sept. 10, 1968; "Humphrey Is Heckled by Students," *Philadelphia Inquirer*, April 19, 1972.
14. *Commencement Address at the University of Pennsylvania, Philadelphia*, May 22, 1977, Sound Recording Collection. Hubert H. Humphrey Papers. Minnesota Historical Society, St. Paul.
15. *Democracy at Work*, p. 190

Chapter 1

1. Wright, *Racial Violence in Kentucky, 1865–1940*, pp. 19, 38, 73, 307.

2. R. E. Farwell, quoted in "We Were Here: African-Americans in Danville and Boyle County, Kentucky," Michael J. Denis.

3. *Battle Creek Enterprise*, Battle Creek, NE, Oct. 31, 1912, and Oct. 26, 1911.

4. Olga Burge oral history, HHAF, Box 1, MHS.

5. "Local and Other News," *Times-Record*, Aug. 10, 1922. Shipman Brothers is identified by name as doing the "dirt work" in "State Highway Construction under Federal Aid," *Times-Record,* Aug. 31, 1922.

6. *South Dakota Hiway [sic] Magazine*, vol. 1, no. 1, Dec. 10, 1925.

7. German-speaking immigrants from Ukraine, to be precise.

8. Humphrey interrupts during Norman Sherman interview of Charles Hyneman, HHAF, Box 1, MHS; interview with Norman Sherman for book, HHAF, Box 148.B.9.11B; Humphrey, *The Education of a Public Man*, p. 344. N.B.: All page citations for *The Education of a Public Man* in my footnotes refer to the 1991 paperback edition of the book (Minneapolis: University of Minnesota Press), which was originally published in hardcover in 1978 by Doubleday.

9. Hubert Humphrey, "My Father," *Atlantic Monthly*, November 1966.

10. Susie Albrecht, ed., *Doland, S.D. Centennial, 1882–1982.*

11. Ibid.

12. Solberg, *Hubert Humphrey*, p. 24.

13. Humphrey, *The Education of a Public Man*, p. 5.

14. Sullivan, "The Peruna Story," in *Bottles and Extras*.

15. Ibid.

16. Author interview, Gregory Higy and Lucas Richert, Nov. 13, 2019.

17. Sannes family history booklet, HHPFP, 148.B.10.10F.

18. "Forty-Year Dream Comes True for H.H. Humphrey In Modern, New Drugstore; Opens Thursday," undated from the *Huronite and Daily Plainsman*, HHPFP, 148.B.10.11.B.

19. Anderson, "Microhistory of South Dakota Agriculture, 1919–20."

20. Thompson, *A New South Dakota History*, p. 229.

21. "Farm Performance in North Central South Dakota, 1930–1939," Agricultural Extension Station, South Dakota State College, Brookings.

22. Hamlin and Noyes, "100 Years of South Dakota Agriculture, 1900–1999."

23. Albrecht, *Doland, S.D. Centennial, 1882–1982.*

24. *Times-Record*, April 16, 1920.

25. Frances Humphrey Howard interview, MCPM Box 1.

26. *Times-Record*, March 5, 1920.

27. Author interview, Harvey Wollman.

28. Ibid.

29. The equivalent of about $85,000 in 2021, when the median home price in Doland was about $50,000.

30. Frances Humphrey Howard, interview for Cosmos Club, in FHHP, Box 9, Schlesinger Library, Harvard University, Cambridge MA.

31. H. H. letter to Hubert, undated from 1945, HHPHP, 148.B.10.10F.

32. The term "World War I" did not come into common use until the late 1930s, as the next global war was building.

33. Humphrey, *Education of a Public Man*, p. 9.

34. Frances Humphrey Howard, text of speech "Straight from the Heartland," FHHP, Box 2.

35. Eugenie Anderson oral history, HHOHP.

36. Humphrey, "My Father," *Atlantic Monthly*, Nov. 1966.

37. Humphrey uses the term as a proper noun, although other longtime residents of Doland recall it as more of a descriptor than a name.

38. Erin Beck, "South Dakota Claim Shanty," https://www.sdstate.edu/south-dak ota-agricultural-heritage-museum/south-dakota-claim-shanty; author inter- views with Don Mendel and Norbert "Tip" Miles, July 18 and 20, 2021.

39. Humphrey, *Education of a Public Man*, p. 8.

40. Webb, *The Great Plains*, p. 8.

41. Author interview, Don Mendel.

42. Webb, *The Great Plains*, p. 478.

43. *Times-Record*, crop price chart, March 12, 1920.

44. Maurice Leven, *Income in the Various States*, p. 256.

45. Curtis Mosher, "The Cause of Banking Failure in the Northwestern States"; in the 1920s, the Minneapolis district of the Federal Reserve also included a few banks in Wisconsin and Michigan.

46. Author interviews Kevin Kephart, Neal Foster, Shaukat Ali, and Sunish Sehgal.

47. A. P. Roelfs, *Estimated Losses Caused by Rust in Small Grain Cereals in the United States—1918–76*, p. 20.

48. Leonard Schrader et al., *South Dakota Weeds*, pp. 14–15.

49. *Dakota Farmer*, June 1, 1922.

50. Leven, *Income in the Various States*, p. 256.

51. *Times-Record*, April 8, 1921.

52. Ibid., April 15, 1921.

53. Ibid., May 28, 1920.

54. In Humphrey's autobiography, *The Education of a Public Man*, he places this event in 1927, and virtually every biographer or historian writing about him has repeated that version. It is, however, plainly incorrect. The warranty deed for the home sale, dated Oct. 27, 1922, remains accessible in the Spink County Courthouse. Records of the Doland City Council confirm that, as of 1923, H. H. was representing the Second Ward, where his family rented a house; earlier, he had represented the First Ward, where the four-square home was located. In an interview for the HHOHP, Julian Hartt emphasizes that the book is incorrect about the year that the Humphrey family lost its home. Hartt recalls only ever visiting young Hubert in the later, rented home.

55. Humphrey, *Education of a Public Man*, p. 15; Frances Humphrey Howard interview in MCPM, MHS.

56. Lundy, G. "Farm Mortgage Experience in South Dakota: 1910–40," p. 30.

57. North American Construction Company, Aladdin Houses, spring 1910, pp. 16–18.

58. Julian Hartt oral history, HHOHP.

59. Humphrey, *Education of a Public Man*, p. 15; Humphrey, "My Father," *Atlantic Monthly*; Humphrey interview with Eiler Ravenholt, HHPFP 148.B.10.10.F.

60. *Times-Record*, July 19, and July 26, 1923.

61. Vanepps-Taylor, *Forgotten Lives*, pp. 160–162.

62. Charles Rambow, "The Ku Klux Klan in the 1920," in Thompson, *South Dakota History*.

63. Benson and Eggers, "Black People in South Dakota."

64. *Times-Record*, Aug. 16, 1923.

65. Ibid., Dec. 13, 1923.

66. Humphrey, *Education of a Public Man*, p. 16.

67. Humphrey, "My Father," *Atlantic Monthly*.

68. Julian Hartt, memoir part 2; Hartt oral history, HHOHP.

69. *Times-Record*, Dec. 10, 1925.

70. Dawson, "South Dakota Farm Production and Price."

71. Steele, "Farm Mortgage Foreclosures in South Dakota, 1921–1932."

72. Hamlin, "100 Years of South Dakota Agriculture."

73. *Times-Record*, May 1, 1924.

74. Description drawn from Frances Humphrey Howard papers, Box 2; Hubert Humphrey audio in collection of Mick Caouette/South Hill Films; and Olga Burge oral history, HHAF Box 148.B.9.10F, MHS.

75. Author interview, Charles Calomiris.

76. The Depositors' Guaranty Fund was essentially a statewide version of the later New Deal program FDIC.

77. "Seventeenth Biennial Report of the Superintendent of Banks," State of South Dakota, 1926.

78. *Times-Record*, Jan. 7, 1926.

79. South Dakota Banking Commission Minutes, 1915–1972, V. 1, pp. 243, 297, 302, 517, 569, 611. South Dakota State Historical Society—State Archives, Pierre.

80. Ravenholt interview.

81. Humphrey, *Education of a Public Man*, p. 12.

82. Julian Hartt interview, MCPM, Box P2826, MHS.

83. *The Evening Huronite*, May 14, 1931.

84. Humphrey, Ravenholt interview, 148.B.10.10F

85. Julian Hartt interview, MCPM, P2826, MHS.

86. Julian Hartt, "Pieties of the Prairie."

87. Ibid.

88. Matthew 5:41, *King James Version.*

89. Julian Hartt, "Pieties of the Prairie."

90. Julian Hartt interview, HHOHP.

91. Julian Hartt interview, MCPM, P2826, MHS.

92. Hartt, "What We Make of the World: Selections from Yankee Preacher, Prairie Son."

93. Hartt, "What We Make of the World: Selections from Yankee Preacher, Prairie Son."

94. Ibid.

95. Humphrey, *Education of a Public Man,* p. 10; Charles L. Garrettson III, *Hubert H. Humphrey: The Politics of Joy,* pp. 12–13.

96. Blount, "The History of the Epworth League," p. 52.

97. Ibid., p. 50.

98. Sudhakanta Roy Choudhury, "Why Is Gandhi a Living Voice?," *Epworth Herald,* July 9, 1927.

99. Mame Mason Higgins, "He's an Honor Man, but—," *Epworth Herald,* Feb. 12, 1927.

100. Harry Emerson Fosdick, "Thrills," *Epworth Herald,* March 24, 1928.

101. Francis H. Case, "Patriotism—Counterfeit and Genuine," *Epworth Herald,* June 13, 1925.

102. Humphrey, *Education of a Public Man,* p. 16.

103. Hartt, "Pieties of the Prairie."

104. Hartt, "What We Make," part 2.

105. Humphrey, *Education of a Public Man,* p. 16.

106. Julian Hartt oral history, HHOHP, MHS.

107. Hubert Humphrey interview by Eiler Ravenholt, HHPFP 148.B.10.10F, MHS.

108. HHPFP 148.A.19.2F.

109. Humphrey, *Education of a Public Man,* p. 17.

110. *Times-Record,* May 9, 1929.

111. Ibid., June 6, 1929.

112. Ibid., May 23, 1929.

113. Humphrey, *Education of a Public Man,* p. 17.

114. *Minnesota Daily,* p. 1., Oct. 3, 1929.

115. Humphrey, *Education of a Public Man,* p. 19.

116. HHPFP 148.A.18.18F.

117. Solberg, *Hubert Humphrey,* p. 47.

118. *Minnesota Daily,* October 18, 1929.

119. Ibid., p. 2.

120. https://www.federalreservehistory.org/essays/stock-market-crash-of-1929; https://www.thebalancemoney.com/black-tuesday-definition-cause-kickoff-to-depression-3305819.

121. *Minneapolis Tribune,* Nov. 1, 1929, p. 1.

122. Ibid., p. 22.

123. *Minnesota Daily*, Oct. 31, 1929.

124. *Minneapolis Star*, Nov. 1, 1929.

125. *Times-Record*, Oct. 24, 1929.

126. Ibid., Nov. 7, 1929.

127. Hubert Humphrey Sr. letter to creditors, July 1930, HHPFP 148.B.10.15B.

128. Solberg, *Hubert Humphrey*, p. 47.

129. Humphrey, *Education of a Public Man*, p. 23.

130. Ibid.

131. Ibid., p. 24.

Chapter 2

1. "Crowd of 3,000 Renews Attack on Negroes Home," *Minneapolis Tribune*, July 16, 1931.

2. Mary Forman oral history, Juergens private collection.

3. Ibid.

4. Kirsten Delegard, "July: Month of Rage," http://historyapolis.com/blog/2014/07/23/july-month-rage/.

5. Maurine Boie, "A Study of Conflict and Accommodation in Negro-White Relations in the Twin Cities," p. 8.

6. "HOME STONED IN RACE ROW," *Minneapolis Tribune*, July 15, 1931; "Police Guard Negro's Home" and "House Smeared with Paint in Row," *Minneapolis Star*, July 15, 1931.

7. Ibid.

8. Boie, "A Study of Conflict and Accommodation in Negro-White Relations in the Twin Cities," p. 13.

9. Raymond Cannon oral history, MHS.

10. Ibid.

11. Boie, "A Study of Conflict and Accommodation in Negro-White Relations in the Twin Cities," p. 13.

12. "Crowd of 3,000 Renews Attack on Negroes' Home," *Minneapolis Tribune*, July 16, 1931.

13. Cannon oral history.

14. Cannon oral history.

15. "Crowds Besiege Negro's Home in Effort to Make Him Move," "2-Day Truce Asked in War to Oust Negro from Home," "Mayor Pleads with Citizens to Remain Away from Home," *Minneapolis Star*, July 16, 1931.

16. Ann Juergens, "Lena Olive Smith: A Minnesota Civil Rights Pioneer."

17. Chatwood Hall, "A Roman Holiday in Minneapolis," *The Crisis*, Oct. 1931.

18. Forman oral history.

19. "Lee Home Again Threatened after Trouble with Boys," *Twin-City Herald*, Sept. 17, 1932; "This World," *Twin-City Herald*, Oct. 1, 1932.

20. Leipold, *Cecil E. Newman*, pp. 63–64; Lori Richardson, "A Dream Comes True."

21. *Twin-City Herald*, Aug. 8, 1931, cited by Boie, "A Study of Conflict and Accommodation in Negro-White Relations in the Twin Cities," p. 38.

22. "Lee Case Again Topic as Assault Case Heard," *Twin-City Herald*, Sept. 24, 1932.

23. Author interview, Tracey Williams-Dillard.

24. In his biography, Newman says that both of his parents attended several years of high school and his father became a chef, but there is no independent confirmation of those assertions.

25. Leipold, *Cecil E. Newman*, p 32.

26. Ibid., pp. 27–28.

27. Ibid., p. 46.

28. Ibid., p. 27.

29. "Editor Backs Up All Minorities," *Minneapolis Tribune*, Aug. 31, 1947.

30. "What of Tomorrow," *Twin-City Herald*, April 30, 1927.

31. "This World," *Twin-City Herald*, Oct. 1, 1932.

32. Ibid.

33. "This World," *Twin-City Herald*, March 25, 1933.

34. "This World," *Twin-City Herald*, June 18, 1932.

35. "We Have Faith and Confidence in Minneapolis and St. Paul," *Minneapolis Spokesman*, Aug. 10, 1934.

36. Minneapolis was founded in 1850, though not chartered until 1867. The municipal boundaries of the time did not include the adjoining city of St. Anthony. The two merged in 1872, forming most of the present-day Minneapolis.

37. *The Free North*, Twin Cities Public Television. The University of Minnesota was founded in 1851, seven years before the state itself joined the United States.

38. Don E. Fehrenbacher, *The Dred Scott Case*, pp. 244–247; "Enslaved African Americans and the Fight for Freedom." https://www.mnhs.org/fortsnelling/learn/african-americans.

39. Fehrenbacher, *The Dred Scott Case*, p. 353. He cites original on pp. 416–417 of the published decision.

40. Earl Spangler, *The Negro in Minnesota*, p. 38.

41. William Green, *Degrees of Freedom*, p. 129.

42. Ibid., p. 222.

43. James Curry, "Hastings, 1907: The Burning of Brown's Chapel AM," https://www.minnpost.com/mnopedia/2021/04/hastings-1907-the-burning-of-browns-chapel-ame/.

44. Spangler, *The Negro in Minnesota*, p. 102; Elizabeth Dorsey Hatle and Nancy M. Vaillancourt, "One Flag, One School, One Language: Minnesota's Ku Klux Klan in the 1920s"; Tina Burnside, "On June 15 1920, a Duluth Mob Lynched Three Black Men," https://www.minnpost.com/mnopedia/2019/07/on-june-15-1920-a-duluth-mob-lynched-three-black-men.

45. *Call of the North*, Nov. 14, 1923, p. 4.

46. Hatle, "One Flag, One School, One Language."

47. "Gompers Speaks to Big Audience," *Minneapolis Journal*, May 24, 1905.

48. Michiko Hase, "W. Gertrude Brown's Struggle for Racial Justice, Female Leadership and Community in Black Minneapolis, 1920–1940," pp. 30–33.

49. Boie, "A Study of Conflict and Accommodation in Negro-White Relations in the Twin Cities—Based on Documentary Sources," pp. 97–98.

50. Harris L. Abrams, *The Negro Population in Minneapolis: A Study in Race Relations*, pp. 36–37.

51. Barbara Cyrus oral history, Juergens private collection.

52. Raymond Cannon oral history.

53. David Vassar Taylor, *African Americans in Minnesota*, p. 39.

54. Ibid., p. 34.

55. Schmid, *Social Saga of Two Cities*, p. 176.

56. Luke Mielke, "Racial Uplift in a Jim Crow Local: Black Union Organizing in Minneapolis Hotels 1930–1940," pp. 21–22.

57. Anthony Brutus Cassius oral history, 20th Century Radicalism in Minnesota Project, MHS.

58. Taylor, *African Americans in Minnesota*, p. 26; Paul Nelson, "National Afro-American Council Meeting, 1902," https://www.mnopedia.org/event/natio nal-afro-american-council-meeting-1902.

59. Taylor, *African Americans in Minnesota*, pp. 15, 30.

60. "United States Census of Religious Bodies, County File, 1926," https://www .thearda.com/Archive/Files/Downloads/1926CENSCT_DL2.asp.

61. Calvin F. Schmid, *Social Saga of Two Cities*, p. 79.

62. Ibid., p. 78.

63. Boie, "A Study of Conflict and Accommodation in Negro-White Relations in the Twin Cities—Based on Documentary Sources," p. 122.

64. Hase, "W. Gertrude Brown's Struggle for Racial Justice, Female Leadership and Community in Black Minneapolis, 1920–1940," p. 131.

65. *Minnesota Messenger*, August 5, 1922, p. 1.

66. Ann Juergens, "Lena Olive Smith: A Minnesota Civil Rights Pioneer."

67. Better-known by her later, married name of Nellie Stone Johnson.

68. Nellie Stone Johnson, pp. 70, 73. *Nellie Stone Johnson: The Life of an Activist*, pp. 70, 73.

69. Boie, "A Study of Conflict and Accommodation in Negro-White Relations in the Twin Cities—Based on Documentary Sources," p. 21.

70. Ibid., pp. 23–24.

71. Ibid., pp. 37–38.
72. Ibid., p. 27.
73. Leipold, *Cecil E. Newman*, pp. 86–87.
74. Author interview, Wayne Glanton.
75. Leipold, *Cecil Newman*, pp. 77–78, 87.
76. Schmid, *Social Saga of Two Cities*, p. 18. The exact numbers he cites as $361 million in 1929 and $171 million in 1933.
77. Raymond L. Koch, "Politics and Relief in Minnesota During the 1930s," p. 154.
78. Ibid., pp. 158–159.
79. Schmid taught at the University of Minnesota from 1931 through 1937, when he took a position at the University of Washington, where he spent most of his academic career.
80. Schmid, *Social Saga of Two Cities*, p. 51.
81. Mielke, "Racial Uplift in a Jim Crow Local," pp. 79–80.
82. Millikan, *A Union against Unions*, pp. 249–250.
83. Gordon Parks, *A Choice of Weapons*, pp. 54–55.
84. "This World," *Twin-City Herald*, Feb. 25, 1933.
85. Philip Foner, *Organized Labor and the Black Worker, 1619–1981*, p. 200.
86. "This World," *Twin-City Herald*, Sept. 9, 1933.
87. "This World," *Twin-City Herald*, Nov. 22, 1933.
88. Bryan Palmer, *Revolutionary Teamsters*, p. 37.
89. Millikan, *A Union against Unions*, p. 12.
90. Palmer, *Revolutionary Teamsters*, p. 33.
91. Ibid., pp. 67, 88.
92. Ibid., pp. 97–101.
93. Ibid., p. 172.
94. "The Strike Situation" and "W.M. Smith," *Minneapolis Spokesman*, Aug. 17, 1934.
95. Paul D. Moreno, *Black Americans and Organized Labor*, p. 102; David Witwer, "Race Relations in the Early Teamsters Union."
96. Mielke, "Racial Uplift in a Jim Crow Local," p. 8.
97. Ibid., p 7.
98. Hase, "W. Gertrude Brown's Struggle for Racial Justice," p. 148.
99. Dewitt, Larry, "The Decision to Exclude Agricultural and Domestic Workers from the 1935 Social Security Act."
100. Ira Katznelson, *Fear Itself*, p. 260.
101. Robert L. Zangrando, "The NAACP and a Federal Antilynching Bill, 1934–1940."
102. "The President's Message," *Minneapolis Spokesman*, Jan. 10, 1936.
103. "Call for a National Negro Conference," *Minneapolis Spokesman*, May 3, 1935.
104. "Is It Fair?," *Minneapolis Spokesman*, May 10, 1935.

105. "Our Fight Is Your Fight," *Minneapolis Spokesman*, May 31, 1935.

106. "The Brewery Situation," *Minneapolis Spokesman*, May 24, 1935.

107. "Editorial Notes," *Minneapolis Spokesman*, April 4, 1935.

108. "The Unions and the Brewers," *Minneapolis Spokesman*, July 7, 1935.

109. Leipold, *Cecil E. Newman*, p. 92.

110. Ibid., pp. 92–93.

111. "Brutal Attack by Mill City Police Stirs Entire City," *Minneapolis Spokesman*, July 23, 1937.

112. Ibid.

113. Juergens, "Lena Olive Smith"; "Officers Involved in Jordan Case Are Penalized," *Minneapolis Spokesman*, Aug. 13, 1937.

114. Ibid.

115. Boie, "A Study of Conflict and Accommodation," pp. 23–24.

116. "This World," *Minneapolis Spokesman*, Nov. 30, 1934.

117. "Familiar Words," *Minneapolis Spokesman*, March 12, 1937.

Chapter 3

1. Hubert interview with Norman Sherman, HHAF, Box 148.B.9.11B.

2. *Evening Huronite*, various articles, Nov. 11, 1933; 11/11/33; Humphrey, *Education of a Public Man*, p. 24.

3. *Education of a Public Man*, pp. 27–28.

4. H. H. letter to Hubert, undated 1933, HHPFP, Box 148.B.10.15B.

5. Solberg, *Hubert Humphrey*, p. 50.

6. Carrie Beatty letter to Hubert, March 17, 1931. HHPFP, Box 148.B.10.15B.

7. FHHP, Box 2, Folder 7

8. Humphrey, *Education of a Public Man*, p. 28.

9. Kumlein, *Graphic Summary of the Relief Situation in South Dakota*, pp. 39, 47.

10. Husse, *Huron Revisited*, p. 216.

11. Lee, *A New Deal for South Dakota*, p. 433.

12. Humphrey, *Education of a Public Man*, p. 27.

13. For this paragraph and the preceding one: "Worst Dust Storm in History," *Evening Huronite*, Nov. 13, 1933; Charles H. Pierce, "The Dust Storm of November 12 and 13, 1933," *Bulletin of the American Meteorological Society*; Hovde, "The Great Duststorm [*sic*] of November 12, 1933," *Monthly Weather Review*; Wolff and Cash, "South Dakotans Remember the Great Depression," *South Dakota History*; Hull, *The Dirty Thirties*; additional newspaper accounts in *Daily Argus-Leader* (Sioux Falls, SD), *Aberdeen* [SD] *Evening News*, and *Daily Capital Journal* (Pierre, SD).

14. A copy of the photograph is in the collection of the South Dakota State Archives.

15. Humphrey, *Education of a Public Man*, p. 34.

16. Lowitt and Beasley, *One Third of a Nation*, p. 83.

17. Ibid., pp. 90–92.

18. Hubert Humphrey draft of speech, March 3, 1958. ADA papers, Series 5, Box 34, legislative file.

19. H. H. letter to Hubert, March 23, 1933. HHPFP, Box 148.B.10.15B.

20. "Deposits in Banks Mount as Institutions Open in Huron," *Evening Huronite*, March 15, 1933.

21. "The Future of the Forest Army," *Evening Huronite*, Sept. 14, 1933.

22. Lee, *A New Deal for South Dakota*, p. x.

23. H. H. letter to Hubert, March 23, 1933. HHPFP, Box 148.B.10.15B.

24. Humphrey, "My Scouting Past, Your Scouting Future," *Scouting*.

25. Hubert Humphrey draft of speech, March 3, 1958. ADA papers, Series 5, Box 34, legislative file.

26. FHHP, Box 9, Folder 3.

27. Harry Humphrey letter to Ralph Humphrey, March 5, 1932. HHPFP, Box 148.B.10.10F.

28. Harry Humphrey letter to Hubert, August 8, 1936. HHPFP, Box 148.B.10.15B.

29. Frances Humphrey letter to H. H., undated, but probably late 1934. HHPFP, Box 148.B.10.10F.

30. Frances Humphrey, letter to H. H., undated, but mid-1930s. HHPFP, Box 148.B.10.10F.

31. Frances Humphrey letter to H. H., undated, but 1935 by context. HHPFP, Box 148.B.10.10F.

32. "Minnesota's 'First Lady' Dies," *Minneapolis Star-Tribune*, Sept. 21, 1993; Humphrey, *Education of a Public Man*, pp. 30–31.

33. Humphrey, *Education of a Public Man*, p. 30.

34. Ibid., p. 31.

35. Andrew Buck letter to Charles Bonesteel, Nov. 6, 1932. HHPFP, Box 148.B.10.15B.

36. *Tiger* yearbook, Huron High School, 1930.

37. H. H. letter to William Shore, Aug. 6, 1948. HHPFP, Box 148.B.10.10F.

38. Solberg, *Hubert Humphrey*, p. 51.

39. Ibid., p. 51.

40. "Scout Jamboree Is Big Affair," *Evening Huronite*, May 16, 1935, and "Tour Arranged during Jamboree," *Evening Huronite*, July 1, 1935.

41. "Substitute Trips Offered to Scouts," *Evening Huronite*, Aug. 14, 1935.

42. Hubert letter to Muriel, Aug. 19, 1935. HHPFP, Box 148B.10.15B.

43. I am indebted to the educator Deborah Meier for that analogy, which I heard her use to describe her brother.

44. Hubert letter to Muriel, undated, but probably Aug. 20, 1935. HHPFP, Box 148.B.10.15B.
45. Muriel letter to Hubert, Aug. 21, 1935. HHPFP, Box 148.B.10.15B.
46. Muriel letters to Hubert, Aug. 22 and 29, 1935. HHPFP, Box 148.B.10.15B.
47. Muriel letter to Hubert, Aug. 22, 1935. HHPFP, Box 148.B.10.15B.
48. Ibid.
49. Muriel letter to Hubert, Aug. 28, 1935. HHPFP, Box 148.B.10.15B.
50. Muriel letter to Hubert, Aug. 24, 1935. HHPFP, Box 148.B.10.15B.
51. Hubert letter to Muriel, Aug. 23, 1936. HHPFP, Box 148.B.10.16F.
52. For this paragraph and the preceding two paragraphs: "F.D.R. Is Greeted by Large Throng in Visit to Huron," *Evening Huronite*, Aug. 29, 1936.
53. "Text of Roosevelt's Speech to Democrats," *Washington Post*, Aug. 25, 1935.
54. Direct quotations in this paragraph from Muriel letter to Hubert on May 11, and Hubert letters to Muriel, June 18, May 5, July 24, and May 28, 1936. HHPFP, Box 148.B.10.16F.
55. Andrew Buck letter to Hubert, Aug. 22, 1936. HHPFP, Box 148.B.10.16F.
56. Humphrey, *Education of a Public Man*, p. 32; Olga Burge interview, HHAF, 148.B.9.10F, Box 1.
57. Robert Osborn interview, HHAF, 148.B.9.10F, Box 1.
58. Humphrey, *Education of a Public Man*, p. 34.
59. Hubert letter to Muriel, May 23, 1936. HHPFP, Box 148.B.10.16F.
60. Hubert letter to Muriel, May 26, 1936. HHPFP, Box 148.B.10.16F.
61. H. H. letters to Hubert, March 23, 1933, and Aug. 9, 1936. HHPFP, Box 148.B.10.15B.
62. Hubert letter to Muriel, June 14, 1936. HHPFP, Box 148.B.10.16F.
63. The slightly varying accounts of the location and exact statements are in Humphrey's *Education of a Public Man*, p. 35, and Solberg's *Hubert Humphrey*, p. 53. The two versions completely agree on the substance of the conversation between H. H. and Hubert.
64. Humphrey, *Education of a Public Man*, p. 35.
65. Humphrey's academic transcript is contained in HHPFP, Box 148A.18.18F.
66. Jane Freeman interview. MCPM, Box P2826.
67. Shively, "In Memoriam: Benjamin Evans Lippincott," in *P.S.: Political Science and Politics*.
68. "A.F.T., Says Lippincott, Asks Freedom," *Minnesota Daily*, Nov. 23, 1938.
69. Lippincott interview by radio station KUOM. Lippincott papers, UMASC.
70. Lippincott oral history, HHOHP.
71. The accounts of Humphrey's verbosity are from, in order of the quotations or paraphrases: Solberg, *Hubert Humphrey*, p. 71; Arthur Naftalin oral history, University of Minnesota Digital Conservancy; Frank Adams interview, HHAF, 148.B.9.10F, Box 1.
72. "Protests Council's Refugee Plan," *Minnesota Daily*, Dec. 3, 1938.
73. Solberg, *Hubert Humphrey*, p. 67.

74. University of Illinois letter to Hubert, March 31, 1939. HHPFP, Box 148.B.10.15B.

75. Charles Hyneman interview, HHAF, 148.B.9.10F, Box 1.

Chapter 4

1. T. G. Wooster letter to Axel Sundborg, July 23, 1938. Thomas Gaddis file, JCRC P445, Box 25.

2. "Report on Silver Shirt meeting," dated Aug. 1, 1938. Gaddis file, JCRC P445, Box 25. See also: Sarah Atwood, "This List Not Complete: Minnesota's Jewish Resistance to the Silver Legion of America, 1936–1940," *Minnesota History*; Laura E. Weber, "'Gentiles Preferred': Minneapolis Jews and Employment, 1920–1950," *Minnesota History* (Spring 1991).

3. Travis Hoke, *Shirts!: A Survey of the New "Shirt" Organizations in the United States Seeking a Fascist Dictatorship.*

4. *Liberation*, Oct. 14, 1938.

5. *Hitler's American Friends*, p. 56.

6. *Pelley's Weekly*, July 29, 1936.

7. "Report on Silver Shirt meeting," Gaddis file, JCRC P445, Box 25.

8. "Silver Shirts Are Organizing in Minnesota," *American Jewish World*, Aug. 5, 1938.

9. "Silver Shirts Rap F.D.R. at Meeting Here," *Minnesota Leader*, Aug. 6, 1938.

10. "Silver Shirts Are Organizing in Minnesota," *American Jewish World*, Aug. 5, 1938. Cordell Hull was FDR's secretary of state, Henry Morgenthau the secretary of the Treasury, and Frances Perkins the secretary of labor.

11. Details in this paragraph are drawn from the previously noted articles in the *Minnesota Leader* and the *American Jewish World*.

12. "Report on Silver Shirt Meeting," Gaddis file, JCRC P445, Box 25.

13. "Silver Shirts Hear National Office," *Minneapolis Star*, July 30, 1938.

14. This phrase is not common in Judaic theology. The rabbi may have been borrowing and altering the terms from the Christian identifications of either Sarah in the Old Testament or Mary in the New Testament as the "mother of Christianity."

15. W. Gunther Plaut, *The Jews in Minnesota*, p. 82; Albert I. Gordon, *Jews in Transition*, p. 151.

16. Plaut, *The Jews of Minnesota*, p. 162.

17. Ibid., p. 293.

18. The description of the economy is drawn from Plaut's *The Jews in Minnesota*, pp. 283–285, and Laura E. Weber, "'Gentiles Preferred': Minneapolis Jews and Employment 1920–1950". The quotation is from Plaut, p. 20.

19. Berman, Hyman, and Linda Mack Schloff, *Jews in Minnesota*, p. 7; Rhoda Lewin, *Images of America: Jewish Community of North Minneapolis*, p. 9; Gordon, *Jews in Transition*, p. 18.
20. Schmid, *Social Saga of Two Cities*, p. 78.
21. Paul Maccabee, "Alias Kid Cann," *Mpls. St. Paul Magazine*, Nov. 1991.
22. Plaut, *The Jews in Minnesota*, p. 274.
23. Michael Gerald Rapp, "An Historical Overview of Anti-Semitism in Minnesota," p. 44.
24. "Jews Still Barred From Country Club by Realty Company," *American Jewish World*, November 23, 1934.
25. "Resort Discrimination Complaints," JCRC2.
26. "FACTS NOT THEORIES," *Saturday Press*, Nov. 19, 1927.
27. Maurice Lefkovits, "Minneapolis Jewry—An Appraisal," *American Jewish World*, Sept. 7, 1923.
28. Berman and Schloff, *Jews in Minnesota*, p. 30; Gordon, *Jews in Transition*, p. 41; Plaut, *The Jews in Minnesota*, p. 217.
29. Editorial, *American Jewish World*, Sept. 22, 1933; "Reasons for Hope," *American Jewish World*, Sept. 7, 1934.
30. Gordon, *Jews in Transition*, p. 11.
31. Sherman, Norman. *From Nowhere to Somewhere*, pp. 13–14.
32. "Discrimination against Jews Adds to Unemployment Severity in Twin Cities," *American Jewish World*, Jan. 8, 1932.
33. "Man about Town," *American Jewish World*, May 25, 1934.
34. Gordon, *Jews in Transition*, p. 50.
35. To be more specific, Coffman authorized two types of tracking. One was drawn from the required physical exams for first-year students and the other from housing records, which were used to identify Jews from New York, as if they were especially subversive.
36. "Political Surveillance of the University," https://acampusdivided.umn.edu/essay/political-surveillance-of-university/.
37. Riv-Ellen Prell, "Antisemitism without Quotas at the University of Minnesota in the 1930s and 1940s," *Jewish Social Studies 105*, nos. 1–2.
38. "Peace: Is It a Prospect or a Propaganda," text for sermon delivered Nov. 11, 1934, WBRP.
39. The article from the *Seattle Star*, undated but probably from 1913, is in Scrapbook #19, WBRP.
40. Lewis Schwartz letter to William Bell Riley, Sept. 7, 1934. Riley folder, JCRC P445 Box 46.
41. "The Protocols and Communism," text for sermon and pamphlet, Feb. 1936, WBRP; "The Jew and Communism," text for sermon delivered Oct. 18, 1936, WBRP.
42. Ibid.

43. Eric Sevareid, *Not So Wild a Dream*, p. 69. Although Eric was Sevareid's middle name, it was the one he used during his illustrious later career for CBS News.

44. Ibid., p. 70.

45. Ibid., pp. 70-71.

46. All articles from the *Minneapolis Journal*: "New Silver Shirt Clan with Incredible Credo," Sept. 11, 1936; "Silvershirts Meet Secretly Here but Come Out Openly in Pacific Coast Drive," Sept. 12, 1936; "Silvershirts Hoard Food in Readiness for Siege Foretold by Pyramids," Sept. 13, 1936; "Silver Shirts Here Elevate Maurice Rose to Status of International Banker," Sept. 14, 1936; "Silver Shirts Say Quarters Are Bought by Morgenthau in Russia at 5 Cents Each," Sept. 15, 1936; "Silvershirts' Dire Prophecy Falls Flat; World Goes On with a Chuckle over Plot," Sept. 16, 1936.

47. "A Pathetic Hallucination," *Minneapolis Journal*, Sept. 17, 1936; "Mingled Reactions," *American Jewish World*, Sept. 18, 1936.

48. The Jacobins were a rarity in the Greek system for having both Christian and Jewish members. They did not have a fraternity house, meeting instead in the student union building.

49. "What Other People Think," *Minneapolis Journal*, Sept. 15, 1936.

50. Details of Olson's experiences with the Jewish community from *American Jewish World* issues of Sept. 26, 1930; March 13, 1931; March 31, 1933. Also see Hyman Berman, "Political Antisemitism in Minnesota during the Great Depression," *Jewish Social Studies*.

51. "Governor Floyd B. Olson," *American Jewish World*, Aug. 28, 1936.

52. Minnesota held its gubernatorial elections every two years until 1966, when it switched to the more common schedule of every four years.

53. See Chapter 2 for the direct quotation and a footnote to the primary source.

54. *American Jewish World*, June 17, 1938.

55. *American Jewish World*, May 13, 1938. See also *Wesley News*, May 13, 1938.

56. "Attended Silver Shirt Meet," *Minnesota Leader*, Aug. 6, 1938.

57. "What Other People Think," *Minneapolis Journal*, Aug. 10, 1938.

58. "A Sorry Spectacle," *Minneapolis Tribune*, Aug. 5, 1938.

59. "Can't Stand the Light," Askov American, Aug. 11, 1938.

60. "Silver Shirts Are Organizing in Minnesota," *American Jewish World*, Aug. 5, 1938.

61. "Hitler in Power," *American Jewish World*, Feb. 3, 1933.

62. "Offers Plan to Cope with Silver Shirt Invasion," *American Jewish World*, Aug. 5, 1938.

63. Charles I. Cooper, "The Minnesota Jewish Council in Historical Perspective—1939-1953." JCRC, 147.A.3.7B Box 1-C.

64. Letter to the editor from "E.D.," *American Jewish World*, Aug. 12, 1938.

65. Cooper, "The Minnesota Jewish Council in Historical Perspective—1939-1953." An urban legend has persisted about Jewish gangsters in Minneapolis

breaking up a Silver Legion meeting and beating the "Shirters" so severely that the group never returned to the city. The source for this anecdote is the memoir *Easy Street* by Susan Berman, daughter of the Minneapolis (and, later, Las Vegas) gangster Davie Berman. Another author, Robert Rockaway, uncritically repeated her account in his book about Jewish gangsters, *But He Was Good to His Mother*, and in an article for the webzine *Tablet*. Berman, however, provides no supporting documentation whatsoever for the brawl she describes, and it took place between seven and nine years before her birth. To explain away the lack of any newspaper coverage of the purported brawls, she claims that the Jewish mobsters bribed police officers not to make any arrests.

66. "175 Hear Report of Local Anti-Defamation Council," *American Jewish World*, Aug. 12, 1938.

67. Berman, "Political Antisemitism in Minnesota during the Great Depression." The cartoon is reprinted in Weber, "Gentiles Preferred."

68. For whatever reason, Chase did not end the title with a question mark.

69. Berman, "Political Antisemitism in Minnesota during the Great Depression"; "Political Surveillance of the University," http://acampusdivided.umn.edu/essay/political-surveillance-of-university/.

70. "Stassen, Minnesota's 'Baby Governor,' Wades into Tough Political Battles," *Des Moines Register*, Feb. 5, 1939.

71. "WE Win with STASSEN," advertisement of *American Jewish World*, Nov. 4, 1938.

72. Cooper, "The Minnesota Jewish Council in Historical Perspective—1939–1953"; Samuel L. Scheiner, "Jewish Community Relations Council of Minnesota: Yesterday, Today and Tomorrow," 1964.

73. Reinhardt was widely identified as a "gypsy" guitarist, when that pejorative time was commonly used. His heritage was part Romani and part Belgian, but he did his most influential musical work in France.

74. "Man about Town," *American Jewish World*, Jan. 12, 1934, and Sept. 24, 1937; Roy Robison oral history, Jazz in the Twin Cities Oral History Project, MHS.

75. Author interview, Susan Druskin.

76. Ibid.

77. Ibid. Also: Henry W. McCarr, "Amicus Curiae," *Hennepin Lawyer*.

78. The correspondence does not indicate which of the Paymar family members had tried to make the reservation.

79. SLSP Box 144.D.10.16F.

80. Samuel Scheiner letter to David Smith, Aug. 4, 1939. JCRC P445 Box 55.

81. Ibid.

82. JCRC P445, Box 16.

83. Ibid. Also: JCRC2, Boxes 116 and 117, and "Ben Cutler, 96, Whose Bands Entertained the Society Set," *New York Times*, Jan. 15, 2001.

84. JCRC P445 Box 4.

85. Albert Cyr affidavit, incorrectly dated to July 27, 1939, because it refers to events that occurred as late as July 29, 1939. JCRC P445 Box 4.
86. "Minneapolis Should Snicker about Decency" and "Comments," both in *American Jewish World*, April 1, 1932.
87. William Anderson and I. S. Joseph typed statement, JCRC P445 Box 4.
88. A copy of the complaint is preserved in the folder, "Anti-Jewish Pamphlet" in JCRC P445 Box 4.
89. A copy of the sentencing memorandum, issued Sept. 8, 1939, is preserved in JCRC P445 Box 8.
90. "A Plague of Intolerance," *Minneapolis Journal*, Sept. 8, 1939.
91. Scheiner letter to unnamed *TIME* editor, Sept. 11, 1939. JCRC P445 Box 8.
92. Dwayne Johnson letter to George Blaisdell, Sept. 27, 1939. JCRC P445 Box 8.

Chapter 5

1. Humphrey letters to Charles Hyneman, May 16, June 29, and August 16, 1939. HHP MSS. 5334, Folder 1.
2. Details of Jim Crow cars from Kornweibel, "Jim Crow Cars," p. 8; Bay, *Traveling Black*, pp. 75, 79, 85; author interview, Kirk Reynolds, author and historian of Illinois Central.
3. Quigley, *Just Another Southern Town*, pp. 130–131.
4. Humphrey, *Education of a Public Man*, pp. 344–345.
5. He would later win a Nobel Prize for his success as a United Nations diplomat in mediating a ceasefire between Israelis and Arabs to end the 1948 war.
6. The term was commonly used by Black intellectuals. It was codified in book form with the university's 1941 publication of *Howard University—The Capstone of Negro Education. A History: 1867–1941* by Howard Dyson.
7. H. H. letter to Edward Nicholson, March 28, 1940. HHPFP 148.B.10.15B.
8. Author interview, Kirk Reynolds.
9. Humphrey, *Education of a Public Man*, pp. 41–42.
10. "Louisiana Kingfish Turns Conservative, Tells Funny Jokes," *Argus-Leader* (Sioux Falls, SD), October 25, 1932.
11. Humphrey, *Education of a Public Man*, p. 40.
12. Under a complicated political arrangement that Long himself engineered, he did not actually take his seat in the Senate until 1932. He had remained governor in order to push through his legislative agenda and ensure that his preferred successor as governor would be elected.
13. While many of those improvements to the university's campus began during Long's years as governor and senator, Leche continued and expanded them in the late 1930s, partly because after Long's assassination, the Roosevelt

Administration resumed WPA aid to LSU, which had been cut off as punishment to the Kingfish.

14. Heilman, *Southern Connection*, p. 38; Williams, *Huey Long*, pp. 493, 780; Kane, *Louisiana Hayride*, pp. 216, 227; "30,000 Expected Here for L.S.U. Grid Season Opener," *Morning Advocate*, September 30, 1939; author interview and email correspondence with Barry Cowan.

15. Sindler, *Huey Long's Louisiana*, p. 137; Kane, *Louisiana Hayride*, p. 271.

16. "Hyneman Says La. Government Not Democratic," *Morning Advocate*, October 20, 1939.

17. Humphrey, *Education of a Public Man*, p. 41.

18. Humphrey interjection in Hyneman oral history, HHOHP.

19. Ibid.

20. In the early decades of the twentieth century, three parishes (counties) in mostly Protestant northern Louisiana recorded the most lynchings of any county in the nation, per p. 9, *Race & Democracy*, Adam Fairclough. In the more Catholic southern portion of Louisiana, the Josephites religious order specifically served the Black population, building churches and schools. Eleven Italian Americans and Italian immigrants were themselves lynched in New Orleans in 1891.

21. Louisiana State University, *The Negro in Baton Rouge*, pp. 104–106, 112.

22. Hendry and Edwards, *Old South Baton Rouge*, pp. 13, 31, 153; *Negro in Baton Rouge*, pp. 116–117.

23. "Negroes Admit Taking Bridge Planks for Fuel," *Morning Advocate*, January 20, 1940; "Fair, Warmer Forecast as Ice Flows By in River," *Morning Advocate*, January 28, 1940.

24. Humphrey, *Education of a Public Man*, p. 41.

25. Isadore Tansil oral history; Hendry, *Old South Baton Rouge*, pp. 59, 74–75; *Negro in Baton Rouge*, p. 36, 96.

26. Ruffin, Thomas F., *Under Stately Oaks*, p. 88.

27. Hyneman oral history, HHOHP.

28. Humphrey interjection in Hyneman interview, HHAF, 148.B.9.10F, Box 1.

29. Ibid.

30. Ibid.

31. Hyneman interview, HHAF, 148.B.9.10F, Box 1.

32. Robert J. Harris in Foreword to Humphrey, *The Political Philosophy of the New Deal*, p. xxiv.

33. Heilman, Robert. *The Southern Connection*, p. 13.

34. Rubin, Janice Ginsberg, "The Non-Legal Alvin Rubin," p. 1381

35. "Leaders of Three Religious Sects Speak at L.S.U.," *Morning Advocate*, October 25, 1939.

36. "Recall Humphrey's Days at LSU," *Morning Advocate*, undated from 1964.

37. Author interview, David Rubin.

38. Rubin, "The Non-Legal Alvin Rubin," p. 1381.

39. "South of the Border," *Daily Reveille*, February 6, 1940.
40. Author interview, David Rubin.
41. Solberg, *Hubert Humphrey*, pp. 75, 78.
42. Heberle, "Reminiscences," p. 137.
43. Heberle, *From Democracy to Nazism*, p. 94.
44. Heberle, "Reminiscences," p. 137.
45. Franziska Heberle letter to Otto Neurath, undated 1942, FHL.
46. Wagner, Rainer, *Rudolf Heberle*, pp. 111–116.
47. Ibid, p. 117; Franziksa letter to Carola Atkinson, November 8, 1938, FHL; F. Heberle letter to Mety and Alfred, November 21, 1938, FHL.
48. F. Heberle letters to Carola, December 6, 1938, and undated early 1939, FHL; F. Heberle letter to unnamed recipient, December 1938, FHL; Antjie Heberle Kolodziej, author interview and email correspondence.
49. Rudolf Heberle letter to Maurice Rothberg, July 8, 1941. RHP, Box 2.
50. "Shunning Involvement," *Morning Advocate*, October 16, 1939; "War Opposition," *Daily Reveille*, October 16, 1939; "Former Student Describes European War Activity," *Daily Reveille*, September 16, 1939.
51. F. Heberle letter to Mety and Alfred, November 21, 1938, FHL.
52. Heberle, *From Democracy to Nazism*, pp. 59, 71–72, 121.
53. Ibid, pp. 39, 52.
54. Author interview, Juergen Heberle.
55. Humphrey letter to Rudolf Heberle, June 28, 1986. HHPFP, 148.A.19.1B.
56. Humphrey interjection in Hyneman interview, HHAF, 148.B.9.10F, Box 1.
57. Humphrey, *The Political Philosophy of the New Deal*, pp. 4–5, 10, 73–75; Humphrey, *Education of a Public Man*, p. 42; Hyneman interview, HHAF, 148.B.9.10F, Box 1.
58. Ibid.
59. Offner, *Hubert Humphrey*, pp. 18–19.
60. Humphrey, *Education of a Public Man*, pp. 41–42.

Chapter 6

1. H. H. letter to Hubert, Nov. 21, 1941. Private collection of William Howard.
2. Humphrey letter to Duluth chapter, American Institute of Banking, May 6, 1941. HHPFP 148.B.9.9B.
3. Humphrey, *Education of a Public Man*, pp. 44–45.
4. Hubert letter to H. H. Oct. 18, 1941; Solberg, *Hubert Humphrey*, p. 88.
5. The sermon, entitled "A Preacher and the Perils of War," was originally delivered on July 20, 1941, at First Baptist Church. Shipstead inserted a version of it with some of the most offensive language redacted into the

Congressional Record on Aug. 14, 1941. It can be found in the appendix to vol. 87 on pp. 4215–4217.

6. "Oppose U.S. Air Help to Britain," *Minnesota Daily*, Nov. 27, 1941.

7. Humphrey letter to Committee to Defend America by Aiding the Allies, May 19, 1941. HHPFP 148.B.9.9B.

8. "One World, One War," *Minneapolis Star Journal*, Dec. 8, 1941. The *Journal* and the *Star* had merged into a single newspaper by this time.

9. See *Minneapolis Tribune*, *Minneapolis Star Journal*, and *Minnesota Daily*, Dec. 7 through Dec. 9, 1941.

10. See *American Jewish World*, Dec. 12 and Dec. 19, 1941.

11. "Five Loyal Men Not Wanted by Army," *Minneapolis Spokesman*, Dec. 12, 1941.

12. "News in Brief from Everywhere," *Minneapolis Spokesman*, Dec. 12, 1941.

13. Hubert letter to H. H., Dec. 14, 1941. HHPFP 148.B.10.10F.

14. "Information—The Strength of Democracy," Oct. 1, 1942. HHSTF 310.G.11.2F, Box 1. The speech was also reprinted in the Dec. 1942 issue of *Minnesota Libraries*.

15. Oz Black letter to Humphrey, Oct. 7, 1942. HHPFP 148.B.9.9B.

16. Unnamed Rotary Club member letter to Humphrey, undated but probably 1942. HHPFP 148.B.9.9B.

17. Unnamed Kiwanis Club member letter to Humphrey, undated but probably 1942. HHPFP 148.B.9.9B.

18. Hubert letter to H. H., Dec. 2, 1943. HHPFP 148.B.10.10F.

19. Arthur Naftalin interview, MCPM Box 2826; Jane Freeman interview, MCPM 2826.

20. Arthur Naftalin interview, HHAF 148.B.9.11B.

21. Arthur Naftalin oral history, University of Minnesota Digital Conservancy.

22. Jennifer Delton, PhD diss., pp. 46, 56–57.

23. "HITLER MUST BE LAUGHING!," *Minneapolis Spokesman*, Sept. 5, 1941.

24. "Giving Aid to Hitler," *Minneapolis Spokesman*, Sept. 5, 1941.

25. Prattis assumed the position after the death of the *Courier's* legendary and longtime publisher, Robert Vann.

26. "Should I Sacrifice to Live 'Half-American?,'" *Pittsburgh Courier*, January 31, 1942; Mark Whitaker, *Smoketown*, pp. 169–170.

27. Ibid.

28. Charles Beasley, Letter to the editor, *Minneapolis Spokesman*, Jan. 16, 1942.

29. Cecil Newman oral history, BJOHP.

30. Newman's official title was advisor in the industrial relations department.

31. After six months, Newman did go on the company payroll.

32. Leipold, *Cecil E. Newman*, p. 97.

33. Ibid., p. 100.

34. "A Letter of Welcome!," *Minneapolis Spokesman*, May 22, 1942.

35. CHP 129.F.4.3B-2.

36. "President's Visit to Twin Cities War Plant Sept. 19 Is Revealed," *Minneapolis Star Journal*, Oct. 1, 1942; "Vastness of Twin Cities Ordnance Plant Amazes Writer," *Minneapolis Star Journal*, Oct. 26, 1942; Photo essay, *St. Paul Dispatch*, Oct. 26, 1942; Photo essay, *St. Paul Pioneer Press*, Nov. 1, 1942; "Democratic Spirit Reigns at Ordnance Plant," *Pittsburgh Courier*, Feb. 20, 1943.

37. "Great Patriot Hawley," *Minneapolis Spokesman*, June 5, 1942.

38. "Minnesota Mining Agrees to Hire Negro Workers," *Minneapolis Spokesman*, Dec. 4, 1942.

39. Equal Justice Institute, "Lynching in America: Targeting Black Veterans," p. 36.

40. "Publisher's Son Beaten," *Minneapolis Star Journal*, Aug. 23, 1940.

41. "War Gets Closer to Home," *Minneapolis Spokesman*, Feb. 5, 1943.

42. Christopher Paul More, *Fighting for America*, pp. 62–64, 88–89; "Negro Surgeon, World Plasma Expert, Derides Red Cross Blood Segregation," *Chicago Defender*, Sept. 26, 1942.

43. "War Gets Closer to Home," *Minneapolis Spokesman*, Feb. 5, 1943.

44. Solberg, *Hubert Humphrey*, pp. 88–89.

45. Humphrey, *Education of a Public Man*, p. 48.

46. "Kline's U Pals Play Politics as Hobby, and Win!," *Minneapolis Tribune*, July 7, 1941.

47. Both photographs are in the Hennepin County Library's digital collection.

48. Harold Seavey interview, HHAF 148.N.9.10F.

49. William Simms oral history, HHOHP.

50. Arthur Naftalin interview, MCPM P2826.

51. "Minneapolis Election," *Minneapolis Spokesman*, April 30, 1943.

52. "New Low Mark in Primary Betting Interest Reported," *Minneapolis Tribune*, May 9, 1943.

53. Ibid.; also Frederick Manfred interview, HHOHP. Feikema legally changed his name to Frederick Manfred in 1952.

54. Feikema letter to the editor, *Minneapolis Star Journal*, April 26, 1943.

55. Solberg, *Hubert Humphrey*, p. 89.

56. Bradley Mintener interview, HHOHP.

57. Thurber, *The Politics of Equality*, p. 19.

58. "Hopefuls for Mayor Sing Same Tune," *Minneapolis Star Journal*, May 6, 1943.

59. "Democratic Speech" (radio), May 9, 1943. HHSTF 310.G.11.2F, Box 1.

60. "Lively Kline-Humphrey Race for Mayor Looms," *Minneapolis Star Journal*, May 11, 1943.

61. A. E. Dahl, letter to the editor, *Minneapolis Star Journal*, May 6, 1943.

62. This newspaper, a comparative latecomer to the journalistic competition in the city, was published only from 1941 through 1947.

63. "Racketeers Back Rival, Kline Claims," *Minneapolis Daily Times*, May 25, 1943; Frederick Manfred oral history, HHOHP. Manfred incorrectly recalls

the article having been in the *Star Journal*, but the headline he refers to was in the *Times*.

64. Manfred oral history, HHOHP.

65. "Humphrey Invades Kline's Office, Stirs Hot Debate," *Minneapolis Daily Times*, May 26, 1943.

66. Cassius oral history, 20th Century Radicalism in Minnesota. In the oral history, Cassius even claimed that he was first person to donate to the Humphrey campaign. While that assertion is dubious, it does reflect the enduring pride that Cassius felt in having supported Humphrey early on.

67. "Working Girls Council to Sponsor Hubert H. Humphrey Meeting Soon," *Minneapolis Spokesman*, June 4, 1943.

68. "Hubert Humphrey Speaks Saturday at Wheatley," *Minneapolis Spokesman*, June 11, 1943.

69. "Thye GOP Group to Aid Kline," *Minneapolis Star Journal*, June 9, 1943.

70. "Indorsement [*sic*] from Dunne Is Scorned by Humphrey," *Minneapolis Star Journal*, June 12, 1943; "Voters Sluggish in Reactions to City Contests," *Minneapolis Times*, June 12, 1943.

71. "Civic Liberalism," *Minneapolis Star Journal*, June 11, 1943.

72. This refers to Rev. Dr. Laurence Nye, the pastor of Hennepin Avenue Methodist Church, one of the most important and influential Methodist congregations in Minneapolis.

73. Hubert letter to H. H., May 28, 1943. William Howard private collection.

74. Ibid.

75. Olga Fredericksen letter to Humphrey, undated but probably June 1943. HHPFP 148.B.9.9B.

76. "Buddies Praise Soldier in Cafe Bias Incident," *American Jewish World*, May 29, 1942. The Tucker case was also covered by the *Minneapolis Tribune* and the Jewish Telegraphic Agency, a news service for Jewish publications.

77. "Inn Manager Apology Brings Case Dismissal," *American Jewish World*, June 5, 1942.

78. "With Our Fighting Men," *American Jewish World*, Aug. 14, 1942.

79. Full text of speech, http://www.charleslindbergh.com/americanfirst/spe ech.asp.

80. Arthur Brin letter to General Robert Wood, Sept. 14, 1941. "Lindbergh, Charles A., Correspondence," JCRC papers P445, Box 34.

81. Anonymous letter to Scheiner, undated but probably Sept. 1941. "Lindbergh, Charles A, Correspondence," JCRC P445, Box 34.

82. Richard Gutstadt letter to Scheiner, Sept. 19, 1941. "Lindbergh, Charles A, Correspondence," JCRC P445, Box 34.

83. "Defense Agency Name Now Jewish Council," *American Jewish World*, July 31, 1942.

84. Scheiner letter to Joseph Sroga, May 19, 1943. "Subversive Activities," JCRC P445 Box 55, Folder 10.

85. Scheiner annual report for 1942, JCRC, P445, Box 63.

86. "America in Jeopardy," *American Jewish World*, July 2, 1943.

87. "This World," *Minneapolis Spokesman*, March 13, 1942.

88. Anonymous letter to Scheiner, Feb. 12, 1943. Scheiner papers MHS.

89. "More of Less Personal," *Minneapolis Tribune*, April 15, 1943.

90. Scheiner letter to Erwin Oreck, April 8, 1943. Scheiner papers UMJA, Box 21.

91. "Equal Rights Bill Finally Passes House," *Minneapolis Spokesman*, April 23, 1943.

92. Rapp, "An Historical Overview of Anti-Semitism in Minnesota, 1920–1960," p. 187.

93. Selden Menefee, "What Americans Think," *The Nation*, May 29, 1943.

94. Scheiner letter to Menefee, June 14, 1943. "Menefee, Selden, Poll on Anti-Semitism, 1943" JCRC2, Box 20.

95. Gideon Seymour letter to Scheiner, Nov. 24, 1943. Scheiner letter to Menefee, June 14, 1943. "Menefee, Selden, Poll on Anti-Semitism, 1943" JCRC2, Box 20.

96. Scheiner letter to Menefee, Dec. 16, 1943. "Menefee, Selden, Poll on Anti-Semitism, 1943" JCRC2, Box 20.

97. "Scheiner Honored by Citizens as He Enters U.S. Service," *Minneapolis Spokesman*, Feb. 4, 1944.

98. Author interview, Susan Druskin.

99. "Letter from Minnesota," *New Republic*, Oct. 11, 1943.

100. David Anderson letter to Humphrey, May 22, 1944. HHPFP 148.B.9.9B.

101. C. E. Ficken letter to Humphrey, Aug. 15, 1943. HHPFP 148.B.9.9B.

102. Humphrey letter to C. E. Ficken, Sept. 1, 1943. HHPFP 148.B.9.9B

103. G. Theodore Mitau oral history, HHOHP.

104. Ibid.

105. Ibid.

106. Mrs. Paul Kunian letter to Humphrey, Dec. 16, 1943. HHPFP 148.B.9.9B.

107. "Black Book of Polish Jewry Estimates 1,000,000 Polish Jews Killed by Nazis," Jewish Telegraphic Agency, Dec. 15, 1943.

108. Humphrey letter to St. Paul branch of American Federation of Polish Jews, May 5, 1944. HHPFP 148.B.9.9B.

109. Reverend Philip Gregory letter to Humphrey, July 24, 1946. HHPFP 148.B.9.9B.

110. First Congregational Church bulletin, Feb. 2, 1941.

111. First Congregational Church bulletins of Feb. 2, 1941; Feb. 15, 1942; May 10, 1942; and Feb. 14, 1943.

112. Riley, "Character Slanders by Pseudo-Communists," *Northwestern Pilot*, Sept. 1940.

113. Riley, "Baptist Modernists and Hitler Methods," *Northwestern Pilot*, June 1943.

114. Deborah Dash Moore, *GI Jews*, pp. 120–123.

115. The sermon was delivered on January 3, 1943, and the full text was published in the January edition of *Chimes*, the monthly newsletter of First Congregational Church.

116. "Report of the Pastor," *Chimes*, Jan. 1943.

117. Glen Jeansonne, *Gerald L.K. Smith: Minister of Hate*, pp. 12, 16, 24; Isabel Price, "Gerald L.K. Smith and Anti-Semitism," p. 33.

118. Jeansonne, *Gerald L.K. Smith: Minister of Hate*, p. 12.

119. Smith FBI file.

120. Jeansonne, *Gerald L.K. Smith: Minister of Hate*, p. 58.

121. Ibid.; Price, "Gerald L.K. Smith and Anti-Semitism," p. 77.

122. Jeansoone, *Gerald L.K. Smith*, pp. 83, 155.

123. As Rachel Maddow revealed in her groundbreaking podcast, "Ultra," Senator Lundeen regularly gave speeches and issued press releases that had been written for him by a Nazi agent, George Sylvester Viereck. Lundeen died in a suspicious plane crash in 1940 that also took the lives of several federal investigators who were on the same flight.

124. Gerald L. K. Smith file, JCRC, P445, Box. 47.

125. Steve Rauch report to Scheiner, Gerald L. K. Smith file, JCRC, P445, Box 47.

126. Report by Ed Ryan on Smith's speech at Gustavus Adolphus Hall on March 22, 1944. Gerald L. K. Smith file, JCRC P445, Box 47.

127. M. L. Bacon letter to city council committee on public buildings and grounds, March 1944. Petition 90498, Minneapolis City Council records, MHS.

128. "Smith in Free-for-All, Plugs for Lindbergh," *Minneapolis Daily Times*, March 24, 1944.

129. Betty Ginsberg postcard to city council committee on public buildings and grounds, March 1944. Petition 90498, Minneapolis City Council records, MHS.

130. Labor Coordinating Committee letter to city council committee on public buildings and grounds, March 1944. Petition 90498, Minneapolis City Council records, MHS.

131. "Smith in Free-for-All, Plugs for Lindbergh," *Minneapolis Daily Times*, March 24, 1944.

132. Ibid.; "Fur Flies at Gerald Smith Hearing on Speech Permit," *Minneapolis Tribune*, March 24, 1944.

133. Walter Rauschenbusch, *Christianity and the Social Crisis*, p. 53.

134. Ida Schoening letter to Humphrey, April 4, 1944. HHPFP 148.B.9.9B.

135. Humphrey letter to Schoening, April 25, 1944. HHPFP 148.B.9.9B

136. "What Can Religion Do in These Days?," April 28, 1944. HHSTF 310.G.11.2F, Box 1.

137. Humphrey letter to Charles Hyneman, April 22, 1944. HHPFP 148.B.9.9B.

138. Ibid.

139. Manfred, "Hubert Horatio Humphrey: A Memoir," *Minnesota History*.

140. Solberg, *Hubert Humphrey*, p. 97; Humphrey, *Education of a Public Man*, p. 56; "Chronology of Vice President Humphrey's Selective Service Records," undated but 1965–1968, HHPFP 148.A.19.1B; notarized statement by navy recruiter Rollo Mudge, undated, HHPFP 148.A.19.1B.

141. Evron Kirkpatrick and Orville Freeman joint oral history, HHOHP.

142. "A Survivor of Kristallnacht Remembers," *Minneapolis Star Tribune*, Nov. 9, 1988; "Anticipating a Return Visit to My Native City of Frankfurt," *Kignston Daily Freeman*, June 3, 2001.

143. Author interviews, Diane Neumaier and Micki Solle.

144. John Neumaier letter to Humphrey, April 12, 1944. HHPFP 148.B.9.9B.

145. Jean Ann Rosenbloom letter to Humphrey, undated but probably mid to late 1944, HHPFP 148.B.9.9B.

146. "Overseas Soldier Writes Editorial," *Minneapolis Spokesman*, Sept. 10, 1943.

147. "Plain Talk!," *Minneapolis Spokesman*, March 31, 1944.

148. Orville Freeman letter to Humphrey, Sept. 27, 1942. HHPFP 148.B.9.9B.

Chapter 7

1. Humphrey provides the details of his itinerary in a memo found in "General Correspondence," MOF, 150.A.5.1B, Box 1.

2. "Minneapolis Labor Groups Unite to Support Humphrey for Mayor," *Minneapolis Tribune*, January 25, 1945; "Wife Files for Humphrey," *Minneapolis Star Journal*, January 25, 1945.

3. For one example among many, see *Minneapolis Star Journal*, April 24, 1945.

4. Humphrey letter to Clifford Rucker, May 4, 1945, "General Correspondence," MOF, 150.A.5.1B, Box 1.

5. Herbert McClosky interview, MCPM, P2826.

6. Scheiner letter to Humphrey, February 13, 1945. "General Correspondence," MOF, 150.A.5.1B, Box 1.

7. Humphrey speech on WLOL, May 1, 1945. HHSTF 310.G.11.2F Box 1.

8. James Eli Shiffer, "Rubbed Out: The Unsolved Murder of Journalist Arthur Kasherman," July 8, 2019, http://www.jamesshiffer.com/rubbedout/category/story/.

9. Ibid.

10. L. B. Nichols memo to Clyde Tolson, in FBI file on Hubert Humphrey. File 62–77485, Section 1, p. 4.

11. Ed Ryan interview, HHAF, 148.B.9.10F, Box 1.

12. "Anti-Semitism in the United States," *Minneapolis Star Journal*, January 18, 1945.

13. "Discrimination, General, 1941–1948," JCRC, P445, Box 17; Stenographer's notes from public meeting on March 26, 1945. RGFP, A.G487, Box 36.

14. "Police Curb Attacks on No. Side Boys," *American Jewish World*, January 26, 1945.
15. The reference is to the vast Ford auto plant named for that river and located in Dearborn, Mich. As most newspaper readers of this time understood, River Rouge was a metaphor for assembly-line scale and efficiency.
16. "Nazi Mass Killing Laid Bare in Camp," *New York Times*, August 30, 1944.
17. Stenographer's notes from public meeting on March 26, 1945. RGFP, A.G487, Box 36.
18. All direct quotations from the meeting are drawn from stenographer's notes from a public meeting on March 26, 1945. RGFP, A.G487, Box 36. Those notes are consistent with, and more detailed than, coverage of the meeting in the *Tribune, Star Journal*, and *American Jewish World*.
19. "Curing Intolerance," *Minneapolis Star Journal*, March 28, 1945.
20. "Everybody's Ideas," *Minneapolis Star Journal*, March 31, 1945.
21. "Humphrey Maps 5-Point Racial Plan," *Minneapolis Star Journal*, March 31, 1945.
22. "Humphrey Calls Positive Program as [*sic*] Answer to Attacks on Jewish Children in Minneapolis," *Minneapolis Spokesman*, April 6, 1945.
23. "Discrimination, General, 1941–1948," JCRC, P445, Box 17.
24. Dwight D. Eisenhower, *Crusade in Europe*, pp. 408–409.
25. "Eide, Humphrey, Kline Lead Poll Survey on Mayoralty," *Minneapolis Tribune*, May 13, 1945.
26. "Humphrey Sets New Records in Lead over Kline," *Minneapolis Star Journal*, May 15, 1945.
27. "GOP Leadership Considers Moving In to Help Kline," *Minneapolis Daily Times*, May 16, 1945.
28. "Fight to End Promised by 2 Candidates," *Minneapolis Star Journal*, May 16, 1945.
29. "Mayor and Rival Issue Final Blasts," *Minneapolis Daily Times*, June 9, 1945.
30. "Rivals Wheel Out Heavy Artillery," *Minneapolis Tribune*, May 27, 1945.
31. "Kasherman 'Hush Cash' Discovered," *Minneapolis Star Journal*, February 27, 1945.
32. "Two in Mayor Race Blast at One Another," *Minneapolis Star Journal*, June 5, 1945.
33. "It Did Happen Here," *Minneapolis Spokesman*, June 15, 1945.
34. "The Chance of a City's Lifetime," *Minneapolis Tribune*, June 13, 1945.
35. Clair Lovelace letter to Humphrey, June 30, 1945, MOF 2.
36. Fern Gosch to Humphrey, undated but probably June 1945, "General Correspondence," MOF 150.A.5.1B, Box 1.
37. Humphrey to Fern Gosch, June 26, 1945, "General Correspondence," MOF 150.A.5.1B, Box 1.
38. Inaugural address, July 2, 1945. HHSTF 310.G.11.2F, Box 1.
39. Hubert Humphrey III interview, MCPM, Box P2826.

40. All of these letters can be found in "General Correspondence," MOF 150.A.5.1B, Box 1.

41. Naftalin interview, MCPM, Box P2826.

42. Julian Hartt, "What We Make of the World," *Soundings* 82, no. 1–2 (Spring/Summer 1999): p. 34.

43. Humphrey, *Education of a Public Man*, p. 60.

44. Sullivan, *The Murder of the Real Jack Ryan*, p. 58.

45. Ibid., p. 80.

46. Ryan interview, HHAF, 148.B.9.10F, Box 1.

47. Mintener oral history, HHOHP; Ryan oral history, HHOHP.

48. Simms interview, HHOHP.

49. Ryan interview, HHAF, 148.B.9.10F, Box 1.

50. Ibid.

51. Leslie Minter letter to Humphrey, March 17, 1946, MOF 150.A.5.4F, Box 4.

52. Naftalin interjects this statement in the course of interviewing Mintener for HHOHP.

53. Simms interview, HHOHP.

54. "Lewis Slaying Background Will Be Pictured to Jury," *Minneapolis Daily Times*, September 4, 1945.

55. Kirsten Delegard, "'Don't Be Fooled by Appearances': A.B. Cassius and the Fight to Integrate Public Spaces in Minneapolis," *The Historiapolis Project* (blog), February 11, 2015, http://historyapolis.com/blog/2015/02/11/dont-fooled-appearances-b-cassius-fight-integrate-public-spaces-minneapolis/.

56. "What Really Happened Last Wednesday Night," *Minneapolis Spokesman*, September 7, 1945.

57. Robert T. Smith column, no other headline, *Minneapolis Tribune*, March 25, 1973.

58. Leipold, *Cecil E. Newman*, p. 166.

59. FHHP, Box 2, Folder 7.

60. Humphrey, *Education of a Public Man*, p. 64.

61. "Mayor Takes Hand; Amity Is Restored," *Minneapolis Star Journal*, August 30, 1945.

62. William Carlson letter to Humphrey, November 18, 1945, "General Correspondence," MOF 150.A.5.1B, Box 1.

63. "The Screen," *New York Times*, October 25, 1945.

64. The entire film can be viewed at https://www.youtube.com/watch?v=ovwHkb1wEfU. The transcript of dialogue is accessible at https://www.americanrhetoric.com/MovieSpeeches/moviespeechthehouseilivein.html.

65. He used the pseudonym Lewis Allan.

66. Gary Cahall, "The House I Live In (1945): Sinatra's Song of Brotherhood," MovieFanFare (blog), December 11, 2015, http://www.moviefanfare.com/?p=48027.

67. Gunnar Myrdal, Introduction, in *An American Dilemma*, pp. xlvii–xlviii.

68. Ibid.
69. Walter A. Jackson, *Gunnar Myrdal and America's Conscience*, pp. 241–242.
70. John Roy Carlson, *The Plotters*, p. 9.
71. The series is archived at www.youtube.com/watch?v=1ol8Gmi57DI&list= PLFC6919BC375F0440.
72. Laura Z. Hobson, *Gentleman's Agreement*, p. 192. See Chapter 4 of this book for the footnoted reference to "silken curtain."

Chapter 8

1. "Wildest Festivity in Five Years to Greet '46 Here," *Minneapolis Daily Times*, Dec. 31, 1945; "2 Killed in Traffic Mishaps," *Minneapolis Star Journal*, Jan. 1, 1946; "Twin Cities Sets New Records in 1945," *Minneapolis Tribune*, Jan. 1, 1945.
2. Humphrey letter to John Seabert, Jan. 7, 1946. "General Correspondence," MOF 150A.5.4F, Box 4.
3. Humphrey letter to Otto Silha, Jan. 3, 1946. "General Correspondence," MOF 150A.5.4F, Box 4.
4. Thurber, *The Politics of Equality*, p. 36.
5. "City Drafts Fair Play Ordinance," *Minneapolis Daily Times*, Jan. 3, 1946.
6. "FEPC Ordinance Still Stalled," *Minneapolis Tribune*, Feb. 14, 1946.
7. McClosky interview, MCPM Box P2826.
8. Ruchames, *Race, Jobs, & Politics*, pp. 156–160.
9. "Reconversion from 1865 Messes Up That of 1945," *Minneapolis Star Journal*, Jan. 23, 1946.
10. Ruchames, *Race, Jobs, & Politics*, pp. 91–92.
11. "Stupid Approach to Negro Voters," *Minneapolis Spokesman*, June 9, 1944.
12. "Jim Klobuchar," *Minneapolis Star*, March 4, 1968.
13. "Mayor's Council on Human Relations," MOF 150.A.6.8F, Box 16.
14. Author interview, Susan Druskin.
15. "With Our Fighting Men," *American Jewish World*, Feb. 1, 1946; Author interview, Susan Druskin.
16. "Mayor's Council on Human Relations," minutes of meetings on March 19, 1946; March 26, 1946; April 11, 1946. HOF 150.A.6.8F, Box 16.
17. Newman letter to Humphrey, March 11, 1946, MOF 150A.5.4F, Box 4,
18. See these and other incidents of police brutality and harassment in "Minneapolis Police Department," MOF 150.A.7.3B, Box 19.
19. Lansing article; *Minneapolis Star*, March 21, 1946.
20. Humphrey letter to MacLean, Dec. 17, 1946, Minneapolis Police Department file, 150.A.7.3B, Box 19, MHS.

21. "AVC Scores Housing Bias," *Minneapolis Tribune*, June 26, 1946; "Veterans Insist on Home Site for Nisei," *Minneapolis Star Journal*, June 26, 1946.

22. "Nisei Couple Plan Fight to Buy Lot," *Minneapolis Tribune*, June 27, 1946; "AVC Scores Housing Bias," *Minneapolis Tribune*, June 26, 1946.

23. "Nisei Bias Fight Gains," *Minneapolis Tribune*, July 2, 1946; "Race Restrictions Bar Thousands from Housing," *Minneapolis Tribune*, July 7, 1946.

24. "Keynote Address to Minnesota DFL Convention," March 30, 1946. HHSTF 310.G.11.2F Box 1.

25. Humphrey letter to Harry Hubbard, Dec. 11, 1944. "General Correspondence," MOF 150.A.5.1B, Box 1.

26. Haynes, *Dubious Alliance*, p. 127.

27. https://shec.ashp.cuny.edu/items/show/1253.

28. Humphrey letter to Freeman, Jan. 10, 1947. "General Correspondence," MOF 150.A.5.5B, Box 5.

29. Scheiner letter to Sidney H. Sayles, July 26, 1946. "Smith, Gerald L.K." JCRC P445, Box 48; "The Demise of a Small-Town Business," *Forward*, March 2, 2007.

30. Youngdahl letter to L. M. Froiland, July 21, 1946; "Smith, Gerald L.K." JCRC P445, Box 48.

31. Jeansonne, *Minister of Hate*, p. 98; "Pickets Break Up Smith Meeting," *Minneapolis Tribune*, Aug. 22, 1946.

32. Jeansonne, *Minister of Hate*, pp. 98, 144.

33. *The Cross and the Flag*, March 1951; *The Letter*, Aug. 28, 1946.

34. Humphrey letter to Will V. Lundquist, August 29, 1946. "Smith, Gerald L.K.," MOF 150.A.7.4F, Box 20.

35. For all description of Aug. 21 events: "Pickets Break Up Smith Meeting," *Minneapolis Tribune*, Aug. 22, 1946; Scheiner memo to file, undated but by context late Aug. 1946; "Smith, Gerald L.K.," JCRC P445, Box 47; "We Don't Want a Hitler Here," http://historyapolis.com/blog/2015/12/09/we-dont-want-a-hitler-here/.

36. *The Cross and the Flag*, Aug. 8, 1946; *The Letter*, July 15, 1946.

37. "Pickets Break Up Smith Meeting," *Minneapolis Tribune*, Aug. 22, 1946.

38. *The Letter*, Sept. 16, 1946.

39. "Mayor Assails Smith, Pickets," *Minneapolis Tribune*, Aug. 22, 1946.

40. "Minneapolis Mob," *Minneapolis Star Journal*, Aug. 23, 1946.

41. Humphrey letter to Will V. Lundquist, Aug. 29, 1946. "Smith, Gerald L.K.," MOF 150.A.7.4F, Box 20.

42. Humphrey letter to Franklin D. Roosevelt Jr., May 13, 1946. "General Correspondence," MOF 150A.5.4F, Box 4.

43. Humphrey letter to Ruth Wallace, Feb. 26, 1946. "General Correspondence," MOF 150A.5.4F, Box 4.

44. Muriel letter to Hubert, undated but probably summer 1946, HHPFP 148.B.10.11B.

45. Peter Richardson, *American Prophet*, pp. 13–14.

46. Laura Weber, "'Minneapolis: The Curious Twin': A Reexaminaton."

47. Carey McWilliams, "Minneapolis: The Curious Twin," *Common Ground*, Vol. 7, no. 1, Sept. 1946.

48. As noted earlier in the book, Sevareid became famous as a CBS news correspondent under his middle name, Eric.

49. "Capital of Anti-Semitism?" *Minneapolis Star Journal*, Oct. 18, 1946.

50. "What Will Minneapolitans Do about Anti-Semitism Charge?" *Minneapolis Star Journal*, Oct. 31, 1946.

51. "Humphrey Asks Attack on Bias," *Minneapolis Tribune*, Oct. 4, 1946; Jeanne Leland letter to Humphrey, Jan. 13, 1948, "Mayor's Council on Human Relations," MOF 150.A.6.8F, Box 16; "Four Urge Minority Aid," *Minneapolis Tribune*, Oct. 8, 1946; "Women Get Summary of City Problems," *Minneapolis Star Journal*, Nov. 22, 1946.

52. "City Government Employment," *Minneapolis Spokesman*, Oct. 4, 1946; Dr. D. W. Pollard letter to Humphrey, April 27, 1946, MOF 3; Martin Friedman letter, Jan. 25, 1947, "Police Department," MOF 150A.7.3B, Box 19.

53. Walter Jones letter to Humphrey, Nov. 19, 1946, MOF 150.A.5.3B, Box 3.

54. Ibid.

55. Manuscript of essay "The American Negro Minority," 1944. CSJC Register T, Box 17, Folder 8.

56. Text for speech to American Council of Race Relations, 1944. CSJC Register B, Box 1, Folder 2.

57. Gilpin dissertation, p. 5.

58. Cited in Gilpin dissertation, p. 514.

59. Long letter to John, Jan. 8, 1947. RRD, Box 103, Folder 1.

60. "Mayor Praises Anti-Bias Group," *Minneapolis Tribune*, Jan. 7, 1945.

61. "Race Relations in Action 1946–1947," report by Race Relations Department of American Missionary Association. CSJC, Register G, Box 7, Folder 15.

62. "Minority Counselor Plan Held Up," *Minneapolis Daily Times*, Jan. 30, 1947.

63. Steefel report to Human Relations Council, undated but late 1946 or early 1947. "Self-Survey of Human Relations," MOF 150.A.6.8F, Box 16.

64. Laura G. Haggerty letter to Humphrey, Sept. 11, 1946. "Self-Survey of Human Relations," MOF 150.A.6.8F.

65. Russell letter to Humphrey, April 1, 1946. "General Correspondence," MOF 150A.5.4F, Box 150A.5.4F, Box 4.

66. "Council Unit Approves Anti-Bias Proposal," *Minneapolis Star*, Jan. 16, 1947.

67. Steefel note to Humphrey, Feb. 19, 1947. "Self-Survey of Human Relations," MOF 150.A.6.8F.

68. "'U' to Punish Race Hatred Instigators," *Minneapolis Star Journal*, Nov. 14, 1946.

69. DNP letter to Humphrey, undated but probably late 1946. FBI file on Democratic Nationalist Party, obtained by FOIA, https://archive.org/details/

DemocraticNationalistParty/Democratic%20Nationalist%20Party-Max%20
Nelsen-Minneapolis-1/.

70. "New Anti-Jewish Slogans at U Intensify Search for Culprits," *American Jewish World*, Jan. 10, 1947.

71. "U Skeptical on Theory of Campus DNP Group," *Minnesota Daily*, Jan. 8, 1947.

72. FBI transcript dated Jan. 3, 1947. FBI file on Democratic Nationalist Party, obtained by FOIA, https://archive.org/details/DemocraticNationalistParty/Democratic%20Nationalist%20Party-Max%20Nelsen-Minneapolis-1/.

73. Quoted in memo from Roy Stuart of FBI field office to FBI Laboratory, Dec. 31, 1946. DNP FBI file.

74. M. B. Rhodes letter to Victor Anderson, Jan. 8, 1947. FBI file on Democratic Nationalist Party, obtained by FOIA, https://archive.org/details/DemocraticNationalistParty/Democratic%20Nationalist%20Party-Max%20Nelsen-Minneapolis-1/.

75. William Simms oral history, HHOHP.

76. Humphrey, *Education of a Public Man*, pp. 65–66; "3 Shots Fired at Humphrey," *Minneapolis Tribune*, March 18, 1947; "Mayor Gives Version of 'Shooting,'" *Minneapolis Star Journal*, March 18, 1947; "Shots Fired at Hubert Humphrey," *Minneapolis Star Tribune*, March 18, 2018.

77. "Mayor Gives Version of 'Shooting,'" *Minneapolis Star Journal*, March 18, 1947.

78. David Winton interview, HHAF, 148.B.9.10F, Box 1.

79. Author interview, Pat Gray.

80. The *Tribune* was a morning paper. In the same day's edition of the *Star Journal*, an afternoon paper, Humphrey did speak on the record, verifying the earlier account.

81. Unsigned letter to Muriel Humphrey, postmarked March 22, 1947. "Threats and cranks," MOF, 150A.6.1B, Box 9.

82. "'Hate Gang' Leader Nabbed; Arsenal Seized," *Minneapolis Star Journal*, April 24, 1947; The sedition case against Dillig ended in a mistrial after the death of the judge.

83. FBI file on Democratic Nationalist Party, obtained by FOIA, https://archive.org/details/DemocraticNationalistParty/Democratic%20Nationalist%20Party-Max%20Nelsen-Minneapolis-1/.

84. "'Hate Gang' Leader Nabbed; Arsenal Seized," *Minneapolis Star Journal*, April 24, 1947; "Hate Leader Agrees to Mental Test," *Minneapolis Star Journal*, April 26, 1947; "Hate Leader Posts Bond, Leaves Jail," *Minneapolis Tribune*, May 17, 1947.

85. FBI file on Democratic Nationalist Party, obtained by FOIA, https://archive.org/details/DemocraticNationalistParty/Democratic%20Nationalist%20Party-Max%20Nelsen-Minneapolis-1/; "I'll Tell the World," *American Jewish World*, Oct. 24, 1947.

86. Newman interview, HHAP.
87. Gwen Owens letter to Humphrey, March 21, 1947. "General Correspondence," MOF 150.A.5.6F, Box 6.
88. Sidney L. Shom letter to Humphrey, March 19, 1947. "General Correspondence," MOF 150.A.5.6F, Box 6.
89. Kramer, "Young Man in a Hurry," *New Republic*, June 16, 1947.
90. "The Mayor of Minneapolis: A New Political Power," *Forward*, June 19, 1947, translated from the original Yiddish.
91. "The Way I See It," *Minneapolis Spokesman*, June 20, 1947.
92. "Mayor's Council on Human Relations," MOF, 150.A.6.8F, Box 16.
93. MFEPC, 116.K.13.11.B, Box 1.
94. Seabron letter George Jensen, Aug. 20, 1947. MFEPC, 116.K.13.11.B, Box 2.
95. "Spitting Bartender to Face Trial," *Minneapolis Tribune*, July 18, 1947.
96. Unsigned letter to Humphrey, Nov. 29, 1947. "Fair Practices in Bowling," MOF, 150.A.6.8F Box 16.
97. Not to be confused, of course, with the Republican Party in the United States. In Spanish, the Republican side was on the left, and it fought against and was ultimately defeated by the Loyalists under Francisco Franco.
98. "Progressives and Communists," *New Republic*, May 13, 1946.
99. Haynes, *Dubious Alliance*, p. 139.
100. Loeb letter to Humphrey, Nov. 12, 1946. "UDA Administrative File," ADAP, Series 1, Box 15.
101. Wechsler, *The Age of Suspicion*, pp. 210–211.
102. Gillon, *Politics and Vision*, p. 21.
103. Ibid., p. 20.
104. "General Purposes" document, March 1947. Found in MPF, 150.A.8.4F, Box 28.
105. "Antidiscrimination in employment hearings," p. 431.
106. Ibid., p. 430.
107. Ibid., p. 445.

Chapter 9

1. Rauh and Loeb telegram to Humphrey, Oct. 15, 1947. "Americans for Democratic Action," MPF 150.A.8.4F, Box 28.
2. Biemiller oral history, HTPL.
3. "Kersten Eyes Biemiller Color, Talks of 'Red' Tinges," *Milwaukee Journal*, Sept. 25, 1946.
4. "Memo on Political Recommendations," July 14, 1947. "Administrative Files," ADAP Series 2, Box 26.

5. Biemiller letter to Loeb, Nov. 18, 1947. "Administrative Files," ADAP Series 2, Box 26.

6. Humphrey letter to Harold Margulies, Oct. 16, 1947. "Americans for Democratic Action," MPF 150.A.8.4F, Box 28.

7. Address to AFL Convention, Oct. 8, 1947. HHSTF 310.G.11.2F, Box 1.

8. Biemiller oral history, HTPL.

9. Humphrey letter to James Roosevelt, Nov. 5, 1947. "General Correspondence," MOF 150.A.5.6F, Box 6.

10. Biemiller letter to Loeb, Oct. 28, 1947. "Administrative Files," ADAP Series 2, Box 26.

11. Christine Humphrey letter to Hubert Humphrey, March 10, 1947. HHPFP 148.B.10.11B.

12. Frances Humphrey Howard letter to Hubert Humphrey, May 18, 1947. HHPFP 148.B.10.11B.

13. Hubert Humphrey letter to Frances Humphrey Howard, May 26, 1947. HHPFP 148.B.10.11B.

14. Gillon, *Politics and Vision*, p. 33.

15. "The Democratic Convention," *Minneapolis Spokesman*, July 28, 1944.

16. "Henry Wallace Throws Hat in Presidential Ring as Independent," *Minneapolis Spokesman*, Jan. 2, 1948.

17. After his early years on the *Spokesman*, Rowan would go on to have an illustrious career as a syndicated columnist, author, and diplomat.

18. "Candidate Wallace," *Minneapolis Spokesman*, Feb. 20, 1948.

19. https://news.gallup.com/poll/116677/presidential-approval-ratings-gallup-his torical-statistics-trends.aspx.

20. Diary entry, Jan. 6, 1948. Truman, *Off the Record*, p. 122.

21. "Congress Hostile," *New York Herald Tribune*, Jan. 8, 1948; "COLD RECEPTION GIVEN TRUMAN," *Des Moines Register*, Jan. 8, 1948.

22. Harry S. Truman, Annual Message to the Congress on the State of the Union Online by Gerhard Peters and John T. Woolley, The American Presidency Project https://www.presidency.ucsb.edu/node/232897.

23. George Elsey oral history, Truman Library; "Congress Cold to Message," *Washington Post*, Jan. 8, 1948.

24. Bernstein, *Politics & Policies of the Truman Administration*, pp. 271–273; Gergel, *Unexampled Courage*, p. 64; McCullough, *Truman*, p. 247; Frank, *The Trials of Harry Truman*, pp. 151–152.

25. Gergel, *Unexampled Courage*, pp. 4, 12, 32–33.

26. Equal Justice Institute, "Lynching in America: Targeting Black Veterans."

27. Gergel, pp. 39–40, 45–46.

28. Ibid., p. 90.

29. White, *A Man Called White*, pp. 330–331.

30. Bernstein, *Politics & Policies of the Truman Administration*, p. 278.

31. Harry S. Truman, Executive Order 9808—Establishing the President's Committee on Civil Rights Online by Gerhard Peters and John T. Woolley, The American Presidency Project, https://www.presidency.ucsb.edu/node/231504.

32. https://www.trumanlibraryinstitute.org/historic-speeches-naacp/.

33. *To Secure These Rights*, pp. ix–x.

34. Ibid., p. 99.

35. Ibid., p. 103.

36. Memo, Clark Clifford to Harry S. Truman, Nov. 19, 1947. Political File, Clifford Papers. HTPL.

37. Dudziak, *Cold War Civil Rights*, p. 37.

38. DuBois, "An Appeal to the World: A Statement on the Denial of Human Rights to Minorities in the Case of Citizens of Negro Descent in the United States of America and an Appeal to the United Nations for Redress." New York: NAACP 1947.

39. Diary entry, Feb. 2, 1948. Truman, *Off the Record*, p. 122.

40. Harry S Truman, "Special Message to the Congress on Civil Rights," February 2, 1948, in *Public Papers of the Presidents of the United States. January 1 to December 31, 1948*. Washington: United States Government Printing Office, 1964, n. 20.

41. "Truman Acts," *Chicago Defender*, Feb. 14, 1948; "The World Today," *Pittsburgh Courier*, Feb. 14, 1948.

42. "South Threatens to Bolt Truman over Civil Rights," Associated Press, published in *St. Louis Post-Dispatch*, Feb. 3, 1948.

43. Harry S. Truman, Address at the Jefferson–Jackson Day Dinner. Online by Gerhard Peters and John T. Woolley, The American Presidency Project, https://www.presidency.ucsb.edu/node/232335.

44. "Arkansans Stage Truman Walkout," United Press International, published in *The New York Times*, Feb. 20, 1948.

45. Gallup Organization. Gallup Poll # 1948–0414: Foreign Policy/States/Civil Rights/Presidential Election, Question 8. USGALLUP.040548.RK10C. Gallup Organization. Cornell University, Ithaca, NY: Roper Center for Public Opinion Research, 1948. Web. Oct-10-2013.

46. Nash oral history, Truman Presidential Library, pp. 331–332; Bernstein, *Politics and Policies of the Truman Administration*, p. 286 and note p. 309.

47. Inaugural address, Jan. 20, 1948. FWP, Speeches, Series 941, Box 1835, RG27/Wright.

48. Wright address to legislature, March 4, 1947. FWP, Speeches, Series 941, Box 1835, RG27/Wright.

49. "Mississippi's Governor Wins Nationwide Fame by Attack on Democrats' Negro Policy," *Memphis Commercial Appeal*, Feb. 8, 1948; "Press Comment on Wright's Address," *Jackson Daily News*, Jan. 29, 1948.

50. It was not widely known until many years later that in 1925 Thurmond had fathered a child named Essie Mae with one of his family's Black servants, Carrie Butler.

51. Crespino, *Strom Thurmond's America*, p. 54.

52. Ibid., pp. 51, 53.

53. "State Unfurls Rebel Flag, Endorses Stand for South," *Jackson Clarion-Ledger*, Feb. 13, 1948.

54. Ibid.

55. "Wright-Thurmond Correspondence," MDAH Manuscript Collection, Z1528f.

56. Strom Thurmond, "Keynote address of J. Strom Thurmond, Governor of South Carolina, before States' Rights Democratic Conference, Jackson, Mississippi, 1948 May 10" (1948). *Strom Thurmond Collection, Mss 100.* 325, https://tigerprints.clemson.edu/strom/325.

57. Frederickson, *The Dixiecrat Revolt and the End of the Solid South, 1932–1968*, pp. 103–106; Hilliard, "A Biography of Fielding Wright," pp. 92–93.

58. In some of the committee's letters and documents, "Jim Crow" is also rendered as "Jimcrow" or "jimcrow."

59. Eisenhower testimony to Senate Armed Services Committee, April 2, 1948.

60. Pfeffer, *A Philip Randolph, Pioneer of the Civil Rights Movement*, p. 133.

61. The entire exchange between Randolph and Truman is taken from Randolph's oral history in the Lyndon Baines Johnson Library. Randolph gave a similar version in an interview for Jervis Anderson's biography. There is also a brief account of the White House meeting in an Associated Press article dated March 22, 1948. It was published in the *New York Times* on March 23, 1948, under the headline "Truman Advised of Hesitancy to Serve without Anti-Bias Pledge." Interestingly, Truman makes no mention of it in his memoirs or the published selection of his personal papers, which include passages from his diary.

62. APRP, Box 17.

63. Universal Military Training: Hearings before the Committee on Armed Services, United States Senate, Eightieth Congress, Second Session on Universal Military Training, pp. 687–688.

64. Ibid., p. 692.

65. Anderson, A. *Philip Randolph: A Biographical Portrait*, p. 279; "Segregation in the Armed Services," *Pittsburgh Courier*, April 10, 1948.

66. "Editor Points War to Better Race Relations in Address to Lions," April 16, 1948.

67. APRP, Box 17.

68. Universal Military Training: Hearings before the Committee on Armed Services, United States Senate, Eightieth Congress, Second Session on Universal Military Training, p. 686.

69. "Bulletin No. 8," League for Non-Violent Civil Disobedience against Military Segregation, undated by probably mid-June, 1948. Also form letter, undated but probably late June or early July 1948. Both items are in the "Committee Against Jim Crow in Military Service and Training," Box 1, Folder 1, in the collection of the Schomburg Center for Research in Black Culture.

70. D. M. Bowman letter to Randolph, June 25, 1948. APRP, Box 17.

71. Universal Military Training: Hearings before the Committee on Armed Services, United States Senate, Eightieth Congress, Second Session on Universal Military Training, pp. 693–694.

72. Loeb letter to Humphrey, March 10, 1948. "Administrative files," ADAP Series 2, Box 53.

73. Bowles letter to Humphrey, March 17, 1948. "Americans for Democratic Action," MPF, 150.A.8.4F, Box 28.

74. Humphrey letter to Leon Henderson, March 25, 1948, "Americans for Democratic Action," MPF, 150.A.8.4F, Box 28; Humphrey letter to Gael Sullivan, April 19, 1948, "Democratic National Committee," MPF 150A.8.3B, Box 27.

75. Humphrey letter to Max Lerner, "Americans for Democratic Action," MPF 150.A.8.4F, Box 28.

76. "The Plight of the Liberals," *Minneapolis Spokesman*, March 12, 1948.

77. Humphrey telegram to Henderson, April 10, 1948. "Americans for Democratic Action," MPF 150.A.8.4F, Box 28.

78. Gillon, *Politics and Vision*, pp. 44–45.

79. Ibid., p. 45.

80. Ancil Payne letter to Loeb, June 11, 1948. "Political File," ADAP, Series 6, Box 1.

81. Moon, *Balance of Power*, pp. 10–11.

82. Frances Humphrey to Hubert Humphrey, Jan. 20, 1948. HHPFP 148.B.10.11B.

83. This term presumably refers to the geographical shape of the District of Columbia.

84. Harry Humphrey to Hubert Humphrey, April 25, 1948. HHPFP 148.B.10.11B.

85. "Mayor's Council of Human Relations: Community Self-Surveys," MOF 150.A.6.8F, Box 16.

86. "Neither Free Nor Equal," July 30, 1947. Both versions of the text are in HHSTF 310.G.11.2F, Box 1. Because no recording of the radio show survives, it remains uncertain which script Humphrey ultimately used.

87. Haynes, *Dubious Alliance*, p. 173.

88. Mondale, of course, went on to win what had been Humphrey's seat in the U.S. Senate. McCarthy broke with Humphrey over the Vietnam War, running for the Democratic presidential nomination against Lyndon Johnson and later Humphrey.

89. Haynes, *Dubious Alliance*, p. 174.

90. Delton, "Forging a Northern Strategy," pp. 246, 249.

91. Haynes, *Dubious Alliance*, p. 180.
92. Offner, *Hubert Humphrey*, p. 47.
93. Editorial column without headline Simmons, *Minnesota Leader*, February 1948.
94. Henry Olson letter to Humphrey, Dec. 22, 1947. "General Correspondence," MOF 150.A.5.6F, Box 6.
95. "DFL Camps Open Separate Parleys," *Minneapolis Tribune*, June 13, 1948.
96. Haynes, *Dubious Alliance*, p. 193. The account comes from Haynes's interview in 1977 with Carl Ross, head of the Minnesota Communist Party during the 1940s.
97. "DFL Refuses to Indorse [*sic*] Truman," *Minneapolis Tribune*, June 14, 1948.
98. Author email exchange with Andrew Biemiller Jr., Aug. 10–12, 2022.
99. Biemiller oral history, HHOHP.
100. Biemiller letter to Humphrey, June 14, 1948. "Civil Rights Correspondence 1948," MPF 150.A.8.1B, Box 25.
101. Gillon, *Politics and Vision*, p. 46.
102. "Americans for Democratic Action," MPF 150.A.8.4F, Box 28.
103. Whitney telegram to Humphrey, June 15, 1948; Marty letter to Humphrey, June 15, 1948; Moore letter to Humphrey, June 28, 1948. All in "Civil Rights Correspondence 1948," MPF 150.A.8.1B, Box 25.
104. "Truman Foes Back Rights Plan," *Minneapolis Star*, July 5, 1948. The statement was reprinted in *ADA Word*, Aug. 7, 1948.
105. "Civil Rights Issue Pushed," *Minneapolis Tribune*, July 5, 1948.
106. R. M. Westcott letter to Humphrey, July 5, 1948. "Americans for Democratic Action," MPF 150.A.8.4F, Box 28.

Chapter 10

1. "100-Degree Heat Due Again Today," *Minneapolis Tribune*, July 7, 1948.
2. "Eisenhower Says He Couldn't Accept Nomination for Any Public Office," *New York Times*, July 6, 1948.
3. Diary entry dated July 6, 1948, reprinted in *Off the Record*, p. 141.
4. Thurber, *The Politics of Equality*, pp. 56–57.
5. "Democrats Rib Themselves," *Minneapolis Tribune*, July 13, 1948.
6. "Matter of Fact: The Straw in the Flood," *New York Herald Tribune*, July 12, 1948; "Matter of Fact: Ghost in the White House," *Washington Post*, July 7, 1948.
7. Harry T. Moore letter to Humphrey, July 8, 1948. Private collection of Steve Hunegs.
8. White telegram to Humphrey, July 5, 1948; Humphrey letter to White, July 7, 1948, both "Americans for Democratic Action," MPF 140.A.8.4F, Box 25.
9. Culver and Hyde, *American Dreamer*, p. 480.

10. Baime, *Dewey Defeats Truman*, p. 139.

11. Acacia, John, *Clark Clifford: Wise Man of Washington*, pp. 132–133; Clifford, *Counsel to the President*, p. 218.

12. "Final O.K. on Platform Will Be Left to Truman; Civil Rights Fight Looms," *Philadelphia Inquirer*, July 8, 1948.

13. Ibid.

14. The written statement from Tobias's coalition and the testimony by Wilkins can be found in "Democratic National Platform 1948," MPF, 150.A.8.2F, Box 26. See also "Civil Rights Plank Debate Is Dodged," *Philadelphia Inquirer*, July 9, 1948, and "Platform Writers Warned against Giving in to South," July 9, 1948.

15. Civil Rights Plank Debate Is Dodged," *Philadelphia Inquirer*, July 9, 1948; "Platform Writers Warned against Giving in to South," July 9, 1948.

16. "News in Tabloid," *Baltimore Afro-American*, July 17, 1948.

17. "Democrats Will Debate Civil Rights Plank Today," *Washington Post*, July 8, 1945; "South Demands States Rights in Party Platform," *New York Herald Tribune*, July 8, 1948.

18. "McGrath Urges Strong Plank on Civil Rights," *New York Herald Tribune*, July 10, 1948.

19. "ADA Will Press Douglas Drive," *Philadelphia Inquirer*, July 11, 1948; "Drive to Stop Truman Collapses, Douglas Says He's Not Candidate," *Philadelphia Inquirer*, July 10, 1948; Truman diary entry dated July 12, 1948, reprinted in *Off the Record*, pp. 141–142.

20. "Gloom at Philadephia," *Washington Post*, July 12, 1948; "Democrats on the Eve," *New York Herald Tribune*, July 11, 1948.

21. The Beechers sold the resort in the mid-1960s.

22. Muriel letter to Hubert, July 10, 1948. HHPFP 148.B.10.11B.

23. "Secret Group Drafting Platform," *New York Herald Tribune*, July 11, 1948; "Civil Rights Stand at Issue as Party Prepares Platform," *Washington Post*, July 12, 1948.

24. "Truman Offering a Platform Draft," *New York Times*, July 11, 1948; Secret Group Drafting Platform," *New York Herald Tribune*, July 11, 1948.

25. The maps actually used red lines, a practice that gave rise to the idiom.

26. "Secret Group Drafting Platform," *New York Herald Tribune*, July 11, 1948; "Platform 'Vigilance' Group Out for Strong Civil Rights Plank," *New York Herald Tribune*, July 12, 1948.

27. "Dems Brawl over Civil Rights," *Chicago Defender*, July 17, 1948.

28. "Give Us Civil Rights Now: It's the South Vs. Negro Vote," *Pittsburgh Courier*, July 17, 1948.

29. Ethridge, "Mississippi's Role in the Dixiecratic Movement," p. 142; "Truman Does Splits on States' and Civil Rights," *New York Herald Tribune*, July 12, 1948; "Dissidents Give Up: Southerners Fail to Get Candidate to Contest Truman on Rights," *New York Times*, July 12, 1948.

30. "Randolph Will Invite Arrest for Treason Saturday," *Pittsburgh Courier*, July 17, 1948.

31. "Committee to End Jim Crow in the Armed Services," APRP, Box 17; "Draft Segregation Foes Picket Convention Hall," *Philadelphia Inquirer*, July 13, 1948.

32. "Committee to End Jim Crow in the Armed Services," APRP, Box 17.

33. "Political File," ADAP, Series 6, Box 1; "Democrats Appear to Have Given Up Hopes of Victory over Republicans," *Washington Post*, July 12, 1948; "What People Are Thinking," *New York Herald Tribune*, July 15, 1948.

34. "Gayety Comes to the Democrats as Mummers Parade and Sing," *New York Herald Tribune*, July 13, 1948.

35. Rev. Charles Engvall letter to Humphrey and James Loeb, July 12, 1948. "Political File," ADAP, Series 6, Box 1.

36. Clifford oral history, HTPL.

37. From the transcript of Humphrey's testimony to Platform Committee, found in "Correspondence April—November 1948," MPF, 150.A.2F, Box 26.

38. Ibid.

39. Biemiller oral history HTPL; Solberg, *Hubert Humphrey*, p. 14; Clifford, *Counselor to the President*, pp. 218–219.

40. From the transcript of Humphrey's testimony to Platform Committee, found in "Correspondence April–November 1948," MPF, 150.A.2F, Box 26.

41. "ADA World" edition of August 7, 1948. "Administrative File," ADAP, Series 5, Box 13; Offner, *Hubert Humphrey*, p. 3.

42. Jeannine O'Connor letter to Hamilton, Dec. 22, 1936; Leonard Golditch letter to Hamilton, Nov. 15, 1944; Louise Charlton letter to Hamilton, Aug. 29, 1938. All letters in CGHP Z/U/2002.001, Box 65.

43. John Lucas Casey letter to Hamilton, March 14, 1948. CGHP Z/U/2002.001, Box 65.

44. "Proceedings of Credentials Committee, July 13, 1948." Proceedings Files 1944–1955, Democratic National Committee, HTPL.

45. "Rebellious South Marks Up Victory, Defeat at Confab," Associated Press article published in *Biloxi Sun Herald*, July 14, 1948; "Mississippi Delegation Seated after Hot Row," *Philadelphia Inquirer*, July 14, 1948.

46. Ethridge, "Mississippi's Role in the Dixiecratic Movement," p. 144.

47. The source for all direct quotes from and paraphrases of Vaughan's speech is the verbatim transcript in *Democracy at Work*, pp. 102–105.

48. "St. Louis Negro Starts Race Row at Convention," *St. Louis Post-Dispatch*, July 14, 1948.

49. "Sidelights: Off the Convention Floor," *Chicago Defender*, July 24, 1948; "Truman Back in Running," *Baltimore Afro-American*, July 24, 1948; "Reverence, Near-Riot, Gavel-Banging and Heat Feature Night Session," *Philadelphia Inquirer*, July 14, 1948.

50. Although the crux of the credentials controversy was about the Mississippi delegation, there had also been alternate slates offered in South Carolina and Virginia. So the decision to accept the majority report applied to the all-white, anti-Truman delegations from those two states, as well.

51. Douglas, *In the Fullness of Time*, p. 1

52. Lamson, *Few Are Chosen*, pp. 165–169.

53. Ibid., p. 171; Dupont, *Mrs. Ambassador*, p. 65.

54. Humphrey, *Education of a Public Man*, p. 77.

55. Ibid.

56. Muriel letter to Hubert, July 12, 1948. HHPFP 148.B.10.11B.

57. Biemiller oral history, HTPL.

58. Ibid.

59. The Republican convention, held in the same hall several weeks before the Democratic gathering, was the first national political convention to be broadcast on television.

60. Biemiller oral history HTPL; Biemiller interview HHOHP.

61. Solberg, *Hubert Humphrey*, p. 16; Rauh interview HHOHP.

62. Humphrey's editing can be seen on the speech text in HHSTF 310. G11.3B, Box 2.

63. The description of the conversation and action on the rostrum is taken from: Biemiller oral history, HTPL; Humphrey, *Education of a Public Man*, p. 78.

64. *Democracy at Work*, p. 179.

65. Ibid., pp. 179–181.

66. Ibid., p. 189.

67. Douglas, *In the Fullness of Time*, p. 133.

68. The text of Humphrey's speech is drawn from the original manuscript in HHSTF 310.G.11.3B Box 2 and *Democracy at Work,* pp. 189–192, as well as the audio recording on YouTube that includes Humphrey's stumbles and ad-libs. Unless indicated otherwise in footnotes, the descriptions of the physical setting and audience reaction are drawn from these video sources: *Decision: The Conflicts of Harry S. Truman; Democratic Convention's Dramatic Highlights— Victory for Truman,* News of the Day; *Democratic Presidential Convention!* News of the Day.

69. HHSTF 10.G.11.3B Box 2 and *Democracy at Work,* pp. 189–192, as well as the audio recording on YouTube that includes Humphrey's stumbles and ad-libs.

70. Ibid.

71. Ibid.

72. All of these details are drawn from telegrams and letters the listeners sent to Humphrey after the speech. They can be found in "Civil Rights Correspondence 1948," MPF, 150.A.8.1B, Box 25.

73. HHSTF 10.G.11.3B Box 2 and *Democracy at Work,* pp. 189–192, as well as the audio recording on YouTube that includes Humphrey's stumbles and ad-libs.

74. Ibid.

75. Ibid.

76. Ibid.

77. Douglas, p. 133.

78. Solberg, *Hubert Humphrey,* p. 19; Thurber, *The Politics of Equality,* p. 62.

79. Clifford, *In the Fullness of Time,* p. 219.

80. "Democrats on the Eve of Convention," *Minneapolis Spokesman,* July 16, 1948.

81. Douglas, *In the Fullness of Time,* p. 134; *Democracy at Work,* pp. 201–202.

82. Truman diary entry, July 14, 1948. Reprinted in *Off the Record,* p. 143.

83. "The One Happy Face," *Montgomery Advertiser,* Aug. 2, 1948.

84. Thurber, *The Politics of Equality,* p. 63.

85. Ibid.; "Platform Strong on Civil Rights, Otherwise Weak," *Philadelphia Inquirer,* July 15, 1948; "Race Vote Whipped Dixiecrats," *Pittsburgh Courier,* July 24, 1948; "In the Nation: Even Grant Left Them Their Horses," *New York Times,* July 15, 1948.

86. "Mississippi and Alabama in Walkout," *Philadelphia Inquirer,* July 15, 1948; "13 Alabamans, Mississippi Quit," *Washington Post,* July 15, 1948; Steinberg, *Sam Rayburn: A Biography,* p. 243.

87. *Democracy at Work,* p. 233.

88. "Dixiecrat Convention in Birmingham," July 20, 1948, story no. 066–084, Fox Movietone, www.itnsource.com.

89. Turnip Day falls on July 25, but that date was a Sunday in 1948, when Congress was not in session.

90. *Democracy at Work,* pp. 304–305.

91. Nash, "Science, Politics, and Human Values: A Memoir."

92. John Barriere oral history, HTPL.

93. "The Army and 'Social Reform,'" *Minneapolis Spokesman,* July 30, 1948; *Chicago Defender,* July 31, 1948.

94. Author interview, Micki Solle.

95. Description of Humphrey return from "Parade Greeting Mayor to Start at Auditorium," *Minneapolis Star Journal,* July 17, 1948; "2,000 Cheer for Mayor," *Minneapolis Tribune,* July 18, 1948.

96. Rev. J. J. Harris telegram to Humphrey, July 14, 1948; C. O. Pearson telegram to Humphrey, July 14, 1948; White telegram to Humphrey, July 14, 1948. All in "Civil Rights Correspondence 1948," MPF, 150.A.8.1B, Box 25.

97. Helen Eberle letter to Humphrey, July 16, 1948; Pruden letter to Humphrey, July 21, 1948. Both in "Civil Rights Correspondence 1948," MPF, 150.A.8.1B, Box 25.

98. Unsigned postcard to Humphrey, July 25, 1948. "Civil Rights Correspondence 1948," MPF, 150.A.8.1B, Box 25.

99. A. M. Joyce letter to Humphrey, July 23, 1948. "Civil Rights Correspondence 1948," MPF, 150.A.8.1B, Box 25.

100. Presumably, Humphrey is referring to his travels with the LSU debate team.

101. Humphrey to R. C. Bohlen, July 28, 1948. "Correspondence, April-November 1948." MPF 150.A.8.2F, Box 26.

102. Newman telegram to Humphrey, July 14, 1948. "Civil Rights Correspondence 1948," MPF, 150.A.8.1B, Box 25.

103. Humphrey letter to Newman, July 30, 1948. "Civil Rights Correspondence 1948," MPF, 150.A.8.1B, Box 25.

Epilogue

1. Truman, *Memoirs*, p. 219. Truman provides the totals of 356 speeches and 31,700 miles for the entire campaign. But at the point he was speaking in Harlem, with four days of campaigning left, he had not reached those totals.

2. "Vote for Gov. Dewey" and "President Truman Ominously Silent on Civil Rights," *Pittsburgh Courier*, October 30, 1948.

3. "Truman Leads in Latest Poll," *Minneapolis Spokesman*, August 13, 1948.

4. Nash oral history, HTPL.

5. Ibid.

6. Harry S. Truman, Address in Harlem, New York, upon Receiving the Franklin Roosevelt Award. Online by Gerhard Peters and John T. Woolley, The American Presidency Project, https://www.presidency.ucsb.edu/node/233997.

7. Ibid.

8. "Truman's Courage about Civil Rights Gives Significance to His Victory," *Pittsburgh Courier*, November 20, 1948.

9. "Spokesman Voters' Guide," *Minneapolis Spokesman*, October 29, 1948.

10. "Dan Burley Says Little Man Won," *New York Age*, November 6, 1948.

11. David A. Bositis, "Blacks & the 2012 Democratic National Convention."

12. Gary A. Donaldson, *Truman Defeats Dewey*, p. 190.

13. Harvard Sitkoff, "Harry Truman and the Election of 1948."

14. H. H. letter to Hubert, November 7, 1948. HHPFP 148.B.10.11B.

15. Humphrey, *Education of a Public Man*, p. 85.

16. He fully recovered.

17. Humphrey speech to National Urban League, August 3, 1965. HHSTF 310.G.12.10F, Box 19.

18. Underlining and capitalization are in the original.

19. *Miami News*, August 4, 1965.

20. D. J. Leary, author interviews; "Hubert Horatio Humphrey: Some Parting Notes," [*sic*] *Minneapolis Star*, January 21, 1978.
21. "Humphrey Gets Joyful Return Home to Senate," *New York Times*, October 26, 1977.
22. Aaron Latham, "The Immortality of H.H.H.," *Esquire*, October 1977.
23. Ibid.
24. "Cecil Newman, Editor and Idealist, Dies." *Minneapolis Tribune*, February 8, 1976.
25. Latham, "The Immortality of H.H.H.," *Esquire*, October 1977; author interviews, Ursula Culver and Pat Gray.
26. Author interview, Walter Mondale.
27. "Ailing Humphrey Returns Home for the Holidays," [*sic*] *Minneapolis Tribune*, December 23, 1977.
28. Author interviews, D. J. Leary.
29. https://www.splcenter.org/hatewatch/2017/10/10/when-white-nationalists-chant-their-weird-slogans-what-do-they-mean.
30. https://www.politico.com/story/2017/08/15/full-text-trump-comments-white-supremacists-alt-left-transcript-241662.
31. Author interview, Susan Druskin.
32. Author interview, Tracey Williams-Dillard.
33. A. Philip Randolph, "The Indictment," *The Messenger*, April 1926.
34. Author interviews, Regina Jones and Trenton Slaughter.
35. It has since been returned to its original Indigenous name, Bde Maka Ska.
36. *Haven in the Heart of the City*, pp. 70–71; "Lakewood Cemetery: A Self-Guided Tour."
37. *Haven in the Heart of the City*, p. 122.
38. "A Stroll in Lakewood Cemetery," *Minneapolis Tribune*, October 3, 1981.

BIBLIOGRAPHY

Archival Sources

Americans for Democratic Action Papers (ADAP), State Historical Society of Wisconsin

A. Philip Randolph Collection (APRC), Schomburg Center for Research in Black Culture, Manuscripts, Archives and Rare Books Division, The New York Public Library

A. Philip Randolph Papers (APRP), Manuscript Division, Library of Congress

Charles Granville Hamilton Papers (CGHP), Mississippi Department of Archives and History (Jackson, MS)

Charles L. Horn Papers (CHP), Minnesota Historical Society (MHS) (St. Paul)

Charles S. Johnson Collection (CSJC), Special Collections, John Hope and Aurelia E. Franklin Library, Fisk University (Nashville, TN)

Committee against Jim Crow in Military Service and Training (CAJC), Schomburg Center for Research in Black Culture, Archives and Rare Books Division, New York Public Library

Fielding Wright Papers (FWP), Mississippi Department of Archives and History (Jackson, MS)

Frances Humphrey Howard Papers (FHHP), Schlesinger Library, Harvard Radcliffe Institute (Cambridge, MA)

Franziska Heberle Letters (FHL), Louisiana and Lower Mississippi Valley Collections, Hill Memorial Library, Louisiana State University Library

Harry Truman Presidential Library (HTPL) (Kansas City, MO)

Hubert Humphrey Autobiography Files (HHAF), MHS (St. Paul)

Hubert Humphrey Oral History Project (HHOHP), MHS (St. Paul)

Hubert Humphrey Personal and Family Papers (HHPFP), MHS (St. Paul)

Hubert Humphrey Papers (HHP), Louisiana and Lower Mississippi Valley Collections, Hill Memorial Library, Louisiana State University

Hubert Humphrey Speech Text Files (HHSTF), MHS (St. Paul)

Mayor's Office Files (MOF), MHS (St. Paul)

Mayor's Political Files (MPF), MHS (St. Paul)

Jewish Community Relations Council Papers (JCRC), MHS (St. Paul)

Jewish Community Relations Council Papers (JCRC2), Upper Midwest Jewish Archives, University of Minnesota

Mick Caouette Production Materials (MCPM), MHS (St. Paul)

Minneapolis Fair Employment Practices Commission (MFEPC), MHS (St. Paul)

Race Relations Department of the United Church Board for Homeland Ministries (RRD), Amistad Research Center, New Orleans.

Robbins Gilman and Family Papers (RGFP), MHS (St. Paul)

Rudolph Heberle Papers (RHP), Louisiana and Lower Mississippi Valley Collections, Hill Memorial Library, Louisiana State University

Samuel L. Scheiner Papers (SLSP), MHS (St. Paul)

University of Minnesota Archives and Special Collections (UMASC)

William Bell Riley Papers (WBRP), University of Northwestern (St. Paul, MN)

Books and Scholarly Papers

Abrams, Harris L. *The Negro Population in Minneapolis: A Study in Race Relations.* Minneapolis, MN: Minneapolis Urban League and Phyllis Wheatley Settlement House, 1926.

Acacia, John. *Clark Clifford: The Wise Man of Washington.* Lexington: University of Kentucky Press, 2009.

Albrecht, Susie, ed. *Centennial Doland S.D., 1882–1982.* Privately published.

Anderson, Grant K. "A Microhistory of South Dakota Agriculture, 1919–1920." In *The Great War and the Northern Plains (1914–2014), Papers of the Forty-Sixth Annual Dakota Conference*, edited by Jasmin Graves, Amy Nelson, and Harry F. Thompson. Sioux Falls, SD: Center for Western Studies, Augustana College, 2014.

Anderson, Jervis. *A Philip Randolph: A Biographical Portrait.* New York: Harcourt Brace Jovanovich, 1972.

Ano, Masaharu. "Loyal Linguists: Nisei of World War II Learned Japanese in Minnesota." *Minnesota History* 45, no. 7 (Fall 1977).

Antidiscrimination in Employment. *Hearings before a Subcommittee of the Committee on Labor and Public Welfare, United States Senate, Eightieth Congress, First Session, on S. 984*, a bill to prohibit discrimination in employment because of race, religion, color national origin or ancestry, June 11–13, 18–20, July 16–18, 1947.

Atwood, Sarah. "'This List Not Complete': Minnesota's Jewish Resistance to the Silver Legion of America, 1936–1940." *Minnesota History* 66, no. 4 (Winter 2018–2019).

Baime, A. J. *Dewey Defeats Truman: The 1948 Election and the Battle for America's Soul.* Boston: Houghton Mifflin Harcourt, 2020.

Bass, Jack, and Marilyn W. Thompson. *Strom: The Complicated Personal and Political Life of Strom Thurmond.* New York: Public Affairs, 2005.

Bay, Mia. *Traveling Black: A Story of Race and Resistance.* Cambridge, MA: Harvard University Press, 2021.

Beck, Erin. "South Dakota Claim Shanty." https://www.sdstate.edu/south-dakota-agricultural-heritage-museum/south-dakota-claim-shanty.

Bedsole, V. L., and Oscar Richard, eds. *Louisiana State University: A Pictorial Record of the First Hundred Years*. Baton Rouge: Louisiana State University Press, 1959.

Berman, Hyman. "Political Antisemitism in Minnesota during the Great Depression." *Jewish Social Studies* 38, no. 3/4 (Summer–Autumn 1976).

Berman, Hyman, with Jay Weiner. *Professor Berman. The Last Lecture of Minnesota's Greatest Public Historian*. Minneapolis: University of Minnesota Press, 2019.

Berman, Hyman, and Linda Mack Schloff. *Jews in Minnesota*. St. Paul: Minnesota Historical Society Press, 2002.

Berman, Susan. *East Street: The True Story of a Mob Family*. New York: Dial Press, 1981.

Bernson, Sara L., and Robert J. Eggers. "Black People in South Dakota History." *South Dakota History* 7, no. 3 (1977).

Bernstein, Barton. *Politics & Policies of the Truman Administration*. Chicago: Quadrangle, 1970.

Blount, Emanuel L. "The History of the Epworth League: A Concept of Youth in Nineteenth Century America." PhD diss., State University of New York at Buffalo, 1996.

Boie, Maurine. "A Study of Conflict and Accommodation in Negro-White Relations in the Twin Cities—Based on Documentary Sources." Master's thesis, University of Minnesota, 1932.

Bositis, David A. "Blacks & the 2012 Democratic National Convention." Washington, DC: Joint Center for Political and Economic Studies, 2012.

Burnside, Tina. "On June 15 1920, a Duluth Mob Lynched Three Black Men." *MinnPost*, July 29, 2019. https://www.minnpost.com/mnopedia/2019/07/on-june-15-1920-a-duluth-mob-lynched-three-black-men.

Calomiris, Charles W., and Matthew Jaremski. "Stealing Deposits: Deposit Insurance, Risk-Taking and the Removal of Market Discipline in Early 20th Century Banks." *Journal of Finance* 74, no. 2 (April 2019).

Carlson, John Roy. *The Plotters*. New York: E.P. Dutton & Company, 1946.

Caro, Robert A. *The Years of Lyndon Johnson: The Passage of Power*. New York: Alfred A. Knopf, 2012.

Clifford, Clark, with Richard Holbrooke. *Counsel to the President: A Memoir*. New York: Random House, 1991.

Cooper, Charles I. "The Jews of Minneapolis and Their Christian Neighbors." *Jewish Social Studies* 8, no. 1 (January 1946).

Crespino, Joseph. *Strom Thurmond's America: A History*. New York: Hill and Wang, 2012.

Culver, John C., and John Hyde. *American Dreamer: The Life and Times of Henry A. Wallace*. New York: W.W. Norton, 2000.

Curry, James. "Hastings, 1907: The Burning of Brown's Chapel AME." *MinnPost.* https://www.minnpost.com/mnopedia/2021/04/hastings-1907-the-burning-of-browns-chapel-ame/#:~:text=Early%20in%20the%20morning%20on,ceilings%2C%20and%20broke%20the%20windows.

Dawson, O. L. *South Dakota Farm Production and Prices, 1890–1926.* Brookings, SD: Agricultural Experiment Station, 1927.

Delton, Jennifer A. "Forging a Northern Strategy: Civil Rights in Liberal Democratic Politics, 1940–1948." PhD diss., Princeton University, 1997.

Delton, Jennifer A. "Labor, Politics, and African-American Identity in Minneapolis, 1930–1950." *Minnesota History* 57, no. 8 (Winter 2001–2002) .

Delton, Jennifer A. *Making Minnesota Liberal: Civil Rights and the Transformation of the Democratic Party.* Minneapolis: University of Minnesota Press, 2002.

Democracy at Work: Official Proceedings of the Democratic National Convention 1948. Philadelphia: Local Democratic Political Committee of Pennsylvania, 1948.

Denis, Michael J. "We Were Here: African-Americans in Danville and Boyle County, Kentucky." https://sites.rootsweb.com/~kydaahs/The-Past/6-Presentations/We%20Were%20Here.pdf.

Dewitt, Larry. "The Decision to Exclude Agricultural and Domestic Workers from the 1935 Social Security Act." *Social Security Bulletin* 70, no. 4 (2010).

Donaldson, Gary A. *Truman Defeats Dewey.* Lexington: University Press of Kentucky, 1999.

Douglas, Paul H. *In the Fullness of Time: The Memoirs of Paul H. Douglas.* New York: Harcourt Brace Jovanovich, 1972.

Dudziak, Mary L. *Cold War Civil Rights: Race and the Image of American Democracy.* Princeton, NJ: Princeton University Press, 2000.

Dupont, Mary. *Mrs. Ambassador: The Life and Politics of Eugenie Anderson.* St. Paul: Minnesota Historical Society Press, 2019.

"Enslaved African Americans and the Fight for Freedom." https://www.mnhs.org/fortsnelling/learn/african-americans.

Equal Justice Initiative. *Lynching in America: Targeting Black Veterans.* Montgomery, AL: Equal Justice Initiative, 2017.

Ethridge, Richard C. "Mississippi's Role in the Dixiecratic Movement." PhD dissertation, Mississippi State University, 1971.

Fehrenbacher, Don. E. *The Dred Scott Case: Its Significance in American Law and Politics.* New York: Oxford University Press, 1978.

Ferrell, Robert H., ed. *Off the Record: The Private Papers of Harry S. Truman.* New York: Harper & Row, 1980.

Foner, Philip S. *Organized Labor and the Black Worker, 1619–1981.* New York: International Publishers, 1982.

Frank, Jeffrey. *The Trials of Harry S. Truman: The Extraordinary Presidency of an Ordinary Man, 1945–1953.* New York: Simon & Schuster, 2022.

Franke, W. H. *The Economy of North Central South Dakota, Bulletin no. 50*. Vermillion: Business Research Bureau, University of South Dakota, February 1957.

Frederickson, Kari. *The Dixiecrat Revolt and the End of the Solid South*. Chapel Hill: University of North Carolina Press, 2001.

Gardner, Michael R. *Harry Truman and Civil Rights: Moral Courage and Political Risks*. Carbondale: Southern Illinois University Press, 2002.

Garrettson, Charles L., III. *Hubert H. Humphrey: The Politics of Joy*. New Brunswick, NJ: Transaction, 1993.

Gergel, Richard. *Unexampled Courage: The Blinding of Sgt. Isaac Woodard and the Awakening of President Harry S. Truman and Judge J. Waties Waring*. New York: Farrar, Straus and Giroux, 2019.

Gillon, Steven M. *Politics and Vision: The ADA and American Liberalism, 1947–1985*. New York: Oxford University Press, 1987.

Gilpin, Patrick. "Charles S. Johnson: An Intellectual Biography." PhD diss., Vanderbilt University, 1973.

Gilpin, Patrick. "Charles S. Johnson and the Race Relations Institutes at Fisk University." *Phylon* 41, no. 3 (1980).

Golay, Michael. *America 1933: The Great Depression, Lorena Hickock, Eleanor Roosevelt, and the Shaping of the New Deal*. New York: Free Press, 2013.

Gonda, Jeffrey D. "Litigating Racial Justice at the Grassroots: The Shelley Family, Black Realtors, and *Shelley v. Kraemer* (1948)." *Journal of Supreme Court History* 39, no. 3 (November 2014).

Gordon, Albert I. *Jews in Transition*. Minneapolis: University of Minnesota Press, 1949.

Green, William D. *Degrees of Freedom: The Origins of Civil Rights in Minnesota, 1865–1912*. Minneapolis: University of Minnesota Press, 2015.

Hamlin, William G., and Stephen W. Noyes. *100 Years of South Dakota Agriculture, 1900–1999*. Sioux Falls: South Dakota Agricultural Statistics Service, 2000.

Hart, Bradley. *Hitler's American Friends: The Third Reich's Supporters in the United States*. New York: Thomas Dunne Books, 2018.

Hartman, Christopher, and Robert Moldwin. "Hubert Humphrey's Bladder Cancer." *Journal of Urology* 191, no. 4S (May 19, 2014).

Hartt, Julian N. "Hubert Humphrey and the Pieties of the Prairie." *Dialog* 23, no. 1 (1984).

Hartt, Julian N. "What We Make of the World: Selections from 'Yankee Preacher, Prairie Son.'" *Soundings: An Interdisciplinary Journal* 81, nos. 1–2 (Spring/Summer 1998).

Hartt, Julian N. "What We Make of the World: Concluding Selections from 'Yankee Preacher, Prairie Son.'" *Soundings: An Interdisciplinary Journal* 82, nos. 1–2 (Spring/Summer 1999).

Hase, Michiko. "W. Gertrude Brown's Struggle for Racial Justice, Female Leadership and Community in Black Minneapolis, 1920–1940." PhD diss., University of Minnesota, 1994.

Hatfield, Edward. "Columbians." *New Georgia Encyclopedia*. https://www.geor giaencyclopedia.org/articles/history-archaeology/columbians/.

Hatle, Elizabeth Dorsey, and Nancy M. Vaillancourt. "One Flag, One School, One Language: Minnesota's Ku Klux Klan in the 1920s." *Minnesota History* 61, no. 8 (Winter 2009–2010).

Haynes, John Earl. *Dubious Alliance: The Making of Minnesota's DFL Party*. Minneapolis: University of Minnesota Press, 1983.

Heberle, Rudolf. *From Democracy to Nazism: A Regional Case Study of Political Parties in Germany*. Rev. ed. New York: Grosset & Dunlap, 1970.

Heberle, Rudolf. "Reminiscences of a Sociologist." *Journal of the History of the Behavioral Sciences* 13, no. 2 (April 1977).

Heilman, Robert Bechtold. *The Southern Connection*. Baton Rouge: Louisiana State University Press, 1991.

Hendry, Petra Munro, and Jay Dearborn Edwards. *Old South Baton Rouge: The Roots of Hope*. Lafayette: University of Louisiana at Lafayette Press, 2009.

Hilliard, Elbert Riley. "A Biography of Fielding Wright: Mississippi's Mr. State [*sic*] Rights." Master's thesis, Mississippi State University, 1959.

Hoke, Travis. *Shirts! A Survey of the New "Shirt" Organizations in the United States Seeking a Fascist Dictatorship*. New York: American Civil Liberties Union, 1934.

Hovde, M. N. "The Great Duststorm [*sic*] of November 12, 1933." *Monthly Weather Review* 62, no. 12–13 (January 1934).

Hruban, Ralph H., et al. "Molecular Biology and the Early Detection of Carcinoma of the Bladder—the Case of Hubert H. Humphrey." *New England Journal of Medicine* 330, no. 18 (May 5, 1994).

Hull, William H. *The Dirty Thirties*. Self-published, 1989.

Humphrey, Hubert H. *The Education of a Public Man: My Life and Politics*. Minneapolis: University of Minnesota Press, 1991.

Humphrey, Hubert H. *The Political Philosophy of the New Deal*. Baton Rouge: Louisiana University Press, 2015.

Husse, Dorothy, et al. *Huron Revisited*. Huron, SD: East Eagle Company, 1988.

Jackson, Walter A. *Gunnar Myrdal and America's Conscience: Social Engineering and Racial Liberalism, 1938–1987*. Chapel Hill: University of North Carolina Press, 1990.

Jeansonne, Glen. *Gerald L.K. Smith: Minister of Hate*. Rev. ed. Baton Rouge: Louisiana State University Press, 1997.

Johnson, Nellie Stone, with David Brauer. *Nellie Stone Johnson: The Life of an Activist*. St. Paul, MN.: Ruminator Books, 2000.

Juergens, Ann. "Lena Olive Smith: A Minnesota Civil Rights Pioneer." *William Mitchell Law Review* 28, no. 1 (2001).

Kane, Harnett T. *Louisiana Hayride*. New York: William Morrow & Co., 1941.

Katznelson, Ira. *Fear Itself: The New Deal and the Origins of Our Time.* New York: Liveright, 2013.

Kellogg, Peter J. "The Americans for Democratic Action and Civil Rights in 1948: Conscience in Politics or Politics in Conscience?" *The Midwest Quarterly* 20, no. 1 (1978).

Kellogg, Peter J. "Civil Rights Consciousness in the 1940s." *The Historian* 42, no. 1 (November 1979).

Kersten, Andrew E. *A. Philip Randolph: A Life in the Vanguard.* Lanham, MD: Rowman & Littlefield, 2007.

Kilgore, Jack. *South Dakota: Our Towns . . . a Pictorial Review.* Dallas, TX: Taylor Publishing, 1989.

Koch, Raymond L. "Politics and Relief in Minneapolis during the 1930s." *Minnesota History* 41, no. 4 (Winter 1968).

Kornweibel, Theodore. "Jim Crow Cars: A Brief History and Census." *National Railway Bulletin* 62, no. 4 (1997).

Kornweibel, Theodore. *Railroads in the African American Experience: A Photographic Journey.* Baltimore: Johns Hopkins University Press, 2010.

Kumlien, W. F. *Graphic Summary of the Relief Situation in South Dakota (1930–1935).* Brookings: Agricultural Extension Station, South Dakota State College, 1937.

Lamson, Peggy. *Few Are Chosen: American Women in Political Life Today.* Boston: Houghton Mifflin Company, 1968.

Landis, Paul. *Rural Relief in South Dakota.* Brookings: Department of Rural Sociology, South Dakota State College, June 1934.

Lansing, Michael J. "Policing Politics: Labor, Race, and the Police Officers Federation of Minneapolis, 1945–1972." *Minnesota History* 67, no. 5 (Spring 2021).

Lee, R. Alton. *A New Deal for South Dakota: Drought, Depression, and Relief, 1920–1941.* Pierre: South Dakota Historical Society Press, 2016.

Leipold, L. E. *Cecil E. Newman: Newspaper Publisher.* Minneapolis, MN: T.S. Denison & Co., 1969.

Lesher, Stephan. *George Wallace: American Populist.* Reading, MA: Addison-Wesley, 1994.

Leven, Maurice. *Income in the Various States: Its Sources and Distribution 1919, 1920, and 1921.* New York: National Bureau of Economic Research, 1925.

Lewin, Rhoda. *Images of America: Jewish Community of North Minneapolis.* Charleston, SC: Arcadia Publishing, 2001.

Long, Herman H. *Segregation in Interstate Railway Coach Travel.* Nashville, TN: Race Relations Department, American Missionary Association, Fisk University, 1952.

Lowitt, Richard, and Maurine Beasley, eds. *One Third of a Nation: Lorena Hickock Reports on the Great Depression.* Urbana: University of Illinois Press, 1981.

Lundy, G. *Farm Mortgage Experience in South Dakota: 1910–40.* Brookings: Agricultural Experiment Station, South Dakota State University, 1943.

Manfred, Frederick. "Hubert Horatio Humphrey: A Memoir." *Minnesota History* 46, no. 3 (Fall 1978).

Mann, Robert. *The Walls of Jericho: Lyndon Johnson, Hubert Humphrey, Richard Russell, and The Struggle for Civil Rights*. New York: Harcourt Brace & Company, 1996.

Mathis, Paul. *The Business Cycle in South Dakota*. Vermillion: Business Research Bureau, University of South Dakota, 1953.

McCullough, David. *Truman*. New York: Simon & Schuster, 1992.

McWilliams, Carey. "Minneapolis: The Curious Twin." *Common Ground* 15 (Autumn 1946).

Mendel, Don. "Doland's Beginnings." Text of speech delivered August 12, 2007, Doland, SD.

Menefee, Selden. *Assignment: U.S.A.* New York: Raynal & Hitchcock, 1943.

Meyers, M. *Farm Performance in North Central South Dakota 1930–1939, Bulletin 343*. Brookings, SD: Agricultural Extension Station, South Dakota State College, June 1940.

Mielke, Luke. "Racial Uplift in a Jim Crow Local: Black Union Organizing in Minneapolis Hotels 1930–1940." American Studies Honors Projects, Macalaster College, 2016.

Millikan, William. *A Union against Unions: The Minneapolis Citizens Alliance and Its Fight against Organized Labor, 1903–1947*. St. Paul: Minnesota Historical Society Press, 2001.

Moon, Henry Lee. *Balance of Power: The Negro Vote*. Garden City, NY: Doubleday, 1948.

Moore, Christopher Paul. *Fighting for America: Black Soldiers—the Unsung Heroes of World War II*. New York: One World, 2005.

Moore, Deborah Dash. *GI Jews: How World War II Changed a Generation*. Cambridge, MA: Belknap Press, 2004.

Moreno, Paul. *Black Americans and Organized Labor: A New History*. Baton Rouge: Louisiana State University Press, 2006.

Mosher, Curtis L. *The Causes of Banking Failure in the Northwestern States*. Minneapolis, MN: Federal Reserve Bank, 1930.

Murphy, John M. "The Sunshine of Human Rights: Hubert Humphrey at the 1948 Democratic Convention." *Rhetoric & Public Affairs* 23, no. 1 (Spring 2020).

Myrdal, Gunnar. *An American Dilemma: The Negro Problem and Modern Democracy*. New York: Harper & Row, 1944.

Nash, Philleo. "Science, Politics, and Human Values: A Memoir." *Human Organization* 45, no. 3 (Fall 1986).

Nathanson, Iric. *Minneapolis in the Twentieth Century: The Growth of an American City*. St. Paul: Minnesota Historical Society Press, 2010.

Nathanson, Iric. "Spokesman for the Community: Cecil Newman and His Legacy of African American Journalism." *Hennepin History* 69, no. 3 (Fall 2010).

"The Negro in Baton Rouge: A Study by the Class in Race and Race Relations (Sociology 204)." Baton Rouge: Louisiana State University and Agricultural and Mechanical College, 1939–40.

Nelson, Paul. "National Afro-American Council Meeting, 1902." https://www .mnopedia.org/event/national-afro-american-council-meeting-1902.

Nelson, Paula. *The Prairie Winnows Out Its Own: The West River Country of South Dakota in the Years of Depression and Dust*. Iowa City: University of Iowa Press, 1996.

Offner, Arnold A. *Hubert Humphrey: The Conscience of the Country*. New Haven, CT: Yale University Press, 2018.

Osteen, Mame. *Haven in the Heart of the City: The History of Lakewood Cemetery*. Minneapolis, MN: Yeager, Pine & Mundale, 1992.

Palmer, Bryan D. *Revolutionary Teamsters: The Minneapolis Truckers' Strikes of 1934*. Leiden, Netherlands: Brill, 2013.

Parks, Gordon. *A Choice of Weapons*. New York: Harper & Row, 1966.

Patrick, Robert Pierce, Jr. "A Nail in the Coffin of Racism: The Story of the Columbians." *The Georgia Historical Quarterly* 85, no. 2 (Summer 2001).

Pfeffer, Paula F. *A Philip Randolph, Pioneer of the Civil Rights Movement*. Baton Rouge: Louisiana State University Press, 1990.

Pierce, Charles H. "The Dust Storm of November 12 and 13, 1933." *Bulletin of the American Meteorological Society* 15, no. 2 (February 1934).

Plaut, W. Gunther. *The Jews in Minnesota*. New York: American Jewish Historical Society, 1959.

Prell, Riv-Ellen. "Antisemitism without Quotas at the University of Minnesota in the 1930s and 1940s: Anticommunist Politics, the Surveillance of Jewish Students, and American Antisemitism." *American Jewish History* 105, nos. 1–2 (January/ April 2021).

Price, Isabel B. "Gerald L.K. Smith and Anti-Semitism." Master's thesis, University of New Mexico, 1965.

Purdum, Todd S. *An Idea Whose Time Has Come: Two Presidents, Two Parties, and the Battle for the Civil Rights Act of 1964*. New York: Henry Holt, 2014.

Quigley, Joan. *Just Another Southern Town: Mary Church Terrell and the Struggle for Racial Justice in the Nation's Capital*. New York: Oxford University Press, 2016.

Rambow, Charles. "The Ku Klux Klan in the 1920s: A Concentration of the Black Hills." *South Dakota History* 4, no. 1 (1973).

Rapp, Michael Gerald. "An Historical Overview of Anti-Semitism in Minnesota, 1920–1960—with Particular Emphasis on Minneapolis and St. Paul." PhD diss., University of Minnesota, 1977.

Reed, Merle R. *Seedtime for the Modern Civil Rights Movement: The President's Committee on Fair Employment, 1941–1946*. Baton Rouge: Louisiana State University Press, 1991.

Reichard, Gary W. "Mayor Hubert H. Humphrey." *Minnesota History* (Summer 1998).

Richardson, Lori. "A Dream Comes True: Saga of Two Crusading Newspapers." *The Negro Digest.*

Riley, W. B. "A Sketch of My Life." In *The Scroll* yearbook. Minneapolis, MN: Northwestern Bible College, 1930.

Rockaway, Robert. *But He Was Good to His Mother: The Lives and Crimes of Jewish Gangsters.* Jerusalem: Gefen Publishing House, 2000.

Roelfs, A. P. *Estimated Losses Caused by Rust in Small Grain Cereals in the United States—1918–1976.* Washington, DC: Agricultural Research Service, U.S. Department of Agriculture, 1978.

Rousselow, Jessie. "The Social Conscience of Fundamentalism as Seen in W.B. Riley." Research paper in partial fulfillment of master's degree, University of Minnesota, 1965.

Rubin, Janice Ginsberg. "The Non-Legal Alvin Rubin." *Louisiana Law Review* 52, no. 6 (July 1992).

Ruchames, Louis. *Race, Jobs, & Politics: The Story of the FEPC.* New York: Columbia University Press, 1953.

Ruffin, Thomas F. *Under Stately Oaks: A Pictorial History of LSU.* Baton Rouge: Louisiana State University Press, 2002.

Russell, C. Allyn. "William Bell Riley: Architect of Fundamentalism." *Minnesota History* 43, no. 1 (Spring 1972).

Schmid, Calvin F. *Social Saga of Two Cities: An Ecological and Statistical Study of Social Trends in Minneapolis and St. Paul.* Minneapolis: Bureau of Social Research, The Minnesota Council of Social Agencies, 1937.

Schrader, Leonard, et al. *South Dakota Weeds.* Rev. ed. Brookings: Agricultural Extension Service, South Dakota State University, 1975.

Schuler, Harold H. "Patriotic Pageantry: Presidential Visits to South Dakota." *South Dakota History* 30, no. 4 (Winter 2000).

Sevareid, Eric. *Not So Wild a Dream.* New York: Atheneum, 1976.

Sherman, Norman. *From Nowhere to Somewhere: My Political Journey.* Minneapolis, MN: First Avenue Editions, 2016.

Shively, W. Phillips. "In Memoriam: Benjamin Evans Lippincott." *Political Science and Politics* 22, no. 1 (March 1989).

Simon, Art. "The House I Live In (1945)." https://www.loc.gov/static/programs/ national-film-preservation-board/documents/The-House-I-Live-In_Simon.pdf.

Sindler, Allan P. *Huey Long's Louisiana: State Politics, 1920–1952.* Baltimore: Johns Hopkins University Press, 1956.

Sitkoff, Harvard. "Harry Truman and the Election of 1948: The Coming of Age of Civil Rights in American Politics." *The Journal of Southern History* 37, no. 4 (November 1971).

Sluss, Jackie. "Lena Olive Smith: Civil Rights in the 1930s." *Hennepin History* 54, no. 1 (Winter 1995).

South Dakota Agricultural Statistics Service. *100 Years of South Dakota Agriculture, 1900–1999*. Sioux Falls: South Dakota Agricultural Statistics Service, February 2000.

Spangler, Earl. *The Negro in Minnesota*. Minneapolis, MN: T.S. Denison, 1961.

State of South Dakota, Eighteenth Biennial Report of the Superintendent of Banks. Pierre, SD: Hipple Printing Co., 1928.

State of South Dakota, Seventeenth Biennial Report of the Superintendent of Banks. Mitchell, SD: Mitchell Publishing Co., 1926.

States' Rights Information and Speakers Handbook. Jackson, MS: National States' Rights Democrats Campaign Committee, 1948.

Steele, H. A. *Farm Mortgage Foreclosures in South Dakota, 1921–1932*. Brookings, SD: Agricultural Experiment Station, 1934.

Steinberg, Alfred. *Sam Rayburn: A Biography*. New York: Hawthorn Books, 1975.

Sullivan, Daniel P. *The Murder of the Real Jack Ryan*. Omaha, NB: Daniel P. Sullivan, 2020.

Szasz, Ferenc M. "William B. Riley and the Fight against Teaching Evolution in Minnesota." *Minnesota History* 45, no. 5 (Spring 1969).

Taylor, David Vassar. *African Americans in Minnesota*. St. Paul: Minnesota Historical Society Press, 2002.

Thompson, Harry F., ed. *A New South Dakota History*. 2nd ed. Sioux Falls, SD: Center for Western Studies, Augustana College, 2009.

Truman, Harry S. *Memoirs, Volume Two: Years of Trial and Hope*. Garden City, NY: Doubleday, 1956.

Vanepps-Taylor, Betti. *Forgotten Lives: African Americans in South Dakota*. Pierre: South Dakota State Historical Society Press, 2008.

Wagner, Rainer. *Rudolf Heberle: Soziologie in Deutschland zwischen den Weltkriegen*. (Rudolf Heberle: Sociologist in Germany between the World Wars). Hamburg: Rolf Fechner Publishing House, 1995.

Webb, Walter Prescott. *The Great Plains*. Boston: Ginn and Co., 1931.

Weber, Laura E. "'Gentiles Preferred': Minneapolis Jews and Employment 1920–1950." *Minnesota History* 52, no. 5 (Spring 1991).

Weber, Laura E. "'Minneapolis: The Curious Twin': A Reexamination." *Middle West Review* 8, no. 2 (Spring 2022).

Weber, Michael. *Don't Call Me Boss: David L. Lawrence, Pittsburgh's Renaissance Mayor*. Pittsburgh, PA: University of Pittsburgh Press, 1988.

Whitaker, Mark. *Smoketown: The Untold Story of the Other Great Black Renaissance*. New York: Simon & Schuster, 2018.

White, Theodore H. *The Making of the President 1972*. New York: Atheneum, 1973.

White, Walter. *A Man Called White*. New York: Arno Press, 1969.

Williams, Harry T. *Huey Long*. New York: Alfred A. Knopf, 1969.

Witwer, David. "Race Relations in the Early Teamsters Union." *Labor History* 43, no. 4 (2002).

Wolff, Gerald W., and Joseph H. Cash, "South Dakotans Remember the Great Depression." *South Dakota History* 28, no. 2 (1989).

Wright, George C. *Racial Violence in Kentucky, 1965–1940: Lynchings, Mob Rule, and "Legal Lynchings."* Baton Rouge: Louisiana State University Press, 1990.

Zangrando, Robert L. "The NAACP and a Federal Antilynching Bill, 1934–1940." *The Journal of Negro History* 50 no. 2 (April 1965).

Magazine Articles

Feikema, Feike. "Report from Minnesota." *New Republic*, October 11, 1943.

Humphrey, Hubert. "My Father." *Atlantic Monthly*, November 1966.

Humphrey, Hubert. "My Scouting Past, Your Scouting Future." *Scouting*, January 1966.

Kramer, Dale. "Young Man in a Hurry." *New Republic*, June 16, 1947.

Latham, Aaron. "The Immortality of H.H.H." *Esquire*, October 1977.

Lefkovits, Dr. Maurice. "Minneapolis Jewry—an Appraisal." *American Jewish World*, September 7, 1923.

Maccabee, Paul. "Alias Kid Cann." *Mpls. St. Paul*, November 1991.

McCarr, Henry W. "Amicus Curiae." *Hennepin Lawyer*, November/December 1974.

"Medicine: H.H.H.'s Cystectomy." *TIME*, October 18, 1976; Dr. W. Britt Zimmerman, author interview.

Rosengren, John. "A Sinister Parade Float." *Minnesota History*, Spring 2020.

Sullivan, Jack. "The Peruna Story: Strumming That Old Catarrh." *Bottles and Extras*, May–June 2007.

Thompson, Hunter S. "More Late News from Bleak House." *Rolling Stone*, May 11, 1977.

Newspapers

Aberdeen Evening News (Aberdeen, SD)
Amsterdam News (New York)
Baltimore Afro-American
Battle Creek Enterprise (Battle Creek, MI)
Chicago Defender
Daily Argus-Leader (Sioux Falls, SD)
Daily Capital Journal (Pierre, SD)
Daily Pennsylvanian (Philadelphia)
Daily Reveille (Baton Rouge, LA)
Des Moines Register
Epworth Herald (Chicago)
Evening Huronite (Huron, SD)
Evening Star (Washington, DC)
Jackson Clarion-Ledger (Jackson, MS)

Jackson Daily News (Jackson, MS)
Louisiana Weekly (New Orleans, LA)
Memphis Commercial Appeal (Memphis, TN)
Memphis Press-Scimitar (Memphis, TN)
Miami Herald
Miami News
Minneapolis Journal
Minneapolis Spokesman
Minneapolis Star
Minneapolis Star Journal
Minneapolis Times
Minneapolis Tribune
Minnesota Leader (St. Paul)
Minnesota Messenger (Minneapolis)
Morning Advocate (Baton Rouge, LA)
New York Age
New York Herald Tribune
New York Times
Northwestern Bulletin-Appeal (St. Paul, MN)
Philadelphia Inquirer
Pittsburgh Courier
Saturday Press (Minneapolis, MN)
Timely Digest (Minneapolis, MN)
Times-Record (Doland, SD)
Twin-City Herald (Minneapolis–St. Paul, MN)
Washington Post

Author Interviews

Berman, Hyman, 6/3/15
Calomiris, Charles, 8/26/21
Cowan, Barry, 4/1/22
Culver, Ursula, 10/22/19
Druskin, Susan, 12/29/17, 7/30/18, and 9/8/22
Faltesek, Mary Culver, 4/21/21
Foster, Neal, 6/7/21
Fraser, Arvonne, and Don Fraser, 7/3/15
Glanton, Wayne, 10/30/18
Joseph, Geri, 7/2/15
Gray Pat, 3/31/21 and 4/12/21
Greenwood, Marsha, 10/23/19
Heberle, Juergen, 10/1/18
Higby, Gregory, and Lucas Richart, 11/13/19
Huft, Dave, 6/12/19
Humphrey, Hubert III (Skip), 6/12/15 and 12/27/16
Humphrey, Hubert III (Skip), and William Howard, 8/20/17, 12/28/17, 12/6/19, 3/19/21, and 7/9/21

Hunegs, Richard, 8/16/18
Jones, Regina, 9/12/22
Joseph, Geri Mack, 7/2/15
Kelman, Eleanor Sussman, 10/5/18
Kephart, Kevin, 8/12/19
King, David, 7/27/19
Kolodziej, Antje Heberle, 10/17/18
Leary, D. J., 12/28/18, and 9/12/19
Mondale, Walter, 8/19/15, 8/16/18, and 11/4/19
Neumaier, Diane, 2/7/19
Reynolds, Kirk, 4/8/22
Rubin, David, 3/28/18
Sherman, Norman, 9/25/18, 8/23/19, and 3/25/20
Skorseth, Ken, email exchanges, 7/5/19 and 4/29/21
Slaughter, Trenton, 9/14/22
Solle, Micki, 7/29/19
Tunheim, Jack, 4/9/21
Williams-Dillard, Tracey, 8/17/18 and 9/9/22
Wollman, Ralph, 11/6/2017
Wright, John, 4/22/21 and 7/2/21
Zimmerman, Dr. W. Britt, 5/27/21

Oral Histories (outside Humphrey Collection)

Barriere, John E. HTPL.
Biemiller, Andrew. Columbia Center for Oral History, Columbia University.
Biemiller, Andrew. HTPL.
Cannon, Raymond W., interviewed by Steve Trimble, MHS.
Cassius, Anthony Brutus. 20th Century Radicalism in Minnesota Project, MHS.
Clifford, Clark. HTPL.
Cyrus, Barbara. Ann Juergens private collection.
Edwards, India. HTPL.
Elsey, George. HTPL.
Forman, Mary. Ann Juergens private collection.
Heberle, Franziska, Hill Memorial Library, LSU.
Johnson, Nellie Stone. Our Gathering Places Oral History Project, MHS.
Johnson, Nellie Stone. 20th Century Radicalism in Minnesota Project, MHS.
Loeb, James. HTPL.
Naftalin, Arthur. University of Minnesota Digital Conservancy.
Nash, Philleo. HTPL.
Newman, Cecil. Black Journalists Oral History Project, Columbia Center for Oral History, Columbia University.
Randolph, A. Philip, Lyndon Baines Johnson Library, Austin, TX.
Robison, Roy. Jazz in the Twin Cities Oral History Project, MHS.
Unthank, Lesley. Eliot Oral History Project, Portland, OR.

Video Sources

Cecil Newman funeral, KSTP 85384, MHS.

Cecil Newman Remembrance: From private collection of Tracey Williams-Dillard.

Cecil Newman retrospective, KSTP 85385, MHS.

Cornerstones: A History of North Minneapolis. https://video.tpt.org/video/tpt-documentaries-cornerstones-history-north-minneapolis/.

Decision: The Conflicts of Harry S. Truman. https://www.historicfilms.com/tapes/6089.

Democratic Convention's Dramatic Highlights—Victory for Truman. News of the Day, Vol. 19, Issue 291. SG14155, UCLA Film & Television Archive.

Democratic Presidential Convention! News of the Day, Vol. 19, Issue 290. SG2729, UCLA Film & Television Archive.

The Heart of Bassett Place: W. Gertrude Brown and the Wheatley House, a film by Mick Caouette.

Hubert Humphrey arrival at airport, December 22, 1978. KSTP T0083-33, MHS.

Hubert Humphrey birthday interview, May 27, 1977. KTSP T0048, MHS.

Hubert Humphrey press conference at airport, December 22, 1978. KSTP T0083-35, MHS.

Hubert Humphrey: The Art of the Possible, a film by Mick Caouette.

This Free North. https://www.tpt.org/this-free-north/.

Online Scholarly Sources

"A Campus Divided: Progressives, Anti-Communists, Racism & Antisemitism at the University of Minnesota, 1930–1942." https://acampusdivided.umn.edu/.

"The Historyapolis Project." http://historyapolis.com/.

"Mapping Prejudice." https://mappingprejudice.umn.edu/.

INDEX

For the benefit of digital users, indexed terms that span two pages (e.g., 52–53) may, on occasion, appear on only one of those pages.

473

INDEX